# Rome and Judae

MW01716610

'Linda Zollschan, by her thorough analysis of the process by which Romans formed international relations as well as her detailed linguistic analysis of the letter at 1 Macc 8:23–32, has provided a new and fascinating understanding of the relations between Rome and the Hasmoneans from the first embassy to Rome in 162 BCE to the arrival of Pompey in Syria in 63 BCE. She concludes that there was no formal treaty between Rome and the Judeans, but a relationship of *amicitia* (friendship). Her findings are invaluable and essential to any further study of this period.'

Professor Robert Doran, *Amherst College, USA*

*Rome and Judaea* explores the nature of Judaea's first diplomatic mission to Rome during the Maccabaean revolt: did it result in a sanctioned treaty or was it founded instead on amity? This book breaks new ground in this debate by bringing to light the 'Roman–Jewish friendship tablet', a newly discovered piece of evidence that challenges the theory Rome ratified an official treaty with Judaea. Incorporating interdisciplinary research and this new textual evidence, the book argues that Roman–Jewish relations during the Maccabean revolt were motivated by the Roman concept of diplomatic friendship, or *amicitia.*

**Linda Zollschan** is an independent research professional based in Israel. She obtained her PhD from Ben-Gurion University of the Negev, Beersheva, Israel.

## Routledge Studies in Ancient History

**Cicero and the Catilinarian Conspiracy**
*Charles Matson Odahl*

**Ancient Graffiti in Context**
*Edited by Jennifer Baird and Claire Taylor*

**Roman Elections in the Age of Cicero: Society, Government, and Voting**
*Rachel Feig Vishnia*

**Time in Roman Religion: One Thousand Years of Religious History**
*Gary Forsythe*

**Banishment in the Later Roman Empire, 284–476 CE**
*Daniel A. Washburn*

**Immigrant Women in Athens: Gender, Ethnicity, and Citizenship in the Classical City**
*Rebecca Futo Kennedy*

**The Tombs of Pompeii: Organization, Space, and Society**
*Virginia L. Campbell*

**The Popes and the Church of Rome in Late Antiquity**
*John Moorhead*

**Imagining Ancient Cities in Film: From Babylon to Cinecittà**
*Edited by Marta García Morcillo, Pauline Hanesworth and Óscar Lapeña Marchena*

**Rewriting Ancient Jewish History: The History of the Jews in Roman Times and the New Historical Method**
*Amram Tropper*

**Forthcoming:**

**Truth and History in the Ancient World: Pluralising the Past**
*Ian Ruffell and Lisa Irene Hau*

# Rome and Judaea

## International Law Relations, 162–100 BCE

**Linda Zollschan**

Routledge
Taylor & Francis Group
LONDON AND NEW YORK

# Contents

# Maps

# Introduction

The most crucial event in the history of Judaea, given its wide-reaching repercussions, was the voluntary approach to Rome for help during the Maccabaean revolt. Judas Maccabaeus could not have foreseen the ultimate tragic consequences of his decision, that Judaea would lose its independence and its temple in Jerusalem. Whether Judaea would have inevitably come under Roman rule without the step of petitioning to become Roman allies is a question in itself. Judas took the risk thinking Rome was a long way from his country, but, in the end, after he had made the request for aid, none came. Judas and his army were left to face the Seleucid army alone and Judas fell in battle.

The reasons why the Romans entered into diplomatic relations with the Jews and why no consequences flowed as a result of the decision taken by the senate, are best explained through an understanding of the actual type of ties formed as a result of that first embassy. The way in which the Romans treated their allies, at least in the second century BCE, varied according to whether the alliance had been formed via a treaty or friendly relations with the Roman people. Allies made by Rome through a treaty were bound permanently through mutual oath taking, whereas friends of Rome had less secure links and were continually under pressure to prove their loyalty, where failure could lead to war.

The vague wording in the First Book of Maccabees chapter 8 to describe the ties formed between Rome and the Jewish people is 'friendship and alliance'. This phrase has generated considerable comment and arguably the longest-running controversy in the study of the history of Judaea. Views divide essentially into two camps: either the Jews entered into a treaty or they received an avowal of friendship. While the entry point to the history of relations between Rome and Judaea is Judas' embassy, it is of vital importance for our understanding of the subsequent history to settle this question. The approach of this study, one that has not been considered to date, is to define the characteristics of both options in the light of the work on Roman International Law (*Völkerrecht*) and to evaluate the diplomatic instrument that best conforms to the historical and legal circumstances.

the Jews would have been problematic because it would have meant, in effect, a declaration of war by Rome against Demetrius.[11]

Viereck brought the debate back from a *philia* relationship to that of a treaty.[12] In his view, the chief arguments in favour of a treaty were the correspondence of certain phrases to other Roman treaties and the renewals of the treaty under Jonathan and Simon.[13] The early years of the twentieth century saw Niese propose that the Jews received only a friendly senatorial decision and not a treaty. In his view, the lack of any consequences flowing from a treaty told against its existence. He also was of the view that the style in which the document was written bore little resemblance to the style of the text of Roman treaties. Niese considered that the divergences from Roman usage were such that they could not be explained by the double-translation process.[14]

Täubler continued to work with the methodology of Mommsen and he compared the text of 1 Macc. 8.23–32 with other extant Roman treaties, notably those with Kibyra and Methymna. His ability to find close textual similarities with these Roman texts was assisted by some judicious emendations of the text of 1 Maccabees.[15] Täubler judged the Jewish document to be an authentic *foedus aequum* and this view has to this day found majority support.[16]

After Täubler, scholars paid more attention to the text of 1 Macc. 8.23–32 in its own right. An anachronism in the text – namely, that the Jews were obliged to assist Rome with ships before they had control of the port of Joppa – convinced Willrich of its inauthenticity.[17] Graetz did not deny the existence of a treaty, but placed it in a later period, during the time of Simon.[18] Further grounds to doubt that the Jews could have entered into a treaty were based on theological prohibitions on such an alliance.[19] Still harsher criticism alleged that the treaty was an interpolation in the text.[20]

The argument that revived the debate briefly during the 1980s was the argument from historical circumstances. The most recent assertion that the text in 1 Macc. 8.23–32 could not be a treaty because it does not accord with Roman international diplomatic practice, came from Sherwin-White: 'To grant the Jews a formal alliance when at war with Demetrius Soter was to rate the king among the enemies of the Roman people by the specific wording of the treaty'.[21] Sherwin-White had resurrected the lines of debate first put forward by Mendelssohn, Niese and Winckler.

An attack on the treaty hypothesis was launched by Gauger, whose 1977 work, *Beiträge zur jüdischen Apologetik*, presented a catalogue of objections. Since its publication, calls have been made for a detailed refutation, which to date has not been forthcoming.[22] In brief, Gauger mounted a two-pronged attack first on the authenticity of the text of 1 Macc. 8 and secondly on the likelihood of a treaty given the senate's response to other rebellious movements at that time.[23] The authenticity of chapter 8 in 1 Maccabees came under suspicion on the basis that Gauger considered it a late interpolation into the book. The Maccabaean treaty text is contained in what Gauger terms a foreign body in the text.[24] He maintains it was inserted in the work at the time of the dispute between Hyrcanus and Aristobulus in 63 BCE. Gauger lists the differences between this document in 1 Macc. 8.23–32 and other Roman treaties. His conclusion is that the text in 1 Maccabees is not a forgery but a document that has been reinterpreted by the author. Perhaps it was derived from a Hebrew or Aramaic original, from which the author freely wrote his version.[25]

Secondly, Gauger rejects the document in 1 Macc. 8.23–32 as a Roman treaty. Better suited to the Roman practice is a declaration of *libertas*, evidence of which Gauger finds in a passage in Justinus (36.3.9) that has an important role in the quest for understanding what the senate granted the Jewish embassy.[26] Gauger argues that *amicitia petita* is separate from *libertatem acceperunt* – that is, although the Jews sought *amicitia*, they did not receive it. In its place, the senate decided to grant them *libertas*.[27] Moreover, he asserts that a declaration of *libertas* formed the beginning of their diplomatic relations with Rome. This act Gauger interprets as an intervention in the sovereignty of the Seleucid Empire. However, he maintains that such an act reflected the point of view of the Romans only. The Seleucids would have taken a different view, considering Judaea was still part of their empire.[28] Gauger then introduces into the debate a few of the known declarations of *libertas*, namely, those granted to Delphi, Heraclea-on-Latmos and the Galatians. The work of Dahlheim is brought into the discussion of freedom declarations and how they were used by the Romans to keep friends and foes within borders acceptable to Rome.[29] Such declarations served as a guarantee without putting Rome under any obligation to defend them. Diplomatic measures that did not bind Rome were also to be seen in the senate's response to the rebel Timarchus, who was granted a *senatus consultum*. Gauger characterises declarations of *libertas* from Rome as statements devoid of legal meaning and political consequence, but which were effective propaganda.[30]

Gauger also finds supporting evidence for a declaration of freedom to the Jews in 161/60 BCE in Diod. 40.2, a passage that records a statement to the effect that in earlier times the senate resolved that Jews should be autonomous and should live according to their own laws. In this statement, Gauger sees a similarity to the declaration of *asylia* to Teos, an action that cost the Romans nothing yet made an impression in the East.[31]

In response, Fischer put forward the proposal that the senate decided on treaty relations with the Jews, but that the specific terms had not been ratified by Judas Maccabaeus, as he fell in battle before the envoys' return. Fischer, however, was forced to concede that no such procedure for such a ratification by the Jews is known from external evidence.[32]

Gruen in his *The Hellenistic World and the Coming of Rome* examines the treaty hypothesis anew. He concludes that it is unnecessary to claim the document was a forgery or a Jewish invention. The fact that the treaty brought no aid to the Jews argues in favour of its authenticity, as the lack of consequences of the treaty concords with his principal conclusion about Roman treaties – namely, that they were merely symbolic diplomatic instruments. He finds sufficient parallels with

24 Gauger (1977) 187–188.
25 Gauger (1977) 223.
26 Zollschan (2008).
27 Gauger (1977) 265.
28 Gauger (1977) 268.
29 Gauger (1977) 267.
30 Id.
31 Gauger (1977) 273.
32 Fischer (1980) 113.
33 Gruen (1984) 43.
34 Stern (1986) 22–26 [20–24]; followed by Gera (1998) 311; Shatzman (1999) 59 n. 35.
35 Stern (1986) 27 [25].
36 Gera (1998) 305, 305–308.
37 Gera (1998) 311.
38 Baltrusch (2002) 94–97.
39 This work not not have been possible without the subtle and astute guiding hand of Miriam Ben Zeev. For five years she encouraged me to develop my ideas. Always with good humour and a smile she read many drafts of each chapter of the thesis. Her advice always bore the marks of wise experience and I was more than happy to follow her suggestions. After the dissertation her help allowed me to make it possible to continue to research, present conference papers and to publish. This book would not have been possible without her. It is a privilege and pleasure to thank the anonymous reviewers for the many improvements they contributed to individual chapters. To Miriam Ben Zeev and Edward Dąbrowa I am grateful for your comments on chapter 7 and my very special thanks to Rochelle Altman and Chris Seeman who heroically read the whole manuscript. I hope that I have incorporated the suggestions of all to everyone's satisfaction. I take full responsibility for any errors that may remain.

# 1 New evidence

## The Roman–Jewish friendship tablet[1]

The First Book of Maccabees records the dispatch of a diplomatic mission to Rome by Judas Maccabaeus in 162 BCE, during the final stages of the Jewish revolt against King Antiochus IV of Syria. Two Greek-speaking Jews, Jason and Eupolemus, were chosen to go to Rome and seek help against Syria from the Romans. They were granted an audience in the senate and were successful in obtaining 'friendship and alliance' (φιλία καὶ συμμαχία). The senate presented them with bronze tablets as a record of their decision and instructed Jason and Eupolemus to take them back to Jerusalem to be set up there as a memorial of the ties between the Romans and the Jews.[2]

### The controversy over friendship for the Jews

The first mention of friendship between the Romans and the Jews in Graeco-Roman sources is to be found in Justinus' summary of a 44-volume work no longer extant called the *Liber Historiarum Philippicarum et totius mundi origines et terrae situs* by Pompeius Trogus, written during the Augustan Principate. In it, he writes:

> *A Demetrio cum desciuissent, amicitia Romanorum petita primi omnium ex orientalibus libertatem acceperunt.* [36.3.9]

The embassy, Justinus writes, was the first from the Eastern peoples to seek friendship with Rome.[3] Other ancient writers corroborate that the diplomatic relations at this time were in the form of *amicitia*. Among these we may include Josephus (*B.J.* 1.38), Justinus (36.3.9), Eusebius (Ol. 155/1, p. 126 Schoene) and Jerome (*Chron.* p. 141, b, 1.23 ff. Helm). On the basis of these passages, Herzfeld in 1863 determined that the Jews entered into a treaty of friendship with the Romans.[4] The fact that the Romans never came to the aid of the Jews during their revolt against Syria was for Mendelssohn and Niese indicative that the two peoples had settled on a friendship rather than a formal treaty.[5] The consensus remains, however, that the Jews entered into a treaty; however, more recently dissenting voices have emerged, proposing that the Romans conferred on the Jews other forms of diplomatic relations.[6]

*Figure 1.1* General view of the Forum of Augustus (photograph by the author).

The remains of the church of San Basilio were uncovered in the course of demolition work to 'liberate' the Forum of Augustus from the accretion of modern construction,[27] a project conceived by Corrado Ricci (in 1911),[28] which came to fruition under the patronage of Mussolini in the years 1924–1932.[29] In the course of Ricci's excavations, in order to reach down 7 metres to the Augustan level,[30] he had to remove nineteenth-century and mediaeval buildings. In the process of this removal, he found the earliest remains of the monastery of San Basilio. The church on the podium of the Temple of Mars Ultor was small, measuring only 15.3m by 13.1m; see figures 1.2 and 1.3.[31]

Ricci dated his finds to the ninth century[32] on the basis of several decorated marble fragments of a ciborium (a permanent vaulted canopy over an altar).[33] Ermini, in his multi-volume study on sculpture in the Middle Ages, dates these to the first half of the ninth century.[34] Against a ninth-century date, Hamilton, in his study on the Greek churches in Rome in the tenth century, considered that architectural styles had not changed with sufficient rapidity to provide a precise dating. He brought forward in favour of his date in the tenth century the fact that the monastery of San Basilio was not mentioned in the *Liber Pontificalis* from 885–891, which records the gifts that the popes made to Roman monasteries. Hamilton is, however, the first to admit that there were monasteries and convents in existence in Rome that are not always mentioned in the literary sources.[35] Bordi, in his study on the mediaeval frescoes in the church of Sant'Adriano in the Forum Romanum, preferred a date earlier than Hamilton's and he suggested the late ninth century.[36] Ermini, in his multi-volume work on mediaeval sculpture in Italy, dates the church to the first half of the ninth century on the basis of both the decorative fragments that Ricci found and the period when Greek monks were fleeing north to Rome.[37]

Plutarch records this event as follows: 'Cicero went up with a great company to the Capitol, and there tore away and destroyed the tablet'.[123] The Romans called this *tabulum refigere*, meaning 'to unfasten something attached to a wall',[124] which they took literally.[125] When Julius Caesar wanted to rescind grants of citizenship, he took down from the wall the bronze tablet recording those rights.[126] Josephus relates that the senate and people of Antiochia petitioned the emperor, Titus, to expel the Jews from their city and, when that failed, they requested that he annul the rights of the Jews and asked that the bronze tablets, on which their rights were inscribed, be removed.[127] In cases where the law or decree was particularly hated, taking the tablets down from the wall was not sufficient: they were also destroyed.[128]

## Modern excavations

The mention of the bronze tablet in the *Mirabilia* has been accorded virtually no scholarly attention. The compiler of the *Mirabilia*[129] knew that it had once existed, but he informed his readers that it was no longer in the church. It was definitely not on the site when the land was given to the Knights of St John of Malta between the end of the twelfth and the beginning of the thirteenth centuries,[130] a date after the circulation of the *Mirabilia*.

The bronze tablet was mentioned in 1140 and continued to be known in the sixteenth century when the guidebook was still sold to pilgrims coming to Rome. The tablet, while still known, had long since disappeared. During the course of Ricci's excavations during the demolition of the buildings on the podium of the Temple of Mars Ultor in the late 1920s, he uncovered fragments of bronze, which had been deliberately broken up into pieces, and which still displayed clear signs of the considerable force that had been used to destroy them.[131] He was surprised at the violence he saw in the marks made from the sharp points of the implements that had been used to break the bronze apart. The bronze pieces that he found bore signs of gilding.[132] The gilding of letters in inscriptions was a well-known Roman practice.[133] Ricci tentatively suggested that the bronze came from thin sheets that he proposed had been used as cladding over the white marble that covered the podium; see Figure 1.4.[134] He also found the remains of iron clamps that had been used to hold the bronze in place. Ricci referred to the *Mirabilia* and the bronze tablet that had once hung in the church of San Basilio. Regrettably these excavations were not fully documented and, to my knowledge, no photograph exists of these bronze fragments. Much material from the Forum of Augustus was simply thrown away.[135]

Various suggestions have been made to explain the presence of these bronze fragments at the podium of the Temple of Mars Ultor found at the Augustan level. Platner and Ashby considered that they were the remains of bronze reliefs that might have decorated the marble cladding of the podium.[136] Traces of the marble cladding that once covered the podium have been published by Ganzert.[137] He rejects the idea that the podium had been clad with bronze. The pattern of plug holes in the marble does not permit such a

## Notes

1 I would like to express my appreciation to professors Miriam Ben Zeev (Ben-Gurion University of the Negev) and Jonathan Price (Tel Aviv University) for their insightful comments on an earlier draft of this chapter. Any errors, here and throughout the book, are the responsibility of the author. Martin Conde gave invaluable assistance in providing the literature in Italian that was hard to obtain. He maintains a photographic collection on the Forum of Augustus on his website: http://imperialfora.blogspot.com (accessed 12 December 2008).

2 1 Macc. 8.17–22. Verses 23–31 purport to be the text inscribed on that bronze tablet.

3 On this passage see Zollschan (2008).

4 Herzfeld (1863) 294.

5 Mendelssohn (1875) 99 and Niese (1906) 824.

6 For the consensus, Gera is representative (1998) 305–311. I have argued elsewhere, in Zollschan (2005), that the Jews did not enter into a treaty, although there I did not explore the question of 'friendship'/*amicitia*, as is the focus of this study.

7 In some editions it appears as chapter 21. Full Latin text available at http://www.thelatinlibrary.com/mirabilia.html (accessed 11 December 2008); English translation of F.M. Nicholls (1889) *The Marvels of Rome or a Picture of the Golden City*, London–Rome is available at https://archive.org/stream/.../marvelsromeorapOOnich-goog_djvu.txt (accessed 11 December 2008). In the latter work, the passage on the bronze tablet may be found on p. 93.The earliest Latin manuscript is from the late twelfth century and is held in the Vatican Library (Cod. Vat. 3973). An English work by a Magister Gregorius, the *De Mirabilibus Urbis Romae*, from the twelfth century, is a work independent of the *Mirabilia*. See Rushforth (1919) 14–15. There was a thirteenth-century translation into 'Roman vulgate' entitled *Le miracole de Roma*: see D'Onofino (1988) 9. Italian, German, French, English and Dutch editions were made in the fifteenth and sixteenth centuries. See Saastamoinen (2006) 3, n. 15. Most editions continued to be in Latin: see Miedema (1996) 95–144. On the question of the political purpose of the *Mirabilia* relating to the *renovatio senatus* of 1143–1144, see most recently Herklotz (2000) 215–217, a view that had been rejected by Miedema (1996) 1–11.

8 Translation by the author. Text: Jordan (1871) 470.

9 Heuss (1933) 35 and Paradisi (1947) 178.

10 Gutman (1963) 77.

11 Shatzman (1992) 32–33, 46.

12 *CIL* $1^2$ 726 = 6.30927 and *CIL* $1^2$ 730 = 6.30922. See Degrassi (1951–1952) 21, 27, 30.

13 Cf. Meyer (2004) 97.

14 Greenlees-Zollschan (2005) ch. 6.

15 Date in fourth or fifth century: Lanciani (1890a) 87. Date in 8th century: D'Onofino (1988) 10. See for example *CIL* 6.1014. For other sylloges of Roman inscriptions prior to the 11th century see Silvagni (1921) 227–229.

16 D'Onofino (1988) 11.

17 Greenhalgh (1989) 172.

18 Greenhalgh (1989) 173.

19 *Mirabilia*, ch. 32.

20 Valentini and Zucchetti (1940–1954) 10.

21 Lanciani (1890a) col. 519.

22 In Kinney (2007) 252.

23 All dates are CE unless otherwise stated. For a date of approximately 1143 see Duchesne (1904) 479.

24 Sources from ninth and tenth centuries: Limentani (1970) 256. That the *Mirabilia* represents Rome in 1000, see Kinney (2007) 235–236.

25 Federici (1899) 272.

26 Hamilton (1961) 11.
27 A project Ricci had advocated in 1911 – see Ricci (1911) 445–455 – but which was put into effect only during the rule of Mussolini.
28 Ricci (1911) 445–455.
29 Leone and Margiotta (2007) 17.
30 Ganzert and Kockel (1988) 157. For a view of the dense maze of buildings that had been built over the forum since the sixteenth century, see Leone and Margiotta (2007) 55.
31 Meneghini and Valenzani (2007) 141.
32 Gerkan (1927) 58.
33 For photographs of the pieces see Leone and Margiotta (2007) 127–128, 132–133.
34 Ermini (1974) 17.
35 Hamilton (1961) 44.
36 Valenzani (2007) 141 and Bordi (2000).
37 Ermini (1974) 68.
38 Ricci (1926) 6.
39 Salvatorelli (1938) 469.
40 Hamilton (1961) 10.
41 Meneghini and Valenzani (1996) 82–83.
42 Salvatorelli (1938) 469.
43 Hamilton (1961) 6.
44 Saastamoinen (2006) 3.
45 Dunbabin (1985) 32.
46 Dunbabin (1985) 35.
47 Dunbabin (1985) 32, 40.
48 John of Antioch, Frg. 202.
49 Religious significance: Coates-Stephens (2002) 289–290.
50 The most recent mention is in Arton (1908) 203.
51 Jordan (1871) 470–472.
52 Rossi (1888) 202–203; Delehay (1961) 84, n. 1.
53 *CIL* 1.198.
54 For the other *elogia* see Degrassi (1937).
55 For a plan of the Forum of Augustus see Ganzert and Kockel (1988) 198. This plan should now be updated to include a third exedra that was demolished to make way for the Forum of Trajan. See Coates-Stephens (2008) 300.
56 Uncle: Elvers (2005) 1055.
57 *CIL* 1.198.
58 Coates-Stephens (2002) 289.
59 Limentani (1970) 254–256.
60 Limentani (1970) 260–261.
61 Cappelli (1928) 194.
62 Toebelmann (1927) 36 and photograph fig. 36.
63 For the route of the *cloaca maxima* under the Forum of Augustus see Lanciani (1890b) plates 7 and 8, between pages 112 and 113.
64 Meneghini and Valenzani (1996) 139.
65 Meneghini and Valenzani (1996) 141–142 and fig. 150.
66 For a plan of the monastery see Meneghini and Valenzani (1996) 140 fig. 148.
67 The thickness of the wall may be gauged from the photo in Leone and Margiotta (2007) 99. See also pp. 88–89, 97 and 112–113.
68 For the purpose of the high wall and a photograph of the enclosure wall from the side of the Suburra, see Platner and Ashby (1929) 222.
69 Toebelmann (1927) 36.
70 Ricci (1930) 176, 181.
71 Ermini (1974) 19.
72 Ferrari (1957) 63; Johannes Diaconus quoted on p. 62.

73 Ganzert in Ganzert and Kockel (1988) 162, fig. 65, p. 160.
74 Hamilton (1961) 10.
75 Caesar: Suet. *Iul.* 44.1. Vow in 42 BCE: Ov. *Fast.* 5. 573.
76 Suet. *Aug.* 29.2; Ovid *F.* 5.569–578.
77 Kockel in Ganzert and Kockel (1988) 156.
78 Suet. *Aug.* 29.2.
79 Suet. *Calig.* 44.2.
80 Suet. 29.1f. Cf. Dio 55.10.2–5; Suet. *Calig.* 44.2.
81 Anderson (1984) 90.
82 *ILS* 18; *ILLRP* 511.
83 *IGGR* 1.118 = *CIL* $1^2$ 588.
84 Crawford (1996) 293–296.
85 Suet. *Vesp.* 8.5.
86 See the *Senatus consultum de Asclepiade* from 78 BCE (RDGE no. 22 = RGE no. 66) l. 25; Pucci Ben Zeev (1998) 385.
87 Examples include the treaty between Rome and Kibyra (*OGIS* 762) ll. 12–15; the treaty with Astypalaia (*IGRR* 4.1028) ll. 6–7 and 12–15; the treaty with Maroneia (*SEG* 35 (1985) 823) ll. 22–26; the treaty with Pergamum (*OGIS* no. 466) ll. 4–61; the treaty with Epidaurus (*SEG* 13.382) ll. 7–8.
88 Mitchell (2005).
89 Mitchell (2005) 167 and plates 29, 40 and 41.
90 Private conversation on 30 August 2008 at University of Lampeter, Wales.
91 Polyb. 3.26.1.
92 See also Jos. *Ant.* 14.188, 14.266.
93 Pucci Ben Zeev (1998) 384.
94 Meyer (2004) 99, n. 31.
95 Temple of Dius Fidius: D.H. *Ant. Rom.* 4.58.4. Temple of Diana: D.H. *Ant. Rom.* 4.26.4–5. Atrium Libertatis: Festus p. 277L. Temple of the Nymphs: Cic. *Mil.* 73. Temple of Castor and Pollux: Livy 7.11.16. Temple of Saturn: Cassius Dio 45.17.3.
96 Cic. *Phil.* 1.7.16.
97 *N.H.* 34.21.99: *Usus aeris ad perpetuitatem monimentorum iam pridem tralatus est tabuleis aereis, in quibus publicae constitutiones inciduntur.*
98 Williamson (1989) 174.
99 Williamson (1987) 169.
100 Pliny *Ep.* 8.6.15: *sic quasi foedera antiqua sic quasi sacrae leges.*
101 *Carm.* 3.30, l. 1.
102 Williamson (1987) 178–179.
103 Cic. *Off.* 3.111. Fraenkel (1916) 187–189; Heinze (1929) 163–166; Boyancé (1964b); Boyancé (1972) 106–109; Freyburger (1986).
104 Tupet (1976) 39–42.
105 Culham (1984) 23; id. (1989) 110.
106 Williamson (1987) 174–176.
107 For examples see Pucci Ben Zeev (1996).
108 Cic. *Off.* 3.1.6, 66.
109 Bonnefond-Coudry (1987) 251–258, 270. For the functions of the Temple of Mars Ultor, see Cassius Dio 55.10.2–5. For centre of the army, see Taylor (1931) 200–202.
110 Anderson (1984) 97.
111 Bonnefond-Coudry (1987) 270.
112 Cic. *Cat.* 3.19; *Div.* 1.12.19.
113 Meyer (2004) 100, n. 36.
114 Suet. *Vesp.* 8.4.
115 Meyer (2004) 101.
116 *CIL* 1.583.
117 Williamson (1987) 162 and n. 6.

118 *CIL* 12.593.
119 Williamson (1987) 163.
120 Meyer (2004) 99.
121 *Dig*. 48.13.10.8.
122 Dio 39.21.1–2; Plut. *Cic.* 34.1.
123 Plut. *Cic.* 34.1. Translation: Perrin (1968) 169.
124 Glare (1982) 1595.
125 Cic. *Phil.* 12.12.
126 Cic. *Fam.* 13.36.1.
127 Jos. *Bell.* 7.106–110.
128 Plut. *Cic.* 34.1.
129 The author of the *Mirabilia* is considered to be Benedict, Canon of St Peter's Basilica. See Kinney (2007) 236.
130 Valenzani (2007) 141.
131 Ricci (1930) 188.
132 These bronze fragments were from the Roman period because of the depth at which they were found. Their purpose remains open to speculation. They were most assuredly not bronze cladding for the podium. See Gerkan (1927) 58 and Ganzert (1996) 40, 99, 223. The podium was clad in marble. For pictures of the fragments of the marble cladding see Ganzert (1996) 97, plate 46, nos. 2 and 3; plate 47, no. 2 and INV 2050, p. 189.
133 See, for example, a shrine on the Sacred Way, excavated in 1878 in Lanciani (1892) 207; Williamson (1987) 166 n. 23.
134 Ricci (1930) 188.
135 Parker (1997) 307. Enquiries about these bronze fragments to the Musei Capitolini, where the material from Ricci's excavations are housed (except for the marble remains), have to date not produced any results.
136 Platner and Ashby (1929) 223.
137 Ganzert (1996) 96–97, plates 46 nos. 2 and 3, 47 no. 2.
138 Ganzert (1996) 99.
139 Ganzert (1996) 40–41.
140 Ganzert (1996) 60.
141 For a reconstruction of what the Imperial Fora may have looked like in the Middle Ages, see Meneghini and Valenzani (1996) 114, showing Trajan's Forum, the Forum of Augustus and the Forum of Peace. One can readily see how little remained of the Forum of Augustus. The two fora standing on either side were left relatively intact.
142 Ricci (1926) 8.
143 Susini (1982) 116–118. Kloos (1979) 893–901. Limentani (1970) 260, n. 42 for examples of false inscriptions.
144 Kloos (1979).
145 See note 143.
146 Extensive extracts from Zollschan (2012b) have been reprinted with the kind permission of Tusculanum Press.

*Map 2.1* Judaea

# 2 The timing of the embassy

When the envoys departed and returned to Jerusalem, cannot be determined from the First Book of Maccabees alone. The question of the timing of the Jewish Embassy has a bearing on what Judas planned to obtain from the Roman Senate. The chronological relationship of the embassy to the final stages of the Maccabaean revolt alters our perspective on Judas' expectations of the mission to Rome. Despite the uncertainty of the dating, there may exist another method that would help to indicate when the envoys were actually in Rome. Before starting that investigation, it is important to review previous scholarly attempts to date the first Jewish Embassy to Rome. Efforts to pinpoint when the envoys set out for the city and the date of their return are hampered by the fact that no date is given in 1 Maccabees 8. Commonly, the chronology of the departure and the return of the envoys is measured according to the placement of chapter 8 in 1 Maccabees. This entails assigning a date to the interval between the end of chapter 7, which tells of the death of Nicanor, and the beginning of chapter 9, which opens with the return of Bacchides to Judaea. Various time periods have been proposed for this interval. The length of time suggested varies from only one or two months, according to Grimm and Abel,[1] to a maximum estimate of up to thirteen months, according to Welhausen.[2] The first estimation, of one to two months, does not permit sufficient time for the long voyage to Rome.[3] The second reckoning has not won general acceptance. However, rather than interpret the position of chapter 8 as marking the date of departure of the envoys, it is possible to consider its position as reflecting the date of the conclusion of the alliance. Grimm first noticed that the narrator of 1 Maccabees bound together the sending of an embassy and the determination of a treaty.[4]

Bévenot attempted a dating based on accounts of sea voyages and from the dates when weather permitted such voyages. He calculated that, according to nautical data, the last favourable date for departure from Judaea would have been 11 November in the autumn of 161 BCE and the first favourable time for departure from Rome would have been 5 March 160 BCE.[5] Between 10 November and 10 March each year the seas were closed to shipping, due not so much to the danger of storms as to the lack of visibility for navigation.[6] The Romans extended these dates: for them, the sailing season did not open until April.[7]

We turn at this point to an entirely different approach. Earlier in chapter 8 of the First Book of Maccabees, a description is given of the Roman political system. In verse 16, it is most puzzling to read that the Romans put their faith in one man to rule over them for a year. How can we reconcile one-man rule with the founding principle of the Roman Republic of collegiality, as exemplified in the two consuls elected for one year?[8] The system was designed to prevent the return of a *regnum* or tyranny, which was incompatible with *libertas* (liberty).[9] It may very well be that this is a reference to the atypical political situation in Rome when the Jewish envoys were there. Some have interpreted this verse as a negative comment on the Hasmonaean kings, looking back from a later era.[10] Another possibility is that this verse is a comment on contemporary politics in Rome, based on the report that the two envoys brought back with them. The principal evidence lies in the fact that in 162 BCE there actually was one-man rule in Rome for a time. It was a constitutional measure with precedent reaching back as far as the days of the Roman kings, where provision was made for one-man rule in specific circumstances.

In 162 BCE the two consuls abdicated. As consul in 163 BCE, Ti. Sempronius Gracchus had presided over the elections for 162 and he went to his province of Sardinia.[11] While there,[12] he was reading the books of the augurs (to which he had access as a member of the augural college[13]) and he realised that the election was invalid because he had crossed the *pomerium* (the sacred boundary of Rome) twice without taking the auspices the second time. Gracchus raised the matter with the augural college, who in turn referred it to the senate, who ordered the two consuls to abdicate.[14] Figure 2.1 shows the names of the consuls for 163 and 162 BCE from the Fasti Consulares, displayed in the Museo Capitolini in Rome. In the third line is found 'vitio facti', meaning that the consuls were elected through a faulty process.

The election in itself was still valid, so that it could not simply be annulled. The problem lay in the mistake or flaw (*uitium*) in the auspices, for which there was no remedy. In a case where the magistrates had entered office and were carrying out their duties, all their actions were tainted by the invalid auspices. This necessitated the abdication of the consuls of 162 BCE. Due to the flaw in their election, they could not preside over the election for their successors, as part of their normal duties. The auspices were tainted and the only solution was to have the auspices revert to the senate as a body who would choose an *interrex*. This was established augural law; the problem had occurred previously in 404 BCE.[15]

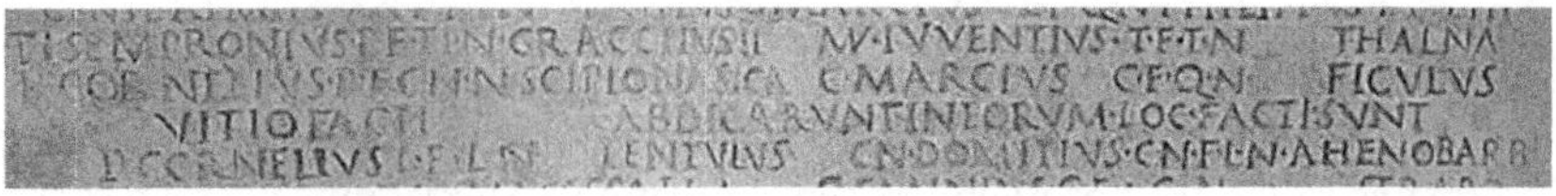


*Figure 2.1* The names of the consuls for 163 and 162 BCE from the Fasti Consulares (photograph by the author with permission from the Musei Capitolini)

In 162 BCE, Rome was without its two consuls during their time in their provinces; and on their return, they abdicated. For a time Rome had only one consul: P. Cornelius Scipio Nasica Corculum in Corsica was but a short distance from Rome. He could return in four days. He would have had to resign on arrival. Meanwhile his colleague, C. Marcius Figulus, had to travel from Gaul. Until he arrived, Rome had only one consul. Once both had resigned, Rome was without its heads of state. In their place, the senate appointed an *interrex*,[16] a position that was a relic from the days of the regal period.[17] His function was to hold consular elections for suffect consuls (substitute consuls). During an *interregnum* the constitution was suspended and the *interrex* presided over the senate and administered the Republic.[18] Patrician senators nominated one of their own to be *interrex*.[19] His *interregnum* was created in order to elect new suffect consuls. The normal procedure for consular elections meant that candidates put their name forward to the presiding consul at least three weeks before the election. The consul would issue a decree announcing the date of the elections, then the names of the candidates would be published.[20] During an *interregnum*, this procedure was replaced by the nomination of candidates by the *interrex*.[21] It may even be said that the *interrex* created the consuls.[22] Given the power of the *interrex* in 162 BCE, it is not surprising that the Jews thought that the Romans obeyed one man. The name of the *interrex* or *interreges* is unknown.[23] Broughton considers the *interrex* was L. Aemilius Paullus, but this cannot be. Plutarch mentions his illness that kept him away from Rome after he had fulfilled his duties as censor in 164 BCE. On the only occasion he returned to Rome, he died within three days.[24]

The question arises as to whether the envoys witnessed the unusual events in Rome in 162 BCE. Perhaps it is time to rethink the timing of the embassy. The underpinnings of a date of 161 BCE are primarily the position of chapter 8 in 1 Maccabees, the date of the Fannius letter in Jos. *Ant.* 14.233 and the sequence in which Josephus placed events. I have argued previously that the placement of the Fannius letter by Josephus among documents dating to 49 BCE should stand and I have rejected Niese's arguments for a date in 161 BCE on the basis of the information internal to the letter.[25] Arguing for a date in the first century BCE is the dangerous situation on Cos, the addressees being the archons of Cos, and the background of the civil war between Pompey and Caesar.

Chapter 8 is inserted after the victory over Nicanor at the end of chapter 7 and before the return of Bacchides in chapter 9. The time interval between these two events has been variously calculated at between one to two months or even thirteen months.[26] The Day of Nicanor is dated to 13 Adar and historians cannot agree whether the year was 161 or 160 BCE.[27] The interval between the Day of Nicanor and the return of the Seleucid army can be extended somewhat if we adopt the suggestion that there may have been an Adar sheni (a second month of Adar) during that year.[28] The return of the Seleucid army under Bacchides is dated to Nisan (April/May) 160.[29]

Josephus gives the following sequence of events: the High Priest Alcimus died and Judas became High Priest, then comes the Jewish embassy and the senatorial decree, after which the death of Judas is recorded.[30] Long ago Grimm suggested that chapter 8 was inserted not at the point when the envoys were despatched, but at the time of their return. Chapter 8 records not only the decision of Judas to send Jason and Eupolemus to Rome, but also the successful outcome of the embassy.[31] A compelling argument against 161 or 160 BCE for the despatch of the embassy to Rome resides in the fact that it would have set off after Timachus gained no military aid from Rome despite having received a senatorial decree in his favour. His revolt was quashed in winter 161/60. Why send an embassy to Rome after learning that the senate was long on words and short on action?

If the embassy returned in 161 BCE, when would they have left Jerusalem and when would they have been in Rome? I propose that Judas was spurred to appeal to the Roman Senate after hearing that Demetrius (later Demetrius I Soter of Syria) had disobeyed the senate, had escaped from Rome, and had landed in Phoenicia. Politically, the timing makes sense. Demetrius had flouted two decisions of the senate that denied his request to be released as a hostage and to leave Rome. Judas could count on using the senate's hostility towards Demetrius in his favour. The future king left Rome in the summer of 162 BCE and his arrival in Phoenicia was in early autumn 162 BCE; he travelled on a regular Carthaginian ship that landed before the heavy autumnal storms.[32] It was clear once he landed in Tripolis that, with the Seleucid army having rallied with him, there was little obstacle to his path to the throne.[33] Demetrius announced that he was acting to avenge the murder of the Roman ambassador in Syria, which he blamed on Lysias.[34] In Antioch, Lysias and Antiochus V were imprisoned and killed. With the death of Lysias came the death of the truce between the Seleucid king and the Jews. It was all too easy to predict that the consequences would be a renewal of fighting in Judaea. In Jerusalem, preparations were being made. In this reconstruction of the chronology, it is suggested that the Jewish envoys left Jerusalem as soon as they had received reports of Demetrius' return. That would place their departure in early autumn – that is, in September 162 (Julian). A voyage at this time of year via Alexandria would take 26 days.[35] They would arrive in Rome in October 162 (Julian).[36]

Now we turn to when the *interregnum* may have occurred. The loss of Livy's account after Book 45 has meant the absence of information on 162 BCE. The consular *fasti* inform us of their abdication and the election of suffect consuls for the remainder of the year.[37] Without Livy's account for this year, we do not know when the *interregnum* happened and we cannot say how long it lasted. Records from previous *interregna* show that an *interregnum* could last from 10 days to 70 days, or even longer.[38]

The information that we do have from Livy about the consuls at the beginning of other consular years, enables a reconstruction of the time that elapsed between the election of the consuls and their abdication so as to demonstrate the possibility that the Jewish envoys were at Rome during the *interregnum*. The consular year at this period of Rome's past began on the Ides of March – that is, 15 March.[39] This date is according to the Roman calendar marked (R). The Roman lunar calendar required the insertion of an intercalendary month of 23 days every alternate year.[40] If this was not done, the calendar could run ahead of the seasons.

In 168 BCE, we can see that the Roman calendar was running ahead of the Julian calendar by two and a half months. A lunar eclipse before the battle of Pydna occurred on 28 June 168 (Julian). Livy dates it to 4 September (R).[41] Between 168 and 162 there were two known intercalations in 167 and 166, with perhaps another in 164.[42] If two intercalations were performed then in 162 the calendar was running 21 days ahead; however, if three were made, it was running six days behind the Julian calendar.

A reconstruction of the consular activity of Marcius Figulus can be suggested from what is known about their general practice and normal duties in Rome before the consuls usually departed for their provinces. The consuls remained in Rome for a month (15 March to 15 April), to be present in the senate when foreign envoys came to plead their cause. A consul had to see to the expiation of prodigies and to levy troops. Only after the two consuls celebrated the *feriae Latinae* were they free to leave Rome and go to their provinces.[43] This Latin festival was celebrated on the Alban mount for four days around the Nones of May to June.[44] Marcius Figulus would not have been able to leave until late May at the earliest. It took 50 days for him, marching with his army, to reach Gaul. His arrival would have been in July/August.

The consuls appeared to have been settled in their provinces when a senatorial letter reached them with the news that they had to abdicate. The return of Ti. Sempronius Gracchus to give evidence would have been necessary in the enquiries that were made into the conduct of the elections under his authority in 163 BCE. Polybius informs us that a few days after the senate learned that Demetrius had escaped from Rome they appointed an embassy to go to the East, naming Ti. Sempronius Gracchus as one of its members.[45] This means Gracchus was in Rome in August 162 (Julian). If a letter was sent in July/August, Figulus would have received it in August/September. It would have taken him 40 days to return by himself or 12 days by sea. By this calculation, he arrived in Rome in late September/early October (R), which translates into early October (Julian) after three months had been intercalated, or early September (Julian) if only two months had previously been intercalated. Figulus resigned and the senate met to choose an *interrrex*. The *interregnum* can be dated to September/October 162 (Julian).[46] If the Jewish envoys had arrived before Figulus, they would have been aware of only one consul. If they had come to Rome after Figulus had abdicated, they would have known only the one-man rule of the *interregnum*.

If the Jewish envoys were in Rome in October 162 (Julian), they could not have been able to stay long, as the sailing season ended on 10 November (Julian) and did not resume until 10 April.[47] Although the Mediterranean was not totally closed to shipping, caution was exercised due to the weather and the short hours of daylight.[48] It would have proved difficult to find private ships willing to take the long voyage in winter from Italy to the coast of the Levant. By the time the Jewish envoys had arrived in Rome, Ti. Sempronius Gracchus had already departed on the embassy to the East. Polybius informs us that Gracchus was 'very kindly disposed to Demetrius'.[49] His absence from the senate cleared the way for a favourable decision for the Jewish ambassadors, Jason and Eupolemus.

A placement of the embassy in 162 BCE results in a new sequence of events: the Jewish embassy is in Rome before the embassy of Timarchus, who also led a revolt from the Seleucids. For the embassy of Timarchus, the dates are not clearly delineated in our sources. Extant is a brief mention of the revolt in Diodorus (31.27a), Appian (*Syr.* 45–47) and Pompeius Trogus Prol. 34. The coins that Timarchus issued during the revolt, cannot assist because they are undated. Cuneiform records pose problems as well.[50] On the evidence at hand, therefore, the sequence of events appears to be that Demetrius came to the throne and deposed Heracleides (Timarchus' brother) from his position of finance minister, which prompted Timarchus not to recognise the new king's authority. Timarchus then sent an embassy to Rome, which returned with a *senatus consultum*, and this emboldened him to commence a full-scale military revolt.[51] Timarchus' embassy is dated to 161 BCE by the placement of the account in the work of Diodorus.[52] The revolt began in spring 161, according to Volkmann.[53] If these calculations are indeed correct, Timarchus was inspired by the example of Judas.

Their return took 20 days. This would place their departure from Rome before 10 November and arrival back in Jerusalem in late November or the beginning of December 162 (Julian). It is frequently assumed that Judas had died before the outcome of his initiative in sending an embassy to Rome was known to him.[54] When the envoys arrived in Jerusalem, Judas was still alive; he was also alive before the battle of Adasa, where he won a decisive victory over the Seleucid general, Nicanor, who was killed in that battle.

Why did Judas not activate the diplomatic agreements made in Rome and use the senate's letter, to prevent the campaign of 161? The envoys returned with a letter from the senate. After the alliance document in the First Book of Maccabees, verses 31–32 recount the contents of a letter to Demetrius. It was not the task of Judas to produce the senatorial letter, which in any case was addressed to Demetrius the king and not to the generals of the Seleucid army. It had to be shown to the king directly and by a Roman ambassador sent by the senate to carry out its instructions. The threat of war demanded that it be conveyed by a Roman ambassador. A letter containing a senatorial decree was expected to be obeyed. It trumped any order from a Roman general, as is revealed in the purpose of Cn. Octavius' embassy to the Greek states in 170/69. He was tasked with informing the Greeks that orders from a Roman general were only to be obeyed if they were based on a decree from the senate.[55] The mechanism to be employed may be seen when Popillius Laenas, the Roman envoy sent by the senate, confronted Antiochus IV at Eleusis, a suburb of Alexandria, in 168 BCE and demanded that he withdraw his army from Egypt or he would no longer be considered a friend of Rome.[56] The consequence of losing the friendship of Rome meant, in effect, a declaration of war (see Chapter 4). The account of the senatorial letter in the First Book of Maccabees follows the same formula. It states that the Jews are friends and allies of Rome and threatens a 'just war' against Demetrius if the Jews come to the senate with further complaints. When confronted with a letter from the senate, a ruler faced a dilemma: if he obeyed there was a degree of humiliation and if he refused the senate's demands he ran the risk that Rome would lose patience and embark on war.[57] Judas died before another embassy could be sent and Tiberius Gracchus only met with the king in person in 160 BCE, by which time Judas had been killed in battle.[58]

The next purpose of the magistrate was, according to Livy, to provide the envoys with lodging and entertainment at the state's expense, as was their right as envoys on Rome's list, the *formula amicorum*.[59] Those *legati* who were registered in the *formula amicorum*, were provided with official lodgings in a *Villa Publica*[60] inside the city boundary, with entertainment, food, utensils and clothing.[61] In the majority of cases, the senate awarded the envoys a sustenance allowance as a lump sum or sometimes as an amount per day.[62] The communities whose business was urgent due to the threat of war, or because an armistice was due to expire, could come at any time of the year.[63] In 190 BCE Aetolians came to Rome seeking a treaty. They were pressed for time because of the shortness of an armistice.[64] In 177 BCE a delegation from Latin communities approached the senate regarding the alarming numbers of their people who were migrating to the city of Rome.[65] In 168 BCE Egyptian ambassadors came to denounce the aggression of Antiochus IV. Their case was considered urgent and their audience in the senate was held before the voting that Aemilius Paullus be sent to Macedonia.[66] In fact, according to some calculations, some 60 per cent of embassies came to Rome outside the usual first month of the consular year.[67] If both consuls were absent from Rome, this did not mean that the senate could not receive ambassadors.[68] It fell then to the praetor peregrinus to introduce the envoys.[69]

In 162 BCE the most powerful man in Rome was M. Aemilius Lepidus: he held two lifelong positions that gave him the powers that the ancient kings of Rome had possessed. Since 179 BCE he had been *pontifex maximus*, the high priest of Rome (a position held for life) and simultaneously *princeps senatus*, the leader of the senate. The man who led the senate had to be one of the *principes ciuitatis* – that is, one of the leading citizens of Rome.[70] His reappointment was virtually automatic: the only way he could be removed was by expulsion from the senate itself.[71] Thus, the *princeps senatus* held tenure for life. In all, he held control of the senate continuously for just over 26 years. This was a rare combination of power, attained by L. Cornelius Lentulus Caudinus before him and P. Cornelius Scipio Nasica Corculum after him.[72] The holder of the office embodied the *grauitas* and dignity of the institution of the senate itself. Not only was it considered a position of high honour, but it conferred a recognition of the holder's personal authority and moral standing. As such, the *princeps senatus* could wield substantial political influence.[73] He exercised considerable control over the day-to-day running of the senate. He decided where in Rome it would meet; he summoned meetings and adjourned them. He set the agenda for each meeting and had the right to speak first in debate (*primus rogatus*). He maintained order and applied the rules, acting as chairman. He was the representative of the senate in meeting with embassies from foreign countries and he wrote official letters on behalf of the senate.[74]

During Lepidus' tenure in office, Polybius records two occasions when he used his influence to obtain the foreign policy result he desired from the senate. In 169 BCE ambassadors from Egypt came to request a renewal of their friendship (*amicitia*) with the Romans. Lepidus anticipated that, if the senators became aware that the Sixth Syrian War had broken out (between Egypt and Antiochus IV), the attempt to renew friendly relations would not go well for the envoys. So Lepidus advised them not to mention in the senate the outbreak of war.[75] The second episode surrounded the visit of Charops, the tyrant of Epirus, to Rome in 160 BCE.[76] Lepidus was disturbed by accounts of his brutal killing of anti-Roman elements in Epirus and refused to admit him to his home. Although the tyrant was granted an audience in the senate, not only were his requests denied, but the senate voted to set up a commission of enquiry into the murders. It would appear that, in the 160s, in order for a foreign embassy to obtain a favourable decision from the senate, the active support of Lepidus was required. The success of the Jewish embassy may be attributed to the support of Lepidus. He decided what would be discussed in the senate and he spoke first on issues and so guided the debate towards the outcome favoured by him. For the Jewish ambassadors, this created the impression that Rome was ruled by one man.

Lepidus was the patron of the Ptolemies. Several versions survive of the story that he was tutor to Ptolemy's child or children.[77] Lepidus did participate in an embassy to Egypt in 200 in order to thank the Ptolemies for their support during the Hannibalic War.[78] We have seen earlier how he helped and advised the Egyptian ambassadors in deceiving the senators in 169 BCE. In 168 BCE the senate had acted to oppose the invasion and almost conquest of Egypt by Antiochus IV. It should not be forgotten that Judaea lay within Coele-Syria, control of which was disputed between Egypt and Syria, and over which six wars had been fought. The Egyptians had an interest if the Jews were wanting to break away from the Seleucids. No doubt the Ptolemies were well informed of events in Judaea. It would be only natural if they passed on what they knew to their patron, Lepidus. He, in turn, would have been only too ready to help the Jewish ambassadors.

Lepidus' rival for power in Rome was L. Aemilius Paullus, the victor of the Third Macedonian War. In domestic politics he was leader of what has come to be called the 'Scipionic faction'.[79] Allied to him was Ti. Sempronius Gracchus, whose mistake in running the consular elections for 162 BCE had resulted in the abdication of the two consuls.[80] Gracchus also had been sent on an eastern embassy to Antiochus IV in 168 BCE and later in 162 he left Rome for the East, chosen, Polybius says, predominantly because he was a friend of the Syrian king from the time that Demetrius had been a hostage in Rome.[81] On each occasion he reported back to Rome favourable accounts of both Seleucid kings.[82] There has even been a modern suggestion that Gracchus' friendship with Demetrius and the voiding of the consular elections may not have been unrelated.[83] Paullus and his sons were patrons of the historian Polybius while he lived in Rome.[84] When Demetrius made his secret flight from Rome, Polybius assisted him. Many historians have seen the hand of Paullus behind the whole plot to escape, although hard evidence is lacking.[85]

The Jewish envoys, in bringing their complaints against the Seleucids to Rome, came straight up against bitter political rivalry in the senate, against two men who advocated completely opposite policies in dealing with Demetrius. It is clear from the favourable outcome for the Jews that the opinion of Lepidus prevailed. The Jewish envoys were fortunate to have arrived when they did; two supporters of Demetrius were no longer available to provide opposition. Gracchus had departed for his eastern mission and Paullus was suffering from a severe illness (which eventually took his life in 160 BCE) and spent most of his time at Velia in Italy.[86] He was not the powerful figure he had once been.

## Notes

1 (1853) 131; (1949) 153.
2 Wellhausen (1907) 250, n. 3.
3 Gauger (1977) 192, n. 72.
4 (1853) 131; Gauger (1977) 243, n. 173 suggests it reflects the date when the envoys returned.
5 Bévenot (1931) 103 relying on Vegetius 4.39; followed by Goldstein (1976) 359.
6 Casson (1971) 271–272. Vegetius (ed. C. Lang) (1885) 4.39: *lux minima noxque prolixa, nubium densitas, aeris obscuritas, ventorum imbri vel nivibus geminata saevitia* were the perils of sailing in winter. Cf. more recent view: Beresford (2013) chs 1 and 4; Morton (2001).
7 Fasti Praenestini, *CIL* 1.316. See De Saint-Denis (1947) 197.
8 Commentators have generally explained this impression of one-man rule as arising from the presence in Rome of only one consul. See for example, Sordi (1975) 102.
9 Livy 1.43.1, 1.47, 1.50.3, 1.55.2, 2.43.5.
10 Most recently see, for example, Regev (2013) 159.
11 After the Second Punic War until 153 BCE, the consular elections were held in January or February. See Pina Polo (2011) 198.
12 Linderski (1986) 2159–2161; Wardle (1998) 89.
13 Since 204 BCE: Livy 29.38.7; Broughton (1951) 1.406; Rüpke (2008) nos. 507, 515.
14 Cic. *de nat.* 2.10–11; *de div.* 1.33, 36; *de leg.* 2.72; Val. Max. 1.1.3; Plut. *Marc.* 5.1–3; Gran. Lic. pp. 8–9 Flemisch; Auct. *uir. ill.* 44.2.
15 Conrad (2004) 174.
16 Gizewski (2005) 871.
17 Staveley (1954) 194.
18 Willems (1887) 2.31. Powers: Staveley (1954) 196.
19 Cic. *de domo* 14.38; Livy 4.43.7. See Staveley (1954) 200–202; Friezer (1959) Interregnum at 306; Gizewski (2005) at 871.
20 Mommsen (1887) 1.471–477; Pina Polo (2011) 205–206.
21 Schwegler (1870) 150–152 proposed that the *interrex* nominated just two candidates and the people could only vote yes or no. Defended most recently by Staveley (1954) 193–199. Against: Jahn (1970) 50–52; Twyman (1984) 289.
22 The language of the sources is indicative. Whereas the people *designare*, the *interrex creare*. See Staveley (1954) 198 with references.
23 *CIL* $1^2$ 1 p. 194 = 11.1829 = Degrassi, *Inscr. Ital.* 13.3.81 = *AE* (2008) 83. No indication of date from this inscription. Mazzotta (2013) 61, n. 58 is correct that L. Aemilius Paullus was not *interrex* in 162 BCE and dates it to 175 BCE but does not bring Plut. *Aem.* 39.1–5 as evidence.
24 Broughton (1951) 1.442. Plut. *Aem.* 39.1–5.
25 Zollschan (2007b) 9–38.
26 One to two months: Grimm (1853) 133. Thirteen months: Wellhausen (1907) 230, n. 3.
27 161 BCE: Seeman (2013) 124. For 160 BCE: Babota (2014) 104, n. 48.
28 Bar Kochva (1989) 372 traces the first mention of a leap year back to 1778.
29 Goldstein (1976) 168; Babota (2014) 105.

30 Alcimus' death: Jos. *Ant.* 12.414; Jewish embassy: Jos. *Ant.* 12.415–418; Judas' death: Jos. *Ant.* 12.434.
31 Grimm (1853) 131; Gauger (1977) 192.
32 Bevan (1930) 518; Schaumberger (1955) 426; Walbank (1979) 3.479.
33 1 Macc. 7.1–4; 2 Macc. 14.1–2; Jos. *Ant.* 389–390; Polyb. 31.15.13; App. *Syr.* 47; Zon. 9.25; Just. 34.3.9.
34 Zon. 9.25; Walbank (1979) 3.478, 3.483.
35 Using the Stanford University programme ORBIS. See the Stanford Geospatial Network Model of the Roman World, at orbis.stanford.edu
36 This by convention refers to dates according to our modern calendar.
37 Degrassi (1937) 81.
38 The longest *interregnum* on record in Livy is in 326, when 14 *interreges* followed one after the other for 5 days each, making a total of 70 days. However, Livy does not say this was the longest *interregnum*. See Gruen (1978) at 64 and n.19.
39 For detailed discussion see Back (2005) 409–411.
40 Bickerman (1968) 43; Michels (1968) 161; Samuel (1972) 159.
41 Livy 44.37.8. See Oost (1953); Samuel (1972) 163; Derow (1973); Marchetti (1976).
42 See Michels (1968) 171–172.
43 On consular duties in Rome before departure see Pina Polo (2011) 17–30.
44 Pina Polo (2011) 34.
45 Polyb. 31.15.9.
46 Broughton (1951) 1.442–443 seems to imply also late in the year.
47 Vegetius, *Epitoma rei militaris* 4.39, written between 388 and 391CE. See Beresford (2013) 14, n. 22.
48 De Saint Denis (1947) 197. Beresford (2013) 137 argues that stronger hulls developed in the Hellenistic period resulted in greater seaworthiness; this is demonstrated by excavated vessels and the sailing of replicas (171).
49 Polyb. 31.33.4.
50 Bar-Kochva (1989) 43, n. 50.
51 For the sequence see Diod. 31.27a: ὁ δὲ ἐπαρθεὶς τῷ δόγματι συνεστήσατο κατά τὴν Μηδίαν στρατόπεδον ἀξιόλογον.
52 Walton (1957) 386–387; Bar-Kochva (1989) 347. For a date of 162/161 BCE see Zeigler (1936); Gera (1998) 303.
53 Volkmann (1925) 393.
54 Volkmann (1925) 399; Schürer (1973) 1.173, n. 35; Goldstein (1976) 368; Gruen (1984) 45, n. 172, where he notes that the chronology is uncertain; cf. 1 Macc. 9.3.
55 Polyb. 28.3–5; Livy 43.17.2–9.
56 Polyb. 29.27.1–8; Diod. 31.2; Livy 45.12.1–6; Cic. *Phil.* 8.23; Val. Max. 6.4.3; Vell. 1.10.1–2; Plut. *Mor.* 202 F; App. *Syr.* 66; Justin. 34.3.1–4; Porph. *FGrH* 260, F 50; Zon. 9.25; Gran. Licin. p.4 Flemisch.
57 Briscoe (1986b) 96.
58 Date early 160: Walbank (1979) 3.517.
59 Bowman (1989).
60 Livy 30.17.4, 30.24.5, 35.23.11, 42.6.11.
61 Mommsen (1887) 3.1152–1153; Bowman (1989) 330, 332.
62 Lump sum in gold: Livy 28.39.19, 31.9.5, 37.3.11, 45.42.11. In sesterces: *Syll.* 241; *CIGr.* 2905. Per day: Val. Max. 5.1.1. See Mommsen (1887) 3.1153 nn. 1,2.
63 Bonnefond-Coudry (1989) 307.
64 Livy 37.1.1.
65 Livy 41.8.5–6.
66 Livy 44.19 1, 44.19.5.
67 Bonnefond-Coudry (1989) 308 using examples from 199–81 BCE.
68 Mommsen (1887) 3.1155 and n. 4.
69 Pina Polo (2011) 71–72, citing two examples: Livy 39.45.3 and 40.34.10.

70 Cremutius Cordus *apud* Seneca *Suas.* 7. See Ryan (1998) 230–231.
71 Ryan (1998) 244.
72 Münzer (1999) 169, 328. Caudinus: Livy 252.1; Zon. 22.2. For P. Cornelius Scipio Nasica Corculum as Pontifex Maximus: Cic. *Cato* 50; *RE* Cornelius 353; *NP* Cornelius I.83.
73 Livy 32.6.5–8; Bonnefond-Coudry (1993) 115.
74 Zon. 7.19; Gell. 14.7.9; Mommsen (1864b) 455–457; Mommsen (1887) 3.835–1271; Badian (1972) 691.
75 Polyb. 28.1.1–9.
76 Polyb. 32.6.5–8.
77 Just. 30.2.8, 30.3.1, 30.3–4, 31.1.2; Val Max. 6.6.1; Tac. *Ann.* 2.67.4. Arguments against: Gruen (1984) 681–682.
78 Polyb. 16.25–27, 16.34; Livy 31.2.3–4, 31.9.1–5, 31.18.1–7. See Bloy (2012) 178–179.
79 Reiter (1988) 129.
80 Alliance: see Briscoe (1968); Briscoe (1969) 65.
81 Polyb. 31.33.1.
82 166 BCE: Polyb. 30.27, 30.30.7–8; Diod. 31.17. 162 BCE: Polyb. 31.15.11, 31.33.4.
83 Walbank (1979) 3.478.
84 Reiter (1988) 32.
85 Badian, (1958) 108; Walbank (1979) 3.9; Briscoe (1969) 61, 67.
86 Plut. *Aem. Paull.* 39. 1–3.

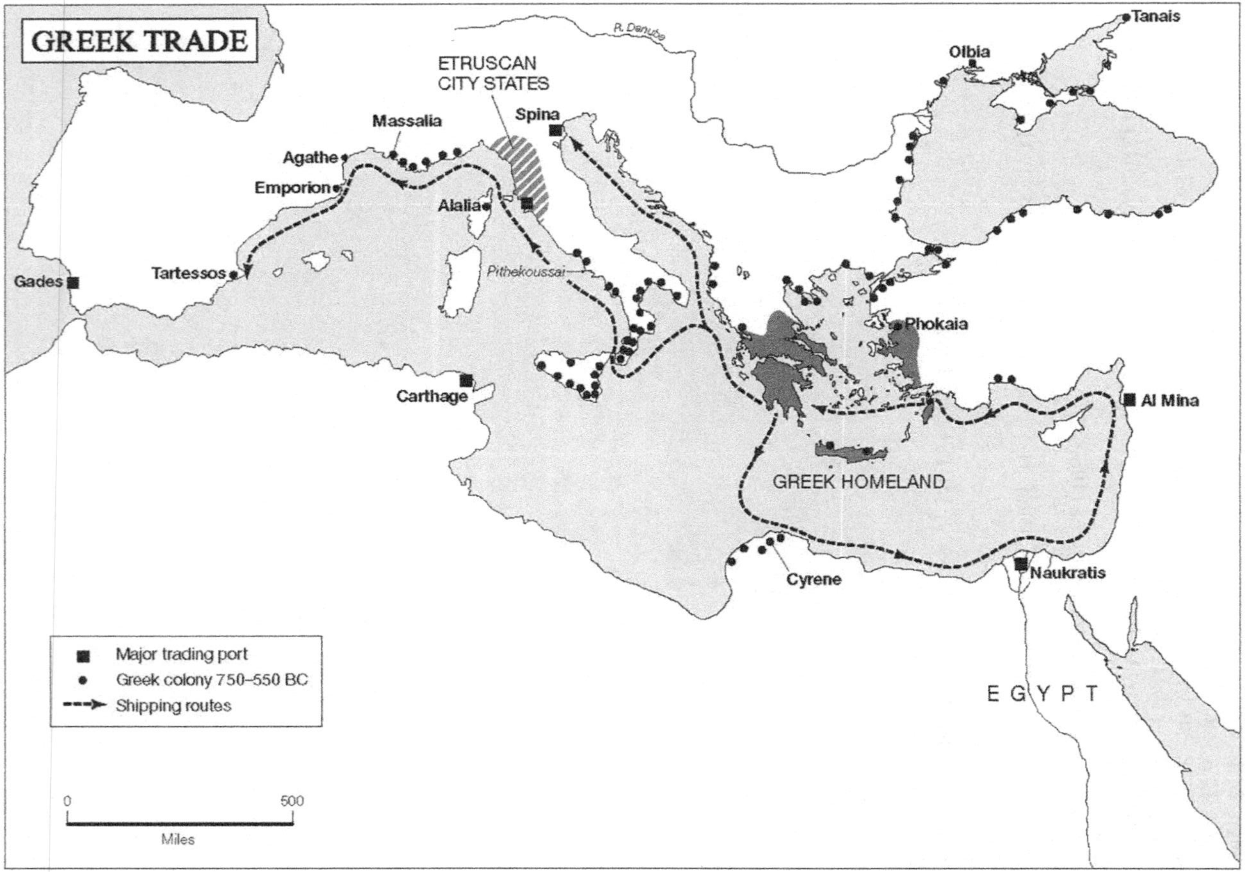


*Map 3.1* Greek trade

# 3 Early Roman ties of international friendship with Hellenistic powers

Diplomatic traffic, not only trade, flowed and developed from east to west and vice versa throughout the ancient Mediterranean.[1] Greek and Roman historians preserved accounts of contacts between Rome and the Hellenistic powers beginning in the fourth century BCE with Alexander the Great. The work of Maurice Holleaux, who maintained that there was no evidence for Roman diplomatic engagement with the Greek East in the period between Pyrrhus and the First Illyrian War, has been challenged by more recent scholarship. Although his legacy remains influential over studies of this period, the tide is turning against such rejectionism.[2]

The issues that drove the sending of embassies included the security of the sea lanes in the Mediterranean, the clash of Greek cities and Italians in Magna Graecia, and the urgent need to unravel the puzzle that was the young conqueror of Asia, Alexander the Great, whether his designs extended further into the East or over the Western Mediterranean as well. Rome addressed these concerns by means of embassies. Holding on to her gains in Italy depended on prudent diplomacy with the rising new powers, that of Alexander the Great, and after him, his successor kingdoms. It is not surprising, therefore, to find that Rome's earliest ties of international friendship (*amicitia*) were formed in the late fourth and third centuries BCE. The Hellenistic powers that had control of Judaea, the Ptolemies and later the Seleucids, each initiated ties of *amicitia* with Rome in the third century and maintained these ties throughout the period, when first the Ptolemies, and from 200 BCE the Seleucids, were the governing power over Judaea. The Jews, therefore, became familiar with their overlords as allies of Rome. The next section argues for the historicity of the early ties between Rome and the following Hellenistic rules: Alexander the Great, his uncle Alexander the Molossian, the Ptolemies of Egypt and the Seleucids of Syria. This information will assist our understanding of how the Jews came to perceive *amicitia* – and not treaty relations – as the salvation of their country and the means to liberation from the Seleucids.

## Roman contact with Alexander the Great

There are traditions that record two separate contacts between the Romans and Alexander the Great.[3] The first came in 335/34 BCE in the form of a threatening letter from the young king. In response, the Romans sent a golden crown of

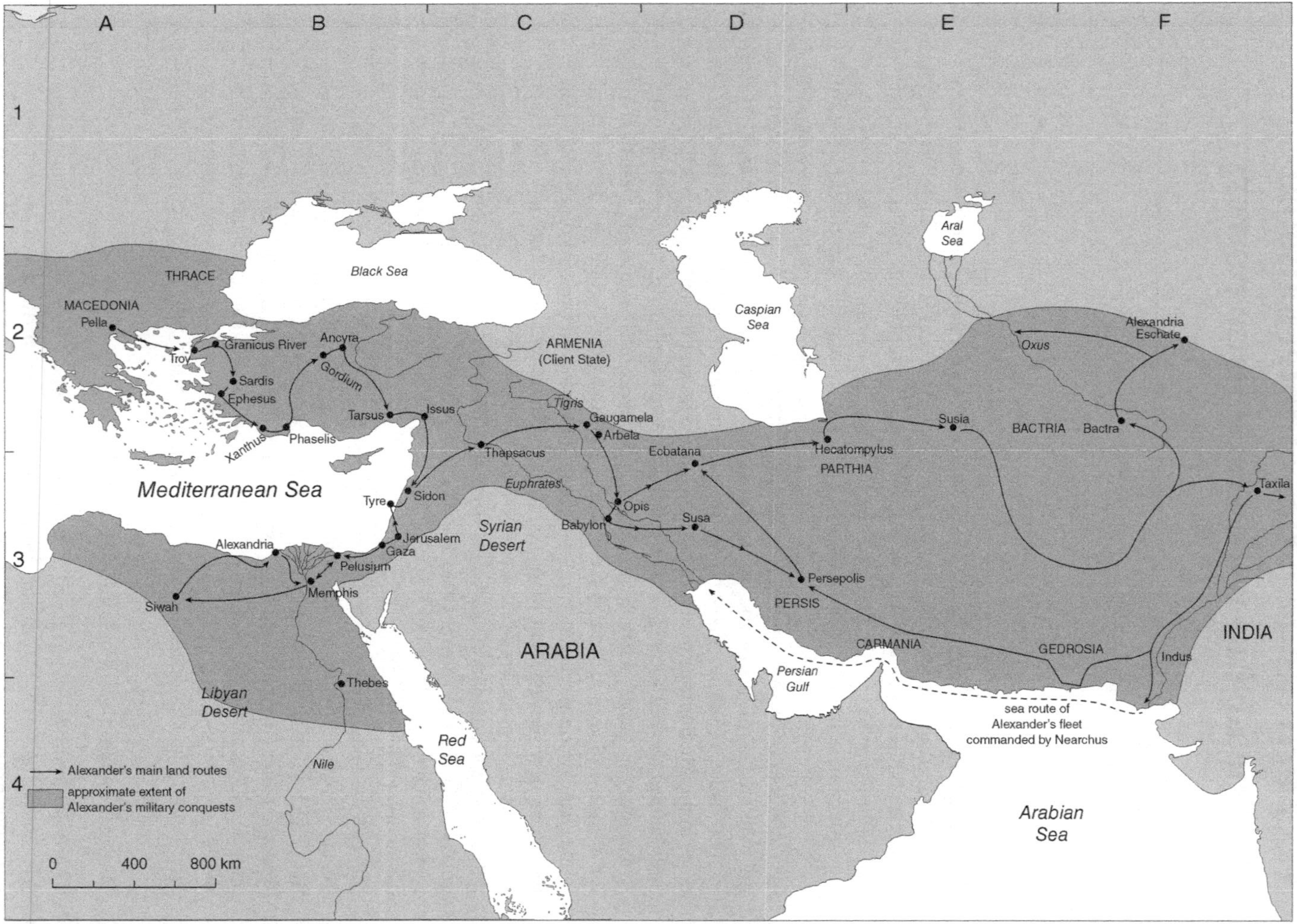
A
B
C
D
E
F
1
2
3
4
THRACE
MACEDONIA
Pella
Troy
Granicus River
Sardis
Ephesus
Xanthus
Phaselis
Ancyra
Gordium
Tarsus
Issus
Black Sea
Mediterranean Sea
Tyre
Sidon
Jerusalem
Gaza
Pelusium
Alexandria
Memphis
Siwah
Thebes
Libyan Desert
Nile
Red Sea
ARMENIA
(Client State)
Thapsacus
Tigris
Gaugamela
Arbela
Euphrates
Syrian Desert
Babylon
Opis
Susa
Ecbatana
ARABIA
Caspian Sea
Hecatompylus
PARTHIA
Persepolis
PERSIS
Persian Gulf
CARMANIA
Aral Sea
Oxus
Susia
BACTRIA
Bactra
Alexandria Eschate
Taxila
GEDROSIA
Indus
INDIA
sea route of
Alexander's fleet
commanded by Nearchus
Arabian Sea
Alexander's main land routes
approximate extent of
Alexander's military conquests
0
400
800 km

considerable weight and value as a sign of submission and willingness to be friends of the Macedonian. The request to the Romans came as part of Alexander's plans to consolidate the position in Europe before embarking on his war against the Persians. This incident ought not to be confused with reports of a later embassy to Alexander in Babylon by Roman ambassadors in 324/23 BCE.[4]

Memnon of Heraclea, writing sometime between the first and second centuries CE (his work is known only from an epitome compiled by Photius in the ninth century CE[5]), mentions Rome's first contact with Alexander in the context of a digression on the development of Roman power. At the heart of the reliability of Memnon's report lies the question of the sources he used. Various historians have been suggested, some of them almost contemporary. These include the Sicilian Greek Timaeus, a popular and learned historian writing at the end of the fourth century (after 317 BCE);[6] Nymphis of Heraclea, whose history ended at 247 BCE;[7] and Domitios Kallistratos, writing in the second half of the second century BCE, whose work was known by Dionysius of Halicarnassus.[8] Others have suggested the Roman historian Acilius, who wrote in Greek c. 143 BCE, as Memnon's source.[9] All of these were reliable historians.

Of Acilius, Memnon writes in his Fragment 18.2: 'He told how the Romans, when Alexander was crossing to Asia and had written to them saying that they would either prevail, if they were capable of ruling, or would submit to stronger forces, dispatched to him a golden crown weighing a considerable number of talents'.[10]

The giving of a crown was a well-recognised gesture of submission and acknowledgement of a superior power.[11] The Romans had received a crown from the Carthaginians after they had heard of the Roman victory in the war against the Samnites in 342 BCE.[12] The sending of a golden crown to Alexander represented a symbol of friendship and thus indicated the desire to form φιλία/*amicitia*.[13] Many examples may be found in Livy: the earliest case mentioned is the golden crown presented by the Latins and Hernici to Rome in 449 BCE.[14]

Why should Alexander have regarded the Romans as being a threat to his interests and an obstacle to his success? Strabo provides the answer when he writes of the threat of piracy in the Tyrrhenian Sea from a colony, Antium, founded by the Romans in 467 BCE.[15] At 5.232 he relates that Alexander demanded Rome put an end to such practices, noting that it was not fitting for the Romans to harm the Greeks considering the bonds of kinship that existed between them. The letter, says Strabo, caused the Romans to put an end to this piracy.

The historical background to the problem of piracy in the Tyrrhenian Sea is that Athens also had complained to Alexander as hegemon of the Corinthian League about the effect of piracy on her commerce.[16] That their vessels were affected, may be seen by the report of a Greek fleet off the coast of Latium in 345 BCE.[17] In 334 BCE (338 Varronian) the Romans destroyed the fleet of Antium and, further, they took active steps to prevent the rebuilding of it.[18] In addition, Alexander included the Tyrrhenians as offenders and accused them of piracy.[19] Four historians – Strabo, Arrian, Livy and Pliny – reported a problem with piracy that resulted in a diplomatic crisis with Alexander, one that was averted only by Rome's agreement to take swift action against the pirates. Her compliance after the giving of the golden crown indicates that Rome was acting as a true friend should.

The bonds of friendship were further strengthened by the sending of a Roman embassy to Alexander the Great in Babylon in 323 BCE. The incident was recorded by the historian Cleitarchus, a contemporary of Alexander, who is mentioned by Pliny in the context of a discussion of which Greek historians were the first to mention the Romans (*NH* 3.57.4 [= *FGrH* 137 F31]):

> Theophrastus, qui primus externorum aliqua de Romanis digentius scripsit – nam Theophrastus, ante quem nemo mentionem habuit, urbem dumtaxat a Gallis captam dixit, Clitarchus, ab eo proximus, legationem tantum ad Alexandrum misssam . . . .
>
> Theophrastus, the first foreigner to write with special care about the Romans – for Theopompus, before whom nobody mentioned them, merely states that Rome was taken by the Gauls, and Cleitarchus, the next after him, only that an embassy was sent to Alexander . . . .

Arrian, writing later than Pliny,[20] poured cold water on the whole story and historians have been arguing about the authenticity of the embassy ever since (Arrian, *Anabasis* 7.15.5–6):[21]

> Aristus and Asclepiades among the historians of Alexander say that even the Romans sent envoys, and that when Alexander met their embassy he prognosticated something of their future power on observing their orderliness, industry and freedom, and at the same time investigating their constitution. This I have recorded as neither true nor wholly credible, except that no Roman ever referred to this embassy sent to Alexander, nor did the historians of Alexander whom I prefer to follow, Ptolemy, son of Lagus and Aristobulus; nor was it suitable for the Roman government, at a time when it enjoyed freedom in the highest degree, to send envoys to a foreign king, especially so far from home, without the compulsion of fear or hope of advantage, given that no other people was so possessed by hatred of despotism and its very name.

Arrian's objections to the historicity of such an embassy are fourfold:

1. the embassy is not mentioned by Roman historians;
2. the historians Ptolemy and Aristobulus do not mention it;
3. Rome would not send envoys to a foreign king;
4. Babylon was too distant from Rome.

Brunt regarded all these arguments as 'worthless'; nevertheless, they can be satisfactorily dealt with.[22] With regard to the first point, the silence among Roman historians may be attributed to a sense of shame that Rome had submitted to Alexander in the face of a humiliating charge of piracy or of condoning piracy.

As to the second point, Greek historians frequently confused the Romans with the Tyrrhenians, who are mentioned as having sent an embassy to Babylon.[23] With the death of Alexander soon afterwards, the friendship so formed was nullified and may have been forgotten.[24] Concerning the third point, there was a very pressing need for the Romans to send an embassy: to demonstrate, in person, that the Romans had abjured any association with piracy. To make accusations of piracy branded the accused as uncivilised and incapable of adhering to diplomatic agreements. Alexander, in accusing the Romans of condoning piracy, signalled that he would wage war if his demand to put an end to the piracy from Antium was not met. Had Rome not disavowed the charge, Alexander was within his rights to have initiated an undeclared war without regard for the standards of the civilised norms of fighting.[25] The fourth point made by Arrian, that the journey to Babylon was too long, neglects the means of travel at that time. Along the Royal Road from Susa to Sardis, soldiers and messengers were travelling back and forth on Alexander's orders. The famous Persian courier system could cover the length of the Royal Road in 7–9 days.[26] Herodotus estimated that it took 90 days to travel from Sardis to Susa; in line with the Helleno-centric tendency to exaggerate the distances with regard to the Persian Empire, his timing was on the high end.[27] Briant has shown that the Royal Road, for example, was to be reserved for the king and his official business, which included its use for ambassadors as approved by the Satraps.[28] At the time of Alexander the Great, the satraps were his appointees and Roman ambassadors would have carried letters of credentials in Greek, thus giving them permission to use royal roads and avail themselves of provisions and fresh horses along the way. With these resources at the way stations, couriers under the Persian Empire could take 7–9 days to travel from Sardis to Susa.[29] As a consequence, the journey for the Romans envoys from Asia Minor to Babylon in all likelihood took less than a month.

Pliny's report was based on information from Cleitarchus, who wrote immediately after Alexander's death, the same year of the Roman embassy.[30] He had no reason to invent the story and may even have been an eye-witness.[31] Arrian's account carries a prophecy that is a later fabrication (probably in late first century BCE) and may be easily detached from the historical core of the arrival of a Roman embassy in Babylon.[32] Arrian says he obtained his report about a Roman embassy from two historians, whom he names as Aristus and Asclepiades.[33] Asclepiades is unknown. Speculation is that he was from Cyprus or Alexandria or Bithynia and estimates concerning when he lived range from the third to the first century BCE.[34] Of Aristus we are no better informed. He was from Salamis on Cyprus and lived in the first century BCE or CE. Pearson dates him to c. 150 BCE on grounds that the prophecy about Rome could not have been manufactured before that date.[35] Evidently the works of these two historians were better known in the time of Arrian.[36]

In Babylon in 324/23 BCE there were many foreign embassies. Some came to congratulate Alexander now that he was king of Asia; among them were the Libyans, Lucanians, Bruttians and Etruscans (Tyrrhenians). Others came to seek friendship, such as the Carthaginians, Ethiopians, Scythians, Celts and Iberians.[37]

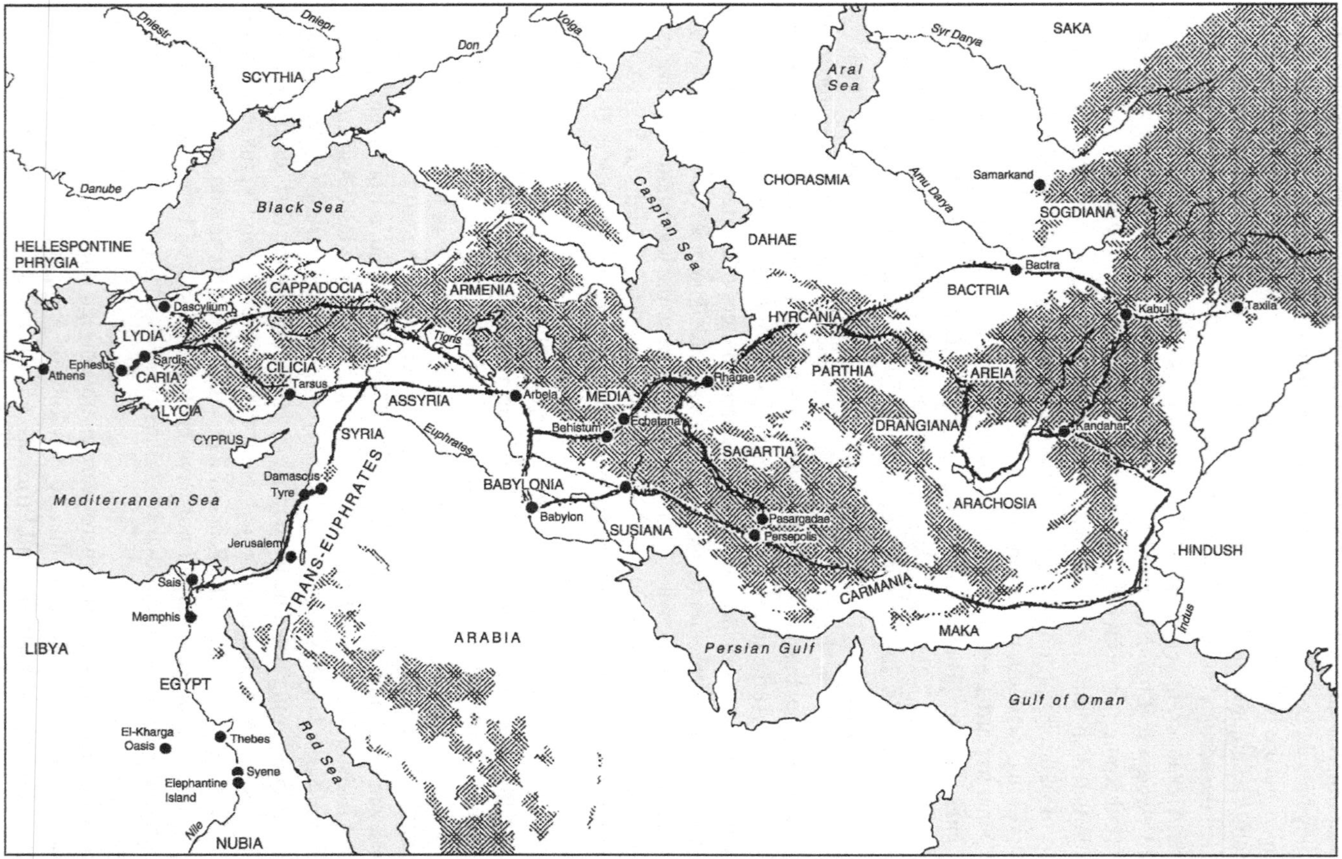


*Map 3.3* Roads of the Persian Empire

The Roman embassy was sent at a significant period in history. The Romans were not to know that Alexander would die very shortly after their visit. As far as they were concerned, they were troubled by the rumours swirling around Alexander's court that he next planned to turn his attention westwards and they could not be sure whether they would be on his list.[38] Many writers wrote of these plans.[39] Arrian chose not to give credence to what some of his sources wrote on this subject.[40] With Alexander, who knew what he would do next? The challenge presented by Carthage and Rome was out there and he was never one to resist a challenge. A precedent of sorts was Timoleon, who liberated the Greeks in Sicily from the Carthaginians, but the job was unfinished. The rallying cry of 'Liberation of the Greeks!' could be used to good effect among the cities of Magna Graecia.[41] An attack on Italy, if Alexander had lived, could be portrayed as a continuation of the campaign of his uncle, Alexander I of Epirus, who had died fighting the Lucanians and Bruttians in 331 BCE on the side of Tarentum.[42]

## Roman *amicitia* with Alexander the Molossian (Alexander I of Epirus)

The entry of the army of Alexander the Molossian into Italy cannot be separated from the events in Babylon. This king of Epirus was put on the throne by Philip II in 342/41 BCE by virtue of the fact that he was the brother of Olympias, the mother of Alexander the Great.[43] In fact, it was at his wedding in 336 BCE to Cleopatra, the daughter of Philip, that Philip was assassinated.[44] In 334 BCE he was invited by Tarentum to lead them in their war against the Lucanians and Bruttians. The chronology points to the connection with Alexander: the letter from Alexander the Great to the Romans in 335/34 BCE complaining about piracy from the fleet of Antium and Rome's consequent apologetic behaviour occurs just before the Epirote army arrived in Italy in 333 BCE. This date has been reached by the fact that we know from Arrian (3.6.7) that, when Harpalus fled to Europe before the battle of Issus in November 333 BCE, Alexander the Molossian was already in Italy.[45] Humm suggests that Alexander instructed his uncle to go to the aid of the Greek cities threatened by the Italians.[46] Justinus 12.2 provides an account of the activities of Alexander the Molossian in Italy. He reports that Alexander wished to emulate Alexander the Great's achievements, but in Italy, Sicily and Africa. He notes that he made treaties and alliances in Italy with the Romans, among others.[47]

As far as Rome was concerned, the arrival of Alexander's uncle in Italy was not a welcome development. It was feared that Alexander the Molossian wanted to restructure the Italian League, taking away the leadership of Rome and putting Tarentum at its head.[48]

The Romans made a pact with Alexander at Poseidonia (Paestum) after his victory over the Samnites and Lucanians in 332 BCE. The agreement reached is recorded as a *pax* in Livy (8.18.10) and as a *foedus amicitiaque* by Justinus (12.2.12). The confusion derives from the use of a Greek source that probably wrote εἰρήνην (peace), which would have been the consequence of forming *amicitia* and was misunderstood.[49] Similarly, Manni suggests that the mention in the summary of Livy of the accord between Rome and Ptolemy II in 273 BCE as *societas* rather than *amicitia* came about through a similar error.[50] The factuality of the agreement reached ought not to be dismissed on the basis that there was no reason for *pax* since there was no war between Rome and Alexander the Molossian.[51]

These two encounters – the letter from Alexander the Great and the accord reached with his Molossian namesake – spurred the Romans to send ambassadors to Babylon in order to affirm their *amicitia* with the Macedonian in person. It was not purely a question of being curious about Alexander himself, but rather of being concerned about his future plans and intentions.

The date of Alexander the Molossian's death factors into the connection with Alexander the Great's view of Italy and the Romans. The Epirote king's death has been variously dated between 332/31 BCE and 331/30 BCE.[52] Alexander was making preparations on the coast of the Levant in preparation for a new campaign in 324 BCE and it is not inconceivable that this build-up was noticed by the Romans. During the same year that the Romans sent ambassadors to Babylon, they were also shoring up their naval defences around Naples and securing their east coast with an alliance with the Lucanians, whose territory was the closest to Epirus.[53] It may have been that Alexander the Great had in mind a plan to take revenge for the death of his Molossian uncle. Whatever the intentions of Alexander the Great may have been, his sudden death put a halt to his next steps.

## *Amicitia* between Rome and Ptolemy II in 273 BCE

The friendship formed by Rome with Alexander was nullified on his death. The fact that Ptolemy II Philadelphus claimed to be his true successor may explain why he considered his embassy to Rome in 273 BC as the renewal of the ties made between Rome and Alexander in Babylon.[54] Three sources report that Ptolemy sent an embassy to Rome.[55] Eutropius supplies the date.[56] The timing of the embassy is significant. Dio provides the reason for the sending of an embassy at that particular time: he states that Ptolemy decided on this diplomatic step after he had learned that Pyrrhus' campaign in Italy had gone badly and that the Romans were growing powerful. The sequence of events is given by the Livian summary: Pyrrhus departed Italy for Sicily, the consul Curius Dentatus having claimed credit for expelling him from Italy in 275 BCE. Only after these events are reported, is the formation of diplomatic relations with Egypt mentioned. The initiative came from Ptolemy and not from the Romans. For some historians, this has presented problems, on the grounds that it was implausible that the powerful Egyptian king should turn to the Romans while the latter were still confined to the Italian peninsula and not yet a power on the international stage.[57] In order to explain Ptolemy's reasons for approaching Rome, some have discounted political motives in favour of economic explanations: a desire for access to Italian ports or to combat piracy.[58] This theory finds no support in the literary tradition or in the archaeological evidence for trade between Rome and Egypt in the early third century.[59] In fact, there was not much commerce between Rome and Egypt in the third century.[60] Neatby suggests that Egypt wanted access to the sea port of Tarentum and other south Italian cities.[61] If that was so, the archaeological evidence implies that Ptolemy was unsuccessful. There may, indeed, have been a more pressing need for an Egyptian embassy to Rome. It was to reach out to this emerging power in the Mediterranean and to mend bridges after the support Ptolemy had given to Pyrrhus.[62] There may have been an element of curiosity about the Romans, but this was not the sole or primary reason.[63] To congratulate Rome may have been part of the normal diplomatic courtesies that could just as effectively have been communicated by letter.

An understanding of the embassy requires that it be situated within the broader context of the foreign policy of Ptolemy II. He had embarked on a policy of expansion that, at its height, saw him control Syria and Phoenicia, Arabia, Libya and Ethiopia, and, in the eastern Mediterranean, Caria, Lycia, Pamphylia, Cilicia and the Cyclades islands.[64] In one of his alliances he misjudged and backed the wrong horse: he had supported Pyrrhus. A close relationship between Ptolemy and Pyrrhus had first formed at the court at Alexandria, where the future Egyptian ruler had met Pyrrhus. Thirteen years his senior, Pyrrhus was serving time as hostage to guarantee the peace with Demetrius of Macedon.[65] On Pyrrhus' return to Macedon in 297 BCE, Ptolemy formed a political friendship (φιλία) between them, sealing it with money and military support in order to recapture Epirus.[66] That friendship continued throughout the joint reign of Ptolemy I and Ptolemy II from 284–282 BCE.[67] A marriage alliance was struck between Pyrrhus and Antigone, the daughter of Ptolemy's wife Berenice by a previous marriage.[68] The son born of this alliance was named Ptolemy in honour of his father-in-law and a new city was built in Epirus by Pyrrhus; this was named Berenicis, after his mother-in-law.[69] Plutarch reported that it was well known that Pyrrhus would obey Ptolemy.[70] That is not all. When Pyrrhus was gathering a force to bring into Italy, he received on loan from Ptolemy II 20 war elephants and a promise of 9,000 troops and 50 elephants to use for the defence of Epirus while he was absent in Italy. These troops stayed for two years. Without this aid, Pyrrhus would not have found it possible to leave Epirus and campaign in Italy.[71] The military aid continued in 280 BCE in Tarentum.[72] It required a degree of trust on the part of Pyrrhus to leave his kingdom in the hands of the troops of Ptolemy II.[73]

By 273 BCE the political situation in Italy, Greece and Asia Minor had changed. Pyrrhus had lost Italy and Sicily and had begun attacking Macedon and Spain. He was Ptolemy's sole remaining ally in Greece. Ptolemy was concerned over Rome's future military intentions, especially whether the senate would decide to pursue Pyrrhus and send an army across to Epirus. If this should occur, Ptolemy would be required by ties of friendship to help him. Rome, however, could find ready allies to work against Pyrrhus: Antiochus Gonatas of Macedon and Antiochus I of Syria. Complicating the picture and negatively impacting on Ptolemy II was the potential for a common front against the Galatians – Antiochus Gonatas, Antiochus I and Rome – from which Ptolemy II would be excluded because he employed Gauls in his army.[74]

The reasons for Ptolemy's embassy to Rome are not obscure:[75] his approach was initiated to allay concerns that the Romans might still consider him an ally of their enemy, Pyrrhus, who was still alive.[76] Under one of the fundamental principles of Roman international law, rendering aid to an enemy of Rome automatically rendered one an enemy (*hostis*), against whom war could be launched without any prior declaration.[77] Being allied to Rome's enemy and giving aid in time of war was an immediate *casus belli*. This may account for the coolness of the Roman reception of the envoys. The purpose of the embassy was to disassociate Ptolemy from Pyrrhus' invasion of Italy.[78] Hence the lavish gifts from Ptolemy to the Romans as described by Zon. 8.6.11:

> And Ptolemy Philadelphus, king of Egypt, when he learned that Pyrrhus had fared badly and that the Romans were growing powerful, sent gifts to them and made a compact. And the Romans, pleased with this, despatched ambassadors to him in turn. The latter received magnificent gifts from him, which they desired to place in the treasury; the senate, however, would not accept them, but allowed the envoys to keep them.

This passage makes clear the causal connection between Pyrrhus and the sending of the embassy to Rome. These generous gifts indicated the desire to form friendship ties with Rome.[79] The Egyptian envoys were successful in turning the senate around and cemented diplomatic relations with an exchange of embassies.

The type of diplomatic relations formed at this time is not identified consistently by the sources: Eutropius reports the resulting ties as *amicitia*, as does Appian (φιλία, *Sic.* 1), while Livy summarises them as *societas* and Dio uses the vague non-technical term ὁμολογία.[80] Eutropius' account here is derived from Livy's history, not the summary.[81] The error in Livy *Per.* 14 was the writing of *societas* rather than *amicitia*, which was a mistake on the part of the Epitomator.[82] The majority of scholars are in agreement that the diplomatic ties made in Rome comprised *amicitia*.[83]

As mentioned, Dio, however, speaks of ὁμολογία, which has two meanings: first, a general compact or agreement; second, terms of surrender.[84] Some have thought the use of this term 'bizarre'; there may, in fact, have been a good reason to use it.[85] Its use reflects the problem presented to Ptolemy of having aided Rome's enemy and how to extricate himself. While the word ὁμολογία in the sense of the terms of surrender may not have been intended to represent a full legally binding *deditio*, it did suggest a certain amount of grovelling in order to nullify any grounds the Romans had for war.

Ties were further cemented by an exchange of embassies in which Roman envoys travelled to Alexandria to meet Ptolemy II. No source provides an indication of the date when the envoys were in Egypt, but they must have returned to Rome no later than autumn 270 BCE because the envoy Q. Ogulnius was elected consul for 269 BCE.[86] Valerius Maximus (4.3.9) provides the names of the envoys: Q. Fabius Gurges, N. Fabius Pictor (the uncle of the historian) and Q. Ogulnius. This information probably derives from Livy and Cicero.[87] Justinus' account of the embassy came from a non-Roman source, Hieronymus of Cardia, and so corroborates the historicity of the event.[88] The surviving accounts concentrate on the refusal of the golden crowns given to the envoys by Ptolemy. Rather than see in this gesture the incorruptibility of the Romans, we should interpret the actions of the envoys according to the norms of diplomatic practice.[89] The Romans had been presented with golden crowns during the embassy of Ptolemy's representatives to Rome a short time earlier. The gifts had softened the senate's attitude to Egypt and inclined them to consider Ptolemy a friend, forgetting his earlier ties to Pyrrhus. Such a short time after this contact, there was no further need for a friend to persist in proving his loyalty, hence the rejection of the gifts: it was not a rejection of the friendship between Rome and Ptolemy II.

## Early ties of *amicitia* with the Seleucid Empire

Suetonius in the pages of his biography of the emperor Claudius reports a brief but intriguing piece of information about the origin of the ties of *amicitia* between the Seleucids and the Romans. He writes (Suet. *Claud.* 25.3):

> recitata uetere epistula Graeca senatus populique Romani Seleuco regi amicitiam et societatem ita demum pollicentis, si consanguineos suos Ilienses ab omni onore immunes praestitisset.
>
> reading an ancient letter of the senate and people of Rome written in Greek to king Seleucus, in which they promised him their friendship and alliance only on condition that he should keep their kinsfolk of Ilium free from every burden.

The veracity of this report is dependent on the sources Suetonius used for it and where Claudius found the letter. The older literature tended to reject Suetonius' account of the old Greek letter; more recent work favours its authenticity.[90]

The report in Suetonius comes several centuries after the events in this undated letter. Mention of the letter is placed among a list of Claudius' deeds. We know from Tacitus that his decision on behalf of Ilium occurred in 53 CE, the last year of his reign.[91] In the modern literature we find reference to three works that may have contained such information: Claudius' autobiography, his *commentarii* and his *acta*. We may eliminate his autobiography (which is not to be confused with his *commentarii*[92]), as it was a lengthy work in eight books (or rolls) and was full of personal anecdotes starting from his childhood.[93] It also included the story of his accession, his triumph over Britain and the *Ludi Saeculares* of 47 CE.[94]

The *commentarii* were of a different nature, containing the deeds of the emperor organised by subject, as well as official correspondence and copies of judicial hearings.[95] Other Julio-Claudian emperors wrote *commentarii:* first setting the example was Julius Caesar with his *Commentarii de bello Gallico* and *Commentarii de bello ciuile*, followed by Augustus and Tiberius.[96] *Commentarii* were detailed by their very nature, but the chapters in Suetonius constitute merely

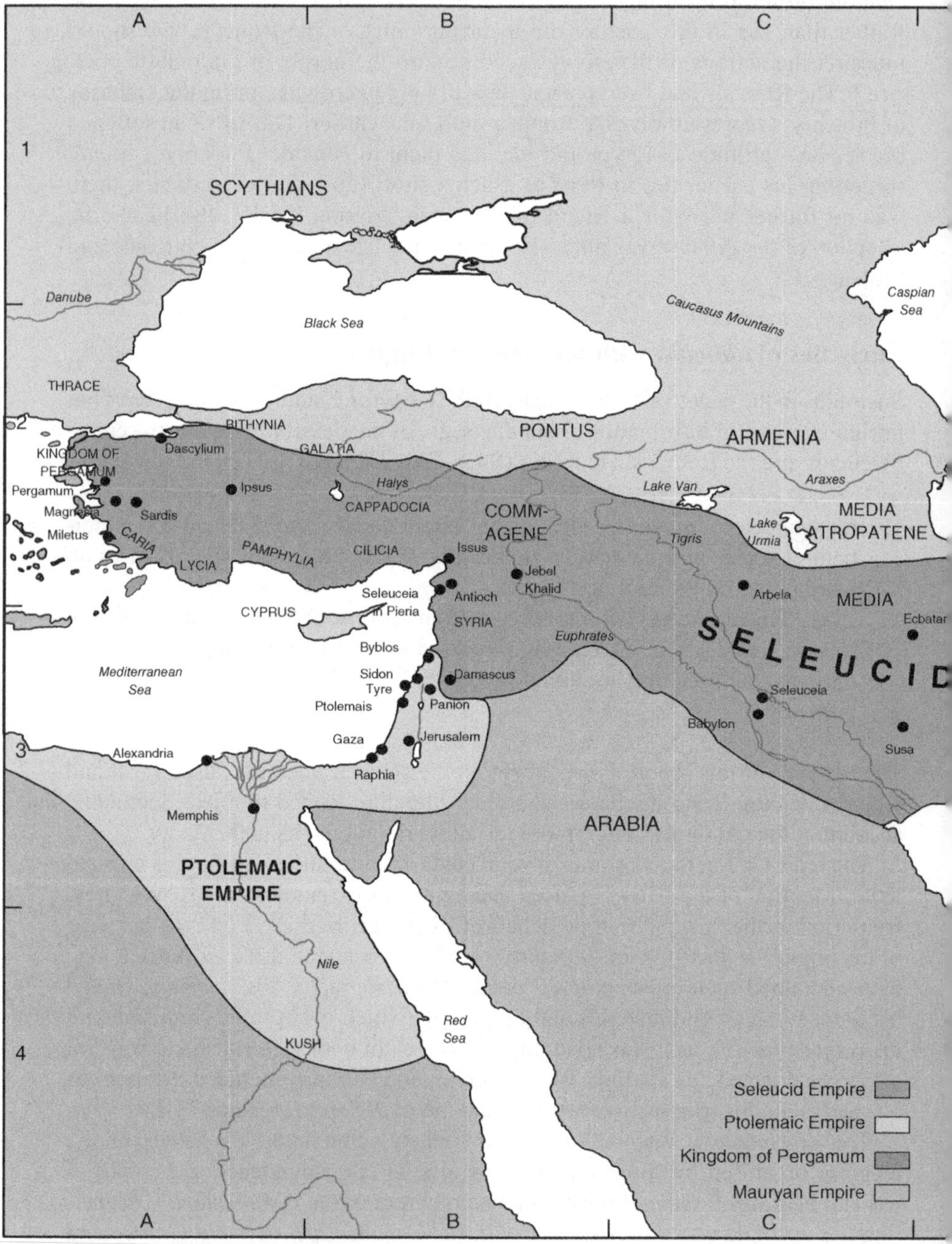


*Map 3.4* Ptolemaic and Seleucids Empires

D
E
F
The six 'Syrian Wars' (between the Seleucids and the Ptolemies)
c. 274–271 First Syrian War (Antiochus I vs Ptolemy II)
260–253 Second Syrian War (Antiochus II vs Ptolemy II)
246–241 Third Syrian War (Seleucus II vs Ptolemy III)
219–217 Fourth Syrian War (Antiochus III vs Ptolemy IV)
202–198 Fifth Syrian War (Antiochus III vs Ptolemy V)
170–168 Sixth Syrian War (Antiochus IV vs Ptolemy VI)
MASSAGETAE
Aral Sea
Jaxartes (Syr Darya)
SAKA HAUMAVARGA
CHORASMIA
Oxus (Amu Darya)
Cyropolis
Maracanda
FERGHANA
SAKA TIGRAKHAUDA
MARGIANA
BACTRIA
HYRCANIA
GANDHARA
EMPIRE
Kabul
Taxila
ARIA
Zagros Mountains
DRANGIANA
ARACHOSIA
Kandahar
Dahan-i Ghulaman
Helmand
Naqsh-i Rustam
SATTAGYDIA
PARSA (PERSIS)
CARMANIA
Indus
MAURYAN EMPIRE
Persian Gulf
GEDROSIA
Arabian Sea
0
500
1,000 km
D
E
F

a list. We know that the *commentarii* were full of detailed information, as Nero was able to halt a court case because he had found definitive evidence in the *commentarii* of his father, Cn. Domitius Ahenobarbus.[97] The literary output of the Caesars themselves constituted a primary source for Suetonius: for example, Suetonius devotes two chapters to the works of Julius Caesar (*Diu. Iul.* 55–56) and cites several works of Augustus (*Diu. Aug.* 85.1–2; *Claud.* 1.10–11). He notes the book of Tiberius entitled *Commentarius de uita sua* (*Tib.* 61.2) and two lengthy *Commentarii et acta* much admired by Domitian (Suet. *Dom.* 20.3).

The brevity of the list of Claudius' achievements in chapters 22 to 25 of Suetonius' Life in which mention of the old letter to King Seleucus is found, is reminiscent of the *Res Gestae Divi Augusti*. It may be that Tiberius prepared his own manuscript of his *Res Gestae*, as Augustus had done, which he then deposited in the imperial archives.[98] With the propensity of Claudius to favour the traditional approach, he may also have been preparing his own list of achievements, in the standard formula as set by Augustus.[99]

By contrast, the *commentarii* of Tiberius were a summary of the emperor's life, not just his deeds.[100] There is now some doubt whether Suetonius used the *commentarii* at all in writing his *Life of Claudius*.[101] What we see in chapters 22 to 25 is a list of achievements similar to the *Res Gestae* of Augustus.[102] It has been remarked upon that Suetonius in all likelihood obtained his material from which to write the *Life of Claudius* from published sources,[103] such as published collections of Claudius' speeches.[104]

As for published sources, it is likely that the *acta diurna* were accessible to Suetonius.[105] Whether at this time the bulletins came out daily or at other various intervals is not known; what is known was that they were issued with a specific day's date.[106] This was the name of the official newspaper-type publication.[107] In his *Life of Claudius*, mention is made of this source in connection with Claudius' introduction of his invented new letter forms.[108] Suetonius refers to *acta diurna* in six places throughout the *Lives*: *Iul.* 20.1; *Aug.* 64.4; *Tib.* 5.2; *Calig.* 8.5 and 36.6; as well as the report in the *Life of Claudius*. It was this source that published the speeches of Claudius used by Suetonius.[109] The imperial bureaucracy operated what was in effect a press office with a procurator in charge whose job it was to publish daily records of government business. The *acta* contained decrees of the senate, the emperor's edicts, results of the votes in assemblies, and news about the imperial family, such as births, deaths and marriages.[110] They were displayed on white boards for the public to read in various locations in the city and copies were later placed in the state archives.[111] This publication was used as a source by both Pliny and Tacitus: the former reveals that it contained verbatim transcripts of the decrees of the emperor.[112] If we want to know where Suetonius obtained his information about Claudius' decision on behalf of the people of Ilium, the *acta diurna* were the most likely and most easily accessible choice for him.[113]

The *Life of Claudius* is thought to have been completed c. 121/22 CE or a little later.[114] Recently it has been proposed that all 12 *Lives* may have been finished by 119 CE.[115] Suetonius may either have ceased to use the imperial archives after he had written the *Life of Tiberius* or he may have used just published sources for the whole of the 12 *Lives*.[116] Various reasons have been proposed for the first view:

either that he was banished from Rome by Hadrian after his fall from favour, some going so far as to say that he lost interest in the project, or that it had now all seemed too much like hard work.[117]

Where had Claudius found this old letter from the senate to King Seleucus? For Claudius, as an historian in his own right, it was natural, with regard to petitions brought to him, that he would investigate the history of the issue.[118] For example, he undertook research by going through the personal papers of Caligula.[119] The old letter written in Greek was written by the senate in the republican period. To find the place where this letter would have been archived, it is necessary to examine how the senate kept its records and how accessible they were. The senate recorded its decisions in the *Liber sententiarum in senatu dictarum*, which is referred to by Cicero, who in a letter to Atticus requested that someone consult it for him regarding the text of a senatorial decree passed in 146 BCE.[120] From this we can verify that the records were publicly accessible. In the records where the information was published (either the *acta diurna* or the *Res Gestae* of Claudius), not every detail would have been included. This may explain the absence of a date.

These senatorial records were held in the *aerarium Saturni* – that is, in the treasury in the Temple of Saturn.[121] If Atticus had access to the senatorial records, the emperor surely could have ordered a search there for the relevant material. The one to do so would have been Narcissus, his *ab epistulis* – that is, his chief secretary who dealt with imperial correspondence and kept a file of past imperial correspondence on the subject of privileges and grants.[122] In Suetonius' account, he does not say that Claudius read from the actual letter. The possibility, then, arises that the letter was quoted in the *liber sententiarum* as it was part of the senatorial decision to send a written reply to King Seleucus.

Magie suggested that the letter was a forgery brought to Rome by the Ilian envoys. The appropriate response is that of Derow, who observes that it is difficult to see how the Ilians could have planted a forgery in the Roman archives and how Claudius could have been fooled.[123] It did not require delegates from Ilium to produce this letter, as it had not been addressed to them: the only proof they required for their plea was the favour bestowed on them by Julius Caesar. The letter cannot be regarded as a forgery produced by the people of Ilium in order to bolster their case for special treatment.[124]

The letter was produced as part of the mission of the representatives from Ilium to request tax immunity from the emperor. This status had first been granted to them by Alexander the Great.[125] Under the Seleucids they had paid tribute and with the Roman defeat of Antiochus III the Romans had included a clause in the peace treaty of Apamea in 188 BCE that Troy (Ilium) be free from taxation.[126] This privilege was restored by Sulla under the general rubric of restoring their freedom.[127] Strabo records that the deified Caesar (that is, Julius Caesar) followed the example set by Alexander and granted them freedom and immunity from taxation. He says that these privileges have been retained by the Ilians up to this day. It is considered that Strabo died in 24 CE.[128] Obviously by 53 CE those concessions had been lost. Somewhere between the latter years of Tiberius' reign (starting with the death of Strabo in 24CE and the death of Tiberius in 37 BCE) and the early part of Claudius' reign, the city of Troy had been without tax exemption.

The city of Ilium is situated in an active seismic region: it lies both on the Troy fault and the Northern Anatolian fault.[129] In 53 CE an earthquake struck Apamea Cibotus (Apamea ad Maeandrum) in Phrygia, which was felt as far away as Philippi in Greece.[130] Tacitus records that the citizens of Apamea came to Claudius for financial assistance and that they were given tax remittance for five years.[131] Bearing this in mind, it is not surprising that other affected cities in Asia Minor requested from Claudius financial relief to deal with earthquake damage. Not all petitions were given a favourable response: the emperor did not dole out such important grants to all.[132] The Ilians were given tax relief because of their sentimental ties to the foundation legend of Rome.[133] The damage and suffering caused by the earthquake of 53 CE was the reason for the petition of the Ilians to Claudius in that year.[134]

The account in Suetonius of an old letter written in Greek from the senate to a king Seleucus deserves to be taken seriously. Its origin in the senatorial records is plausible and the publication in the *acta diurna* of Rome of the grant to Ilium and Claudius' discovery of the letter are indicated and suggested by the use of mainly published sources by Suetonius for his *Life of Claudius*. As the letter is undated and the name of the king is very vague, it is now necessary to provide some chronological framework.

The name Seleucus presents several problems. It needs to accord with the appropriate time when the Seleucids had control over Ilium in order to guarantee to the Romans that they would keep its tax-free status. No available kings readily fit the description. Seleucus I (ruled between 312 and 281 BCE) had acquired control over Ilium only one year prior to his death.[135] Moreover, this monarch's reign may be too early for the myth of Rome's Trojan foundation to have become prominent.[136] Seleucus II (ruled from 246 to 225 BCE) had possession of Ilium from 246 until 240 BCE, when it was taken from him by his brother Antiochus Hierax. A consensus has formed around Seleucus II as the king to whom the senate wrote.[137] The date of 242 BCE makes sense from the Roman standpoint, as the Romans had just defeated the Carthaginians in the naval battle that decided the First Punic War, and the letter displays a newfound sense of international power and willingness on the part of Rome to engage in issues relating to the Greek East.[138]

## Apollonia

Valerius Maximus and Dio relate an incident that is undated: envoys from Apollonia in Epirus had travelled to Rome where they were attacked by two *aedilicii* – that is, men who had been aediles, and therefore were senators. For their actions, the two senators were punished. The details are not relevant here.[139] The question is, what had prompted the envoys to come to Rome? Also, when did this incident occur? After the death of Pyrrhus in 272 BCE, the city of Apollonia was still part of the Epirote kingdom.[140] A chronology may be reached from the account in the *Periochae* of Livy 15, where the events are listed in chronological order. The Apollonian envoys are placed between the revolt of Rhegium and the suppression of the Picentes. The revolt had ended by 270 BCE, when the Romans celebrated a triumph over their defeat of the Tarentines, and the triumph over Picenum was celebrated in 268 BCE. We can, therefore, date the envoys' stay in Rome to 270/69 BCE.[141] What was the purpose of this embassy? Many scholars have seen this embassy as an example of Rome reaching out to the Greek world.[142] This disregards the lack of evidence of any initiative on the part of Rome to invite the envoys to visit: rather, it appears that the envoys approached Rome. The timing was just after the death of Pyrrhus, under whose control Apollonia had been during the war with Rome.[143] The embassy occurred before the Romans occupied Brundisium, so any theory about control over the Adriatic is inappropriate.[144] The clue to understanding this embassy is the defeat of Pyrrhus and the desire of both Ptolemy II and

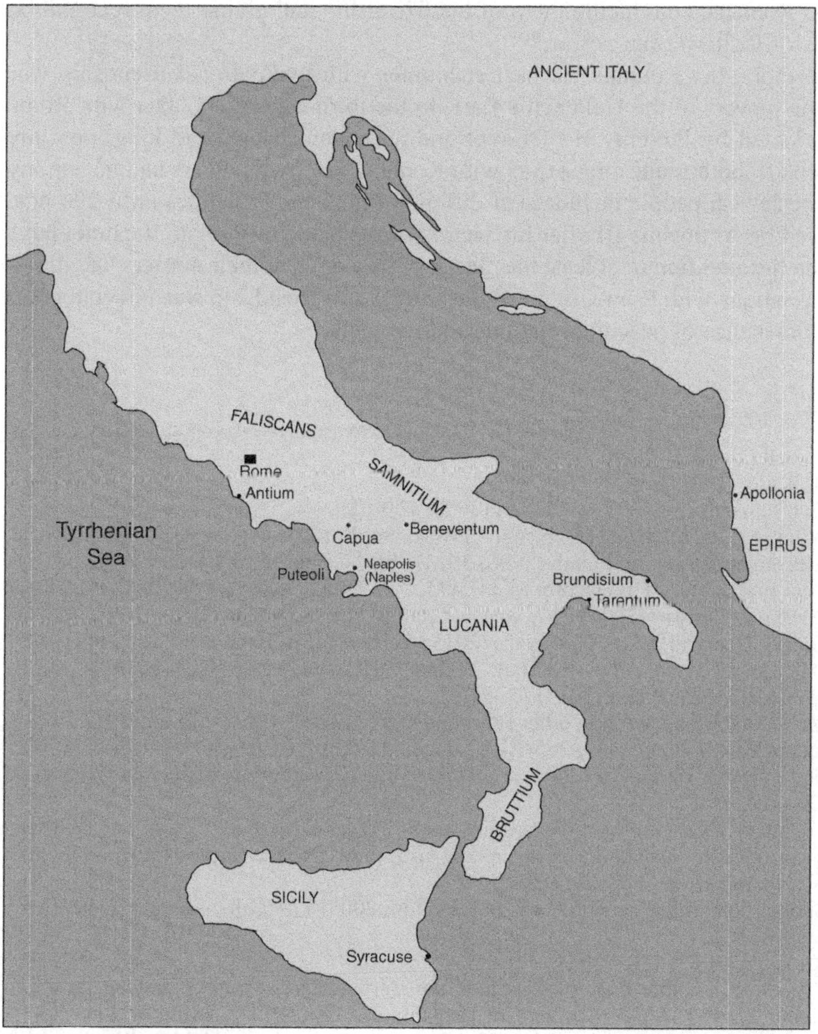


*Map 3.5* Ancient Italy

Apollonia to distance themselves from Pyrrhus and proclaim themselves friends of Rome. What may have occasioned the assault by two senators was the fact that Apollonia had been on the side of Pyrrhus during his campaign against Rome. The Roman action of handing over the two to the Greeks is an indication that friendly relations had come to exist between Rome and Apollonia.[145]

In summary, the Roman war with Pyrrhus brought Rome to the notice of much of the Hellenistic world.[146] The Egyptian patronage shown to Pyrrhus put Ptolemy II in an awkward position when the Romans defeated Pyrrhus at Beneventum and drove him from Italy. The unexpected Roman victory over the one who considered himself the successor to Alexander the Great necessitated a diplomatic change in direction for Ptolemy; thus his embassy to Rome was aimed at appeasing the Romans, convincing them of his friendship and giving them recognition as a new Mediterranean power.[147]

Therefore, the Romans' earliest encounter with international friendship was with the powers of the Hellenistic East. In the third century, contact with Rome was initiated by Ptolemy II of Egypt and an unnamed Seleucid king, possibly Seleucus II, both requesting φιλία with Rome. These two powers had hegemony over the Jewish people in Judaea at different times, the Ptolemies until 200 BCE, followed by Antiochus III after his victory at the battle of Panion. It cannot have escaped the attention of at least the elite in Jerusalem that their masters had diplomatic relations with Rome. In the Hellenistic world friendship was understood as the maintenance of peaceful relations and goodwill.

## Notes

1 Purcell (2013) 367–390.
2 Holleaux (1921) i–iv.
3 Two separate episodes: see Humm (2006) 179–180.
4 Wilcken (1931) 213–214; Nenci (1958); Sordi (1965); Braccesi (1975) 16–24; Alessandrì (1994) 30; Prandi (1996) 30–31; Sisti-Zambrini (2004) 619–620.
5 Date first century CE: Jacoby *FGrH* 434, 3.267–283; Janke (1938) 7–8, 11; Bittner (1998) 4; Yarrow (2006) 357. Second century CE: Laqueur (1926) 1099; Meister (1999); Henry (1965) 177; Davaze (2013) 67. On date of Photius see Ziegler (1941).
6 Date, learned and popular: Polyb. 12.25a.3, 12.25c.1, 12.26d.1–6, 12.28.6; Jacoby *FGrH* IIIb. 526; Baron (2013) 53–54.
7 Memnon used his work in other surviving extracts: *BNJ* 434 T3, T4 and F10.
8 Jacoby *FGrH* 3c, no. 433, 265–270; Laqueur (1926) 1101; Desideri (2007) 47.
9 Janke (1938) 18; Dueck (2006) 53. Acilius' life and works: Bispham and Northwood (2013) 224.
10 Fragment 18.2: (2) ὅπως τε ἐπὶ τὴν 'Ασίαν 'Αλεξάνδρωι διαβαίνοντι, καὶ γράψαντι ἢ κρατεῖν, ἐὰν ἄρχειν δύνωνται, ἢ τοῖς κρείττοσιν ὑπείκειν, στέφανον χρυσοῦν ἀπὸ ἱκανῶν ταλάντων 'Ρωμαῖοι ἐξέπεμψαν'.
11 Submission: Yarrow (2006) 142–143; Humm (2006) 179. Gifts: see pp. 78–82.
12 Livy 7.38.2.
13 Rutledge (2012) 148–150.
14 Livy 3.57.7. Other examples include the Carthaginians giving a golden crown to Rome: Livy 7.38.1–3. Attalus I of Pergamum: Livy 32.27.1. Philip V: Livy 36.35. Alabanda and Lampsacus: Livy 43.6.5–6. Pamphylia: Livy 44.14.3. Rhodes: Livy 45.25.7. See Östenberg (2009) 119–127.

15 Memnon and Strabo writing of the same incident: Davaze (2013) 412.
16 Worthington (2014a) cxxx.
17 Polyb. 2.18; Claud. Quad. fr. 12 Peter; Livy 7.25–26; D.H. 15A.
18 Destruction: Livy 8.14.12; Pliny *NH* 34.20; Flor. 1.5.10. Prevent rebuilding: Livy 8.14.8, 8.14.12.
19 Arrian, *Anab.* 17.5.4.
20 Arrian fl. c. 85–168 CE: see Bosworth (1972) 181.
21 Against: Mommsen (1903) 1.383; Niese (1903) 1.182, n. 2; Tarn (1921) 13; id. (1948) 2.21–26; Hoffmann (1934) 59; F. Jacoby *FGrH* Kommentar on no. 137, F 31; Nenci (1958); Bengston (1950) 1.335n.; Pearson (1960) 232–233; Hammond (1983) 74; Gruen (1984) 318. For authenticity: Kornemann (1920); Pais (1920) 487–494; De Sanctis (1907) 2.426–427; Meyer (1924) 2.529, n. 2; Berve (1926) 1.326; Mederer (1936) 108–110; Schachermeyr (1949) 456, 526, n. 286; Brown (1950) 151, n. 131; Treves (1953) 27–29; Manni (1956); Hamilton (1961) 454; Sordi (1965) 445ff; Cassòla (1962) 39–41; Brunt (1983) 2.498; Flower (2002) 132–134; Humm (2006) 176–184; Grainger (2007/2009) 99–100; Yardley and Hoyos (2013) 341; Worthington (2014a) cxxx; id. (2014b) 289, nn. 27 and 28.
22 Brunt (1983) 2.497.
23 Humm (2006) 177 and n. 17.
24 Bosworth (1988) 90, 92.
25 See Chapter 7.
26 Herod. 8.98.
27 See Briant (1991) 67–69.
28 Briant (1991) 70–72.
29 Herod. 8.98 266–267.
30 Bosworth (1988) 88. Cf. Tarn (1950) 2.19: not before 280 BCE.
31 An invention by Cleitarchus: Tarn (1948) 25. Eye-witness: Badian (1965) 5–11. Cf. Pearson (1962).
32 Brown (1950) 152, n. 131.
33 Arrian 7.15.5–6.
34 Cyprus or Alexandria: Jacoby *FGrH* 144 F1. Bithynia: Bosworth (1988) 83. Cf. Radicke (1999) 586–589.
35 Worthington (2014–2017) 143 T2 and F 1.
36 Worthington (2014–2017) 143 F2 Commentary.
37 Arrian 7.15.4.
38 Brunt (1983) 2.497; Roller (2013) 60.
39 Plut. *Alex.* 68.1–2; Curtius 10.1.17–19; Diodor. 18.4.4.
40 Arrian 7.1.3–4.
41 Grainger (2007/2009) 100.
42 Just. 12.2.1–5; Livy 8.3.6–7; Strabo 6.1.3; Flower (2002) 133, n. 154.
43 Diod. 16.72.1.
44 Diod. 16.91–95.
45 Werner (1987) 352–354 and Yardley and Heckel (1997) 1.192. Livy records the crossing of the Epirote army into Italy in 340 BE. Forsythe (1999) 104 estimates that the army was in Italy from mid-summer 336 till spring 330 BCE.
46 Humm (2006) 181.
47 Other accounts in Livy 8.3, 8.17, 8.24 and Gell. 17.21.
48 Zorat (1966) 100.
49 Manni (1962) 351.
50 See Manni (1949) 81.
51 Not historical on this basis: Braccesi (1974). Followed by Gruen (1984) 61.
52 Livy 8.3.6–7; Just. 12.2.1–3 (quoted previously). Modern estimates: Manni (1962) 347.
53 Humm (2006) 186.
54 Bingen (2007); Erskine (2002).

55 Dio fr. 41 [= Zon. 8.6.11]; Livy *Per.* 14; Eutrop. 2.15.
56 Eutrop. 2.15: *Anno urbis conditae quadringentesimo sexagesimo.*
57 Fraser (1967) 1–3. Against: Westall (2011) 358.
58 Bandelin (1853) 8; Mommsen (1903) 1.429; Droysen (1877/1878) 3.297; Bouché-Leclercq (1913) 319; Colin (1905) 33; Reinach (1911) at 403; Ciaceri (1918) 1–5; Walek (1925); Preaux (1931) 265; Manni (1949) 81–82; Dahlheim (1968) 142 and n. 46; Cimma (1976) 34, 36 n. 12.
59 'Admittedly we do not know of any Roman trade agreement, and it is equally true that we lack evidence of any regular Romano-Egyptian trade in the third century', Lampela (1998) 48. Not commercial ties: Mattingly (1950); Schmitt (1957) 40–42; Volkmann (1959a) 1651; Huzar (1966) 345–346.
60 Peremans and van't Dack (1972) 667.
61 Neatby (1950) 96.
62 Emerging power: Mommsen (1868) 429; Lehmann-Haupt (1902) 347–348; id. (1903) 537; Täubler (1913) 203; Colin (1905) 32.
63 Curiosity: Pliny *NH* 6.58; Holleaux (1921) 81; Lampela (1998) 33–34, 48.
64 Gruen (1984) 672.
65 Plut. *Pyrr.* 4.
66 Paus.1.6.8; Plut. *Pyrr.* 5.1.
67 Adams (2008) 94–95.
68 Plut. *Pyrr.* 4.
69 Plut. *Pyrr.* 6.1.
70 Plut. *Pyrr.* 6.2.
71 Just. 17.2.13; that Ptolemy II offered troops and not Ptolemy Ceraunus of Macedonia: Hammond (1988) 406–408. Cf. Lampela (1998) 40–41.
72 Adams (2008) 95–96.
73 Hammond (1988) 409.
74 Grainger (2002) 6–8.
75 For the opposite view that the Romans initiated the contact, see Westall (2011) 356.
76 He died in autumn 272 BCE in Argos: Holleaux (1921) 62, n. 2.
77 Livy records an episode during the Second Punic War in Spain when, in 206 BCE, two Spanish cities (Illiturgi and Castulo) went over to the Carthaginian side after the Romans had suffered defeats and the death of the two Scipio brothers. At the lowest point for the Romans in the war, one of the cities (Illiturgi) betrayed and killed the Roman soldiers who had managed to escape the battlefield. The immediate reaction of the Roman commander was to launch a two-pronged attack against the two cities without any declaration. The Spanish inhabitants were conscious of the legal repercussions of their decision to ally with the Carthaginians and realised that their action constituted a declaration of war against Rome. Livy writes: 'so completely had the consciousness of what they deserved produced the same effect as a declaration of war against them' (28.19.1–3 and 5). They understood why no declaration of war had been made by the Romans. Other examples: the Vestini in 325 BCE (Livy 8.29.1 and 6) and Pyrrhus in 280 BCE. See Rich (2011) 206.
78 Grainger (2002) 8; Hammond (1988) 412.
79 Reinach (1911) 402–403. See Chapter 4, p. 79.
80 Eutrop. 2.15: *primo legati Alexandrini a Ptolemeo missi Romam uenire et a Romanis amicitiam, quam petierant, obtinuerunt.*
81 Gensel (1907) 1523; Westall (2011) 350. Cf. Bird (1983) xlv–xlvi.
82 Manni (1949) 81.
83 Holleaux (1921) 60–83; Manni (1949) 80–81; Nenci (1953) 183, n. 200; Lévêque (1957) 582; Badian (1958) 44; Volkmann (1959a) 1651; Walbank (1963) 2; Dahlheim (1968) 141–146; Heinen (1972) 634; Peremans and van't Dack (1972) 660–667; Baronowski (1982) 245; Gruen (1984) 62–63, 673–676; Errington (1989) 83; Vollmer (1990) 24; Beyer-Rotthoff (1993) 199; Huss (2001) 201. Those who argue for a treaty:

see Lampela (1998) 34, n. 35. Her conclusion that *societas* in Livy means a treaty takes no account of Mommsen (1887) 1.593, n. 2 and 1.660, 724–725; Matthaei (1907) 192–193; Heuss (1933) 26; Dahlheim (1968) 269–274. See Passerini (1935b) 318–324.

84 *LSJ* 1226 C3 and C3b; Herod. 7.156, 8.52; Phillipson (1911) 375.

85 Holleaux (1921) 65.

86 Lampela (1998) 34.

87 Westall (2011) 353. See also D.H. 20.14 and Dio fr. 41.

88 Lévêque (1957) 58–59.

89 Inexperience: Campbell (2001) 22, n. 71.

90 Account rejected: Niese (1903) 2.153, n. 4 and 2.281; Willrich (1903) 404; Täubler (1913) 203; Holleaux (1921) 46–58; Beloch (1925) 663; Magie (1950) 2.943–944; Schmitt (1964) 291, 293; Heurgon (1969) 224–226; Weber (1972) 217–218; Will (1982) 296; Walbank (1979) 3.182; Sordi (1983) 726–727; Mottershead (1986) 103; Ferrary (1988) 25, n. 81. Account historical: Alföldi (1957) 33; Badian (1958) 44; De Sanctis (1923) 269; Derow (1970) 94–102; Rizzo (1974) 85–87; Gabba (1976) 100; Coppola (1994) 180–182; Erskine (2001) 175; Grainger (2002) 11–12. Non-committal: Elwyn (1993) 280–282.

91 Tac. *Ann.* 12.58.1; Weber (1972) 217.

92 Lewis (1993) 629; Levick (2013) 511.

93 Suet. *Claud.* 8.2; Bardon (1968) 129.

94 Suet. 41.1–3.

95 Millar (1992) 259–265; Corcoran (2013) 174–190. It is known that the correspondence was collected according to subject and arranged chronologically from the Tabula Banasitana, where letters granting Roman citizenship were collected going back to Augustus. See Millar (1992) 359–360; Corcoran (2013) 190. For the Tabula Banasitana, see Sherwin-White (1973b) 90–91.

96 Augustus: Suet. *Aug.* 85.1; Tiberius: Suet. *Tib.* 61.1.

97 Tac. *Ann.* 13.43.3.

98 Cichorius (1922) 388–390.

99 Traditional: Momigliano (1961) 1–19. Preparing *Res Gestae*. Lewis (1993) 695.

100 Schanz and Hosius (1935) 421.

101 De Coninck (1991) 3686.

102 Peter *HRR* 2. cxviiii.

103 Gascou (1994) 14. It was not by rummaging through the archives that Suetonius found his material. See Birley (1984) 249; De Coninck (1991) 3688–3690; Hurley (2001) 7–8.

104 Baldwin (1983) 170.

105 Nomenclature: *diurna urbis acta*, Tac. *Ann.* 13.31; *diurna*, Suet. *Claud.* 41.3; *acta urbis*, *CIL* 8. 4874 = *ILS* 1410; *acta publica*, Suet. *Tib.* 5; *acta populi Romani*, Pliny *NH* 8.61.145. Accessible to Suetonius: Gascou (1994) 12.

106 Baldwin (1979) 191–192.

107 De Coninck (1991) 3677.

108 Suet. *Claud.* 41.6.

109 Talbert (1984) 324.

110 Contents: Mastino (1978) 40–41.

111 *Procurator ab actis urbis*: *CIL* 8. 11813 and 27573. See Mastino (1978) 19. Display: Kubitschek (1894) 291–294. Forged fragment of the *acta diurna*, known as the fragmenta Dodwelliana (*CIL* 6.3403, i–xi*): Mastino (1978) 74. Older literature on its authenticity: Mastino (1978) 75, n. 3. Placed in the *aerarium*: Serv. *ad Georg.* 2.502; Schol. *Iuven.* 9.84f. See De Ruggiero (1961–1962) 1.50.

112 Baldwin (1979) 197.

113 Newspaper: Mastino (1978) ch. 1. Valuable source: Pliny *Ep.* 7.33.3 considered them a valuable historical source and recommended them to Tacitus.

114 Syme (1980) 121 [= Birley (1984) 1268]; id. (1981) 117 [= Birley (1984) 1349].
115 Power (2010) 159.
116 Power (2010) 160.
117 Fall from favour: appears to have occurred while travelling with Hadrian to Gaul, Germany and Britain in spring or early summer in 121/22 CE and he became too close to the emperor's wife. See SHA, *Hadr.* 11.2–3. Date: 119–122 CE, van't Dack (1963) 183–184; 128 CE, Crook (1956–1957) 18–22. Banished: Townend (1959) 290; Syme (1980) 117 [= Birley (1984) 1263]. Lost interest: Macé (1900) 360–361; Wallace-Hadrill (1983) vii. Loss of access: Wallace-Hadrill (1983) 62. Hard work: Wallace-Hadrill (1983) 62; Birley (1984) 249. Archives not needed: De Coninck (1991) 3688–3690.
118 He composed a history of Rome from the death of Julius Caesar to the death of Augustus, probably entitled *A pace ciuile*, an 8-volume history of Carthage, a 20-volume history of the Etruscans and an 8-volume autobiography. See Huzar (1984) 621–623; Briquel (1988); Malitz (1994); Levick (2013). Encouraged by Livy to write history: Suet. *Claud.* 41.1; Last and Ogilvie (1958).
119 Dio 60.4.5.
120 Cic. *Att.* 13.33.3.
121 Tac. *Ann.* 3.51; Corbier (1974) 682; Nicolet (1994).
122 Wallace-Hadrill (1983) 90.
123 Forgery by the Ilians: Magie (1950) 2.943–944, n. 40; Rizzo (1974) 87. Not fooled: Derow (1970) 95, n. 1.
124 Magie (1950) 2.943–944, n. 40.
125 Strabo 13.1.26.
126 Livy 38.39.6–8.
127 App. *Mith.* 61; *OGIS* 8870; *RDGE* 53. See Santangelo (2007) 59–60 and n. 38.
128 Dueck (1999).
129 Kürçer et al. (2012).
130 Acts 15.36–16.40.
131 Tac. *Ann.* 12.58.2.
132 Higgins (2009) 106.
133 See Russo (2014) 589–590.
134 Scramuzza (1971) 125.
135 Mehl (1986) 301–307; Erskine (2001) 173.
136 Derow (1970) 95, n. 1.
137 Holleaux (1921) 47; Rizzo (1974) 85–87; Gabba (1976) 100.
138 Derow (1970) 97–99.
139 Val. Max. 6.6.5; Dio fr. 42 [= Zon. 8.7.3].
140 Holleaux (1921) 3, n. 2.
141 Korn (1972) 572–573. For earlier scholarship, which mainly argued for 266 BCE, see Korn (1972) 570–571.
142 Early literature: Holleaux (1921), nn. 1–7.
143 Control: Cabanes (2008) 179–180.
144 Occupation 269–264 BCE: Cabanes (1976) 83. Trade: Cabanes (1976) 85, nn. 105, 106.
145 Holleaux (1921) 4.
146 Lampela (1998) 48.
147 Successor: Garoufalias (1979) 24. Recognition: Forsythe (2005) 358.

# 4 Roman international friendship

The two major types of diplomatic relations employed to cement ties with other states or communities by the Roman Senate were friendship (*amicitia*) and the treaty (*foedus*). These also represent the two sides of the scholarly debate over the nature of the diplomatic ties formed between Rome and Judaea in 162 BCE. This chapter sets out the now accepted position that the Romans conducted their diplomacy according to norms of ancient international law and practice.[1]

## The reality of *Völkerrecht* (Roman international law): not just a label

Interstate relationships were formed by the Romans, not on some *ad hoc* basis, but in accordance with, if not rules, then precedents and well-understood concepts. Those underlying principles, which we call international law, need to be grasped as the Romans would have recognised them, rather than overlaying them with modern concepts such as state sovereignty. With the proviso that we recognise 'international law' as modern, it remains a useful and concise way of referring to the rules by which the Romans' interstate diplomacy was conducted. Those rules can be legitimately applied to ancient circumstances when the following conditions are present:

1 when they are exercised between two independent states;
2 when diplomatic relations are conducted between those states;
3 when those states undertake to observe agreements under customary law;
4 when there are consequences for not upholding agreements entered into.[2]

For diplomacy to exist between international peoples, there needed to have been in place modes of statecraft – that is, agreed-upon basic principles, such as rules for the conduct of embassies, the protection of and immunity for ambassadors, the sanctity of treaties, and rules governing warfare.

The early Roman community, through the fetial law (*ius fetiale*), considered that its inter-community regulations were upheld by a system of rules sanctioned by religious bonds. The Romans and their neighbours shared these rules and believed that consequences would follow should they break the execration oath and be the first to violate the terms of treaties concluded through the fetial priests' ritual. Separate from the fetial law was the *ius gentium* (law of nations), which is not to be confused with international law. The law of nations was a collection of unwritten laws and customs first articulated in the Late Republic, principally but not exclusively by Cicero.[3]

Thus in referring to international law in a Roman context, I do not refer to the modern field of International Relations with its two competing theories, the Realist and Constructionist schools.[4] The former is based on the principle that actions are driven by the dictum that 'might is right'; the latter sets its focus on the factors that drive states to co-operate, holding that states make decisions on the basis of shared past experiences.[5] The present study raises questions about the utility of such theories for analysing Roman diplomacy.

The study of *amicitia* has been influenced by modern theories based on early modern and modern history. This chapter returns to first principles and discusses *amicitia* on the basis of the Romans' understanding of the concept exemplified by their words and actions. Studies by historians have not as a rule engaged the research on *amicitia* to be found in the field of Roman *Völkerrecht*, where it might be valuable in throwing light on our understanding of historical events, especially in those involving the formation of Roman friendship in international relations.

At the outset, it is important to note that *amicitia* will be studied here only in the sphere of international relations and not in the context of interpersonal political relationships among the Roman nobility. It is true that the Romans applied to international relationships the cohesive social principles from their internal societal workings. It is not surprising, therefore, to see that the principles of friendship were extended into the international sphere.[6] Nor is it the concern of this study to explore theories of Roman imperialism, although it is acknowledged that the formation of ties of *amicitia* has played a pivotal role in the discussion of the main theories.[7]

The Romans themselves had texts in Greek and Latin to which they could refer on the subject of international law. Only a few of these treatises on statecraft, setting out the rules for statecraft, are known by name.[8] Demetrius of Phaleron was the author of three books dealing with three aspects of diplomacy. He fled Athens and came to reside in Egypt at the time of Ptolemy I, where he composed three works, Δίκαια ('Justice'), Πρεσβευτικὸς ('On Ambassadors') and Περὶ Εἰρήνης ('On Peace'). Varro in his *Antiquitates Rerum Humanarum* included a book entitled, *De Bello et Pace* ('On War and Peace'). Among other subjects, it presumably covered the rules concerning the declaration of war and treaties. These would have clarified for us the rules and workings of Hellenistic and Roman diplomacy. Unfortunately none of these works has survived. We are thus left with the works of historians (which only allude to the workings of international law) and copies on stone of actual diplomatic documents.

How *amicitia* was established and the reasons the senate would choose this diplomatic method over a *foedus*, are key to understanding that *amicitia* was the outcome of Judas' embassy. *Amicitia* could lapse or be terminated. The possibility of its re-establishment permits a better comprehension of the diplomatic relations between Rome and Judaea under the later Hasmonaeans, a subject explored in Chapter 7.

This chapter will deal with our understanding of what *amicitia* entailed: how it was formed, what were the conditions of *amicitia* for the ally, what were the obligations to Rome, and how *amicitia* could be severed. Much of our evidence is derived from observing how *amicitia* operated in practice from the third to the first centuries BCE.

The First Book of Maccabees reports (8.17–18) that the Jewish envoys were tasked with obtaining φιλία καὶ συμμαχία (literally, 'friendship and alliance'). The account continues (8.20) that in their audience with the senate the envoys pleaded their case and asked for συμμαχίαν καὶ εἰρήνην (literally, 'alliance and peace'). Verse 22 notes that the senate decided to grant their request and expresses the outcome as εἰρήνης καὶ συμμαχίας ('peace and alliance'). At 1 Macc. 8.31, the Jews are referred to as τοὺς φίλους ἡμῶν τοὺς συμμάχους' Ιουδαίους ('your friends and allies, the Jews'). Jews would have interpreted such language in terms of how their Seleucid (and earlier Ptolemaic) overlords were bound to Rome. *Amicitia*, not treaties, was the method by which Rome formed her first connections with Hellenistic leaders.

## The Jewish concept of friendship

A friend was expected to show loyalty, reliability and trustworthiness at all times. For example, in the Book of Ben Sira (Ecclesiastes) we find, 'Love a friend and keep faith with him' (27.17a).[9] The Romans, as we saw before, would not have disagreed with these sentiments of keeping faith, which corresponded with the Latin, *fides*. A friend is also thought of as a 'sturdy shelter' (Ben Sira: 6.14), which was exactly what Judas was hoping to find in the Romans. The views expressed in the Book of Ben Sira are of great relevance to what Judas may have thought about friendship, as they reflect those from the first quarter of the second century BCE.[10] Unlike the Greek concept of friendship, the Jewish semantic range did not confine itself to kinship relations or to ties with family, nor did the Hebrew language have a noun for 'friendship'.[11] A very important association for Jews was that friendship was a relationship between equals.[12] To the Roman mind, there was no such thing as equality with Rome through *amicitia*. Dietrich has considered perhaps some influence of Aristotle on the views current during the period.[13] Many scholars do find similarities between Greek writings and the views in Ben Sira.[14] One can see Ben Sira navigating between Hellenistic ideas and those of the Torah to find some middle ground in adapting to a society where cultural and social norms emphasised relationship of friendship.[15] In particular, he tried to reconcile the view from the Old Testament that friendship was based on equality with the Hellenistic notion of φιλία, which was not contractual but based on gift exchange. Ben Sira thought that a man had to know the rules of gift giving.[16] For the gift was the conventional way of gathering friendships.[17]

In Proverbs, friendship is expected to last from one generation to the next: 'Do not abandon your companion or your father's companion' (Prov. 27.10a). The friendship between David and Jonathan was also pledged for eternity and bound their children.[18] In international relations, throughout the Ancient Near East, friendship was a legal institution.[19] For example, the friendship between Jonathan and David was formed by a covenant.[20] Contrast this with the extra-legal nature of Roman international friendship, which, although without legal form, was considered by them to be just as binding. Did the Jews regard such a non-legal form of diplomatic relations as less binding because there were no oaths? In Rome, friendship forms the basis for a treaty at some later point. In the Ancient Near East, friendship represented the treaty.[21] The alliance between King David and Hiram, the king of Tyre, uses the language of friendship. At 1 Kgs 5.15, we learn, 'Hiram was always a friend to David.' This alliance continued between Hiram and David's son, Solomon.[22]

In these differences lay a wide range of possibilities for misunderstanding. The principal question, however, is, when the Roman Senate spoke to the Jews of friendship, did the Jewish envoys assume that they had a treaty with Rome? The Jewish envoys and Judas knew that friendship was broken by treachery and by abandoning old friends.[23] In the conduct of later Hasmonaeans they should have been aware that their friendship with Rome could be nullified by their treachery – that is, their friendly relations with states apart from Rome.

## The meaning of friendship in Greek diplomacy

The text of 1 Maccabees provides the term for 'friendship' in Greek; this necessitates a discussion of its meaning in Greek international relations before we can move to its use in Roman international relations. The Greek concept of φιλία covered a wider semantic range than did the Latin *amicitia*. The Romans translated φιλία as *amor*.[24] In Greek, φιλία certainly could denote 'friend' in terms of an emotional relationship, but it was also used for kinship and civic relations.[25] For the Greeks, φιλία, while translated as 'friendship', is derived from the Indo-European root *bheid-, meaning 'good faith'. Thus, φιλία is a pact formed on the basis of good faith between the parties.[26] It carries the assumption that underlying the friendship is a reciprocal arrangement and that carries mutual obligations.[27] It bears the meaning of a partnership without necessarily implying friendship on an emotional level.[28] It was kept deliberately vague to enable communities to maintain their own autonomy.[29] Friendship ties could in this way be used to bind allies tightly in the Delian League in the fifth century.[30] The concept of interstate friendship evolved from the archaic period based on the concept of ξενία (guest friendship or hospitality) that served as a mechanism for forming connections between the stranger and the host (πρόξενος). The reciprocal benefits between guest and host comprised protection during the stay, shelter and favours, with the whole relationship based on loyalty and trust.[31]

From the classical period, φίλος spilled out of the private realm and came to be used as a term for the foreign ally of a Greek city, one who enjoyed peaceful relations and who was not an enemy.[32] The conclusion of friendship was accompanied by the formation of ties of kinship (συγγένεια).[33] Thus, in the classical period, φιλία had a narrow meaning, restricted to the type of agreement that was reciprocal in the sense that each would have the same friends and enemies (οἱ αὐτοὶ φίλοι καὶ ἐχθροί).[34] In time of war, if the host and his guest friend should find themselves on opposing sides, it was expected that the interests of the state would prevail over these personal ties.[35]

In the Hellenistic period, evidence from decrees shows that φιλία comes to be associated with kinship and goodwill.[36] According to Dionysius of Halicarnassus (4.25.3), these are the bonds that cement good relations between states.

## Terminology of Roman international *amicitia*

Roman international *amicitia* between states first and foremost indicated the formation of a state of peace between them and the absence of hostilities.[37] What resulted was a state of favourable, cordial relations. The ties thus formed were not defined in a concrete or specific manner.[38] Whether they were legally formed and legally binding is a subject that divides scholars.[39]

The question of how to characterise *amicitia* has in most cases been dealt with by reference to situational analysis. Some view *amicitia* as a transitional stage between the absence of relations with Rome and the status of *amicus et socius*. This was the conclusion of Sherwin-White, who considered that states referred to their first dealings with Rome as the time 'when a people first entered into friendship with Rome.'[40]

In the sources, we find an unfortunate amount of terminological confusion between the terms *amicus*, *socius* and *amicus et socius*. Livy, in particular, has been considered unreliable when it comes to discriminating between these terms.[41]

It was once thought that Roman *amici* (friends) were separate and distinct from *socii* (allies). Mommsen had divided Roman allies into either *socii* or *amici*. In his view, *socii* were Roman allies in Italy who supplied military contingents to the Roman army and *amici* could be divided into either *amici* or *amici et socii*.[42] The *amici* were bound to Rome by a treaty and *amici et socii* were the friends who were obligated to send troops to Rome. The *socii* were in fact subjects of Rome. A *socius* had to send to Rome a fixed number of soldiers to the Roman army every year, whereas an *amicus* gave military help only on a voluntary basis.[43]

The terms *amicitia* and *foedus* became interchangeable in Livy as a consequence of the usage of the early principate, when all allies irrespective of their technical status had been subsumed into a form of subjection to Rome.[44] One finds inconsistencies – for example, the Aetolians are called *socii* and have *societas* in Livy[45] yet they are also described as *amici* and have *amicitia*.[46] The Achaeans are mentioned as *socii* and have *societas*.[47] They are labelled as *amici* and have *amicitia*.[48] Then in other places they are called *socii et amici*.[49] Matthaei found 24 places where Livy uses *amicitia* and also *societas* to describe an alliance.[50] In Livy 45.25.9 *societas* indicates the absence of a *foedus* when the Rhodians describe their previous diplomatic relations with Rome:

> nam ita per tot annos in amicitia fuerant, ut sociali foedere se cum Romanis non illigarent: tunc utique petenda societas uidebatur.
>
> For all those years they had maintained friendly relations with Rome without binding themselves by an express treaty of alliance.

Polybius (30.5.6) distinguishes between φιλία and συμμαχία: the former had existed between Rome and Rhodes, but the Rhodians had never sought the latter because they did not want to be tied to Rome by means of oaths and treaties. In another example, Livy (39.11.1–2) mentions that none of the states in Asia had *societas*, but the Romans already had friendship with Attalus of Pergamum. From these passages Matthaei concluded that Roman writers did recognise a distinction between *societas* and *amicitia*.[51]

Matthaei also addressed the question as to whether *amici* could have a *foedus* with Rome. Livy does mention that the Aetolians, the Achaeans, Messene and Philip had both *amicitia* and a *foedus* with Rome. Athens is mentioned with both a *foedus* and *amicitia* by Tacitus.[52] Matthaei was able to conclude, contrary to Mommsen, that *amicitia* was not created by a treaty. Fundamental is Livy 33.30 (which is based on Polybius 18.44), where Philip already has a peace treaty but was seeking friendship.[53] Another example illustrates this distinction: the Aetolians had both *amicitia* and a treaty with Rome in 211 BCE, which was cancelled in 205 BCE. In 200 BCE only the friendship is restored and not their treaty.[54] When some *amici* are called *foederati* – that is, allied by a treaty – this refers to allies who have a peace treaty with Rome.[55] *Socii et amici* have a defensive alliance with Rome in which they are bound to assist Rome. The *amicus*, however, has an independent foreign policy and freedom from conscription terms defined in a senatorial decree and not in a treaty.

Matthaei emphasised that the imprecision of terms in the literary sources necessitated priority be given to the use of inscriptions that are official copies of Roman senatorial decrees and so are the best forms of evidence. The expressions used in them may be formulaic, but they do preserve the accurate language of Roman diplomacy.[56] The epigraphic texts are not mediated through the works of historians at second or third hand and provide a window into the actual speeches that took place in the senate. The senatorial decree that is epigraphically preserved to settle a land dispute between two Thessalian cities, Narthakion and Melitaia,[57] speaks of 'entering into the friendship of the Romans'[58] and Greek states considered it advantageous to remind the Romans of long-standing ties of friendship. They made mention of having always been in the friendship of the Romans or having been *amici* of the Romans from the beginning. Some said they enjoyed ancestral friendship with the Romans.[59] Others announced that they had preserved their friendship with the Romans always.[60]

Cimma found the contexts in which *amicitia* is found to be so diverse as to defy categorisation.[61] Cimma in her reliance on passages from Livy did not take into account sufficiently the inconsistency with which that historian used terms such as *amicitia*. From her collected examples, she proposed a division of *amicitia* into two strictly separate usages.[62] The first is a general usage in the sense of good relations. The second is a technical sense of *amicitia* as a legal relationship with mutual obligations, a relationship that has been established through *ad hoc* accords. Such a division has not found universal acceptance.[63]

In addition, Cimma argued against the shift in the meaning and use of the term due to the development of Roman power in the East in the first third of the second century BCE, as was pointed out by Dahlheim. The only categories made by Dahlheim were the *amicitia* that came about through international contact, for example through trade, for which he uses the term *Interessengemeinschaft* (a community of interest), and the *amicitia* as a result of treaties.[64]

The most recent treatment of these classifications by Zack proposes that *amici* were private persons who enjoyed *hospitium* in Rome, as distinct from *socii*, who may be states or peoples (*ciuitates* or *populi*). *Socii et amici* are foreigners or strangers with no personal privileges in Rome, who resemble *socii*.[65] The introduction of *hospitium* into the definition of *amici* is belied by the letter of Cicero to Crassus in 54 BCE, where the two concepts are kept separate.[66]

## The formation of *amicitia*

In the debate over how *amicitia* was concluded or formalised between Rome and her allies, two main views have emerged. The older is that friendship was made through a treaty.[67] The second view is that friendship came about through cordial gestures, such as an exchange of embassies. These two proposals are the subject of this section, bearing in mind the context of the question of the Jewish embassies to Rome in the second century BCE. As such, the *amicitia* formed between Rome and communities and not kings is the primary focus. The Jews in the revolt from the Seleucid Empire came into contact with the Romans for the first time and came to understand how the Seleucids' ties of *amicitia* with Rome could benefit them. While most of the kings who had friendship with Rome are not dealt with in any detail, the Seleucids kings are discussed at length.

### *A friendship treaty?*

The whole issue of whether one could become a friend of Rome involves the question as to whether *amicitia* was formed by a treaty.[68] The Greek term φιλία καὶ συμμαχία has been construed to mean a 'friendship' treaty, on the one hand, and solely 'friendship', on the other. To understand the phrase φιλία καὶ συμμαχία, it is necessary to examine its appearance and use in a Greek context.

In Greek interstate relations, a distinction was made between an alliance (συμμαχία) and friendship (φιλία). As early as the second half of the sixth century BCE, we find an extant copy of an alliance between the Greek city of Sybaris in southern Italy and the Serdaioi (an indigenous people living on the Tyrrhenian coast).[69] The text speaks of 'the Sybarites and their allies and the Serdaioi united in friendship, faithful without guile forever.'[70] Already in this document the friendship, newly established, is distinguished from existing alliances with Sybaris.[71] The Greek text of the Romano-Carthaginian alliance of 509 BCE also shows a distinction between φιλία as the result of the agreement and συμμαχία as the treaty itself.

Polybius explains: 'There is to be friendship between the Romans and their allies and the Carthaginians and their allies on these terms' (3.22.4). The treaty established respective spheres of influence and φιλία was formed between the two states without any mention of military assistance to either side.[72]

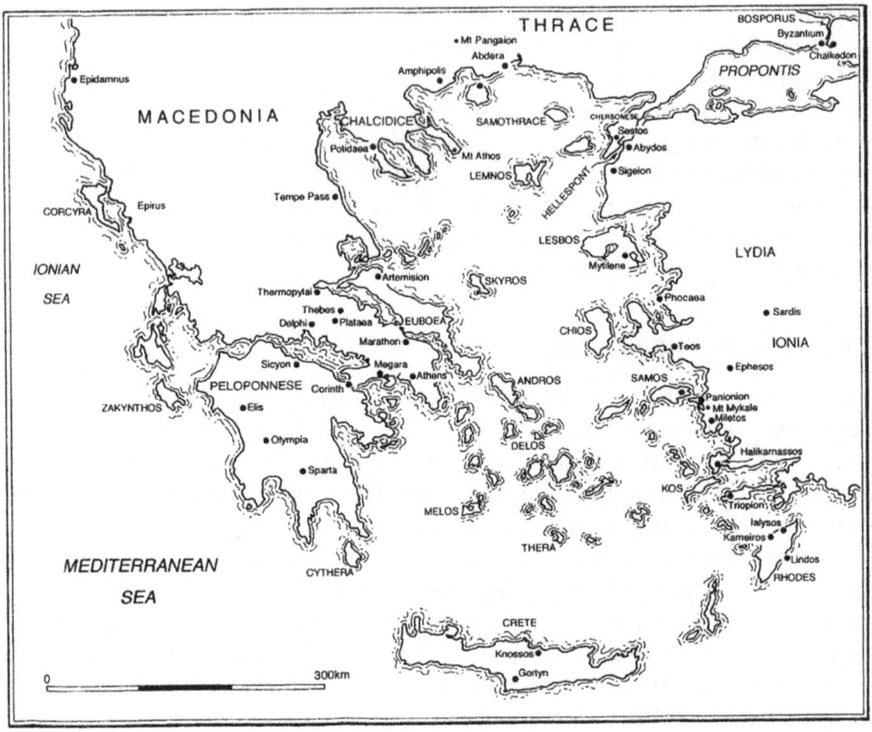


*Map 4.1* The Greek world

The reason the two concepts are separate, is their differing functions. When diplomatic relations are made for the first time there are certain obstacles to be overcome – for example, previous hostility or just the foreign character of the new ally. The role of φιλία is to negate prior unfriendly relations and to establish common ties as though with a community that shares a similar culture and language. Φιλία becomes the first step to provide a basis for relations with communities with dissimilar religious or ethnic characters.[73] The συμμαχία is the agreement itself containing the obligations to which both sides are bound.[74] The first two mentions of φιλία and συμμαχία being linked together comes from Herodotus. In the first example, Croesus wants to become an ally of Sparta (Hdt. 1.69.2): φίλος τεθέλων γενέσθαι καὶ σύμμαχος ἄνευ τε δόλου καὶ ἀπάτης . . . .

The second example is the friendship and alliance made between Amasis of Egypt and Cyrene (Hdt. 2.181.1): φιλότητά τε καὶ συμμαχίην . . . . Both of these alliances were between Greeks and foreigners. In the fourth century, there are two examples from Xenophon of treaties between two parties that have had no prior diplomatic ties. Both are with foreigners: Seuthes and Pharnabazus.[75] The φιλία in these instances was designed to overcome the foreignness of the new ally to offset the lack of common values.[76]

Another and important use of φιλία as a precondition to συμμαχία is to be found in the treaty of 422 BCE between Athens and the cities of the Bottiaeans in Thrace.[77] The inscription mentions that they will forgive past wrongs. This represents the putting of past hostilities behind them so that a new relationship may begin. In the late-fourth-century relationships of φιλία between Rome and Alexander the Great, the need for forgiveness coloured the sending of the Roman envoys to Babylon. Their aim was to erase the complaints of Alexander of piracy emanating from a Roman colony that should have been under Roman control. The need for forgiveness also underlay the embassy of Ptolemy II to Rome, as the ruler sought to make amends for the support he had given to Pyrrhus, whom Rome had just defeated. Φιλία also carried this idea of wishing to remove past hostile associations with the embassy from Apollonia that had been part of Pyrrhus' kingdom.

Originally the expression φιλία καὶ συμμαχία was not a pleonasm or hendiadys: it expressed two notions that came into effect in time of war. The first was that a friend did not provide help to the enemy in line with the requirement to have the same friends and enemies and the second that a friend should provide military aid. By the Hellenistic period, however, the expression lost this second component and became a term to indicate friendship, which in wartime guaranteed to the ally that their friend would remain neutral at the very least.[78]

It is now generally accepted that φιλία καὶ συμμαχία does not denote a treaty in the sense of a *foedus*. The idea that there existed in Roman *Völkerrecht* such a concept as a 'friendship treaty' was put forward by Mommsen, who coined the term 'Freundschaftsvertrag'. A treaty was necessary, he argued, in order to overcome and annul the 'natural state of enmity' that he believed existed between Rome and all those who were not her allies. This doctrine he called 'natürlich Feindschaft' or 'natürlich Rechtlosigkeit'. In other words, according to Mommsen's principle, Rome considered everyone an enemy until such time as they had proved otherwise by making a treaty with Rome.[79] The term *socius* was considered by Mommsen as sufficient evidence to indicate a treaty relationship.[80] Mommsen's theory was further developed by Täubler.[81] He varied Mommsen's interpretation by suggesting that the Roman treaty developed not out of the treaty over *hospitium* but from the war treaty.[82] Matthaei in 1907 challenged Mommsen's doctrine and maintained that *amicitia* was not formed through a treaty; rather it was a separate diplomatic instrument entirely.[83] Since the terminology in the literary sources had mutated over time, Matthaei turned to inscriptions, especially the *Senatus Consultum de Narthaciensium et Meliteensium litibus*, for an understanding of *amicitia*. She found that *amicus et socius* does not refer to *socius*, but is the official title for a friend of the Roman people.[84] She concluded that *amicitia* was a state of diplomatic relations that could be terminated by the Romans at will, unlike a *foedus*, which was permanent and could not be unilaterally annulled.[85]

## *'Formless' amicitia*

For Täubler, *amici* had a 'friendship treaty' with Rome and *amici et socii* had surrendered to Rome and then had formed a military alliance.[86] Refuting this concept of the friendship treaty, Heuss and Paradisi have shown that *amicitia* was not created by a treaty.[87] According to Heuss, at the beginning of a relationship characterised as friendship there was no need for a *Freundschaftsvertrag* principally because the *amicitia* relationship was considered enduring and not bound by time.[88] As the relations between Rome and Judaea in 162 BCE are still described as a friendship treaty, even after the publication and wide acceptance of the researches of Heuss,[89] the arguments against such a type of treaty need to be covered in some detail.

The only treaty held to be a treaty of friendship in the literature is the peace treaty with Antiochus.[90] Thus, the discussion on the validity of the nomenclature 'friendship treaty', centres on this treaty in particular. The reliance on one treaty to denote a general type is, in itself, methodologically weak.[91] It should be noted at the outset that our sources for this treaty, Polybius and Livy,[92] transmit this treaty in a form that no longer exhibits the original character of the treaty. Indeed, some scholars have even thrown doubt on how much of the document cited by Polybius was his own work or part of the treaty.[93] The transmission of the Polybian text has left some textual difficulties at crucial points.[94] Given the state of the text that one has to work with, the question remains whether this treaty was in fact a 'friendship treaty'. According to Heuss,[95] the structure of the Antiochus treaty is in the form of a condition. The opening sentence of the treaty (Polyb. 21.42 [43].1) sets out the basic condition: φιλίαν ὑπάρχειν 'Αντιόχῳ καὶ 'Ρωναίοις εἰς ἅπαντα τὸν χρόνον ποιοῦντι τὰ κατὰ τὰς συνθήκας ('There shall be friendship between Antiochus and the Romans for all time if he fulfils the conditions of the treaty'). The entire treaty rests on this condition. There shall be *amicitia* if this and that happens. The *amicitia* is bound indissolubly to the fulfilment of the specific conditions that follow in sections 2–26. Thus, the Antiochus treaty is negative in character and the *amicitia* so formed is not found together with positive clauses. Otherwise, one would find the treaty opening with only positive words or sentiments, such as these: φιλίαν ὑπάρχειν 'Αντιόχῳ καὶ 'Ρωναίοις εἰς ἅπαντα τὸν χρόνον ('There shall be friendship between Antiochus and the Romans for all time'). The fact that the treaty with Antiochus opens with a condition indicates that what follows – that is, the conditions – is the important part of the treaty. The setting out of the obligations to Rome is the purpose of the treaty. Once doubt is thrown on the identification of the single example as a 'friendship treaty', the existence of the very category itself comes into question.

The researches of Paradisi brought to light another aspect of *amicitia* that was not related to the *Freundschaftsvertrag*. *Amicitia* that comes about as a result of a treaty does not necessarily indicate the existence of a 'friendship treaty' as such. Thus, for example, when Livy speaks of *in foedere atque amicitia* (4.7.14) or of *cum amicitiam ac societatem petentes* (7.27.2), this simply means that the ally will be loyal and abide by the literal interpretation of the treaty.[96] The combined work of Heuss and Paradisi has caused the old category of *Freundschaftsvertrag* to disappear among the work of Roman historians; nevertheless, the term is still found in discussions of the document in 1 Macc. 8.23–32 and continues to permeate the discussion of the word *amicitia* in connection with Roman–Jewish relations.

In particular, *amicitia* in Justinus 36.3.9 is often taken to mean a treaty.[97] The characteristics of *amicitia* as understood today would exclude such an interpretation. Rather than being formed by means of a treaty, *amicitia* was a relationship between states of equal power that was formed through non-legal methods and was derived from *amicitia* in the private sphere.[98] *Amicitia* did not require a specific act of establishment.[99] A relationship of friendship could be brought about by the exchange of ambassadors and the giving of gifts.[100] An older view that *amicitia* could be divided into a relationship established either *de iure* or *de facto* involves a distinction that is no longer made.[101] Just as *amicitia* was formed in an informal way, so equally informal was its manner of dissolution, which could be due to any behaviour deemed unfriendly by Rome.[102]

It was Heuss who, in his published dissertation in 1933, laid out the case for an international law instrument of *amicitia* formed not by a treaty but through more informal means – for example, the exchange of embassies or military co-operation. For Heuss, there was no 'treaty of friendship': *amicitia* was formed not through any legal act and so was formless (meaning without legal form). Roman friendship denoted an international law relationship of cordial relations. This has become the prevailing view.[103] He argued that by the third century this had become the most common form of diplomatic relations used by the senate. His work remains the consensus position on the nature of *amicitia* as a form of international relations.[104]

Heuss thought that, although originally Roman alliances were for military purposes, the same effect later could be achieved without a treaty. He also took issue with Bickerman for asserting that *socius* could be equated with συμμαχος.[105] Such a parallel may have held for the fourth century, but it did not take sufficient consideration of the linguistic changes that followed the shift in political relationships over time. Dahlheim argued that precisely this factor had to be taken into account: that by the second century a *socius* could refer to a treaty partner, but it need not.[106]

Key texts in this context are two passages from Livy (29.11.2 and 45.25.9) referring to the Rhodian embassy that came to Rome in 167 BCE to seek an alliance. In this passage the terms *amicitia* and *societas* are distinguished one from the other. The same distinction is found in Polyb. 30.23.4, where the senate left their *amicitia* unaltered but refused to grant an alliance.[107] According to Heuss, in inscriptions φίλος καὶ σύμμαχος is a pure pleonasm and carries no legal meaning other than an indication of a relationship of friendship.[108] This was recognised by both Mommsen and Matthaei.[109] Furthermore, *amicitia et societas* could be used interchangably with *amicitia*.[110] The use of φιλία καὶ συμμαχία not to refer to a treaty but to indicate merely φιλία, has been a finding of Heuss and Dahlheim.[111]

The important contribution made by Dahlheim was to show that the form and content of *amicitia* began to diverge. Originally *amicitia* had been a relationship of parity between powers sharing common interests. Under such a relationship, it was impolitic to attempt to suppress one partner. Concomitant with *amicitia* was the legally empowered obligation to respect the sovereignty of the *amicus*.[112] The subordination of *amici populi Romani* to Roman decisions had already occurred in the Second Macedonian War, in the matter of the deployment of their troops and later in their power to make political decisions.[113] As an example, the declaration of war on Antiochus by Pergamum was considered incompatible with its *amicitia* with Rome.[114]

According to Dahlheim, the result was that after the First and Second Macedonian wars Rome changed from reliance on relationships expressed as *amicitia* to relationships expressed as *amicitia et societas*. This change was necessary to accommodate the Roman need for military support from her allies.[115] The wars against Antiochus and Perseus only increased the number of allies on the Roman side and hence caused a broadening of the circle of Roman *amici et socii*. According to Dahlheim, it was at this point that *amicitia* and *societas* became indistinguishable.[116] There was little difference, as these allies were now bound to follow Roman foreign policy.[117] The new facts on the ground are illustrated by the treaty between Pharnaces and Chersonnesus (180–179 BCE), which contained, as one of its clauses, the stipulation that both would continue in *amicitia* with Rome and would conduct their activities in accordance with Roman wishes.[118] After 168 BCE the reality of Roman power obliterated any pretence of equality in the relationship. *Amicitia* with the Romans was maintained only on the conditions of the utmost loyalty to Rome. Even the suspicion that Rhodes and Pergamum had thought of changing sides at the end of the war with Perseus was sufficient grounds for Rome to question their continuing existence.[119]

When Rome ordered an end to the war between Prusias II and Attalus in 156 BCE and her demand was ignored, Rome sent an embassy to cancel the *amicitia*. This step brought Prusias into line and he accepted a peace whose terms had been dictated by Rome.[120] As a consequence it was clear (if it had not been before) that every political action in the foreign policy arena of an *amicus* had to be sanctioned by Rome.[121] By the end of the second half of the second century BCE virtually all the Hellenistic states were in a relationship of *amicitia* with Rome. Military allies could be called upon without having to rely on formal state treaties (*foedera*)[122] and with the factual superiority of Rome only non-judicial forms of diplomacy were needed by her.

In essence, *amicitia* signified the presence of voluntarily established diplomatic relations formed after diplomatic contact through embassies. In times of war this *amicitia* assumed greater importance in that Rome expected her friends to remain neutral – that is, to desist from helping her enemies and to refrain from action that would hurt the Roman cause. In addition, more positive help in the form of military aid was usually expected from the *amici*. At the conclusion of a war, the defeated enemy came to Rome asking for friendship and then followed the act of *deditio*. After the surrender there arose *amicitia* between Rome and her former enemy, which was embedded in the subsequent peace treaty in a clause designed to make the friendship permanent.

## The formation of amicitia through *appellatio*

The process of *appellatio*, whereby the senate named an ally as 'friend and ally of the Roman people', is clear cut for the kings who became friends of Rome.

Being named by the senate as a 'friend' or 'friend and ally' was the decisive act;[123] the public naming and identifying a state as a 'friend' made it so. For example, when Vermina, the son of Syphax, sent an embassy to Rome in 200 BCE with the request to become a friend and ally of Rome, although this request was denied, the need for an act of naming by the senate is recorded by Livy: the embassy asked that Vermina be named king and ally and friend by the senate.[124] The impression from this account is that the Romans were schooling Vermina on the principles of statesmanship and international relations.[125] In this passage, the senate expounds on the principle that a precondition for the naming as friend is that there must be peace between Rome and the applicant before he can be named a friend and ally: *ut rex sociusque et amicus a senatu appellaretur*. In this context it was natural that the senate should state that the conditions were that the prospective friend should have undertaken some great service on behalf of the Romans. Almost all the known occasions of the conferral of the title friend and ally were in response to a request from the king. A great exception was made for Ariobarzanes III of Cappadocia, who had not sought the honour but for whom Cicero successfully raised the matter in the senate.[126]

If the agreement was made by a general in the field, it had to be ratified in Rome by the senate.[127] We can see this in operation in the case of Massinissa, king of Numidia, who became a friend first by Scipio and then later by the senate. Livy 30.15.11 reports,

> Addressing Massinissa as king and eulogising him in the highest possible terms, he presented him with a golden crown, curule chair, an ivory sceptre and also with a purple-bordered toga and a tunic embroidered with palms.

A later example is that of Ariovistus, king of the Suebi in Gaul, who was declared a friend of the Romans first by Julius Caesar and then later by the senate in Rome. In Caesar's own report, he states (*BG* 1.35.2) that 'he [Ariovistus] had been named as king and friend by the Senate.'

In all these cases the king is *appellatus*: he was named or declared a friend of the Roman people. The equivalent in Greek was προσαγορεύω.[128] Its meaning in this context is to name someone – that is, it is in the form of a salutation that the *amicitia* is formed.[129] For example, Zonaras (our only source for this incident) relates the declaration for Ariarathes IV of Cappadocia in 188 BCE. Zonaras states (9.24): 'But the fact that Ariarathes had been declared a friend and ally by the Romans enabled him subsequently to make the entire domain his own.'

In 55 BCE Ptolemy Auletes was restored to his throne in Egypt and Suetonius records the prior granting of friendship and alliance. Suetonius relates (*Div. Iul.* 11), 'because the citizens of Alexandria had deposed their king, who had been named by the senate an ally and friend of the Roman people'.[130] Dio (39.12.1) uses a different verb, ὀνομάζω; it bears, however, the same meaning of 'to name' or 'to address by name'.

During the first year of the civil war, Juba, king of Mauretania in 49 BCE, was also made a friend of the Romans by 'naming' (*appellatio*) by the alternate government that Pompey had established in Macedonia when most of the senate left Rome to Julius Caesar.[131] Dio reports (41.42.7): 'And Juba received honours at the hands of Pompey and the senators who were in Macedonia, and was named as king; but by Caesar and those in the city he was called to account and declared an enemy, while Bocchus and Bogud were named kings, because they were hostile to him.' In the early empire, during the reign of Tiberius in 24 CE, the senate named Ptolemy of Mauretania as friend and ally of the Romans.[132]

The naming procedure entailed a request; this, if successful, resulted in a senatorial decree and enrolment in the list of friends (*formula amicorum*, see below), followed by the deposition of the bronze tablet containing the decree on the Capitol. The most complete account of the whole procedure is given by Josephus (*Ant.* 14.388–389) for the *appellatio* for King Herod in 40 BCE:

> When the senate adjourned, Antony and Caesar left with Herod between them, preceded by the consuls and other officers, to offer sacrifices and to deposit their decrees in the capitol. Antony held a feast for Herod on the first day of his reign; and that is how he received the kingship . . . .

Not only kings but other individuals who had given service to the Romans could be named as friend and ally. A bilingual inscription records a senatorial decree from 78 BCE honouring three Greek sea captains who had distinguished themselves in services to Rome in the Social War.[133] The three men were designated officially by *appellatio* as friends: *uiros bonos et ameicos appellari* (line 6 in the Latin) and (in the Greek) ἄνδρας . . . φίλους προσαγορεῦσαι (lines 10–11).

The same procedure was used for communities and evidence for the naming of communities as friends and allies by the senate comes from a number of inscriptions. The first was found in a partially preserved state at Erimupolis in Crete in 1919 and relates to a land dispute between the two cities of Itanos and Hierapytna in 112 BCE.[134] Only a narrow strip down the whole right side is completely legible and this accounts for the much-restored state of the text.[135] In the inscription it is told how envoys from Hierapytna came to Rome to the senate to plead their case. The text gives their speech to the senate followed by the decree that the senate passed the consul's decree to set up an arbitration tribunal and a letter by the consul to the Hierapytnians. Especially pertinent is a statement by the envoys from Hierapytna in their speech to the senate. In line 11 they state that some cities in Crete, including Knossos, had not been named or declared friends and allies: οὔτε συμμάχους αὐτοὺς προσηγόρευσε οὔτε Κνωσίους οὔτε τοὺς. The Hierapytnians renew the friendship they made with Rome earlier in 115 BCE. Here we see the same verb, προσαγορεύω, used to express the *appellatio*, the nomination or declaration of the community as friend and ally of the Roman people.

The second inscription concerns the celebration of games in honour of the governor of the province of Asia, Q. Mucius Scaevola, in 98 or 94 BCE.[136] Writing to Ephesus, Scaevola begins his letter with a reference to the friendship existing between Rome and the Ephesians.[137] The inscription at part of this line reads, τῶν ἐν τῇ φιλίαι κριθε͂τωῦ δῆμων τε, where the verb κρινώ expresses the notion of being judged or estimed. A similar turn of phrase is to be found in another inscription from Asia from the early first century.[138] In line 2 it speaks of those judged individually to be in friendship with the Romans: καὶ οἱ καὶ ἄνδρα κεκριμένοι ἐν τῆι πρὸς Ῥωμαίους φιλίαι. Again, we see the verb κρινώ. Here it is a technical expression equivalent to the Latin *appello* – that is, the naming of individuals or communities as friends and allies of the Romans.[139]

The procedure for establishing friendship was not a treaty: it came about through a decision of the senate to declare or name either a king, an individual or a community as a friend and ally. The senate then ordered a senior magistrate, either a consul or the praetor peregrinus, to have the new ally inscribed in the list of allies (the *formula amicorum*) in order to record to what privileges their envoys were entitled when in Rome (see below). Following this decision, the senate could decide to give permission for a bronze tablet recording the friendship to be placed on the Capitol (see below).

## The formula amicorum

States (and individuals) who entered into the friendship of the Romans were then registered on a list of friends. When the Jewish embassy was sent to Rome by Judas Maccabaeus, its members are reported in 1 Maccabees 8.21 as having requested from the senate that we might 'be registered as your friends and allies' (γραφῆνας ἡμᾶς συμμάχους καὶ φίλους ὑμῶν). This form of words is also found in Plutarch when he reports the friendship that Sulla granted to Archelaus of Cappadocia.[140] In the second century BCE extant examples mentioning the *formula* for individuals and communities refer to the *formula sociorum*.[141] The term *formula amicorum* is strictly found only in the first century and is also used for individuals and communities.[142] The combined name of the list, *formula amicorum et sociorum*, is confined to the first century.[143] Bowman sees a chronological progression from the second century, when those registered were entitled to the same benefits to a differentiation concerning entitlements that led to a combined list.[144] Many see the *formula amicorum* and the *formula sociorum* as being variants on the name for the one list.[145] Others consider that there existed two separate lists.[146]

An important question arises over the list: was the list an official register of the friends of the Roman people or was the list a means of assigning various privileges to foreign envoys when they were in Rome? The common opinion holds that the *formula amicorum* was an official list of Rome's friends. Entry in the list would appear not to have been the legal act that created friendship with the Romans. The earlier theory of Mommsen explained *formula* as representing technical language for a list of allies who have legal relations in Rome.[147] In so doing, he was advancing his now discredited theory that Roman international law relations for *amicitia* and for treaties evolved from the guest right (*hospitium*).[148]

The senate made the foreign policy decision to admit a community into the friendship and the senate ordered a magistrate with *imperium*, either a consul or the praetor peregrinus, to have the new friend written into the list.[149] Both decisions were made by the senate. In the case of Lampsacus, Livy reports (43.6.10) that the praetor, Quintus Maenius, was ordered to enrol the people of Lampsacus as allies. In the bilingual inscription, the *Senatus consultum de Aeslepiade* (line 17) indicates that the senate gave the order and the consul was to see to it that the friend was enrolled in the *formula amicorum*.[150]

'Formula' in the Latin part of the *Senatus consultum de Asclepiade* (line 17) is translated in the Greek part (line 24) as διάταγμα.[151] While *formula* means a 'list' or 'register', διάταγμα is actually a decree or edict.[152] The Greek preserves the notion of the official means of communication by a magistrate who spoke *dicere* to convey the senatorial decision.[153] The purpose of this list was to enable the praetor peregrinus to make arrangements for receiving foreign envoys. The status of being enrolled conferred the right to accommodation, food and clothing at state expense, and the right to approach the senate.[154] The deposition of this list in the *aerarium* (the treasury), together with financial records such as records of state debt and contracts for public works, indicates that the purpose of the list was primarily to facilitate the disbursement of state funds. In other words, this document was a financial one.

## Bronze tablet of friendship

Not all decrees of the senate were routinely engraved and displayed on the Capitol in Rome.[155] The purpose in making them visible was not so that they were archived for reference purposes.[156] Their presence on the walls of temples testified to their authority as a legal document.[157] The tablets appear to have been regarded as a witness to the historical circumstances that created the senatorial decree.[158] The engraved decree served as a memory of the event and a guardian of that memory.[159] We are informed about senatorial approval to erect bronze tablets regarding *amicitia* from inscriptions on stone found on the Capitol, from Josephus and from an inscription from the time of Augustus.[160] By the Late Republic, the whole of the Capitol was covered in such tablets.[161] The tablets were attached to the outside walls of temples, the most important of them to the Temple of Jupiter Optimus Maximus.[162] Typically the bronze tablet recorded in its text the location in which it was to be placed.[163] It was illegal to tamper with the bronze tablets in any way.[164] The tablet was intended to be permanent and an eternal witness to the friendship with the Romans.[165] As long as the friendship endured, the tablet remained on the wall of the Temple of Jupiter Optimus Maximus on the Capitol. If the friendship were renounced, the tablet was taken down, as the act of removal constituted the cancellation of the decree.[166]

## Gifts of golden crowns and golden shields

The exchange of gifts was an integral part of international friendship in antiquity.[167] When we read in Livy and other sources of foreign embassies arriving in Rome with gifts, this was not bribery, as many examples in the first century BCE have been interpreted. Nor was it a case of ambassadors complying with diplomatic courtesies or being pleasant and showing goodwill towards the Romans. The fact that, when seeking friendship, embassies invariably brought to Rome the same gift, demonstrates that a mutually understood exchange was taking place. Friendship was formed through an exchange of embassies and an exchange of gifts.[168]

Embassies that came to Rome from the Greek-speaking East (of which Judaea was a part) frequently are recorded in the sources as having brought with them a symbolic but extravagant gift of a golden crown. Gift giving was part of Greek diplomatic practice and the following examples from the Hellenistic period bear this out. The friendship between Xenophon and Seuthes from Thrace in the early fourth century was formalised through the exchange of gifts and Agesilaos concluded friendship with Egypt through gift exchange.[169] The presentation of gold crowns to a Hellenistic king by ambassadors was a widespread practice.[170] Arrian (7.23) reports that envoys came from Greece to Alexander the Great and crowned him with golden crowns.

As far as the evidence is available, the first recorded instance of the practice of giving golden crowns to the Romans occurred following the Roman settlement in 449 BCE of the strife between patricians and plebeians. Representatives of the Latins and the Hernici came to Rome with a golden crown, which they dedicated to Jupiter Capitolinus. Livy reports (3.57.7): 'they brought an offering to Jupiter Optimus Maximus, in the shape of a golden crown. It was not a large one, as they were not wealthy States'.

The first recorded instance of a Hellenistic Greek embassy bringing gifts to Rome is that of the embassy of Ptolemy II to Rome in 273 BCE.[171] Ptolemy II, having initiated the contact, was the one who began the gift exchange. In Greek practice, taking the first step signified that one was the higher or superior in status. The details in Dio's account reveal the Romans' unfamiliarity with the custom. The recipient continued in an indebted state until he reciprocated the gift.[172] The Romans did not present gifts to Ptolemy's envoys. The gifts appear not to have presented any difficulty to the senate when the Egyptian envoys presented them in Rome; yet, when the Roman envoys in Alexandria were each presented with a gold crown, the senate did not comprehend this as a gift to the state, but mistakenly understood the crowns as a gift to the three individual envoys. The account in Dionysius is fuller and gives the names of the envoys, the first of whom was the uncle of the Roman historian Fabius Pictor. The senate was the body that gave or withheld permission for the crown to be deposited.[173] A gold crown was brought to Rome from the Carthaginians on the occasion of Rome's victory over the Faliscans in 342 BCE.[174] Two recurring statements are to be found in Livy's account. First, the weight of the crown is listed, thereby denoting its monetary value. Contrary to Auliard, the crown to be donated was not the subject of bargaining or haggling.[175] The weight and therefore the value of the crown were determined by the giver, according to their financial situation. Secondly, Livy notes that the crown was to be placed in the Temple of Jupiter on the Capitol. In 193 BCE Attalus I of Pergamum sent a golden crown to Rome in thanks for their intervention that saved his kingdom from the invasion of Antiochus III.[176] Once again we read in Livy's report the weight of the crown and its deposition on the Capitol. Philip V of Macedon sent his envoys to Rome bearing a gold crown in acknowledgement of the Roman victory over Antiochus III in 191 BCE.[177] Just as Dionysius of Halicarnassus reported how the gifts from Ptolemy II required the authorisation of the senate before they could be dedicated in the Temple of Jupiter Capitolinus, so too Livy writes of the need for the senate's permission.

In the triumphal parade celebrated for the victory over Antiochus, there were 45 golden crowns, gifted from allied cities.[178] Eventually, when all the gifts came in, he was able to display in his procession a total of 200 gold crowns.[179] In addition, the Roman general was visited by cities west of the Taurus river in Asia Minor; these brought congratulations and gratitude to the Romans for their freedom and each gave a gold crown whose value varied according to their ability to pay.[180] The number of gold crowns grew in leaps and bounds with the Roman victory over Perseus in the Third Macedonian War. Four hundred gold crowns were carried in the triumphal procession of L. Aemilius Paullus.[181] The sheer amount of gold accumulated in dedications may be seen in figures from the next century after the Temple of Jupiter Capitolinus had been destroyed in 83 BCE.[182] Marius took from there and the other temples on the Capitol a total of 14,000 pounds of gold for safekeeping to Palestrina. All of these crowns received from Rome's friends served as a visual testimony to the many friends Rome had gathered to her side.[183]

At this point, it is important to observe that each of these legations brought golden crowns to Rome followed a Roman victory in war, either internal or external. International states came to acknowledge Rome's military strength and success; the gift they brought symbolised rule or royal power and since Rome was not a monarchy they had no one person to crown. The golden crowns were then dedicated to the chief Roman god, Jupiter, but only with the permission of the senate. The Temple of Jupiter on the Capitol came to represent a symbol of Rome's world empire as expressed in the legend of the human head (*caput humanum*) buried under the temple.[184] Due to its commanding position over the city, the temple was thought of as *caput urbis Romae*, the head of the city of Rome, and, with the expansion of Roman domination, as the *caput terrarum*, the head of the world.[185] Crowns were the symbol of rule; when they were deposited in the Temple of Jupiter Capitolinus, they provided visual recognition of Roman strength and Roman superiority.[186]

In 170 BCE, ambassadors from Lampsacus came to Rome asking to be admitted into the friendship of the Romans (*ut in amicitiam populi Romani reciperentur*). They brought with them a crown weighing 80 pounds. Their request was successful.[187] At the same time ambassadors came with a gift of a gold crown from Alabanda requesting *amicitia* with Rome. Livy states that they sought permission to place their gift of a crown on the Capitol. The senate's reply to their requests is not given, the only hint being that the senate replied favourably to all the legations that came to the senate. The same sentiments were used by Livy to express the agreement of the senate in the case of the Pamphylians.[188] In 169 BCE envoys came from Pamphylia asking to renew their friendship with Rome. (The meaning of this phrase *amicitiam renouare* is discussed later.) In acknowledgement of Rome's power and to show their loyalty to Rome during the war against Perseus, Livy reports (44.14.3–4),

> ambassadors from Pamphylia, brought into the senate-house a golden crown, of the value of twenty thousand Philippeans, and requested permission to deposit it, as an offering, in the shrine of Jupiter supremely good and great, and to offer sacrifice in the Capitol, which was granted. The said ambassadors having expressed a wish to renew friendship, a gracious answer was given, and a present was made to each of two thousand *asses*.

Ariarathes V of Cappadocia required Roman support for his accession to the throne under unstable circumstances. He despatched an embassy to Rome with a crown of some 1,000 gold pieces. His petition was successful.[189] He was later deposed and Orophernes was installed in his place. The new king, in turn, sent envoys to Rome who knew to bring a gold crown with them.[190] Envoys wanting Roman friendship, and to be protected by this world power, came to Rome bringing with them a gold crown. By doing so they acknowledged Rome's position in the world and demonstrated their desire to be part of Rome's orbit, with the hope that Rome's influence and might would be available to protect them. The cost of the shield was noted by the senate and the wealth status of donating states was estimated on the basis of the weight in gold of the crowns that they presented to the Romans. In the context of friendship, the gift of a gold crown was a tangible representation of that friendship and a witness to the ties with Rome.[191]

So far we have discussed the gift to Rome of golden crowns. When they brought gifts to Rome, Jewish envoys did not bring golden crowns, but donated golden shields. The outward symbolism of golden gifts is manifest, yet in the practice of the Jews the form itself differs. The symbolism of the shield bears a slightly different connotation. For the Jews, the shield was not only an emblem of protection, but also, fundamentally, the symbol of divine protection. 'But you, O Lord, are a shield for me; my glory and the lifter up of my head.'[192] The shields of the rulers and the nobles of the earth who protect the earthly nations in the end derive their power to protect from God. 'God reigns over the nations: God sits upon the throne of his holiness. The nobles of the peoples are gathered together, the people of the God of Abraham: for the shields of the earth belong to God: he is greatly exalted.'[193]

It is recorded that shields covered in beaten gold were placed by King Solomon on the internal walls of his palace. These would have been made of wood and then covered with sheets of beaten gold. We learn from the First Book of Kings that there were in the palace 200 large shields using 600 shekels of gold each, an amount that would have weighed 15 pounds.[194] There were in addition 300 smaller shields made with three minas of gold, which would equate to 4.5 pounds of gold. In all, it has been estimated that 2 tons of gold went into making these shields.[195]

The Jews, in sending embassies to Rome bearing golden shields, were conforming to the Hellenistic Greek practice that by the second century was recognised and expected by Rome. Their gift of a golden shield conveyed to the senate a none-too-subtle message. It was an outward symbol of their desire to have friendship with the Romans and a sign of the Jews' preparedness to acknowledge Rome's might. A golden crown would have served the same purpose. By their sending a shield, it was clear to the senators that the Jews were imploring Rome for her protection. In the first embassy of the Jews to Rome, Judas and his envoys continued to think of Roman friendship in terms of their own Jewish concept of friendship. They did not bring from Jerusalem gifts of any kind. The reason may lie in the Jewish expectation that those who keep faithfully to friendship (which was brought into being by a covenant) were rewarded with gifts bestowed on them. They were not accustomed to having to be the giver of gifts. They may have been unaware of the Roman idea of gifts and their significance.[196]

## Conditions for the formation of *amicitia*

In general terms, there were four circumstances in which friendship with the Romans could come into being. It could be formed to secure military co-operation in war or through exchanges of diplomatic embassies. *Deditio* (unconditional surrender) played its part: a friend could secure that status through voluntary surrender or surrender after having suffered a military defeat. Since at the time of Judas' embassy to Rome there had never been military action between the Jews and the Romans, the last two categories are not relevant to this present study.

*Amicitia* for the purposes of military co-operation in wartime is presented through three examples: Attalus of Pergamum, Sparta and Syphax.

### *Attalus*

In 205 BCE it is reported in several sources that Attalus I of Pergamum gave help to Rome when the sacred stone of the Magna Mater was taken from its temple in Galatia and transported to Rome. Of all the accounts, only Livy states the nature of the relationship between Rome and Pergamum.[197] He writes (29.11.2): 'also . . . a friendship had already commenced between them and King Attalus, on account of the war which they waged in common against Philip'. When these ties of *amicitia* were formed, they appear to have been forged because of the First Macedonian War. Attalus had been admitted into the Roman alliance with Aetolia and had served a general for the Aetolian League in 210–109 BCE.[198] The Livian account (26.24.8) is at pains to indicate that Attalus and the other allies were not bound fast by this treaty and would participate in the war only on a voluntary basis. This is reflective of the principle of friendship that aid to Rome was offered to Rome, not compelled by Rome. The lack of obligation was not taken into consideration among those scholars who believed that Attalus was bound to Rome by a *foedus* or *Bündnis* (league or confederation).[199] Possibly, the inducement of being able to purchase the island of Aegina for 30 talents brought Attalus into the united front against Philip. Later, according to Polybius, Eumenes of Pergamum proclaimed that Rome had no greater friend than Attalus.[200]

### *Sparta*

Sparta was said to have first become a Roman ally through a 'most ancient treaty' (*uetustissimum foedus*).[201] Such was the claim made in 197 BCE during the war with Philip. If one wants to push the diplomatic ties back to the fifth century, one might connect this treaty with a Roman embassy sent to Greece to investigate the laws of the Greek states before the drawing up of the XII Tables.[202] Such a reconstruction of events must remain speculation. Flamininus considered that the reference to a treaty belonged to that treaty which had brought Messene into the Roman alliance: *nam et Messenem, uno atque eodem iure foederis quo et Lacedaemonem in amicitiam nostram acceptam* (Livy 34.32.16). Here is found the first mention of *amicitia*. This friendship was said to have been formed with the Spartan boy king Pelops, who ruled from 210–199 BCE.[203] In 197 BCE Nabis, the tyrant ruler of Sparta, approached Flamininus and offered to abandon his alliance with Philip in the midst of the war and come over to the Romans bringing Argos with him.[204] If the reports in Diodorus were true, Nabis had ordered the murder of Pelops, an *amicus* of Rome, so that he could seize power: a story not mentioned by Polybius and so doubted by some scholars.[205] Nonetheless he had seized power and was not a Spartan king; Flamininus did not accept him without certain conditions. He was to send auxiliary troops to supplement the Roman army to fight Philip and to make peace with the Achaean League, a condition that Nabis negotiated down to a temporary truce. Nabis was accepted into the friendship of the Romans, although later in 195 BCE Flamininus was to argue that the friendship was with Sparta and not Nabis.

Nabis referred to his alliance with the Romans as *amicitia ac societas* (Livy 32.31.5) and separately as *societas* (Livy 32.31.7, 8, 10, 12, 15) and also as *amicitia* (Livy 32.31.16, 19). Flamininus equally in Livy described the ties as *amicitia et societas* (Livy 32.31.1, 14), as *societas* (Livy 32.32.19) and as *amicitia* (Livy 32.32.4, 14). It is only in Livy that there is mention of a *foedus* (treaty) with Rome (Livy 34.31.5; 34.32.16). This has been accepted by many scholars.[206] Clarification of whether the Spartans had a *foedus* or *amicitia* with Rome may be achieved by looking at how the relationship operated in practice. The first account of Roman international law relations with Sparta is a stipulation in the treaty with the Achaean League in 211 BCE that provided for the addition of the Spartans and others to have the same rights of friendship (*eodem iure amicitiae*) that is reminiscent of Flamininus' words in Livy 34.32.16: *eodem iure foederis*. His words could be construed as a reference to the treaty with the Achaean League, which brought about friendship with the Spartans.[207] Then in 205 BCE Sparta appears as one of several states added on to the Peace of Phoenice, which would indicate some form of participation of Sparta in the war against Philip.[208] If the relationship with Rome began somewhere between 210 and 199 BCE with the friendship with Pelops, it could predate the Peace of Phoenice. It would permit a date of 210–207 BCE.[209]

The *amicitia* formed in 197 BCE would be a revival of the friendship, necessary because of the violent changeover of leadership in Sparta and formed at this time because of the necessity for war co-operation against Philip.[210]

The second occasion when Rome sought allies to bring them into Roman friendship was during war, when the Roman army was distant from Italy. To illustrate this point, the next section comprises a case study of the friendship formed by Scipio with Syphax of Numidia during the Second Punic War.

### *Syphax*

In 213 BCE, during the Second Punic War, the Scipio brothers in Spain, P. and Cn. Cornelius Scipio, sent envoys to Syphax, king of Numidia, hoping to establish *amicitia et societas* with him.[211] They wished Syphax to continue his war with Carthage, so that Carthage would be fighting a war on two fronts.[212] No formal treaty was made at this time as a result of the embassy and Livy reports that *amicitia* was formed.[213] His account is not an annalistic fiction but from a reliable source: Livy does not use the term *foedus sociale*, as found in propaganda.[214] The diplomatic relations cannot have been formed by a treaty, as the senate and the assembly in Rome were not involved.[215] In 210 BCE Syphax sent an embassy to Rome to seek friendship (*petere Romanam amicitia*); he was given a favourable reply and gifts by the senate.[216] This example of *amicitia* shows that it was formed in this case through military co-operation and then reinforced through an exchange of embassies. The gift exchange is also a feature of *amicitia*.[217] The presenting of gifts is seen in 206 BCE when Scipio sought to encourage Syphax to break his treaty with the Carthaginians and re-form friendship. He sent Laelius as his envoy to sound out the king, but the king would only undertake to make ties of friendship with Scipio himself.[218] Later these ties would be referred to as ones of *societas*, both by Livy from Scipio, who when hearing of the marriage alliance between Syphax and the Carthaginians sent the king a letter reminding him of his *societas* with Rome, and by Hasdrubal, who recalled that Syphax had formed *societas* with the Romans.[219] The Romans' relationship with Syphax from its origins was grounded in *amicitia* going back to 213 BCE, not from later ties made in Rome. Thus, *amicitia* could be made by a general in the field or by a decree of the senate as a result of the visit of a foreign embassy.[220] In the case of Syphax, we see both uses in operation.

Sometimes friendship formed in time of war was a matter of some coercion and hard bargaining. Such was the case when the general Cn. Manius Vulso met the tyrant of Kibyra during his campaigning in the war against Antiochus III. Polybius and Livy have the story.[221]

### *Moagetes of Kibyra*

In 189 BCE Vulso sent an advantage troop of soldiers to judge the attitude of Moagetes. The tyrant begged them not to damage his territory because he was a friend of the Romans and he offered them 15 talents. He was referred to Vulso and duly sent ambassadors to the Roman commander carrying a crown as a gift. There they met an angry Vulso, who accused Moagetes of being an enemy of Rome. The most the envoys could obtain was a meeting between the tyrant and Vulso. For the meeting, Moagetes dressed in a humble manner; he pleaded poverty and offered the 15 talents. Vulso threatened to lay waste to the tyrant's lands unless he paid 500 talents. In the end, the sum was bargained down to 100 talents and 10,000 medimni of wheat, to be collected in three days. On those conditions, Moagetes was accepted into the Roman friendship.[222]

After a war, the Romans were known to use their victory as a platform for seeking out allies to join them in friendship. As a case study, Athens forms a useful example.

### *Athens*

The earliest reference for friendship between the Romans and Athens comes from Appian (*Mac.* 4.2), who reports that in the summer of 200 BCE Philip V of Macedon, who was laying siege to Abydos, was presented with the Roman demand not to harm Roman friends, among them Athens. While Appian probably derived this information from Polybius and Livy, these historians omit Athens in the list of friends to be protected.[223] Moreover, in the accounts of the three embassies that Athens sent to Rome between 201 and 200, there is no mention of Athens as an *amicus* of Rome.[224] The Peace of Phoenice in 205 BCE contained several allies who were tacked on to the treaty (*adscripti*), including Athens.[225] Holleaux dismissed the peace as the starting point for Roman–Rhodian relations because these are not mentioned when the Romans come to Philip with their ultimatum in 200 BCE.[226] This argument has generally been accepted.[227] Burton has recently discussed just this point. He suggests that Philip considered that the treaty of Phoenice had already been broken by the Athenians in 201 BCE with their execution of two Acarnanians for violating the Eleusinian mysteries. In turn the Acarnanians appealed to Philip, who launched an attack on Athens.[228] In 200 BCE the Macedonian king was warning the Romans not to side with treaty breakers. Philip's attack on Athens is alluded to in Polybius (16.27.2 and 34.3) The Romans did not need to invent Athens as an *adscriptus* to justify going to war against Philip: they only had to cite Philip's attack on Pergamum, whose king, Attalus, was undisputedly a friend of Rome and an *adscriptus* to the Peace of Phoenice. Athens had not participated in the First Macedonian War and it is possible that her *amicitia* came about at a time unrelated to this war.

The date 228 BCE has won some adherents.[229] This is based on a mention in Zonaras (8.19.7) regarding a Roman embassy to Athens (and other Greek states) after the Roman victory in the First Illyrian War in which envoys came to Athens and made friendship: 'Moreover they formed a friendship with the Athenians (πρὸς Ἀθηναίους φιλίαν ἐπεποιήκεσαν) and were admitted by them to citizenship and to the Mysteries.' Polybius, however, fails to mention this, which has caused some historians to doubt that friendship ties were formed at this time. It would be unusual for the historian to have passed up the extraordinary honours given to the Romans of *ispoliteia* with Athens and admission into the Eleusinian mysteries. More telling is that there is no evidence of the implementation of these ties for twenty years. At the time, Athens was keen to maintain a position of neutrality, as seen in her refusing to join the Achaean League the year before.

Burton suggests that *amicitia* was formed during the attempts at mediation made between 209 and 208 BCE to settle a truce during the Second Macedonian War. Only at one of these sessions were Romans present: in 208 BCE.[230] Burton's reconstruction of events is that the Romans established diplomatic contact in 228 and this was followed by the Athenians forming *amicitia* in the context of attempting to end the Second Macedonian War in 209 or 208 BCE. Having become friends of the Romans, they were added to the Peace of Phoenice in 205 BCE. When the Athenians found themselves under attack by the forces of Philip, they appealed to the Romans as their friends for help in 201–200 BCE. At the meeting with Philip at Abydos in 200 BCE, the Roman envoy resented the ultimatum to refrain from harming her ally, Athens.[231] A slightly different reconstruction may be possible taking into consideration some important information from Zonaras. What he records is the offer of citizenship and membership in the Eleusinian mysteries. De Sanctis rightly interprets this as an offer of προξενία – that is, of guest friendship, which, as we have seen, is a Greek form of friendship.[232] There was no equating this with Roman friendship, hence the confusion of Zonaras. It was only later, during the mediation in 208 BCE, that the Roman form of friendship was consolidated.

*Amicitia* could be formed by a direct approach to Rome by a state with no previous contact with the Romans that also had not been defeated by the city. This was the situation of the Jews in 162 BCE. We see this in operation with the Ptolemies and the Seleucids in the third century BCE, who approached Rome on their own initiative. It was seen before that φιλία was used to bring into alliance those who were foreigners or strangers to the Romans and that on first contact the Romans did not conclude treaties.

## Obligations of the *amicus*

Roman international *amicitia* involved more than the formation of peace with Rome: it also entailed positive requirements. These could be summarised as non-hostility towards Rome and the giving of mutual support. A friend of Rome was expected to maintain a favourable attitude towards Rome. Concrete obligations were primarily to abstain from hostilities against Rome, not to provide any help to Rome's enemies and not to permit free passage through one's territory for an enemy of Rome.[233] To render aid to an enemy of Rome when she was fighting a war rendered one an automatic enemy and there was no requirement to make a formal declaration of war.[234] This principle appears early, at least from the fourth century, in the Second Samnite War: the Vestini joined the Samnites after the war had begun and the senate and people of Rome in 325 BCE voted for war without any declaration of war.[235] When Pyrrhus of Epirus accepted the call of Tarentum to help them in their war against Rome, he too became an enemy without any declaration of war from Rome.[236] Later the Romans began to formalise this principle in the provision to 'have the same friends and enemies as the Roman people' (*hostes eodem habeto quos populus Romanus*).[237]

Those entering into the friendship of the Romans became liable only for voluntary obligations, for the Romans expected that help would be forthcoming but unsolicited by them. In providing unsolicited assistance, the ally was displaying their goodwill towards the Romans. A friend of Rome was not obliged to supply troops or ships; however, a good friend was expected to make the offer. Rome did not coerce her friends to provide assistance in war.[238] Rhodes, for example, readied 40 warships in case they would be needed in the war against Perseus.[239] This was in line with one of the main principles of friendship as outlined by Cicero: friends do not wait to be asked for help.[240] Friends of Rome are on record as having offered Rome troops, supplies, money and ships. Eumenes could boast that Pergamum had taken part in all of Rome's wars with troops and supplies.[241] When Rome was readying herself for war against Antiochus III, unsolicited offers of supplies came from her friends; the most generous was from Egypt, which offered Rome 1,000 pounds of gold and 20,000 pounds of silver – however, this was declined.[242] Yet in the war against Mithridates, Rome did request troops from her allies, and inscription records indicate that the proconsul Q. Oppius praised the people of Aphrodisias as good friends and allies in promptly sending troops following his request, 'as it was incumbent on good allies and friends of the Roman people to do'.[243]

On the news of Roman victory, *amici* would send an embassy to congratulate Rome. Several examples may be found in the section earlier on gift giving to the Romans. A true friend of Rome was expected to show steadfast loyalty.[244] For a community with multiple alliances, the friendship with the Romans had first priority.[245] The preservation of peaceful relations with Rome entailed not joining a third party in any hostile actions against Rome.[246] In other words, they were to have no independent foreign policy. Allies felt that they had to seek Roman approval before making a new alliance with a third party. Thus, for example in 192 BCE BCE Chalcis was being urged by the Aetolians to become a friend of Antiochus III, informed that they could be a friend both of Rome and of Antiochus. Chalcis repudiated the notion and told the Aetolians that they would only form a new alliance with the authorisation of the Romans.[247] In the late summer of 200 BCE, Ptolemy V's envoys reported to Rome that Athens had sought his help against Philip, but the king would not attack without Roman authorisation.[248] In 191 BCE Thyrrheion, when also faced with the demand to become an ally of Antiochus III, replied that they too would only make an alliance with the authorisation of the Roman commanders.[249] Polybius (33.16.7–8) reports that in 154/53 BCE the Achaeans would not favour any side in the war between Crete and Rhodes without taking the advice of Rome.[250] The claim of the Aetolians that one could be a friend of Rome and at the same time be friends with another third party was false. Any state that did so had its relationship with Rome terminated immediately.

For example, when the Aetolians in 206 BCE made a separate treaty with Philip, the Romans considered that their alliance with the Aetolians was cancelled. Polybius writes: 'For the alliance had been dissolved, when, deserting the Romans, they made terms with Philip'.[251] To make an alliance with a third party without consulting Rome was regarded as having deserted the Roman alliance. Such conduct broke the rule of steadfast loyalty to Rome. By c. 155 BCE it had become ingrained in the *amici* of Rome that both their loyalty to Rome and the proof of it in not opposing Rome were a keystone of their interstate relationship. It is even found enshrined in a treaty between Pharnaces I of Pontus and the city of Chersonnesus of that period, a copy of which was found on stone in Chersonnesus. In it, the people of Chersonnesus took an oath that 'we will assist in guarding his kingdom with all our power, as long as he remains with us in friendship and maintains his friendship with the Romans and does nothing in opposition to them'.[252] The principle of not having dealings with the enemies of Rome was clearly laid out by Flamininus to Nabis in the speech that Livy inserted in the year 195 BCE. He writes (34.32.15): 'In what ways, then, is friendship violated? Chiefly, no doubt, in these two ways: if you treat my allies as enemies, and if you associate yourself with my enemies'. The context in this passage is that the *hostis* is another Greek state. The treaty with Pontus is also between two states, both of which enjoyed relations with Rome. Suppose, however, that one state has relations with Rome and the other does not. How did the Romans refer to powers that were inside the Roman *imperium* and those that were outside it? *Hostis*, which we have translated as 'enemy', originally carried no such connotation. It is found in the XII Tables from the fifth century BCE to mean a 'stranger' or a 'foreigner'.[253] Cicero (*de off.* 1.37) mentions a letter of Cato the Elder to his son in which he refers to the fact that *hostis* is what we now call *peregrinus* (stranger/foreigner):

> There is extant, too, a letter of the elder Marcus Cato to his son Marcus, in which he writes that he has heard that the youth has been discharged by the consul, when he was serving in Macedonia in the war with Perseus. He warns him, therefore, to be careful not to go into battle; for, he says, the man who is not legally a soldier has no right to be fighting the foe. This also I observe – that he who would properly have been called 'a fighting enemy' (*perduellis*) was called 'a guest' (*hostis*), thus relieving the ugliness of the fact by a softened expression; for 'enemy' (*hostis*) meant to our ancestors what we now call 'stranger' (*peregrinus*). This is proved by the usage in the Twelve Tables: 'Or a day fixed for trial with a stranger' (*hostis*). And again: 'Right of ownership is inalienable for ever in dealings with a stranger' (*hostis*). What can exceed such charity, when he with whom one is at war is called by so gentle a name? And yet long lapse of time has given that word a harsher meaning: for it has lost its signification of 'stranger' and has taken on the technical connotation of 'an enemy under arms.'

When the change of meaning occurred is not known. The two meanings continued to exist side by side in the works of the playwright Plautus (c. 254–184 BCE).[254]

Likewise L. Cincius (in Gellius NA 16.4.2–4) quotes a document from 190 BCE that uses the word *hostis* in the sense of both 'enemy' and 'foreigner'.

Some would hold that the meaning changed to 'enemy' in the first half of the second century BCE as a consequence of the growth of Roman power. As Rome expanded the number of her allies (to the extent that they comprised most of the inhabited world), there were few enemies left.[255] This view is based on two premises, one literary and the other geo-political. First, in the literature, the meaning of foreigner for *hostis* persisted into the principate as Lucan and Pliny use it to refer to 'foreign parts'.[256] In traditional areas of Roman life, such as religion and law, the usage of *hostis* for 'foreigner' persisted.[257] Second, the geo-political circumstances were that, until the first century BCE, there were large swathes of inhabited world outside the Roman imperium, most notably the Parthian Empire.

In sum, the rules for Roman friends were, first, not to oppose Rome and form ties with Rome's enemies, a condition that came into prominence in times when Rome was at war (which was often). The second rule was not to have dealings with *hostes*. How one interprets this depends very much on the context. In the context of inter-Greek rivalries, Rome would be referring to her enemies within Greece. To others further away from Rome, with the opportunity to have contact with peoples outside Roman control or external to the Roman imperium, it would mean that an ally of Rome would not make an alliance with those with whom Rome herself had no ties without first seeking the advice of Rome. When combined with the need for a friend to have Roman authorisation for any alliance they may make, it makes it most unlikely indeed that the Romans would have given sanction to an ally to have diplomatic relations with peoples that were not themselves Roman allies.[258]

## Rome's obligations to her *amici*

The Roman Senate heard requests from the *amici* and attempted to satisfy them, listened to long speeches by their ambassadors, and sent out numerous delegations on fact-finding missions. When in Rome, the ambassadors from *the amici* were given privileges to honour their status, money, gifts and free accommodation. They consulted with their allies, sometimes protected them, and were judicious in their use of their friends' troops.

The foremost duty of Rome towards the *amici* was to guarantee their territorial integrity.[259] According to Dionysius of Halicarnassus, the principle was in evidence in Roman relations with the Latins and the Hernici in the fifth century. A proposal to expand their territory from parcels of land conquered by the Romans met opposition on the grounds that this territory had belonged to Rome at the time when the two peoples had entered into friendship.[260] In this case, what was being safeguarded was the territorial integrity of Rome, as one of the friends. The principle was that the status quo as at the time on entering into the friendship of the Romans was to remain unchanged. An example of protecting the territory of an ally as it was when entering into the friendship of the Romans, is the decree epigraphically preserved relating to Melitaia and Narthakion c. 140 BCE.[261]

Envoys from Melitaia in Thessaly sought arbitration from the senate over land they claimed that the Narthakieians had unjustly taken. Envoys from Narthakion referred to court decisions that had been made in their favour. The arguments that both sides put to the senate requested that each should keep their territory in the same borders as it had been when they entered into the friendship of the Romans. In the *lex agraria* of 111 BCE the lands in Africa belonging to those who had remained in the friendship of the Romans during the Third Punic War would not be included in the lands to be redistributed.[262] In 100 BCE the governor of Macedonia was instructed by law to ensure that the friends of the Romans were not attacked by any enemy such that they were expelled from their territory.[263] Sumner sums up the tenor of the law as follows: 'The whole tone of the document suggests an intent to reassure friends and subjects in the East that Rome regarded their protection and the security of the area as a primary concern.'[264]

Benefits accrued to friends of the Roman people: namely, they were chosen to govern communities that had surrendered to Rome. Such was the situation of Coronaea in 171 BCE and in Thisbae in 170 BCE when during the war with Perseus they had been on the Macedonian side and had surrendered after being put under siege by Rome. They had the *amici* of Rome from their cities imposed as rulers for ten years because these men had come over to the Romans before the siege had begun.[265] Individuals who were *amici* could be nominated as rulers because they were friends of the Romans. Such was Hermadoros, priest of Amphiaraos, who was given control of certain lands by Sulla. We only know of his privileges because they were challenged in 73 BCE in the senate by the *publicani*, the Romans contracted to collect taxes. The senate decided for Hermadoros because he had 'consistently remained in the friendship of the Roman people.'[266]

For states and communities considering moving over to the Romans, there was no better incentive than the promises from the senate that whatever laws, institutions and privileges they already possessed would be maintained as they were at the point of becoming *amici*.[267] For peoples and states with special religious or political institutions, there existed the reassurances and further the guarantees that what they enjoyed and what was essential to their community would be preserved.

Many requests for Roman intervention came from ambassadors to the senate from friends in situations where they were faced with armed attack. The Romans felt a moral duty to help because of the bonds of *fides* that bound them to these existing friends.[268] The response of the senate was in most cases to send out an embassy on a fact-finding mission. The example of Pergamum is instructive. Eumenes sought Roman help against Pharnaces of Cappadocia and the Romans sent four different embassies. Their response was to engage in third-party negotiation. First, they brokered a truce; when that broke down, they negotiated a peace settlement. When the negotiations in turn failed, the Romans gave up.[269] At no stage were Roman troops sent or deployed against Pharnaces. Direct aid, by contrast, was sent to Apollonia in 214 BCE, when the Romans sent a fleet to aid the city.[270]

## Renewal of *amicitia*

The naming of a person or community as a friend of the Roman people was intended to be permanent simply because it lacked a fixed time component.[271] It was understood by the Romans, at least by the mid-second century, that the friendships they formed were to endure unless terminated by them because of a breach of *fides*.[272] In this, Roman friendship was unlike Greek friendship, which was specified as being formed to last 'for all time'. This formula was used in the treaty of Apamea with Antiochus III, which opens with such a statement.[273] Friendship with individuals was also permanent. In the *senatus consultum* for the three Greek sea captains, the grant of *amicitia* is to be in force *in perpetuo* – that is, the benefits accrue to their descendents.[274] Why, then, do we encounter reports that *amicitia* was renewed?

The renewal of *amicitia* (*amicitiam renouare*) was not a regular practice; however, it would be hard to endorse the position that there was no necessity for any renewals.[275] In the case where friendship was made with an individual, usually a king, there are recorded instances where on his death his successor would seek to renew the friendship.[276] Heuss makes the point that it was not compulsory.[277] The examples that we do have represent more a desire for an affirmation of the friendship due to new and changed circumstances.

The first category of changed situations was typically when the ally feared that Rome might be 'unfriendly' to them due to how their actions towards Rome had been interpreted or were in danger of being interpreted in the senate. By way of examples, there are the embassies of Antiochus IV, Egypt and Rhodes. In 173 BCE Antiochus sent an embassy to the senate, two years after he had come to the throne. Livy (42. 6.85–10) reports as follows:

> [6] Envoys from Antiochus arrived about the same date. Their leader, Apollonius, when introduced to the senate, alleged many valid reasons why the king was paying his tribute after the appointed day. He had, however, brought the whole amount, so that no favour need be shown to the king beyond excusing the delay. [7] He had, in addition, brought a present of golden vases weighing 500 pounds. [8] The king asked that the friendship and alliance which had been formed with his father might be renewed with him, and that the people of Rome would look to him for all that a friendly monarch could supply; he would never be lacking in any service he could render them. [9] During his stay in Rome, he reminded the House, it was due to the kindness of the senate and the friendliness of the younger men that he was treated as a prince more than as a hostage. [10] The deputation received a gracious reply and the City praetor, A. Atilius, was ordered to renew the alliance with Antiochus which had existed with his father. This embassy was sent to make amends for the failure for some years to pay the annual tribute that had been a condition of the peace treaty of Apamea.[278]

In 170 BCE an embassy from Egypt arrived in Rome in order to answer any charges that the envoys of Antiochus had made against Egypt. Polyb. 28.1 reports: 'Timotheos and Damon came to renew their master's friendship with the Romans, and to offer their mediation for putting an end to the war with Perseus; but, above all, to watch the communications made by Meleager's [Antiochus'] embassy . . . but after formally renewing the friendly relations between Ptolemy and Rome, and receiving a favourable answer, they returned to Alexandria.'

Diod. 30.2 emphasises the war: 'Ptolemy, however, also sent off envoys to speak in his defence, and to inform the senate that Coelê Syria had belonged to his forebears and that its subjection to Antiochus was contrary to all justice. He also instructed them to renew friendly relations with the Romans and to try to bring about peace with Perseus.'

In 169 BCE Rhodes sent an embassy to Rome worried about adverse reports that might be reaching the senate about them. Polybius reports (28.2.1–2): [1] 'At this period towards the end of summer Hagesilochus, Nicagoras, and Nicander arrived as envoys from Rhodes [2] to renew friendly relations and obtain permission to export corn and also to defend their town from the false accusations brought against it.'

Another circumstance that tended to prompt the request for renewal of *amicitia*, was during the onset of war, when Rome sent embassies to her friends to shore up their loyalty in the face of the coming campaign. The best example of this was the travels of the Roman ambassadors to ascertain the support of their *amici* in the imminent war with Perseus. They called in at Alexandria, Crete and Rhodes. Livy (42.6.4) gives the details: 'The same were ordered to proceed to Alexandria to Ptolemy, to renew the friendship.'

Embassies were sent to Rome to congratulate Rome after a successful war and often couched these praises in terms of a renewal of friendship. Many examples may be found in the earlier section on gifts. In 167 BCE Prusias wanted territory in Asia Minor, as Livy relates (45.44.8):

> [8] He further desired that the alliance with him might be renewed; and that the territory taken from king Antiochus, and not granted to any other, but now in possession of the Gauls, might be given to him.

Similarly, during the course of a war, friends would want to renew their friendship in order to make clear their loyalty to Rome. So in 172/71 BCE Thebes, in the midst of civic strife, overcame the pro-Macedonian party and in reward for the Thebans' loyalty the Romans informed them that they should send an embassy to Rome requesting a renewal of their friendship.[279] In 170 BCE Alabanda sent an embassy to Rome with gifts; an inscription speaks of renewal.[280] In 169 BCE envoys from Pamphylia came to the senate requesting the renewal of their friendship (first established in 189 BCE) and offering a gift of a golden crown.[281]

## The renunciation of international friendship (*amicitiam renuntiare*)[282]

The Romans could unilaterally renounce their friendship through a decision of the senate and, by their own actions, a friend of Rome could be found in breach of their friendship. The revocation of friendship led to war unless the friend of Rome abided by certain conditions. This may be seen in the case of the Aetolians.[283] In 191 BCE the senate consulted the fetial priests over the proper procedure for declaring war on Antiochus III. One of the problems to be resolved was whether the Aetolian League would be covered by one declaration against the king or would require a separate declaration because Antiochus had been invited to become the head of their league. Livy (36.3.7–12) reports the consultation of the fetial priests:

> [6] The consul Acilius, in compliance with a resolution of the senate, submitted two questions to the College of Fetials. One was whether the declaration of war had to be made to Antiochus personally, or whether it would be sufficient to announce it at one of his frontier garrisons. [7] The other was whether a separate declaration of war must be made to the Aetolians and whether in that case the alliance and friendship must first be renounced. [8] The Fetials replied that they had already on a previous occasion, when they were consulted in the case of Philip, decided that it was a matter of indifference whether the declaration were made personally or in one of his garrison towns. [9] As to the friendship and alliance, they held that it was obviously renounced, seeing that after the frequent demands put forward by our ambassadors the king had neither surrendered the towns nor given any satisfaction. [10] In the case of the Aetolians, they had actually declared war on Rome by taking forcible possession of Demetrias, [11] a city belonging to the allies of Rome, by going to attack Chalcis by land and sea, and by bringing Antiochus into Europe to levy war on Rome.[284]

This account indicates that there had been some debate in the senate that remained unresolved and a *senatus consultum* was passed instructing the consul, Glabrio, because he was to have the command in Greece, to submit several questions to the fetial college for their opinion. The fetial college was asked to give its advice on three questions (not two, as the Livian passage states). The questions were:

1. whether a declaration of war had to be made to Antiochus in person or whether it would be sufficient to make it at the nearest borderpost;
2. whether two declarations need be made – one to Antiochus and a separate one to the Aetolians; and
3. whether a declaration of war required Rome also to renounce her *amicitia* with the Aetolians.

The fetial priests gave a *responsum* (36.3.9: *fetiales respondereunt*) that for the first question followed the precedent they had set in 200 BCE for the Second Macedonian War.[285] In answer to the third question about *renuntiatio amicitiae*, the fetial college's decision was that more than once the king had rejected Roman demands for satisfaction (*res repetere*) by Roman envoys, which had produced an automatic break in Antiochus' friendship with Rome.[286] As for the Aetolians, they had themselves renounced their *amicitia* by declaring war on Rome by various hostile acts, most importantly by inviting Antiochus into Greece to be *strategos* of the Aetolian League and to join them in their war on Rome.[287]

The unprecedented nature of having to deal with the renunciation of a friendship that the Romans themselves had established has been highlighted by Frezza.[288] The fetial rite had provisions for *res repetere* and *indictio belli*, but not for *renuntiatio amicitiae*. Such a step fell under the authority of the senate, hence their issuance of a *senatus consultum* requesting advice on the matter. A *renuntiatio* was an entirely new issue arising out of diplomatic relations with Greek states. The issue that had to be resolved was the nature of the alliance that Rome had made with the Aetolians in 212 BCE.[289] The Romans claimed that the Aetolians had voided the treaty in 206 BCE when they made a separate peace with Philip.[290] The specificity of the treaty's stipulations suggests that the Romans had not intended a long-time or permanent alliance.[291] The fetial college did not have to rule on a mechanism for renouncing friendship, as they ruled that the friendship had been broken by the hostile acts of the other party.[292] The senate's request for advice to the fetials did involve, as the senators suspected it might, a possible analysis of the Aetolian treaty; and since the fetial priests were responsible for Rome's state treaties, this too fell within their competency.[293]

In the case of the Aetolians, they were deemed to have voided their friendship with Rome by their hostile actions. If, however, the senate made the decision to renounce the friendship, the former ally was left in a precarious position. No longer a 'friend', it did not know what would follow and often panicked. The action of Prusias II in 156 BCE is a good example of this. Rome had wanted Prusias II and Attalus II to stop their war and come to terms. Ten commissioners were sent by the senate to deliver an official message to this effect. Polybius reports that they did so before the king in a threatening manner. Prusias would only agree to a few of their terms and rejected the majority. The Romans then renounced their 'friendship and alliance' and left. Prusias' reaction was immediate regret that he had spurned the envoys and he chased after them, wanting to appeal. The Romans would not listen and kept on going, for their renunciation of Roman friendship was final. The envoys separated: some returned to Rome to report to the senate and the rest travelled to the allies of Prusias urging them to forego their alliance with Prusias and go over to Attalus. Back in Rome, the senate heard the envoy's report and decided to despatch a new embassy to Prusias, this time with a treaty of peace drawn up ready for the two kings to sign – this they both did.[294]

In other circumstances, without friendship and any other ties to replace it, an ally could feel vulnerable. Such was the situation of Rhodes from 167 to 164.

First, however, it is necessary to explore the issue of when Rhodes first became a friend of the Romans.

### *Rhodes*

Our knowledge of international relations between Rome and Rhodes comes from Polybius, who reports that there had been ties going back 140 years, ties he describes as having never been formed through a treaty.[295] Polybius reports (30.5.6–8):

> [6] For the policy of Rhodes had been so little dictated by sentiment, that although that state had from nearly a hundred and forty years taken part in the most glorious and finest achievements of the Romans, they had never made an alliance with Rome. [7] The reason of their action in this respect should not be ignored. It was this. [8] As they wished none of the kings and princes to despair of gaining their help and alliance, they did not desire to run in harness with Rome and engage themselves by oaths and treaties, but preferred to remain unembarrassed and able to reap profit from any quarter.

The context is the immediate aftermath of the Third Macedonian War. Before the war the Rhodians had professed their loyalty to Rome and offered ships to Rome if they should be required.[296] The Rhodians had ties of friendship with both the Romans and Macedonians and in the course of the war their behaviour brought forth charges of disloyalty to Rome. Her ships spent most of the war inactive or protecting their own trade.[297]

The whole subject of whether and, if so, when Rhodes enjoyed *amicitia* with Rome has been the subject of some controversy. We are fortunate in having contemporary evidence for the fact that the Rhodians had *amicitia* with the Romans. A fragment survives of Cato's speech *pro Rhodiensibus*, where he is quoted as saying: 'Shall we, then, of a sudden abandon these great services given and received and this strong friendship?'[298]

Livy and Polybius report that in 172 BCE Perseus turned to Rhodes to see whether they would be willing to help mediate if Macedonia should be attacked by Rome. Their reply was not outright rejection of his proposal, but only that he not ask them to do anything against the wishes of the Romans that would lead to putting their relationship with Rome in jeopardy.[299] Livy (42.46.6) adds: 'if there was war, the king need not expect or ask for anything from them, since he was trying to break up the long-standing friendship between them and the Romans, a friendship which was the fruit of many valuable services rendered in both peace and war.'

A further offer in 169 BCE, according to Livy,[300] was made by the Rhodians while in Rome: it was to mediate along with Prusias of Bithynia. Their biggest blunder was to offer to mediate peace with Perseus, the Macedonian king, in an approach to Aemilius Paullus while he was in the midst of preparing for the battle that would win the war for Rome, the battle of Pydna.[301] The reaction was so furious that the Rhodians were almost clapped into chains.[302] The Livian account (44.14.12) has the Rhodians demanding peace and threatening military action if their demands are not met.

In 169 BCE any Greek leaders who advocated for a stance of neutrality in the war were regarded by Rome as enemies.[303] At this point it ought to be understood that the Greeks and the Romans had two different concepts about not taking a stance in time of war. For the Greeks the concept of neutrality was well known and well respected. The Romans, by contrast, had no such concept. A friend who tried to be neutral was a contradiction in terms. The whole concept of neutrality was very much opposed by the Romans.[304] It was precisely when war broke out that Rome expected her *amici* to demonstrate their loyalty to Rome and Rome's other allies. There was no space to be neutral: an ally of Rome could not choose to sit this one out.[305] Polybius' more mild version that the Rhodians came to Rome just to renew friendship and to ask permission to import grain from Sicily appears similar to the official version put out to the public after the senate's session, while Livy's account reads like an eyewitness account.[306]

The next year, 168 BCE, the Rhodians approached not the senate in Rome but the Roman general in the field with an offer to mediate. This was meddling of the first order and the officers were all for kicking them out of the camp.[307] As soon as the war was over the Roman Senate expressed their view on the behaviour of the Rhodians, accusing them of only having had one aim in mind – and that was to help Perseus.[308] For a state with *amicitia* with Rome, this was a severe charge. A friend of Rome who aided Rome's enemy at the time of war was immediately regarded as an enemy. The crux of the matter was simply that the senate considered that the Rhodians had not behaved as proper *socii et amici* during the Third Macedonian War.[309] In the words of Livy (45.20.8): 'The conduct of the Rhodians during the war had not been such that they deserved to be counted amongst the friends and allies of Rome.'

After Rome's victory in 167 BCE the Rhodians sent an embassy to Rome, concerned at the hostility towards them, where they narrowly escaped being declared enemies of Rome.[310] When the two Rhodian ambassadors arrived in the city, they were shocked to experience both publicly and privately a palpably hostile reception. Things came to a head when one of the praetors jumped up on the rostra and advocated that the people declare war on Rhodes. The ambassadors implored the audience to treat them as though the people were still their *amici*, their friends. The motion was only halted by the veto of a tribune of the plebs. A few days later, the envoys spoke in the senate; after this, the senate informed them that only because they had a few powerful friends in the city, such as Cato, had war been averted. Livy gave the decision of the senate that the Rhodians were not to be declared enemies, but they were no longer to be allies of Rome: *Rhodiis responsum ita redditum est, ut nec hostes fierent nec socii permanerent*.[311] One of the envoys later published the speech he gave in the senate, as Cato also did, on behalf of his homeland.[312] Polybius had read it and was not impressed. When the news reached Rhodes that there would not be war with Rome, there was a great relief. It was decided that they wanted to put their relationship with Rome on a more stable footing and so they sent another embassy empowered to request and to make a treaty (*foedus*). Their admiral was sent to make the request armed with a crown of 10,000 gold pieces as a gift to the Romans.[313] Livy reports that the Rhodians first approached the Roman naval commander seeking treaty ties with Rome. He adds (45.25.9–10) (from Polybius) that they mentioned that they had been *in amicitiam* with the Romans for many years. The key aspect of Livy's account is that the Rhodians thought that the Romans no longer trusted them. Some historians suggest that this account is tainted because it is derived from a pro-Roman account showing Rhodes in the wrong in order to justify Rome's conduct.[314] For this present study it is precisely the Roman mindset that is most relevant in the need to understand Rome's rationale for considering that the friendship with Rhodes was broken.

In Dio's account (Book 20 frg. 68.2) the Rhodians explain not that they had never had *amicitia* with the Romans, only that in making such ties with the Romans they had not done so through oaths. Dio states that the Rhodians had valued their loose ties of friendship with Rome because they thought it gave them greater manoeuvrability. Their crime was arrogance (*superbia*) in thinking that, after the Roman victory at Pydna, a motivating factor in Roman foreign policy would still be fear of what Rhodes might do.[315] From this extract we learn that the Rhodians characterised their relationship with Rome as friendship (φιλία/*amicitia*). They had previously rejected treaties, but after the Roman defeat of the Macedonian kingdom they embraced the idea. The Romans, it is clear, were not so willing. Once trust had broken down, it required time for Rhodes to prove her loyalty to Rome. The Romans kept the Rhodians in a state of diplomatic limbo between 167 and 164 BCE. It was only in c. 164 BCE, on their fourth attempt, that they obtained a *foedus* with Rome.[316]

### *The Thracians*

The Rhodians were not the only Roman allies who had been accused of supporting Perseus in the recent war, leaving themselves open to charges of disloyalty to Rome. Diodorus informs us (31.5.1) about a delegation in Rome from the Thracians, who came to avert war being declared on them by the Romans. They were only able to retain their friendship with the Romans by begging for mercy and forgiveness.

It is clear from these examples that, if the Romans renounced their friendship with one of their allies, the way lay open, if the senate decided, for war. The battle for war or peace was fought out in the senate house. Cato was able to use his rhetorical skills to plead the case for the Rhodians and although the senate decided not to declare war on Rhodes it did not agree to maintain friendship.[317] In the case of the Thracians, they too feared war, but the grovelling of their envoys averted the prospect. The sheer terror that comes through in the sources after charges that an ally has aided the enemy shows how real was the threat of war once Rome had withdrawn her friendship from an ally.

In sum, after the Roman intervention in 168 BCE, which prevented the Seleucid takeover of Egypt, the Romans were receptive to making new friends in the area. *Amicitia* was used to bring foreigners into a Roman alliance as a first step before a treaty was considered by the senate. Those requesting friendship sent embassies to Rome with other requests for assistance, military or political. In return, the Romans demanded constant loyalty, with the result that association with Rome's enemies could lead to a unilateral renunciation of friendship. Renewals of *amicitia* were requested when circumstances changed. Jews came to Rome to renew the friendship after it had been annulled by a Seleucid military victory and they had in turn been victorious over the Syrians.

## Notes

1 See Bederman (2001) 4–15 for the critics. See his chapter 2 for response.
2 On the first three principles see Preiser (1963) 20–21, 54–56. On the last, see Badian (1984) 401. Further to the history of the debate on the applicability of *Völkerrecht* to Roman international relations and the accompanying literature, see Baldus (2002) 313–327.
3 Cic. *de off.* 3.17.69; also Dig. 1.1.9. Imprecise: Lombardi (1947) 61.
4 See Ramsey (2013) for the discussion that has ensued since Eckstein's book first appeared in 2008 on the application of International Relations (IR) theory of Realism and theory of Constructivism to ancient history.
5 Burton (2011) 1–17.
6 Paradisi (1947) 180; Badian (1984) 414; Billows (2007) 320.
7 See Badian (1958) and critiques, most recently Burton (2011).
8 Leech (1877) 22–23.
9 Dietrich (2014) 158.
10 Collins (1998) 23.
11 Beentjes (2013) 55.
12 Schwartz (2005) 24; Dietrich (2014) 160–161.
13 Aristotle *Eth. nic.* 9.8.2 §1168b. Dietrich (2014) 171, n. 49. Unlikely: Corley (2002) 10.
14 See Middendorp (1973); Kieweler (1992); Wischmeyer (1995) 8–13.
15 Schwartz (2005) 32–34; Beentjes (2013) 55.
16 Ben Sira 20.13.
17 Ben Sira 20.16.
18 1 Sam. 20.42.
19 Schwartz (2009) 21.
20 1 Sam. 18.3.
21 Weinfeld (1973) 192.
22 1 Kgs 5.26.
23 Ben Sira 23.22, 9.10.
24 Fest. 15L; Cic. *Lael.* 26; Konstan (1997) 122.
25 Burton (2011) 35.
26 Panessa (1999) vi, n. 6. Cf. Taillardat (1982) 9–10.
27 Panessa (1999) xviii.
28 Mitchell (1997) 29–30.
29 Bolmarcich (2010) 119.
30 Mitchell (1997) 43.
31 Herman (1987) 69–74; Konstan (1997) 33.
32 Konstan (1997) 83.
33 Gruen (1984) 73.
34 Thuc. 3.70.6; Xen. *Hell.* 2.2.20.

35 Herman (1987) 2–5.
36 Panessa (1981) 243.
37 Paradisi (1947) 179.
38 Paradisi (1947) 187; Burton (2011) 265–266. Cf. Holleaux (1921) 40, who divided *amicitia* into *de facto* and *de iure* friendship.
39 Legal but not a treaty: Paradisi (1947) 187. Revival of a treaty of friendship and legal form of *amicitia*: see 28–34.
40 (1984) 66.
41 Sands (1908) 24.
42 (1887) 3.593.
43 See App. *BG* 13; Livy 32.8–10.
44 Matthaei (1907) 188. Examples: Livy 1.1.8f., 4.7.4, 7.27.2, 8.25.3, 9.41.20, 42.12.5. See Zack (2007) 171, n. 768.
45 Livy 31.1.9, 31.29.3, 33.6.33–35, 33.11.5, 33.12.2, 33.13.2, 34.23.7, 35.32.6.12, 35.33.4, 38.8.6, 38.10.5.
46 Livy 26.24.3, 33.35.9.
47 Livy 32.1.6, 32.1.31, 32.1.34, 32.1.37, 32.22.3, 32.22.12, 32.22.25, 32.1.11, 32.1.32–37, 33.2.9, 33.29.8, 39.36.11, 39.7.9, 41.24.2, 42.69.9.
48 Livy 32.19.1, 32.21.30.
49 Livy 32.21.4, 32.25.3, 39.37.10, 41.24.9.
50 (1907) 186.
51 (1907) 188.
52 Aetolians: Livy 26.24.14, 29.12.4, 33.34.7, 34.23.7. Achaeans: Livy 39.37.10, 41.23.5,9. Messene: Livy 34.32.16. Philip: Livy 33.35.5, 42.25.4, 42.62.5, 44.16.5. Athens: Tac. *Ann.* 2.53.3. For a discussion of Roman *amicitia* with Rome, see pp. 85–86.
53 Matthaei (1907) 189.
54 Restoration of *amicitia*: Livy 31.31.20; App. *Mac.* 3. Cf. Livy 33.35.9, 35.32.6, 36.3.8. Treaty not restored: Livy 36.27.6. See Matthaei (1907) 190.
55 Polyb. 21.45.1 6–10 = Livy 38.38.2, 38.38.6, 38.38.15; Polyb. 18.39, 18.44; Livy 33.30.2–10.
56 Matthaei (1907) 185; Burton (2011) 24–25; Snowdon (2014) 426.
57 First published: Laticheff (1882). See Sherk (1969) 9. For the most recent treatment, see Snowdon (2014) 422–444.
58 Ll. 21–22, 46–48.
59 Always: Sherk (1969) 18, l.79 and 22, l. 20. From the beginning: *SEG* 3.710, l.10; *SEG* 9.7 ll. 15–16, *SIG*[3] 694, l. 11. Ancestral: Sherk (1969) 18, l.3; *SEG* 23.489, l. 5.
60 Snowdon (2014) 443.
61 Cimma (1976) 28.
62 Cimma (1976) 84.
63 Criticism of Cimma on her treatment of *amicitia*: Ziegler (1982) 63–64.
64 (1968) 147.
65 Zack (2013) 66–67.
66 Cic. *ad Fam.* 5.8.5. See Williams (2008) 40.
67 A revival of the concept of *amicitia* formation through a 'Vertrag' by Zack (2015b). Against: Coşkun (2008).
68 Those who agree that there existed *societas sine foedere* include: Horn (1930) 10–15; Heuss (1933) 26–27; Kienast (1968) 350–351, 354–356; Dahlheim (1968) 163–170, 226–229 and Gruen (1984) 55, 79. Against: Sherwin-White (1984) 63–69; Hammond (1972) 3.601–610; Ziegler (1972) 84; Derow (1991); Petzold (1992) 87; Baldus (2002) 317.
69 Horsnaes (2002) 121.
70 Fornara (1983) $1^2$.31–32.
71 Bauslaugh (1991) 159–160.

72 David (1946) 231, 233–234.
73 Paradisi (1951) 349.
74 Bolmarcich (2010) 117.
75 Xen. *Hell.* 4.8.26 and 4.1.32, 4.1.37.
76 Bolmarcich (2010) 122–123.
77 *IG* $1^3$, 76 where although in ll. 23–25 φιλία and συμμαχία is restored, the previous l. 17 has, 'we shall be friends and allies to the Athenians': φίλοι ἐσόμε [θα' Αθεναίοις καὶ χσύμ]μαχα. See Bolmarcich (2010) 120.
78 Panessa (1999) xxii–xxiii with examples of neutrality.
79 (1887) 3.590–595.
80 (1887) 1.593, n. 2 and 1.660, 1.724–725.
81 (1913) 423–425.
82 (1913) 402ff., 408, 411ff.
83 Matthaei (1907) 190–191.
84 Matthaei (1907) 185.
85 Matthaei (1907) 191.
86 (1913) 3–6; 44–66.
87 Heuss (1933) 35; Paradisi (1947) 178ff.
88 Heuss (1933) 46.
89 For example: Martola (1984) 63.
90 Täubler (1913) 254ff. Mommsen (1887) 1.599 gave no examples.
91 Heuss (1933) 18.
92 Polyb. 21.42 [43]; Livy 38.38.
93 Täubler (1913) 263.
94 For example the section (42 [43].5) on the territorial provisions.
95 Heuss (1933) 12–18.
96 Paradisi (1951) 345, n. 2.
97 For example Gutman (1963) 77.
98 Heuss (1933) 12–59; Paradisi (1947) 178 ff.; Timpe (1962) 351; Frezza (1969) 355; Dahlheim (1968) 136–146; Gruen (1984) 55.
99 Heuss (1933) 46; Ziegler (1972) 87.
100 Ambassadors: Heuss (1934) 20–30; Paradisi (1951) 346, n. 1; Gruen (1984) 55.
101 Distinction first made by Holleaux (1921) 40, 45, n. 2. Followed by Brassloff (1928) 24; Bickerman (1936) 471–472; Wegner (1936) 48, 61.
102 Frezza (1969) 9–11; Ziegler (1972) 89.
103 See Zack (2007) 169–170 for the supporters and critics of Heuss' theory.
104 Badian (1958) 36ff.; Kienast (1968) 330ff; Dahlheim (1968) 136ff., 163ff., 238ff.; Gruen (1984) 54ff., 76ff.
105 (1933) 59, n. 1 where he uses the examples of the treaty of Apamea (Polyb. 21.42) and *OGIS* 221, 58.
106 (1968) 163–164.
107 See also Livy 5.27.6, 10.12.1–2, 31.32.16, 44.23.8. The wording of the treaty of alliance of Heraclea preserved by Memnon (*FGrH* 434 F 1, 18.10) speaks of φιλία καὶ συμμαχία. See also Livy 34.57.9–11 and Justin. 43.3.4.
108 Heuss (1933) 26, n. 1.
109 Mommsen (1887) 3, 1.593, n. 2 and 1.660, 724–725; Matthaei (1907) 192–193.
110 Heuss (1933) 26–27.
111 Heuss (1933) 26; Dahlheim (1968) 269–274. In Livy 42.6.8–10 a renewal of friendship and alliance may not necessarily refer to the renewal of a treaty. The point of my comments is to separate *societas* from *amicitia et societas*. Heuss has shown that this passage in Livy refers to a verbal request and a verbal response that cannot be construed as the renewal of a treaty. See Heuss (1933) 50–51. Gruen (1984) 88 notes that the phrase 'to renew friendship' was an 'accompanying gesture' of embassies that came to Rome on other business.

112 Dahlheim (1965) 281.
113 Dahlheim (1965) 284. Attalus in 198 BCE had to plead in front of the senate for permission to withdraw his troops from Greece to defend Pergamum from Antiochus: Livy 32.8.9–16.
114 Livy 35.48–50.4.
115 (1968) 260.
116 Dahlheim (1965) 286.
117 (1968) 266.
118 *IPE* I$^2$ 402, ll. 3–4, 25–26: τήν τε πρὸς Ρωμαίους φιλίαν διαφυλασσόντων.
119 Polyb. 30.5.6; Livy 45.29.9. See Dahlheim (1968) 270. Against: Schmitt (1957) 11.
120 Polyb. 33.13.4–10; *OGIS* 327, l. 4; Dahlheim (1968) 271.
121 Welles (1966) 290, 293, no. 72.
122 Dahlheim (1965) 289–290.
123 Kienast (1968) 338, 341, n. 34.
124 Livy 31.11.14–16.
125 Comparison with Caes. *BG* 1.43.4, see Boas (1931), followed by Klotz (1953) 63; Briscoe (1986a) 86. Not an exact match between the two texts and Vermina's case may well have been the first.
126 Cic. *Fam.* 2.17.7, cf. 15.2.8, 15.4.6. For how instrumental Cicero may have been, see Braund (1982) 37–39.
127 Kienast (1968) 340.
128 Lewis and Short 141 s.v. *appello*, D. *OLD*$^2$ 1.166, s.v. *appello* 7 and 9 give no Greek equivalents.
129 Ritter (1965) 90, n. 3.
130 *quod Alexandrini regem suum socium atque amicum a senatu appellatum expulerant resque uulgo improbabatur*. Also Dio 39.12.1.
131 See Zollschan (2007b) 22–24.
132 Tac. *Ann.* 4.26.2.
133 *RDGE* 22.
134 For literature see Sherk (1969) 78, no. 14.
135 Kienast (1968) 343 brings this document forward to substantiate his thesis. Photograph: Guarducci (1942) 109.
136 Inscription: *OGIS* 437 = *RDGE* 47. For the date of 94 BCE see Badian (1956).
137 *RDGE* 47, l. 28.
138 *OGIS* 438.
139 Kienast (1968) 339 and n. 28.
140 Plut. *Sulla* 23.
141 Examples given by Bowman (1989) 331 include the Aetolians in 200 BCE (App. *Mac.* 4), some Greeks in 196 BCE (App. *Mac.* 9.4); Livy reports Lampsacus in 170 BCE (43.6.5–10), a Macedonian noble in 169 BCE (44.16. 5–7).
142 Bowman (1989) lists Ilium, Chios, Lycia, Rhodes, Magnesia and others in 84 BCE (App. *Mith.* 61) and the three Greek sea captains in 78 BCE (*CIL* 1$^2$ 588 = Sherk (1969) 22).
143 Bowman (1989) gives the examples of Mithridates (Plut. *Sull.* 23), Tigranes (Dio 36.53.5), Pharnaces (Dio 37.14.2), Ariovistus (Dio 38.34.3), Cleopatra (Dio 43.27.3) and Polemo (Dio 53.25.1).
144 Bowman (1989) 333, 336.
145 Badian (1958) 12, n. 4 and 143, n. 1; Marshall (1968) 54, n. 35; Bowman (1989) 332; De Martino (1973) 34; Valvo (2001) 140; Burton (2011) 82.
146 Mommsen (1887) 3.593, 3.651; Ferrenbach (1895) 62–64; Sands (1908) 40–42; Kienast (1968) 343, 345, 351, 359; Zack (2013) 98–100.
147 Mommsen (1887) 3, 1.1153, n. 3.
148 Mommsen (1864a) 319–320, 328–329. Followed by Täubler (1913) 395–406. Overturned by Heuss (1933) 1–59.

149 Senate: Livy 43.6.7–10; 44.16.4–7; Sherk (1969) 22; App. *Mac.* 4.2, 9.4. See Zack (2013) 99.
150 *CIL* 1.203 = *CIL* $1^2$ 588. New edition: Raggi (2001).
151 Valvo (2001) 138–139.
152 List: Meyer (2004) 63. Decree: Zack (2013) 94 and n. 100.
153 Zack (2013) 95 and n. 104.
154 Gallet (1937) 280–282; Bowman (1989) 332; Burton (2011) 83; Zack (2013) 94.
155 Williamson (1987) 172.
156 Williamson (1987) 167.
157 Cic. *Phil.* 1.26, 2.97, 3.30. Williamson (1987) 168.
158 Williamson (1987) 168–169.
159 Williamson (1995) 250.
160 Second century BCE: see p. 19; *S.C. de Aesclepiade*, Sherk (1969) no. 22, l. 25; Jos. *Ant.* 14.146–147; *AE* (1976) no. 678 ll. 5, 34. See Gallet (1937) 262–263, 401–402.
161 Cic. *Phil.* 2, 36, 92: *toto Capitolio tabulae figebantur*.
162 See pp. 18–21.
163 Williamson (1987) 168–169.
164 Williamson (1987) 177.
165 Eternal: Williamson (1987) 170.
166 Cic. *Fam.* 13.36. See Williamson (1987) 167.
167 Zack (2015b) 150–156 maintains that the acceptance of gifts by Rome constituted a legal act, the formation of a treaty. This fails to take into account the symbolic nature of the gifts and the expectation of the giver of return on his investment: *gratia* followed by *beneficium*.
168 Heuss (1933) 29.
169 Xenophon: Xen. *Anab.* 7.3.20. Agesilaos: Plut. *Agesilaus* 31. See Trundle (2008) 110.
170 On this custom see Klausner (1974) 292–309.
171 Dio frg. 41.1.
172 Domingo Gygax (2013) 53 and n. 38.
173 D.H. 20.14.1–2. See also Val. Max. 4.3.9.
174 Livy 7.38.2.
175 Auliard (2009) 69.
176 Livy 32.27.1.
177 Livy 36.35.12–13.
178 Livy 37.46.4.
179 Livy 39.7.1.
180 Livy 38.37.2–4.
181 Plut. *Aem.* 34.5.
182 Flower (2008) 74–92.
183 Domingo Gygax (2013) 56, n. 38.
184 For the legend see Thein (2014) 284–319.
185 Florus 1.7.9; Serv. *ad Aen.* 8.345.
186 Rutledge (2012) 148.
187 Livy 43.6.–10. Rejected by Magie (1950) 2.1064–1065, n. 48 as an annalistic fiction citing Nissen (1863). Briscoe (1986a) 408 rejects the Livian account on the basis of an error in reporting that Lampsacus had been subject to Macedonia.
188 Livy 43.6.6–10.
189 Polyb. 31.32.2; Diod. 31.19.8; Zon. 21.
190 Polyb. 32.10.4.
191 Rutledge (2012) 150.
192 Ps. 3.3, 28.7.
193 Ps. 47.9–10.
194 1 Kgs 10.17.
195 Milard (1994) 286–310.

196 Weinfeld (1973) 195.
197 Livy 29.10.4–11, 29.10.8, 14.5–14; Ovid *Fasti* 4.247–348; Cic. *har. resp.* 27–28; Sil. Ital. 17.1–43; Auct. *uir. ill.* 46.1; Varro *LL* 6.15. See Broughton (1951) 1.304.
198 Treaty: Livy 26.12.9. General: Livy 27.29.10.
199 Täubler (1913) 215; Larsen (1935) 210f; id. (1937) 16f; id. (1970) 218; Hansen (1972) 46–48; Sherwin-White (1984) 60f. Not a treaty: Badian (1958) 57–58; Dahlheim (1968) 210f. n. 75, 223, 252; Gruen (1984) 20, 77; Burton (2011) 84–87.
200 Polyb. 21.20.1.
201 Livy 34.31.5. For the earlier literature on Rome and Sparta see Dahlheim (1968) 221–229.
202 Livy 3.31; D.H. 10.52, 54. See Walbank (1967) 1.166; Ehrimes (1949) 26, n. 6.
203 Livy 34.32.1; Diod. 27.1.
204 Livy 32.39.9–11; Zon. 9.16.
205 Diod. 27.1; for the literature see Burton (2015) 225–228, n. 16.
206 Larsen (1935) 210–212; Badian (1958) 59; Walbank (1979) 3.516; Briscoe (1981) 98.
207 Burton (2015) 229–230.
208 Livy 29.12.14. Considered annalistic fiction: Holleaux (1921) 264.
209 Burton (2015) 229.
210 Gruen (1984) 82.
211 Date: 214/13 BCE: Eckstein (1987) 204. 213 BCE: Broughton (1951) 1.265. 212/11 BCE or 129 BCE: Lazenby (1978).
212 Livy 24.48. Episode historical: Eckstein (1987) 204–205. Not historical: Kahrstedt (1913) 254–255, 513, n. 2; Gsell (1913–1929) 3.181; Holleaux (1921) 171, n.2. Followed by Lazenby (1978) 129. Doubted on the basis that it may be a doublet of a later meeting between Scipio (later Africanus) and Syphax in 206: Livy 28.17.2ff. Against this: independence evidence for 213 BCE from Appian (*Ib.* 15–16) and the difference between the two Scipio brothers dealing with Syphax in 213 BCE and only Scipio Africanus in 206 BCE meeting with Syphax.
213 Livy 24.48.2, 13. No treaty: Heuss (1933) 30; Eckstein (1987) 204–205; Burton (2011) 95.
214 Eckstein (1987) 204.
215 Heuss (1933) 30.
216 Livy 27.4.5–7.
217 Burton (2011) 64–67.
218 Livy 28.17.5–8.
219 Livy 19.23.3, 19.23.6, 19.24.3. Cf. Zack (2015a) 33.
220 Sherwin-White (1984) 59. Cf. Zack on *Feldherrnverträge*: (2007) 187–191. Against this, the joining of right hands (Livy 29.24.3) is not evidence of the oath concluding a *foedus*: see Livy 1.24.4–8.
221 Polyb. 21.34; Livy 38.14.4–14.
222 This friendship does not refer to the epigraphically extant text of a treaty. See Gruen (1984) 731–732. For the text of the treaty, see Chapter 5.
223 Polyb. 16.34.3; Livy 31.18.2.
224 Livy 31.1.10–12, 31.5.2, 5–8, 31.14.3.
225 Livy 29.12.14.
226 (1921) 54, 56, n. 1, 259–260.
227 Larsen (1937) 15–31; Dahlheim (1968) 209–221; Habicht (1982) 138–142; Ferrary (1988) 25, n. 81; id. (1990) 220; Habicht (1997) 195; Eckstein (2008) 113–114, 210–211, 248, n. 62.
228 Livy 31.14.6–10; Burton (2013) 211–213.
229 Briscoe (1973) 9; Rich (1984) 75, n. 187; Warrior (1996) 99–100.
230 Livy 28.7.13–16.
231 Burton (2013) 218.
232 De Sanctis (1903) 3,2.438, n. 98.
233 Lesaffer (2002) 80–81.

234 See Kostial (1995) 81–82.
235 Livy 8.29.1, 8.29.6.
236 Rich (2011) 206.
237 Livy 38.11.3. On this principle see Dahlheim (1968) 221–224; Klose (1972) 98 and n. 330; De Libero (1997).
238 Gruen (1984) 81.
239 Polyb. 27.3.3; Livy 42.45.3.
240 Cic. *de amic.* 44.
241 Polyb. 21.20.4.
242 Livy 36.4.1–4.
243 Reynolds (1982) no. 3, ll. 26–29.
244 Cic. *de senec.* 12.4. See De Visscher (1945) 41; Marshall (1968) 46, n. 14.
245 Livy 35.48.8.
246 Neumann (1934) *RE* 1.2, s.v. *amicus* (3), col. 1832.
247 Livy 35.36.13.
248 Livy 31.9.1–2. Date: Briscoe (1973) 44, n. 3.
249 Livy 36.12.8.
250 Date: Walbank (1979) 3.558.
251 Polyb. 18.38.8.
252 Sherk (1969) 30. For date see Burstein (1980). Quotation: ll. 1–5.
253 XII Tables: Cic. *de leg.* 2.59; Fest. 372fL. Cato: Cic. *de off.* 1.37.
254 For examples see Zack (2012).
255 Zack (2012) 107–108.
256 Lucan *BC* 1.622; Pliny *NH* 2.143.
257 The *carmen* of the Arval Brothers: *ILS* 5039. The augurs: Varro *LL* 7.8. Roman Law: Gaius *Inst.* 4.11–30. See Zack (2012) 109–110, nn. 137–140.
258 Relevant in discussing the Roman reaction to Jewish ties with the Parthians in the last third of the second century before the Romans had any, which was not until the first century BCE. See below pp. 259–264.
259 Kallet-Marx (1995) 174.
260 D.H. 8.74.2.
261 Sherk (1969) no. 9 with references to the literature to which can be added Snowdon (2014).
262 *CIL* $1^2$ 585, ll. 75–76, 79–80. See Saumagne (1927); Hinrichs (1966); Mattingly (1969); Johannsen (1971); Lintott (1992) 171–201, commentary 202–284.
263 *Lex de prouinciis praetoriis* (the piracy law): Crawford (1966) no. 12, Knidos IV, ll. 21–24.
264 Sumner (1978) 225.
265 Coronea: Sherk (1969) no. 3, ll. 1–5. Thisbae: Sherk (1969) no. 2, ll. 22–24.
266 Sherk (1969) no. 23, ll. 50–51.
267 Sherk (1969) 70, ll. 14–18. A happenstance discovery that enshrines principles that enabled the Romans to gather *amici* in the second century.
268 Burton (2011) 229 lists communities who formed *amicitia* with Rome in the face of imminent danger.
269 Four embassies: Polyb. 24.1.2, 24.1.3, 24.5.1. Truce: Polyb. 24.14.1. Negotiations failed: Polyb. 24.158. Gave up: 24.15.12.
270 Livy 24.40.7–8; Zon. 9.4; Plut. *Arat.*; Gruen (1984); Eckstein (2008) 86; Burton (2011) 229.
271 Mommsen (1887) 3.593.
272 Dahlheim (1968) 228; Burton (2011) 92.
273 Polyb. 21.42.1; Livy 38.38.2. For other Greek examples see Gruen (1984) 33, n. 106.
274 Raggi (2001) 80: Latin, ll. 14, 82; Greek, l. 22.
275 Regular: Cimma (1976) 92. Not necessary: Heuss (1933) 46–53.
276 Gruen (1984) 88.

277 Heuss (1933) 48.
278 Also Polyb. 33.18.7; App. *Mac.* 11.4.
279 Livy 42.44.3–5. Cf. Polyb. 27.2.6.
280 Livy 43.6.5–6. Inscription: *REG* 11 (1898) 258–266, ll. 12–15, 18–21.
281 189 BCE: Livy 38.15.6, 39.17; Gruen (1984) 90, n. 204.
282 Modern writers commonly use the expression *renuntiatio amicitae* for the renunciation of friendship. The verb *renuntiare* in classical Latin means 'to revoke' or 'to renounce'; the noun, *renuntiatio,* means a 'declaration' or 'announcement'. See Rogers (1959) 224, n. 2.
283 The case of Perseus is not discussed as the evidence for *renuntiare* comes from Livy 42.25.1, which is not considered historical. See Gruen (1984) 411 and n. 75.
284 Passage reliable: Rich (2011) 228. See also Turelli (2011) 208–210; Burton (2011) 275–278.
285 At that time, when their advice was innovative, the fetial college issued a *decretum.* See Turelli (2011) 206.
286 Turelli (2011) 211–213 suggests possible embassies for *res repetere* 196 BCE of Cn. Cornelius and 193 BCE T. Quinctius Flamininus.
287 *Strategos*: Livy 35.45.5–9; App. *Syr.* 12. That *societas et amicitia eis* at 36.3.8 refers to that of both Antiochus and the Aetolians see Rich (1976) 61; Briscoe (1981) 223; Giovannini (2000) 90, n. 25 and 110, n. 45. Cf. Turell (2011) 204, n. 77.
288 (1969) 349–353.
289 Treaty: Livy 26.24.8–11; *SEG* 13.382.
290 Livy 29.12.1,5 and referenced again later in Livy 35.33.4.
291 Heuss (1933) 37–44; Dahlheim (1968) 206–207; Burton (2011) 90–92.
292 For mechanisms to break friendship, see the episode in 190 BCE: Livy 42.25.12. See Turelli (2011) 209–210.
293 Cf. Turelli (2011) 214.
294 Polyb. 33.12.1–9, 13.4–10. See Dahlheim (1967) 270–271; Gruen (1984) 588.
295 The question of the date of the beginning of Rhodian–Roman relations is fraught with difficulty. By Polybius' reckoning 140 years prior would have been 306 BCE, the date that marks the beginning of *amicitia* between Rhodes and Rome. This period was an important stage in Rhodian history. Diodorus (20.81) specifies the date according to both the Greek and Roman manner. The consular year was 305 BCE. See Livy 9.44.2. Many scholars have done violence to the text to make it accord with their view that diplomatic relations only began c. 200 BCE. This necessitates changing Polybius' text from 140 years to 40 years. See Holleaux (1902); Holleaux (1921) 44–46. This is followed by Täubler (1913) 204–206; Heuss (1933) 31; Badian (1958) 33. No emendation: Schmitt (1957) 1–48; Berthold (1984) 234–236. Taken against the background of Roman diplomatic encounters in the late fourth and early third centuries, it is not inconsistent that Rome should have made ties of friendship with Rhodes: Bleicken (1959) 440–441. Between 306 and 304 BCE is the most likely date, as 304 BCE saw the end of Demetrius' siege of Rhodes, after which Rhodes had other issues. See Schmitt (1957) 30–31. The purpose of the ties with Rome at this stage has generally been thought to be concerned with trade or with Rhodian complaints over piracy. Trade: Schmitt (1957) 32–49; Walbank (1963) 2–3. Pirates: Schmitt (1957) 3–46; Ormerod (1924) 127–130; Berthold (1984) 236, n. 15. This would tie in with the reports of Alexander the Great sending a letter to the Romans complaining about piracy. Those who hold for the validity of *amicitia* between Rome and Rhodes from 306 BCE point to the possibility that the formation of ties was spurred by mercantile considerations. See Mommsen (1903) 417; Täubler (1913) 204; Cimma (1976) 171ff.; Sherwin-White (1984) 69 and n. 39; Zack (2007) 216. Further evidence for Roman ties with Rhodes is said to be found in an undated fragmentary inscription from Rhodes. First published in 1983 by Kontorini, the relevant section is l.2, which reads, ? Ῥωμαίοις τε καὶ Ῥοδίοις καὶ τοῖς Ῥωμαῖων συμμάχοις. Unfortunately, the crucial word συμμαχία

is restored and cannot provide evidence of any diplomatic relations between the two states. The date of the inscription has been estimated to be c. 200 BCE. See Kontorini (1983); Robert and Robert (1984) 461, n. 294. It remains most likely that *amicitia* with Rome was established around 306–305 BCE.

296 Polyb. 27.3.1–5; Livy 42.45.1–7.

297 They sent only six ships, which arrived too late and were sent back by the Roman commander: Polyb. 27.7.14; Livy 42.56.6. Another fleet never engaged the Macedonians: Livy 44.28.1–3.

298 Cato fr. 95e, Peter = Gell. *NA* 6.3.26

299 Polyb. 27.4.9.

300 Rejected as an annalistic fabrication: Walbank (1979) 3.327; Gruen (1975) 9–60.

301 For a history of Rhodian mediation with other Greek states, see Ager (1991) 12–29.

302 Livy 44.35.4–6; Zon. 9.2.3. For Roman anger see Scafuro (1987); cf. Eckstein (1988). Chains: regarded by Gruen (1975) 76, n. 6 as an annalistic fiction.

303 Polyb. 28.3.3–6; Gruen (1975) 77.

304 Poddighe (2013) 4760.

305 See note 303 above. Bauslaugh (1991) 243: a clear legal definition of neutrality existed in the fifth century BC in Greece. Examples of neutral states: 252–253.

306 Embassy: Polyb. 28.2.2–6. Response: Polyb. 28.2.5–6, 16.9. This account preferred over that of Livius: Gruen (1975) 59, 71.

307 Livy 44.35.4–5.

308 For a pro-Rhodian view that does not deal with the international law implications, see Ager (1991) 34–35.

309 Gruen (1975) 81: the Roman charges of disloyalty was a pretext.

310 Polyb. 30.4; Livy 45.20–25; Diod. 31.5.

311 Livy 45.25.4.

312 Gell. *NA* 6.3.

313 Polyb. 30.4.

314 Schmitt (1957) 211–217; Gruen (1975).

315 *Superbia*: Burton (2011) 284–285.

316 Polyb. 30.31.19–20; Livy *Per.* 46. Fourth attempt: Gruen (1984) 40.

317 Gabrielson (1993) 134; this work was written before the explosion of studies on *amicitia* between 2005 and 2015, which now indicate that it was not possible for Rome to have preserved its friendship with Rhodes while she thought Rhodes was collaborating with Perseus.

# 5 The treaty hypothesis revisited

The view that the Jews received a *foedus* at the time of Judas Maccabaeus has a long history and remains the current consensus. The treaty hypothesis has to be judged against what is known about Roman treaties, but generally there has been little discussion of the Roman State treaty or how it was formed. In the field of Roman *Völkerrecht* there is considerable material to enable a treaty to be recognised by its distinguishing characteristics, by the circumstances and methods in which it was concluded.

## The Roman state treaty: the *foedus*

A legal basis for diplomatic relations between Rome and other states was established by the *foedus* (*Staatsvertrag*), the formal Roman state treaty. A *foedus* is commonly understood as an agreement between two or more peoples that imposed obligations and rights without negating the sovereignty of the treaty partners. The Romans only concluded treaties with independent communities that were fully empowered to make their own foreign policy decisions.[1] The treaty partner had to be under its own power (*in sua potestate*) and not subordinate to another, more powerful entity.[2] The treaty carried lasting obligations for the future and was intended to be permanent.[3]

The Roman State treaty (*foedus*) is characterised by two aspects: written documentation and a religious ceremony of conclusion replete with mutual oath taking. The treaty has, therefore, a legal and sacral element.

The *foedus* placed the whole Roman community as bound to the terms and conditions of the treaty through the execration oath. Through this means, peace was ensured.

What distinguished the *foedus* from other types of diplomatic relations was the ceremonial form and religiously sanctioned oaths with which it was concluded. The Roman treaty ceremony and its ritual words are preserved in Livy's account (1.24.6–8) of the formation of a treaty between Rome and Alba Longa in the reign of King Tullus Hostilius, traditionally dated to the first half of the seventh century BCE:[4]

> The *pater patratus* [the head of the fetial college of priests] is appointed to pronounce the oath, that is, to make the treaty inviolable; and he executes it with many words, that are fixed in a long incantation which it is not worthwhile to quote. Next, after having read out the clauses, he says, 'Hear, Jupiter; hear, *pater patratus* of the Alban people: hear you, People of Alba. As soon as they have been publicly read out from beginning to end, from these tablets or wax tablets without fraud, and as they have been this day most clearly understood, the Roman People will not be the first to violate these conditions. If he shall first violate them, by public intention, with malice aforethought, then on that day do you, great Diespiter, so strike and kill the Roman People as I shall here today strike and kill this pig: and so much the harder smite them as your power and your strength are greater.'

The terms of the treaty were read aloud from wax tablets (*legibus recitatis*) in the manner of an oral contract.[5] Jupiter was called on to witness the treaty and to inflict punishment on the Roman people should they break it.[6] Any breach of the treaty was a breach of trust with Jupiter.[7] Then a pig, the symbol of the perjurer, was sacrificed with a flint knife to symbolise the blow of punishment that would come from Jupiter.[8] So connected was the pig sacrifice with the concept of *foedus* that the grammarian, Servius, could use it as a basis for an etymology of the word *foedus* itself.[9] The verb *ferire* referred to the striking down of the animal and one view found the origin of the word *foedus* in this verb.[10]

The necessity to invoke religion was twofold. First, the gravity and solemnity surrounding this ceremony can be readily explained by the fact that a treaty with another people created an indissoluble bond; its permanence necessitated that it was sanctioned by both the Roman gods and by the gods of the other party to the treaty. Secondly, the bond so formed was lasting and the religious ceremony resulted in a sanction that was meant to enforce compliance with the treaty terms on both sides. The constant problem of ensuring the future adherence of the treaty parties to its terms was handled by imposing religious sanctions that were intended to compel compliance.

An integral part of the ceremony was a recitation of the text of the treaty clauses, an act indispensable in the ceremony to ensure the validity of the treaty formation.[11] The treaty clauses are called *leges* (laws). The word *lex* (law) is cognate with *lego* (I read), which means to read out in a loud voice. The *lex* was a solemn pronouncement and in this case a verbal enunciation of the clauses designed to impose them on the parties to the treaty.[12] The Livian text, by using the word *lex*, indicates that this was how this stage of the ceremony was conducted.

This recitation ensured that both parties were aware of what they were agreeing to and that they were bound to each treaty clause without any omissions. This prevented any partial adherence to the treaty. A full reading in public of the clauses of the treaty from beginning to end (*prima postrema*) also acted to prevent any of the parties at a later date from altering the treaty.[13] This reading aloud was a most necessary feature for compliance with the treaty, for once the words had been heard and listened to, one was henceforth bound to uphold them.

The reading aloud of laws also bound those who heard, even those forming an audience, to be liable to the provisions of the law.[14] Livy (1.24.7) reports that the reading was designed to show that the terms of the treaty were clearly understood by all the people. Fearsome consequences were to befall the Romans if they were the first to violate the treaty. Jupiter was called upon to hear and to witness: *Audi, Iuppiter* . . . ('Hear, Jupiter. . .'). The blow to the sacrificial pig represented a blow to the perjurer[15] and Jupiter stood as the guarantor.[16] The Romans thought that such treaties could not be repudiated when they were solemnised in this way with religious sanction.[17]

The execration oath took place at an altar on which an animal was to be sacrificed. It was accompanied by gestures.[18] The typical hand gesture when swearing an oath was to stretch out the arm with the palm turned down. In this case, the palm would have touched the altar.[19] This oath was, in effect, an uttered curse with the words containing the magic that would bring about the conditions stipulated. The oath was uttered in conditional form so that, if taken falsely, the event stipulated would come about. If the conditions being sworn were broken, then the event would irrevocably come to pass.[20] After the oath had been solemnly uttered by the *pater patratus*, he commenced the ritual of the sacrifice of the pig. It should be borne in mind that only priests could make such oaths.[21]

This sacrifice, an integral part of the ceremony, was held in the open in front of a temple in a cultic space, near a raised altar.[22] Watching would be the community that was involved (in Livy's account, the Romans and the Albans). Immolation of the animal signalled the conclusion of the treaty and the end of the ceremony. The purpose of the sacrifice was to make concrete the self-cursing oath with the striking down – that is, the killing – of an animal as an indication that a similar fate would await the party that was the first to break the treaty. The pig symbolised the one who would break the oath.[23] Pigs were used for expiation.[24]

Through this ritual, the Romans secured good relations with the god who was invoked. This ritual action of sacrifice was in many ways the most important part of the ceremony in terms of its religious significance. The conclusion of a Roman treaty was not a pure legalism. The ceremony was imbued with religious symbolism that invoked magical powers. The ceremony created a treaty that was *sacer*, a treaty that became the possession of the gods, in this case of Feretrius-Diespiter. Ritual was performed not for its own sake but in order to create a divine bond between the Roman state and its treaty partner. With the immolation of the sacrificial animal, a *pax deorum* was established and an indissoluble bond was created with another people. Invoking Jupiter created a religious sanction that made the treaty once formed sacrosanct, eternally permanent, and inviolable.

It may be that a coin from a series of *denarii* minted by a moneyer of the *gens Veturia* in 137 BCE depicts such a ceremony.[25] On the obverse is a youthful head wearing a feathered helmet; this might belong to either Mars or Roma.[26] Crawford[27] suggests that it was the head of Mars chosen as a reference to the Veturius who was Flamen Martialis in 204 BCE. On the reverse are two armoured men, one bearded, both with spears and swords in their hands. The tips of their swords touch a pig, which is being held by a kneeling boy. Above the scene is the legend ROMA. Mommsen suggested that the coin depicted the *sponsio* of the Caudine Forks.[28] The consul at the time was from the *gens Veturia*, one T. Veturius Calvinus; herein lies the connection with the moneyer of 137 BCE. Crawford[29] saw the minting in the following light. In 137 BCE, when news reached Rome that Mancinus had surrendered his army to the Numantines, controversy erupted over whether to ratify the agreement made in the field. The events of 321 BCE at the Caudine Forks were revived to bolster each side. Those who thought it was a *foedus*, for example Veturius, were of the view that the Romans were bound and could not break it. On the other side, others considered that the deal reached to save the Roman army had been merely a *sponsio* and that it could be repudiated. Against the view that the coin made reference to the Caudine Forks disaster, is the suggestion that it would have been unlike the Romans to have made reference on their coinage to such a disgraceful defeat.[30] Nonetheless, the scene on the *denarius* provides us with a good facsimile of the ceremony.

The use of the image of the fetial rite on coins of the late second century BCE may indicate that the *fetiales* maintained their function in the conclusion of treaties, a function still existing in the time of Varro in his *De lingua latina* (47–43 BCE).[31]

In the older literature it was doubted whether both parties of a treaty bound themselves to the terms by oaths.[32] In the treaty ceremony, as quoted by Livy, after the Romans had sworn the oath, the officiating guests from the Alban people followed and also took their oaths. Täubler asserts that oath taking in a treaty accepted by the Roman people appears to be the rule.[33] Polybius mentions (3.25.6) that, in concluding its first treaty with Rome, the Carthaginians swore an oath by

*Figure 5.1* Ti. Veturius. 137 BCE. AR Denarius (19mm, 3.86g, 11h). Rome mint. Helmeted and draped bust of Mars right; TI • (VE) downwards and X (mark of value) to left / Oath-taking scene: youth kneeling left, head right, between two soldiers, each of whom holds a spear and sword that touches pig held by the youth; ROMA above. Crawford 234/1; Sydenham 527; Veturia 1 (image courtesy of the Classical Numismatic Group, Lot 80, No. 171).

their ancestral gods.[34] Likewise, the *foedus Cassianum*, preserved by Dionysius (6.95.3), has both the Romans and the Latins confirming the treaty with oaths. From the Greek copies of Roman treaties found on inscriptions from the Greek East, treaties (oaths) ὅρκια are mentioned in those extant sections where, in the standard format, the mention of oaths is usually placed. The treaties that mention oaths are those from Kibyra (line 5), Methymna (line 15) and Astypalaia (line 43).

The oath swearing could take place in Rome if foreign representatives of the other party were present in Rome, in which case the full college of the *fetiales* would be present.[35] If the oath swearing had to take place in the territory of the treaty partner, a group of *fetiales* would travel with their ceremonial rod, the sceptre of Jupiter Feretrius, the guarantor of treaties and oaths, as well as sacred herbs and vessels in order to conduct the ceremony.[36] This would seem to indicate that both parties were required to swear oaths to uphold the treaty.

The importance of the oath in international treaties is set forward by Cicero, who remarked that the Roman ancestors considered that a bond guaranteed 'good faith' when it was sealed with an oath. His example was the treaty concluded with an enemy. 'For our ancestors were of the opinion that no bond was more effective in guaranteeing good faith than an oath . . . by the treaties in which good faith is pledged even to the enemy'.[37]

The *foedus* was characterised by the requirement that it be ratified by the *comitia centuriata*.[38] In its preamble, the treaty with Lycia in 46 BCE records that it was ratified by a law of the assembly.[39] Polybius, in his discussion of the Roman constitution, says that the people hold the power to ratify or reject treaties.[40] The first known example of a treaty ratified by the people was the alliance with the Mamertines (264 BCE), followed by the treaty with the Aetolians (212 or 211 BCE), the two treaties with Philip V in 205 BCE and 197 BCE, the treaty with the Carthaginians (202 BCE), the treaty with the Aetolians (189 BCE) and the treaty with Antiochus (188 BCE).[41] The process of ratification through the popular assembly is reflected in the literary sources, such as Caesar (*B.C.* 3.107.2: *Quod et lege et senatus consulto societas erat facta*. Against this, such a step was considered by Gruen a mere formality.[42] Yet the ratification by the passing of a law was the exact feature that the Romans regarded as having endowed the *foedus* with its permanency. This can be seen in the following juristic opinion: *Foedera legibus firmiora sunt, nam leges impugnantur aliis legibus* (Scolia Bern. *Ad Lucanum* 2,2 ed. Usener).[43]

Attempts at a typology of Roman treaties have yielded many different schemes, most of which are not faithful to Roman terminology. The most elaborate classification of Roman treaties came from Täubler, who divided them into *Deditionsvertrag*, *Waffenstillstandsvertrag*, *Grundvertrag*, *Klientelvertrag*, *Feldherrnvertrag*, *Senatsvertrag*, *Gastvertrag*, *Schwurvertrag*, *Friedensvertrag*, *Freundschaftsvertrag*, *Volksvertrag* and *Kaiservertrag*.[44] Baronowski considered that many typologies of treaties were 'overly speculative, elaborate, and dogmatic.'[45]

The *locus classicus* for the types of Roman categories of treaties comes from Livy 34.57.7–9:

> [7] There were three kinds of treaties, he said, by which states and kings concluded friendships: one, when, in time of war, terms were imposed upon the conquered; for when everything was surrendered to him who was the more powerful in arms, it is the victor's right and privilege to decide what of the conquered's property he wishes to confiscate; the second, when states that are equally matched in war conclude peace and friendship on terms of equality; [8] under these conditions demands for restitution are made and granted by mutual agreement, and if the ownership of any property has been rendered uncertain by the war, these questions are settled according to the rules of traditional law or the convenience of each party; [9] the third exists when states that have never been at war come together to pledge mutual friendship in a treaty of alliance; neither party gives or accepts conditions; for that happens when a conquering and a conquered party meet.

In this passage are set out three types of treaties: those imposed on the defeated after war, a peace treaty between equals after a war, and a treaty of alliance between those who have never waged war on each other. From this passage, a common typology of treaties has been constructed, principally by Täubler and Horn.[46] The difficulty with this passage is that it comes in a speech reported from Menippus, the envoy of Antiochus III. The reply of Flamininus is more instructive.[47] With sarcasm he explains that the envoy might delight in making nice distinctions and in listing the different types of alliances of friendship. The implication is that the Romans require no lesson in how to form diplomatic relations and are not interested in categorisations. The passage by Livy cannot be relied upon to reflect Roman thought on classifications of treaties. It is better to follow the approach of Ziegler, who also rejects this Livian passage on different grounds as a benchmark for classification. His objection is that the speech reflects the political pragmatism of the Syrian envoy rather than any deep insight into Roman Law.[48]

In the modern literature, there are technical terms for different types of treaties derived from attempts by scholars to construct some systemisation of treaties that find no mention in the ancient sources. The first of these is the *deditio* treaty, a construction devised by Täubler.[49] This concept has fallen into disuse since Horn showed the internal inconsistency of Täubler's concept: since *deditio* legally annihilated the party with which Rome was to make a treaty, there was no independent treaty partner with which to make a contract. The two examples that Täubler presented of a *deditio* treaty (Tac. *Ann.* 3.73 and Tac. *Agric.* 18) cannot be reconciled with *deditio*.[50] That *deditio* was separate from a treaty was shown by Heuss and Dahlheim.[51]

The second modern type of treaty is the *Senatsvertrag*, or the senatorial treaty, also proposed by Täubler.[52] This type fell into two subcategories: the treaties that appear as the text of a *senatus consultum* and those that appear as the draft of a senatorial decision. For the first type, Täubler brought forward one example only – the Roman–Jewish treaty in 1 Macc. 8.23–32. For the second type, Täubler gave as his examples the treaties of Kibyra, Astypalaia and Mytilene.[53]

Additionally, an argument against a treaty is that, according to 1 Macc. 8.20–32, all the decisions were made solely by the senate, whereas in fact the senate did not have the competency to conclude a treaty. It could only decide for a treaty and send advice to the people's assembly to vote in favour.[54] Gruen finds no evidence of the treaty made solely by the senate with anyone in the East and there is no basis in fact for a category of a 'senatorial treaty' as suggested by Täubler.[55]

In Horn's estimation, it was not sufficient to delineate such categories only on the basis of the postscripts of the inscriptions. These postscripts concern the publication of the treaties, and the actual publication would seem to form an inappropriate step if these were drafts.[56] What Täubler considered a draft was found published on its own without the senatorial decision, as in the inscription from Thyrrheion.[57] Ultimately, Täubler himself came to the conclusion that what in fact is extant in the epigraphically preserved treaties is a *senatus consultum* and a treaty text.[58] The prescripts were not composed in Rome and the details, such as the names of the consuls, serve to authenticate the treaty document.[59] In Täubler's three examples of draft senatorial treaties (Kibyra, Astypalaia and Mytilene), the treaty is referred to as συνθήκη. That the treaty is not referred to as a ὅρκιον (that is, a sworn treaty) reinforced his suggestion that this was a senatorial treaty; yet, by Täubler's own definition, ὅρκιον refers to a 'basic treaty'.[60] The label 'draft senatorial treaty' ought to be treated with some scepticism after Horn's analysis.[61] Finally, Täubler had to admit that there were no extant examples of a 'senatorial treaty'.[62]

Täubler proposed another category of treaty that he named 'the client treaty' (*Klientelvertrag*).[63] Such a treaty required the treaty partner to affirm its inferior status *vis-à-vis* Rome by affirming that it would uphold the *maiestas* of the Roman people. Certainly treaties are found with the *maiestas* clause in them, such as, most notably, the Aetolian treaty and the treaty with Gades, but the term *Klientelvertrag* has no Latin equivalent.[64] Scholars now avoid such overclassification of treaties as set out by Täubler.

When the granting of treaties by Rome in response to foreign embassies to the senate became a widespread practice, is a matter of some debate. Gruen maintains the minimalist approach, stating that before 167 BCE Rome was reluctant to conclude formal alliances.[65] A majority opinion holds that there were many treaties from the late third century through the first half of the second century.[66] The issue is hard to resolve for two reasons: the first is the difficulty of assigning a *foedus* where only the term φιλία καὶ συμμαχία or σύμμαχοι is employed; the second reason is the difficulty of dating the treaties known from the epigraphic record with any precision.[67] For these two very reasons it is not sustainable to use a renewal of φιλία καὶ συμμαχία, with Pharos mentioned in an inscription, to substantiate Roman *foedera* in the early third century BCE.[68] The question at issue here is the granting of a treaty by Rome at the request of a foreign embassy before the senate. Neither the treaty forced on the Aetolians in 189 BCE nor the treaty of Apamea with Antiochus III fits into this category of alliances.[69] The earliest known inscriptional *foedus* in the Greek East remains the treaty with Kibyra dated shortly after 188 BCE or after 167 BCE.[70] For treaties with minor Greek states before 148 BCE, there are differing opinions.[71]

One of the more frequent circumstances under which treaties were granted, was after a Roman war had been fought in the area of the treaty partner. The reason for the request for a treaty was the need to confirm good relations with Rome.[72] This was the case with Rhodes (c. 164 BCE), Byzantium (c. 140s BCE) and Elea (c. 120s BCE).[73] These treaties were sought because they expressed Rome's goodwill and satisfaction with the treaty partner's behaviour. Most importantly, the treaty was a guarantee of local sovereignty.[74] The treaties from the second half of the second century BCE, according to Dahlheim, were bestowed as an act of grace on favoured communities by the senate.[75] This comes across clearly in the form in which the Greek copies were published in the East. Heuss showed that the attachment of *senatus consulta* to the treaty text along with copies of letters from consuls indicated that the favour of the senate as displayed by these documents was just as important, or even more so, than the treaty itself.[76]

For those treaties from extant inscriptions, Täubler devised a category that he called the *Bundesgenossenschaftsvertrag*, or 'treaties of alliance', as examples of which he named the treaties of Kibyra, Methymna and Astypalaia.[77] From the inscriptions of Roman treaties there emerges a marked uniformity and rigidity in the order and wording of their clauses. From a comparison of the extant treaties, a canonical or stylised form becomes clear.

## Foedus aequum

In dealing with the Hasmonaean period, a consensus has been reached that Judas Maccabaeus received not merely a treaty from Rome, but a *foedus aequum*.[78] Nowhere in these works is reference made to the extensive literature on how the Romans used these words or whether they should be regarded as technical terms with any legal weight.

A technical categorisation of treaties into either *foedus aequum* or *foedus iniquum* was made by Mommsen and is a matter of some dispute.[79] In his magisterial *Römisches Staatsrecht*, Mommsen set out two broad categories of treaty: one called the *foedus aequum* (the equal treaty), which as he defined it denoted a treaty between states with equal sovereignty; this was to be distinguished from a *foedus iniquum* (an unequal treaty), which was a treaty made after *deditio* (unconditional surrender). Since his time, the description of the two categories has broadened so that a *foedus aequum* is understood as a bilateral defensive alliance, one that permitted to each party the discretion when to act.[80] The *foedus iniquum* was characterised as a unilateral treaty that bound the ally to aid Rome in times of war. Luraschi has lamented the extent to which the classification of Roman treaties into one or other of these types has become quite dogmatic.[81] Mommsen meant something quite different by his two categories: calling a treaty either *aequum* or *iniquum* was merely how the Romans managed to sugar-coat a bitter pill of being subject to Rome. When the Romans used the word *aequum*, the contracting ally still acknowledged the hegemony of Rome and the lack of reciprocal recognition of the full sovereignty of both parties; that is to say, the

Romans did not recognise that the ally enjoyed equal sovereignty with Rome. Such a treaty created dependence without the insertion of the *maiestas* clause that stipulated *maiestatem populi Romani comiter conseruare*. Both types of treaty, according to Mommsen, had implicit in their formation the understanding that the ally would respect the *maiestas* of the Roman people, the distinction being whether the clause was written in or tacitly implied.[82] Mommsen held that the *foedus aequum* also came to indicate a relationship of dependence.[83] Essentially, between these two "types" of treaties there was, in practice, little to distinguish one from the other.[84] Despite the caveat of Mommsen and modern criticism of their use, the terms are still found with the failure to note the euphemistic nature of the vocabulary employed by the Romans.

Over the past sixty years, one half of this classification, the *foedus iniquum*, has been subject to some probing scrutiny, with the result that its position as a legal, technical term to denote a category of treaty is no longer considered valid. To continue to use the term in any technical sense would be unhelpful. In a system of classification with only two parts, the invalidation of one half should be sufficient to demolish the edifice. Nevertheless, the first half remains and continues to be found in the literature, in the context of Judas Maccabaeus' embassy to Rome.

A wholesale reconsideration of the term *foedus iniquum* was undertaken by Badian, who questioned the value of using it in a technical sense. He began by noting that the Romans would not have used the term 'unequal treaty' because the words were hardly conducive to successful diplomacy.[85] This perspective has found wide acceptance.[86] Modern opinion considers that the Roman propensity to resort to polite language with their allies would have made them avoid such a harsh term as *iniquum*.[87] The validity of the term *foedus iniquum* is questionable when one understands that it is a *hapax legomenon* and is found only in Livy 35.46.10:

> For his part he knew not any state in Greece which either contained a garrison, or paid tribute to the Romans, or was bound by a disadvantageous treaty, and obliged to submit to terms which it did not like.

Most consider its meaning to be 'disadvantageous' or 'unjust'.[88] Livy's main source for this passage was Polybius, who had little reason to use technical language in this context.[89]

To the Romans, all allies were unequal; yet they deferred to the sensibilities of those who sought alliances.[90] There lay only the difference between a greater or lesser measure of importance of the ally to Rome.[91] Many scholars now admit that political reality dictated that all Roman treaties were based on the superiority of Roman power. 'After this time [340–338 BCE], the Romans normally controlled the foreign policy of all their Italian allies, whether their *foedera* were *aequa* or not.'[92] Badian's rejection of the term *foedus iniquum* was followed by many.[93] Toynbee understood that once the term *foedus iniquum* became invalidated, the artificial division of treaties into two categories could no longer be maintained:

> Foedus iniquum is not, however, a term that was ever used by the Romans themselves, so far as we know, and it may have misled its modern inventors into representing the distinction between two classes of treaties as being sharper than it was in reality. It is, indeed, probably a mistake to assume that there were two standardized forms of treaty.[94]

No ancient writer proposed a dichotomy between a *foedus aequum* and a *foedus iniquum*. Using the words in this way is misleading and should be avoided.[95] The Romans did not confine themselves to the use of two adjectives to describe their treaties: a treaty could be *par* ('suitable' in Sil. Ital. 6.487), or *inferius* ('lesser', referring to a treaty with a *maiestas* clause in Cic. *Balb.* 35), or *superius* ('stronger' in Livy 1.52.4), as well as *turpe* ('dishonourable' in Vell. 2.1.4), *infidum* ('treacherous', Livy 7.42.8), *honestum* ('respectable', Cic. *de inv.* 2.92), *pium et iustum* (Cic. *Phil.* 37). It cannot be said that these adjectives represent legal categories.[96]

Several Livian passages that mention a *foedus aequum* derive from an unreliable annalistic source[97] or are examples of rhetorical embellishment.[98] Much has been made of the phrase *sub umbra foederis aequi*, which is to be found in Livy 8.4.2. The words are taken from a speech of Annius, the leader of the Latin League. Further into the speech in section 3, Annius throws down the challenge to Rome that *foedus* could be *aequum* when he says, 'if a treaty, an alliance, an equality of rights really exists'. The Romans were attempting to dictate foreign policy to their Latin allies by demanding they cease the war against the Samnites. The Latin refusal led to war. In this instance, the Romans were clear about their concept of a *foedus aequum*: it gave them the right to set the policy. It is clear that the Romans did not treat the Latins as equals.[99]

It is only possible to understand the phrase *foedus aequum* in the context of each passage where it occurs. Livy uses the phrase more than any author: it is found in eight places.[100] Mommsen considered that only four of these passages attest to a *foedus aequum* in any legal sense.[101] These four passages require further elaboration.

1 In the passage at 9.4.4, we find that the Samnites refer to the terms they offer to the Roman army as 'a just and honourable treaty'.
2 At 9.20.8, Livy writes of a treaty to the Teates in Apulia that was *neque . . . aequo*. In other words, to express 'unequal', he did not use *iniquum*, indicating that the latter was not a technical term. In this context Livy made reference to the fact that the Teates had put themselves into the power of the Romans, *in dicione populi Romani*, a vague term.[102]
3 The next passage is 23.5.9, where Livy gives a speech of the Roman consul to the Capuan envoys during the Second Punic War. The consul reminds them that they had previously been bound to Rome by a treaty 'on equal terms'. The aim of his words is to entice the Capuans away from their alliance with Hannibal by offering them a treaty on favourable terms.
4 At 28.45.20, Livy reports the call by Scipio for volunteer recruitment in his campaign to invade Africa. Among those cities that contributed troops was Camerinum, a city in Umbria that had been allied to Rome with a treaty on

> the basis of 'equal rights'. The claim that this phrase carries nothing more than a general goodwill expression is substantiated by the words that Cicero used to refer to this treaty when he called it *aequissimum*.[103]

In 34.57.7–9, Livy reconstructs a speech of the ambassador of King Antiochus III, who enumerated the three types of treaties that states and monarchs entered into with one another. Many scholars comment on this speech as if the Seleucid was so well versed in Roman *Völkerrecht* that we should construct legal theory from his words. Livy has him speak of one type of treaty, which he describes as 'a league of peace and amity on equal terms'. It was shown that this cannot be considered a *locus classicus* for Roman terminology on types of treaties. The second type of treaty that Menippus mentions is the league of peace and friendship 'on equal terms'. Counterbalancing the Livian account is another version by Diodorus.[104] Both derive from Polybius.[105] We can be confident that Livy inserted the words *foedus aequum* into the speech, since the Greek equivalent is absent from the account in Diodorus (and possibly was not to be found in Polybius either).[106] Appian (*Syr.* 6) has an account with the words of the speech of Menippus:

> They were sent really to find out the intentions of the Senate, but for the sake of appearances Menippus said, 'King Antiochus, while strongly desirous of the friendship of the Romans and willing to be their ally if they wish, is surprised that they urge him to give up the cities of Ionia and to remit tribute for certain states, and not to interfere with certain of the affairs of Asia and to leave Thrace alone, though it has always belonged to his ancestors. Yours are not the exhortations of friends, but resemble orders given by victors to the vanquished.'

Here too there is no mention of a discourse on the three types of treaties. Appian's account also derives from Polybius, leading to the conclusion that in the missing portion of Polybius there was to be found no such content. We must assume that the words of the speech are a Livian composition and, therefore, carry no weight for any evaluation of the types of Roman treaties.[107]

The next example derives from a passage of Livy (39.37.13) that reports a speech of Lycortas, as head of the Achaean League in 184 BCE at a time when the Achaeans and Sparta were in conflict. Lycortas, the father of the historian Polybius, protested to the Roman delegation that, in their attempt to mediate with Sparta, Rome was showing greater solicitude towards Sparta. The report of the speech is derived from Polybius, so we may be assured that the speech, as reported, contains the elements of the speech as delivered.[108] Lycortas said that the treaty 'looks as if' it is between equals, whereas, in reality, the Romans only want to take away Achaean sovereignty. His remarks about the appearance of equality do not illuminate the legal status of a *foedus aequum*. Most consider the reference to an 'equal treaty' to be just a rhetorical embellishment.[109]

The remarks on a *foedus aequum* in many of these Livian passages appear in speeches that can only be regarded as the work of Livy himself, schooled as he was in the art of rhetoric. The reliability of these passages for defining Roman international law principles cannot be trusted. After all, Livy was not an expert in Roman jurisprudence.[110]

The term *foedus aequum* should not be thought of in the sense of an 'equally balanced' treaty where each side has equal rights and equal status.[111] Rather it carries the meaning of 'favourable' or 'advantageous'.[112] Four Livian passages refer to a treaty that is 'favourable', two of which (9.4.4 and 23.5.9) also describe a treaty that is 'generous' and 'humane'.[113]

## The underpinnings of the treaty hypothesis

As applied to 1 Maccabees 8, the treaty hypothesis typically contains five elements:

1 The Jews had been granted a special type of treaty that did not require the religious ceremonies of the fetial priests and the mutual sworn oaths.[114] The Jewish treaty, it is maintained, was formalised simply by a decision of the senate.
2 There is such a clear correspondence between the text in 1 Maccabees and the texts of epigraphically extant Roman treaties that this constitutes sound proof of a treaty.
3 The Maccabaean document represents a genuine *senatus consultum*.
4 It is an actual letter from the Roman Senate.
5 The extent of the discrepancies between the document in 1 Macc. 8.23–32 and examples of Roman treaties has caused a fifth component to be added in response. In its defence, it is maintained that each and every deviation from the texts of Roman treaties can be laid at the feet of the many translations that the document has undergone before it reached the form in which we see it today. It originated from Rome, according to this view, where it was translated from Latin to Greek. The Greek copy arrived in Jerusalem, where it was translated into Hebrew for its use in the first edition of the First Book of Maccabees. This Hebrew translation was rendered once more into Greek when the First Book of Maccabees became the version we have today. I have named this process 'the multiple translation hypothesis'.

Needless to say, all five of these elements are seriously flawed.

## A comparison of the text in 1 Macc. 8.23–32 with extant Roman treaties

The shadow of Mommsen still falls over scholarly views on the question as to whether or not the Jews did indeed enter into a treaty with Rome. Mommsen pioneered the method of comparing the content of the Jewish alliance with the treaty of Astypalaia, extant in the form of an inscription on stone, thus developing the methodology of choice for the adherents of the treaty theory.[115] Even those scholars who do not hold to this theory still feel bound to continue following the method of Mommsen.[116] The apparent similarities Mommsen found between the Jewish document and the treaty of Astypalaia remain the chief argument in favour of a treaty and account for the widely held acceptance of his view today.

The lynchpin of the treaty hypothesis is the correlation of the wording of 1 Macc. 8.23–32 with known Roman treaties. The treaties that provide the most accurate comparison are those of the mutual defence type. More inscriptions containing treaties have come to light since Mommsen's day. Treaties cited by Graeco-Roman historians are not similar to mutual defence treaties, nor are they comparable to the Jewish document. Polybius cites the treaties between Rome and Carthage that delineated their respective commercial and territorial spheres.[117] Dionysius of Halicarnassus cites the *foedus Cassianum*, a treaty between Rome and the Latins.[118] None of these is comparable to the Jewish document.

What distinguishes the citation in 1 Macc. 8.23–32 from the citations of treaties in the works of Graeco-Roman historians, is the statement in 1 Macc. 8.22 that this is a copy (ἀντίγραφον) of a senatorial letter. In 1 Maccabees, other cited documents, but not all, are introduced as 'a copy'. These are the letter of Jonathan to the Spartans (1 Macc. 12.5), the letter of the Spartan king to the Jews (1 Macc. 12.19), the letter of the Spartans to Simon (1 Macc. 14.20) and the letter of the people to Simon (1 Macc. 14.27). A 'copy' implies that the cited document is a replica and not a *précis*. In a copy, one expects that no elements are omitted. By contrast, when Polybius cited the Roman–Carthaginian treaty of c. 306 BCE, he introduced it with these words: this treaty is more or less as follows (εἰσὶ δὲ τοιαίδε τινές).[119] He also introduces the Roman–Carthaginian treaty of 509/508 BCE in the same way.[120] He makes no claim that he is presenting exact copies. The citation of the *foedus Cassianum* by Dionysius of Halicarnassus is thought to have been from a text reconstructed almost 300 years after the event.[121] This treaty is also not an authentic copy. The author of 1 Maccabees has included no fewer than eight cited documents. This is in line with Hellenistic Jewish historiography, which considered that cited documents were important aids in making one's case. So 2 Maccabees has four cited letters: three from Seleucid kings, and one from two Roman envoys to the Jews concerning negotiations with the Seleucid king during the Maccabaean revolt.[122] Josephus in his *Antiquities* considered it important to show the standing of the Jews in the eyes of pagans by quoting official correspondence.[123]

The copy of an official decision or decisions of the Roman Senate in favour of the Jews as cited in 1 Macc. 8.23–32 is in the form of an agreement made by the senate. Inscriptions from the Greek-speaking East provide examples of official copies sent from Rome in Greek. In order to ascertain whether the Jews entered into a treaty, one needs to compare the text, as Mommsen did, with these official texts on inscriptions. With the discovery of more complete texts than the treaty of Astypalaia, there is the potential for a more precise and considered comparison between the Jewish alliance document and the treaties of Maroneia and Lycia.[124] With these texts, a more accurate delineation of the parts of a typical Roman mutual defence treaty is possible.[125]

The six elements common to a treaty are:[126]

1 the prescript;
2 the peace and alliance stipulation;
3 the clause obligating neutrality;
4 a defensive support obligation;
5 the amendment clause;
6 the publication clause.

In all, there are seven extant copies of Roman treaties in Greek. These treaties are between Rome and Kibyra, Maroneia, Astypalaia, Methymna, Thyrrheion, Callatis (the only treaty recorded in Latin) and Lycia. In order to determine whether these six parts of a Roman treaty occur in the same order in all known Roman treaties, the six parts are laid out according to the material extant in each treaty. Table 5.1 presents the order of the six parts are identical across the board. The form of the treaty remained remarkably constant.[127]

The content of these mutual defence treaties was formulaic, rigid and standardised.[128] Their wording shows remarkably little variation. Here follows a description of each of the six parts, with quotations from the Greek inscriptions.

### *The prescript*

Part 1, the prescript, is found in the treaties with Astypalaia, Thyrrheion and Lycia. Its first component is the heading of the document: for example, in the treaty with Thyrrheion it has Συμμαχία ποτὶ Ῥωμαίους (line 1) and in the Lycian treaty Ὅρκος (line 1). Then the names of the two consuls are listed: in the case of Thyrrheion, Gaius Coelius Caldus, son of Gaius, and Lucius Domitius Ahenobarbus, son of Gaius (lines 4–5); in the Lycian treaty of 46 BCE, the names are Gaius Iulius Caesar, dictator, and Marcus Lepidus, Master of the Horse (lines 2–3). The prescript gives the date (day and month): in the treaty with Lycia, the date is given as the ninth day before the Kalends of Sextilius (lines 4–5). The place of meeting is given: in the treaty with Lycia, this is the assembly. Next mentioned

*Table 5.1* The six parts of a Roman treaty as found in extant Roman treaties[a]

| *Maroneia* | *Kibyra* | *Astypalaia* | *Methymna* | *Callatis* | *Thyrreion* | *Lycia* |
|---|---|---|---|---|---|---|
| 1 | | 1 | | | 1 | 1 |
| 2 | | 2 | | | 2 | 2 |
| 3 | | 3 | 3 | 3 | | 3 |
| 4 | 4 | 4 | 4 | 4 | | 4 |
| 5 | 5 | 5 | 5 | 5 | | 5 |
| 6 | 6 | 6 | | 6 | | |

Note

a 1, prescript; 2, the peace and alliance clause; 3, the neutrality clause; 4, the defence support obligation; 5, the amendment clause; 6, the publication clause.

are those senators who comprised the committee responsible for committing the decree to writing: in the treaty with Thyrrheion, the leading name is L. Gellius, son of Lucius (lines 5–6), followed by the names of the ambassadors (lines 7–8).

## *The alliance clause*

The alliance clause, in part 2, mentions φιλία καὶ συμμαχία, but only the treaty of Astypalaia mentions εἰρήνη, perhaps because the text says it is a renewal of a treaty. Both the treaties of Maroneia and Astypalaia contain the same expression: πόλεμος δὲ μὴ ἔστω. The treaty with Thyrrheion has τῷ δήμῳ [τῷ Ῥωμα]ίων [κα]ὶ τῷ δήμῳ τῷ Θυρρεί[ων] εἰρήνη καὶ φιλία καὶ συμμαχία ἔστω. In the treaty with Lycia it is expressed somewhat more fully:

> τῷ δήμῳ τῷ Ῥωμαίων καὶ τῷ κοινῷ τῶν Λυκίων φιλί[α καὶ συμμαχία κ] αὶ κοινωνία τὸν ἅπαντα χρόνον ἀσφαλὴς καὶ ἀμετάθετος ἔστωι ἄ[νευ δόλου πο]νηροῦ. εἰρήνη τε κατὰ γῆν κατὰ θάλλασσαν αἰώνιος ἔστω τῷ τε δήμῳ τῷ Ῥω[μαίων καὶ] τῶι κιονῶι τῶν Λυκίων.

## *The neutrality clause*

In part 3, the neutrality clause, the wording also is fairly standardised. In the treaty of Maroneia is found, μήτε ὅπλοις μήτε ναυσὶν μήτε χρήμασιν χορηγείτωσαν δημοσίᾳ βουλῇ δόλῳ πονηρῷ τοῦ δήμου τοῦ Ῥωμαίων (lines 27–29), while in the treaty of Methymna is found, μήτε ὅπλοις μήτε χρήμασιν μήτε ναυσὶν βοηθείτωσαν δημοσίᾳ βουλῇ δόλου πονηροῦ (lines 8–9). The treaty of Astypalaia has the same wording: μήτε ὅπλοις μήτε χρήμασι μήτε ναυσὶν βοηθείτω [ο] δημοσίᾳ βουλῇ δόλῳ πονηρῷ (lines 38–40). In the Lycian treaty, it is expressed very much the same way: καὶ μήτε χρήμασιν μήτε ἐφοδίοις μήτε ὅπλοιη μήτε πλοίοις συνυπηρετείτωσαν δημοσίαι βουλῆι δόλῳ πονερῷ. While not fully extant, as in the treaty of Maroneia, the prohibition against allowing enemies of the other to pass through one's territory (διὰ τῆς ἰδίας χώρας) is found in the treaties of Astypalaia and Methymna.

## *The defensive clause*

In part 4, the defensive clause from the Roman side, for example, is expressed in the treaty of Maroneia as, Ἐάν τις πρότερος ἐκφέρῃ τῷ δήμῳ τῶν Ῥωμαίων ἢ τοῖς ὑπὸ Ῥωμαίους τασσομένοις, τότε ὁ δῆμος ὁ τῶν Μαρωνιτῶν τῷ δήμῳ τῶν Ῥωμαίων κατὰ τὸ εὔκαιρον βοηθείτω (lines 30–33), and finds echoes in the treaty with Kibyra, [ἐ]ὰν δέ τις πρότερος πόλεμον ἐπιφέρῃ τῷ δήμῳ τῶν Ῥωμαίων ἢ τὰς συνθήκας παραβῇ, τότε ὁ δῆμος ὁ τῶν Κιβυρατῶν τῷ δήμῳ τῷ Ῥωμαίων βοηθείτω κατὰ τὸ εὔκαιρον (lines 2–5), and in the treaty with Methymna, ἐάν τις πόλεμον πρότερος ἐπιφέρῃ τῷ δήμῳ τῶν Μηθυμναίων, τότε ὁ δῆμος ὁ Ῥωμαίων τῷ δήμῳ τῷ Μηθυμναίων βοηθείτω ὡς ἂν ᾖ εὔκαιρον (lines 10–12). In the treaty of Astypalaia, the text is not wholly extant at this point. The words, however, πρότερος πόλεμον ἐπιφέρῃ, can be read without difficulty. The fullest text is to be found in the treaty with Lycia:

> ἐάν τις τῷ δήμῳ τῷ Ῥωμαίων ἢ καὶ τοῖς συμμάχοις αὐτοῦ πολέμου προκατάρξηται τὸ κοινὸν τὸ Λυκίων βοηθείτω τῶι δήμωι τῷ Ῥωμαίων κατὰ τὸ ἐνδεχομενον. ἐάν τις τῶι κοινῶι τῶν Λυκίων ἢ τοῖς ὑποτασσαμένοις τούτωι καὶ τοῖς συμμάχοις τοῖς τούτων πολέμου προκατάρξηται ὁδῆμος ὁ Ῥωμαίων τῶι κοινῶι τῶν Λυκίων βοηθείτωι κατὰ τὸ ενξδεχόμενον (lines 23–260).

### *The amendment clause*

In part 5, the amendment clause shows a remarkable similarity between different treaties. In the treaty of Maroneia, the clause is expressed in this fashion: Ἐάν τι πρὸς ταύτην τὴν συμμαχίαν προσωεῖναι ἢ ἐξελθεῖν ὁ δῆμος ὁ τῶν Ῥωμαίων καὶ ὁ δῆμος ὁ τῶν Μαρωνιτῶν βούλωνται, κοινῇ βουλῇ ἑκατέρων βουλομένων ἐξέστω καὶ ὃ ἂν προσθῶσιν τοῦτο ἐν τῇ συμμαχίᾳ ἐνέστω, ὃ δὲ ἐὰν ἐξέλωσιν, τοῦτο ἐν τῇ συμμαχίᾳ μὴ ἐνέστω (lines 36–40). The same clause in the treaty of Kibyra reads: καὶ ἐάν τι πρὸς ταύτας τὰς συνθήκας ὁ δῆμος ὁ Ῥωμαίων καὶ ὁ δῆμος ὁ Κιβυρατῶν κοινῇ βουλῇ προσθεῖναι ἢ ἐξελεῖν βούλωνται, κοινῇ βουλῇ δημοσίᾳ ἑκατέρων θελόντων ἐξέστω. ἃ δὲ ἂν προστιθῶσιν ἐν ταῖς συνθήκαις, ἐνέστω ἐν ταῖς συνθήκαις, ἃ δὲ ἂν ἀφέλωσιν τῶν συνθηκῶν, ἐντός ἔστω (lines 7–11). Similarly, in the treaty of Methymna: ἐὰν τι πρὸς ταύτας τὰς συνθήκας κοινῇ βουλῇ προσθεῖναι ἢ ἆρᾳ βούλωντᾳ, δημοσίᾳ βουλῇ ἑκατέρων ἐξέστω˙ ἃ δὲ ἂν προσθῶσιν ἢ ἄρωσιν ἐν ταῖς συνθήκαις, ἐκτὸς ἔστω ταῦτα προσγεγραμμένα ἐν ταῖς συνθήκαις (lines 17–20). The same clause in the treaty of Astypalaia reads: Ἐὰν δέ τι πρὸς ταύτας τὰς συνθήκας κοινῇ βουλῇ προσθεῖναι ἢ ἀφελεῖν βούλωντᾳ δημοσίᾳ βουλῇ ὃς ἂν θελήσῃ εξέστω˙ ἃ δὲ ἂν προσθῶσιν ἐν ταῖς συνθήκαις ἢ ἃ ἂν ἀφέλωσω ἐκ τῶν συνωηκῶν, ἐκτὸς ἔστω ταῦτα ἐν ταῖς συνθήκαις γεγραμμένα (lines 45–48). The treaty with Lycia has an amendment clause also remarkably similar but written almost seventy years later. It reads: ἐὰν τι κατὰ τὴν ἑκατέρων γνώμην φαίνηται προσθεῖναι ἀφελεῖν ἐντάξαι περιγράψαι ἐξέστωι, ἐάν τι προστεθῆι γραφῆι ἐνταγῆι πρὸς τοῦτο τὸ ὁρκωμόσιον ἐξέστωι. ἐὰν τι πάλιν ἐξαιρεθῆι ἢ περιγραφῆι ἐκ τούτου τοῦ ὁρκωμοσίου καὶ τοῦτο ἐξέστωι. τούτωι τῶι ὁρκωμοσίωι καὶ τῇ συνθήκηι δόλος πονηρὸς ἀπέστωι. τούται τῶι ὁρκωμοσίωι καὶ τῇ συνθΎκηι δόλος πονηρὸς ἀπέστωι (lines 69–74).

### *The publication clause*

In part 6, the publication clause also is expressed with a certain degree of conformity. For the treaty of Maroneia, the clause reads as follows: Ταύτην τὴν συμμαχίαν γραφῆναι εἰς χάλκωμα καὶ ἀνατεθῆναι ἐν μὲν Ῥώμῃ ἐν τῷ Καπετωλίῳ ἐν δὲ Μαρωνείᾳ ἐν τῷ Διονυσίῳ. The treaty of Kibyra reads, ταύτας δὲ τὰς συνήκας εἰς χάλκωμα ἀναγραψάτωσαν καὶ ἀναθέτωσαν ἐμ μὲν ʽΡώμῃ ἐν τῷ ἱερῷ τοῦ Διὸς τοῦ Καπετωλίου, and the treaty of Astypalaia reads, ἀναθέντων δὲ ἀνάθημα ἒμ μὲν ʽΡωμαίων ἐν τῷ Καπετωλίῳ ναῷ τοῦ Διός, ἒν δὲ ʼΑστυπαλαιέων ἐν τῷ ἱερῷ τῆς ʼΑθηνᾶς καὶ τοῦ ʼΑσκληπιους καὶ πρὸς τῷ βωμῷ . . . τῆς ʽΡώμης.

The treaties of Maroneia and Lycia have provided an almost complete text with which to compare the other examples of Roman treaties found in various states of completion. A comparison of the treaty of Maroneia with other examples enables the following conclusions to be formed. There were six parts to a treaty and they occurred in the same order. In other words, the form of the treaty was consistent. The content of these treaties was expressed in remarkably similar vocabulary and phraseology. As a result, there is no difficulty in speaking, as have many scholars, of a standard Roman treaty that was rigidly formulaic.[129]

Due to the fact that the Roman treaty had a standard sequence of clauses and formulaic phrasing, a Jewish treaty ought to conform to the Roman formula. For purposes of demonstrating the relative points of correlation, Table 5.2 provides a synopsis of the verses in the text of 1 Maccabees that bear some correspondence with certain lines of the text in the Maroneia treaty.[130]

The first feature to notice about the alliance document in 1 Maccabees is that the order of the clauses varies from the order of clauses in the treaty of Maroneia. In order to preserve the same order of a Roman treaty, the verses in 1 Macc. 8 would have to be sequenced in the following order: 23, 26, 28, 24, 25, 27, 30. Clearly, the alliance document in 1 Maccabees does not follow the strict order of clauses in a Roman treaty. A Roman treaty began with (1) a prescript, followed by (2) a peace and alliance stipulation, (3) a neutrality clause, (4) a defensive support obligation, (5) an amendment clause, and then (6) a publication clause. Moreover, the order of the clauses in Roman treaties was remarkably uniform. Table 5.3 places the order of these six parts of a Roman treaty as they occur in the Jewish document alongside the order of the constituent parts of a Roman treaty in the six extant texts of Roman treaties. This arrangement shows at a glance that the order in the Jewish document deviates from the standard Roman sequence of clauses.

The reason the order of clauses in the Jewish document is different is because it groups the alliance and neutrality clauses of the Jews and then the alliance and neutrality clauses of the Romans. The Jewish text lists the alliance decision first and only then lists the neutrality clause. What explanations have been offered for this difference in the sequence of the clauses? Täubler explained that this order corresponded to the order in which the senate voted on the clauses.[131] Against this, the extant Roman treaties bear evidence that the senate (if it dealt with clauses *seriatim* – which is doubtful – and not as a block) dealt with clauses in a consistently identical order. This raises the question of why a Jewish treaty should display a remarkable singularity in the order of its clauses when the Roman pattern is remarkably consistent.

*Table 5.2* A comparison between the text of 1 Macc. 8.23–32 and the text of the treaty of Maroneia

| *1 Macc. 8.23–32* | *The Treaty of Maroneia (SEG 35.823, pp. 218–219)* |
|---|---|
| | 1 ἱ]ερέῳ[ς Διὸς καὶ Ῥώμης Διονύσου καὶ Μὰρωνος]<br>πρεσβε[υσάντων (δεῖνος), τοῦ (δεῖνος)],<br>Ἐπιγόνου τọ]υ (δεῖνος), (δεῖνος) τοῦ<br>4 Μητροφάνου,τ[ọ] [(δεῖνος), τοῦ (δεῖνος), (δεῖνος)<br>τοῦ 'Αθήνεω, 'Αγαθοḳ[λέọυς τοῦ (δεῖνος)]<br>Πυθίωνος τοῦ 'Ηραγόροụ [ποιεῖν τὸν δῆμον τὸν]<br>Ῥωμαίων καὶ τὸν δῆμον τὸν [Μαρωνιτῶν καὶ]<br>8 Αἰνίων τοὺς κεκριμένους ὑπὸ Λευκίο[υ Παύλου<br>ἐλευθέρους καὶ πολιτευομένους με[τ' αὐ ]–τῶν·<br>10 φιλία καὶ συμμαχία καλὴ ἔστω |
| 23 Καλῶς γένοιτο Ῥωμαίοις καὶ τῷ ἔθνει 'Ιουδαίων | |
| ἐν τῇ θαλάσσῃ καὶ ἐπὶ τῆς ξηρᾶς | καὶ κατὰ γῆν καὶ κατὰ θάλασσαν |
| εἰς τὸν αἰῶνα | εἰς τὸν ἅπαντα χρόνον, |
| καὶ ῥομφαία καὶ ἐχθρὸς μακρυνθείν ἀπ' αὐτῶν. | 12 πόλεμος δὲ μὴ ἔστω· |
| | Ὁ δῆμος ὁ τῶν Μαρων[ι]τῶν τοὺς πολεμίους καὶ ἀντιπολεμίους τοῦ δήμου τοῦ Ῥωμαίων διὰ τῆς ἰδίας χώρας καὶ η[ς [ἂν] αὐτοὶ κρατῶσιν μὴ διιέτωσαν δημοσίαι βọυ–<br>16 λῆι δὸλωι πονηρῶι, ὥστε τῶι δήμωι τῶι Ῥω–<br>17 μαίων |
| 26 καὶ τοῖς πολεμοῦσιν οὐ δώσουσιν οὐδὲ ἐπαρκέσουσι σῖτου, ὅπλα, ἀργύριον, πλοῖα | καὶ τοῖς ὑπ' αὐτοὺς τασσομένοις πόλεμọυ<br>18 ἐκφέρωσιν, μήτε αὐτοὺς σίτωι μήτε ὅπλοις μή–<br>19 τε ναυσὶν μήτε χρήμασιν χορηγείτωσαν |
| 26 καὶ φυλάξονται τὰ φυλάγματα αὐτῶν οὐθὲν λαβόντες. | δημοσ [ίαι]<br>20 βουλῆι δόλωι πονηρῶι, |
| | ὥστε τῶι δήμωι τῶι Ῥω-<br>μαίων πόλεμον ἐκφέρωσιν· Ὁ δῆμος ὁ τῶν Ῥωμαί– |

| | |
|---|---|
| [28]καὶ τοῖς συμμαχοῦσιν οὐ δοθήσεται σῖτος, ὅπλα, αργύριον, πλοῖα, . . . καὶ φυλάξονται τὰ φυλάγματα ταῦτα καὶ οὐ μετὰ δόλου. | ων τοὺς πολεμίους καὶ ἀντιπολεμίους τοῦ δήμου τοῦ Μαρωνιτῶν διὰ τῆς ἰδίας χώρας καὶ ἧς ἄν αὐτοὶ [24]κρατῶσιν μὴ διιέτωσαν δημοσίαι Βουλῆι δόλωι πονηρῶι, ὥστε τῶι δήμωι τῶι Μαρωνιτῶν καὶ τοῖς ὑπ᾽αὐτοὺς τασσομένοις πόλεμον ἐκφέρωσιν, μήτε αὐτοὺς σίτωι μήτε ὅπλοις μήτε ναυσὶν μήτε χρήμασιν χορηγείτωσαν |
| [24]ἐὰν δὲ ἐνστῇ πόλεμος Ῥώμῃ προτέρᾳ ἢ πᾶσι τοῖς συμμάχοις αὐτῶν ἐν πάσῃ κυρίᾳ αὐτῶν, | δημοσίαι βουλῆι δόλωι πονηρῶι |
| [25]συμμαχήσει τὸ ἔθνος τῶν Ἰουδαίων, ὡς ἂν ὁ καιρὸς ὑπογράφῃ αὐτοις, καρδίᾳ πλήρει. | [29]τοῦ δήμου τοῦ Ῥωμαίων, ὥστε τῶι δήμωι τῶι Μαρωνι-[31]τῶν πόλεμον ἐκφέρωσιν· Ἐάν τις πρότερος ἐκφέρηι τῶι δήμωι τῶν Ῥωμαίων ἢ τοῖς ὑπὸ Ῥωμαίους τασσομένοις, |
| [27]κατὰ τὰ αὐτὰ δὲ ἐὰν ἔθνει Ἰουδαίων συμβῇ προτέροις πόλεμος, συμμαχήσουσιν οἱ Ῥωμαῖοι ἐκ ψυχῆς, ὡς ἂν αὐτοῖς ὁ καιρὸς ὑπογράφῃ. | [32]τότε ὁ δῆμος ὁ τῶν Μαρωνιτῶν τῶι δήμωι τῶν Ῥωμαίων κατὰ τὸ εὔκαιρον βοηθείτω· Ἐάν τις πρότερος πόλεμον ἐκφέρηι τῶι δήμωι τῶν Μαρωνιτῶν ἢ τοῖς ὑπὸ Μαρωνίτας τασσομένοις, τότε ὁ δῆμος ὁ τῶν Ῥωμαίων τῶι δήμωι τῶι Μαρωνιτῶν κατὰ τὸ εὔκαιρον βοηθείτω· |
| [30]ἐὰ δὲ μετὰ τούς λόγους τούτους βουλεύσωνται οὗτοι καὶ οὗτοι προσωεῖναι ἢ ἀφελεῖν, ποιήσονται ἐξ αἱρέσεως αὐτῶν, καὶ ὃ ἐὰν προσθῶσιν ἢ ἀφέλωσιν, ἔσται κύρια. | Ἐάν τι πρὸς ταύτην συμμαχίαν προσθεῖναι ἢ ἐξελεῖν ὁ δῆμος ὁ τῶν Ῥωμαίων καὶ ὁ δῆμος ὁ τῶν Μαρωνιτῶν βούλωνται, κοινῇ βουλῆι ἑκατέρων βουλομένων ἐξέστω καὶ ὃ ἂν προσθῶσιν τοῦτο ἐν τῆι συμ<μ>αχίαι ἐνέστω, ὃ δὲ ἐὰν ἐξέλωσιν, τοῦτο ἐν τῆι συμ<μ>αχίαι μὴ ἐνέστω· |
| | Ταύτην τὴν συμμαχίαν γραφῆναι εἰς χάλκωμα καὶ ἀνατεθῆναι ἓν μὲν Ῥώμῃ ἐν τῷ Καπετωλίῳ, ἐν δὲ Μαρωνείαι ἐν τῶι Διονυσίωι |

*Table 5.3* The sequence of clauses in Roman treaties and in 1 Macc. 8.23–32[a]

| *Maroneia* | *Kibyra* | *Astypalaia* | *Methymna* | *Callatis* | *Thyrreion* | *Lycia* | *1 Macc. 8.23–32* |
|---|---|---|---|---|---|---|---|
| 1 | | 1 | | | 1 | 1 | |
| 2 | | 2 | | | 2 | 2 | 2 |
| 3 | | 3 | 3 | 3 | | 3 | 4 |
| 4 | 4 | 4 | 4 | 4 | | 4 | 3 |
| 5 | 5 | 5 | 5 | 5 | | 5 | 5 |
| 6 | 6 | 6 | | 6 | | | |

Note

a 1, prescript; 2, the peace and alliance clause; 3, the neutrality clause; 4, the defence support obligation; 5, the amendment clause; 6, the publication clause.

The second significant feature arising from the comparison is just how much of the content from a standard treaty is absent from the document in 1 Maccabees 8. These omissions have been noted by many scholars. Yet the deviations from a Roman treaty text so caused do not appear to alter their perception that the Jewish document is, for all that, still a Roman treaty.

What are the items that have been omitted? Left out entirely is any prescript. This section would usually have included the names of the consuls, the date of the meeting, the place, and the names of the witnesses. In the treaty of Thyrrheion this prescript gives the names of the consuls of the year when the treaty was concluded (lines 1–9). This omission in the Jewish treaty has been remarked upon by Mommsen, Täubler, Abel and Gauger. Both Mommsen and Täubler maintained that the prescript had become jumbled with the text standing before verse 23 and found reference to this missing prescript in 1 Macc. 8.16. A translation of this verse reads as follows: 'They entrusted their government and the ruling of all their territory to one man each year, everyone obeying him, without any envy or jealousy among themselves.' However, this verse is well outside the purported text of the letter, which commences in verse 23 and, by its own admission, is not part of the alliance document itself.

An indication of the success of the mission is usually to be found in the prescript that contained authenticating information, such as the date, the place where the senate met, the president of that particular session of the senate and the names of witnesses.[132] One could make the omission of a prescript less significant than it ought to be by neglecting to include the prescript as a standard feature of a Roman treaty; but this would be to go against the evidence of the treaties of Maroneia, Astypalaia, Thyrrheion and Mytilene, all of which include a prescript.[133] The only other two extant treaties, those of Methymna and Callatis, have texts that are not extant at the point where a prescript would be found.

There are other significant omissions. A copy of a senatorial letter should have no items missing. The Jewish document, however, lacks a standard provision in these types of treaties; that is, a prohibition against the transit through each other's territory of the forces of the enemy. This omission Täubler found most striking.[134] The Jewish alliance document does not speak of 'the Jews and their allies' or, as in the treaty of Maroneia, 'those marshaled under' the Jews. It speaks only of 'the Jews', whereas the mention of 'the Romans together with their allies' is documented in Roman treaties. The Maccabaean document combines the neutrality and treaty decision clauses and, in so doing, shortens both and omits details.[135] The defensive clause is omitted. Such a detail would not be missing in a copy of a senatorial letter. Täubler suggested that the missing clause might be rebuilt from verses 24, 26, 27 and 28.[136] For πολεμοῦσιν in verse 26 Täubler read πολευμίοις. For συμμαχουσ̂ιν in verse 28 he read συμμαχήσουσιν.[137]

There is no publication clause contained within the text of the Maccabaean document. Such clauses are known from the treaties between Rome and Maroneia, Astypalaia and Methymna.[138] A reference, however, is made to certain bronze tablets in 1 Macc. 8.22: καὶ τοῦτο τὸ ἀντίγραφον τῆς ἐπιστολῆς ἧς ἀντέγραψεν ἐπὶ δέλτοῖς χαλκαῖς . . . . In Roman treaties this section was included as part of the treaty itself and formed the final clause, which also contained the consent of the senate to set up a bronze tablet on the Capitol in Rome and in a local temple in the partner city.[139] The Jewish document, however, claims that the text of the alliance with Rome was sent from Rome to Jerusalem in the form of bronze tablets, a practice otherwise unattested. The usual procedure was to have the *senatus consultum* and the treaty text engraved on bronze and set up on the Capitol, then a copy of the same was set up on a temple in the community's own city at their own expense.[140] The text for the latter was taken from the letter sent to the city concerned. Some envoys carried their senatorial letter back from Rome with them.[141] The treaty with Lycia, while it is indeed engraved on a bronze tablet, is not a Roman copy.[142] It was in all likelihood made to be placed in the Letoon, the sanctuary outside Xanthos that served the Lycian Confederacy, where other decrees have been found.[143] Mitchell suggests that bronze and not stone was used for the inscription due to the Lycians' desire to imitate the Romans (the Lycians being the most philo-Roman of the peoples in Asia Minor).[144]

In order to explain these omissions, Täubler suggested that the Jews received not a final treaty but a *senatus consultum*, which had contained merely the proposal of a treaty. He maintained that the Maccabaean document was, in fact, a senatorial protocol given in a letter to the envoys to take back with them from Rome.[145]

Let us examine the extent to which the Maccabaean document conforms to the standard form of a senatorial decree. Using the format pioneered by Moehring, the results are set out in Table 5.4.

When the text of 1 Macc. 8.23–32 does not fit easily into the treaty paradigm, scholars have resorted to convoluted efforts to accommodate the difficulties while retaining the paradigm. By way of example, one may cite Goldstein, who claims that the treaty is a 'novel form' made out of stereotyped clauses but modified to accommodate the religious scruples of some Jews towards a rebellion against the Syrian king. He notes, 'a special terminology and procedure had to be invented when the Jews could not subscribe to the friendship section of the standard Roman treaty'.[146]

For Täubler, the decisive evidence that this document was actually a Roman treaty is the correspondence in 1 Macc. 8.23–32 between various expressions

*Table 5.4* 1 Macc. 8.23–32 compared with a senatorial decree

| *Standard form for senatus consultum* | *Degree of compliance*[a] |
|---|---|
| 1 Prescript | |
| (a) name and rank of the presiding magistrate/s | 0 |
| (b) *senatus consuluit* τῃ συγκλήτῳ συνεβουλεύσατο | 0 |
| (c) day and month of meeting | 0 |
| (d) place | 0 |
| (e) names of the witnesses introduced by the phrase *scribendo adfuerunt* γραφομένῳ παρῆσαν | 0 |
| 2 Theme | |
| (a) *relatio: quod [*name of *relator] uerba fecit de [*or *ut]* περὶ ὧν ὁ δεῖνα ἐποιήσατο περὶ ̔ορ ὅπωξ | 0 |
| (b) résumé of the events or motives that prompted the *relator* to bring the matter before the senate | 0 |
| (c) concluding formula *d(e) e(a) r(e) i(ta) c(ensuereunt)* περὶ τούτου τοῦ πράγματος οὖδοξεν serves as an introduction to | 0 |
| 3 The Decree Proper | |
| In indirect speech or introduced by *ut (uti)* | 0 |
| 4 Mark of approval: formal expression of the vote c(*ensuere*) ἔδοξεν | / |

Note

a 0, nil; /, partial.

found there as well as in extant Roman treaties. He showed in chart form similarities in wording between the Maccabaean document and a collection of Roman documents. The number of similarities with a Roman treaty is not large. Täubler's chart, although it was intended to show similarities, reveals by its gaps the differences between known Roman treaties and the wording of 1 Macc. 8.26 and 27. The difficulty with Täubler's chart is that it does not compare each verse with a Roman treaty. He could not refer in 1913 to a very full text of a Roman treaty, such as the texts now available of the treaty of Maroneia and of Lycia. For ὡς ἂν ὁ καιρὸς ὑπογραφ ̂η in 1 Macc. 8.25 he found its parallel in ὡς ἂν εὔκαιρον in the treaty of Astypalaia and twice in the treaty with Methymna. The phrase ἐκ ψυχ ̂ης in 1 Macc. 8.27 is also found in the treaties of Astypalaia and Methymna. *Sine dolo malo* finds its echo in καὶ οὐ μετὰ δόλου in 1 Macc. 8.28.

To account for the lack of numerous elements in the content usually found in a Roman treaty, especially of a prescript at the beginning of the Jewish document, it has been suggested that the text was not taken from a full transcript of an official Roman document. Indeed, Martola is one scholar who does not consider the Maccabaean document to be a true transcript.[147] Against this, 1 Macc. 8.22 does not say that it is giving a partial transcript; it is quoting a copy of a senatorial letter.

## Does 1 Macc. 8.23–32 represent a genuine senatorial decree?

This section examines the document in 1 Macc. 8.23–32 in terms of what it claims to be. 1 Macc. 8.22 states that a text of a copy (ἀντίγραφον) of a letter is quoted, a text that the Romans engraved on bronze tablets and sent to Jerusalem. The author of 1 Maccabees quite distinctly states that he is quoting from an official Roman document. This document is not presented as a piece of literature or a *précis* or a summary. Therefore, we must examine it on the terms in which it is presented in the book. In analysing the claim that 1 Macc. 8.23–32 is a letter from the senate, we need to set it against the thesis advanced here that the document was written in Aramaic by the Jewish envoys themselves. The procedure for coming to an estimation of whether this was a Roman or a Jewish document is not difficult. The yardstick is a comparison of this document with the material that is available in standard Roman practice.

### *The form and content of a senatorial letter*

The claim that this document, preserved in 1 Macc. 8.23–32, was written down by Roman officials, may be tested by comparing its content and style with known examples of letters from the senate. A number of such letters have survived in the form of stone inscriptions written in Greek that have been found in cities throughout the Aegean region and Asia Minor. Consequently, the form and content of letters originating from the senate in Rome is known and they follow a pattern established and continued according to custom.[148]

Typically, senatorial letters open with a salutation that takes the form of the name of the sender in the nominative (usually a consul, praetor or pro-magistrate – the last of these is not relevant in a letter sent *from* Rome, as the document in 1 Macc. 8.23–32 purports to be).[149] The name or title of the addressee was given in the dative, with the city in the genitive. It was followed by a greeting formula, such as χαίρειν. The senate could be writing to the *boule* or magistrates, for example to the archons of the city.[150]

The greeting χαίρειν[151] was a wish for good health (a *formula ualetudinis*), as for example in Sherk, no. 23, εἰ ἔρρωσθε, εὖ ἂν ἔχοι, which is not found in Roman letters until 62 BCE.[152] In official Roman letters written in Greek, the *formula ualetudinis* is placed after χαίρειν. Therefore, in a senatorial letter of 161 BCE, one would expect that the greeting would be simply χαίρειν.

If a senatorial letter was prompted by requests from foreign envoys, those envoys were named after the salutation together with details of where their meeting with Roman magistrates had taken place. Then followed the instructions they had been given from their home community concerning their mission and the name of the Roman magistrate who wrote the letter and who frequently remarked on how well the envoys had spoken and conducted their mission.[153] From the name of the sender of the letter to the praise of the envoys, all formed the prescript to the main body of the letter. A farewell formula – for example, Ερρωσθε – closed the letter. In the case of letters that conveyed the text of *senatus consulta*, the farewell formula may have been omitted.[154]

The most common reason for the sending of a letter was to convey a decision of the senate to the community in response to a request from a petitioning community.[155] In such cases, the letter contained a formal statement, such as Συγκλήτου δόγμα τόδε εστίν.[156] Where the decision results from an appeal from ambassadors, they are often referred to as 'fine and good men'.[157] The style of such letters is generally businesslike and informative.[158] Such letters have been known to include a statement of Rome's goodwill to the city but more frequently the goodwill of the city to Rome.[159] Both the content and the order of material in senatorial letters were standard and formulaic.

### *Discrepancies between a senatorial letter and 1 Macc. 8.23–32*

Acceptance of 1 Macc. 8.23–32 or 23–29 as a senatorial letter has been widespread.[160] Many of those scholars who are prepared to accept the text as a senatorial letter are not unaware that the Maccabaean passage lacks many features of a typical letter from the senate. There is no salutation and there is no mention of to whom the letter was addressed and in whose name the letter was sent, be it consul or praetor. There is no mention of the city or its governing bodies. The letter is undated too. There is no mention of senatorial decisions or resolutions (συγκλήτου δόγμα). A fair number of elements of a senatorial letter are not present in 1 Macc. 8.23–32. The document in 1 Maccabees is not consistent with the rigid form of senatorial letters. In the face of this lack of conformity with a genuine senatorial letter, those who wish nevertheless to maintain that it is a letter from the senate have proposed a number of ways around the problem.

The first attempt was that of Mommsen, who sought to find some of the preamble of a *senatus consultum* in the earlier part of chapter 8 of 1 Maccabees. He was of the view that the names of the ambassadors could be found in verse 17, that the name of the chairperson of the meeting of the senate in which the Jewish envoys made their case could be read in verse 16, and a reference to the number of senators present at that meeting could be seen in verse 15.[161] Is his case convincing?

Any attempt to find the missing elements of a senatorial letter in 1 Macc. 8.15–22 is confronted with a problem that was pointed out by Heuss.[162] In Roman communications that have a letter preceding the text of a *senatus consultum*, there exists a division between the ambassador's request and the actual senatorial decision. Heuss brought forward the examples of *Syll.*[3] 646 and 674. The first inscription dates from 170 BCE and records a letter from the praetor, Q. Maenius. In lines 5–7, it is mentioned that the Thisbaeans spoke about their situation; then lines 11 onwards record the various senatorial decisions that resulted from the envoys' representations. The division between the pleas of the envoys and the senatorial decisions is marked by the words, 'and about this matter it was decreed as follows'.[163] The second inscription dates from c. 140 BCE and records a *senatus consultum* concerning a land dispute between Melitaia and Narthakion. It records the representations from both cities (lines 14–15 and 35–39). The senatorial decree is introduced in the same words: 'about this matter it was decreed as follows'.[164]

In order to maintain that the Jewish alliance was contained in a senatorial letter, scholars have had to disregard the fact that the Romans used a text divider. So, for example, Täubler would like to find the greeting formula of the letter in verse 23 where it says, Καλῶς γένοιτο ῾Ρωμαίοις καὶ τῷ ἔθνει ᾿Ιουδαίων.[165] This line is at the start of the text of the senatorial decision *after* verse 21 where it is recorded that the senate agreed to the proposal of the Jewish envoys; the greeting formula should appear *before* verse 21. To find the salutation of a senatorial letter in verses after verse 21 flies in the face of the order of the content as found in inscriptions.

Others maintain that the document in 1 Macc. 8.23–32 has not been quoted in full and this would account for the fact that parts of a senatorial letter are missing.[166] This suggestion fails to account for the material being placed out of order, an order that is found so frequently in inscriptions. Other typical items of content in a letter are left unexplained, such as the addressee and the name of the magistrate who wrote the letter on behalf of the senate; see Table 5.5. At least two scholars have gone on record that in their view the text in 1 Macc. 8.23–32 is not a senatorial letter.[167]

A Roman letter from the senate that recorded the text of a *senatus consultum* was full of information: the prescript to the senatorial decree included the date, the place the senate met, and the names of the witnesses. The text of 1 Macc. 8.23–32 has none of this information. The Roman letter was businesslike in tone. The text of 1 Macc. 8.23–32 is poetic, as may be seen in the following examples. In verse 23 is a metaphor, 'may the sword and enmity be far from them', and hyperbole is found in verse 26, 'The Jews shall carry out their obligations incorruptibly'.

*Table 5.5* Compliance of 1 Macc. 8.23–32 with a standard senatorial letter

| *Standard form and content of a Roman senatorial letter* | *Degree of compliance of 1 Macc. 8.23–32*[a] |
|---|---|
| 1 Salutation | |
| (a) name of sender | 0 |
| (b) name of addressee | 0 |
| (c) greeting formula: χαίρειν | 0 |
| 2 Names of envoys | 0[b] |
| 3 Senate | |
| (a) meeting place | 0 |
| (b) date of meeting | 0 |
| 4 Envoys' instructions from their community | 0[c] |
| 5 Name of Roman magistrate who authored the letter | 0 |
| 6 Senate's parise of the envoys | 0 |
| 7 Text of the *senatus consultum* introduced by Συγκλήτου δόγμα τόδε εστίν | 0 |
| 8 Farewell formula: Επτωσθε | 0 |

Note

a 0, nil; /, partial.
b Names found in v. 17 outside the senatorial letter.
c Found outside the letter in v. 20.

Such phrases do not convey the same businesslike tone that is seen in genuine letters from the senate.

A certain level of doubt arises about the identification of this Maccabaean document as a senatorial letter. Treaties known to us from inscriptions in different degrees of completeness show evidence that a senatorial letter was the vehicle by which treaties were passed on to the allied city. Signs of such letters may be traced in the treaties of Maroneia in lines 1–10, of Astypalaia in lines 1–23, of Thyrreion in lines 1–8 and of Mytilene in lines 1–2.[168]

Suggestions that the document in 1 Macc. 8.23–30 quotes a *senatus consultum* or *senatus consulta* rest on two foundations. The grounds for finding a senatorial decision in this document is based on the evidence from the Fannius letter and on the phrase in verses 26 and 28, ὡς ἔδοξε ῾Ρώμῃ. In the first instance, the Fannius letter must be regarded as far from certain evidence for the year 161 BCE.[169] The expression ὡς ἔδοξε ῾Ρώμῃ may also be far from a clear reference to a *senatus consultum*.

For Täubler the presence of the phrase ὡς ἔδοξε ῾Ρώμῃ was proof that this text was a *senatus consultum*. Certainly, the phrase does not occur in the texts of treaties. Täubler equated this phrase with *censuere*. By this, he meant a notation of agreement in the voting process in the senate chamber.[170] Grimm saw that a problem arose with the word ῾Ρώμῃ. For in Roman documents they do not mention anything other than the statement that it was decided and certainly not that it was decided *in Rome*. Grimm explained its presence as a substitute for ῾Ρωμαίοις. According to Grimm's interpretation, the phrase in Latin would have been *ut Romanis uisum fuerit*.[171] However, this phrase comes, as Heuss and Timpe pointed out, in mid sentence and not at the end of a clause as one sees in Roman documents.[172] Timpe claimed, 'Diese Wendung hat mit dem Abstimmungsvorgang im Senat nichts zu tun'.[173] Likewise Goldstein in his commentary on verses 26 and 28 does not agree with Täubler that ὡς ἔδοξε ῾Ρώμῃ means *censuere*.[174]

In the search for the origin of this phrase in the Maccabaean document, Gera put forward the following suggestion:

> It is better to assume that the phrase ὡς ἔδοξε ῾Ρώμῃ is in fact a mistranslation of the original text. The words appear in our treaty after the obligation, taken by both parties, not to furnish strategic assistance to the other side's enemies, and before their commitment to act without fraudulent intent. In the Roman pacts with Maronea, Astypalaea, and Methymna, we find the formula δημοσίαι βουλῇ ('by public consent'), at exactly the same place.
>
> Since the Hebrew translator of the treaty between Rome and the Jews was not familiar with Roman procedure, and his knowledge of Greek was less than perfect, it is possible that he understood the word βουλῇ as referring to the Roman Senate. In other words, the translator wrongly perceived that it was the Senate (and possibly also the Roman people, if he took the expression to be the equivalent of δήμῳ καὶ βουλῇ) who decided that neither party would assist the other's enemies. He chose to translate this by the phrase 'as was decided in Rome.'[175]

Someone, although not necessarily the translator, may have made this error in understanding the Greek. Such an error could have had its origin in the fact that the transmission of the content of the *senatus consultum* to the envoys was made orally. The conclusion to be drawn from the misuse of the phrase ὡς ἔδοξε Ῥώμῃ is that the document was not made from an original Roman document sent from Rome where the phrase would have occurred in the correct position. If Gera's interpretation is accepted, it could also provide indications that the document was written by a Jew.

The divergences from the usual form of a Roman senatorial letter are so many that as a result the very origin of the letter is called into question as a document that emanated from the senate. The order of the content varies widely from a senatorial letter and the style betrays the hand of a Jewish writer. Those who still wish to maintain that this is a senatorial decision commonly refer to another letter to hold onto their position.

### *Is the Fannius letter in Jos. Ant. 14.233 evidence that the Jews in 162 BCE received a senatorial letter?*

This letter speaks of the handing over of 'senatorial decisions' (συγκλήτου δόγματα) that the Jews had requested and which are appended to the letter. Scholars have held that these decrees refer to the conclusion of a treaty with the Jews. A problem with making such an identification has long been recognised. Viereck and Mendelssohn noted that, whereas the letter speaks of senatorial decisions in the plural, only one senatorial decision would be required for contracting a treaty.[176] Several suggestions have been made to overcome this problem. Timpe explained that the plural form included the senatorial decision for a treaty and another decision to give the envoys a safe-conduct letter.[177] The difficulty here is that the senatorial decisions in the plural are also referred to in the statement that they are appended to the letter (ὑποτέτακται δὲ τὰ δεδογμένα). Would the decision to give the Jews a safe-conduct letter be one of the senatorial decisions that the Jews requested? The sequence of events works against such a possibility. The Jews sent an embassy to request certain decrees concerning them, which were passed by the senate. *After* they make their request, the senate decides on a safe-conduct letter. We cannot be sure which senatorial decrees are being referred to in this letter; however, the order of events would seem to exclude the possibility that a decree concerning safe conduct was one of them. That leaves only a decision for a treaty or for some other diplomatic instrument. There were no embassies to the senate from the Jews prior to 162 BCE (or at least no evidence exists concerning them), so there can have been no previous *senatus consulta* on behalf of the Jews emanating from that body. If this letter was written by the consul Fannius of 161 BCE then only the decision for diplomatic relations can be intended.

Niese too sought to reconcile the plurality of senatorial decisions by saying that in senatorial negotiations a matter was voted on along the lines of its various parts.[178] The inscriptionally extant decree for Thisbae from 170 BCE shows signs of several voting processes.[179] The difficulty with this explanation is that a senatorial decision that has multiple parts is referred to *in the singular*. Cicero (*ad Fam.* 8.8.4) refers to a *senatus consultum* that has various themes and he uses a singular noun.[180] Gauger came to the conclusion, after searching for citations of decrees in the plural from inscriptions, that he could find no evidence for the use of the plural for a *senatus consultum* that was made up of many parts.[181]

Attempts to argue that the Fannius letter refers to the voting of a treaty despite the mention of 'senatorial decisions' (συγκλήτου δόγματα) fail to convince. The plain meaning of the text ought to prevail. There are two points to be emphasised here. The first is that a treaty was so rigidly formulaic in its clauses that the senate had no reason to conduct a multiple vote on it. The second point is that the order of events is that the Jews were sent to obtain senatorial decrees that had been passed *before* they arrived in Rome. On this question, the sequence of events adds further weight to doubts surrounding Niese's dating of the letter to 161 BCE that I have enumerated elsewhere.[182]

Gauger reached the conclusion that the senatorial decrees mentioned in the Fannius letter must be senatorial decisions 'of the usual type'.[183] Timpe has suggested that one such decision might have been the enrolment in the *formula sociorum* for the Jews.[184] To decide whether this was the correct procedure, one needs to look at the available evidence on the procedure for enrolment in the *formula sociorum* to determine whether a *senatus consultum* was required to be enrolled as an ally of the Romans.

Livy reports the presence of a Macedonian nobleman, Onesimus, in the senate in 169 BCE. His advice to Perseus not to go to war with Rome was ignored and so he defected. Livy reports that he told the senate about the help he had given to the Roman commander. Livy then informs us of the procedure: *senatus in formulam sociorum eum referri iussit* (44.16.7). In other words, there was no vote, and therefore no *senatus consultum*. The mechanism was to instruct a magistrate to carry out an order from the senate. *Iubere* means to order or to direct that something be done.[185] Willems shows that the verb means an order.[186] This order was given orally, as in Livy 2.27.5, 3.25.9 and 29.33.8.[187] Another example would be Livy 27.28.13, where the consuls were ordered (*iussi*) to enrol the city legions. Also in *CIL* $1^2$ (1529), the censor is carrying out an order of the senate. In Suet. *Tib.* 2.2, *iubere* is used where the senate appointed a dictator. In contradistinction, when the senate decrees that something be done, the verb *decerno* is used, as in Livy 27.28.3.

The magistrate being ordered by the senate in this case was the praetor peregrinus. The same procedure was used to enrol the Lampsacenes in the *formula sociorum*, according to Livy 43.6.10. Later examples have the general in the field inscribing the ally on the list.[188] There is no mention in our sources that a *senatus consultum* was required to enrol an ally in the *formula sociorum*. To suggest that the Jews needed a senatorial decree in order to be enrolled, as the author of 1 Maccabees says they were in verse 20, goes against the evidence. Timpe's explanation cannot stand. Several senatorial resolutions may indeed have been needed for the type of diplomatic relations formed in 162 BCE, but a plurality of decisions was not needed for treaty relations.

In summary, the document in 1 Macc. 8.23–32 is neither a senatorial letter nor an official Roman document. It ought not to be inferred that the position taken here is a denial that the senate made a decision. Rather, given that a *foedus* would have been conveyed in an official letter, one would expect the document in question to show signs of being an official letter from the hand of a Roman official. Its claim to be a letter from the senate cannot be reconciled with what we know of the form and content of senatorial letters.

The arguments listed cast doubt on the identification of 1 Macc. 8.23–32 as a senatorial letter and so cast doubt on the treaty hypothesis itself. The identification of the Maccabaean document as the genuine text of a senatorial letter, quoted in full, that conveys the content of a treaty between Rome and the Jews, lies at the very heart of the treaty hypothesis. The identification of 1 Macc. 8.23–32 as a letter from the senate is problematic because its form, content and language do not correspond to what we know of senatorial letters.

## The multiple translation hypothesis

Adherents of the treaty theory are aware, as they cannot fail to be, that the wording of 1 Macc. 8.23–32 from the Greek text extant today varies greatly from the Greek texts of Roman treaties extant from inscriptions. It is recognised that a great number of expressions and points of grammar with a Semitic influence are present in the document in 1 Macc. 8.23–32. The appearance of Semitisms, however, because inconvenient, is usually brushed aside. The profusion of Semitisms has not been fully appreciated because they have not been previously collated. The section below presents the many Hebraisms that have been identified already by various scholars in the Maccabaean document. Scholars have found 18 Hebraisms in all in the text of the Jewish document.

### *Semitisms in 1 Macc. 8.23–32*

v.23 Καλῶς γένοιτο Ῥωμαίοις καὶ τῷ ἔθνει Ἰουδαίων ἐν τῇ θα–
λάσσῃ καὶ ἐπὶ τῆς ξηρᾶς εἰς τὸν αἰῶνα, καὶ ῥομφαία καὶ ἐχθρὸς
μακρυνθείν ἀπ' αὐτῶν. v.24 ἐὰν δὲ ἐνστῇ πόλεμος Ῥωμῃ προτέρᾳ ἢ
πᾶσι τοῖς συμμάχοις αὐτῶν ἐν πάσῃ κυρίᾳ αὐτῶν, v.25 συμμαχήσει τὸ
ἔθνος τῶν Ἰουδαίων, ὡς ἂν ὁ καιρὸς ὑπογράφῃ αὐτοῖς, καρδίᾳ πλή–
ρει. v.26 καὶ τοῖς πολεμοῦσιν οὐ δώσουσιν οὐδὲ ἐπαρκέσουσι σῖτον,
ὅπλα, ἀργύριον, πλοῖα, ὡς ἔδοξε Ῥώμῃ, καὶ φυλάξονται τὰ φυλάγ–
ματα αὐτῶν οὐδὲν λαβόντες. v.27 κατὰ τὰ αὐτὰ δὲ ἐὰν ἔθνει Ἰου–
δαίων συμβῇ προτέροις πόλεμος, συμμαχήσουσιν οἱ Ῥωμαῖοι ἐκ
ψυχῆς, ὡς ἂν αὐτοῖς ὁ καιρὸς ὑπογράφῃ. v.28 καὶ τοῖς συμμαχοῦσιν οὐ

δοθήσεται σῖτος, ὅπλα, ἀργύριον, πλοῖα, ὡς ἔδοξε Ῥώμῃ, καὶ φυλάξονται τὰ φυλάγματα ταῦτα καὶ οὐ μετὰ δόλου. v. 29 κατὰ τοὺς λόγους τούτους οὕτως ἔστησαν Ῥωμαῖοι τῷ δήμῳ τῶν Ἰουδαίων. v. 30 ἐὰν δὲ μετὰ τοὺς λόγους τούτους βουλεύσωνται οὗτοι καὶ οὗτοι προσθεῖναι ἢ ἀφελεῖν, ποιήσονται ἐξ αἱρέσεως αὐτῶν, καὶ ὃ ἐὰν προσθῶσιν ἢ ἀφέλωσιν, ἔσται κύρια. v.31 καὶ περὶ τῶν κακῶν, ὧν ὁ βασιλεὺς Δημήτριος συντελεῖται εἰς αὐτούς, ἐγράψαμεν αὐτῷ λέγοντες Διὰ τί ἐβάρυνας τὸν ζυγόν σου ἐπὶ τοὺς φίλους ἡμῶν τοὺς συμμάχους Ἰουδαίους; v.32 ἐὰν οὖν ἔτι ἐντύχωσι κατὰ σοῦ, ποιήσομεν αὐτοῖς τὴν κρίσιν καὶ πολεμήσομέν σε διὰ τῆς θαλάσσης καὶ διὰ τῆς ξηρᾶς.

*Commentary*

Καλῶς γένοιτο
This Semitism was first noted by Roth (1914) 14.

ἐν τῇ θαλάσσῃ καὶ ἐπὶ τῆς ξηρᾶς
An identical expression is found in lines 10–11 of the treaty of Maroneia. However, in the Maccabaean alliance document, the order is reversed and 'on sea' is mentioned first. In the wording of the Jewish alliance ξηρᾶς replaces γῆν. A difference in meaning results from this change. Instead of 'on land', the Jewish treaty says 'on dry land'. Timpe (1974) 139 dismisses this change as merely the use of a metaphor by the translator of 1 Maccabees into Greek. However, the expression 'on land and sea' is such a non-technical and proverbial one that there is no immediate reason to alter it unless the author is using an idiolect. Elsewhere in the book, the phrase 'on land and sea' is rendered using γῆς. See 1 Macc. 15.14: ἀπὸ τῆς γῆς καὶ ἀπὸ τῆς θαλάσσης. The expression used in verse 23, 'on sea and land', is a Semitic turn of phrase and is reminiscent of certain phrases that recur in the Septuagint. In Ex. 14.16 and 22 is found, εἰς μέσον τῆς θαλάσσης κατὰ τὸ ξηρά. Equally the expression may be found in Ex. 15.19; Ps. 65(66).6; Jn 1.9; Hg. 2.7(6); 2.22(21). The order 'on sea and land' as given in these verses from the Septuagint is the chosen mode of expression in 1 Macc. 8.23. In addition, the preposition used is ἐν and not κατά as in the Roman treaty. This is a Semitic usage that translates ב as ἐν. See Martin (1974) 5.

ῥομφαία καὶ ἐχθρὸς μακρυνθείν ἀπ' αὐτῶν
It has been suggested that this phrase corresponds to πόλεμος δὲ μὴ ἔστω in the treaty of Astypalaia (line 29) and in the treaty of Maroneia (line 12).[189] Two difficulties have been noted if one wants to maintain a direct line of translation. The first is the change of 'war' into 'sword' (ῥομφαιά). Such a usage is found in the Septuagint in Lev. 26.36. In several places ῥομφαία is used as a metaphor

for 'war'. See 1 Kgs 15.33; 2 Kgs 2.26, 12.10; 2 Chr. 20.9; Ps. 21(22).20; Jer. 4.10; Ho. 2.20(18), 11.6; Amos 1.11, 7.9; Na. 2.13(14), 3.15; Ezek. 5.17, 6.3, 6.8, 11.8, 12.16, 21.9(14), 29.8, 33.2, 33.3, 33.4, 33.6.[190] The expression also occurs in 1 Macc. 9.73: καὶ κατέπαυσε 'Ρομφαία ἐξ'Ισραήλ. The second difficulty is that a direct translation from Greek into Hebrew would keep the active voice, yet 1 Macc. 8.23 has rendered the expression into the passive. Goldstein preferred to read ἔχθος (enmity) for ἐχθρὸς (enemy); however, such a reading would provide additional grounds that the document dealt not, as he asserted, with a specially worded treaty for the Jews, but with *amicitia*. The phrase καὶ'ρομφαία καὶ ἐχθρὸς μακρυνθείν ἀπ' αὐτῶν clearly imitates biblical language and it is difficult to find its equivalent in a Roman treaty.

ἐὰν δὲ ἐνστῇ πόλεμος 'Ρωμη προτέρα

This clause is said to be paralleled in the treaty of Astypalaia (lines 43–44), 'Εὰν δέ τιξ πρότερος πόλεμον ἐπιφέρῃ τῷ δήμῳ τῷ'Ρωμαίων, and similarly in lines 33–34 of the treaty of Maroneia: 'Εάν τις πρότερος πόλεμον ἐκφερη τῷ δήμῳ τῶν Μαρωνιτῶν. The misunderstanding of this Roman clause as evidenced by its formulation in 1 Macc. 8.24 was recognised by Täubler (1913) 242. Dancy (1954) 130 drew attention to the fact that the author or the translator misunderstood the usual formula where the alliance was activated only in a situation of a defensive war. As Goldstein (1976) 367 pointed out, the object in the sentence has been turned into the subject in order to accommodate the Hebrew idiom.

ἐν πάσῃ κυρίᾳ αὐτῶν

In this sense is found κυρεία, used in the Septuagint. See Dan. Bel. 11.4 and 5: ἔχουτα πάσνς σαρκὸς κυρείαν.

καρδίᾳ πλήρει

καρδίᾳ πλήρει is recognised as a rendering of the Hebrew בלבב שלם. See Roth (1914) 13; Gauger (1977) 220–221; Wacholder (1974) 18, n. 79. Grimm noted the use of this expression in the Septuagint in 4 Kgs 20.3: ἐν ἀληθείᾳ καὶ καρδίᾳ πλήρει. Also found in 2 Chr. 16.9, 19.9, 25.2; 1 Es. 1.23; Si. 25.13. In 1 Maccabees this is the only occurrence of this expression.

ὡς ἔδοξε 'Ρώμῃ appears together with οὐθὲν λαβόντες

In Roman treaty texts, two phrases are found side by side: namely, δημοσία βουλῇ with δόλῳ πονηρῷ. See the treaty of Maroneia lines 15–16, 19–20, 28–29; the treaty of Methymna lines 2, 5, 9; and the treaty of Astypalaia lines 34, 37. Gera (1998) 307 proposed that the Hebrew translator saw the phrase δημοσία βουλῇ and translated βουλῇ as 'the senate'. Hence the translator translated the phrase to mean 'as was decided in Rome'.

καὶ φυλάξονται τὰ φυλάγματα αὐτῶν

This expression was recognised by Grimm (1853) 129 and Roth (1914) 13 as a Hebraism. Parallel expressions may be found in the Septuagint at Lev. 8.35, φυλάξεσθε τὰ φυλάγματα κυπίου; Lev. 22.9, φυλάξονται τὰ φυλάγματά μου; Deut. 11.1, φυλάξῃ τὰ φυλάγματα αὐ; and Mal. 3.14, ἐφυλάξαμεν τὰ φύλαγμα αὐ. The expression, as found in the Septuagint, represents a Greek translation of שמר את-משמרת.[191] The Semitic nature of this phrase in the Maccabaean alliance document was noted by Abel (1949) 156.

οὐδὲν λαβόντες
This phrase, although literally meaning 'having taken nothing', is generally translated as 'incorruptibly'. It is found in this sense in the Septuagint in Ps. 14.5. See Goldstein (1976) 368.

ἐκ ψυχῆς
The meaning in this verse is 'wholeheartedly'. It is a common expression used in the Septuagint translation of Deut. 4.29, 6.5 and 10.12, among other places. It is also found three times in Isaiah, notably in Is. 42.25: οὐδὲ ἔθεντο ἐπὶ ψυχήν. The expression in question is also found in Ps. 36.(37).15: ἥρομφαία αὐτῶν εἰς ψυχὴν. Variant readings for ψυχὴν are given. In the manuscripts, A and B is written τὴν καρδίαν and in manuscript S$^2$ τὰς καρδίας, which harks back to verse 24, καρδία πλήρει. In Ps 26.5 one finds the expression ἐν τῇ ψυχῇ with a variant reading in the Codex Alexandrinus, καρδιᾳ. The expression ἐν ψυχῆς is not found in 1 Maccabees outside chapter 8.

οὗτοι καὶ οὗτοι
This expression, meaning 'both sides', was recognised by Joüon as a Hebraism, translating the Hebrew אלה ואלה: Joüon (1922) 206.

Διὰ
Identified as a Hebraism by Beauchamp (1976) 82, n. 7.

τὸν ζυγόν
Grimm (1853) 129 compares the expression 'to make the yoke heavy' with 2 Chron. 10.10, 10.14 and Is. 47.6: הכביד עול or הכביד שוט.

ποιήσομεν αὐτοῖς τὴν κρίσιν
According to Grimm (1853) 129, ποιεῖν κρίσιν = עשה משפט.

In other parts of chapter 8, Hebraisms have been found: 8.1, 2, δυνατοὶ ἰσχύι;[192] 8.6, ἀπό;[193] 8.15;[194] 8.31, ἐβάρυνας τὸν ζυγόν; and 8.32, ποιήσομεν αὐτοῖς τὴν κρίσιν.[195] This brings the total of Hebraisms to 23 in 1 Macc. 8. One should note that the quantity in 1 Macc. 8 far outnumbers those noticed in any other chapters of the First Book of Maccabees. Hebraisms that have been found by Joüon in 1 Maccabees outside chapter 8 number 22.[196] Grimm noted phrases taken from the Septuagint translation of the Bible in other parts of 1 Maccabees, among them verses 7.9, 9.23 and 14.9.[197] But these are few in number compared with the concentration of such phrases in 1 Macc. 8.23–32. The instances found by Joüon and Grimm bring the total of instances of Hebraisms in 1 Maccabees (excluding chapter 8) to 42; that is, 42 out of 888 verses. To put this into perspective, in the 32 verses of chapter 8, 25 Hebraisms have been identified. The number of Hebraisms appears in a significantly higher proportion in 1 Macc. 8 than in any other part of the book.

The presence of these Hebraisms in the text of 1 Macc. 8.23–32 is commonly explained by a process of at least three translation stages in the following manner.[198] A document sent from Rome to the Greek-speaking East was usually already translated from Latin into Greek. The original edition of 1 Maccabees was in Hebrew, so the author translated it (or had it translated) into Hebrew. When at some later unknown date the book was translated into Greek, the document in 1 Macc. 8.23–32 was also translated from Hebrew into Greek for the second edition of the book. For ease of reference, I propose to call this process 'the multiple translation hypothesis'. According to this hypothesis, the document underwent three translation processes. The multiple translation hypothesis provides essential underpinning for the treaty theory. It is used to explain away any and all deviations in 1 Macc. 8.23–32 from the standard wording of a genuine Roman treaty. The deviations in phraseology from a Roman treaty are all satisfactorily explained, according to its adherents, by the reshaping that took place in the translation from Latin to Greek to Hebrew and back to Greek.[199] The following is an exposition of the way in which the hypothesis is used to evade the question of why the Semitic elements should be present in a Roman senatorial document:

> While much of the formula of a genuine treaty may be found in the covenant, there are certain elements that are unlike a Roman treaty. However, if this document was written in Latin and then was translated by or for the author of *First Maccabees*, who probably wrote in Hebrew, and then the Hebrew version was translated into the Greek of the Septuagint, whence our rendition is made, much must be ascribed to literary adornment.[200]

The question arises as to whether this explanation is sufficient to account for the heavy presence of Hebraisms in chapter 8, more than in all other chapters in 1 Maccabees. Surely if the Hebraisms were a result of the translation processes, one would find Hebraisms scattered in equal measure throughout the book. The issue then becomes why chapter 8 should have a more Semitic character than other chapters in 1 Maccabees and what can account for this linguistic phenomenon. A re-examination of the multiple translation hypothesis is needed in order to assess whether it is capable of supplying satisfactory answers to these questions.

In the first stage of the multiple translation hypothesis, it is regarded as axiomatic that the document was translated first from Latin into Greek. The Latin stage in the translation process is assumed because Roman treaties derived from a Latin original, so if 1 Macc. 8.23–32 is a treaty it must *ipso facto* also have come from a Latin original text. As a first step in the re-examination of the multiple translation hypothesis, the assumption that the Jewish document had a Latin original needs to be tested.

What is the state of our knowledge on treaties written in Latin? Only one specimen of a treaty in Latin has come to light: namely, the treaty of Callatis. This treaty, found in Chorzum in Asia Minor c. 1905, has only a small portion (46 words) extant.[201] The size of the stele suggested that it was originally very large, so it could also have carried a Greek version of the same text.[202] The importance of this treaty in this context is that it gives a unique picture of what the original texts in Latin may have, all the other texts of Roman treaties being Greek translations. With this in mind, the multiple translation hypothesis will be put under the microscope.

One test to determine whether the Maccabaean document could have originated from the senate would be to determine whether any Latin underlay the Greek text. Several scholars have attempted to find such a Latin *Vorlage* (textual foundation). There have been several attempts to reconstruct what may have been a Latin original text of 1 Macc. 8.23–29. A consensus seems to have developed around the identification in verse 23 of the words Καλῶς γένοιτο Ῥωμαίοις καὶ τῷ ἔθνει Ἰουδαίων with a rendition of the Roman official phrase, *quod bonum, faustum felixque sit populo Romano et genti Judaeorum*.[203] A comparison between the opening words of the Jewish alliance document and the treaty of Callatis is not possible, as the latter is not extant at this precise point. On closer examination, there would seem to be no strong grounds for finding a Latinism in verse 23. The expression *quod bonum* . . . is not found in the text of Roman treaties. Indeed, this formula was not used until the imperial period, when it was used by the senate as a greeting to the *princeps*.[204] Cicero preserves a somewhat similar expression, *Quod bonum, faustum, felix fortunatumque esset*.[205] Closer inspection shows that this wish for good omens was, according to Cicero, uttered before entering into business transactions. Two points here reveal some significant differences. The first is that the phrase was used in the context of business and not in official state diplomacy. The second difference is that the phrase was spoken before the business transaction began. In other words, it could not be part of any alliance document because it came before the text. For these reasons, the use of the phrase must be ruled out as an explanation for the wording in verse 23. Other Latinisms have been suggested by scholars, but they are Latin translations of phrases that are not attested in the Greek copies of Roman treaties. Examples include *longe absit* for μακρυνθείη in verse 23, *corde integro* for καρδίᾳ πλήρει in verse 27, and *ut quod populo Romano uisum fuerit* for ὡς ἔδοξε Ῥωμαίοις in verse 27.[206]

Mommsen extensively sought the Latin *Vorlage* that he thought should underlie the text in 1 Macc. 8.23–32. The assumption behind his method was that 1 Macc. 8.23–32 was a genuine document that went back to an authentic text. He thought that, for verse 25, the Latin original would have been phrased along the following lines: *et militibus non daturos neque praebituros esse frumentum, arma, stipendium, naves placuit Romanos eorumque dicto audientes eos esse cum nihil accipiant*. Verse 26 would have been as follows: *et militibus non suppeditari neque frumentum neque arma neque stipendium neque naves placuit a Roma eosque dicto obtemperaturos esse sine mal dolo*.[207] A glance at the extant portion of the treaty of Callatis that covers this section of the treaty reveals only *p]ẹqu[n]ia adioua[n]to* (line 4), which does not accord with Mommsen's translation. These attempts to find Latinisms in the text have not yielded satisfactory results.

In the next step of our analysis, the methodology of Mommsen and his assumption that 1 Macc. 8.23–32 is a citation of an authentic document will be probed by comparing the Jewish alliance document with an authentic Roman treaty, this time a treaty in Latin. The awkwardness of the text in 1 Macc. 23–32 as a translation into Latin may be seen by looking at Walton's translation.[208] According to the multiple translation hypothesis, the Semitisms evident in the Latin would be attributable solely to the translation into Hebrew for its insertion in the original version of the First Book of Maccabees. Some of the stilted language may be seen, for example, in verse 23, *ab eis* at the end of the sentence; verse 25, *corde pleno*, to translate 'wholeheartedly'; the use of *constituerunt* without an object in verse 29; *hii aut illi* in verse 30; and *quare* in verse 31. A comparison of a Latin text of a treaty that has not undergone any retranslation will be made with the Vulgate of the Jewish alliance document, which is considered by many scholars to have gone through several translations.

Based on what survives of the treaty of Callatis, and combined with the known Greek text of treaties, such as that of Maroneia, the full Latin text of the former may be reconstructed.[209] The restoration used here is that of Avram, who used the extant Greek copies of Roman treaties to complete the inscription. A comparison of verses 23–32 of the Jewish document with the reconstructed text of the treaty of Callatis will show how far this Jewish document diverges from an authentic Roman treaty. The methodology used here does rely on a reconstructed text of the treaty of Callatis; however, that reconstruction is based on good epigraphic evidence. I have confined my comparison of the Callatis treaty to two of the four parallels – that is, only to the words and phrases of the Callatis treaty that are extant.

The comparison of the treaty of Callatis with the Latin Vulgate of 1 Macc. 8.23–32 is made easier by a comparison in the same language, Latin to Latin (Table 5.6).

First, let us consider points of divergence; secondly, we shall pose the question of whether these differences could be the result of retranslations. In the Latin Vulgate of 1 Macc. 8.23, the Jews as *ethnos* is translated as *gens*, while the people of Callatis are a *populus*. The Latin Vulgate refers to Rome and all her allies (*omnibus sociis eorum*), while the treaty of Callatis refers to those under Roman control (*sub inperio*). In the list of supplies that are not to be provided to the enemy of the other, the Latin Vulgate mentions *triticum*, which is omitted in the treaty of Callatis. There would not be space on the stone to include it, so it is not a question of whether there was a lacuna at this point. The *corde pleno* in the Jewish document becomes something different in the restored text of the treaty of Callatis as *utei e tempore dato adiouanto*.

Are these differences the result of the multiple translation process in 1 Maccabees? One might attribute the divergences of the Vulgate of 1 Macc. 8.23–32 from the treaty of Callatis to the Hebrew rendering of the Greek version of 1 Maccabees on which the Vulgate was based. Looking again at the points of

*Table 5.6* A comparison of Walton's Latin translation of 1 Macc. 8.23–32 with a reconstruction of the text of the treaty of Callatis (according to Avram (1999) 53–54)

| *1 Macc. 8.23–32* | *Treaty of Callatis* |
|---|---|
| v. 23<br>bene sit Romanis et genti Iudaeorum in mari et in terra in aeternum gladiusque et hostis procul sit ab eis | |
| v. 24<br>quod si institerit bellum Romanis prius aut omnibus sociis eorum in omni dominatione eorum | Sei quis prior faxit poplo Romano queiue sub inperio eius |
| v. 25<br>auxilium feret gens Iudaeorum prout tempus dictaverit corde pleno | erunt poplus Callatinus poplo Romano utei e tempore dato adiouanto. |
| v. 26<br>et proeliantibus non dabunt neque subministrabunt triticum arma pecuniam naves sicut placuit Romanis et custodient mandata eorum nihil ab eis accipientes | |
| v. 27<br>similiter autem et si genti Iudaeorum prius acciderit bellum adiuvabunt Romani ex animo prout eis tempus permiserit | Sei quis bellum prior faxit poplo Callatino queiue sub inperio eius erunt poplus Romanus poplo Callatino utei e tempore dato adioutanto. |
| v. 28<br>et adiuvantibus non dabitur triticum arma pecunia naves sicut placuit Romanis et custodiant mandata eorum absque dolo | queiue sub inperio eius erunt bellum facerent neue eos armis necque nauibus necque pequnia adiouanto poplico consilio sc. dolo malo p. R. |
| v. 29<br>secundum haec verba constituerunt Romani populo Iudaeorum | |
| v. 30<br>quod si post haec verba hii aut illi addere vel demere ad haec aliquid voluerint facient ex proposito suo et quaecumque addiderint vel dempserint rata erunt | Sei quid as hance societatem poplus Romanus ac poplus Callatinus adere eximereue uelint communi poplico consilio utriusque uoluntate liceto quodque adiderint id inesto quodque exemerint id societati ne inesto. |

difference, several items in the version in 1 Maccabees are not found in the Callatis treaty. Would a translator omit material? Why does the Jewish treaty omit any phrase equivalent to *sub inperio* in the Callatis treaty? These differences go beyond what could be attributable to the process of retranslation or even linguistic misunderstandings. They reveal a difference not in style or vocabulary *but in the actual content*. For these reasons, the Jewish document seems to be too far removed from the Callatis treaty to have had a Latin *Vorlage*.

If the document were an authentic Roman treaty, one would expect the possibility of retranslating it into Latin and still discerning some hallmarks of a Latin original text found in the treaty of Callatis. The opposite is the case. However much one tries to render the Greek from 1 Macc. 8.23–32 into Latin, one comes back to a document that differs in content.

In trying to square the language of the document in 1 Macc. 8.23–32 with the form of a typical Roman treaty, time and again experts have remarked upon the impediment of its Semitic flavour. Typical would be this comment: 'While much of the formula of a genuine treaty may be found in this covenant, there are certain elements that are unlike a Roman treaty.'[210]

Several authorities have drawn attention to the Hebrew style of the Greek in the Jewish alliance document in 1 Macc. 8.23–32. Its wording has been explained as a product of the way the translator of the book into Greek had worked.[211] Others have thought the Greek was an 'idiomatic rendering' of an original document.[212] It has been called a 'hybrid'.[213] Another suggestion is that this document had been reworked by the author of the Hebrew original of 1 Maccabees.[214] Still others have characterised this document as a 'uniquely Jewish recasting'.[215]

Perhaps one ought to be open to another and quite different reason for this Jewish style. That reason may be found in the original language of the Jewish document. Any translation process leaves traces of the original language. 'It is extremely difficult to make any translation without leaving traces of idiom, syntax or vocabulary from the original'.[216] The first task is to show the extent of this Jewish rendering of the document in 1 Macc. 8.23–32. Some work has already been carried out in identifying Semitic words and phrases in the Maccabaean alliance document. The issue here is whether these traces of a Semitic language underlying the current Greek text are the product of the multiple translation process or whether there was an original document written in a Semitic language.

That the original language of the First Book of Maccabees was Hebrew is widely accepted. One might expect to find some Hebrew style renderings in the process of translation from Hebrew into Greek. It must be borne in mind that the document in question presents itself in verse 22 as a quoted senatorial letter that emanated from Rome. Yet, in this document, many Hebraisms have been noticed. What is a Hebraism? 'A Hebraism may be defined as a Greek word, phrase or syntagma which transfers certain characteristic Hebrew elements into Greek in an un-Greek fashion'.[217] In addition, in the text of 1 Macc. 8.23–32 there are phrases and vocabulary borrowed from the Septuagint translation of the Bible.

The question remains why only parts of a book (that is, chapter 8, verses 23–32) written in Greek display obvious Semitic influences. The answer provided by Grimm was that the translator slavishly reproduced the Hebrew of the Old Testament. The translator, he stated, was so well versed in the Old Testament that he unintentionally inserted phrases from the Bible into 1 Maccabees.[218] This explanation is unsatisfactory, however, because it does not address the problem of the uneven distribution of the Hebraisms that are concentrated in one chapter – namely, chapter 8. One finds, for the same reason, other claims equally unsatisfactory, such as that, in first century CE Judaea, 'the Septuagintal translation of Greek so full of Hebraisms must have exerted a powerful influence on the style of Greek spoken by Jews.'[219]

Another explanation given for the Hebraisms is that the translator wrote in a 'Jewish Greek' or a style of Greek common in Judaea.[220] This was a view that had widespread currency in the nineteenth century.[221] With the study of Greek papyrus fragments from Hellenistic Egypt, this view had to be revised, for many of the words that had previously been considered Hebraisms were in fact common in the Greek used in Egypt.[222] However, the two arguments used to explain away the Hebraisms do not account for the imbalance of occurrences of Hebraisms heavily concentrated in one chapter alone. If, indeed, it were the case that the translator used a 'Jewish Greek' or that he unconsciously imitated the language of the Septuagint because he knew it so well, one would expect to see an even distribution of Hebraisms throughout the First Book of Maccabees.

An alternative explanation presents itself on other grounds. Could the Semitic elements have been present from the beginning in the Urtext? That is to say, could the Hebraisms indicate evidence of a Semitic original underlying the Greek? Is it at all necessary to assume that there was a Latin original? Scholars no longer dispute the fact that the First Book of Maccabees was originally written in Hebrew; however, that may not be the specific Semitic language that underlies this Maccabaean alliance document. Aramaic suggests itself as another and different possibility for the original *Vorlage* of 1 Macc. 8.23–32.

The possibility that this document (1 Macc. 8.23–32) was originally written in Aramaic deserves serious consideration. Grimm noticed that in several places in 1 Maccabees there occur, not Hebraisms, but Aramaisms.[223] Other scholars have found additional examples of Aramaisms.[224] Grimm noticed Aramaisms in 1 Macc. 1.5, 8.5, 6.8, 2.19, 11.28, 13.26 and 14.10.[225] Nelis noticed that in 1 Macc. 4.19 the expression πληροῦντος was a translation of the Aramaic *mĕmallē*.[226] Martola found that six of the nine letters cited in 1 Maccabees contain an Aramaism. There is a structural marker found in Aramaic letters that introduces the subject of the letter. That marker in Aramaic is *wᵉ-atta*, which in Greek is translated as νῦν. Martola considered this marker as a sign of the influence of Hebrew or Aramaic epistolography.[227] However, this Aramaic word *wᵉ-atta* does not appear in 1 Macc. 8.23–32. The question needs to be asked whether Aramaisms of a different kind and variety occur in the Maccabaean Roman diplomatic document.

The Aramaisms in the Maccabaean alliance document are highlighted below.

## *Aramaisms in 1 Macc. 8.23–32*

v. 23 Καλῶς γένοιτο Ῥωμαίοις καὶ τῷ ἔθνει Ἰουδαίων ἐν τῇ θα–
λάσσῃ καὶ ἐπὶ τῆς ξηρᾶς εἰς τὸν αἰῶνα, καὶ ῥομφαία καὶ ἐχθρὸς

μακρυνθείν αἀπ'αὐτῶν. v. 24 ἐὰν δὲ ἐνστῇ πόλεμος ʽΡω'μῃ προτέρᾳ ἢ πᾶσι τοῖς συμμάχοις αὐτῶν ἐν πάσῃ κυρίᾳ αὐτῶν, v. 25 συμμαχήσει τὸ ἔθνος τῶν ʼΙουδαίων, ὡς ἂν ὁ καιρὸς ὑπογράφῃ αὐτοῖς, καρδίᾳ πλήρει. v. 26 καὶ τοῖς πολεμοῦσιν οὐ δω'σουσιν οὐδὲ ἐπαρκέσουσι σῖτον, ὅπλα, ἀργύριον, πλοῖα, ὡς ἔδοξε ʽΡω'μῃ, καὶ φυλάξονται τὰ φυλάγματα αὐτῶν οὐδὲν λαβόντες. v. 27 κατὰ τὰ αὐτὰ δὲ ἐὰν ἔθνει ʼΙουδαίων συμβῇ προτέροις πόλεμος, συμμαχήσουσιν οἱ ʽΡωμαῖοι ἐκ ψυχῆς, ὡς ἂν αὐτοῖς ὁ καιρὸς ὑπογράφῃ. v. 28 καὶ τοῖς συμμαχοῦσιν οὐ δοθήσεται σῖτος, ὅπλα, ἀργύριον, πλοῖα, ὡς ἔδοξε ʽΡω'μῃ, καὶ φυλάξονται τὰ φυλάγματα ταῦτα καὶ οὐ μετὰ δόλου. v. 29 κατὰ τοὺς λόγους τούτους οὕτως ἔστησαν ʽΡωμαῖοι τῷ δήμῳ τῶνʼΙουδαίων. v. 30 ἐὰν δὲ μετὰ τοὺς λόγους τούτους βουλεύσωνται οὗτοι καὶ οὗτοι προσθεῖναι ἢ ἀφελεῖν, ποιήσονται ἐξ αἱρέσεως αὐτῶν, καὶ ὃ ἐὰν προσθῶσιν ἢ ἀφέλωσιν, ἔσται κύρια. v. 31 καὶ περὶ τῶν κακῶν, ὧν ὁ βασιλεὺς Δημήτριος συντελεῖται εἰς αὐτούς, ἐγράψαμεν αὐτῷ λέγοντες Διὰ τί ἐβάρυνας τὸν ζυγόν σου ἐπὶ τοὺς φίλους ἡμῶν τοὺς συμμάχους ʽΙουδαίους; v. 32 ἐὰν οὖν ἔτι ἐντύχωσι κατὰ σοῦ, ποιήσομεν αὐτοῖς τὴν κρίσιν καὶ πολεμήσομέν σε διὰ τῆς θαλάσσης καὶ διὰ τῆς χηρᾶς.

A total of 13 Aramaisms appear in the passage (ἔδοξε appears twice). They are:

1 καλῶς γένοιτο
2 τῆς ξηρᾶς
3 εἰς τὸν αἰῶνα
4 κυρίᾳ
5 καρδίᾳ
6 πολεμοῦσιν
7 ἔδοξε
8 οὐδὲν λαβόντες
9 ψυχῆς
10 κύρια
11 τὸν ζυγόν
12 ποιήσομεν αὐτοῖς τὴν κρίσιν
13 Διὰ τί

*Commentary*

Καλῶς γένοιτο

A common Aramaic salutary wish is 'peace with me and also with you': wkʿt bznh qdmy šlm ʿp tmh qvdmyk šlm yhwy. γένοιτο may be considered a translation of the Aramaic הוה.[228] The Aramaic הוה means 'come to pass', as may be seen in Dan. 2.28, 29, 45, or 'come to be', as in Dan. 4.24 and 5.29. A close parallel with 1 Macc. 8.23 may be found in LXX Is. 39.8: γενέσθω δὴ εἰρήνη. Similar usage is found in the following places in the LXX Dan. 2.35, ὁ λίθος . . . ἐγενήθη ὅρος μέγα; II Es. 4.20 γίνονται ἐπὶ Ἱερ. . . . In commenting earlier on the Hebraisms in the Jewish alliance text, I reported that Roth considered the phrase Καλῶς γένοιτο to be a Hebraism. My research has led me to conclude that this Semitism is actually from Aramaic and not Hebrew.

τῆς ξηρᾶς

This is used instead of γῆ, that is, writing 'dry land' (יבשה) rather than simply 'land'. ξηρά is a translation of the Aramaic יבשה as used in Dan. Th. 2.10: οὐκ ἔστιν ἄνθρωπος ἐπὶ τῆς ξηρᾶς.[229] The whole expression ἐν τῇ θαλάσσῃ καὶ ἐπὶ τς ξηρᾶς was considered a Hebraism above, but the language in the Book of Daniel suggests that it is from Aramaic not Hebrew.

εἰς τὸν αἰῶνα

Translating Aramaic עלם.[230] In Dan. 3.33 and 7.18 αἰών means 'perpetuity'. In Dan. 4.31 and 7.18 it means 'for ever'.

κυρία

This is a translation of Aramaic שלטן as found in LXX Dan. 11.4 Bel, οὐδὲ κατὰ τὴν κυρείαν αὐτοῦ and 11.5 κυριεύσει κυρείαν πολλήν, in addition to Bel. 5: ἔχοντα πάσης σαρκὸς κυρείαν.[231] Its parallel use in 1 Macc. 8.24 suggests that this is an Aramaism and not a Hebraism.

καρδία

καρδία may be considered a translation of לבב, which is Aramaic.[232] See LXX Dan. Th. Su. 2.30, ἵνα τοὺς διαλογισμοὺς τῆς κ. σου γνῷς; Dan. Th. Su. 3 (41), ἐξακολουθοῦμεν ἐν ὅλῃ κ.; Dan. Th. Su. 3 (87), ὅσιοι καὶ ταπεινοὶ τῇ κ.; Dan. 4.13, ἡ κ. αὐτοῦ ἀπὸ τῶν ἀνθρώπων ἀλλοιωθήσεται καὶ καρδία θηρίου δοθήσεται αὐτῷ; Dan. Th. Su. 5.20, ὅτε ὑψώθη ἡ κ. αὐτου; Dan. Th. Su. 5.21, ἡ κ. αὐτοῦ μετὰ τῶν θηρίων ἐδόθη; Dan. Th. Su. 5.22, οὐκ ἐταπαίνωσας τὴν κ. σου; and Dan. 7.4, καρδία ἀνθρώπου ἐδόθη αὐτῇ.

πολεμοῦσιν

This is a translation from Aramaic, מלחמה - לחם, according to Gauger.[233] 'Denkbar ist eine unterstützende Deutung, die die *Möglichkeit* einer aramäisch-hebräischen Vorlage – in welcher Form auch immer – berücksichtigt. πολεμεῖν–πόλεμος in der LXX kann z.B. zurrückgehen auf hebr. לחם-מלחמה; איש מלחמה(1) bzw. מלחמה

אנשי (2): (=Mann, Männer des Krieges, Kriegsleute) kann je nach Kontext auch den Asekt “Feind” annehmen, so etwa bei 1 Chr. 18, lo ἀνὴρ πολέμιος + Dat. (1) oder Jes. 41.12 ἀντιπολεμοῦντες + Akk. (2). Ich erinnere zudem auch an 1.Kge 12, 21 ποιοῦντες πόλεμον (=πολεμοῦντες) von hebr. מלחמה עשה. Es ist nicht auszuchliessen, dass eine hebräisch-aramäische Vorlage eine solche oder ähnliche Form aufwies, die der Verfasser des Makkabäertextes mit der neutralen Form πολεμοῦντες wiedergab.’

ἔδοξε

ἔδοξε may be considered a translation of the Aramaic נדב.[234] The Aramaic verb means ‘to become voluntarily obliged to do’.[235] See LXX Ex. 25.2, οἷς ἂν δόξῃ τ῀ῃ καρδίᾳ; Ex. 35.21 ὅσοις ἔδοξε τ῀ῃ ψυχ῀ῃ αὐτ῀ων; and Dan. Bel. 6, οὐ δοκε῀ι σοι Βὴλ εἶναι ζ῀ων θεός. Gera considered the phrase ὡ̔ς ἔδοξε Ῥω'μῃ a Semitic construct by the hand of the Hebrew translator.[236] The linguistic evidence presented here indicates that it is derived from Aramaic and not Hebrew.

οὐδὲν λαβόντες

It was noted earlier that Goldstein considered this expression a Semitism. But ο῀υθὲν is a translation of the Aramaic הל.[237] The expression should more properly be considered as deriving from Aramaic than Hebrew. Examples include the following verses from the Septuagint: Dan. Bel. 6, οὐθὲν βέβρωκε πώποτε ο῀ὑτος; Dan. Bel. 13, οὐθενὸς τ῀ων ἐκτὸς αὐτο῀υ εἰδότος. λαβόντες from λαμβάνω, which is used to translate the Aramaic לבק.[238] This translation may be seen at work in Dan. Th. Su. 2.6, τιμὴν πολλὴν λήψεσθε παρ’ ἐμο῀υ. Also in the sense of ‘receive’, it is found in Dan. 2.6 and 7.18. Its parallel use in 1 Macc. 8.26 would indicate that λαβόντες is an Aramaism and not a Hebraism.

ψυχῆς

This means ‘faithfully’ and is a translation of בבל, which was seen above to be Aramaic.

κύρια

The meaning here is ‘valid’ and is a translation of the Aramaic ממשל.[239] One finds it used in this sense in LXX Dan. 11.3: κυριεύσει κ. πολλῆς. The parallels from the Book of Daniel would indicate that κύρια is an Aramaism and not a Hebraism.

τὸν ζυγόν

It was noted earlier that Grimm considered this a Semitism. The use of the word ‘yoke’ to denote oppression or slavery is found also in 1 Maccabees, in 8.18 and 13.41. It is found in LXX Dan. Th. 5.27, ἐστάθη ἐν ζυγῷ, and Dan. 8.25, ὁ ζυγὸς τοῦ κλοιοῦ αὐτοῦ κατευθυνεῖ.[240] This is an Aramaism for מטה.[241]

ποιήσομεν αὐτοῖς τὴν κρίσιν

According to Muraoka, this expression derives from Aramaic. κρίσιν is the Aramaic equivalent of נקם, as is found in LXX Is. 1.24.[242]

Διὰ τί
This is the equivalent of Aramaic למה.[243]

If one places the Hebraisms and the Aramaisms together in the one chart, one is better able to see the hand of a Jewish author in this document (Table 5.7).

There appear 13 Aramaisms and between 1 (definite) and 4 possible Hebraisms. The table was compiled from published sources from scholars such as Grimm, Roth, Täubler, Dancy, Goldstein, Gauger, Wacholder, Joüon and Beauchamp, who all noticed the Semitic influence on the Greek language used in 1 Macc. 8.23–32. Most of the scholars listed above remarked on the Semitic influence in the text and/or commented that various expressions reflected Hebrew idioms. While individually these scholars commented on only one or two expressions, there has been until now no systematic attempt to collate all the previously noted Semitic phrases or Hebraisms. This resulted in the appearance in Table 5.6 of 15 Hebraisms. Once presented in the form of a table, the quantity of words and phrases that show a Semitic hand becomes quite prominent.

In this present study, the next step undertaken was to examine each of the Hebraisms that have been remarked upon in previously published studies and to examine whether they might, in fact, derive from Aramaic and not from Hebrew. Listed below are those words and expressions that at first glance appear as

*Table 5.7* The Hebraisms/Semitisms and Aramaisms in 1 Macc. 8.23–32[a]

[v. 23] Καλῶς γένοιτο 'Ρωμαίοις καὶ τῷ ἔθνει 'Ιουδαίων ἐν τῇ θα–
λάσσῃ καὶ ἐπὶ τῆς ξηρᾶς εἰς τὸν αἰῶνα, καὶ ῥομφαία καὶ ἐχθρὸς
μακρυνθείν ἀπ' αὐτῶν. [v. 24] ἐὰν δὲ ἐνστῇ πόλεμος 'Ρώμῃ προτέρᾳ ἢ
πᾶσι τοῖς συμμάχοις αὐτῶν ἐν πάσῃ κυρίᾳ αὐτῶν, [v. 25] συμμαχήσει τὸ
ἔθνος τῶν 'Ιουδαίων, ὡς ἂν ὁ καιρὸς ὑπογράφῃ αὐτοῖς, καρδίᾳ πλή–
ρει. [v. 26] καὶ τοῖς πολεμοῦσιν οὐ δώσουσιν οὐδὲ ἐπαρκέσουσι σῖτον,
ὅπλα, ἀργύριον, πλοῖα, ὡς ἔδοξε 'Ρώμῃ, καὶ φυλάξονται τὰ φυλάγ–
ματα αὐτῶν οὐδὲν λαβόντες. [v. 27] κατὰ τὰ αὐτὰ δὲ ἐὰν ἔθνει 'Ιου–
δαίων συμβῇ προτέροις πόλεμος, συμμαχήσουσιν οἱ 'Ρωμαῖοι ἐκ
ψυχῆς, ὡς ἂν αὐτοῖς ὁ καιρὸς ὑπογράφῃ. [v. 28] καὶ τοῖς συμμαχοῦσιν οὐ
δοθήσεται σῖτος, ὅπλα, ἀργύριον, πλοῖα, ὡς ἔδοξε 'Ρώμῃ, καὶ φυλά–
ξονται τὰ φυλάγματα ταῦτα καὶ οὐ μετὰ δόλου. [v. 29] κατὰ τοὺς λόγους
τούτους οὕτως ἔστησαν 'Ρωμαῖοι τῷ δήμῳ τῶν 'Ιουδαίων. [v. 30] ἐὰν
δὲ μετὰ τοὺς λόγους τούτους βουλεύσωνται οὗτοι καὶ οὗτοι προσθεῖναι
ἢ ἀφελεῖν, ποιήσονται ἐξ αἱρέσεως αὐτῶν, καὶ ὃ ἐὰν προσθῶσιν ἢ
ἀφέλωσιν, ἔσται κύρια. [v. 31] καὶ περὶ τῶν κακῶν, ὧν ὁ βασιλεὺς Δημή–
τριος συντελεῖται εἰς αὐτούς, ἐγράψαμεν αὐτῷ λέγοντες Διὰ τί ἐβά–
ρυνας τὸν ζυγόν σου ἐπὶ τοὺς φίλους ἡμῶν τοὺς συμμάχους 'Ιου–
δαίους; [v. 32] ἐὰν οὖν ἔτι ἐντύχωσι κατὰ σοῦ, ποιήσομεν αὐτοῖς τὴν κρίσιν
καὶ πολεμήσομέν σε διὰ τῆς θαλάσσης καὶ διὰ τῆς χηρᾶς.

Note

a Aramaisms, underlined; Hebraisms/Semitisms, shaded

Hebraisms or Semitic-influenced Greek, but which may prove to be Aramaisms following further investigation.

1 κα λῶς γένοιτο
2 τῆς ξηρᾶς
3 ἐν πάσῃ κυρίᾳ αὐτῶν
4 καρδίᾳ πλήρει
5 ὡς ἔδοξε ʽΡώμῃ
6 ψυχῆς
7 οὐδὲν λαβόντες
8 Διὰ τι
9 τὸν ζυγόν
10 ποιήσομεν αὐτοῖς τὴν κρίσιν

A total of 10 expressions that appear in Table 5.7 as Hebraisms are in fact Aramaisms. This reduces the number of Hebraisms in the passage to just 4. These Hebraisms are:

1 καὶ ʽρομφαία καὶ ἐχθρὸς μακρυνθείν ἀπ᾽αὐτῶν
2 ἐὰν δὲ ἐνστῇ πόλεμος ʽΡώμῃ προτέρᾳ
3 καὶ φυλάξονται τὰ φυλάγματα αὐτῶν (in verse 26 and repeated in verse 28)
4 οὗτοι καὶ οὗτοι

What is it about these expressions that has led scholars to single them out as Hebraisms? καὶ ʽρομφαία καὶ ἐχθρὸς μακρυνθείν ἀπ᾽αὐτῶν was considered a Hebraism because it metaphorically uses 'sword' for 'war' in imitation of biblical language. However, this does not rule out Aramaic. ἐὰν δὲ ἐνστῇ πόλεμος ʽΡώμῃ προτέρᾳ is considered Hebraic because the object has been turned into the subject of the sentence in imitation of a Hebrew idiom. However, this could just as well be a characteristic of any Semitic language, including Aramaic. καὶ φυλάξονται τὰ φυλάγματα αὐτῶν is considered a Hebraism because it renders into Greek שמר את-משמרת. This is a Semitic phrase. οὗτοι καὶ οὗτοι is considered a Hebraism translating the Hebrew אלה ואלה.

From this discussion, it may be seen that the evidence that Hebrew is the Semitic language from which the Greek was derived is ambiguous in the case of καὶ ʽρομφαία καὶ ἐχθρὸς μακρυνθείν ἀπ᾽αὐτῶν, ἐὰν δὲ ἐνστῇ πόλεμος ʽΡώμῃ προτέρᾳ and καὶ φυλάξονται τὰ φυλάγματα αὐτῶν. This leaves only one phrase that may unequivocally be attributed to Hebrew. The other three could just as well be Aramaisms.

The presence in 1 Macc. 8.23–32 of several Hebraisms does not necessarily reinforce the view that the document was translated into Hebrew from Greek. This argument does not take sufficient account of the appearance of Hebraisms in Qumran Aramaic.[244] In fact, marked Hebraisms are a feature of Aramaic from at least the fifth century BCE, if not earlier.[245] To find Hebraisms in a document in

Aramaic from the second century BCE would be quite unexceptional.[246] It is more consonant with the linguistic evidence to consider that the Semitic expressions in 1 Macc. 8.23–32 indicate that the copy of the senatorial letter was composed originally in Aramaic.

The existence of such a quantity of Aramaisms in the Maccabaean alliance document as compared with the rest of the book has significant implications. Any multiple translation process can be ruled out as a hypothesis because it supposes a translation from Latin to Hebrew, that being the original language of the First Book of Maccabees. The book was not written in Aramaic. The proof of this may be seen in the syntax of verses 1.28, 29; 2.8, 34; 3.3, 15; 4.19, 24; 10.72; 11.39; 14.5 and 16.3 – this is Hebrew and not Aramaic.[247] Many errors in the Greek text of the First Book of Maccabees can be accounted for by a misunderstanding of Hebrew and not Aramaic.[248] The multiple translation theory never envisaged a translation from Latin or from Greek to Aramaic. To suggest that 1 Macc. 8.23–32 was written in Aramaic directly contradicts the evidence shown by the many errors in the Greek translation that go back to a misunderstanding of Hebrew words and expressions. An Aramaic alliance document is not compatible with the multiple translation hypothesis.

To suggest that the document was originally written in Aramaic opens up the possibility that this document is a late forgery. That is not the claim being made here; quite the opposite. The forgery claim was made by Gauger, who considered that the original document was written in Aramaic and interpolated into the book c. 63 BCE. Its purpose, he maintained, was to provide support for the delegation that appealed to Pompey not to impose a monarchy on Judaea of either Aristobulus or Hyrcanus.[249] In order to determine whether a document in Aramaic from the middle of the second century could be authentic, one must establish that Aramaic was in use in Judaea in 162 BCE at the time of the sending of the Jewish embassy to Rome or soon thereafter.

It is known that Achaemenid Imperial Aramaic was still in use in southern Palestine in the first half of the third century from ostraka found at el-Kom near Hebron.[250] This Imperial Aramaic was used in the Book of Daniel, which was written c. 165 BCE and in the oldest manuscript of 1 Enoch.[251] However, by 142 BCE Hasmonaean Aramaic replaced Imperial Aramaic.[252] From the Dead Sea Scrolls material a significant body of texts in Aramaic has emerged, dating from between c. 200 BCE and 122 CE.[253] The situation in 162 BCE for the written language used in Judaea at this time would have been that Hebrew was considered the language of sacred texts, but speech and secular writings were conducted in Aramaic.[254] Further to this, Aramaic was by this time the language of empire, the language with which the Jews had communicated with the Persians, where it was the lingua franca of that empire. Its use in this way is reflected in its use in the Book of Daniel.[255] Aramaic was used by the Jews as the language for dealing with international powers and for foreign relations.[256] It is not surprising, therefore, to see the shadow of Aramaic all through the document in 1 Macc. 8.23–32.

Turning to the spoken language in Judaea at the time of Judas Maccabaeus, scholarly opinion is in a state of flux. It used to be thought that from the beginning of the Hellenistic period Hebrew was replaced as the spoken language by Aramaic.[257] From 300 BCE to 70 CE Aramaic was widely considered to have been the spoken language of ancient Palestine.[258] Important conclusions that affect this picture have come from the Aramaic texts found at Qumran. The picture that is emerging is that Aramaic was well established, as evidenced in the names of persons and places, but that it was not completely dominant in Judaea.[259]

Thanks to the work of Kutscher, it can now be shown that Qumran Hebrew was a living spoken language. There were probably two Hebrew dialects.[260] One dialect was used for traditional readings from the Bible in synagogues and the other dialect was for colloquial use.[261] Qumran Hebrew displays signs of a language that, while trying to maintain tradition, is being modified in a multilingual environment. The studies of Qimron into the nature of the Hebrew used in the Dead Sea Scrolls showed that it was not an imitation of classical Biblical Hebrew but has morphology that differs from both Biblical and Mishnaic Hebrew. He found independent features that are not found in Aramaic and which developed from a spoken language.[262] Scholars are coming to realise that in Judaea a vernacular form of Hebrew was spoken, whereas in Galilee and in Samaria people held onto Aramaic as their spoken language.[263]

The issue of Judaea's linguistic milieu was raised for the purpose of assessing whether an alliance document written in Aramaic in 162 BCE could be considered genuine or a forgery. In order to provide an answer to this question, one needs to consider the language that in Judaea would have been used for written documents of this type. Aramaic was the language in which politics was conducted.[264] The official language for commercial contracts, personal contracts, marriage and divorce documents was Aramaic.[265] The legal and official documents in the Book of Ezra are quoted in Aramaic.[266] Additionally, Aramaic served as the language in which Jews in Judaea communicated with the outside world.[267] One can assert with some surety that, if a document on Roman–Jewish relations were written by Jews, a document that showed to the outside world their status as new Roman allies, it would have been written in Aramaic. Therefore, the possibility exists that such a document was not a later forgery but actually a contemporary document.

If it was the case that the Maccabaean document was originally written in Aramaic, can the authors of this document be identified? That this document originated from a Jew and not a Roman (or a state functionary) has long been recognised, for example by Roth.[268] That the document may have been written by a Jew is also supported by the testimony of Josephus. At the conclusion of his citation of the Jewish alliance document, he appends a statement not attested in other sources. He states that Eupolemus, the son of John, and Jason, the son of Eleazar, wrote it: ἐγράφη τὸ δόγμα ὑπὸ Εὐπολέμου τοῦ Ἰωάννου παιδὸς καὶ ὑπὸ Ἰάσονος τοῦ Ἐλεαζάρου (*Ant.* 12.419). In his translation, Marcus renders the verb ἐγράφη as 'signed' but notes that it literally means 'written'.[269] The literal meaning has also been removed by Wieseler, who interpreted it to mean that the decisions had been achieved through the agency of Jason and Eupolemus, but this interpretation was only achieved by emending ἐγράφη to ἐπράχθη.[270] Neither of these interpretations is acceptable as they both distort the plain meaning of the text. Some might consider that Josephus' remarks in 12.416, to the effect that this is a copy of a senatorial decree, contradict the statement of the authorship in 12.419. It is well known that Josephus tidied up the details of Roman procedure in his account from what he found in 1 Maccabees. Moreover, attention should be paid to 12.419, as it may have been part of the document that Josephus was quoting from his version of 1 Maccabees either directly or indirectly.

This statement has been generally overlooked in the literature and dismissed as unhistorical.[271] Possibly two factors may account for this neglect. First, doubt surrounds its acceptance because 1 Maccabees does not corroborate the information. Secondly, the report in Jos. *Ant.* 12.419 continues as follows: 'Judas being high priest of the nation, and his brother Simon commander.'[272] This statement is regarded as erroneous and so it is generally considered that the accompanying claim about the authorship of the document about Roman–Jewish relations must also be unhistorical.[273]

How did Josephus arrive at his report regarding the authorship of the Roman–Jewish agreement? One possible explanation is that he inserted the information about the authorship of the text (but not the text itself) from memory based on his own knowledge. When Josephus looked back on his own education, he took pride in his reputation for an excellent memory.[274] The type of instruction used in the education system was based on learning texts that first had to be committed to memory. Gerhardsson made a study of the educational techniques in such schools of learning.[275] According to his researches, the student was expected to make a literal repetition from memory of his teacher's words.[276] The words were to be quoted exactly and were not to be given in summary form.[277] In order for the student to master the memorisation, the teacher was enjoined to repeat the material to his pupil four times.[278] Pedagogy had two stages: first the material had to be memorised and then the text was expounded. First memory, then understanding. An important component of Jewish education was to convey the transmission of the Oral Torah to the next generation by memorisation of the text. The Mishna was recited by heart, using melody to aid memory.[279] Students were trained to remember texts with precision. The memorisation of religious texts using mnemonic devices reveals the capacity of educated Jews to commit lengthy passages to memory.

The necessity for accurate recall of material has been stressed by Zlotnick. 'Painstaking exactness was a matter of necessity, not pedantry, in conveying the oral law. The links between ministering to the master, memorisation, study and the transmission of an accurate text of Mishnah had to be firm. The reliability of the law depended on it. Learning inaccurate dicta could undermine the entire structure of the law.'[280] Rubin states: 'Oral traditions depend on human memory for their preservation. If a tradition is to survive, it must be stored in one person's memory and be passed to another person who is also capable of storing and retelling it. All this must occur over many generations'.[281] The Sages said that students had to master oral mnemonics so that the oral tradition could be retained and passed on with precision.[282] R. Hisda, the head of the Babylonian academy at Sura, would say, 'The law can be acquired only through mnemonics.'[283]

So the possibility exists that the information in *Ant.* 12.419 that Jason and Eupolemus wrote the document could have been added by Josephus from what he had learned or read. He may have obtained this information either from an oral tradition about the Hasmonaeans from his own family or from his education, which involved memorising large quantities of text, a skill in whose mastery he took pride. A man with his education would have been accustomed to retrieving information that was stored in his memory. The information that Josephus added about the authorship and date of the document may have come from something he remembered he had read.

An alternative possibility is that Josephus added this information from his own knowledge. Feldman remarks that Josephus was in possession of oral traditions, being a descendant of the Hasmonaeans, and that this was the source of the information that he added from his own personal knowledge.[284] For example, Josephus adds the name of the officer, Apelles, who was slain by Mattathias in *Ant.* 12.270, information that does not appear in the corresponding account in 1 Macc. 2.25. Josephus did add details to aid his Greek readers.[285] He wanted to make the text more interesting or more acceptable to his Greek audience.[286] Josephus added glosses or small pieces of information to make clear for his Greek readers details that would not be familiar to non-Jews. The type of information Josephus thought would add clarification were geographical and topographical details.[287] For example, Josephus gives the distance between two places. In *Ant.* 12.369, he writes that Beit Zachariah is 70 stades from Beit Zur and in *Ant.* 12.408 that Adasa is 30 stades from Beit Oron.[288] In addition, Josephus added the Macedonian names of the months to the Hebrew names so that his non-Jewish readers would understand.[289] For example, in *Ant.* 12.248 Josephus explains that the month of Kislev is the Macedonian month, Apellaios, information that is not found in 1 Macc. 1.54. Again, in *Ant.* 12.412 Josephus adds to his account that he based on 1 Macc. 7.43, that the month of Adar is the Macedonian month Dystros. Other changes to the account in 1 Maccabees were made for ideological reasons. One such example would include those changes made to de-emphasise the Maccabaean revolt as a struggle for the Temple and replace that with a fight for the Law and the Commandments.[290]

In summary, we have cast doubt on the possibility that there had been a Latin original of the text of 1 Macc. 8.23–32 and showed, in addition, the possibility that it was composed in Aramaic. The evidence of Jos. *Ant.* 12.419 (which was considered to be possibly an authentic colophon) informs us that the authors were the envoys themselves. Coupled with these arguments, we have presented evidence that the whole of 1 Macc. 8.23–32 ought to be considered as a single piece of text and therefore from the hand of the same authors. Whoever wrote the letter to Demetrius, as it appears in verses 31 and 32, also wrote the copy of the document in 1 Macc. 8.23–32 (for more on this, see pp. 199–201).

## Jewish treaty formation

The Torah expressly prohibited the Jews from making treaties with the peoples in Eretz Israel.[291] These people were to be exterminated, not made into allies. Treaties were permitted with cities lying outside this area but not on an equal basis: the treaty partners were to become tribute-paying subjects.[292]

There existed a fundamental conflict between the ceremonies that governed the formation of treaties (*foedera*) for Jews and for Romans. We saw before that the Romans employed priests (the *fetiales*) to conduct the treaty formation ceremony, a set of rituals that included an execration oath and an animal sacrifice. The Romans permitted their treaty partner to use their own priests and their own choice of sacrificial animal, and to swear by their own gods.

The Jews had in biblical times made treaties (*britot*) with foreigners. The ceremony is described in the Book of Joshua with reference to the treaty with Zedekiah. In Joshua 9.18–20 we learn that the participants in the ceremony were the leaders, priests and peoples (possibly a representative group) of both sides. The procedure entailed taking the sacrificial animal and cutting it in half. Next the two pieces were placed so as to allow space to walk between them. Passing through this space came the leaders, priests and people of one party to the treaty and then those of the other treaty partner.[293]

The Jews also had a firm tradition of honouring sworn treaties. A well-known example is the treaty that Joshua concluded with the Gibeonites, as told in Joshua 9.6–20. It is clear from Joshua's behaviour, when he negotiated with the Gibeonites who had come to request a treaty, that he aimed to comply fully with the Torah prohibition on treaties. He asked who they were and where they had come from. The Gibeonites insisted that they lived in a far country and, as proof, offered to show their shoes, which were worn out from walking, and their stale provisions. Convinced that they were not neighbours, Joshua made the treaty, only to discover later that they had lied and were indeed dwellers in the Land of Israel. Joshua was counselled to abandon the treaty as it had been made and sworn under false pretences. He refused on the grounds that it was impossible to renounce the oath that he had sworn to the Lord God of Israel. Joshua exclaimed that the Gibeonites had deceived him and therefore they were cursed.[294]

Both cultures, Roman and Jewish, sealed their treaties with oaths that they were loathe to break. Both conducted religious rituals to sanctify the treaty, though the forms of their ceremonies differed. In deciding that the Jews entered into a treaty, one has to account for the absence of any mention of these ceremonies or oath taking.[295] The resort to defining this alleged treaty as a 'senatorial treaty' (which is said not to have required oaths) does not take into account the scholarly consensus in the sphere of Roman *Völkerrecht* to reject such a category. An additional factor to consider, is how empowered the two Jewish envoys were to participate in such ceremonies. They were not priests and there is no evidence that, even if a treaty were being offered, they could have participated with the fetial priests in a public sacrifice and oath taking. The whole question of Jewish sacrifices outside the Temple in Jerusalem is fraught with difficulties. In the end, we must conclude that the Roman method of concluding treaties made it highly unlikely for the Jews to have been able to participate.

## Lack of consequences of a treaty

Several authorities have drawn attention to the dissonance between the conclusion of a Roman–Jewish treaty at this time and the lack of any Roman aid under the terms of a treaty to Judas and his followers.[296] The conspicuous lack of any aid from Rome resulting from the sending of an embassy to Rome, is an argument against a treaty's having been concluded. This argument, while not new, remains valid.[297]

Some scholars consider that a treaty gave Rome the option to decide whether the circumstances were appropriate for them to send aid. Gruen maintains that Roman treaties contained an 'escape clause'.[298] The so-called 'escape clause' in Roman treaties is the phrase κατὰ τὸ εὔκαιρον. εὔκαιρον literally means 'well timed'. When one finds in the literature that the phrase κατὰ τὸ εὔκαιρον is translated, for example, in the following manner, 'as appropriate',[299] it becomes a small step to conclude erroneously, as Gruen does, that this phrase is a standard escape clause.[300] From a translation that omits the time element, Gruen goes on to consider that the clause κατὰ τὸ εὔκαιρον allowed the Romans to back away from their commitment in treaties to send aid to an ally. So, for example, Gruen says: 'The senate, as usual, refrained from bargaining away its freedom of action.'[301] This interpretation is based on an omission of the aspect of time that is contained in the word εὔκαιρον. This time element was pointed out in 1913 by Täubler. He understood the phrase κατὰ τὸ εὔκαιρον correctly: it is a restriction on the commitment to send aid only to the extent that the treaty partner, be it Rome or its ally, did not have to arm itself immediately and move forces into the field. Täubler supported the intent behind this phrase by reference to the offer of the Achaeans to help Rome in the war against Perseus. Polybius (28.13.5) reported that the Roman consul informed the Achaean delegation, led by Polybius himself, that they need not send aid immediately.

As a consequence, the phrase κατὰ τὸ εὔκαιρον is more properly to be understood in the sense that 'help may not come immediately, but when we can get there'. As such, it is correctly understood by Dahlheim.[302] It is noteworthy that the phrase κατὰ τὸ εὔκαιρον does not appear in the *foedus Cassianum*[303] where within Italy the Romans did not have far to travel and so could respond more immediately than to faraway Kibyra, Methymna or Maroneia, in whose treaties this phrase occurs.[304] In the alliance document between the Romans and the Jews in 1 Macc. 8.23–32, the Jewish rendition of this time restriction phrase is ὡς ἂν ὁ καιρὸς ὑπογράφῃ αὐτοῖς, which occurs in verses 25 and 27.[305] Keil translated this as 'the time with its circumstances'.[306] Bévenot understood it as, 'Wie die Zeit vorschreibt'.[307] Gutberlet considered that its Latin equivalent would be *prout tempus permiserit*.[308] Earlier scholars noticed and commented on the time element and rightly did not call the phrase a 'loophole' or an 'escape' clause. The purpose of the phrase was to indicate, purely and simply, that practical considerations for amassing a force to be sent to an ally could take some time.

Returning to the basic question of the lack of consequences that would have flowed if the Jews had entered into a treaty at this time, it needs to be reiterated that a *foedus* was permanent.[309] Breaking a treaty was not without terrible consequences.[310] If Rome defaulted on a treaty, the Romans considered that the deities that had heard the treaty being sworn would visit punishment on the Roman people.[311] The permanent *foedus* bound Rome to act if called upon by her ally. The fact that we do not hear of the Jews requesting Roman aid or complaining that no Roman aid was sent to them in the fight against Demetrius' army is suggestive that there was no *foedus*.

The question that remains, however, is why do we not hear of the Jews invoking the treaty if they had one available? In other words, the Jews could have made an appeal to Rome. If the Jews had appealed to Rome and been rebuffed then the subsequent history of Roman–Jewish relations would not consist of more embassies to Rome to renew relations without any hint of criticism of Rome. The proponents of the treaty theory have striven to counter the argument that no Roman aid came to the Jewish rebels. They try to excuse Roman inaction in several ways, despite the premise of a treaty between Rome and the Jews. The lack of any consequences flowing from a 'treaty' has been explained as rather the lack of opportunity of Rome to help due to the apparently quick response of Demetrius in crushing the rebellion and thereby forestalling any Roman action. The question of timing enters into this argument, as it is based on the calculation accepted by the majority of scholars that *before* the envoys had returned to Judaea, Judas had been killed at the battle of Elasa.[312] However, it is equally possible that Judas was killed *after* the envoys had returned from Rome.[313] The return journey was much speedier due to the favourable winds. The whole trip could have taken approximately three weeks.[314] The likelihood exists that Judas did know of the outcome of the embassy before he went into the battle where he lost his life. Both propositions – that either the Romans did not have time to come to the aid of the Jews, or that Judas did not have a treaty in hand before his death – are not possible under the new chronology.

A resort to Roman perfidiousness is commonly made to explain the non-response of the Romans. According to this view, the Romans abandoned a treaty partner when it suited them.[315] Against this, however, Sherwin-White emphasised that a Roman state treaty (*foedus*) was a diplomatic instrument not designed to be at all 'nominal'.[316] The etymology of *foedus* is bound up with the word *fides*.[317] The whole 'glue' that held together Roman diplomacy was the notion of *fides*, 'good faith'.[318] We can see this exemplified in the fetial priests who concluded treaties and made declarations of war: these priests, according to Varro, were the guardians of *fides*.[319] Richardson considered that *fides* was a fundamental notion and that it was 'a norm of Roman behaviour', 'deserv[ing] more widespread examination as one of the formative ideas of Roman imperialism.'[320] *Fides* is not a secular notion; it was a fundamental moral value.[321] *Fides* was an ingredient of all diplomatic relations that involved binding the parties through oaths. The *fides* was the good faith of the swearer of the oath to the gods.[322]

Such oaths were involved in both treaties and in *deditio*. *Fides* was involved in the unconditional surrender (*deditio*) of an enemy to Rome where the enemy was said to give themselves over to the good faith of the Romans (*deditio in fidem*). The general proclaimed orally that he was bound to offer the enemy military protection.[323] The act was sealed by a clasping of hands between the Roman and the defeated general.[324] This was the act requiring the Romans to act in good faith; namely, that when the enemy surrendered and laid down its arms, it would not be slaughtered by the Roman soldiers.[325] The general's oath was accepted because it was sanctioned by the gods.

This may be an opportune point at which to discuss a question raised by Watson concerning the nature of Roman oaths. He considered that Roman oaths were, in act, merely 'quasi-oaths'.[326] Following from this view, one might consider that 'quasi-oaths' had not the same strength as oaths that had the force of religious sanction, as discussed. The idea is expressed by Euripides' famous line (*Hipp.* 612), 'My tongue swore, but not my mind'. The whole issue of the dichotomy between the words (*verba*) and intention (*voluntas*) is not at stake in the question of any oaths in a Roman treaty in 162 BCE. In Roman law, the 'quasi-oath' was not yet in existence in the second century BCE; it only came into being in the post-classical period, as Wheeler and many jurists have pointed out.[327] Thus, in 162 BCE, when the Jewish embassy was in Rome, if the senate had agreed on a treaty for the Jews, this would have been sealed by oaths with the binding force of religious sanction. That the oath was religiously binding for Jews also, may be seen below.

The Roman state treaty was upheld by the bonds of *fides*. The *foedus* was an institution of sacral law and was imbued with sanctity.[328] It was a contract between man and the gods that was sealed by a sacrifice where the animal served as the intermediary.[329] The *foedus* is an act of *sacrosanctum* – that is, it is instituted with the oath.[330] In the case of treaties, the binding nature of the oaths that sealed them incurred divine wrath, in Roman eyes, if they were violated. The violation of a treaty was regarded as a violation of *fides*.[331] Just as the Romans considered that the gods intervened in their affairs on Earth, so they believed they punished those who did not keep their oaths.[332] The maintenance of the *pax deorum* was vital to the state.[333] To repudiate treaties was problematic because a vow had been made. The gods had heard the solemn vow in the *sponsio* of the general.[334] In effect, to renege on the *sponsio* would be a *scelus impium* (Livy 9.10.9), 'a crime against the gods' (or if we take the Sanskrit origin from the word *skhal* into account, it would mean 'deceiving the gods').[335] Such a crime required expiation.[336] The senate might repudiate an agreement made by oaths, but a remedy was required to atone for deceiving the gods.

The remedy the Romans employed for a breach of *fides* with the gods was extreme.[337] The known cases involve commanders in the field who negotiated a surrender sworn by oaths that were later repudiated by the senate. The commander responsible for the oaths was handed over to the enemy, bound and naked. This meant he was to be the sacrifice, the *deuotio*, to be consecrated to the infernal gods. He was to be the instrument of purification, a *piaculum*, to atone for any religious crime involved in reneging on *fides* to the gods.[338] In 321/20 BCE, the consuls responsible for the Roman surrender at the Caudine Forks were handed over to the Samnites; in 236 BCE, the legate M. Claudius Clineas was handed over to the Corsicans; and in 135 BCE, Hostilius Mancinus was handed over to the Numantines.[339] This practice operated both before and after 162 BCE, thus revealing that this traditional practice was in continuous use and was not an archaic custom that had fallen into abeyance. The conclusion by oath was the act that made a treaty difficult to repudiate.[340] The seriousness with which an oath was treated was related to the fact that the oath bound Rome through *fides* to keep to the treaty.[341]

Cicero regarded *fides* as the trustworthiness without which one's promises could not be taken seriously.[342] In the final analysis, what was a sworn treaty if not a promise to the gods, and if one's promises could not be trusted, no one would clamour to obtain a treaty.[343] The Romans had a reputation for fidelity. King Hiero of Sicily was said to have commented that the Romans continually talked of fidelity.[344] When the *fides* of a Roman treaty was broken by the other side, the immediate consequences were clear. Rome considered the breach a *casus belli*. War was the result.

The question at issue here is Rome's faithfulness in sending aid to an ally, aid that had been stipulated in a treaty that had been made with the proper ceremony and oaths. It is instructive to note that, in the debate over whether to aid Saguntum against Hannibal prior to the Second Punic War, the senate did not consider that a treaty with Saguntum might be broken or ignored. Rather, the issue revolved around whether Saguntum was allied to Rome by a *foedus* or allied by some other method. The senate was careful in its debate to clarify the city's status: whether it was *foederati* or allied to Rome in a manner that did not involve an oath to the gods – or in a treaty in which *fides* was involved. The senate knew that a treaty would bind it to send aid, whereas other types of alliances that did not involve oaths gave Rome some discretion to refuse the request for help. In the end, they held that the city's status was one of an ally without a treaty. The bonds with Saguntum were not ones made by sworn oaths but were diplomatic relations formed by *senatus consulta*.

Rome's reliability and her reputation for keeping friendships was something remarked on in the digression in 1 Macc. 8.1 and 12 in praise of the Romans. Obviously, Jews who supported Judas Maccabaeus' policy in seeking Roman aid thought that they could hold Rome to her promises if they became friends and allies of the Romans.

Roman faithfulness to agreements made by religiously sanctioned oaths contributed to the sense that treaties were designed to be permanent. Violation of a sworn treaty brought down the wrath of the gods through the execration oath, whose terms mentioned the destruction of the Roman people should they be the one to first break the treaty. Consideration of the permanent status of treaties concluded in this manner induces us to give thought to the Roman preference for informal *amicitia* from the second century BCE, which provided them with greater flexibility in changing circumstances. Friendship could be annulled without any ceremony. When one examines the localities that entered into treaties with the Romans, one finds that treaties were granted only to states that presented no instability in their region. A common reason for seeking a treaty with Rome was after a war in the area. Their purpose was to advertise and affirm Roman *imperium*.[345] In concluding a treaty, the Romans wanted from their future treaty partner assurances of political and military stability; they avoided treaties in areas where conflict was ongoing.

The situation in Judaea in 162 BCE was fluid and Judas Maccabaeus, lacking any official position or title, did not have the unanimous support of the Jewish people. His envoys could not produce evidence of stability and a treaty under those circumstances was full of risk for the Romans. Better to arrange friendship, which could be terminated by the will of the senate. Its continuance was incumbent solely upon the friend of the Roman people.

The lack of consequences flowing from a sworn treaty, if one had indeed been concluded with the Jews, has given rise to the need to supply several explanations; without some clarification, the treaty hypothesis fails to convince. Grimm concluded that, had Demetrius thought a treaty had been concluded between the rebel Jews and Rome, he would have immediately ceased his military offensive against them.[346] Fischer attempted to reconcile the apparent ineffectiveness of the 'treaty' by suggesting that, although one had been proposed in Rome, it had not in fact been ratified.[347] There is no indication in the account in 1 Maccabees that the whole process had not been completed. On the contrary, 1 Macc. 8.21 states that the senate accepted the proposal of the Jewish envoys. In other words, the mission was a success. The envoys received a letter to take back to Jerusalem (verse 22) as a record of 'peace and alliance'. There is no evidence here of negotiations in mid-course. The solemn, binding nature of a Roman *foedus* with oaths is absent from the events surrounding the Jewish treaty of 162 BCE.

Finally, lack of Roman military support for the Jews does not support the existence of treaty relations. One wonders why no Jewish criticism is ever found of the Romans for this lack of help.[348] Additionally, if the Jews had a treaty with Rome, why did they not press for its fulfilment?[349] To say that there was no time in which to do so is not consistent with the date of 162 BCE for the sending of the embassy.

Gauger brought into the argument the situation of the rebel Timarchus.[350] His embassy received not a treaty but a mere *senatus consultum*. Gauger concludes that, if the senate, despite its negative feelings towards Demetrius, was not prepared to aid the rebellion of Timarchus, then it is even less likely that the same senate would have been inclined to give a fully valid Roman state treaty to the Jewish envoys who appeared in Rome as representatives from what was, from the senate's point of view, a not exactly impressive rebellious movement.[351] According to the new dating of the Jewish embassy, the order presented by Gauger is now reversed: the first delegation was that of the Jews, followed by that of Timarchus.

In short, Demetrius, having angered the senators with his secret escape from Rome in 162 BCE, had undertaken no diplomatic contact with Rome until 160/159 BCE. These circumstances made it possible for Judas Maccabaeus to request aid from Rome, which he hoped would lead to Roman intervention in the war against the Seleucids. A treaty, however, was not possible while the Jews were not yet independent from the Syrian kingdom. The senate found an alternative diplomatic instrument to overcome the obstacle of not being autonomous. Once they had granted the Jews a declaration of *libertas*, there had to be an interval of time before a *foedus* (treaty) could be given. It was against all Roman precedent for the Romans to have made the Jews free with a unilateral declaration of *libertas*, then grant a treaty to the same legation.[352]

## Notes

1 Phillipson (1911) 46, 48; Horn (1930) 7; Badian (1952) 76; Meyer (1964) 228–229; Polay (1964) 106, 124; Dahlheim (1968) 22, 132; De Martino (1973) 35; Sherwin-White (1973*a* 176; Sherwin-White (1984) 66; Baronowski (1982) 21; Reynolds (1982) 8; Schmitt (1988) 531–532; Nörr (1989) 17; Baronowski (1990) 346–347; Eckstein (1999b) 415; Avram (1999) 90; Hölkeskamp (2000) 236. Against: Mommsen (1887) 3, 2.1150.
2 Wegner (1968) 91; Nörr (1989) 17; Eckstein (1999b) 415.
3 Täubler (1913) 91–93; Heuss (1934) 14–15, 50–51; Dahlheim (1968) 22; Bederman (2001) 192. Against: De Martino (1954) 38–39; Paradisi (1957) 200–202; Ziegler (1972) 91.
4 Turelli (2011) 55–82; Rich (2011) 193–195.
5 Watson (1993) 31.
6 The oath did not contain the terms of the treaty as Mommsen thought, at (1887) 1.251, n. 3, as shown by Heuss (1934) 20–22.
7 For Jupiter as the guarantor of order and stability and as the deity in control of the judicial–religious order, see Fiori (1996) 523.
8 Pig as symbol: Ogilvie (1965) 112.
9 Serv. *Aen.* 1.62: *uel a porca foede, hoc est, lapidibus caesa* . . . . The ritual of the pig sacrifice in connection with the conclusion of a treaty is shown on coins from the Augustan period: Grueber (1910) 56, 98, nos. 4492, 4493, 4660.
10 Paulus Festus 81L; Phillipson (1911) 395. Others tied the origin of the word to *fides*: Varro *de LL* 5.86.
11 Liou-Gille (1998) 198.
12 Albanese (2000) 56.
13 Liou-Gille (1998) 204.
14 Cic. *Rab.* 6.14.
15 Perjurer: Ogilvie (1965) 112.
16 Guarantor: Fiori (1996) 523.
17 Boyancé (1964b) 429–430.
18 Lasch (1908) 10.
19 See Cic. *Pro Flacco*, 36. See Instinsky (1964).
20 Silving (1959) 1330–1335.
21 Cic. *Rosc.* 46; Ov. *Ep.* 20 (21) 135ff.; Gell. 5.19.6–7.
22 Scheid (2007) 263.
23 Ogilvie (1964) 112.
24 Scheid (2007) 264.
25 Crawford (1974) 1, no. 234/1.
26 Mommsen (1860) 555 no. 169.
27 (1973) 4–5.
28 Mommsen (1860) 556, n. 384. Followed by Crawford (1974) 1, nos. 234, 266.
29 (1973) 6.

30 For discussion on the scene on this coin, see Zollschan (2011) 51–52.
31 Coins: references in Ogilvie (1965) 110. See Varro *L.L.*5.86; Wiedemann (1986) 488; Ferrary (1995) 417. Broughton (1951) 3.59 considers it a mistake to assume that the *fetiales* became obsolete. See Zollschan (2012a).
32 That both parties swore oaths: Polay (1964) 128; Baronowski (1982) 114–115, 156–157; Bederman (2001) 195; Baldus (2002) 317. Against: Täubler (1913) 369; Accame (1946) 87–89.
33 (1913) 128–129.
34 Ziegler (1995) 244. Carthaginian oaths: Barré (1983) 90, 101–102; Bickerman (1952b) 3–5; Matthaei (1907) 182, 202.
35 Livy 37.55.
36 Livy 1.24.8, 30.43; Wissowa (1912) 550–554.
37 Cic. *de Off.* 3.111.
38 Livy 29.12, 30.43, 33.25, 37.55; Sall. *Iug.* 39; Cic. *Balb.* 34. Cf. Mommsen (1887) 3, 1.343–345.
39 Mitchell (2005) 167, ll. 4–5.
40 Polyb. 6.14.10, 1.62 (the treaty with Carthage of 241 BCE): 'subject to the ratification of the Roman people' (ἐὰν καὶ τῷ δήμῳ τῶν 'Ρωμαίων συνδοκῇ.).
41 Mamertines: Polyb. 1.11.2. Aetolians in 212 or 211 BCE: Livy 26.24.14 (for the literature on the date, see Lehmann (1967) 34–66). Philip in 205 BCE: Livy 29.12.15. Philip in 197 BCE: Polyb. 18.4.2; Livy 33.24. Carthage: Livy 30.44.12. Aetolians in 187 BCE: Polyb. 21.32.2–14. Antiochus: Polyb. 21.17.9; Livy 37.55.3.
42 Gruen (1984) 51, n. 189.
43 As quoted by Heuss (1934) 49.
44 Täubler (1913) table of contents.
45 Baronowski (1990) 346.
46 Täubler (1913) 2ff.; Horn (1930) 6.
47 Livy 34.58.1.
48 Ziegler (1972) 85.
49 (1913) 3.
50 Horn (1930) 17–19 also brings into the argument against Täubler two passages from Appian *Lib.* 64 and *B.C.* 1.475.
51 Heuss (1933) 112; Dahlheim (1968) 22.
52 (1913) 99–157; followed by Accame (1946) 75–101.
53 Kibyra: *OGIS* 762; *Syll.*[3] 763. Astypalaia: Sherk (1969) no. 16 B; *IGRR* 4.1028. Mytilene: *IG* 12.2.35; *IGRR* IV.33.
54 Senate's competence: Mommsen (1887) 3.1158–1163. Assembly: Polyb. 1.62.8–63.1, 6.14.11, 21.30.6; Livy 32.23.2, 37.19.2; Mommsen (1887) 3.340–341.
55 Gruen (1984) 51, n. 189.
56 Täubler (1913) 366, 370; Horn (1930) 76–77.
57 *IG* 9, $I^2$, 2, 242; *Syll*[3], 732.
58 (1913) 368.
59 Horn (1930) 79.
60 Täubler (1913) 49, 101 n. 6, 360 n. 1.
61 Horn's treatment of Täubler's category of the *Senatsvertrag* (whose sole example he gave was the Roman–Jewish treaty in 1 Macc. 8.23–32) is to be found on p. 122.
62 (1913) 112.
63 (1913) 3–6, 62–66. Followed by Horn (1930) 28–31; Badian (1958) 84–87; Gundel (1963) 289–290; Dahlheim (1967) 38–39; Sherwin-White (1973a) 120–123, 184; Bauman (1976).
64 Aetolian treaty: Polyb. 21.32; Livy 38.11. Gades treaty: Cic. *Balb.* 35; Gruen (1984) 26–27, 30, 40.
65 (1984) 50–52. Followed by Kallet-Marx (1995) 184–197.

66 Sherwin-White (1984) 50–70; Hammond (1972) 3.601–610; Derow (1991); Avram (1999) 98, 144–145. Followed by Coppola (1993) 123–127; Heftner (1997) 186; Habicht (1997) 185.
67 Whether 'friendship and alliance' can mean a treaty, see above, pp. 69–71. Difficulty of dating the epigraphic treaties, see, for example, the problem of dating the Pharos inscription from letter forms: Eckstein (1999b) 402.
68 Eckstein (1991) 395–418.
69 Aetolian treaty: Polyb. 21.32; Livy 38.11. Treaty of Apamea: Polyb. 21.43.
70 On the date of the treaty of Kibyra, see Ferrary (1991) 224. For the later date: Sherwin-White (1984) 50–51; Gruen (1984) 731–733; Errington (1987) 107–110.
71 Kallet-Marx (1995) 189.
72 Kallet-Marx (1995) 189.
73 Rhodes: Polyb. 30.5.6–8; Byzantium: Tac. *Ann.* 12.62; Elea: *Syll.*[3] 694.
74 Dahlheim (1977) 179–186.
75 Dahlheim (1965) 289.
76 Heuss (1934) 244ff.
77 (1913) 44–47.
78 Representative would be Gera (1998) 307: 'The basis for our text of the Roman–Jewish alliance was a standard *foedus aequum*, which presented the equal, complementary obligations of the Roman Republic and the Jewish nation towards one another'. Followed by Shatzman (1999) 62; La Rocca (2014) 54. None of these works references the post-Mommsen research on Roman *Völkerrecht*.
79 (1887) 3,1.650–653, 663–664; followed, among others, by Horn (1930) 7, 30; Paradisi (1951) 344; De Ruggerio (1962) 3.174–176; Polay (1964) 124, 126; Toynbee (1965) 261–265; Dahlheim (1968) 49, n. 58; Ziegler (1972) 92; Petzold (1972) 397–381, 402–405; Sherwin-White (1973a 122, 184; Schmitt (1988, 531–532; Gera (1998) 307; Bederman (2001) 189–191. Principal critics of these categories: Luraschi (1979) 25–40; Baronowski (1982) 350–357 and (1990) 345–369. Also Hantos (1983) 156; Gruen (1984) 14–15, 26; Avram (1999) 87–88.
80 Expanded by Täubler (1913) 44–46. Representative: De Ruggiero (1962) s.v. *foedus*, 3.174.
81 Luraschi (1979) 26.
82 Mommsen (1887) 3, 1.664, n. 2.
83 (1887) 3, 1.663–665.
84 Polay (1964) 124.
85 Badian (1958) 26.
86 Mayer (1961) 229, 513–514, n. 94; Gabba (1973) 567; Toynbee (1965) 262; Cassola (1968) 350; Ilari (1974) 39–41 and nn. 35–37; Galsterer (1976) 101; Baronowski (1982) appendix 2.
87 Badian (1958) 26; Meyer (1964) 229–236, 513; Dahlheim (1968) 120, n. 21; Ziegler (1972) 92, n. 206; Briscoe (1981) 209.
88 Sherwin-White (1973a) 112, n. 5; Luraschi (1979) 31; Baronowski (1990) 347.
89 Nissen (1863) 174–175; Klotz (1940) 13.
90 Schmitt (1988) 532; Baronowski (1990) 365.
91 Frezza (1967) 357.
92 Baronowski (1990) 353.
93 Mayer (1961) 229, 513–514, n. 94; Toynbee (1965) 262; Cassòla (1968) 350; Gabba (1973) 567; Ilari (1974) 39–41 and nn. 35–37; Galsterer (1976) 101; Baronowski (1982) appendix 2; id. (1990) 347 n. 6.
94 (1965) 1.262.
95 Gruen (1984) 15.
96 Luraschi (1979) 31; Baronowski (1982) 350–351.
97 Livy 42.25.11. See Baronowski (1982) 355.

98 Livy 39.37.9–11, 13: speech of Lycortas. See Täubler (1913) 223–224; Baronowski (1982) 214–215.
99 Cf. Baronowski (1990) 353.
100 Livy 8.4.2, 9.4.4, 9.20.8, 23.5.9, 28.25.20, 34.57.8, 39.37.13 and 42.25.11.
101 (1887) 3.664, n. 2.
102 Badian (1958) 28.
103 Cic. *Balb.* 46.
104 Diod. 28.15.
105 Livy: Nissen (1863) 162–164; Klotz (1940) 11. Diodorus: Schwartz (1903).
106 Baronowski (1990) 358–359.
107 Appian's account based on Polybius: Rich (2015) 82. Livian composition: Grainger (2002) 134.
108 Lehmann (1967) 197–202.
109 Täubler (1913) 223–224.
110 Sherwin-White (1984) 60.
111 *OLD* s.v *aequus*, 4c, 68.
112 *OLD* s.v *aequus*, 7b, 68.
113 Baronowski (1982) 352.
114 The fetial priests had not disappeared after the Second Punic War but were still carrying out their functions. See Zollschan (2012a).
115 Gera (1998) 306.
116 Gauger (1977) 197–203; Sherwin-White (1984) 71.
117 3.22.1–13, 3.24.
118 6.95.
119 3.24.2.
120 3.22.4.
121 Petzold (1972) 393.
122 2 Macc. 11.16–38.
123 Jos. *Ant.* 14.185–189, 14.218, 14.265, 14.267, 16.160–161, 16.174–178. See Pucci Ben Zeev (1998) 357–373.
124 Text of treaty with Lycia: Mitchell (2005) 167–169, with translation at 170–172.
125 Lists of the epigraphically preserved treaties: Mitchell (2005) 173–174; Schuler (2007) 67–74.
126 Täubler (1913) 44–51; Fischer (1980) 106–108; Gauger (1977) 195–98; Ferrary (1990) 222–223; Gera (1998) 305–306.
127 Gera (1998) 306, 309: although the text has been rearranged and some of its sections are missing, this does not detract from identifying it as a genuine Roman treaty. Kallet-Marx (1995) 191 considers that the treaties were so standardised that the terms were not even a matter for negotiation or discussion. Goldstein (1976) 362 opines that the form of the Jewish document was so removed from the form of a Roman treaty that this would have aroused suspicions that it was a forgery. The jumble of clauses in the Jewish document cast doubt on the well-worn view that this text represents a treaty between the Romans and the Jews.
128 Heuss (1933) 56 remarked on the firm schema and consistent order of the individual clauses in Roman treaties.
129 See notes 115 and 127 above.
130 A similar diagram was tabulated by Roth (1914) 10–13, but in his day the best text of a Roman treaty at one's disposal was the treaty of Astypalaia.
131 Täubler (1913) 243.
132 Gauger (1977) 195.
133 Omission of a prescript: Gera (1998) 305–306.
134 Täubler (1913) 242.
135 Täubler (1913) 242.

136 (1913) 243.
137 (1913) 243.
138 Fischer (1980) 108.
139 Treaties that report the consent of the senate to set up bronze tablets in Rome and in the temple of the allied city include Maroneia (ll. 41–43), Kibyra (ll. 13–15), Astypalaia (B. ll. 48–50), Callatis (ll. 14–15).
140 Example of the treaty with Pergamum (*SIG.*³ 2.694). See Sherk (1969) nos. 11–12.
141 Sherk (1969) no. 10B, l. 1.
142 Mitchell (2005) 183.
143 Mitchell (2005) 183–184.
144 My thanks to Stephen Mitchell for this suggestion.
145 Täubler (1913) 243–244.
146 Goldstein (1976) 362–363.
147 Martola (1984) 227.
148 Sherk (1969) 189.
149 Praetor: Sherk (1969) nos. 8, 15, 34; consul: Sherk (1969) nos. 16, 86; proconsul: Sherk (1969) nos. 50, 57, 59b.
150 *Boule*: Sherk (1969) nos. 8, 34, 57, 59b, 62, 63, 83, 86. Magistrates: Sherk (1969) nos. 15, 16, 50, 59b, 80, 83, 86.
151 Sherk (1969) 190.
152 Cic. *Fam.* 5.2; Pucci Ben Zeev (1998) 34.
153 Sherk (1969) 190–191.
154 Sherk (1969) 197.
155 Sherk (1969) 196–197. For example, Sherk (1969) nos. 8, 15, 16, 37, 63, 83; Pucci Ben Zeev (1998) 118.
156 Sherk (1969) 196.
157 Sherk (1969) nos. 38, 45, 62, 63, 66, 83, 86.
158 Pucci Ben Zeev (1998) 116.
159 For example, Sherk (1969) nos. 8 (both goodwill of Rome and to Rome), 63, 86.
160 Mommsen and Grimm in Grimm (1874) 235; C.F. Keil (1875) 143; Knabenbauer (1907) 156; Täubler (1913) 244; Abel (1949) 155; Dancy (1954) 129; Goldstein (1976) 364.
161 Grimm (1874) 235.
162 (1934) 48.
163 Ll. 9–10: περὶ τού|του τοῦ πράγματος οὕτως ἔδοξεν·
164 Ll. 59–60: περὶ τούτου τοῦ πράγματος οὕτως ἔδοξεν·
165 (1913) 49, n. 1.
166 Abel (1949) 155.
167 Niese (1906) 824; Martola (1984) 63.
168 Maroneia: *SEG* 35.823. Astypalaia: *IGRR* 4.1028. Thyrreion: *SIG*³ 732. Mytilene: *IGRR* 4.33.
169 See Zollschan (2007a).
170 (1913) 243. Followed by Bévenot (1931) 105; Abel (1949) 156; Dancy (1954) 130; Stern (1986) 24 [22], n. 77.
171 (1853) 129.
172 Heuss (1934) 47–48; Timpe (1974) 137.
173 Timpe (1974) 138.
174 (1976) 363.
175 (1998) 307.
176 See Gauger (1977) 171.
177 Timpe (1974) 144.
178 Niese (1906) 826.
179 Sherk (1969) no. 2.
180 Gauger (1977) 171.

181 Gauger (1977) 172.
182 See Zollschan (2007b).
183 Gauger (1977) 173.
184 Timpe (1974) 145.
185 OLD, s.v. *iubeo* 3.977. Examples of this usage with regard to the senate are Livy 27.28.13; Sall. *Iug.* 35.9; Suet. *Tib.* 2.2.
186 (1968) 2.231, n. 2.
187 *TLL* (1990) vol. 72, fasc. 4. 576.
188 Sulla: App. *Mith.* 61. Pompey: Dio 36.53.5. Caesar: Dio 38.34.3. Augustus: Dio 53.25.1.
189 See Abel (1949) 155; Gera (1998) 306 n. 138.
190 See Hatch-Redpath (1998) 1253–1254.
191 See Grimm (1853) 129; Hatch-Redpath (1998) 1441.
192 Nelis (1972) 157.
193 Joüon (1922) 206.
194 Nelis (1972) 162.
195 Examples in 1 Macc. 8.31–32: Nelis (1972) 166.
196 1 Macc. 1.1, 3.52, 5.7, 9.17, 9.58, 9.62, 9.63, 9.65, 9.67, 9.70, 9.73, 10.3, 10.72, 11.10, 11.67, 11.69, 12.33, 12.37, 13.3, 13.6, 13.13, 13.20. Joüon (1922).
197 Grimm noticed the slavish reproduction of the Hebrew in verses 1.16, 1.36, 2.57, 3.9, 3.32, 4.3, 13.17, and errors in translation in verses 1.28, 2.8, 2.34, 3.3, 4.19, 4.24, 11.28, 14.5, 16.3. He noted errors in translation in verses 6.1, 6.37, 9.15, 9.36.
198 Gera (1998) 306.
199 Expressed in its classic form by Timpe (1974) 135.
200 Johnson et al. (1961) 2.32.
201 *ILLRP* 2, no. 516. For the most recent treatment of the treaty of Callatis: Avram (1999). For various reconstructions of the text: Avram (1999) 1–10. For Avram's reconstruction of the text: (1999) 53–54.
202 Passerini (1935a) 71; Gruen (1984) 740, n. 52; Avram (1999) 106.
203 Grimm (1853) 128. Followed by Keil (1875) 144; Knabenbauer (1907) 156; Gutberlet (1920) 134–135; Abel (1949) 155; Zeitlin (1950) 151. Reported by Timpe (1974) 139, n. 11 without comment.
204 Gauger (1977) 201.
205 Cic. *de Div.* 1.102.
206 Keil (1875) 144–145.
207 Grimm (1874) 235–236.
208 Walton (1964) 27.
209 Avram (1999) 53–54.
210 Johnson et al. (1961) 32.
211 Ettleson (1925) 373–375; Timpe (1974) 139, 'false level of style'.
212 Goldstein (1976) 367.
213 Heuss (1934) 34 (47).
214 Roth (1913) 13.
215 Fischer (1980) 109.
216 Gehman (1953) 141.
217 Tov (1988) 179.
218 (1853) xvi.
219 Grundy (1964) 408.
220 See Gehman (1951) 90.
221 Ros (1940).
222 Deissmann (1895); id. (1897). History of the debate: Tov (1988).
223 (1853) xvii.
224 Nelis (1972) 16; Gauger (1977) 213; Goldstein (1976) 140.
225 Grimm (1853) xvii.

226 Nelis (1972) 167.
227 1 Macc. 10.20a, 10.27a, 10.29a, 11.37a, 12.18a, 12.22a. See Martola (1984) 61–62.
228 See Hatch-Redpath (1998) 266; Muraoka (1998) 40.
229 See Muraoka (1998) 53.
230 See Hatch-Redpath (1998) 39; Muraoka (1998) 111.
231 See Muraoka (1998) 151.
232 See Hatch-Redpath (1998) 719; Muraoka (1998) 73.
233 Gauger (1977) 213.
234 See Hatch-Redpath (1998) 339; Muraoka (1998) 93.
235 See Koehler and Baumgartner (2001) 671.
236 Gera (1998) 307.
237 See Muraoka (1998) 74; Hatch-Redpath (1998) 1029.
238 See Hatch-Redpath (1998) 847, 852; Muraoka (1998) 127.
239 See Muraoka (1998) 83.
240 See Hatch-Redpath (1998) 599.
241 See Muraoka (1998) 81.
242 See Muraoka (1998) 99.
243 See Muraoka (1998) 75.
244 See Fassberg (1993) 68.
245 Zimmermann (1975) 1.
246 Lapide (1975) 485.
247 If the book had been a translation into Greek from an Aramaic original, one would expect to find many examples of the construction of a participle with εἶναι: Grimm (1953) xvii. For lists of the verses where mistranslations from Hebrew into Greek occur, see Grimm (1853) xv; Kautzsch (1900) 25; Torrey (1913) *Enc. Bibl.* 3, cols 2858–2889.
248 1 Macc. 1.28, 2.8, 2.34, 3.3, 4.9 and 24, 14.5, 16.3.
249 Gauger (1977) 339 reviving an earlier view of Willrich (1895) 69–71; id. (1900) 63, 71–75; id. (1924) 44–50.
250 Geraty (1975).
251 Beyer (1986) 37.
252 Beyer (1986) 20–21 gives the starting date of 142 BCE and notes the following points that distinguish Hasmonaean Aramaic from Achaemenid Imperial Aramaic: 'even unaccented final *–ā* and medial *ọ* are often represented in writing. At the end of a word an unpronounced א is sometimes added to the vowel-letters ה ו י.ז for **d_* is only found in the pronouns in early texts; ס already appears for **ś* repeatedly in Targum Job . . . . Assimilated **n* is increasingly not written.' Hasmonaean Aramaic is found, according to Beyer (1986) 20 in 'the Aramaic theological literature from Qumran (excluding the testament of Levi from the Cairo Geniza and the two oldest Enoch manuscripts) and the comtemporary inscriptions. In addition, one can mention the private documents from the Judaean desert . . . and (with some qualification) the sentences quoted in the Mishna (2nd cent. A.D.) and Tosefta (3rd cent. A.D.) from private documents. Finally, Hasmonaean is attested in the older layer of Babylonian and Galilean Targumic and Babylonian Documentary Aramaic.' Beyer (1986) 21 states that Hasmonaean was replaced by Old Judaean 'as the Aramaic written language in 37 BCE except in private documents'.
253 van de Water (1999–2000) 424.
254 Spolsky (1985) 43.
255 Portier-Young (2010) 107, n. 45, 112.
256 Sérandour (2000).
257 Dalman (1902) 11–13; Altheim and Stiehl (1966).
258 Representative: Fitzmyer (1979) 61–62, 71–74; Bickerman (1988) 165; Schwartz (1995) 3, 15 and n. 22.
259 Sáenz-Badillos (1993) 170.

260 Kutscher (1974) 1583–90 and (1982) 93ff. For further literature, see Reymond (2014) 13, n. 2.
261 Sáenz-Badillos (1993) 133.
262 Qimron (1992) 354–355.
263 Sáenz-Badillos (1993) 113.
264 Casey (1998) 66.
265 Spolsky (1985) 40.
266 Spolsky (1985) 35.
267 Sáenz-Badillos (1993) 112.
268 (1914) 13–14.
269 Marcus (1933) 219, n. g.
270 Wieseler (1877) 293 n. 2; In the edition of Niese (1955) 145 the apparatus criticus shows no ms. variations in section 419.
271 Willrich (1900) 71; Timpe (1974) 142; Gauger (1977) 325.
272 Translation: Marcus (1933) 219, ἐπὶ ἀρχιερέως μὲν τοῦ ἔθνους Ἰούδα, στρατηγοῦ δὲ Σίμωνος τοῦ ἀδελφοῦ αὐτοῦ.
273 Gauger (1977) 206, 235; Fischer (1980) 112; Annandale-Potgieter (1991) 415–416. Judas as High Priest: Smith (1996) 320–325.
274 Jos. *Vita* 2: μνήυη . . . διαφέρειν.
275 Gerhardsson (1961) 132–134.
276 Avod. Zar. 19a.
277 Gerhardsson (1961) 130–131.
278 Eruvin 54b.
279 Megillah 32a.
280 Zlotnick (1988) 61.
281 Rubin (1995) 9–10.
282 Eruvin 53a.
283 Eruvin 54b.
284 Feldman (1984b) 222.
285 That Jason and Eupolemus *drafted* (*sic*!) the treaty is the type of information Josephus' Greek audience would expect, is the view of Goldstein (1976) 366.
286 Drüner (1896) 35–50 with examples cited.
287 Cohen (1979) 46.
288 Drüner (1896) 42.
289 Gafni (1979) 127, 131, n. 47.
290 Tuval (2013) 194–197.
291 Ex. 23.32–33; Judg. 2.2. See Rosenne (1999) 78.
292 Deut. 20.20ff.; Smith (1978) 3.
293 Jer. 9. 18–20.
294 Josh. 9.8–22.
295 La Penna (1965) 155; Rosenne (1999) 80.
296 Sherwin-White (1984) 72–75; Gauger (1977) 188–190.
297 Cf. Gruen (1984) 38, 42, 43, 46, who, because he considers treaties only symbolic (a view that is not universally accepted), sees in the ineffectiveness of the Jewish 'treaty' an argument for its historicity.
298 Gruen (1984) 44.
299 Kallet-Marx (1995) 190.
300 Gruen (1984) 44, 49, 738.
301 Gruen (1984) 44.
302 (1968) 158, n. 1.
303 D.H. 6.95.2.
304 Kibyra: *OGIS*, 762, l. 5; Methymna: *IGRR*, IV.2, l. 15; and Maroneia: *SEG* 35.823, l. 36.
305 Täubler (1913) 57, Dahlheim (1968) 158, n. 1.

306 (1875) 144.
307 (1931) 106, n. 27.
308 (1927) 135.
309 Frezza (1938) 366.
310 Matthaei (1907) 190, 202.
311 Watson (1993) 32.
312 Täubler (1913) 253, n. 1; Juster (1914) 131, n. 2.
313 See Chapter 2.
314 Casson (1950) 51.
315 Roman perfidy first mentioned: Michaelis (1778) 178; Wellhausen (1907) 262, 268. Followed by Winckler (1902) 3, 1, 97ff.; Niese (1906) 824; Täubler (1913) 253, n. 2; Juster (1914) 131, n. 2; Willrich (1924) 44–46; Kolbe (1926) 38, n. 1; Bévenot (1931) 106; Sordi (1952) 511; Zeitlin (1950) 469, n. 104.
316 (1984) 72.
317 Freyburger (1986) 83–84. Contra: Mommsen (1887) 1, 3.249, n. 3, who thought its etymology lay in *fundere*.
318 Phillipson (1911) 394–346; Badian (1958) 34–36, 51, 60, n. 2; Badian (1984) 410–414.
319 Varro *LL* 5.86.
320 Richardson (1992) 241.
321 Boyancé (1964b) 419.
322 Livy 1.19.13; Tac. *Ann.* 13.15.
323 Caes. *B. G.* 2.15.1; Heuss (1933) 62–63; Freyburger (1986), 144; Eckstein (1999b), 276–77, n. 16.
324 Boyancé (1964b) 427; (1964a).
325 Livy 30.7.2 shows the different treatment given to cities who surrendered to Rome and those who continued to be hostile and were captured.
326 Watson (1993) 44.
327 Wheeler (1984) 260. See n. 28 for references.
328 Virg. *Aen.* 12.200; Magdelain (1943) 6. The difficulty with the brief treatment in Watson (1993) 46–47 is that he ignores or seems to be unaware of the religious dimension involved in the formation of *foedera*, which was the focus of Magdelain's study in 1943.
329 Magdelain (1943) 45.
330 Livy 3.55.10; Cic. *Balb.* 14.33; Magdelain (1943) 49–51.
331 Magdelain (1943) 129.
332 See Livy 1.21.1.
333 Plaut. *Poen.* 253; Lucretius, *De rerum natura* 5.1229; Livy 3.5.14; Verg. *Aen.* 3.369–373. For the role of *pax deorum* in the state, see Sordi (1985), 146–147.
334 The *sponsio* was regarded as being a solemn pledge before the gods. In *De Legibus* (2.41) Cicero says: *sponsio, qua obligamur deo*. That the problem was religious: Cic. *Pro Caecina* 98; Livy *Ep.* 56; Plut. *Ti. Gracchus* 7.2.
335 Lewis and Short (1966) s.v. scelus, 1640.
336 Livy 9.10.4; Visscher (1946a) 88.
337 That primarily religious reasons underlay the ceremony: Cic. *Caec.* 98; Livy *Epit.* 56; Plut. *Ti.Gr.* 7.2.
338 See Michel (1980), 685–687. On *deuotio* see Dumézil (1974), 103–105, 149–150 and 239. On *piaculum* see Visscher (1947), 114–118.
339 The influence of the Numantia episode on the recording of the Caudine Forks disaster: Nissen (1870) 50–60; de Visscher (1946a) 82–83; Crawford (1973) 6–7. Clineas: Dio, fr. 45; Zon. 8.18; Val. Max. 6.3.3. Mancinus: Plut. *Ti. Gr.* 5–7; App. *Iber.* 80, 83; Rosenstein (1986) 232–235.
340 Boyancé (1962) 334.
341 Kienast (1968) 348.

342 *de off.* 1.34–36.
343 For the view that the Romans were careful not to break treaties: Walker (1899) 47.
344 Diodor. 23.1.
345 Kallet-Marx (1995) 189–192.
346 (1853) 131; also Ginsburg (1928) 48.
347 (1980) 114–115.
348 Fischer (1980) 115.
349 Sordi (1952) 5.
350 (1977) 243–247.
351 Gauger (1977) 245–246.
352 See below, pp. 178, 180–182, 185–186.

# 6 The outcome of the embassy in 162 BCE

The chapter opens with the background to the Jewish experience of Roman *amicitia*, as it had been applied by Rome in the immediate vicinity of Judaea in the Fifth and Sixth Syrian wars between the Ptolemies and the Seleucids. An understanding of the events that framed the clash of these empires and the Roman action that it prompted helps to reach an appreciation of why Judas instructed his envoys to seek *amicitia* from the Roman Senate, and not a treaty. Distinct advantages accrued for Judas in having Roman *amicitia* in the struggle with the Seleucids and in the internal political conflict. The Hasmonaean faction could use *amicitia* as a weapon against both groups.

This chapter acknowledges the pioneering work of Mendelssohn in isolating *amicitia* as the successful outcome of the embassy. In the following pages, documentation is presented to validate his statement that, on first contact with Rome, the senate did not conclude a treaty (*foedus*): *amicitia* was the first step in diplomatic relations. It was a matter of the Romans employing prior stages to a treaty. It has always been maintained that a treaty did not fit the historical circumstances in 162 BCE. The question is, how could Rome make diplomatic relations with rebels from the Seleucid Empire and still maintain friendship with them?

This chapter sets out the case for *amicitia* as constituting the diplomatic relations decided upon by the senate in 162 BCE for the breakaway Jewish community in Judaea.[1] As a preliminary step, the previous arguments that have been made for *amicitia* are reviewed; this is followed by some fresh considerations based on the Roman principles of international law. As will be laid out in this chapter, the senate made four decisions concerning the Jewish community in Judaea: that the Jews should be free and autonomous through a unilateral declaration of *libertas* (freedom), that the Jews should become friends of the Roman people, that they should be enrolled in the *formula amicorum/sociorum* and that they should erect a bronze tablet in Jerusalem testifying to the new ties with Rome.

## The Jewish witness to *amicitia* before 162 BCE

Judaea had been part of the Ptolemaic Empire until 200 BCE and then the Seleucid Empire. It had a direct interest in the clashes between the two powers because they fought invariably over control of Judaea, as it was part of Coele-Syria. The kings of both of these empires had enjoyed a relationship of *amicitia* with the Romans.[2] The friendship between the Romans and the Seleucids went back to the time of Antiochus' father, Seleucus II.[3] Inheriting the throne after Seleucus was Antiochus' brother, who ruled as Seleucus III Ceraunus (or Soter) for only two years before he was murdered by his own troops. In effect, Antiochus III was the inheritor of the ties with Rome formed by his father; that is to say, the friendship with the Romans was permanent unless renounced by Rome.[4] Yet the early part of his reign was spent far from areas of Roman hegemony, so the ties of friendship were not exercised and there ensued no clash of interests.

Antiochus was in Babylon in 223 BCE when he heard of the death of his brother. As newly ascendant to the throne, his first project, and one that would come to occupy a great deal of his reign, was to wrest Coele-Syria from the possession of the Ptolemies. He began with an attack on Syria, but more urgent problems in the empire demanded his attention. He turned back to put down a rebellion in Media and Persis, then returned to Syria and began a campaign that is known as the Fourth Syrian War from 220 to 217 BCE. Antiochus suffered defeat at the battle of Raphia in 217 BCE. He used his army to put down a rebellion in Central Asia (216–212 BCE) before turning farther east to emulate the achievements of Alexander the Great. He was successful in campaigns in Bactria, India and Arabia. None of these areas brought Antiochus into conflict with the Romans.

The clash came in 200 BCE, in the course of the Fifth Syrian War. This war had the same aim; that is, for Antiochus to regain control of Coele-Syria from Egyptian rule. The war had erupted when Antiochus took advantage of the turmoil in Egypt following the death of Ptolemy IV Philopater in 204 BCE. This death left a five-year-old boy to reign as Ptolemy V and an internecine struggle between contenders for the post of regent to the boy king. The instability was so great that the king's death was kept secret for a year.[5] In 202 BCE Antiochus invaded Coele-Syria, sweeping down the coast and laying siege to Gaza. He then defeated the Egyptian army in 200 BCE at Panion, near the head of the Jordan river in the Golan Heights.[6] Justinus reports that the people of Alexandria sent ambassadors to the Romans, asking the Seleucid king to defend Egypt.[7] Both Polybius and Appian frame the concern for Rome and others over the rumoured secret pact between Philip V of Macedon and Antiochus III to carve up Egypt and its overseas territories among themselves.[8] The Romans sent an embassy to meet with Antiochus and Ptolemy to find a negotiated settlement to the war.[9] The chronology is given by Polybius, who informs us that the Roman envoys in Athens, after having conveyed to the Macedonian commander their ultimatum to Philip, sailed off to meet the two kings. We know that the envoys were in Athens in 200 BCE.[10] Justinus explains that the aim of the embassy was to warn both Philip and Antiochus to abstain from attacking Egypt.[11]

It is said that this was the first time Rome had attempted to mediate between two major Greek states.[12] The question is, what gave Rome the justification to intervene? Both the Ptolemies and the Seleucids had made friendship with the Romans earlier in the third century. It is known that prior to 198 BCE the Romans already regarded Antiochus as a friend and ally.[13] The Romans were averse to a situation where two Roman allies were at war: they would intervene to put a halt to the hostilities. The Romans expected that any dispute between their friends would be brought to the Romans for arbitration.[14] This principle may be seen in action in 198 BCE, during the conflict between Attalus of Pergamum and Antiochus III, where Livy states, 'it was proper that kings who were allies and friends of the Roman people should likewise be at peace with one another' (32.8.16). In other words, the *amicitia* between Rome and Antiochus and Rome and Egypt legally entitled Rome to order a halt to hostilities as part of the terms of the diplomatic relations that she held with both parties in the Fifth Syrian War.[15] This was quite different from mediation. The *amicitia* with Rome compelled Antiochus to halt his progress towards Egypt.[16] The Roman warning to Antiochus appears to have been successful, for it had two consequences. In 198 BCE Gaza fell to Antiochus and the way lay open to Egypt; Antiochus held back and did not invade. A rapprochement between Ptolemy V and Antiochus came about in the form of a marriage alliance negotiated in 198/97 BCE.[17] Jerome calls this pact *amicitia* and dates it to the seventh year of Ptolemy's reign, which would place the alliance in 198/97 BCE while the marriage itself was not celebrated until the thirteenth year of his reign – that is, in 192/91 BCE.[18] The events of 200 BCE showed to the Mediterranean peoples the action Rome took when two of her friends engaged in hostilities. Between friends of Rome there should only be peace. Here was the Roman doctrine that all of her friends now learned, if they had not done so previously.

Rome took the same action in the Sixth Syrian War. In 169 BCE Antiochus, taking advantage of the succession to the throne of a five-year-old boy, invaded Egypt and conquered most of the country, with only Alexandria left to fall to him. Putting the city under siege in 168 BCE, he was in his camp in the suburbs of the city at Eleusis when a Roman envoy, Popillius Laenas, approached with a message from the senate. We do not have the text of the senate's demand, but the envoy's task was to prevent two *amici* of Rome from fighting each other; to intervene to prevent the collapse of Ptolemaic Egypt. The encounter demonstrates the mechanics of friendship in action. Polybius gives a contemporary account in which he states that Antiochus greeted Popillius from a distance and held out his hand. Antiochus was giving Popillius the gesture that bound friends through *fides* (good faith).[19] The right hand and *fides* are found joined in a hendiadys, *per fidem . . . per dexteram*, in literature from Terence to Ovid.[20] Livy 23.9.3 reports that one of the Campanians explained that his fidelity to Hannibal was based on the 'swearing by every deity, and joining right hands'. The gesture of the *dexterarum iunctio* was a formal one, not to be confused with a salutation.[21] The joining of right hands constituted part of the formality in becoming a friend of the Romans. The ties of friendship formed between the Romans and Syphax during the Second Punic War were sealed by the joining of right hands.[22]

Antiochus was expecting the same gesture of friendship from Popillius and that in extending his hand he would complete the joining of the right hands. However, Popillius, instead of taking his hand, placed a copy of the message from the senate in his hands. This gesture was an unmistakable sign that there was no longer any friendship between Antiochus and the Romans. The letter contained the conditions on which it could be restored. Diodorus specifically states that putting the document in the king's hands was designed to avoid clasping the king's hand until it could be determined whether he was a friend or an enemy.[23] Popillius told the king to read the letter and would not make 'the conventional sign of friendship before he knew if the intentions of him who was greeting him were friendly or hostile.'[24]

Overshadowing the rejection of Antiochus' friendship has been what happened next: the king's request to have time to consult with his advisors was denied and Popillius drew a circle around the king, ordering him to remain within it until he had come to a decision.[25] The reaction of Antiochus is given by Polybius as one of astonishment.[26] Appian and Zonaras describe it as one of fear or even being terrified.[27] What could be said to have caused the king to be afraid? The answer is that he was afraid of the consequences if the Romans had unilaterally renounced their friendship with him. Renunciation was a preliminary step to a possible war with Rome. The letter in the king's hand gave him conditions on which the friendship could be restored. The king announced only after a moment's hesitation that he would meet all the senate's demands. The reaction was the gesture that Antiochus had hoped for at the beginning: Popillius and his retinue 'all grasped him by the hand and greeted him warmly.'[28] The king knew at that moment that he was still considered an *amicus* of the Romans. Although the king complained later about the conditions on which he had held onto his friendship with the Romans, he complied nevertheless and within the short span of time specified he and his troops evacuated Egypt.[29] Twice the Seleucids had been warned by Rome not to attack her friend, the Ptolemies. The justification for issuing the ultimatum, first to Antiochus III and later to Antiochus IV, concerned Egypt's rights as a friend of the Roman people. This diplomatic status entitled the Romans to step in when the territorial integrity of Egypt was threatened and in imminent danger of collapse. The rapid retreat of the Seleucid army through the delivery of a letter from the Roman Senate to Antiochus was a powerful lesson that was not lost on the Jews in Judaea.

Judaea was the near neighbour of Egypt and what happened there had consequences for their small territory, wedged as it was between the Ptolemaic and Seleucid empires. The Jews had seen that the power of holding Roman *amicitia* had made the imperial powers cease to fight and to cause an invading army to retreat. If only they could have *amicitia*, it could be used to leverage Roman intervention in their armed revolt from the Seleucids and force the armies of their enemy to leave Judaea.[30] The embassy of 162 BCE set out to acquire this valuable diplomatic tool.

## What did Judas hope to achieve by this embassy?

One of the chief benefits to having *amicitia* with Rome, was that it obliged the Romans to guarantee the territorial integrity of her ally. For Judas, his territory was the area already won that included the Judaean hills, Hebron, Maresha to the south, and Jerusalem and the Temple. In any disputes, the Romans upheld the claim of their *amici* to the territory they held at the time they entered into the friendship of the Romans.[31] This was an extremely valuable privilege to have, as it meant that Rome would guarantee the maintenance of the territory won through Judas' recent victories. Whether Judas realised this before the embassy or whether his ambassadors were instructed regarding the rights and obligations of *amici*, we do not know. Should there occur any military reverses in the future, Judas' *amicitia* with Rome permitted him to appeal to Rome to intervene with the Seleucids. His death prevented the implementation and activation of his *amicitia* with Rome.

Internally, Roman friendship gave governing rights to the side in civil strife with whom she had friendship. Other parties or factions not holding *amicitia* with Rome were to be subordinate to the friends of Rome. The entrenchment of the Hasmonaean faction would be made possible over the 'Hellenisers' and the party of Alcimus with the Roman *amicitia* in the hands of Judas Maccabaeus. *Amicitia* provided the maintenance of the local constitution and political system, meaning a legitimisation of Judas' leadership, and the continuance of local law, in this case the Torah and the daily sacrifices in the Temple without any compromise with Roman religion or politics.

## *Amicitia* for the Jews in 161 BCE from Graeco-Roman sources

Justinus reports in Book 36.3.9 that the Jews sought *amicitia* and received *libertas*. Justinus' testimony states that the Jews did not receive a treaty (*foedus*).

Furthermore, Justinus preserves the order of diplomatic relations, namely that before a non-autonomous community could receive *amicitia* they had to be declared free. Justinus informs us in this passage that the Jews received *libertas* as a first step towards *amicitia*. Justinus was quite careful in his use of legal language. This may be seen in his use of *exhibere* in 9.2.7, 11.10.9 and 22.1.3. He also used other legal phrases, such as *possessio uacua* in 19.3.6 and *bona inuadere* in 21.2.10.[32] One can be certain that Justinus did not confuse *libertas* or *amicitia* with a *foedus*. When the occasion called for it, he was quite capable of using the term *foedus*.[33] Yet *libertas* and *amicitia* are the terms used by Justinus. In addition, as I have previously suggested (see Zollschan (2008)), this passage may be translated as follows: 'When they had revolted from Demetrius, having sought the friendship of the Romans, they were the first of all Eastern peoples to receive liberty, at that time the Romans willingly granted [liberty] from a foreign [power].' Justinus speaks of the Jews being the first of all Eastern peoples to receive liberty from a foreign power. I venture to suggest that what makes this the first example in the East of this Roman practice, is the use of the two-stage process against the Seleucid Empire. In other words, it is proposed here that what Justinus is saying is that the Jews were the first to be made free from the Seleucids so that diplomatic relations with Rome could be formed.

One was accustomed in the past to dismiss Justinus as a careless historian, but his reputation for soundness has been growing in the last few decades, principally as a result of the work of Jal and Franga.[34] Their work on the methods of making epitomes and what Justinus meant by *brevitas* has resulted in a new appreciation of Justinus' work. His value too, in preserving Trogus and his sources, is now appreciated.[35] So the words of Justinus convey a precise meaning that cannot be summarily dismissed. The importance of this passage for our understanding of the embassy of 162 BCE was highlighted by both Gauger and Stern.[36]

For another reference to the embassy of 162 BCE, mention is made of Judas Maccabaeus and his embassy to Rome in the work of Eusebius, written in the early fourth century CE. Eusebius used as his source 'the history of the Maccabees'; presumably, here he is referring to the books of Maccabees. Writing in Greek, he says that this embassy achieved the enrolment of the Jews as 'friends and allies' by the Romans. The Armenian version mentions that the Jews received a decree of the senate, which was published by Judas Maccabaeus; in this, the Jews were to be regarded as *amici et auxiliatores Romanorum*. The same terminology is used in Hieronymus' translation of the Greek text of Eusebius' work into Latin. According to Hieronymus (*Chron.* p. 141,b, Helm), *Decreuit senatus Iudaeos amicos et auxiliatores Romanorum habendos*. The word *auxiliatores* is a new entry into the terms used to categorised Roman–Jewish diplomatic relations at the time of Judas Maccabaeus. What does *auxiliatores* mean and is it the same as *foederati*? *Auxiliator* is a term confined to war and refers to war allies or σύμμαχοι.[37] An *auxiliator* is one who has a relationship of *societas* with Rome and who is a *socius* of Rome.[38] In fact, the study of Wegner, on the concept of *socius* and *societas*, found that *socius* carried the meaning of 'one who aids'.[39] The interpretation by both Eusebius and Hieronymus of the account in Maccabees was not that the Jews were *foederati* but in fact *socii*. In their work, it was indeed possible to be *socii Romani* and not to possess a treaty with Rome. This type of diplomatic relations Kienast has identified as *societas sine foedere*.[40]

In the *Bibliotheca*, from the late first century BCE, Diodorus Siculus wrote an account of a deputation of Jewish notables to Pompey. Their speech made reference to an earlier Jewish embassy to the senate that had won freedom and autonomy (τῶν Ἰουδαίων ἐλευθέρων καὶ αὐτονόμων) for the Jews at a time when they were in revolt. The source for this account may have been Theophanes of Miletus, himself an eyewitness to these very events, who did not categorise Roman diplomatic relations with the Jews as treaty but rather in terms of 'freedom and autonomy'. This type of diplomatic relations, forming the stage *before* a *foedus* or *amicitia*, could be concluded with a community whose independence had not been universally recognised.[41] In the First Book of Maccabees, when referring back to the embassy of 162 BCE and in three Graeco-Roman sources – namely, Justinus, Eusebius and Hieronymus – there are aspects in these texts that support *libertas* followed by *amicitia*. This corroboration in sources, such as Justinus, that were not derived from 1 Maccabees and thus were independent of Jewish sources, is an important confirmation that *amicitia* was the form of diplomatic relations chosen by the senate in response to the embassy sent by Judas.

## Mendelssohn's identification of Roman *amicitia* for Judaea in 162 BCE

That the Jews received *amicitia* from the Roman Senate in 162 BCE, was the argument made by Mendelssohn in 1875, and many of his arguments remain valid. His work was overlooked after Mommsen and Täubler had used epigraphically preserved Roman treaties to show that the document in 1 Macc. 8.23–32 could be interpreted as a genuine Roman treaty. This section opens with a reprise of Mendelssohn's case for *amicitia*, which was based on statements without documentation. In many aspects his judgement was correct and information in this section shows that our knowledge of Roman *Völkerrecht* supports his view.

Mendelssohn launched his argument with the quotation of a passage from Josephus' *Jewish Wars* (1.38): 'Now Judas, supposing that Antiochus would not lie still, gathered an army out of his own countrymen, and was the first that made friendship with the Romans'. This passage contains mention only of friendship (φιλία) and not of a treaty of any kind.[42]

Mendelssohn stated that the usual practice of the senate was to respond kindly to foreign envoys who came asking for help. Additionally, if the senate judged the time to be opportune in terms of their own policy or stance, they would decide to enter into friendship with the foreign community. It was not the practice of the senate to conclude a permanent treaty (*foedus*) upon dealing with a first-time embassy to Rome.[43] He acquainted his readers with the key principle in Roman international law that a treaty with Rome was possible only with an independent entity.[44] It was actually in the power of the senate whether it chose to believe that the Jews were living under their own laws or were still under Seleucid rule. In determining whether the Jews were sufficiently free from the Seleucid king, the senate reserved the right to decide.[45] Unlike a treaty, mere *amicitia* did not oblige Rome or make it necessary for the city to send military aid. Mendelssohn brought forward a passage from Eusebius stating that Judas hoped both for *amicitia* and to have *auxilium* (military aid) as a result of this embassy. This will be discussed later in the chapter. In a brief remark, Mendelssohn provided an important historical sketch of the later relations between the Romans and the Jews: the Maccabaean document conforms with *amicitia*, which the later Hasmonaeans vitiated by their attack on the friendship of the Romans. This chapter deals with the first half of his statement and the following chapter concentrates on the second half of his statement by showing how the Jewish leadership actually broke the terms of friendship with the Romans.[46]

Niese agreed with Mendelssohn in so far as acknowledging that certain factors made a treaty with Rome at that time impossible under Roman international law. Jews in Judaea were still subjects of the Seleucid Empire, whose kings were themselves friends of the Roman people. No matter how ruthless the Romans may have been in their internal political dealings, said Niese, when it came to international relations, they held to the accepted norms. He added that, to undermine the Seleucid king, a friend of the Roman people with a treaty with the Jews, would have been unthinkable.[47]

## Modern arguments for *amicitia*

For the senate in Rome, presented with an embassy from Jerusalem that represented a group that had never been to Rome and were seeking diplomatic relations for the first time, the usual procedure was to offer *amicitia* in order to bring a community that was foreign to the Romans closer to them.[48] A treaty (*foedus*) was out of the question in this early stage of relations with Rome. The second obstacle was that the Jews were in a state of rebellion against the Seleucids and, therefore, did not fulfil the requirement that they were autonomous and legally capable of undertaking an independent course and having their own foreign policy.[49] Dating the embassy to 162 BCE on the evidence of 1 Macc. 8.16 (see Chapter 2) places the discussion in the senate at a time when there was turmoil in the Syrian court and turmoil in Rome after both consuls had resigned (see Chapter 2). Demetrius had escaped, leaving Rome furtively without senatorial approval, and was in Antioch by the time the envoys arrived in Rome. Antiochus V and his guardian Lysias were dead on the orders of Demetrius, who had no diplomatic connections with Rome. Within this hiatus, until Demetrius declared himself king, the senate could act and declare the Jews autonomous and not subject to the Seleucids. The declaration of *libertas* had been used by the Romans to free Greek cities from the Macedonians and from the Seleucids. How it operated in practice and the benefits it brought to the Jews in terms of religious freedoms, is the subject of the next section.

Before discussing these matters, a preamble is necessary to draw together what has been stated previously about terminology. We have seen the interchangeability of the terms *amicitia* and *societas*, especially after 168 BCE, when all allies, irrespective of the label, supplied troops to Rome in time of war and all allies lost their capacity to operate a foreign policy independent of Rome.[50] The term φιλία καὶ συμμαχία was known in the Greek-speaking world as a relationship capable of being easily terminated.[51] Kienast and Dahlheim independently arrived at the conclusion that the concept of φιλία καὶ συμμαχία (*amicitia et societas*) was decidedly elastic in that it could encompass the separate meanings of *amicitia* – that is, a friendly relationship with Rome – and also *societas*, help in arms. Additionally, together they could simply mean *amicitia*.[52] The vagueness of these concepts, especially after 168 BCE, is important when probing how the First Book of Maccabees describes Roman–Jewish relations.

The etymology of the word *socius*, reveals that its sense is very near to that of friendship. According to Wegner, *socius* is derived not from *sequor*, and thus does not have the meaning of 'one who follows', but rather from the Sanskrit *sakhi*, meaning 'a friend'.[53] *Societas* is the state of being a *socius*.[54] Since a *socius* can be the same as an *amicus*, *societas* can accommodate the meaning of *amicitia* and does not necessarily carry with it the idea that it is formed solely through a *foedus*. The *socius* enters *into* a *societas*. One finds the verbs *uenire*, *trahere* and *accipere* associated with *in societatem*.[55] This is the same choice of words used for *amicitia*. The *amici* are said to enter into (*uenire*) the Roman friendship.[56] *Societas* is distinct from a *foedus*.[57] *Societas* in Greek would be rendered as συνθῆκαι, while a *foedus* as ὅρκοι because of the sworn oaths that were used to conclude a Roman State treaty.[58] The advantage of a *societas* is that it was a more flexible foreign policy instrument than a *foedus* simply because the former may be altered without necessitating another set of oath taking. The rendering of *societas* in Greek as συνθῆκαι can also mean the agreement or understanding to have a *societas*.[59]

Consequently, there was very little to distinguish *societas* from *amicitia*. When Kienast isolated his three-stage process of first a declaration of *libertas*, followed by a declaration of *societas* and enrolment in the *formula amicorum*, he found no label in the Latin literature to describe this phenomenon. To fill this gap he coined a term, *societas sine foedere*, to mean a treaty-less alliance.[60] For all this, Kienast is describing the formation of *amicitia* in circumstances where the Romans granted as a preliminary step a declaration of *libertas*.[61] His third stage, that of being enrolled in the *formula amicorum*, was not a new or exceptional step: it was just the normal process undertaken by the senate after they had named the person or community as a friend.

## A problem of prior stages

The issue of whether the Jews received a treaty from the Roman Senate in 162 BCE has remained confined and limited to studies in Jewish history, with the result that any connections between different forms of diplomatic relations have been ignored. This narrow focus has meant that certain patterns in Roman practice have not been discerned and given the prominence they deserve. By surveying the communities who received *libertas* and by tracing the subsequent history of their diplomatic relations with Rome, the relationship, for example, of *libertas* to *foedus* and *libertas* to *amicitia*, becomes clear and a sequential pattern emerges.[62] By this is meant that one type of relationship follows another, though not always immediately. Consequently, one can see that the senate, when responding to the requests of embassies, had a limited number of options available to them because of the need to take into account some necessary preconditions, one of which was that a community was required to be independent in order to form *amicitia* or conclude a *foedus* with Rome.

## Relations with independent communities

A basic principle for the formation of diplomatic relations with Rome was that the community under consideration by the senate for such ties should meet the requirement that it be autonomous and so be empowered to conduct its own foreign policy. In this chapter, the interrelationship between the three main diplomatic categories (*amicitia*, *societas* and *libertas*) is explored. This section has as its focus the basic principle of autonomy as a precondition for formal diplomatic relations with Rome. This precondition was important above all for the formation of both *amicitia* relations and treaty relations.

The Roman State concluded diplomatic relations with independent communities by ties of *amicitia*, a type of diplomatic relations not based on legal forms. *Amicitia* of this type basically established good relations. Such a situation between Rome and her *amicus* was expressed as a state of peace existing between them.[63] This *amicitia* existed only between partners who were formerly independent.[64] *Amicitia* could be established only with an independent community, as was shown in the studies by Heuss and Kienast.[65]

In the case of treaty relations, the position is unambiguous: a treaty could not be concluded between a non-independent state and Rome. In fact, it was a fundamental principle from the Republic into the imperial period that a *foedus* be concluded with an autonomous community.[66] The evidence comes from the Digest, which states: 'That people is free, which is subject to the authority of no other people, whether it is bound by a treaty or not'.[67] Mommsen, when he published his edition of the Digest, deleted the first 'whether' (*siue*) in this sentence and derived from this passage the meaning that a free people is also bound by a treaty.[68] In the sentence as quoted here can be seen the definition of a free people – that is, a people who are not under the power of any other people – and, moreover, the passage informs that a free people could be under a treaty. The Digest was compiled from sources that went back to the Republic and the criterion for the inclusion of material was simply whether the precepts were still in use. Each ruling was ascribed to the appropriate source. In this case, the passage was ascribed to a jurist of the Julio-Claudian period, Proculus. All this tells us is that the principle whereby treaties were made with autonomous peoples was still in effect in the Julio-Claudian period, not that it originated at that time.[69]

Further evidence that alliances were only made with free peoples, can be demonstrated by Roman conduct. When a Roman magistrate entered the city or territory that was *foederata*, he had to do so without any lictors as a sign that he had no authority there.[70] Moreover, the wording of such a treaty was based on the assumption that the future treaty partner of Rome was free to conduct its own foreign policy in choosing Rome as its ally. Mommsen saw that the treaty required the potential partner to be autonomous in order to negotiate conditions with Rome and that the bilateral treaty was a mutual act of recognition of each other's autonomy. For communities that were subject to Rome, the conclusion of a treaty in which Rome dictated the terms was a sign of their quasi-autonomy.[71] Most authorities today are of the view that independence was a precondition to entering treaty relationships with the Romans.[72] Consequently, for relations of *amicitia* or for a state of treaty relations to exist with Rome, a state, people, city or community needed to be independent, whether *de facto* or after Rome had taken steps to ensure that state of independence by means that satisfied her criteria.

### *Relations prior to a foedus*

The question at issue is how Roman diplomatic practice handled situations such as that of the Jews in 162 BCE, where a community on its first visit to Rome requested establishment of diplomatic relations with the city. Sherwin-White visualised a sequence that involved first *amicitia* and then an official ratification of that status with a formal state treaty that, through subsequent visits to Rome, could be nominally renewed.[73] However, his scenario is difficult to maintain. In the case of a state that was not independent, neither *amicitia* nor a *foedus* could be entered into. In these circumstances, the declaration of *libertas* came into play, as will be seen later.

Sherwin-White observed a certain diplomatic procedure accompanying the first formulation of relations between Rome and other states. It applied, he maintained, in cases where that state had been the subject of a Hellenistic monarchy and with whom Rome had not had direct contact. In order to conclude a treaty, there needed to be, as has been shown, two independent parties. In circumstances where Rome did not consider her potential contractual partner to be an independent community, by a unilateral declaration of *libertas* from the senate, that community, for Rome's purposes, became autonomous and therefore eligible to be a treaty partner at some later date.[74]

As proof for the two-stage process (first *libertas*, then later a *foedus*), Sherwin-White brought one example only, that of the city of Utica in North Africa.[75] His choice of Utica was determined, in part, by his view that all declarations of freedom postdate the First Mithridatic War.[76] Evidence that Utica was a *ciuitas libera* may be found in the *lex agraria* of 111 BCE where, in line 79, the people of Utica are named *inter alia* as 'free': *quei ager intra finis populorum leiberorum Uticensium* . . . .[77] That in Cicero's time Utica had a treaty with Rome may be understood from the fact that Cicero refers to it as a *ciuitas foederata*.[78] This was the only example brought forward by Sherwin-White, although he did note further possible examples.

Furthermore, it can be shown that there existed an actual expectation that, after *libertas*, a community could proceed at some later date to a *foedus* with Rome. This expectation is evident in the example of Agassae, which decided to shift its allegiance away from Rome when it became clear that the Agassaeans were not going to achieve the next stage. In 169 BCE, following the surrender of that city to the Romans, it was given its autonomy and freedom from tribute and garrisons.[79] Two years later, the Agassaeans sought an alliance; after receiving none, they went over to the side of Perseus. Consequently, as a punishment for disloyalty, Paullus ordered the city to be sacked.[80] Some further examples of the sequence where declarations of *libertas* exist prior to a *foedus* have been brought together in my earlier treatment of the subject.[81] Yet these examples do not necessarily exhaust the total number of instances in which the Romans used this two-stage procedure. Literary and epigraphic testimonia reveal several further such probable cases of declarations of *libertas* prior to a *foedus*. Our knowledge of Roman treaties in the second century is essentially limited to the accidental discovery of inscriptions.[82] Owing largely to the nature of the evidence, the possibility exists that further examples of *foedera* await discovery.

The city of Heraclea Pontica was subject to this two-stage process. In 190 BCE, it received a letter from the Scipio brothers that granted its citizens their freedom.[83] A fragment from the historian Memnon relates that the city entered into a treaty with Rome some time after 188 BCE.[84] Cnidos obtained its freedom under the treaty of Apamea in 188 BCE and this grant was renewed by Julius Caesar in 48 BCE. A treaty was concluded with Rome in 29 BCE.[85]

The city of Alabanda in northern Caria also received a grant of *libertas* as a preliminary step to its *foedus* with Rome. The city was an important religious centre in Caria and was probably free between 189 and 170 BCE.[86] Its status as *foederata* is bound up with an inscription, which records two separate embassies to Rome.[87] According to Willrich's reconstruction of events, Alabanda sent an embassy to Rome after the Mithridatic War seeking a συμμαχία.[88] Once having enjoyed its independence, the city's leaders sought the next stage in diplomatic relations with Rome. Whether they returned from Rome with a treaty is not recorded. They may not have achieved their alliance since Pliny records that the city in his day was considered *libera*.[89] There is evidence that the city of Elea was also subject to this two-part process. There is inscriptional evidence (*OGIS* 335, line 144) that it was an independent city at the time of Antiochus I.[90] Under the terms of the treaty of Apamea, the freedom of Elea was confirmed, as was that of all the cities that had enjoyed that status under Antiochus III.[91] Later it received an alliance. The inscription (*SIG*[3] 694) mentions τῆς συνθήκης in line 29. In addition, the setting up of bronze tablets on the Capitol and in the Temple of Demeter in the Greek city is mentioned. A further example is the city of Maroneia, which first received its freedom in 196 BCE as part of the Thracian cities, according to Livy 33.35.2. The senate declared the city free after the war with Perseus.[92] The settlement of Macedonia in 167 BCE placed Maroneia outside the new borders of Macedonia Prima.[93] Later, Maroneia received a *foedus*.[94] Hephaestia on Lemnos received a declaration of *libertas* in 196 BCE, as both Polybius and Livy testify.[95] That there was a treaty may be assumed from epigraphic evidence.[96] This may be considered evidence for a treaty with Rome c. 165 BCE, although some reservations have been expressed.[97]

Methymna was free under the treaty of Apamea in 188 BCE and its treaty with Rome is well known.[98] Mytilene was free until the war with Mithridates. Its status was restored by Pompey in 63 BCE. A treaty with Rome was concluded in 25 BCE.[99] Amisus was freed by Lucullus in c. 70 BCE and that status was restored by Julius Caesar in 47 BCE.[100] A treaty with Amisus was concluded by Trajan.[101] Aphrodisias was freed by Caesar, a decision that was implemented by Antony after Caesar's assassination. A treaty came in the period between 39 and 35 BCE.[102] Another example is perhaps the Carian city of Tabae, whose freedom is known from a *senatus consultum* from the time of Sulla in lines 10–11 of the inscription (*OGIS* 2.442), which have been variously restored. The preferred reading is that of Bean, to the effect that the city was allowed to make its own laws and decisions.[103] On the basis of this inscription, a case may be made for the granting (or reconfirming) of the right of Tabae to make its own laws and decisions. The method by which the Romans granted this privilege was through a declaration of *libertas*. That Tabae had an alliance with Rome, is easier to prove. It is known from an inscription set up by Asiatic communities, among them Tabae, that the city had an alliance with Rome. The text of *IG* 14.696 reads: ὁ δῆμος ὁ Ταβη ῶν, φίλος καὶ σύμμαχος Ῥωμαίων. The dedication in Rome should date not long after the freedom granted to these Lycian cities in 167 BCE.[104]

While the examples so far have been confined to cities, there are, in addition, some examples of *libertas* and then *foedera* given to peoples. Two examples will suffice to demonstrate the existence of the practice. The first case concerns the Vocontii in Gaul, whose autonomous status is mentioned in Strabo 4.6.4 and who are called a *gens foederata* by Pliny (*N.H.* 7.78). The second case involves the Dentheletae in Macedonia, whose *libertas* is mentioned in Pliny *N.H.* 4.40 and whose *foedus* is attested by Dio 51.23.4.

In addition to these 12 examples of *libertas* followed by a *foedus*, one further example is available. In a later edition of his 1954 publication of the inscriptions from the Capitol, Degrassi added two further inscriptions, the first of which is of interest here.[105] Only the Greek copy of the inscription is extant, a dedication from Attaleia in Pamphylia.[106] The city describes itself as φίλη καὶ σύμμαχος of Rome. The city was considered *libera* in 133 BCE, at the time of the bequest of Asia to Rome, and in 85 BCE was counted as an ally of Rome.[107] The dedication Degrassi considers belongs to the imperial period, possibly to the time of Vespasian, according to the form of the letters. However, his dating cannot be held to be sure, as Vespasian had many of the bronze tablets recopied after the fire on the Capitol.[108] This inscription may be one such copy and date from an earlier period.

## The stages after a declaration of *libertas*

After a community had received a declaration of *libertas*, the possibilities for the future would be one of the following: *amicitia*, maintenance of *libertas*, abolition of *libertas*, *libertas* lost when the community had been conquered, status changed from a free city to a Roman *colonia*, or procession from *libertas* to a *foedus*. Examples of some of these trajectories follow.[109]

### *Amicitia*

In his study on the international law principles of Roman foreign policy, Heuss proposed that, after it granted a community *libertas*, the Republic brought the freed community into an international law relationship of *amicitia*. He reached this conclusion through the assumption that in each case the community had effected an act of surrender to Rome. From *deditio* followed, he argued, the annulment of the community's laws or constitution, which the Romans then restored (*leges restituere* or *reddere*). This act of restoration brought into being the recreation of the community's situation that had existed before the war.[110] The restitution of the community's constitution was achieved through Rome's withdrawing her forces; that is, by relinquishing power. This Roman withdrawal signalled the commencement of an international law relationship of *amicitia*. In other words, once hostilities ceased through surrender to Rome, peace and friendship resulted.[111]

However, Kienast refuted this and asserted that, for *amicitia* to occur after a declaration of *libertas*, a further step was required. Magie also considered that the formation of *amicitia* was a definite act, reference to which is found in the inscriptional record. In Latin it is referred to as *in amicitiam venire* and Magie cites *CIL* $1^2$ 585. In Greek the act is referred to as εἰς τὴν φιλίαν παραγίγνεσθαι (*Syll.*$^3$ 674 and 679) or τῇ φιλίᾳ προσέρχεσθαι (*Syll.*$^3$ 785).[112]

The separation into two stages is made clear from the testimony of Appian (*Mithr.* 61) whereby, first, Sulla freed the cities that had remained faithful to Rome in the war against Mithridates, such as Lycia, and after that step, he wrote down that the Lycians, for example, were now friends of the Romans.[113] For Kienast, this passage argued against the view of Heuss that *amicitia* was the immediate effect of being freed.[114]

### *Maintenance of libertas*

The majority of communities that had been granted *libertas* by the senate continued to possess that status, as far as the evidence permits us to determine. This evidence falls into two types. First, there are the recipients who are mentioned in the sources only once, on the occasion of their *libertas* grant, which means that the subsequent developments are not known. Secondly, it is possible to compile a list of communities both known to be 'free' and which are attested as having retained that freedom over centuries. Only the second list has been included in this category. A total of 35 communities maintained their *libertas*. The information is listed in Table 6.1.

### *Abolition of libertas*

The most serious breach of the conditions of *libertas* that resulted in its abolition occurred when the free community joined the side against whom Rome was at war. Known examples include Phocaea, which was granted *libertas* in 190 BCE, but lost it when the Phocaeans supported the revolt of Aristonicus.[115] Another example is Agassae, which assumed that once it had *libertas* from Rome it would automatically receive a treaty, an error that it made in 169 BCE to its cost, for the Roman refusal to grant a *foedus* prompted it to join the side of Rome's enemy.[116] Two years later, Paullus sent his son to sack the city. What merited this punishment? The city had voluntarily asked for an alliance and, having not received it, they changed allegiance and went over to Perseus.[117]

Phocaea also lost its *libertas* when it went over to the side of Aristonicus against Rome and then took the side of Mithridates.[118] In fact, the war with Mithridates divided the loyalties of many a free city in Asia Minor. Other cities whose *libertas* was abolished because they had supported Mithridates included Mytilene and Heraclea Pontica.[119] The flogging and execution of Roman citizens in Cyzicus resulted in the abolition of its *libertas* in 20 BCE, but *libertas* was restored five years later. In the reign of Tiberius, they lost it again because they had imprisoned some Romans and also because they had not completed the shrine to Augustus that they had commenced.[120] Several other cities lost their *libertas* for reasons that are not

*Table 6.1* Communities that maintained their *libertas*

| *Location* | *Sources* | *Location* | *Sources* |
|---|---|---|---|
| Vellavi | Strabo 4.2.2 | Dardanus | Livy 38.39.10; Strabo 13.1.27 |
| Issa | Livy 45.26.13 | Ilium | Livy 38.39.10; App. *Mithr.* 61; Strabo 13.1.27; Suet. *Claud.* 25.3; *Dig.* 27.1.17.1 |
| Risinium | Livy 45.26.13 | Magnesia ad Sipylum | Strabo 13.3.5 |
| Olcinium | Livy 45.26.13 | Chius | Polyb. 31.45.5; Livy 38.39.11; App. *Mithr.* 61, 46; Plut. *Luc.* 3.3; Pliny *N.H.* 5.136 |
| Apollonia | App. *Ill.* 8 | Mylasa | Polyb. 30.5.11; Livy 45.25.11; Pliny *N.H.* 5.108 |
| Pirustae | Livy 45.26.13 | Stratonicea | Polyb. 30.21.3; 24.1–2; Sherk *RDGE* no.18; Pliny *N.H.* 5.109 |
| Orestae | Polyb. 17.47.6; Caes. *BC* 3.34 | Cos | Tac. *Ann.* 12.61 |
| Scotussaei | Caes. *BC* 3.34. | Cnidus | Plut. *Caes.* 48.1; Pliny *N.H.* 5.104 |
| Amantini | Caes. *BC* 3.34 | Heraclea Chersonesus | Polyb. 25.2.13; Strabo 7.4.3; Pliny *N.H.* 4.85 |
| Thessalia | Polyb. 18.46.5; Livy 33.32.5; App. *B.C.* 2.88; Plut. *Caes.*48 | Thermessus Maior | Polyb. 21.35.4; *CIL* 1.204 |
| Pharsalus | Polyb. 18.47.8; Livy 33.34.7; Pliny *N.H.* 4.29 | Seleucia Pieria | Strabo 16.2.8; Pliny *N.H.* 5.79 |
| Aenus | Livy 45.29.6; Pliny *N.H.* 4.43 | Leptis Minor | *CIL* 1.200; Pliny *N.H.* 5.25 |
| Thasus | Polyb. 18.48.2; Livy 33.35.2; Pliny *N.H.* 4.73 | Thapsus | *CIL* 1.200; Pliny *N.H.* 5.25 |
| Corcyra | App. *Ill.* 8; Strabo 7, fr. 8; Pliny *N.H.* 4.52 | Theudalis | *CIL* 1.200; Pliny *N.H.* 5.25 |
| Delphi | Sherk *RDGE* No.s 1 and 5 | Usalis | *CIL* 1.200; Pliny *N.H.* 5.29 |
| Thespiae | Pliny *N.H.* 4.25; *CIL* 8.7059 | Sicyon | Cic. *ad Att.* 1.19.9; *Verr.* 2.1.44 |

known. They include Smyrna, Miletus, Clazomenae, Carystos, Caunus, Acarnania, Rhodes and Antiochia Epidaphnes.[121] The Atrebates, although given *libertas* by Caesar (B.G. VII.76.1), had no rights in the Augustan period.[122] Tenedos lost its *libertas* in 54 BCE because it did not have enough defenders in the senate.[123]

Augustus removed the free status of Tyre and Sidon because they were not able to govern themselves without 'fractious quarrelling' (διὰ τὰς στάσεις ἐποίησεν).[124] The emperor Claudius did the same to Lycia, for the same offence. Lycia, whose *libertas* had been granted in 167 BCE, maintained that privilege through the Republic and Early Empire. This status was withdrawn by Claudius on the grounds that the Lycians were prone to too many internecine feuds.[125] In the Imperial period, 'free cities' had to demonstrate that they were capable of maintaining their own internal stability.

The change in status of these cities occurred during the 140s BCE, 80–78 BCE, in the time of Cicero and Augustus, and under the emperors Tiberius, Vespasian and Septimius Severus. Although the reasons for the abolition of *libertas* is not known in all cases, for those that are known, the reasons were extremely serious and clearly showed a breach of loyalty to Rome. In other cases, the cities had proved unable to govern themselves with stability and without internal upheavals.

### *Libertas void when conquered*

A 'free' city was expected to be able to maintain its own physical independence. Once it came under the power of another state, it could no longer be considered 'free' by the Romans. The definition of a free people was that it was *in sua potestate*.[126] Thus, the cities of Caria, Iasus, Pedasus and Bargylia, which had been freed in 196 BCE, were given to Rhodes in 188 BCE.[127] These cities considered that their *libertas* had been taken away by Rhodes and protested to Rome in 178 BCE.[128] In 167 BCE, these cities of the Euronus were captured by Mylasa[129] (itself a free city[130]) and became incorporated in a *sympoliteia* with Mylasa, with the result that they lost their independent status.[131] The case of Sinope illustrates the fact that conquest eradicated *libertas*. The city had been captured by Sulla in 70 BCE and given its freedom.[132] It was captured subsequently by Pharnaces but regained for Rome on Caesar's orders.[133] Whether it was granted its freedom again, is not known.

### *Procession to a foedus*

The sequence of *libertas* followed by a *foedus* is one that is of some importance to the problem addressed by this current study, namely the issue of whether the Jews received a *foedus* from the Romans in 162 BCE. The material presented here confirms that this sequence existed. Is it possible that *libertas* and a *foedus* could follow immediately, one upon the other? In the situation of the Jews, could it be argued that they received both *libertas* and then a *foedus* in the period when the envoys, Eupolemus and Jason, were in Rome? The question then becomes, what was the length of the time interval between *libertas* and *foedus*?

The scattered nature of the evidence makes chronological precision difficult, as often dates are given for only one of the two stages. Nevertheless, there are some examples that may be referred to with some degree of surety. Mytilene was granted its *libertas* c. 192 BCE, lost it in 80 BCE during the Mithridatic War, recovered it in 63 BCE, and concluded a treaty with Rome in 45 or 25 BCE.[134] The city of Aphrodisias received *libertas* in 43 BCE and then concluded a *foedus* with Rome in 39–35 BCE.[135] A longer interval awaited Amisus, which received *libertas* c. 70 BCE and again in 47 BCE; however, a *foedus* was not concluded until the time of Trajan.[136] One may conclude that there seems to have been no set time interval between the two stages of first *libertas* and then a *foedus*. Nevertheless, the evidence shows that a certain time interval was maintained in each case between the two stages.

The findings made regarding prior stages in Roman diplomatic relations may now be summarised. Certain forms of diplomatic relations are found preceded by a requisite preliminary stage, as some preconditions needed to be met. One of these was that friendship and treaty relations with Rome could only be made with independent entities. Where a community did not have its independence universally recognised, the senate granted a unilateral declaration of *libertas* that resolved, from the Roman side, any ambiguity regarding the status of that community's independence. The sequence of diplomatic relations – of *libertas*, followed (not necessarily immediately afterwards) by *amicitia* or a *foedus* – is more widespread than was previously thought. Examples may be found in Sicily, the Aegean, Asia Minor, Gaul, Africa and Syria. The data given here provides the explicit evidence that was lacking in Mendelssohn's suggestion that the Roman Senate did not decide for a treaty as the first step in diplomatic relations with Rome.[137]

The sequence now in doubt is that of *deditio* preceding all declarations of *libertas*. Several examples exist of *libertas* granted to communities who were not *dediticii*. Such a finding has an impact on the prevailing theories of *libertas*. The existence of *libertas* without *deditio* calls into question the position of Heuss that the immediate consequence of liberation was *amicitia*. This theory of Heuss proposed a sequence of *deditio–libertas–amicitia*. According to this scheme, *libertas* followed surrender to Rome, which marked the end of hostilities. When the Romans relinquished their power over the defeated, Heuss saw this as the initiation of *amicitia* relations. Where there was *libertas*, however, in the absence of war, *amicitia* was not necessarily the immediate stage after the liberation.

Rather, the position of Kienast is better documented. His view was that, after *libertas*, a separate declaration of *amicitia* could be made by the senate. Following this stage, the *amicus* could be enrolled in the list of friends and allies of the Roman people. In other words, the establishment of *amicitia* and registration in the list do not constitute a single process but, in fact, formed two separate processes.

The status of communities before *amicitia* had been formed with Rome, is an aspect of Roman diplomatic relations that has not previously been sufficiently treated in the literature. Equally, the status of communities *after* they received *libertas* has not been treated in any systematic way.

The stages highlighted here serve to provide background information on which to base an evaluation of the nature of the senate's response to the Jewish embassy in 162 BCE. The impact of this study, on the question of the nature of Jewish relations in 162 BCE, is highly significant. The conclusion that both *amicitia* and *foedera* were entered into only with independent entities exerts considerable influence on the interpretation of the senate's response to the Jewish embassy.

## The historical circumstances

The assignment of the status of *foedus* to the document in 1 Macc. 8.23–32 does not sit well with the historical circumstances at the time of the Jewish Embassy, as was noted by Mendelssohn.[138] There are two issues at stake here. First, is whether in 162 BCE the Jews could be considered independent; second, there is the problem of both the Jews and the Seleucids having treaty relations with Rome. Briefly stated, the Jews were not eligible to conclude a treaty with Rome as they were still subjects of the Seleucid Empire; the Seleucids themselves, moreover, had their own treaty relationship with Rome.[139] This was the position in international relations as stated by Niese, namely that an alliance could only be concluded with an independent community, which the Jews were not as they were legally subjects of the Seleucids. The latter were friends and allies of Rome and both they and their territory stood in a firm treaty relationship with the Republic. In addition, an alliance with the rebellious Jews would have caused severe formal difficulties with Rome, which the Romans did not view lightly. Despite all the ruthlessness in politics, the Romans held themselves exactly to the decorum and forms of international law.[140] Moreover, Roman recognition of the Jewish rebels as allies of the Romans would have been close to a declaration of war by Rome on Demetrius.[141]

The main response to the argument that the issue of sovereignty and independence posed a problem with regard to a Jewish treaty came from Täubler. He maintained that there was a break in Seleucid sovereignty over the Jews and that the friendship with Rome was terminated on the death of each Seleucid ruler and had to be renewed.[142] He believed that each king required recognition by Rome. In the case of Demetrius, Täubler held that, at the time of the Jewish embassy, Demetrius had not yet had the friendship with Rome renewed. This happened only with Demetrius' own embassy to Rome in 160/59 BCE. Consequently, in Täubler's view, Rome at the time of the Jewish embassy was not bound in friendship to the Seleucids and there existed no impediment to Roman recognition of autonomy to parts of Syrian territory. This view has found majority support.[143] Objections may be made to Täubler's hypothesis by first examining whether in fact friendship and alliance between Rome and the Seleucids did expire on the death of each Seleucid ruler. A second objection, raised by several scholars, is that the Romans had no set practice of recognising kings. The third question is whether Demetrius was recognised by Rome as king.

There exist differing views on the durability of diplomatic relations with kingdoms, specifically whether they were for the lifetime of the ruler only or not.[144] Additionally, there is scholarly debate over the issue of whether Rome made a regular practice of recognising kings at all.[145] In the older literature, it was held with confidence that friendship and alliance between Rome and a king was extinguished on the death of a king. This was once a widely held view.[146] Certainly, the basis of relations between Rome and the Seleucids in this period, the treaty of Apamea, was to be for all time.[147] Similarly, the Roman treaty with Massinissa, according to Diodorus 28.7, was not limited in time. The one clear reference to the renewal of a treaty is to be found in Livy 42.25.4, where he reports the renewal of the treaty between Rome and the king of Macedonia. Most now accept Heuss' discussion on this passage, in which he remarks that the renewal was made by Perseus under duress from Rome to test his loyalty because the senate wanted to force him to declare his hand in the build-up to the Third Macedonian War.[148]

This single and singular example is commonly cited to uphold the proposition that the alliance with Macedon expired with the death of Philip V, but it does not provide a basis for the formulation of any general principle outside the field of the special circumstances surrounding the situation of Perseus.

Heuss also pointed out that, while it is true that the expression *amicitiam renouare* is found in our sources, the meaning of the expression only becomes clear in each individual context. The passage in Livy 42.6.8, 10 is a verbal request from Apollonius, the envoy of Antiochus IV. This is likewise the case in the request of Ariarathes in 163 BCE.[149] If it were a correct theory that friendship with Rome was a purely personal tie, one would anticipate a reference in the sources to justify the new relationship, whereas the sources refer to an already-existing relationship. The appearance of Eumenes before the senate is frequently used to support this theory. Heuss examined the report in Polyb. 21.20.6 concerning this incident with Eumenes and concluded that, because the king tells the senate he has maintained the same policy as his father towards the Romans, this assurance makes a renewal unnecessary. In another example, a renewal of friendship is mentioned in 173 BCE during the course of a Roman legation to Egypt.[150] Its purpose was to confirm Egypt's loyalty in the lead-up to the Third Macedonian War and it was not connected with the coming of age of Ptolemy Philometer.[151] One might also mention in this context the embassy of Attalus to Rome in 152 BCE, seven years after he came to the throne. If one holds to Heuss' position, there was, in fact, no break in diplomatic relations with Rome on the death of a ruler. Applying this to the situation with the Jews in 162 BCE, it would mean that on the death of Antiochus IV (and Antiochus V) the *amicitia* relationship established by the treaty of Apamea (which was for all time) was not terminated, and that any treaty between the Romans and the Jews would have interfered with this *amicitia*.

The second premise of Täubler is that Rome had an established practice of recognising new kings when they first came to the throne. This view has been followed by several scholars.[152] When a new ruler came to the throne, Rome naturally wanted to know whether he would follow the same policies and whether he would uphold the existing treaty provisions with Rome. The issue for Rome was, in effect, whether or not the king would follow the previous policy of loyalty to Rome or break diplomatic ties.[153] In two places, Polybius reports that foreign kings – namely, Hiero of Syracuse and the Ptolemaic king – had to give Rome assurances that they would take over the alliances and policies vis-à-vis Rome of their predecessor.[154] The passages commonly cited to demonstrate a 'renewal of friendship' or renewal of a treaty, do not bear out this theory. Rather, they show that kings came to Rome to demonstrate their loyalty to an already-existing and continuing relationship.[155] The timing of these embassies has more to do with crises for the rulers and their need to be reassured that Rome supported them. Their embassies sought to intensify an alliance, one that continued to be in force.[156] By his secret escape from Rome, Demetrius had overruled the senate's decisions that he remain a hostage. Under these circumstances, there could be no *amicitia* between Demetrius and Rome.

The third question raised by Täubler was Roman recognition of Demetrius as king. Apart from the fact that the whole practice of Rome recognising kings was discounted previously, what, in fact, Demetrius' status in Rome was as king of Syria is a subject much debated.[157] Demetrius' first embassy to Rome occurs after the Jewish mission in 160/59 BCE and finds mention in Diodorus (31.30) and Polybius (32.3.11–13), both of whom say that the senate left the matter open so that in the future Rome would have some hold over the king. These statements would seem to indicate that, prior to 160 BCE, Rome was not on cordial terms with Demetrius. Nor do the actions of Ti. Sempronius Gracchus (cos. 177, 163) as envoy on Rhodes imply any recognition, although he may have considered himself a 'kingmaker'.[158] The senate may not have welcomed the news that Demetrius had proclaimed himself king, but neither did it launch a war against him, showing that it was not yet prepared to go back on its friendship and alliance with the Seleucids, a bond that remained unbroken. There was a distinct chill in relations between Rome and the Seleucids, whether the friendship was renounced or just put in abeyance as Rome did with Rhodes between 167 and 164 BCE. Our sources do not discuss any contact with Demetrius until after Judas' death. Therefore, from the Roman point of view, the Republic still had formal diplomatic relations with Syria, which any treaty with the Jews would have called into question. The Jews were still labouring under the military forces of the Seleucids and were not universally recognised as free. Heuss, in his study of the relationship between Hellenistic rulers and the cities under them, concluded that sovereignty lay *de facto* with the ruler who held military control over them.[159]

The situation in Judaea in 162 BCE was that, after a truce had restored to the Jews their right to practise their own religion, renewed fighting broke out over the imposition of Alcimus, a Seleucid appointee, as High Priest. Control of Jerusalem was still not totally in the hands of the Jews, as they had not yet been able to expel the Seleucid garrison from the Akra. This garrison had been imposed by Antiochus IV after the failed revolt of Jason in 168 BCE and it was not removed until 141 BCE.[160] In 162 BCE the Jews could not claim sovereignty over Jerusalem and the Seleucids still had sovereignty over them. A prior condition for formal diplomatic relations was that one be *in sua potestate*, which the Jews were not. Herein lies the reason a treaty was not possible and a declaration of *libertas* was required. An interval of time occurred between *libertas* and a *foedus* at a later stage. In the course of one embassy, only *libertas* or *libertas* with *amicitia* would have been possible in 162 BCE.

## Declaration of *libertas* prior to *amicitia*

The informal (meaning without legal form) *amicitia*, which resulted from an exchange of embassies, was confined to friendship between equally ranked partners. For *amicitia* to be formed with a community, whose independence was not universally recognised, a prior step of a unilateral declaration of *libertas* was required in order to overcome the ambiguous status of the petitioning community. *Amicitia* between Rome and an inferior community whose status as autonomous was questionable required a declaration of *libertas*. After this step, a declaration of *amicitia* by the senate could be made, followed by registration in the list of friends and allies.[161] The threefold sequence operated in practice for states whose independence was not universally recognised. Kienast used the Spanish city of Saguntum as one of his examples of this three-stage process. In his view, the city had received *libertas* as part of the terms of the treaty between Rome and Carthage in 226 BCE, according to Livy (21.2.7), who reports *duorum populorum libertas seruaretur*; that is, that both sides swore to uphold the state of independence of the Saguntines that had previously existed. Then in 218 BCE, Cn. Cornelius Scipio renewed old alliances in Spain and formed new ones – *renouandis societatibus, partim nouis instituendis*, as recorded in Livy 21.60.3 – in an area that also included Saguntum. In this place, we see that Livy has used *societas* when it equally conforms with *amicitia*.[162] Appian (*Ill.* 11) reported the debate in the senate; here the view prevailed that the Saguntines had not been inscribed as allies and so were merely free and autonomous. Appian's report mentions the concluding stage in the sequence of diplomatic relations; namely, enrolment in the list of friends and allies. What Kienast was able to show was a three-stage process that moved from a declaration of *libertas* to *societas* without a treaty and moving on to enrolment in the *formula amicorum*. In essence, the process of three stages, all of which could be achieved at the same time, was followed by an enrolment in the list of the friends and allies of the Roman people.

For the Jews, if they wished to have diplomatic ties with Rome, they first were required to be free and autonomous with the freedom to have their own foreign policy. The Romans were able to grant them that autonomy through a unilateral declaration of *libertas* in the senate. This was a diplomatic procedure that had become very common for the Romans to use in the Greek East in the second century.

## A declaration of *libertas*

Declarations of *libertas* were the instruments of diplomacy *par excellence* for the Romans in their dealings with the Greek East.[163] To be sure, the very word *libertas* was hard to quarrel with and the wild scenes of joy at Corinth when Flamininus announced the freedom of the Greeks may be a measure of how such declarations were received. Declarations were made to cities and to peoples alike. Most commonly they were a means around which to arrange a peace settlement and the concomitant redistribution of conquered territory over which Rome did not want direct rule. Not all declarations were alike in their wording and not all declarations conferred the same rights. The central feature argued in this section is that declarations of *libertas* conferred real rights and were not in every case mere slogans or instruments of propaganda. This is not to say that the Romans failed to make use of them to disseminate the view that they were not conquerors but benefactors. How these declarations were used can be found in our sources, but has not been highlighted in discussions about *libertas*. Finally, the publication of these declarations on the Capitol in Rome has been known for some time, but has not been incorporated into the debate on *libertas*. If the work of Gauger is to be assessed fully, his introduction of declarations of *libertas* into the debate over how the senate responded to the Jewish request in 162 BCE has to be measured against the yardstick of what is known about such declarations.

### *The constituent elements of a declaration of libertas*

The principal constituent elements of a declaration of *libertas* were that the city, or community, or people, be free and autonomous and that it, or they, be free from garrisons, tribute and kings. All were declared free, but not all were declared autonomous. Of those declarations listed in Table 6.2, autonomy was only given in 196 BCE to the Greeks of Asia Minor, Lampsacus, Illyria and the Galatians. From this it is clear that *libertas* and *autonomia* were not synonymous.

Freedom from garrisons was not common to all declarations. This provision occurs in the freedom of the Greeks proclamation in 196 BCE, where it is clear that the removal of Roman garrisons is meant.[164] However, Appian (*Mac.* 3), using a source independent of Polybius, gives the more universal version of this right, which is simply freedom from foreign garrisons. In the case of the freedom of the Greeks of Asia Minor, the removal of the garrisons of Antiochus is meant.[165] When in 167 BCE Rome speaks of the removal of garrisons from Macedonia, the garrisons of the king are meant.[166]

Exemption from tribute was a sign of being free. Only subjects paid tribute. The opposite of a *populus liber* is *populus stipendiarius* or *subjectus*.[167] When Flamininus announced the freedom of the Greeks and of the Greeks of Asia Minor, he declared that they were subject to no tribute (ἀφορολογήτους).[168] So strong was this association that the case of Macedonia was hard to fit into this pattern, yet it was made to conform. The importance of Macedonia is precisely because it broke this pattern.[169] Badian considered that the Macedonian settlement was the first known case of the disassociation of *immunitas* from *libertas*.[170]

A declaration of *libertas* provided freedom from monarchy. In Livy there is often found a theme of two opposing political systems – namely, monarchy and republic – in order to highlight the Roman Republic. Livy quotes from the letter of Antiochus to Prusias (37.25.5) that Rome stood opposed to monarchy, but it is in the general nature of things that this should be so and that others viewed the Romans as the common enemies of all kings.[171] The Rhodians contrast the freedom of their democratic island state with kings who bring only enslavement to their will.[172]

In the case of Macedonia, the aristocratic supporters of the king had to be deported because, as Macedonian heads of the kingdom, they represented *regnum* that stood opposed to *leges* and especially the Roman law that Aemilius Paullus introduced. Livy (45.32.5) makes this connection between *libertas* and *leges* on the one hand, and monarchy and its aristocratic supporters on the other. Especially noteworthy in this context is the expression *aequa libertas*, which for the Romans represented the equality before the law of the patricians and the plebeians.[173] Only the Roman constitution – that is to say, a republic – guaranteed *libertas*, and it is this freedom that the Romans bestowed on those they have conquered – that is,

*Table 6.2* Declarations of *libertas* in the East 196–165 BCE

| *Date* | *Place/people* | *Sources* |
|---|---|---|
| 196 BCE | 'The Freedom of the Greeks' | Polyb. 18.46.5,15; Livy 33.32.5, 33.5–7, 34.41.3, 39.37.10; Plut. *Flam.* 10.4, 12.2; App. *Mac.* 9.4 |
| 196 BCE | 'The Freedom of the Greeks of Asia' | Polyb. 18.44.2, 67.1, 50.7; Livy 33.20.2, 34.3; Plut. *Flam.* 12.1; App. *Syr.* 3 |
| 196 BCE | Euromus, Pedasa, Iasus, Abydos, Thasos, Myrina, Perinthus | Polyb. 18.44.4 |
| 196 BCE | Bargylia | Polyb. 18.44.4, 48.2; Livy 33.30.3, 35.3 |
| 196 BCE | Thessaly | Livy 33.34.7 |
| 196 BCE | Magnesians, Perrhaebians and Dolopians | Livy 33.34.6 |
| 196 BCE | Oreus, Eretria and Carystus | Livy 33.34.10 |
| 196 BCE | Hephaestia | Polyb. 18.48.2; Livy 33.35.2 |
| 196 BCE | The Orestae | Livy 33.34.6 |
| 196 BCE | Lampsacus | Livy 43.6.7–10; *Syll.* 2.591 |
| 196 BCE | Kios | Polyb. 18.44.5 |
| 193 BCE | Teos | *Syll.* 2601 |
| 192 BCE | Chalcis | Livy 35.46.9–11, 35.39.3 |
| 192 BCE | The Magnetes | Livy 35.31.8–15, 39.6 |
| 191 BCE | The Ciani | Livy 33.30.4 |
| 190 BCE | Phocaea | Polyb. 21.45.6; Livy 37.32.1, 38.39.12 |
| 190–189 BCE | Mytilene | Vell. Pat. II.18 |
| 190–189 BCE | Smyrna | Polyb. 21.22; Livy 35.42; Polyb. 21.48; Livy 38.39 |
| 189 BCE | Priene | *Syll.*[4] 588 |
| 189/88 BCE | Soli | Polyb. 21.24.10–15 |
| 189 BCE (?) | Tabae | Livy 38.13.11–13; *OGIS* II.442 |
| 189 and 186 BCE | Delphi | Plin. N.H. 4.7; Sherk, *RDGE* No. 1 |
| 188 BCE | Cyme | Livy 37.11.5; Polyb. 21.48 ;Livy 38.39 |
| 188 BCE | Heraclea-by-Latmos | *SIG* II.618 |
| 188 BCE | Dardanus | Livy 38.39.10 |
| 188 BCE | Tenedos | Livy 38.39.10 |
| 188 BCE | Clazomenae | Kaibel, *Inscr.Gr. Sic. et Ital.* 951 |
| 188 BCE | Erythrae | Polyb. 21.48; Livy 38.39.11 |
| 188 BCE | Chios | Polyb. 21.48; Livy 38.39.11 |
| 188 BCE | Colophon and Notium | Polyb. 21.48; Liv. 38.39 |
| 188 BCE | Miletus | Polyb. 21.48; Liv. 38.39; *Syll.* I.240 |
| 188 BCE | Antiochia in Pisidia | Strabo 12.8.14 |
| 188 BCE | Mylasa | Polyb. 30.5.11–15; Livy 45.25.11 |
| 187 BCE | Ambracia | Livy 38.44.4 |
| 179 BCE | Cyzicus | Polyb. 25.2.13 |
| 170 BCE | Abdera | Livy 43.4.8–13 |
| 170 BCE | Lampsacus | Livy 43.6.8–10 |
| 171–169 BCE (?) | Alabanda | *REG* 11 (1898) 258–266, lines 25–32 |
| 169 BCE | Agassae | Livy 44.7.5 |
| 167 BCE | Taulantii | Livy 45.26.12 |

| | | |
|---|---|---|
| 167BCE | Dassaretis | Livy 27.32.9, 45.26.13–15; Strabo C 316 and 318 |
| 167 BCE | Macedonia and Illyria | Livy 45.18.1–3, 26.12–15, 29.4; Diod. 31.8 |
| 167 BCE | Issa | Livy 45.26.12 |
| 167 BCE | Risinium and Olcinium | Livy 45.26.14 |
| 167 BCE | Dyrrhacium | Livy 42.48.8; 45.43.10 |
| 167 BCE | Daorsei | Livy 45.26.14 |
| 167 BCE | Pirustae | Livy 45.26.12 |
| 167 BCE | Carians and Lycians | Livy 45.25.6; Polyb. 30.5.12; *ILLRP* I.174 |
| 167 BCE | Magnesians and Dolopians | Livy 41.22.4, 23.13, 24.8; 54.13.8 |
| 167 BCE | Ainos and Maronea | Polyb. 30.3.7 |
| 167 BCE | Rhodos | Liv. 44.14.9; 45.25.7 |
| 166 BCE | Stratonicea and Caunus | Polyb. 30.21.3 |
| 166/65 BCE | The Galatians | Polyb. 30.19, 28, 30.6 |

the freedom from tyranny. It is clear that the Cappadocians understood *libertas* as such, for they refused the Roman gift of *libertas* because they could not live without a king.[174]

The declaration of *libertas* included 'the right to use one's own laws', which encompassed both law and custom. This privilege was granted by the senate to the Greeks in 196 BCE at the Isthmian Games. Both Livy and Appian purport to be quoting from the text of the *senatus consultum*, whose wording they transmit in this manner. Livy uses what became a much-repeated phrase, *suis legibus esse iubet* (33.32.5), whereas Appian gives more detail, ἰδίοις ἤθεσι καὶ νόμοις χρῆσθαι. Here Appian has elaborated to indicate that *leges* or *nomos* are to be interpreted not just as law but also as custom. Polybius, while claiming to quote only the chief points, does use two modes of expression.[175] In the first place (18.46.5) he speaks of the right to be 'governed by their countries' laws' (νόμοις χρωμένους τοῖς πατρίοις), which can also be translated as 'ancestral law'. In the second location (18.46.15), he uses the expression the right to be 'governed by their own laws' (νόμοις χρωμένους τοῖς ἰδίοις). Plutarch, however, understands what was granted by the Romans as νόμοις χρωμένους τοῖς πατρίοις (*Flam.* 10.4). As regards what was granted to the Greeks of Asia, Polybius only uses the one form of words in two passages. In 18.44.2 he says they were granted νόμοις χρῆσθαι τοῖς ἰδίοις and in 18.46.15 he says νόμοις χρωμένους τοῖς ἰδίοις. When it comes to the freedom declaration for Phocaea in 188 BCE, we find both Livy and Polybius in agreement as to what was meant. Livy (38.39.12) writes, *ut legibus antiquis uterentur permissum*. Polybius more interestingly writes of the 'ancestral constitution', τὸ πάτριον πολίτευμα (21.45.7).

The declarations of *libertas* for the Orestae and for Phocaea mention the restoration of laws.[176] The reason Rome granted the Orestae the privilege of the restoration of their laws was because they had been the first to revolt from the Philip V. Phocaea in 190 BCE had their laws restored, which are termed 'ancient laws'. This phrase, *legibus antiquis*, is not commonly used by Livy; it is found in only two other places.[177]

Our sources equate 'one's own laws' with ancestral custom or ancestral constitution. Where it was not possible to revive the ancient laws, Rome imposed on the freed community a constitution that allowed for elections. From the point of view of Rome, those who did not live under the domination of a king and who were allowed a constitution by Rome were considered free.[178] Pompeius Trogus shows how Roman control first brought elections and then law. In Justinus' Epitome of his work, it is reported, *Ita cum in dicionem Romanorum cessisset, magistratibus per singulas ciuitates constitutis libera facta eat legesque, quibus adhuc utitur, a Paulo accepit* (33.2.7). Examples of the Roman introduction of a constitution include Magnesia, Lampsacus, Teos and Alabanda. In Macedonia in 167 BCE the Romans imposed a new constitution to replace the monarchy that they abolished.[179] Another example of an imposed constitution, though one that proved more popular and long lasting, comes from Thessaly. We learn from an inscription that the constitution that Flamininus put in place for Thessaly was still in place half a century later. The Narthakieins in c. 140 BCE invoke these Thessalian laws in their land dispute with Melitaia. They claimed that previous arbitration in this matter had been in their favour 'in accordance with Thessalian laws which they enjoy up to the present moment and which the consul T. Quinctius Flamininus had granted them on the advice of the ten *legati*, approved by a decree of the senate.'[180]

In summary, *libertas* was characterised by some or all of the following: autonomy, freedom from garrisons, immunity from tribute, and freedom from kings.[181] The history of Rome, in having overthrown her own kings, gave credence to her ability to uphold freedom from monarchy. Law was an important component of *libertas* and the declaration from the republican government of Rome, for *libertas* was the symbol of self-government as opposed to the rule of a king. The right to live according to one's own laws included law, ancestral custom and ancestral constitution. *Libertas* provided political and religious autonomy and was underwritten by the power of Rome. Roman power after 168 BCE demonstrated that Rome was able to guarantee the *libertas* that the senate granted.

### *The use of declarations of libertas by the Romans*

When Rome used freedom declarations after her victories over Philip V and Antiochus III, she was making the statement that she did not intend to rule simply on the basis that she was the victor. Those states that received their freedom from Rome came under an obligation to the city. In two places Livy refers to *libertas* as a gift given by Rome where *libertas* is a *beneficium*.[182] Trogus also refers to *libertas* as a gift with regard to the senate's handling of the settlement of Cappadocia.[183] Evidence such as this caused Badian to describe cities and peoples with *libertas* as independent but morally bound to Rome, demonstrating their thanks to Rome by supplying her with material and military aid.[184]

In the second century, declarations of freedom became the means to keep both friends and enemies within the boundaries that Rome wished. How Rome used this depended on the situation. A declaration of freedom could be used to designate a sphere of influence that could be used to keep an opponent under control.[185] The freedom declaration was a guarantee to those threatened by Rome's opponent, but not a watertight one, as Rome could decide arbitrarily whether to regard violations of these freedoms as a *casus belli* or not.

The declaration of *libertas* could also be used to punish a friend or ally whose expansion Rome wished to halt.[186] Generally, these were Greek cities that still had some sort of dependency on a Hellenistic monarch. When Polybius spoke of Antiochus III's neutrality towards Rome (21.43.2), he also included the cities that were his subjects and their territories.[187] Although these cities were legally sovereign, they still had to bow to the indirect will of the king. Yet this relationship varied according to the degree of strength of the monarch or according to the rise and fall of his power. Hence, in periods of weakness or if the monarch were distant and preoccupied elsewhere in the empire, such states took the opportunity to expand their territory and increase their regional power.[188]

Indeed, the threat that *libertas* posed to the Seleucid Empire should not be underestimated. It was a potent weapon that the Romans used against Antiochus III and which he could not ignore. The 'autonomous' cities of Asia Minor received their status from Antiochus as a privilege to be held on condition of their loyalty. They were not members of the Seleucid Empire, bound as Crete or Lydia were, and so were vulnerable to the Roman declaration that they be free. Other cities such as Smyrna and Lampsacus would soon have followed this example. Ultimately, in order to hold on to his empire, Antiochus had to go to war with Rome.[189] After defeating Antiochus, the Romans assumed the role of arbiter, taking the place of the king, over complaints from the Seleucid cities.[190] Examples of seeking complaints against the Seleucids include the embassies of P. Sulpicius Galba, and the legation that offered to support the cause of the Jews before the Seleucid king.[191] Just one successful revolt from Hellenistic monarchy would have precipitated a wholesale dissolution of such empires. Roman policy exploited this situation. Their success may be seen in the concern expressed by King Eumenes in 189 BCE that Rome's freedom programme was detrimental to the very existence of monarchy.[192]

An example of a declaration of *libertas* to a state that had indirect ties to the Seleucids was Teos. We can see that Teos wanted to present its independent status to the international community because it also arranged other *asylia* decrees with Greek and Cretan communities. Rome was ready to agree to the request of the Teans because in 193 BCE it was anxious to portray itself as the defender of Greek liberty in Asia Minor and Antiochus III as the oppressor of Greek freedom. In the declaration of ἀσυλία for Teos, the term did not confine itself to mean only asylum in the temple precincts but rather the inviolability of the whole city and its territory. There exists no example where a temple was first given ἀσυλία and then following this precedent the privilege was extended to the city and lands.[193]

Another purpose of Roman unilateral declarations of *libertas* was to provide a guarantee of territorial integrity. This idea was raised by Dahlheim,[194] who meant by this that such declarations defined the Roman sphere of interest. In the second century, Rome used this as her diplomatic means to hold both friends and enemies within the boundaries that the Romans desired. Dahlheim suggests that there were two possible ways in which *libertas* worked to further Rome's aim to set territorial limits in the Greek East. First, the declaration was used against an opponent who also wanted possession of the city or territory that the Romans declared free and by doing so Rome declared her own sphere of interests.[195] Secondly, as a consequence, it could be used to limit the possibility of expansion of a friend or ally.

A third purpose was to free a city or people from Hellenistic monarchy. Sherwin-White strongly argues that this was the chief reason for a declaration of *libertas* by Rome. 'Freedom means freedom from a king, and the sign of this freedom is the abolition of the royal tax and the withdrawal of the royal garrison.'[196] So the Greeks also understood that freeing meant freedom from the control of a king or from a certain king.[197] The Romans also saw *libertas* as the means to free from royal control.[198] That Rome had freed herself from her kings and had became a republic leant considerable weight to this claim of Rome to be opposed to monarchy.[199] The once-popular view that Rome's hatred of *regnum* stemmed from her own regal period has now been revised to a date in the late third to early second centuries BCE and reflects Rome's feelings not towards her own distant past but towards Hellenistic monarchy.[200] The first reliable use of the word *rex* as an invective comes from Cato in the year 190 BCE.[201] The turning point came when Rome faced the ambitions of Philip V. The Romans soon gained a reputation for wanting to depose kings and eliminate monarchies. This can be seen in the fear of Prusias of Bithynia, which the Scipio brothers tried to allay by giving him a letter setting forth how Rome had helped many kings.[202] Perseus of Macedon claimed that Rome wanted to remove all kings whose kingdoms were near the area of Roman power.[203] That Rome put fear into all kings is the message of a Sibylline oracle from the late 2nd century.[204] Both Polybius and Livy wrote on the theme that *libertas* and *regnum* were incompatible.[205] Rome's image as the defender of the freedom of the Greeks was credible precisely because Rome herself was a republic, having eradicated her earlier monarchy.[206]

The fourth reason Rome why used declarations of liberty was to free a state already under another's sovereignty so that there would be no legal problem in later concluding further diplomatic relations with them. Only *amicitia* could be formed after the declaration of *libertas* in the same session of the senate and without an interval of years.

In Roman diplomatic relations, the unilateral declaration of *libertas* issued by the senate served several valuable functions, not all of them propagandistic. They could effect a settlement of peace, as, for example, the settlement for Macedonia and Illyria in 167 BCE, or designate spheres of influence, or settle territorial disputes. They were utilised to alter the division of territory made after the treaty of Apamea. Functionally, they could break up hostile federations, guarantee territorial integrity, free a people or city from Hellenistic monarchy, or prepare the legal grounds for a later *foedus*. Such *senatus consulta* declared the city or people free and autonomous and gave them freedom from tribute and garrisons. These were concrete rights and not mere slogans. These declarations were often, but not always, granted after the act of *deditio* or surrender to Rome. Declarations of *libertas* were often published on bronze tablets on the Capitol and several examples have been found in Rome.[207]

## Indications of a declaration of *libertas* for the Jews

The declaration of *libertas* came into play when the prospective ally was not autonomous in an internationally recognised sense. The process by which a unilateral declaration of *libertas* by the senate was made and published was as follows. The senate passed a resolution, which was generally in response to a petition from a delegation of envoys. In other cases, a senator raised the matter. Where the declaration of *libertas* was in response to the petition of foreign envoys, the senatorial decision was conveyed in a letter. There are extant examples of letters that convey the fact that the senate has granted *libertas*. These include the letter to King Prusias of Bithynia regarding *libertas* to the Ciani in 196 BCE, the letter of M. Valerius Messala to Teos, and the letter of the Scipio brothers to Heraclea-on-Latmos in 190 BCE.[208]

Senatorial declarations of *libertas* were not lengthy. The words to look for were fairly simple. It was enough to say, as Gauger suggested: 'Was den Senat anginge, so sei es ihm recht, dass die Juden autonom und frei sein und nach ihren eigenen Gesetzen leben sollten.'[209] Explicit testimony for a declaration of *libertas* may be found in Justinus 36.3.9, where we translate the passage as follows: 'When they had revolted from Demetrius, having requested the friendship of the Romans, they, the first of all Eastern peoples, received liberty; whereupon, the Romans willingly granted it, [that is, liberty] from a foreign power.'[210] In this passage Justinus separates *amicitiam petere* from *libertatem accipere* – that is, between the wish of the Jews to obtain friendship and the reaction of the senate in offering *libertas*.[211] Corroborating evidence is also found in Diodorus 40.2, which reports that the Jews had received 'freedom and autonomy' prior to 63 BCE from the Roman Senate. There is no talk here of a treaty when the envoys went to Rome at the time of Demetrius, being Demetrius I.[212]

In addition to these two extracts, there are indications of a declaration of *libertas* from within the text of 1 Macc. 8.18–32. The plea of the envoys, as given in verse 18, was that Rome might 'lift the yoke' of Seleucid slavery from them (καὶ τοῦ ἆραι τὸν ζυγὸν ἀπ' αὐτῶν). Then verse 31 refers to the yoke upon our (the Romans') friends in the senatorial letter to Demetrius (Διὰ τί ἐβάρυνας τὸν ζυγόν σου ἐπὶ τοὺς φίλους ἡμῶν τοὺς συμμάχους Ιουδαίους).[213] The word 'yoke' was both a Jewish and Roman metaphor for slavery and servitude. The

Septuagint has many references to the yoke of slavery.[214] Attention has been drawn in verse 31 to the Hebraism of הכביד עול.[215] The Romans referred to the yoke of slavery when they spoke of the rule of Philip V, according to Polybius 4.35.7. Likewise, in the freedom declaration for Macedonia and Illyria, those still ruled by kings were likened to slaves.[216] The juxtaposition of *seruitudo* and *libertas* is a favourite theme of Livy.[217]

From verses 18 and 31, it is clear that there was a mutual interest on the part of the Romans and the Jews to liberate Judaea from Seleucid rule.[218] The Romans themselves saw the freedom declaration as a means to free peoples from Hellenistic monarchy. This is asserted by Strabo, when he mentions the freedom of Antiocheia in Pisidia that occurred in 188 BCE.[219] The message from the eulogy to the Romans in 1 Macc. 8.1–16 is that the Romans are feared by kings and that they can make and break kings.[220] So the embassy of the Jews, in using an expression familiar to the Romans, 'the yoke of slavery', was indicating their desire for *libertas*, in the same way that a slave was liberated. In asking to be freed of Seleucid rule, they are using the biblical language with which the envoys were familiar and also language that the Romans themselves tended to use. Such a petition fell on receptive Roman ears. The senate, in hearing such words, would have responded with the diplomatic instrument that they had been using against Hellenistic kings consistently from at least 196 BCE – namely, the declaration of *libertas*.

Other indications that the Jews may have received such a declaration from the senate may be found in 1 Macc. 8.23–32. In verse 26 there is mention of the Jews' obligation to supply weapons (ὅπλα) in the event that Rome should call on them for military aid. This mention of the Jews supplying arms in a conflict in the international sphere of action meant that the Romans already had granted to the Jews the *right* to use weapons. Such a right, by its very nature, is a recognition of the independence of the Jews.[221] Therefore we may see verse 26 as an indication that, prior to the declaration of *amicitia*, the Jews had received *libertas*, whose definition in the context of *amicitia et societas* incorporated the right to bear arms. This verse is one illustration of the reason why the Romans required a community to be independent before concluding most forms of diplomatic relations. The obligation to supply military aid to the Romans necessitates certain aspects of autonomy to be able to fulfil this requirement.

It was shown above that the chief obligation attendant on those with *libertas* was the maintenance of unquestioned loyalty and any failure to fulfil this duty was punished severely. In 1 Macc. 8.23–32 there occur quite frequently clauses that pledge loyalty. Thus in verse 25 is written καρδίᾳ πλήρει, while in verse 26 there is καὶ φυλάξονται τὰ φυλάγματα and οὐθὲν λαβόντες. In the Roman treaties preserved in Greek, these phrases are not found. If one compares such phrases with what is found in inscriptionally extant Roman treaties, a different picture emerges. For purposes of comparison, the fullest treaty, that of Maroneia, will be used. In lines 16, 20 and 28 the same phrase is repeated 'with wicked deceit' (δόλῳ πονηρῷ). No other loyalty phrase is employed.

The loyalty clauses in the Jewish document are expressed in much stronger language. The expression καρδίᾳ πλήρει in verse 25 has been translated literally by Abel and Schunck.[222] Bévenot was probably closer to the mark when he gave as a translation 'mit voller Hingebung' ('with complete dedication'). The degree of compliance to Rome's wishes implicit in this phrase was made clear by Knabenbauer, who translated καρδίᾳ πλήρει as 'corde pleno i. e. sincero, ut scil. toti se impendant utilitati Romanorum'.[223] In verse 26 καὶ φυλάξονται τὰ φυλάγματα is a biblical phrase.[224] Schunck conveys the obligations the Jews owe the Romans in his translation: 'und sie werden ihre Verpflichtungen halten'.[225] The binding nature of such a clause is made clear by Knabenbauer: 'Praeterea Iudaei φυλάξονται τὰ φυλάγματα αὐτῶν obseruabunt quae obseruanda erunt, quae ipsis a Romanis praescribentur'.[226] The phrase οὐθὲν λαβόντες has been variously translated as 'without taking anything from them' or 'sans recevoir de garantie'.[227] The force and impact of these loyalty clauses goes far beyond what is found in extant Roman treaties. Their inclusion is more typical of the loyalty to Rome demanded from *ciuitates liberae*.

However, the principal evidence from the text itself of 1 Macc. 8.20–32 that the Jews received a declaration of *libertas*, remains the last two verses, 31 and 32. Before discussing them, one needs to make a small digression in order to explain the reasons for considering these verses an integral part of the text from verse 23 to verse 32. This is not the accepted opinion. This letter is considered a 'rider' to the so-called Roman–Jewish treaty.[228] Generally, it is considered to have been written by the envoys themselves. Evidence for the authorship comes from the Semitic expressions in the letter. Grimm remarked on these and has been followed by most scholars ever since.[229] Goldstein considers the letter authentic, whereas others do not.[230] Chapter 5 devoted some space to discussing the Semitisms and Aramaisms in the whole of the text from 1 Macc. 8.23–32. Perhaps now is the time to explain why the letter in verses 31 to 32 should more properly be regarded as belonging to the one piece of text that begins with verse 23. Literary analysis has given scholars a number of tools with which to approach texts. Williams is the first to apply these techniques to the First Book of Maccabees. In his work on the structure of 1 Maccabees, Williams took as his starting point the little-remarked-upon feature of repetition in the book. This feature provides signals for unravelling the structure of a work.[231] While Williams applied literary analysis on a macro scale in his investigation of the structure of the whole of the First Book of Maccabees, he understood that it was possible to employ the same techniques on a micro scale, the micro in this case being the passage 1 Macc. 8.23–32.[232]

The letter to Demetrius has been included as proof, but its authenticity has been questioned, most recently by Gauger.[233] One problem with the letter regarding its authenticity is that it was not reproduced in the version of 1 Macc. 8 in Jos. *Ant.* 12.414–418.[234] The majority of scholars follow Grimm, who held that the letter has been transmitted orally.[235] Others who also acknowledge the letter's authenticity believe that it is a letter to the Jewish ambassadors or instructions to the Jews.[236]

In 1 Macc. 8.23–32, a repetition of one phrase in particular catches the eye. In verses 23 and 32 the phrase 'on sea and land' (ἐν τῇ θαλάσσῃ καὶ ἐπὶ τῆς ξηρᾶς) is repeated. This is a unique phrase not found elsewhere in 1 Maccabees. Exact repetition of this sort is called a lexical repetition – that is to say, the recurrence of the same words.[237] When exact repetition occurs, it is done with intent and is worthy of notice.[238] What could be the purpose of this repetition? Repetition was a technique that was used to order material. Technically, in literary analysis, this is known as an *inclusio* (meaning 'a shutting up' or 'a confinement') or 'envelope' structure.[239] The envelope construction brackets a piece of text.[240] It helps to define the parameters of a single passage.[241] The repeated elements act as a frame or border around the unit of text and serve to indicate its limits.[242] An outer envelope delineates the beginning and end of a piece of text. Thus, the *inclusio* in verse 23 and in verse 32 denotes the parameters of the text. That is to say, the text starts ἐν τῇ θαλάσσῃ καὶ ἐπὶ τῆς ξηρᾶς in verse 23 and ends with διὰ τῆς θαλάσσης καὶ διὰ τῆς ξηρᾶ ῖς in verse 32.[243] The conclusion drawn is that the letter to Demetrius in verses 31–32 forms an integral part of the text that contains the Roman–Jewish agreement. The *inclusio* shows that it was originally part of the text and that the letter was written by the same hand as verses 23–32.[244] The repetition of ἐν τῇ θαλάσσῃ καὶ ἐπὶ τῆς ξηρᾶς can in no way be linked to or derived from any known text of a Roman treaty. Many of them do mention 'on land and sea', which one may readily see is the not the same order of the words in 1 Macc. 8 verses 23 and 32 but in fact is phrased in the reverse order. In the treaty of Maroneia in lines 10–11 is found, καὶ κατὰ γῆν καὶ κατὰ θάλασσαν.[245] No repetition of the phrase ἐν τῇ θαλάσσῃ καὶ ἐπὶ τῆς ξηρᾶς occurs in the inscriptions that record Roman treaties or, for that matter, Greek treaties. In other words, there is no *inclusio* in the inscriptionally extant copies of Roman treaties in Greek.

In the Graeco-Roman tradition, the proverbial expression is 'on land and sea'. In the Latin language, the phrase *terra marique*, 'on land and sea', is proverbial and a stock expression.[246] Livy habitually writes *terra marique* in as many as 81 places.[247] In Greek also, the same expression 'on land and sea' is a trope.[248] Treaties between Greek states used the expression μήτε κατὰ γῆν μήτε κατὰ θάλατταν.[249] The reversal of the order of the words is a Semitic turn of phrase, not a Greek or a Latin one.[250] It may be found as early as the Gilgamesh epic. The Jewish expression ἐν τῇ θαλάσσῃ καὶ ἐπὶ τῆς ξηρᾶς in 1 Macc. 8.23 is an imitation of the biblical usage as found in LXX Ex. 14.16 and 22, where it is written as εἰς μέσον τῆς θαλάσσης κατὰ τὸ ξηρά.[251] In Hebrew, especially in poetry, we find a high frequency of 'fixed word pairs', of which 'sea and land' would fall into this category.[252] The Semitic tradition with regard to the motif 'on sea and land' continued into Aramaic, Syriac and Arabic.[253] These word pairs occur not only in poetry but also in other written material.[254] It has been remarked upon that such word pairs are common as a formulaic device in biblical Hebrew in the transfer from oral to written record, especially in the encoding of legislation.[255]

The text in 1 Macc. 8.23 preserves the idiolect of the original idiom. The writer used the language variation that was characteristic to him. From this, we can see that the author was familiar with the Semitic motif. If this document is a re-translation of a Roman treaty then the extant Greek copies show that the Latin motif *terra marique* would have stood in this place in verse 23. The reversal of the word order appears to indicate that ἐν τῇ θαλάσσῃ καὶ ἐπὶ τῆς ξηρᾶς in verse 23 was written by a Jew. Further evidence of a Semitic hand may be seen in the use of the preposition ἐν instead of κατά, which one sees in the Greek copies of Roman treaties. The use of the preposition ἐν is a translation of the Hebrew ב.[256] In only one other place in 1 Maccabees[257] is the expression ἀπὸ τῆς γῆς καὶ (ἀπὸ) τῆς θαλάσσας found, and it is in the narrative concerning the Seleucid king's siege of Dora. This expression is not found in a document that claims to be a cited senatorial letter, a letter from the Romans, which would have used the proverbial expression, *terra marique.* In 1 Macc. 15.14, the work of a translator using a Greek idiolect may be observed. In 1 Macc. 8.23, we can see the careful work of a Jew translating a document word by word without altering its word order. The difference in translation methods can be explained quite simply. 1 Macc. 8.23 is part of a legal document and for legal documents the type of translation used was very literal. Legal language is concerned with precision. Tov remarks that the language of the Septuagint in translating Jewish law reflects the close adherence of the translators to the source language, which was Hebrew.[258] They adhered to the source language to the extent that the word order was preserved.[259] Thus, in 1 Macc. 8.23, as a legal document, the word order is retained as given so that the phrase is written as 'on sea and land'. In 1 Macc. 15.14 this is not a passage from law and so a return to the Greek idiolect is to be expected.

The *inclusio* brackets the text and provides strong grounds for beginning the document of the Roman–Jewish agreement in verse 23 and for concluding it at verse 32, at the end of the letter to Demetrius. The document does not end at verse 30. This would appear to make the letter an integral part of the Roman document and not an addendum.[260]

The search for signs of a declaration of *libertas* remains focused on verses 31 and 32. In these verses is quoted a letter to King Demetrius from the senate, which informs him that the Jews are friends and allies of the Romans and threatens war if the Jews make any further complaint to Rome. This threat falls in the period of the cooling of *amicitia* relations with Rome, when Demetrius, like Rhodes in 167–164 BCE, found himself in limbo: he was neither a friend nor an enemy of Rome. It is not clear whether Demetrius had his friendship with Rome restored in 160/59 BCE. In Chapter 4, we saw the ability of Rome to initiate a war with one who has lost the friendship of the Romans, without any formalities. The letter to Demetrius preserves the correct state of affairs in terms of Roman international law. The example of what happened to Antiochus IV at Eleusis shows that the senate's decision was communicated to the king by letter. The practice of the Roman Senate when it freed a community from the control of a monarch, was also to write to the king concerned. The letter to Demetrius accords with the usual custom of the senate in its communication of threats to kings. That there were no consequences to the letter, may be explained by the attitude of Demetrius at the time: being out of favour in Rome, he sent no embassy to repair the damage. His *amicitia* with Rome was fractured and he may not have considered himself bound any longer by it such that the Roman precept that two friends should not fight each other did not apply to him. He may have thought that the Romans had no authority to order him to cease his war in Judaea.

Another example of a letter from the Roman Senate, is their missive to King Prusias over the freeing of the Ciani.[261] The *senatus consultum* that laid down the terms of the settlement of Greece in 196 BCE instructed Flamininus to write to Prusias about restoring the freedom of Cios.[262] The city of Cios had been disputed between Philip V and Prusias. With the Roman victory over Philip, his former territories were freed. Cios, by the end of the war, was in the possession of Prusias.[263] The Jews, meanwhile, were in Coele-Syria, territory also disputed, in this case between the Ptolemies and the Seleucids. The treaty of Apamea had not mentioned this territory in the peace settlement, as the Ptolemies had hoped. It was not until the underage Ptolemy VI Philometor came solely under the control of his tutors, Eulaeus and Lenaeus, that military preparations were put in train to retake what they considered as their territory.[264] When the campaign threatened to lose them their kingdom, the Romans intervened. Habicht considered that the ultimatum delivered to Antiochus IV at Eleusis to quit Egypt was a modification of the treaty of Apamea. In other words, the boundary of the Taurus Mountains was now supplemented by a boundary to keep out of Egypt and her overseas possessions.[265] In a similar manner, it is possible that the Romans, in response to the petition of the Jewish ambassadors, may have made another adjustment to the treaty of Apamea. Judaea, formerly omitted from the peace settlement of 188 BCE, might now have been included among the other peoples freed by or from that treaty.

Additionally, the text of 1 Macc. 8.20–32 mentions the right of the Jews to bear arms, a right sanctioned by Rome that, in effect, indicated Jewish independence in Roman eyes. Further evidence includes the loyalty clauses in the document in verses 25 and 26 and the letter to Demetrius in verses 31–32.

Why *libertas* was not explicitly stated in 1 Macc. 8.20–32, is bound up with the aims of the author of 1 Maccabees. Two major studies on the literary structure of the First Book of Maccabees have concluded that the main story centres on the theme of liberation.[266] This theme runs through chapters 3–7, 9–11 and 12.24–14.15.[267] In 1 Maccabees the author was concerned with the liberation of the Temple in Jerusalem and liberation from the ‘abomination of desolation’ and the restoration of ancestral worship.[268] The second type of liberation was the liberation of Jerusalem from the control of the heathens.[269] A third type of liberation in the book is the liberation of both the Temple and the Akra, achieved respectively by Judas and by Simon.[270] For Martola, the theme of the book is the liberation of Jerusalem.[271] ‘Seen from the horizon of the first chapter, [1 Maccabees is] above all, the story of the liberation of Jerusalem, in the first hand the liberation of the temple temporarily occupied by foreign powers, secondly the liberation and sanctification of [the citadel] built and inhabited by foreign heathens.’[272] The stance of the book is pro-Hasmonaean.[273] The author displays a tendency to exaggerate the heroic deeds of the Hasmonaeans.[274] Perhaps to attribute liberation to anyone or any power other than Judas and Simon would run contrary to the editorial stance of the book. The author of 1 Maccabees was not interested in detracting from the achievements of the Hasmonaeans, if the liberation of Jerusalem were attributed solely to a grant of *libertas* from the Roman Senate.[275] The evidence for *libertas* may be indicated in the text of 1 Macc. 8.23–32 itself. One has to understand the techniques of composition and the nuances of language. Roman practice of writing to kings accords with the letter to Demetrius.

## Declaration of *amicitia*

Zeitlin believed that the friendship was made in the senate because the senate was not empowered to make a treaty and that the motive was primarily to weaken Demetrius (later Demetrius I of Syria). The senate used the same procedure of a declaration of *amicitia* to make a declaration of friendship with Simon.[276] The declaration became the formative act through a naming, *appellatio*, of the community as a friend of the Roman people, which brought the friendship into being, as was seen in Chapter 4. The capacity to enter into *amicitia et societas* (which means *amicitia*) with Rome necessitated the precondition that the potential ally be formally independent. The naming of a community as an *amicus et socius* meant in the eyes of the Romans that community was a political unity.[277]

The second half of the phrase *amicitia et societas* carries with it the idea of military capacity placed at the disposal of the other *socii*. It was seen in Chapter 4 that this was the prime obligation of the *amicus* towards Rome. The *societas* displays a mutuality or commonality of purpose. Those entering into a *societas* have made their interests coalesce. An external threat by stronger armies would oblige communities to seek military support from Rome. Then, in order to receive Roman aid, they were obliged to enter into an agreement that bound them to reciprocate with military aid when called upon to do so.[278]

To explain the lack of practical aid from the Romans, it has been suggested that the Romans had an escape clause that permitted them to make a treaty and then not abide by its provisions. However, the document in 1 Macc. 8.23–32 does not posses an ‘escape’ clause that permitted the Romans to renege on agreements made. They did make it clear, nevertheless, that aid might not always be assembled and despatched immediately. If the Romans had concluded a treaty with the Jews, they were bound by solemn oaths to adhere to that agreement. It is noteworthy that the Jews never appealed for military assistance from Rome on the basis of a treaty. The new chronology of the embassy, now at 162 BCE, permitted ample time for the envoys to return, for Judas to understand the nature of agreements reached in Rome and to make an appeal for military aid before his death.

States faced with a threat appealed to Rome, trusting in the *fides et societas* of the Romans. The promise of common mutual defence drew foreign embassies to Rome. The wavering of the senate, until it was too late, over whether to defend Saguntum from the Carthaginians, had repercussions. When early in the Second Punic War the Romans attempted to gain allies in Spain, the Volciani told other Spanish tribes not to put their trust in the Roman *fides et societas*.[279]

In foreign policy terms, the acquisition by Rome of allies meant that, in theory at least, the borders of their allies' territory marked the point at which the common external threat lay. Thus, as Rome acquired more and more allies, the territory threatened by enemies became increasingly distant from Rome itself.[280]

## *Amicitia* for the Jews

The Jews in 162 BCE claimed independence from the Seleucid Empire, but their freedom was not recognised outside their own circle. Entry into formal Roman diplomatic relations required that the Romans recognise that independence as a prior step and a precondition, as diplomatic relations with Rome required that the prospective ally be autonomous. In this way, the Romans could justify their policy should any adverse reactions arise. The focus of this enquiry is squarely on the Roman perspective, as they, after all, held the decision as to what type of diplomatic relations, if any, they would grant. The aim is to understand the options available to the senate according to the patterns they set from their own past practice.

After the declaration of *libertas*, one would expect to find traces of a senatorial declaration of *societas et amicitia* or φιλία καὶ συμμαχία. By the middle of the second century BCE, this phrase was similar in all respects to *amicitia*. The reality of Roman power rendered the *amicitia* relationship into an expression without any pretence of equality. After 168 BCE Rome only had to cancel or threaten to cancel her *amicitia* for the community to prefer to return to the Roman fold, rather than face a lonely future. The case of Prusias II suffices to prove the reality of Roman displeasure.[281] His refusal to terminate his war with Pergamum and his treatment of Roman envoys so angered the ten legates sent to end the war that they renounced their friendship and alliance.[282] The effect was to cause Prusias to follow after the legates and beg them to reconsider. The legates refused and Polybius reports that Prusias was at a loss what to do.[283] In the end, he made peace with Pergamum on terms determined by the Romans. The *amici*, in effect, were bound to serve Rome's wishes, which were, in actuality, commands and which left no doubt where the power lay in this relationship. Thus, in the second half of the second century BCE, Rome could use her *amici* in the same way as her military alliance partners without being bound by sworn permanent *foedera*.[284]

After c. 168 BCE, any sharp distinction between a *socius* and an *amicus* had ceased to exist. Both had to render to Rome the services of a *socius*.[285] *Societas* was designed to be a mutual defence pact. It called for material contributions from the partnership with Rome. *Socii*, therefore, were bound to Rome. After Apamea, the undisputed position of Rome in the eastern Mediterranean turned *societas* into a one-sided agreement to supply military aid.[286]

*Societas* was used as a foreign policy instrument to develop relations with communities that were not at war with Rome and which were not *in dicione sub imperium populi Romani*, meaning that they had not made a surrender to Rome.[287] A non-sworn *societas* had no international law validity and was, in fact, virtually similar to a relationship of *amicitia*.[288] This correspondence in practice of *amicitia* to *societas* conforms to the origin of the word in 'friendship', as shown by Wegner.[289] This type of *societas* was voluntary in nature and was between Rome and those who had never been enemies of Rome.[290] In political terms, such an arrangement provided for the *socius* a means to assure its independence under the protection of Rome.[291]

*Societas* involved supplying aid in war.[292] Livy used the expression *societas armorum* (21.60.4) and *societas belli* (33.13.9). From the first, the word *socius* was concerned with the recruitment of allies in war.[293] The *societas* between Rome and the Jews gave the latter the right to wage a defensive war against its enemy. In other words, it legitimised the Maccabaean revolt.[294] For Rome, *societas* was used to bind communities to her that had previously stood outside her control and which were located near actual or potential enemies.[295] At the time of the embassy, Demetrius I was in danger of being an enemy with Rome in the absence of any diplomatic ties with the city. The letter of the Roman *legati* to the Jews in 164 BCE in 2 Macc. 11.34–38 and the Jewish embassy in 162 BCE were not unconnected with the senate's watchfulness over the Seleucids.[296] The status of *socius populi Romani* (and thus *amicus et socius populi Romani*) conferred a validation by Rome of political unity.[297] The embassy was on behalf of Judas Maccabaeus and his brothers and so the meeting in the senate had decided to acknowledge the leadership of Judas and Jonathan and Simon. Certainly, recognition of Judaea as a political unity was determinative if the Jews were to throw off the Seleucid yoke.

From 1 Macc. 8.20–32, the evidence for *amicitia* may be found first and foremost in verse 20, where it is recorded that the envoys asked to be enrolled as 'your friends and allies'. Verse 21 shows that the senate accepted their proposal. The ambiguity between *societas* and *amicitia* after 168 BCE is clear in the phrase *amicus et socius* or φιλία καὶ συμμαχία.[298] It is accepted that, at the time of this embassy in Roman parlance, this φιλία καὶ συμμαχία represented the informal *amicitia* with Rome that was current throughout the Greek-speaking East.

The same expression is found in the letter to Demetrius in verse 31, where the Jews are referred to also as our friends and allies (τοὺς φίλους 'υμῶν τοὺς συμμάχους 'Ιουδαίους). Evidence for the military aid that was expected may be found in verses 24–28.[299] These verses catalogue the material aid that the Jews were expected to provide: items such as food, weapons, money and ships were listed here.[300]

*Amicitia* was a voluntary pact and the Jews initiated the approach to the senate asking to become friends and allies. *Amicitia* was formed with a community friendly to Rome and the Jews had had friendly contact with Rome since possibly 174 BCE and certainly from 164 BCE, when the Roman envoys in Syria wrote to the Jews (2 Macc. 11.34–38). The Jewish obligations are set out in verses 25 and 26. The obligations of a friend of the Roman people were primarily to provide troops and material to Rome in time of war and not to give aid to Rome's enemy. Many of the provisions in the Maccabaean document were designed to provide for aid in time of war. The similarities, which occur for the most part only in verse 26 and the first part of verse 28, are the standard requirements of allies – that is, anyone with *amicitia et societas* with Rome. The Roman obligations are to be found in verse 28. Roman protection for the Jews is pledged in verses 27 and 31–32. Being a friend of the Roman people brought with it the greatest benefit: that the Romans would guarantee one's territorial integrity.

## Enrolment in the *formula amicorum*

After allies had been named as friends of the Roman people, they were enrolled in the *formula amicorum*. Verse 20 recorded the wish of the Jewish envoys for such an enrolment. In the second century BCE, the correct term for this list of allies was the *formula sociorum*, according to Bowman's study.[301] The enrolment did not constitute a legal act.[302] The purpose of the list is given in the decree in favour of the three Greek sea captains who assisted Sulla.[303] In this decree, the enrolment in the *formula* provided them with the rights to gifts, food and lodging at the expense of the Roman state, as well as the right to approach the senate.[304] Bowman considered that the *formula* was a useful list for reference purposes so that it could be determined to which foreign envoys state assistance was required. The benefit of being enrolled was the right of individuals or communities to a formal diplomatic reception in Rome, but the most important right was that of approaching the senate.

The wording in 1 Macc. 8.20 is that the envoys wish to be enrolled as 'your friends and allies'. If the language is technical, this would refer to being inscribed in the *formula amicorum et sociorum*. The earliest extant request for an enrolment as 'friend and ally' comes during the Mithridatic War, from a general of Mithridates.[305] This would make the Judaean request the earliest-attested mention of the *formula amicorum*. As far as a date is concerned, there are broadly two options. The first is to concur with the generally accepted date for the composition, in the time of John Hyrcanus, in the last quarter of the second century. The second is to consider the proposal in this volume that the Maccabaean account of the embassy, especially the cited document in 1 Macc. 8.23–32, was composed by the envoys themselves, and thus is contemporaneous with the events. Whether one takes c. 130 or 162 BCE as the date of verse 20, this posits the above reference to a *formula amicorum et sociorum* as the earliest that we have available.

## *Amicitia* in later embassies to the Romans

In later embassies, the Jewish envoys request a renewal of the ties they had formerly enjoyed with Rome. This renewal was a verbal act, with no connection to a treaty.[306] Subsequent embassies requested the relationship they had enjoyed previously with Rome, which they refer to as φιλία. The first reference to these relations after 1 Macc. 8.23–32 comes in 1 Macc. 12.1, where Jonathan, Judas' successor, is said to have sent an embassy to Rome to renew the former friendship (where φιλία και συμμαχία means friendship); this refers back to the relations under Judas.[307] Josephus (*Ant.* 13.163) makes it clear that it was friendship that Jonathan's envoys requested when he states that Jonathan wanted 'to renew/revive the friendship which his nation had formerly had with them'.[308]

Simon's embassy in 142/41 BCE (in 1 Macc. 14.16–18) was sent as a consequence of Romans' invitation to renew the φιλία καὶ συμμαχία that they had enjoyed under Judas and Jonathan, his brother. In the letter of the consul Lucius, the envoys are said to have renewed the longstanding friendship and alliance (1 Macc. 15.17). The language in which the stated aim of this embassy is expressed is instructive. Its purpose is pronounced in these words: 'to confirm and renew the friendship with Rome'.[309] Treaties were permanent and not renewed, unless perhaps they needed to be modified. Friendship, however, could be renewed.[310] This passage, secondly, mentions φιλία (*amicitia*) as the nature of the previous state of diplomatic relations with Rome.[311] The only previous formal diplomatic relations with Rome were those established by Jason and Eupolemus. The author of the First Book of Maccabees clearly interpreted the relationship formed in 162 BCE as one of φιλία. Josephus (*Ant.* 13.227) reports in his summation of the life of Simon that, 'He also made an alliance (συμμαχίαν) with the Romans.' Here Josephus uses general language referring to the second half of φιλία καὶ συμμαχία, that is, *amicitia et societas* where *societas* is indistinguishable from *amicitia*. We read of further renewals, attributed to the time of John Hyrcanus.[312] There is no mention of a treaty.

## Bronze tablet of friendship in 162 BCE

After the ally had received an *appellatio* by the senate – that is, he was named a friend of the Roman people – he was to be written in the list of Roman friends and, if the senate so decreed, he could erect a bronze tablet on the Capitol commemorating the new ties. Independent evidence confirms that the Romans did inscribe the terms of friendship decrees from the senate on bronze tablets. The *senatus consultum* for the three Greek sea captains specifies that a 'bronze tablet of friendship' (*tabulam aheneam amicitiae*) be erected on the Capitol.[313] The Greek translation on the inscription reads: πίνα<κα> χαλκοῦν φιλίας.[314] Compare this with the wording in 1 Macc. 8.22: ἐπὶ δέλτοις χαλκαῖς. The account in verse 22 is variation on Roman practice, which Josephus thought so flawed, he corrected it in his own version.[315] Scholars have suggested for a long time that Josephus altered the account in 1 Macc. 8.23–32 so that it would conform to official Roman style.[316] He wrote that the Romans sent a copy to Judaea, while the original was engraved on bronze tablets and deposited in the Capitol.[317] The document in 1 Maccabees does not say this. The procedure for the Jewish people was that the diplomatic agreement was to be carved on bronze tablets and sent to Jerusalem as a memorial of the peace and alliance.[318] This does not accord with the way in which the Romans proceeded, which was to set up bronze tablets on the Temple of Jupiter Optimus Maximus on the Capitol in Rome and to give the envoys an official copy in a letter.[319] It is noticeable that the Maccabaean account has scrubbed any reference to temples either in Rome or in Jerusalem.[320] For religious reasons, it was forbidden for the two Jewish envoys to enter the pagan temple on the Capitol in Rome and also to place such a bronze tablet in the Temple in Jerusalem. The usual custom was for the new friend of the Roman people, with the authorisation of the senate, to take part in sacrifices and a dedication in the Temple of Jupiter. Back in the East, the friend was enjoined to set up a stone inscription in a prominent place in the city.[321] With no dedication of a bronze tablet in Rome, there was no witness and guarantee of the terms of the agreement in perpetuity. Here lies the explanation for the change in procedure: the memorial to the agreement would be erected in Jerusalem in a location in consonance with the Jews' religious traditions. How a bronze tablet testifying to friendship between the Romans and the Jews at this time came to be located in the church of San Basilio in the Middle Ages, is a mystery. As we saw in Chapter 1, the tablet was a testimony to *amicitia* in the time of Judas Maccabaeus, once located where the Temple of Mars Ultor had stood. Augustus wished to supersede the Temple of Jupiter Optimus Maximus on the Capitol with regard to international diplomacy. It may have been reinscribed from a tablet taken from the Capitol.[322] However, this can only be speculation. What we do know, is that not only treaties and military diplomas were inscribed on bronze, but also decrees of friendship.

## The order of the diplomatic arrangements in 1 Macc. 8.20–32

The order in which the three arrangements made by the senate are stated in 1 Macc. 8.20–32 merits some discussion. They occur in reverse order. Verse 20 mentions the enrolment in the *formula*, verses 24–28 contain the *amicitia et societas* (that is, *amicitia*) and verses 31–32 the letter indicating *libertas*. The correct order should be *libertas*, *amicitia*, and the enrolment as friend and ally. Why has the order been reversed? The author/s of this document, who may have been the envoys themselves, placed what they considered to be the most important achievement of their embassy in the final position. In Hebrew literature, this final position gave emphasis.[323] What was mentioned last left the final impression.[324] An example would be in the Bible in the Book of Kings, where the final position of demarcated units usually contains the climax, conclusion, outcome or resolution.[325] What we find occupying this last place in chapter 8, is the letter to King Demetrius; its position there indicates that it represents the climax of the diplomatic mission in 162 BCE. The letter is highlighted by being the final act and it may be considered in the minds of the envoys to have been the outcome of their embassy to Rome.

From the last-mentioned feature, working backwards was a pattern of memory recall. Students were trained to start at any point in a text that had been committed to memory and to work forwards or backwards from that point.[326] The question is, why should *libertas* have been given the emphasis? The answer may be that the letter to Demetrius was the actualisation of the aim of the embassy: the Jews sought to have the Romans place pressure on Demetrius to leave the Jews alone.

## The differing understandings of the Romans and the Jews of diplomatic terminology

What understanding did the Romans and the Jews have of the obligations that they had mutually undertaken in 162 BCE? What were the perceptions on both sides? The Romans expected any new ally to be under an obligation to them arising from the new diplomatic ties. They would have expected no less from the Jews as a consequence of their having sought assistance from the senate and as a result of their request to become Roman allies.

One ought to bear in mind that the Jews had never before had any dealings with the senate. In 164 BCE their contact with Romans had been with two *legati* who were on their way to Antioch and who offered to arbitrate the outstanding issues surrounding the ceasefire negotiations between the Jews and the Seleucids.[327] The embassy in 162 BCE was the first approach to the Roman Senate.

It would be fair to say that the Jews were unfamiliar with Roman diplomacy. Whether they realised to what extent they would be permanently bound to Rome is an interesting question. Could the Jews, for instance, have known the future implications of becoming allies of the Roman people? They must have recognised that something was expected in return for help against Demetrius. Yet the question of whether the Jews shared a perception with the Romans of their mutual obligations is one that has not been fully explored in the literature.[328]

It was proposed earlier that there were three steps in the diplomatic relations that the Romans formed with the Jews: a declaration of *libertas*, followed by a declaration of *amicitia* and then enrolment in the *formula amicorum*.[329] This was an agreement into which the Jews voluntarily entered. By accepting these decisions of the senate, how were the Jews obliged to the Romans? First, the Romans had certain specific expectations from those to whom they had granted *libertas*. A good deal is known about the obligations incurred by those who were freed by the Romans. The consequences of a grant of *libertas* placed the freed community in a position of permanent obligation to Rome. Conversely, for their part, the Romans considered themselves as not bound by it.[330] *Libertas* did not guarantee Roman military protection. The freed city had to maintain its own territorial integrity. If it were conquered, Rome regarded its grant of freedom as null and void. Once the formerly freed city threw off its outside ruler, the Romans were usually well disposed to restoring the grant of freedom.

The obligations of a city freed by Rome were henceforth to act with steadfast loyalty towards Rome. As Holleaux expressed it: 'Their [the Greeks'] freedom was a gift, which depended on Rome's good pleasure: this meant both humiliation and insecurity, for Rome's good pleasure might change.'[331] That 'good pleasure' of Rome was guaranteed by steadfast loyalty. The consequences of any breach of loyalty resulted in the destruction of that city, not necessarily immediately, but when a Roman force next came into the area. Any betrayal of Rome was not forgotten.[332]

Equally, the freed city, according to Storm, was expected to act with Roman interests in mind.[333] When the Romans granted *libertas*, they did not confer on the recipient community the right to have an independent foreign policy with the power to declare war and to make peace. In the words of Last: '*Libertas* was not, like *eleutheria* according to some accounts, an unfettered freedom, but rather . . . freedom from arbitrary rule. In particular it did not imply a community's untrammeled control of its international relations, with the right to declare peace and war at will'.[334]

The concept of *libertas* to the Romans implied a hierarchical structure. Yoshimura found that the Romans did not see themselves as equal with those that they recognised as free.[335] The Roman notion of freedom was based on a constellation of power with Rome at the centre.[336] Their hierarchical view of this power relationship was a reflection of the hierarchical structure of Roman society itself.[337] This freedom concept set the Roman notion at odds with the Greek idea of ἐλευθερία, based as the latter was on the principle of equality. The Roman Senate expected that the very *auctoritas* through which *libertas* had been granted would in return be respected (and obeyed).[338] In a formal sense, *auctoritas* was advice only, but in practice it enabled the will of the senate to be followed as if it were an order.[339]

Hellenistic kings, with whose practices the Jews were familiar, made a display of granting freedom, but they put less emphasis on the character of the freedom they granted. By contrast, the conditions and the reality of the freedom that the Romans granted were more important to them. The Romans interested themselves in the type of laws they bestowed, showing a marked preference for timocracies.[340] The Greeks feared that the Romans were establishing oligarchies. By contrast, for the Greeks, liberty and democracy went hand in hand.[341] In contradistinction to this idea, the Romans considered the declaration of *libertas* a mechanism with which to rule over the freed communities. Yoshimura observes that the Romans took seriously the declarations of *libertas* that they made.[342]

For the Romans, the eradication of monarchy was a necessary precondition for freedom. When this was achieved by Roman troops, occupation of Greek cities did not negate freedom, according to Storm, but rather the act of occupation was seen as the agent of liberation from monarchy.[343] While the Romans had a negative definition of freedom – that is, 'freedom from' –, the Greeks had in mind the positive concept of 'freedom to', or freedom of action, which to their mind was the same as political autonomy. Forte expressed this in the following way:

> Doubtless to avoid possible ambiguity, the Romans thus attempted to define in Greek terms the nature of the freedom which they bestowed on the Greeks. Nevertheless, the Roman concept of liberty greatly influenced Rome's treatment of her Greek protegés. The Roman idea of *libertas* had developed from the political and social experience of the Roman people and from Roman law. As a people the Romans associated *libertas* negatively with the absence of royal control (such as that once exercised by their kings) or domination by a master. Positively, they associated freedom with stable government under law (specifically with their own form of government,

> controlled by citizens of wealth and property) . . . . For the Greeks, on the other hand, the terms liberty and democracy had become almost synonymous. Misunderstandings arose . . . .[344]

Out of this misunderstanding grew the dissatisfaction and cynicism of the Aetolians, among others.[345] The disappointment of the Greeks may be best expressed in the cry that *libertas* was only an empty name.[346]

To suggest that *libertas* was an empty slogan, as does Gruen, for example, would be to miss its real significance to the Romans.[347] 'We might draw the conclusion that it [*libertas*] was an empty slogan with no real meaning. Nothing, however, could be further from the truth. The difficulty we have in defining the exact content of *libertas* is indicative not of its insignificance but of its fundamental importance'.[348]

To the Greek mind, *libertas* was understood as autonomy; however, in reality, a grant of *libertas* from the Romans senate meant the loss of autonomy.[349] The freed community owed Rome *gratia* in return for the *beneficium* of freedom.[350] These ties, though informal, had binding force and once broken incurred severe penalties.[351] However, the Greeks found it hard to come to grips with such intangible obligations to the Romans and preferred to put their relations with Rome on a more concrete footing through a treaty.[352]

To what extent did the Jews realise how binding the obligations resulting from *libertas* were and how their foreign policy position would be circumscribed by Rome? *Libertas* would not have given the Jews the right to conduct their own foreign relations. Rome's enemies and friends would henceforth be Judaea's enemies and friends. In practice, Roman *libertas* did not provide freedom from Roman interference; rather, it constituted the preliminary stage to annexation.[353] Through *libertas*, communities were integrated into the Roman *imperium*. Dahlheim rightly points to the lasting subject status of those who surrendered to Rome and were subsequently freed.[354] In this chapter, the stages after *libertas* were listed, ranging from maintaining that status within a Roman *provincia* to treaty relations or conversion into a *colonia*.

The possibility exists that the Jews were seduced by the attraction of Rome's reputation for being opposed to monarchy. Praise for Rome on this point is featured in 1 Macc. 8.14, where it is stated that not one Roman aspired to symbols of kingship; that is, to put on the diadem or to wear purple. After all, Rome was a republic[355] and she had recently abolished the monarchy in Macedonia and taken its king captive back to Italy. Rome's victory over Antiochus the Great and her humiliation of Antiochus IV at Eleusis were all signals that Rome had the power to humble Seleucid kings. Reflections of the Jews' view of Roman superior power over the Seleucids may be seen in the eulogy to the Romans in 1 Macc. 8.7, where it is related, quite erroneously, that the Romans captured Antiochus III. Primarily, the Jewish mission went to Rome with the purpose of achieving freedom from the rule of Demetrius I.[356] The Romans may have used their grant of *libertas* to indicate to the Jews (and perhaps to others) their sign of support for the rebel movement of Judah Maccabee that had fought to throw off the control of the Syrian king over Judaea.

When Rome conquered King Perseus, *libertas* was used to abolish the monarchy. This conquest was known to the Jews and is mentioned in 1 Macc. 8.5. The power of Rome began to spread somewhat closer towards the vicinity of Judaea in 168 BCE, when Popillius Laenas came to Alexandria to deliver the ultimatum to Antiochus IV at Eleusis. To the Jews, this action made concrete the realisation (if it had not occurred to them earlier) that Rome was stronger than the Seleucids. Then in c. 164 BCE contact was made with Roman *legati* on their way to Syria.[357] The Jewish envoys in 162 BCE sought and beseeched the senate that they be freed from Seleucid slavery.[358] The reputation of the Romans in their eyes was of a people who made and unmade kings.[359]

Negotiations in Rome with Jason and Eupolemus would have been conducted in Greek. When the Romans would have spoken of *libertas*, they would have used the word ἐλευθερία to the Jewish envoys.[360] By the Hellenistic period, ἐλευθερία had become synonymous with αὐτονομία, which was confined to the right to internal self-government.[361] So the Roman use of the Greek word ἐλευθερία did convey adequately what the Romans meant by *libertas*.[362]

Autonomy in the experience of the Jews had meant the 'right to live according to ancestral law'. Eupolemus' father, John, according to 2 Macc. 4.11, was the diplomat who won from Antiochus III the privilege to live according to ancestral law.[363] One might be able to see a continuity in policy from that of the father to the son who sought the same privileges from the Romans. The edicts of Antiochus IV had prohibited the practice of Jewish Law. The rallying cry of the Maccabaean revolt had been the preparedness to fight to the death in defence of Jewish Law.[364] The logical step was for the Jews to send an embassy to Rome in 162 BCE to plead that the might of this power newly arrived in the East would guarantee the permanence of Jewish Law. The Roman mechanism for the guaranteeing of local law was one of the elements of declarations of *libertas*.[365]

The identification by Gauger of *libertas* as the type of Roman–Jewish relations concluded in 162 BCE sits well with one of the aims of the rebellion, namely the freedom to live under ancestral law.[366] *Libertas* was required of a future treaty partner of Rome not already independent. However, from the Jewish side *libertas* accorded with what the Jews had sought from previous imperial powers that had ruled over them – that is to say, the right to live according to ancestral law.[367]

When Diodorus (40.2) reported that the Jews had been given αὐτονομία by the Romans, this term meant internal self-government; that is, government headed by a High Priest.[368] For the Jews the right to live according to ancestral law did not mean, as it did for the Romans, merely the right to live under the constitution that was in operation before the Romans came. Ancestral law was religious law. Ancestral laws, by definition, were the Written and Oral Law.[369] The chief official was the High Priest and so government was inseparable from religion. It may be that ancestral law gave the Jews permission both to follow Mosaic Law and to have their own constitution or political system.[370]

The fact that Jerusalem was a major cult centre would have inclined the Romans to grant *libertas*, as they had already in the first half of the second century shown their willingness to respect local cults. In 193 BCE the praetor,

M. Valerius Messala, wrote to the Teans and expressed 'the highest importance to the reverence of the gods' (lines 12–13) and 'our own high respect for the divine' (line 13). In 189 BCE the senate granted *libertas* to the temple, city and territory of Delphi in accordance with its inherited right.[371] In 146 BCE an unnamed Roman magistrate wrote to the guild of the Dionysiac Artists expressing respect for the local cult, saying, 'I grant you for the sake of Dionysos and of the other gods and of the way of life which you have preferred'.[372] In addition, the Romans also were accustomed to re-endorse the rights of local cults that had been granted by the Seleucids.[373] One may cite the examples of the cities of Tyre and Sidon, which, according to Josephus (*Ant.* 15.95), had been free before the Roman era, and which were freed by Augustus.[374] Askalon also was an autonomous city under the Seleucids, minting its own coins.[375] It was made a free city by Augustus, according to Pliny.[376] These examples have been drawn from geographical locations near Jerusalem. Their freedom decrees are somewhat later than the freedom decree proposed for the Jews. An example from the second century would include the decree for Teos.[377]

A misunderstanding then seems to be manifest in the differing definitions of the right to live according to one's own laws. For the Romans, a system of laws, as they understood them, referred to a system of government, but the idea of law for the Jews encompassed religion, customs and the practice of Jewish Law in everyday life. While both sides understood that *libertas* brought freedom from monarchy, there was probably not a common agreement as to what *libertas* brought in the area of law giving.

Additionally, the Romans used declarations of *libertas* as a means to accumulate loyal allies in the East whose foreign policies would follow Roman interest. The Jews saw their *libertas*, as mentioned in Justinus (36.3.9), as independence from Seleucid monarchy and as Roman recognition of the independence of the Jewish *ethnos*.[378] The Jews seem to have believed that the Romans sent a letter to Demetrius, according to 1 Macc. 8.31–32, in which they stated that the Jews were their allies and as such were under Roman protection. To that extent, the Jews received what they wanted from Roman *libertas*. Nevertheless, did the Jews fulfil their part of the bargain? The Romans would have looked for signs of loyalty from the Jews in return. The subsequent renewal of relations with Rome seems to indicate that the Jews maintained their loyalty under Jonathan and Simon.

The second stage for a community whose autonomy was not internationally recognised was a declaration of *amicitia*. What understanding could the Jews have had of *amicitia*? They had seen how it operated in practice, when a senatorial envoy could order the retreat of a Seleucid army. As far as the obligations of a *socius* to Rome are concerned, by 162 BCE the Jews saw this as an agreement that worked in their favour for the moment. What were the obligations of Roman *amici*? To be called *socii et amici populi Romani* entailed the obligation to help Rome militarily and to maintain a friendly relationship with Rome.[379] Military aid was called upon in time of war.[380] Entire communities, and not just cities, were made *amici* of Rome.[381]

It is important to bear in mind that the Jewish envoys were conducting their mission in Greek and, therefore, any mention of *societas* would need to be translated. A corresponding expression in Greek was lacking.[382] In 1 Macc. 8.17 and 20 συμμαχία is mentioned. However, συμμαχία does not mean the same as the Latin *societas*. The Greek συμμαχία carried the meaning of a pact between those who considered themselves equal, while *societas* always had one party standing at the head of the pact.[383] The subordinate role of the *socii* may be seen by the Greek rendering of the term by the words, ὑποτασσόμενοι and ὑπήκοοι.[384] One may readily appreciate how the Jews then may have been mislead as to the nature of the agreement they entered into simply by having the negotiations conducted in Greek. It would be fair to say that the Jews thought that they were entering into diplomatic relations not as subjects of Rome, but as equal partners.

Judaea was some distance from Rome. 1 Macc. 8.19 emphasises just this fact. The last occasion when any Roman troops were anywhere near Judaea was in 168 BCE, when Popillius Laenas had issued the ultimatum to Antiochus IV to leave Egypt. Judas Maccabaeus and his advisors could gamble on the likelihood that Roman forces would not be waging a war in their vicinity in the near future. Without the possibility of war in their region, their obligation to help Rome with troops and weapons would not become operative. For the Jews, the formation of diplomatic relations with Rome, no matter what the cost on paper, was considered essentially a bargain in their favour (or Judas and his successors wanted it portrayed in this light). The shadow side of relations with Rome could be overlooked in their haste to get aid against Demetrius.[385] They believed in the Roman reputation for looking after her 'friends', as expressed in 1 Macc. 8.12, but they did not realise that they had become autonomous, though dependent, allies of Rome.[386]

The final stage in the formation of *amicitia* was the enrolment in the *formula amicorum*. In verse 20 this enrolment is stated as one of the aims of the embassy and one to which the senate agreed. The impression given in verse 20 is that enrolment in the list of Rome's allies was the act that brought this relationship into being, but the enrolment in the list was done by a magistrate on the instruction of the senate. The enrolment was not the step that brought a state of *amicitia* between the Romans and the Jews into existence. The enrolment in the list of allies, however, had a more mundane purpose, a purely administrative function to determine whether the Roman state was obliged to look after (and pay for) the housing, food, clothing and entertainment of the envoys.[387] The list had no legal status.[388] It was not the instrument that created diplomatic relations. The wording in 1 Macc. 8.20 shows that the Jews misunderstood the meaning of their inclusion on this list. They took their inclusion on the list as the formative act that made them allies of the Romans. 1 Macc. 8.20 states that the envoys were sent to establish ties of friendship and peace and to gain enrolment as allies and friends of the Romans. The success of their mission is that the senate accepted this, as noted in 1 Macc. 8.21.

When one compares the expectations of the Romans with what can be gleaned of those of the Jews, it becomes clear that there was a misunderstanding. The Jews had only a partial understanding of the process and the consequences of their first formal diplomatic relations with Rome. The Jews thought that they would receive a promise of military aid from the Romans against Demetrius and could use their newly won ties with the Romans to hold off further threats from Demetrius. They feared that their victory over and killing of Nicanor in battle would not go unpunished. The mutuality of their obligation to Rome – that is, the sending of military aid to the Romans – they probably preferred to defer to some distant and, at this stage, improbable future.

Until 162 BCE, the Jews had had experience only with Roman envoys who had been dispatched to Syria and had had no direct contact with the senate in Rome. They did not realise that the senate's decisions bound them to obey the *auctoritas* of the senate in the future. The Jews did not perceive that the Romans could use *libertas* as the first stage leading eventually to annexation of their territory.

The Jews thought *libertas* was basically the type of autonomy with which they were familiar, having experienced self-rule under the Seleucids until Jason became High Priest. The Seleucid rights gave the Jews the right to live according to Jewish Law. Considering that *libertas* was associated with the right to enjoy one's own laws, the Jews may have equated *libertas* with religious autonomy while not fully appreciating that those with *libertas* were considered dependent allies by the Romans. Finally, they mistakenly thought that enrolment in the *formula sociorum* made them Roman allies.

Only on two points did the Roman and the Jewish views reach any consensus. Both sides were opposed to Hellenistic monarchy for their own reasons. The Romans saw declarations of *libertas* as the means to abolish monarchies and the Jews (as well as others in the Greek world) were happy to sign on to it.[389] Mutual interests combined also in the Roman recognition of the independence of the Jewish *ethnos*. Both parties aimed to strike a blow against Demetrius. For this reason, the majority of Roman senators were happy to vote to assist the Jews with certain senatorial resolutions. In return, Rome gained an ally in the East. The Jews, whether they realised or not, were bound to Rome and were expected to follow Rome's wishes with unquestioning loyalty.

## Advantages to Rome of *amicitia* over a *foedus*

One might ask, what did it matter if the Jews received *amicitia* or *societas*? After all, each was a type indistinguishable from the other in the era after Pydna. Rome was the undisputed master of the eastern Mediterranean, which meant that, in any case, all her allies were subordinate to Rome. There was, however, a clear distinction between a treaty and a friendship in the method of formation, which accounted for the greater frequency of *amici* of the Romans. First, in its setting up *amicitia* could be achieved in a single session of the senate. It required no ratification by the popular assembly. It required no elaborate ceremony by the *fetiales* and it required no swearing of oaths. The establishment of a *foedus*, by contrast, was a slow process.

The declaration of *libertas* followed by *amicitia* had the advantage of not restricting with whom Rome could conclude formal diplomatic relations. Rome could make allies from within the sphere of influence of other powers. In Spain before the Second Punic War Rome made allies this way with Spanish chiefs and Spanish cities. By this method, Rome formed relations with Lampsacus from within the Seleucid sphere of influence. The Jews still within the Seleucid Empire could be made allies of Rome by using *amicitia*. For Rome, this method gave her the potential, unlimited by the sovereignty of other powers, to extend the range of her allies. Then, once relations were formed, Rome was more loosely bound by the ties of *amicitia*. In comparison to the annulment of a *foedus*, the renunciation could be made by the senate. The community requesting an alliance received a fast response and were entitled to call themselves friends and allies of the Roman people.

The position of the Jews was that only they themselves claimed independence from the Seleucid Empire. For Rome to commence diplomatic relations with both of them, the senate would have needed to make their condition correct in law so that they could be legally independent, autonomous allies, according to Roman criteria. To obtain this, a declaration of *libertas* would have been needed before any further stage of diplomatic relations could have been discussed. Such declarations could form a preliminary stage to either *amicitia* or a *foedus*. The previous chapter outlined the reasons a *foedus* seems unlikely and inappropriate for the situation of the Jewish rebels. *Amicitia* enabled the senate in a show of international law correctness to make allies inside the Seleucid Empire (or at least in areas that the Seleucid king still considered his own territory). Judas required a quick response from the senate and *amicitia* could be arranged in one sitting of the senate if need be. In the circumstances facing the senate, when presented with an embassy representing a rebel movement from within the Seleucid Empire, according to Roman practice, the mechanism of *amicitia* best suited the circumstances of the Jews. The category of *amicitia* fits the historical circumstances much better than the treaty hypothesis and conforms to the legal forms to which the Roman Senate adhered. The three stages can be seen in the actual text of 1 Macc. 8.23–32. Consequently, this identification of *amicitia* for the Jews in 162 BCE becomes once again a serious challenge to the prevalent treaty hypothesis.

## Conclusions

A replacement for the treaty hypothesis is offered: alternatively, *amicitia* was the method of diplomatic relations offered by the senate. The Jewish envoys came to Rome voluntarily and they were not *dediticii*; they did not surrender to Rome. A treaty was unlikely in these circumstances. The situation in Judaea was pressing because they feared a renewed attack by the Seleucid army. In urgent situations, *amicitia* was ideal. The senate could pass the necessary decrees and issue instruction to a magistrate to enrol the Jews as allies simply and quickly in a single session without having to convene an assembly of the people to vote on it. Contrast this with the lengthy procedure of a *foedus*, which required months to establish with the ritual of oath taking supervised by the fetial priests and the ratification by the popular assembly. *Amicitia* permitted Rome to intervene in the spheres of influence of other powers, for example that of the Carthaginians and the Seleucids. The mechanism that allowed them to do so was the declaration of *libertas*, which created the conditions of autonomy. From that point, formal diplomatic relations could proceed at a later date. The Jews were keen to be rid of Seleucid overlordship and to have the right to use their ancestral laws. Just such rights were contained in a declaration of *libertas*.

This chapter has shown from the text itself of 1 Macc. 8.23–32 (and not just from the historical circumstances, as Gauger's study had done) that indications exist of a declaration of *libertas* to the Jews. The use of the letter to Demetrius as evidence for *libertas* is made possible by the use of literary analysis (which has not previously been brought into service for the debate on the treaty hypothesis) that shows this letter to be part of 1 Macc. 8.23–32. The senate did not need to give the Jews a letter, as their diplomatic relations were based on declarations and not a formal treaty text. Therefore, a record of the senatorial declarations was made, as is the conclusion reached here, by the envoys themselves. The envoys were on their first visit to Rome and were unfamiliar with the city, the senate and its politics. Their attitude of naiveté is reflected in many statements in 1 Macc. 8.1–16. In their speech to the senate, they would have spoken Greek with the Romans. The possibility for linguistic confusion was without doubt present. The difference between *libertas* and *eleutheria* was bound to be open to confusion between Latin and Greek speakers.

Just how much freedom the Jews considered they would retain under Rome, and how much freedom the Romans gave, is an important issue, which this study has addressed. After 168 BCE, all allies were dependent and their freedom in foreign policy matters was restricted. Storm expressed this situation most aptly when he said that Roman allies were free in the sense of free to carry out Rome's interests. Diplomatic ties with Rome involved risk, a risk of Roman intervention in Judaea. Rome considered after 168 BCE that Greek states should submit their disputes to her for arbitration. Roman legates had a roving brief to solicit complaints against kings. The submission of Antiochus IV to the senate's ultimatum to leave Egypt in 168 BCE sent a powerful message throughout the Seleucid Empire. It did not take long for revolts to break out from Aradus to Judaea, from Commagene to Media. The Maccabaean revolt was one among a series of rebellions. Timarchus, the rebel satrap of Media, was emboldened by his embassy to Rome to declare himself king. Judas' embassy could very well have returned in time to report in person to Judas before the battle of Elasa. The power of a decree of the senate had stopped Antiochus IV's army in its tracks. The Jews may have thought that a letter to Demetrius from the senate would have the same effect. *Amicitia* may have been seen by the Jews as quite an effective weapon against the Seleucids.

The actual Maccabaean document does not claim that it was a treaty. References to what the senate granted the Jews are contained in verses in chapter 8 outside the cited text of the agreement. Verse 22 speaks of εἰρήνη καὶ συμμαχία. Verse 29 speaks of ἔστησαν Ῥωμαῖοι, but the object of the verb is missing so that it is not clear what the Romans set up or established. The Jewish envoys in verse 20 state that the aim of the embassy was στῆσαι μεθ᾽ ὑμῶν συμμαχίαν καὶ εἰρήνην and verse 21 indicates that the senate agreed to their requests. In order for the Maccabaean text to present itself unequivocally as a treaty, the Greek term ορκοι would need to be present. To simply use the word ορκοι does not convey the sense of a sworn written treaty.

## Notes

1 Growing number of scholars are considering the document in 1 Macc. 8.23–32 as evidence of Roman friendship and not a treaty. See Nagy (2010) 110 and Dąbrowa (forthcoming) 2.
2 See Chapter 3.
3 See Chapter 3.
4 See Chapter 4.
5 Walbank (1936).
6 For the chronological issues over the battle of Panion, see Holleaux (1908).
7 Just. 30.2.8.
8 Polyb. 3.2.8, 15.20.2, 16.1.8; App. *Mac.* 4; Livy 31.14.5; Just. 30.2.8. There is a vast literature on the subject, but the most recent discussions that also cover the earlier literature are Gruen (1984) 387–388; Eckstein (2008) 121–180; Grainger (2010) 240–242.
9 Polyb. 16.27.5.
10 For the chronological issues see Holleaux (1921) 50; Broughton (1951) 1.322, n. 4.
11 For the various views on the function of this embassy, see Walbank (1967) 2.533, with references to the older literature.
12 Eckstein (2006) 286.
13 Livy 32.8.12. Annalistic fiction: Niese (1899) 2.607, n. 4; Holleaux (1921) 50–51; Ma (1999) 279–281. Historical: Schmitt (1964) 269–270; Badian (1959a) 82–83; Grainger (2002) 31–32.
14 Polyb. 18.50.1; Livy 33.39.1; Dimitriev (2011b) 126.
15 This answers Badian's point (1959a) 82 that the senate had neither the right nor the power to give orders to Antiochus. I was pleased to read Dmitriev (2011b) 128 in the final stages of the preparation of the manuscript and to see that I had independently come to the same conclusion.
16 Burton (2011) 107.
17 Held back: Grainger (2002) 29–30; Eckstein (2008) 309. Cf. Gruen (1984) 616. Marriage alliance: Polyb. 18.51.10, 28.20.9; Livy 33.40.3, 35.13.4; App. *Syr.* 3, 5.
18 Hieron. *In Dan.* 3.11.17a. Cf. Walbank (1967) 2.623.
19 Polyb. 29.27.1. See Boyancé (1964a) 104; Hölkeskamp (2000) 228.
20 Ter. *Andr.* 289; Cic. *Pro Deiotaro* 8; Ovid *Met.* 14.297.
21 Boyancé (1964a) 107.
22 Livy 29.24.3, 30.13.8.
23 Diod. 31.2.1.
24 Polyb. 29.27.3.
25 Polyb. 29.27.5. Similar accounts: Livy 45.12.1–6; Cic. *Phil.* 8.23; Val. Max. 6.4.3; Vell. 1.10.1–2; Plut. *Mor.* 202F; App. *Syr.* 66; Just. 34.3.1–4; Zon. 9. 25.

26 Polyb. 29.27.6.
27 See note 25.
28 Polyb. 29.27.6–7.
29 Polyb. 29.27.7–8.
30 Dmitriev (2011a) 119, where I had independently also made the linkage.
31 Snowdon (2014) 431.
32 Yardley and Heckel (1997) 18, n. 51.
33 Eichert (1882) 71 'foedus' cites nine entries: 3.7.2, 12.2.12, 7.3.3, 24.1.2, 32.4.2, 41.4.9, 42.3.4, 43.5.3, 48.5.10.
34 Jal (1983) 42 and (1987) 200; Franga (1988) 872.
35 Pulci Doria (1975) 468–477.
36 Gauger (1977) 263; Stern (1974) 333 and (1986) 22–23 [20–21].
37 *TLL* vol.2, s.v. *auxiliator*, col. 1615.
38 *TLL* vol. 1.5, col. 1893.
39 Wegner (1969) 29.
40 Kienast (1968) 350, 352, 354–364.
41 See pp. 178–183, 185–186, 189–191.
42 Shatzman (2012) 69, n. 149: this passage is based not on 1 Maccabees but on a Hellenistic source without documentation.
43 (1875) 99.
44 Mommsen (1879) 1.333–334.
45 Mendelssohn (1875) 99–100, n. 1.
46 (1875) 100, n. 1.
47 Niese (1906) 825.
48 Zack (2015a) 31–32, 34.
49 A community had to be independent in order to enter into foreign relations with Rome see Mommsen (1887) 3.590, n. 1.
50 Dahlheim (1968) 286.
51 Walbank (1979) 3.281.
52 Heuss (1933) 26–27; Dahlheim (1968) 163–164, 286.
53 Wegner (1969) 15–17.
54 Wegner (1969) 33.
55 For these and other verbs: Wegner (1969) 34, nn. 52–55.
56 See Snowdon (2014) 428–430.
57 Cf. Snowdon (2014) 434–435 and n. 52.
58 Wegner (1969) 80 and n. 20.
59 Wegner (1969) 81.
60 Kienast (1968) 350, 352, 354–364.
61 I had earlier considered Kienast's *societas sine foedere* a separate category of diplomatic relations: see Greenlees-Zollschan (2005). In Zollschan (2008) 167 I made the point that Kienast was actually describing *amicitia*.
62 See Zollschan (2003).
63 Dahlheim (1968) 137.
64 Kienast (1968) 335.
65 Heuss (1933) 53–56; Kienast (1968) 335; Sherwin-White (1984) 66.
66 Badian (1952) 76; Sherwin-White (1984) 68; Luraschi (1979) 32, n. 24; Nörr (1989) 17; Eckstein (1999a) 415. Mommsen indicated that bilateral international treaties recognised the autonomous status in a reciprocal way of the two contracting parties: (1887) 3,2.1159.
67 *Dig.* 49.15.7.1: *Liber autem populus est is, qui nullius alterius populi potestati est subiectus: siue is foederatus est [sive non foederatus]* . . . . Text according to Baronowski (1990) 346. The passage is attributed to the first-century CE jurist, Proculus. In the compilation of the Digest only laws still current were included, which shows that this principle endured and secondly the sources used for the Digest go back to the

Republic. See Robinson (1997) 105–106. For recent analysis of this passage, see Zack (2007) 224–228.

68 The word *sive* was restored in the edition of the Digest by P. Bonfante as cited by Baronowski (1990) 346, n. 2.

69 The sources used went back to the Republic and the longevity of this principle is attested by its attribution to Proculus. The c. 200 years between the 160s BCE and Proculus should not be taken to mean that the principle came into being 200 years after 162 BCE.

70 Kunkel (1966) 38.

71 Mommsen (1887) 3, 2.1159.

72 Phillipson (1911) 46, 48; Polay (1964) 106, 124; Meyer (1964) 228–229; Dahlheim (1968) 22, 132; Sherwin-White (1984) 66; id. (1973a) 176; de Martino (1973) 35; Reynolds (1982) 8; Baronowski (1982) 21; id. (1990) 346–347; Schmitt (1988) 531–532; Nörr (1989) 17; Avram (1999) 90; Hölkeskamp (2000) 236.

73 (1984) 69.

74 Sherwin-White (1973a) 176.

75 (1973a) 176; 181, n. 5.

76 Sherwin-White (1984) 69–70.

77 Warmington (1935) 424, also see note 86, 97.

78 Cic. *Balb.* 50–51.

79 Livy 44.7.5.

80 Livy 45.27.1.

81 See Zollschan (2003). Note that this paper was written before my research on the embassy's date.

82 The most recently discovered *foedus* between Rome and Maroneia was discovered in 1972 in the tower of a Byzantine fortress: *BCH* (1978) 102, 726. Hammond in Hammond and Walbank (1988) 608: 'It is obvious too that the inscriptions which have survived are only a small fraction of the sum of such inscriptions at the time'.

83 Sherk (1969) no. 35.

84 Memnon 26.4 (*FGrH* 3 p. 539). Date: Täubler (1913) 99–100.

85 Apamea: Magie (1950) 2.958; Caesar: Plut. Caes. 48. Treaty: Täubler (1913) 450–451. Date: Täubler (1913) 453–454.

86 Magie (1950) 2. 994–995; Holleaux (1898) 259, ll. 25–32; Schmitt (1957) 87, n. 1; Ferrary (1988) 153, n. 89.

87 Holleaux (1898) 260–266; Bickerman (1937) 221, 228, 239; Gruen (1984) 733–735.

88 Willrich (1899) 305–311.

89 *N.H.* 5.109.

90 That Elea had self-government during the Seleucid period: Allen (1983) 67–68. See Magie (1950) 2.734.

91 Livy 37.56.3–6; Kallet-Marx (1995) 186; Ma (1999) 160.

92 Polyb. 30.3.3–7; Livy 45.20.2–3.

93 Livy 45.29.6.

94 Freedom: Polyb. 30.3.7; Livy 39.27.2. Treaty: *SEG* 35.823.

95 Polyb. 18.48.2; Livy 33.35.2.

96 *IG* 2, 2, 1224, ll. 9–10, which read as follows: τοὺς κοινοὺς εὐεργέτας ἀπάντων [῾Ρωμαίους . . . συμ]μαχίαν καὶ καταστὰς πρός τοὺς ἀδι [κοῦντας].

97 Gruen (1984) 738, n. 40 discusses the possibility that συμμαχία in ll. 9–10 may refer to a treaty between Athens and Rome because Athenian cleruchs had erected the decree, but he rejects the idea.

98 Freedom: Magie (1950) 2.958. Treaty: *Syll.*[3] 693.

99 Freedom lost: Suet. *Iul.* 2. Treaty: Sherk (1969) no. 26d.

100 Lucullus: *FGrH* 3, p. 550; App. *Mith.* 83. Caesar: Dio 42.48.

101 Pliny *ep.* 92, 93.

102 Freedom: Viereck (1888) 5. Treaty: Sherk (1969) no. 28.
103 Bean (1956) 196. His reading of lines 10–11 is ὅπω [ς κύριοί ἐφ αὐ] τοῖς (?) τοῖς νόμοις αιρέσεσίν τε ω]σιν [χρῆσθαι]. Regardless of the various restorations, all agree that the sense should be that the city was autonomous. See Sherk (1965) 298.
104 Sullan date of this inscription from Mommsen; now thought that the reference is to Mithridates IV, who came to the throne between 159 and 156 BCE. For a full discussion and the older material, see Magie (1950) 2.954–955.
105 (1954) 45–46.
106 *IG* 14.2229.
107 *Libertas:* Degrassi (1951–1952) 45. Allied: Magie (1950) 2.1169.
108 Suet. *Vesp.* 8 speaks of *restituenda* of the bronze tablets but does not mention whether they were restored on bronze or stone.
109 Except colonies, which is not relevant to the Jewish situation.
110 Heuss (1933) 94, 69–72.
111 Heuss (1933) 80, 84.
112 Magie (1950) 2.960, n. 76.
113 Kienast (1968) 349; Petzold (1992) 238.
114 Heuss (1933) 110–112.
115 But regained *libertas* at the hands of Pompey in 49 or 48 BCE. For references, see Henze (1892) 41.
116 Livy 44.7.5.
117 Livy 45.27.1.
118 Mommsen *R.G.*[8] 2.53; Henze (1892) 41.
119 Mytilene: Suet. *Iul.* 2; cf. Livy *Per.* 89. Heraclea Pontica: *FGrH* 3.545, 558; Strabo 12.3.
120 20 BCE: Dio 54.7. Tiberius: Tac. *Ann.* 4.36; Suet. *Tib.* 37; Dio 57.24.6.
121 Smyrna: Cic. *Flacc.* 71. Miletus, Clazomenae, Carystos: Kaibel *Inscr. Gr. Sic. et It.* 951; Henze (1892) 43, 46–47. Caunus: Cic. *ad Fam.* 12.56.3. Acarnania: Strabo 10.2. Rhodes: Suet. *Vesp.* 8. Antiochia Epidaphnes: *FGrH* 3.716.
122 Because of its absence from Pliny's list of 'free' cities: Henze (1892) 21.
123 Cic. *ad Q. Fr.* 2.11.2 (10 or 11 Feb. 54 BCE).
124 Dio 54.7.6.
125 For *libertas*: Polyb. 30.5.12; App. *Mith.* 61; Strabo 14.3.3; Dio 40.60.17. *Libertas* withdrawn: Suet. *Claud.* 25.
126 *Dig.* 49.15.7.1.
127 Polyb. 30.5.11, 15; Livy 45.25.11; Henze (1892) 54; Berthold (1984) 166.
128 Protest: Polyb. 25.4.1–4; Livy 34.6.8–10; Schmitt (1957) 118–119.
129 Capture: Polyb. 30.5.11; Livy 33.25.11; Reger (1999) 89–90.
130 Polyb. 21.46(48).4; Livy 38.39.8.
131 *Sympoliteia*: *BCH* (1898) 22, no. 9, 384.
132 App. *Mith.* 83.
133 App. *Mith.* 120.
134 Vell. Pat. 2.18. Lost *libertas*: Suet. *Iul.* 2. Restored by Pompey: Vell. Pat. 2.18; Plut. *Pomp.* 42. Date of the treaty depends on which C. Caesar is referred to (Julius Caesar or Octavian).
135 Henze (1892) 52–54.
136 Henze (1892) 64–65.
137 (1875) 99.
138 (1875) 99–100, n. 1.
139 Those who used this argument against the historicity of the treaty of 162 BCE almost 100 years ago were Mendelssohn (1875) 91–100; Willrich (1900) 62–85; Niese (1906) and Winckler (1901) 3.1, 113.

140 Niese, as cited in Täubler (1913) 249.
141 Willrich (1924) 45–46; Sherwin-White (1984) 72.
142 (1913) 249–250.
143 Sordi (1952) 509–512; Liebmann-Frankfort (1969) 101–120; Timpe (1974); Stern (1986) 9–10; Hadas-Lebel (1987) 724, n. 34; Gera (1998) 304, nn. 131, 132; Shatzman (1999) 59, n. 35. Against: Gruen (1984) 45–46, n. 173.
144 Heuss (1933) 50–51.
145 Renewals were sought from each new king: Täubler (1913), 249–251; Ferrenbach (1895) 75ff. and Larivière (1892) 44. That treaties and not friendship had to be renewed with each new ruler, see Mommsen (1887) 3, 1.594, n. 4; Bohn (1908) 42–47, 66; Heuss (1933) 47; and Cimma (1976) 92, 95.
146 Mommsen (1887) 3.594, n. 4; Sands (1908) 42–47, 66; Tarn (1952) 352; Cimma (1976) 92, 95.
147 Polyb. 21.42.1; Diod. 31.8.1; App. *Syr.* 38. Cf. Roman treaty with Massinissa for all time: Diod. 28.7. The only reference to a renewal of a treaty is that of the treaty with Perseus, which was made under duress: Heuss (1933) 50–51.
148 (1933) 50–51.
149 Polyb. 31.3.1–5; Livy *Per.* 46; Diod. 31.19.8.
150 Polyb. 28.1.7–8; Livy 42.6.4; Diod. 30.2.
151 Heuss (1933) 48.
152 Accepted Ferrenbach (1895) 75ff; Larivière (1892) 44; Kienast (1968) 335–342; Cimma (1976) 92.
153 Heuss (1933) 48–51.
154 Polyb 7.3.1 and 7.5.1; Heuss (1933) 50–51.
155 Eckstein (1999a) 416.
156 Giovannini-Müller (1971) 166, n. 36.
157 Demetrius not recognised: Täubler (1913) 253–54; Meyer (1925) 2.236f.; Bevan (1930) 519; Ginsburg (1928) 44, 49; Momigliano (1931) 159; Abel (1949) 152; Walbank (1979) 3.521; Badian (1958) 108, n. 1.
158 Polyb. 31.33.3. For the position that Demetrius was recognised by Tiberius but not by the senate: Niese (1903) 3.247; Otto (1934) 82–83; Briscoe (1969) 52–53.
159 Heuss (1937) 180–182.
160 1 Macc. 13.51.
161 Some clarification is required regarding the separation of the step of the grant of *libertas* and the declaration of *amicitia*. By the Late Republic, the dividing line between *amicitia et societas* and *libertas* became somewhat blurred. However, to assume, as does Bernhardt, that this situation also applied in earlier times is without foundation: Bernhardt (1971) 29–30.
162 That Saguntum had a *foedus* with Rome was argued by Täubler (1921) 42–44; refuted by Badian (1958) 293, note H.
163 For a list of declarations of *libertas*, see Zollschan (2002) 190–192.
164 Polyb. 18.46.5 and Plut. *Flam.* 10.4.
165 Polyb. 15.2.44.4, 15.2.46.15; Plut. *Flam.* 12.2.
166 Diod. 31.8.7.
167 Wirszubski (1950) 4.
168 Polyb. 18.46.5; App. *Mac.* 9.4; Plut. *Flam.* 10.4, 12.1.
169 A more detailed explanation of the declaration of *libertas* for Macedonia may be found in Zollschan (2002).
170 Badian (1958) 97.
171 Livy 44.24.2.
172 Livy 37.54.6.
173 Wirszubski (1950) 12–19; Storm (1992) 81, n. 22.
174 Just. 38.2.8.

175 Polyb. 18.44.2. See Walsh (1996) 356.
176 Orestae: Livy 33.34.6, 37.32.14.
177 26.32.2 and 45.36.5.
178 Bernhardt (1971) 21.
179 See Zollschan (2002) 187–188.
180 *Syll.*[3] 674, ll. 50–53.
181 The emphasis here is on the Roman concept of *libertas* contemporary with the Maccabaean revolt, not that of Josephus influenced by Nicolaus of Damascus almost 160 years later. For the latter see Schwartz (2002).
182 Livy 34.49.11, 35.31.8.
183 38.2.6ff., 5.9.
184 (1958) 40–42.
185 Dahlheim (1968) 100.
186 Dahlheim (1968) 101.
187 Heuss (1933) 288–289.
188 Heuss (1933) 288–290; Bickerman (1938) 133–134; Dahlheim (1968) 101, n. 65.
189 Bickerman (1932) 61.
190 Livy 35.17.1.
191 2 Macc. 11.34.
192 Polyb. 21.19.9.
193 Rigsby (1996) 20.
194 (1968) 100–101.
195 Dahlheim (1968) 100.
196 (1973a) 178.
197 Isoc. *Phil.* 64, 123, 129, 139; *Peace* 42.
198 Forte (1972) 26.
199 Livy 37.25.5.
200 Erskine (1991) 106–111; Ferrary (1988) 167–168; Classen (1965); Rawson (1975); and Grimal (1986) 32, 233–273.
201 *ORF* 3 Cato F58.
202 Polyb. 31.11; cf. Livy 37.25; App. *Syr.* 23.
203 Livy 42.52.16. Gruen (1984) 335 n. 91 dismisses this passage as evidence for Roman aims towards monarchy.
204 *Orac. Sib.* 3.175–179.
205 Polyb. 29.4.9 and Livy 45.24.2.
206 Ferrary (1988) 158–170.
207 *CIL* $1^2$ 726 = 6.30927; *CIL* $1^2$ 730 = 6.30922. See Degrassi (1951–1952) 21, 27, 30.
208 Ciani: Polyb. 18.44.5; Livy 33.30.4. Teos: *Syll.*[3] 601. Heraclea-on-Latmos: *SIG*[3] 618.
209 (1977) 272.
210 Zollschan (2008).
211 Gauger (1977) 265.
212 See Walton (1956) 413–414.
213 There is only one other place in 1 Maccabees outside chapter 8 where ξυγὸν occurs: see 1 Macc. 13.41. Cf. Thompson (2002) 241.
214 Gen. 27.40; Lev. 26.13; Isa. 9.4, 10.27, 14.5, 14.25, 14.29; Ezek. 34.27. See Doran (1977) 106.
215 Parallel expressions in 2 Kgs 1.10, 1.14; Josh. 47.6. Grimm (1853) 129; Nelis (1972) 166.
216 Livy 45.18.2.
217 See for example Livy 2.37.2, 3.56.4, 3.57.5, 34.58.11, 41.6.9, 42.23.9, 43.4.13, 45.15.4.
218 Fischer (1980) 116.
219 Strabo 12.8.14.

220 A contemporary date for the eulogy: Täubler (1913) 244, 248; Sordi (1952) 514–515 and (1975) 98–99; Momigliano (1980) 563. Post-146 BCE: Wernsdorff (1747) 127–128. Followed by Grimm (1853) 125; Gutberlet (1920) 131; Bévenot (1931) 102; Abel (1949) 149–150, n. 9; Schunck (1980) 331, n. 10a; Delcor (1991) 21–22. Date of 63 BCE: Laqueur (1904) 234–235; Gauger (1977) 314–317.
221 Mommsen (1887) 3.739; Kienast (1968) 364, n. 103.
222 Abel (1949) 157 'de tout coeur'; Schunck (1980) 332 'aus vollem Herzen'.
223 Knabenbauer (1907) 156.
224 See pp. 137–138.
225 Schunck (1980) 332.
226 Knabenbauer (1907) 156.
227 Schunck (1980) 332; Abel (1949) 157.
228 Smallwood (1976) 6, n. 11.
229 Grimm (1853) 129; Knabenbauer (1907) 157; Abel (1949) 157; Timpe (1974) 141; Dommershausen (1985) 61–62; Doran (1996) 107.
230 Goldstein (1976) 368–369. Inauthentic: first to doubt the authenticity of the letter because of the many Hebraisms was Wernsdorff (1747) 80. For recent views similar to Wernsdorff see Gauger (1977) 250–252; Gera (1998) 312–313.
231 Williams (1999) 6.
232 Williams (1999) 8, 14.
233 The first to question its authenticity was Wernsdorf: see Grimm (1853) 130. The most recent doubts on the letter have come from Gauger (1977) 250–252.
234 Dancy (1954) 130.
235 Grimm (1853) 130; C.F. Keil (1875) 146; Gutberlet (1920) 137; Fischer (1980) 111; Rappaport (2001) 723.
236 Letter: Bévenot (1931) 106. Instructions: Goldstein (1976) 364.
237 Parunak (1978) 64.
238 Walsh (2001) 9.
239 First isolated by Moulton (1899) 56–58, 65–66, 543.
240 Wilson (1997) 38.
241 Wilson (1997) 40.
242 Walsh (2001) 57.
243 The preposition changes from ἐν in verse 23 to διά in verse 32, so that διά may open and close the letter to Demetrius, thus another *inclusio* appears in the text of 1 Macc. 8.23–32.
244 It should be noted that the literary device of *inclusio* is absent from all inscriptionally extant Roman treaties and also absent from the other cited documents in 1 Maccabees that relate to Roman–Jewish diplomatic relations.
245 The same phrase is found in the treaty of Astypalaia, l. 28.
246 Momigliano (1942) 53–64. For examples see (1743) s.v. *terra*, 4. 410–412. Examples include: Cic. *leg. Manil.* 48; *ad Att.* 7.22; *ad Fam.* 5.9; Sall. *Cat.* 13.3; *Hist.* 69 (K). 13; *ep.* 1.7.1; Virg. *Aen.* 1.598, 9.492 and 10.161, 10.162; Caes. *Bell. Afr.* 24.4, 93.3; *Bell. Alex.* 44.5.
247 Packard (1968) 937–938.
248 Homer *Il.* 14. 24; motif in Thucydides: Rood (1998) 2; Liddell and Scott, s.v. γῆ, p. 347. Examples include Sappho *Supp.* 5.2; Hesiod, *Works and Days*, 2.492; Thuc. 1.2.2, 1.24.6, 2.62.2, 5.18.3, 5.42.1; Xen. *Hell.* 2.2.10.
249 Treaty between the Achaean League and Antigonos Doson (224 BCE): Schmitt (1969) no. 506. Isopolitia decree from Naupactos to Keos (223/22 BCE): *Syll.*$^3$ I.522. Isopolitia decree between Aetolian League and Trikka (c. 206 BCE): *IG* 9, $1^2$, 1, 136, ll. 5–6. Treaty between Rhodes and Hierapytna (c. 201/200 BCE): Schmitt (1969) no. 551. Asylia decree between Aetolian League and Miletus (2nd half of third cent. BCE): Schmitt (1969) no. 564. Treaty between Itanos and Hierapytna (3rd cent.): Schmitt (1969) no. 578.

250 The expression in Latin of *terra marique* is such a cliché that, when Knabenbauer translated verse 32 into Latin, he switched the expression to *terra marique* when instead it should have read *mari terraque*. Knabenbauer (1907) 157.
251 The expression is also found in the LXX in Ex. 15.19; Ps. 65(66).6, 96.10–13; Jn 1.9; Hg .2.7(6), 2.22(21).
252 Yoder (1971) 472.
253 Inscription from Aksum, Ethiopia (pre-Christian), 'I sent an expedition by sea and land'. Syriac: *Against Mani*: 97. Arabic: Tirmidhi, transl. A. Williams (1971) 320.
254 Watters (1976) 60–80.
255 Urbrock (1972) 459, 471–472.
256 Martin (1974) 5.
257 1 Macc. 15.14. See Thompson (2002) 143.
258 Tov (1988) 180.
259 Rife (1933) 246.
260 Additional arguments for oral composition: Zollschan (2007b).
261 Polyb. 18.44.5; Livy 33.30.4.
262 Polyb. 18.44.4: ἐλευθέρας ἀφεῖναι τὰς φρουρὰς ἐξ αὐτῶν μεταστησάμενον.
263 Strabo *NH* 12.563–564.
264 Gera (1998) 122–123 with bibliography.
265 Habicht (1989) 344; Will (1967) 2.272.
266 Martola (1984) 204–207; Williams (1999) 136.
267 Williams (1999) 133.
268 1 Macc. 3.10–4.61.
269 1 Macc. 5–7, 9–11, 12.24–14.3; Williams (1999) 133.
270 For Simon: 1 Macc. 12.24–14.15.
271 Martola (1984) 279.
272 Martola (1984) 109.
273 Dancy (1954) 7; Habicht (1976) 188–189; Attridge (1984) 171–176; Delcor (1989) 460; Williams (1999) 98. Against: Doran (1996) 22.
274 Grabbe (2000) 59.
275 Gauger (1977) 285.
276 Zeitlin (1950) 39–41. See also Smallwood (1976) 5; Grant (1973) 29.
277 Wegner (1969) 91.
278 Wegner (1969) 88.
279 Livy 21.19.6–10.
280 Wegner (1969) 88.
281 Polyb. 33.12.2–9, 33.13.4ff.; Dahlheim (1968) 270–271.
282 Polyb. 33.12.5.
283 Polyb. 33.12.7.
284 Dahlheim (1968) 273.
285 Dahlheim (1968) 265.
286 Avram (1999) 87.
287 Avram (1999) 90.
288 Avram (1999) 91.
289 Wegner (1969) 15–17.
290 Avram (1999) 92.
291 Avram (1999) 95.
292 Sherk (1984) no. 59b, ll. 26–28 and no. 63, ll. 4–14, 37–39.
293 See Plaut. *Cist.* 197b–202 for allies in the war against Carthage; Wegner (1969) 72–74.
294 *Societas* in this sense may be found in Cicero *rep.* 3.34, 35. See Wegner (1969) 84.
295 Livy 2.48.4, 3.8.4, 4.9.1; Wegner (1969) 88.
296 Greenlees-Zollschan (1997) 22–28. Against: Gruen (1976).
297 Wegner (1969) 91.

298 As discussed on pp. 67–71.
299 Nelis (1972) 163 identifies in 1 Macc. 8.24–28 a *senatus consultum*.
300 Whether one should take the mention of ships as an argument against a treaty because the Jews in 161 BCE did not control the port of Joppa, is decisive for Willrich (1895) 73 and (1924) 45. That this is standard and formulaic phraseology: Kallet-Marx (1995) 191.
301 Bowman (1989) 336.
302 Badian (1958) 12; Kienast (1968) 341, n. 34.
303 Sherk (1969) no. 22.
304 Ll. 12–13.
305 Plut. *Sull.* 23.
306 Kallet-Marx (1995) 185.
307 See pp. 229–233.
308 See pp. 230, 269.
309 1 Macc. 12.16.
310 Sherk (1969) no. 9 ll. 18ff., 42ff. and 60ff. Other examples: Heuss (1933) 26.
311 Martola (1984) 63: 1 Macc. 8.23–32 did not 'exert any apparent influence' on the rest of the book and so this passage is classified as one of the 'islands' in the text (231). He was looking for references to treaties; if one looks for evidence of *amicitia*, it may be found elsewhere in 1 Maccabees.
312 For the discussion of the authenticity and dates of the following three documents, see pp. 242–258.
313 Raggi (2001) 80, l. 17 in the Greek.
314 Raggi (2001) 82, l. 25.
315 Gera (1998) 308–309, n. 146: 'As a resident of Rome for many years who had access to many of the Roman documents which he quotes, Josephus knew the right procedure'.
316 Mendelssohn (1875) 96–98; Täubler (1913) 242.
317 Jos. *Ant.* 12.416.
318 1 Macc. 8.20.
319 Raggi (2001) 88–89.
320 Frederiksen (1965) 185 calls 1 Macc. 8.22 'a tissue of misconception'.
321 Inscriptions prescribe setting in the Agora, in temples and in the hall of the Boule. Examples: Pucci Ben Zeev (1998) 383.
322 My thanks to John Rich for this suggestion.
323 Dorsey (1999) 40.
324 Parunak (1979) 45–46.
325 Beekman et al. (1981) 135.
326 Yates (1966) 17–41.
327 2 Macc. 11.34–38.
328 On whether the Jews fully understood what they had received from Rome: Mandell (1991).
329 Kienast (1968) 348, 352, 354–356.
330 Badian (1958) 99; Dahlheim (1968) 100.
331 Holleaux (1930) 196.
332 See p. 185 for the examples of *libertas* lost.
333 Storm (1992) 75–76.
334 Last (1954) 436.
335 (1984) 2.
336 Yoshimura (1984) 10.
337 Yoshimura (1984) 1.
338 Yoshimura (1984) 2.

339 For examples and references see Yoshimura (1984) 4–5; for the role of the senate in general in foreign affairs in the second century BCE see Millar (1984) 4.
340 Yoshimura (1984) 13.
341 Forte (1972) 27.
342 Yoshimura (1984) 14.
343 Storm (1992) 68.
344 Forte (1972) 26–27.
345 Storm (1992) 82.
346 Livy 38.23.8–9; out of this statement has come the many studies that maintain that *libertas* was only a slogan. See Grant (1946) 402; Accame (1946) 50; Calderone (1964) 97–98; Gruen (1984) 151–157; Storm (1992) 78–79.
347 Calderone (1964) 97–98; Gruen (1984) 156–157; Storm (1992) 78–79.
348 Mouritsen (2001) 11. While his discussion concerns *libertas* in the context of Roman domestic politics, his remarks cannot be divorced from *libertas* in Roman external policy.
349 Storm (1992) 86.
350 Kienast (1968) 348–349.
351 The case of Agassae, which was sacked by the Romans: Livy 45.27.1.
352 Forte (1972) 27.
353 Grant (1946) 402.
354 Last (1954) 437; Dahlheim (1968) 109.
355 Ferrary (1988) 158–170.
356 Bévenot (1931) 106–107.
357 2 Macc. 11.34–38.
358 1 Macc. 8.18.
359 1 Macc. 8.13.
360 On the differential meanings of *libertas/eleutheria* and the Jews' understanding of these words, see Schwartz (2002) in the context of their use by Josephus. In 1995 I worked independently on the implications for the Jews of having a different understanding of these concepts while at Deakin University in Melbourne. See Greenlees-Zollschan (1997).
361 Such autonomy accepted subordination to a superior power. See Bickerman (1958) 327.
362 Sherk (1969) 24.
363 Jos. *Ant.* 12.142.
364 That is, if the speech in 2 Macc. 13.14 is to be believed.
365 Eleutheria as the reacquisition of lost privileges: Dąbrowa (2010) 28, n. 78.
366 (1977) 266–271.
367 Hekataios refers to πατρία νόμοι under the Persians and Macedonians. See Stern (1974) 20–25, fr. 11.
368 Kippenberg (1986) 58.
369 Pucci Ben Zeev (1998) 416.
370 Rajak (1984b) 108.
371 Sherk (1969) no.1 A, ll. 4–6.
372 Sherk (1969) no. 44, ll. 4–5. Translation: Sherk (1969) no. 37.
373 Kasher (1990) 182–183; Pucci Ben Zeev (1998) 410.
374 Dio 54.7; Henze (1892) 76.
375 Spaer (1984) 230–231.
376 Pliny *N.H.* 5.68.
377 Sherk (1969) no. 34; Dahlheim (1968) 103.
378 Roberto (2003) 801.
379 Kienast (1968) 334.

380 Sherwin-White (1984) 59–60.
381 See the example of Lampsacus and Hierapytna cited by Kienast (1968) 343. Also Dahlheim (1968) 163–164.
382 Henze (1892) 6.
383 συμμαχία: Avram (1999) 87.
384 Horn (1930) 11.
385 Grimm (1853) 127.
386 Kienast (1968) 350.
387 Livy 42.26.5.
388 Badian (1958) 12.
389 Dahlheim (1968) 101.

# 7 Epilogue

## From 160 to 100 BCE

This study, on the much-debated question of how to classify the diplomatic agreement brought back to Jerusalem by the Jewish ambassadors sent by Judas Maccabaeus, would be incomplete without a treatment of what transpired after 162 BCE. The years 143 to 100 BCE confirm the grant of Roman *amicitia* to Judas' envoys. At no time after the rule of Judas did the Jews receive a treaty. The bonds of friendship were remade and revived several times because of the changing military and political situation until the friendship was nullified, when the Jewish leadership rendered themselves no longer friends of Rome.

### Revival of diplomatic relations[1]

It has been discussed earlier in this volume that, in order to have diplomatic relations with Rome, a people had to show that they were independent and not under the power of another state.[2] In considering the necessary conditions of 'independence', the defining characteristics need to be established and understood as the Romans themselves understood them, for the ambassadors sent by the Judaean rulers sought to convince the Roman Senate that they could meet the Roman criteria for independence. The senate made the necessary decision. The attitude of the Seleucid kings was not relevant. It may have been that in the Seleucid Empire there was no concept of independence;[3] the Romans, nevertheless, had their own perception of *libertas* (see Chapter 6) which was not the same as Greek *eleutheria*.[4] The Roman definition of 'freedom' was that a state had to be free and autonomous, ungarrisoned and not subject to tribute.[5] When conditions in Judaea offered freedom from Seleucid taxation, military victories over Seleucid armies and freedom from Seleucid garrisons, all or most of these developments could persuade the senate that Judaea was independent. Judas' envoys to Rome in 162 BCE had received a declaration of *libertas*, only to have it rendered null and void by the conquest of Judaea by the Seleucid army at the battle of Elasa.[6] This chapter will trace the means by which each of the Judaean leaders attempted to forge their independence from the Seleucids. Hand in hand with these political and military shifts, is the unravelling of the Seleucid Empire and the changing political landscape of the Near East. How the relationship between Rome and the Hasmonaeans fared under these conditions, forms the background to this chapter.

When Judas Maccabaeus was killed at the battle of Elasa in 160 BCE, by the Seleucid army led by Bacchides,[7] the diplomatic ties with Rome came to an end, not because the friendship of the Roman people died with the death of the Jewish leader. Friendship was intended to be permanent.[8] When a country had been reconquered and was no longer *in sua potestate* (under its own power), it lost the freedom and autonomy that the senate had given it. Once the Seleucid army had eliminated the independence of Judaea, diplomatic ties with Rome no longer existed. Until the time that the Judaeans could show themselves once more to be independent, a new embassy to Rome to restart and re-form diplomatic relations was not possible. Diplomatic relations had to be established afresh, revived and re-constituted, not renewed. Unlike the first relations concluded with Judas, there is no evidence of a declaration of *libertas* being made in the senate for Jonathan and Simon. The only opportunities that presented themselves to convince the Romans of Judaean independence were those made by the efforts of the Judaean leadership and their armies. Their *libertas* was cancelled out through conquest of their territory and military victories were necessary to restore their formerly granted Roman autonomy.

## *Jonathan (160–142 BCE)*

Jonathan could only turn to Rome when his envoys could report that they had beaten the army of Demetrius in the field and thus had returned to the status quo ante. Initially, Jonathan allied himself with the pretender to the throne, Alexander Balas, who, in turn, made Jonathan High Priest and later made him his 'First Friend'.[9] This allegiance was in line with Roman policy to support Balas. In 153 BCE the senate had recognised Balas as the son of Antiochus IV and pledged their help.[10] Jonathan remained loyal to him throughout until Balas' death in 145 BCE. During this period, Jonathan could not approach Rome as he had become a vassal of the man the Romans had recognised as king of Syria.[11] On Balas' death, Jonathan could take action to rid Jerusalem of the hated Seleucid garrison and laid siege to the Akra, the symbol of subjection to the Seleucids.[12] Demetrius II objected and Jonathan journeyed to Ptolemais to the king and brought him gifts. This was a sign of submission.[13] Thus, Jonathan was still not free of the Seleucids. He was confirmed as High Priest, given some tax relief, all for the price of 300 talents.[14]

Jonathan broke with Demetrius II when the king reneged on a deal he made, that all Seleucid garrisons would be removed from Judaea and that, in return, Jonathan would send Jewish soldiers to help him put down a rebellion in Antioch. Jonathan kept his side of the bargain, but the king did not. When another pretender arose, Antiochus VI, Jonathan joined his campaign against Demetrius II.[15] That Rome favoured Antiochus VI is revealed in an incident told by Diodorus. Some time after 142/41 BCE, when Tryphon had Antiochus VI murdered so that he could take the throne, he had a gold statue of Victory weighing 10,000 gold staters sent to Rome. The statue was accepted, but the Romans had it inscribed with the name of Antiochus VI. Jonathan's allegiance to Antiochus VI was in line with Roman policy. Jonathan was treated by Antiochus not as a vassal, but as a high court official, as shown by his being given the right to wear purple and drink from gold cups.[16] These constitute the signs of recognition that Jonathan had been promoted to the highest levels of court rank.[17] With the military victory near Hazor around 143 BCE, he was a ruler in his own right and had scored a decisive victory over Demetrius II.[18] He had achieved the necessary conditions to make an approach to Rome. Josephus elaborated on the account in 1 Maccabees and called this a 'brilliant victory', one that had caused Jonathan to believe that God's providence had been behind his success and would bode well for the future.[19] With the defeat of Demetrius II, his envoys could argue in Rome that they had thrown off Seleucid control and defeated an enemy of Rome.

There had been an absence of diplomatic relations with Rome, a cessation of the arrangement gained by Judas, as is clear from 1 Macc. 12.3. Here the envoys speak in the senate of the 'former' friendship and alliance. Hence, for Jonathan there was a need to revive diplomatic relations with Rome. 1 Macc. 12 explains that Jonathan thought the time was ripe to send an embassy to Rome: 'And Jonathan saw that the circumstances were working in his advantage, and he chose men and sent them to Rome to establish and revive friendship with them.' Verse 2, regarding his sending of an embassy to Sparta, seems out of place, interrupting the narrative between the sending of an embassy and their arrival before the senate in Rome. The verse also anticipates what is to come in verse 16 in Jonathan's letter to the Spartans.[20]

Doubts have been expressed about the authenticity of the letter to the Spartans.[21] Indeed, there exists a considerable literature on the question of the historicity of Judaean ties with Sparta.[22] Three letters are cited: the letter of Jonathan to the Spartans (1 Macc. 12.6–18); the Spartans' reply to the High Priest Onias (1 Macc. 8.20–23); and later the letter of the Spartans to Simon (1 Macc. 14.20–23). To judge the letter authentic or false does not preclude the possibility that authentic information may be embedded in the letter.[23] The letter of Jonathan to the Spartans, while found in the context of Roman–Judaean relations, mentions the names of the two envoys sent to Rome only at the end of the document. It would appear that the author of the First Book of Maccabees combined his knowledge that there had been an embassy to Rome under Jonathan and the existence of this letter, and clumsily tried to integrate the two.[24] There exists a vast literature on the authenticity of the Spartan correspondence. Many judge the correspondence authentic,[25] but there are those who consider them to be a literary invention.[26] Ties between Judaea and Sparta are testified in the Second Book of Maccabees at an earlier date, when the ousted High Priest Jason fled and chose as his place of refuge Sparta.[27] It is not essential to enter into the debate on the authenticity of the Jewish–Spartan correspondence to accept the names of Jonathan's envoys to Rome that are contained in the letter of Jonathan to the Spartans.[28]

Gruen maintains that the timing of such an embassy to Rome was inappropriate in the middle of a war.[29] There may be an explanation. Jonathan, now allied to the pretender, Antiochus VI (supported by Tryphon), had augmented the borders of Judaea to include Ashkelon in the south, Ekron to the west, and Jaffa on the coast.[30] The Seleucid army under Demetrius II withdrew, and Jonathan wanted Roman acknowledgement of these new borders to gain legitimacy in the region. The extent of new territory is significant due to the benefits that diplomatic relations with Rome could bring regarding the new borders of Judaea. The Romans, by granting diplomatic relations, guaranteed those borders. That is what was meant by friends of the Romans having a guarantee of their territorial integrity at the time they entered into the friendship of the Romans.[31] Additionally, it was important in the context of long-held Roman views regarding when a war could be commenced without a declaration of war,[32] that when the Romans made allies, it then became part of their laws of war that an attack on an ally was regarded as if it were an attack on Rome itself.[33] In order to determine whether an attack had actually occurred on the territory of an ally, the precise boundaries of the territory of that ally needed to be recognised by Rome.

A discussion of Jonathan's renewed ties with Rome would be incomplete without addressing certain suggestions that this embassy is a doublet of the embassy of Simon.[34] There are similarities: both embassies were headed by a certain Numenius and both were tasked with establishing friendly relations with Sparta. The fact that the same name occurs in both missions speaks for its authenticity. There was, in fact, a strong tradition of a dynasty of Jews who specialised in foreign negotiations. Stern traced these relationships but did not use them as an argument for the historicity of the embassy of Jonathan.[35] The series of embassies began, as far as is known, with that to Antiochus III over the freedoms granted to the Jews in 200 BCE. Judas Maccabaeus sent Eupolemus to Rome in 162 BCE; Eupolemus' own father had negotiated with Antiochus III and may have been an envoy to the Romans in 174 BCE.[36] The other envoy of Judas was Jason, whose own son was charged with the responsibility to go to Rome for John Hyrcanus.[37] Jason, one of the two representatives at Rome for Judas, had a nephew, Antipater, and he is present in the embassy of Jonathan and Simon. Diodorus, son of Jason participated in the embassy to Rome under John Hyrcanus in 128 BCE.[38]

This continuity of the same family members acting as foreign envoys for Judaea may point to nothing more than a scarcity of a diplomatic corps at the Hasmonaean court, of men with the necessary language fluency and knowledge of Roman practices and government to make them suitable envoys,[39] or their recurrence may reflect an intentional concentration of diplomatic activity within the same families. The practice of using the members of the same families for diplomatic work reflects the practice among Hellenistic kings. Its origin may lie in the guest friendship (ξενία) existing between Hellenistic kings and the leading citizens of Greek cities.[40] The two Numenii may be one and the same man, as the embassies are close enough in time to permit this. Good reasons existed to send the same man: the Romans would have been more receptive to someone previously known to them and one who had already established contacts among the Roman nobility. Another possibility was offered by Fischer, who suggested that the two embassies were one and the same. He proposed that the embassy set out during the leadership of Jonathan, but did not return until after Simon had taken over from his brother (held as prisoner of Tryphon and later murdered).[41]

The date of the embassy has been placed at c. 144/43 BCE.[42] It is necessary to explain at this point that the senate gave *amicitia* and not a treaty. Jonathan's letter to the Spartans speaks of a revival of the former friendship and alliance, while Josephus in *The Jewish War* (1.48) mentions only friendship. Elsewhere, Josephus reports that Jonathan received from the Romans a ratification of the senate's former decrees concerning friendship, which can only mean what Judas had been given.[43] This would lead the reader to assume that Jonathan's envoys went to Rome to request exactly what Judas had achieved. In the previous chapter, it was argued that Judas had received not a treaty but *amicitia* (friendship), which could be formed by the senate. For the outcome of Jonathan's embassy, 1 Maccabees 12.3 and 12.16 speak of the formation of friendship and alliance (φιλίαν καί συμμαχίαν).[44] Josephus (*Ant.* 13.164) reports more fully than the author of 1 Maccabees. He writes: 'Accordingly, when they [the envoys] came to Rome, they appeared before the senate and delivered the message of the High Priest Jonathan, saying that he had sent them to establish[45] the alliance (συμμαχίας), whereupon the senate ratified its former decrees concerning friendship (φιλίας) with the Jews'.[46] Josephus elsewhere (*BJ* 1.48) speaks simply of ties of 'friendship'. It is important to note that Jonathan was securing friendship on the basis of what had gone before under Judas Maccabaeus. The latter had not received a *foedus* (for the defining characteristics of a *foedus*, see Chapter 5; for no *foedus* struck by Rome after the embassy of Judas, see Chapter 6) and the senate in reissuing its previous decision was also not offering Jonathan a *foedus* but friendship.[47]

### *Simon (143–134 BCE)*

When Tryphon, the guardian of Antiochus VI, killed his ward and claimed the throne for himself in c. 142/41 BCE, Simon switched his allegiance to Demetrius II. The Romans had an interest in the defeat of Tryphon and in aligning himself with Demetrius II Simon was in effect supporting the Ptolemies (friends of Rome), who had placed Demetrius on the throne. Simon gained independence from the Seleucids, as evidenced by the king's decision to free Judaea from tribute and taxation.[48] 1 Maccabees 13.41 presents Simon as the liberator, having lifted 'the yoke of the gentiles' from Judaea. Josephus writes in the same vein, linking liberation with freedom from tribute.[49] This conformed to one part of the Roman definition of *libertas*. The obstacle of still having the Akra in Jerusalem was removed, with the siege lasting two years and with the surrender of the Seleucid troops. The date of this final liberation is disputed, depending on the length of the siege, placed variously at spring 142 or April 141.[50] This satisfied another of the prerequisites of Roman *libertas* – namely, to be ungarrisoned. Simon had now obtained real liberty from the Seleucids.[51] This change was commemorated with a new dating system heralding a new era based on the first year of liberation from the Seleucids.[52] A yearly celebration was also held to mark liberation from the Seleucid garrison.[53] Such a change in the calendar was not unprecedented: other cases include Aradus, Tyre and Ashkelon, when they too freed themselves from Seleucid rule.[54]

Having met the Roman preconditions for diplomatic relations, Simon was ready to send an embassy to Rome. Before that could occur, there is mentioned, but not cited, a document in the First Book of Maccabees. The text of 1 Macc. 14.16–18 is as follows:

> [16] And it was heard in Rome and as far as Sparta that Jonathan had died, and they grieved greatly. [17] But when they heard that Simon his brother had become High Priest in his place and that he himself had gotten control over the country and the cities within it, [18] they wrote to him on bronze tablets in order to renew with him the friendship and alliance which they had established with Judas and Jonathan his brothers.

This communication does not conform at all to Roman practice and there is a wide consensus against its authenticity.[55] The Romans had no need and did not in practice send messages abroad seeking alliances. The senate waited for embassies to arrive in Rome, in this period in February each year, to make such requests.[56] The most damning part of the text is the erroneous claim that the Romans sent out this communication on bronze tablets. The whole use and significance of bronze tablets has been dealt with in Chapter 2. In brief, bronze was used for its magical properties and for its longevity. It was used for legal documents, such as laws, senatorial decrees, treaties and diplomas of discharge from the Roman army. The metal, moreover, was too expensive to be used for epistolary communication where papyrus would suffice. The purpose of this falsification was to justify Simon's decision to turn to Rome because it could be said that he had been prompted by Roman goodwill.

As a result of this Roman 'invitation', 1 Maccabees (14.24) reports the sending of an embassy to Rome under Numenius, who took with him a great shield weighing 1,000 mina to present to the Romans.[57] This was a gift of submission, acknowledging Rome's power and requesting protection in the same way that ambassadors brought crowns of gold to the Romans as was discussed in Chapter 4.[58] Variants in manuscripts give only a higher figure of five times one thousand (πεντακισχιλίων).[59] Previous Jewish embassies sent by Judas and Jonathan had not brought gifts: in other words, previously the Jews had not felt the need to give proof of submission to the Romans. In the short period from 162 to 142 BCE, Judaea had lost its independence twice, resulting in the absence of ties with Rome. The Romans had to be persuaded that this time ties would last and the best way to convince them was with a substantial gift, costlier than the gifts brought by the Seleucid rulers or pretenders. Since, however, both Jonathan and Simon had acted in accordance with Roman policy towards the Seleucids in the sides that they chose in the internecine rivalries within the Seleucid kingdom, the Romans looked favourably on the envoys.

The embassy is dated to no later than the end of 141 BCE.[60] The letter in 1 Macc. 15.16–24 reads as follows:

> [16] Lucius, consul of the Romans, to King Ptolemy: greetings. [17] The envoys of our friends and allies the Judaeans have come to us, having been sent from Simon the High Priest and the Judaean people, reviving the original[61] (ἀρχῆς) friendship and alliance [18] and they have offered a golden shield worth 1,000 minas. [19] Therefore, it was pleasing to us to write to the kings and countries that they not seek evil against them and that they not make war against them, neither against their cities nor against their country, and that they not fight as allies of those who make war against them. [20] We have decided to accept the shield from them. [21] Therefore, if any pernicious men flee from their country to you, hand them over to Simon the High Priest, so that he may punish them in accordance with their Law. [22] The same things wrote he likewise unto King Demetrius, and Attalus, to Ariarathes, to Arsaces, [23] and to all the countries and to Sampsame, and the Lacedaemonians, and to Delos, and Myndus, and Sicyon, and Caria, and Samos, Pamphylia, Lycia, Halicarnassus, Rhodes, Phaselis, Cos, Side, Aradus, Gortyna, Cnidus and Cyrene. [24] They also wrote a copy of this to Simon the High Priest.

The letter is placed in the narrative at the point when the envoys return. It was not necessarily misplaced, nor should it have to come after 1 Mac. 14.24, which speaks of the sending of the embassy.[62]

At the outset it is important to deal with a point raised by Mendelssohn that this letter is a duplicate of a document cited by Josephus at *Ant.* 14.145–147 and is a later interpolation into the text.[63] There are several divergences in the letter in 1 Maccabees from that in Josephus' *Antiquities*. Some of the details differ and not all information is found in both documents. The shield is said to weigh 1,000 pounds in 1 Maccabees and in the *Antiquities* it is worth 50,000 gold pieces. In 1 Maccabees the Roman official is Lucius, the consul, but a praetor in the *Antiquities*. The embassy is sent representing the High Priest Simon and the Jewish people in 1 Maccabees and in the *Antiquities* they represent the Elders of the Jewish people. The extradition clause in 1 Maccabees is absent from the document quoted in the *Antiquities*.[64] The similarities are only superficial and do not justify the rejection of the Maccabaean document as a doublet of the document from the time of John Hyrcanus.

The letter is widely held to be inauthentic despite the brief mention by Josephus of an embassy by Simon to Rome (*Ant.* 13.227).[65] Several features regarding the content of the letter have fuelled suspicions that the letter might be a forgery: the manner in which the addressee is identified, the value of the golden shield, the extradition clause and the itinerary of the circular letters, in particular, to the king of the Parthians and to an unknown place, Sampsame.

The letter opens with the name of the writer, a Roman official identified only by his *praenomen*. Stern suggests that in the manuscript the *nomen* had disappeared.[66] The standard manner in extant Roman letters in Greek to the East was to open with the name of the addressee with the *praenomen*, followed by *nomen* and filiation, for example, Spurius Postumius, son of Lucius, praetor of the Romans.[67]

*Table 7.1* Comparison of the Lucius Letter with the Valerius Decree[a]

| *1 Macc. 15.16–24* | *Jos. Ant. 14.145–148* |
|---|---|
| Letter of the Roman consul Lucius | Decree of the senate presided over by the praetor Lucius Valerius, son of Lucius |
| The envoys are sent by the High Priest Simon and by the Jews | The envoys are emissaries of the Jews and Simon is not mentioned |
| A short preamble addressed to King Ptolemy | A detailed preamble giving the date, place where the senate met, names of the witnesses and names of the Jewish envoys in accordance with the details in epigraphically preserved *senatus consulta* |
| Only one envoy named – Numenius, son of Antiochus | Three envoys are named – Alexander, son of Jason, Numenius, son of Antiochus and Alexander, son of Dorotheus |
| Golden shield valued at 1,000 minas | Gold shield valued at 50,000 pieces of gold |
| Letters are sent directly to kings, cities and countries, with a copy to Simon | Jewish envoys request copies of letters to various states |
| Main goal of the embassy is to renew the formerly existing friendship | Main goal of the embassy is to renew the formerly existing friendship |

Note

a Adapted Shatzman (2012) 59. Other charts showing the similarities of the two documents side by side: Rappaport (2004) 340 and Seeman (2011) 192.

Sherk provides countless examples of the typical formula.[68] How the letter should be set out, its structure and content, cannot be compared with other letters: the extant letters from Roman magistrates written to the Greek East present no standard model.[69]

Lucius is described in verse 16 as ὕπατος Ῥωμανίων. This provides a clue to the date of the document. Generally in the second century BCE we find in inscriptions that the Greek translation for consul was στρατηγὸς ὕπατος. Only in the first century BCE did it become common to write just ὕπατος to designate a consul.[70] Greek writers on Roman history, for example, Dionysius of Halicarnassus, also followed this convention, writing ὕπατος for consul.[71] When could this letter have been composed? The terminus post quem is the date of composition of the First Book of Maccabees. Estimates range from 104 to 63 BCE.[72] The term στρατηγὸς ὕπατος as a Greek translation for 'consul' is last attested in 92 BCE.[73] The letter, therefore, would fit with a date from 91–63 BCE. This indicates that the letter is not contemporaneous with the rule of Simon.

Attempts to identify the Lucius who is consul in 1 Maccabees have settled on the only consul between 143 and 137 BCE who is attested in the consular Fasti with the *praenomen* Lucius: L. Caecilius Metellus Calvus, who was consul in 142.[74]

The single word 'Ptolemy' to address the King of Egypt in the Lucius letter (1 Macc. 15.16) is typical of the way kings were addressed in official correspondence by the Romans. In the letter of the praetor M. Valerius Messala in 193 BCE to Antiochus III, he is simply mentioned as 'Antiochus the king'. In a *senatus consultum* of c. 156 BCE the king of Cappadocia is mentioned as 'Ariarathes, the king'. The king of Pergamum in a similar manner is addressed as 'Eumenes, the king' in a letter from 171/70 BCE.[75] The ruler of Egypt in 142 BCE was Ptolemy VIII Euergetes II. Outside of Roman correspondence, we find in an inscription that this Ptolemy is called Euergetes the second, so that there is no confusion with Ptolemy III Euergetes.[76]

The inclusion of the high value of the shield given in the Lucius letter has led to the common opinion that this document is inauthentic. It was seen in Chapter 4 that the senate was accustomed to noting the value of the golden crowns donated by foreign envoys. While it is known that states sent representatives with fabulously costly gifts, such as Rhodes in 167 BCE, Ariarathes in 161 BCE and Demetrius I in 160,[77] these states were far wealthier than Judaea. By comparison, Simon's gift to the Romans was far costlier than that brought to Rome by Demetrius I's envoys or by Tryphon.[78] The Romans listed the weight and, therefore, the value of the gold crowns that ambassadors presented to Rome.

The Lucius letter contains an extradition clause that, in terms of international law, in fact means that a country formally surrenders an alleged criminal to another country having jurisdiction over the crime charged. This clause, asking Ptolemy and all the other states mentioned to hand over Jews, has caused some concern over its authenticity. The 'renegades' or 'traitors' (λοιμοὶ) are said to be those fleeing from their country and being punished under their law, which would indicate that the clause refers to Jewish renegades. What is the nature of their crime? These λοιμοὶ are used in 1 Macc. 15.3 to refer to the supporters of Tryphon, the pretender to the Seleucid throne, which supports the view that the λοιμοὶ were guilty of political crimes.[79] Was this a special provision or was it a clause routinely used? Rappaport suggests that it was a special clause inserted at the request of Simon or his representatives to return political exiles to Judaea. Such exiles may have been the Tobiads and their supporters in Egypt, the Oniads and their followers in Egypt, Hellenising Jews, and political opponents of the Hasmonaeans.[80] The decree of the assembly in Jerusalem confirmed Simon as ruler and gave the right to punish anyone who opposed any of the decree's provisions.[81] The fact that both the Lucius letter and the decree for Simon both address the problem of political opposition and the desire to punish, indicates a worrisome level of political opponents to the Hasmonaean regime scattered outside Judaea.[82]

Momigliano interpreted this clause to refer also to the Romans' obligation to hand over criminals and insists this was contrary to Roman law.[83] Greek and Roman customs regarding hospitality and the protection of guests were based on a belief that the gods provided for asylum. Violations of the right of asylum, they believed, brought down retribution from the gods. Often, asylum was based on an individual's proximity to certain powerful symbols. In Rome, refuge was available at two places: the Asylum between the Capitol Hill and the Arx (also known as *inter duos lucus*) and the Temple of Ceres Liber et Libera. The former was said to have been in operation from the time it was instituted by Romulus.[84] The second site in Rome where an individual could seek refuge was built in 493 BCE and was located on the slopes of the Aventine near the Circus Maximus.[85] The right of asylum was a *ius*; that is, a religiously ordained right, not one granted through legislation.[86] In fact, the extradition clause cannot be dismissed on the grounds of Roman law. There is no conflict between the extradition clause and the religious law at Rome. The *ius asyli* is not analogous to the extradition clause as we find it in the decree. The extradition law dealt with a class of people, while the right of asylum in Rome was confined to individuals. If the circular letter had wanted the Romans to extradite Jews, they would have required a list naming each individual wanted for extradition. By contrast, those who were the target for extradition are called λοιμοί, which can be variously translated as 'traitors' or 'renegades' or, more literally, 'pestilential enemies'.[87] Most of the discussion of the identity of these enemies is located within the chronological framework of 142 BCE.[88] The authority of a leader in Judaea to have power over Jews no matter where they were located, given the geographical reach of the distribution of the letter, was not acknowledged by the Romans until the time of Julius Caesar. Grants of such legal jurisdiction by the Romans were given first to Hyrcanus II and later to Herod by Augustus.[89] While it is not impossible that the Romans gave Simon this power, it is most implausible.

Following the Lucius letter is a list of 23 named kings and countries to whom this letter was sent. Momigliano considered that this section of the letter had been added onto the end to provide details that are lacking in the *senatus consultum*, which merely states that letters are to be sent 'to the free states and to the kings'.[90] Goldstein considers it was a common practice among the Romans to send a copy of the text of a letter – in this case, to Simon – that had been despatched to many people and places. The number of copies would show to Simon and the others how wide ranging was this new decision.[91]

First on the list is Demetrius II of Syria. Next are King Attalus of Pergamum (a key Roman ally), Ariarathes of Cappadocia, and Arsaces, the king of the Parthians, with whom Rome had no diplomatic relations. There follows a list of Greek states: Sparta, Delos, Myndos, Sicyon. States in Asia Minor come after this: Caria, Pamphylia and Halicarnassus, followed by Rhodes, Phaselis, Cos, Sidon, Aradus, Gortyna, Cnidus, Cyprus and Cyrene.[92] The top four destinations, showing their importance, are Syria, Pergamum, Cappadocia and Parthia, all in the East (that is, east of Cyprus). It was not unknown for the Romans to send copies of their diplomatic decisions to other cities. The Piracy Law of 100 BCE was circulated to various states by letter.[93] Philo provides an example of a circular letter that was despatched around Greece. The destinations were Thessaly, Boeotia, Macedonia, Aetolia, Attica, Argos, Corinth, most of the Peloponnese, and the islands of Euboea, Cyprus and Crete.[94]

The name 'Arsaces' is not a reliable chronological indicator because the Romans used it as a generic term for all Parthian kings.[95] The time could well be 143 or 47 BCE. If the letter belongs to 142 BCE, the evidence for contact between

Rome and the Parthians depends on a verse from the satirist, Lucilius, who was a close friend of Scipio Aemilianus.[96] He was said to have owned the house in Rome that was originally built at public expense to house the future Demetrius I when he was a hostage in Rome.[97] He was given a rare honour with a public funeral.[98] His work, known only in fragments, contains the following words, which he puts in the mouth of Scipio Aemilianus (14.464–465):[99] 'I will go as envoy to the king, to Rhodes, to Ecbatana and Babylon. I will take a small ship.' These words were intended as satire of a boastful Roman noble about to head off to the East. It is written in the future tense (*ibo* 'I will go') and by itself does not indicate that Scipio realised his plans. It is inherent in the text that Scipio did not attain his exaggerated goals, otherwise there would be no satire centred on Scipio's hubris. Book 14 was published posthumously between Scipio Aemilianus' death in 129 BCE and Lucilius' in 103/102 BCE.[100] No offence was made to Scipio in his lifetime. No longer part of the Seleucid Empire by the time of the embassy, Ecbatana and Babylon had been taken over by the Parthians in the campaigns by Mithridates I. The border of the Parthian Empire was now the Euphrates.[101] The route of Scipio's embassy took him first to Egypt, then to Cyprus and Syria.[102] Between Syria and the next stop in Asia Minor, there may have been time to visit Parthian territory.[103] The majority of scholars consider it unlikely that Scipio proceeded so far east.[104] Added to their opinion is the nature of the evidence, a few verses of satire that do not reflect well on the personality of Scipio Aemilianus. A more fitting explanation for the sending of a letter to the Parthian king, if the letter is genuine, might be the recent conquest by the Parthians of Media and Babylonia where sizable Jewish communities were situated, some in closed rural settlements and some in the large cities, such as, Seleucia.[105]

If the reference to the Parthians belongs in a letter dated to 47 BCE, diplomatic relations between Rome and Parthia had been attempted; these started in 94/93BCE when a Parthian envoy met with Sulla, a meeting that ended in failure.[106] Under Lucullus an agreement was reached with Phraates to mutually lay down the western border of the Parthian Empire at the Euphrates in 69 BCE.[107] Pompey in 65 BCE was met by Parthian ambassadors, but nothing emerged from the talks except a letter that Pompey sent to Phraates in which he refused to address the Parthian king as the 'King of Kings'.[108] Two further embassies to Pompey were rebuffed, as was their request that the Euphrates border still stand.[109] There may have been an agreement reached in 64 BCE, which some late sources report was in effect until Crassus launched his ill-fated campaign ending in the disaster at Carrhae in 53 BCE.[110] Certainly the allegations against Crassus that he had embarked on an 'unjust war' lend weight to the existence of diplomatic ties at that time, which Crassus had breached by his unprovoked attack.[111] Strabo reports that, prior to Crassus' campaign, the Parthians had a favourable view of the Romans.[112] Cicero informs us that between 51 and 49 BCE there was talk in Rome of sending either Pompey or Caesar to make war on the Parthians to avenge Crassus' death.[113] Nothing came of this. The anti-Caesarean faction in the senate talked about a Parthian campaign in the first period of the civil war in 49–48 BCE.[114] By 47 BCE Julius Caesar was already thinking about a Parthian campaign, although active preparations did not get underway until 44 BCE.[115] As the danger to Syria from Parthian incursions subsided in 46 BCE, talk of a Parthian war had died down.[116] In summary, throughout the first century BCE there had been many confirmed diplomatic contacts, but in 142 BCE we cannot say with any certainty that there had been any diplomatic contact between Rome and the Parthians, which only serves to show that the Late Republic fits the period of the Lucius letter. One could suggest that the date 47 BCE best fits the atmosphere in Rome between 51 and 47 BCE, when there was talk of a Parthian war. In 46 BCE the war was no longer a current topic.

Included also in the list of places to which the letter is to be sent is Sampsame (Σαμψάμη), which has roused doubts about the authenticity of the list.[117] In a bid to prove the list is not a forgery, several attempts have been made to identify this location, presenting several possibilities. The manuscripts have various readings: Samsani, Samsamae, Samsake, Sampsace and the Syriac *smsnws*.[118] Michaelis in 1778 was the first to suggest the city may be Samsun on the south Black Sea coast (which at this time was not part of Pontus).[119] The suggestion of Amisos, based on the legend on coins from Amisos reading 'Samisos', was rendered ineligible when Reinach showed that 'Samisos' came from είς Ἄμισον.[120] Reinach proposed instead Samosate, the capital of Commagene, which had strategic importance being on the Euphrates and controlling the caravan routes to the East. Reasoning that in Hebrew the name would be Samsat, Reinach postulated confusion between the final *tav* or *tet* with a *mem* that would result in the name being written as Samsam and being transcribed by the Greek translator of 1 Maccabees as Sampsame.[121] Against this, Reinach's suggestion does not account for the *-p* sound in the name as we have it in Greek.

The inclusion of the place name Sampsame would be more credible if a location could be shown to exist closer to Judaea. Stephanus of Byzantium, the author of *Ethnica* (a geographical gazetteer in over fifty books), writing in the sixth century CE, mentioned Σάμφη (Samphe), a city-state in Phoenicia whose inhabitants were called to ἐθνικὸν Σαμψηός (Sampseos).[122] It may be that the people of Samphe were on the list, rather than a town in the Black Sea. How reliable is this information? While only fragments of his work are preserved mainly from an epitome by Hermolaus (a grammaticus and subordinate of Stephanus),[123] it is known that the original work contained quotations from authors such as Polybius, Herodotus, Thucydides, Xenophon and Strabo.[124] This extract from Stephanus is from the epitome and part of the original Book 46.[125] The mention of this Phoenician city may be derived from one of his sources, that of Philo Erennius (Herennius), who was from Byblos and wrote a 30-volume work, *On Cities and on the glorious Persons each of which has offered*. Also known as Philo of Byblos, he lived a long life from the time of Nero until c. 104 CE.[126] In any event, it is to be regretted that we have only this brief mention from Stephanus and not the full text, which gives no indication of the date of the foundation of the city.

Schwartz links Scipio's embassy, which he dates to 140–139 BCE, with the return in 139/38 BCE of Jewish envoys who elicited Roman involvement throughout the East on behalf of the Hasmonaeans. He maintains that it took the Jewish ambassadors a year or two to return to Judaea. If the senate decided to send letters supporting Simon around the Mediterranean, he speculates that Simon's envoys had to deliver them.[127] Schwartz's suggestion that Simon's envoys travelled with Scipio or in its wake is problematic because he accepts 140–139 BCE as the date for the embassy of Scipio based on Diodorus.[128] Cavaignac first brought awareness of the problems with the chronological sequencing of the Diodorus fragments.[129] Moreover, Diodorus used Athenian archon years, which he tried unsuccessfully to reconcile with Roman consular years, and this has given rise to chronological anomalies.[130] His source for this period, Posidonius, tended to insert blocks of text out of their true chronological position. All of these factors should give rise to a certain amount of caution when using Diodorus for dating in this period.[131] To maintain the later date requires a dismissal of the evidence of Cicero, who corrected his earlier error that the embassy fell between his censorship in 142 BCE and his second consulship in 132 BCE and later confirmed that the embassy left Rome before Scipio's censorship, which was in 142–140 BCE.[132] By 45 BCE, Cicero was correcting his earlier mistakes on the chronology of material in the 140s that he had written previously.[133] For these reasons, Mattingly correctly places the embassy in 144/43 BCE.[134] Sherwin-White has remarked on the silence of the ambassadors (if they travelled in 140–139 BCE) concerning the conquests of the Parthians of the eastern portions of the Seleucid Empire, criticism only relevant after 140 BCE. Mesopotamia was taken over in 141 BCE and Babylonia soon after 140, both events occurring during the time accepted for the embassy by Schwartz.[135]Additional arguments for an earlier date were brought by Astin, who noted that Marx's provisions of travel times were overestimated. This led to the supposition that the whole journey of Scipio lasted two years, whereas Astin gives a timetable in which the envoys left Rome in March 144 BCE and returned in August/September 143 BCE.[136]

In summary, the Lucius letter must postdate the period of Simon. Suspicions of inauthenticity are fuelled by the manner in which the consul is named (simply as Lucius), which flies in the face of firm Roman custom. His office is given in Greek as ὕπατος, which was not the standard Greek translation used for 'consul' until 91 BCE. This feature alone is cause for concern. If we add to this the legal jurisdiction over Jews everywhere, which was not given by the Romans to Jewish leaders until the time of Hyrcanus II, the conclusion must be reached that this document is suspect.[137] The list of kings and cities to whom a circular letter is to be sent is unprecedented for this period and is not attested until 100 BCE in the Piracy Law. Whenever this letter was composed, it was not in the time of Simon. The suggestion of Momigliano that, while the letter of Lucius is false, an authentic letter had once existed, must be rejected.[138] It is not possible to reconstruct such a letter from details of the *senatus consultum* quoted by Josephus, as the date of the Lucius letter could fall between 91 and 63 BCE and the senatorial decree belongs to 47 BCE, as we shall see later. Such a date for the decree puts it outside the range of dates for the composition of the First Book of Maccabees.

In terms of evaluating the letter, the senatorial decree must be distinguished from the forged letter of the consul Lucius (which Josephus omits). The decree is genuine and is datable to 47 BCE. There are individual features of the letter that can only be authentic for the year 47 BCE. As a result, evidence for Roman diplomatic relations at the time of Simon cannot be reconstructed on the basis of the Lucius letter or the senatorial decree of the praetor Lucius Valerius. The only evidence comes from Josephus *Ant.* 13.227, which simply says in summing up Simon's achievements that he 'did also himself make an alliance with the Romans.'

## *John Hyrcanus I (134–104 BCE)*

Hyrcanus was the first or second son of Simon. On the death of his father, he marched to Jerusalem, having been commander of the troops in Gezer. He inherited his father's position as High Priest.[139] In the first year of his reign, Antiochus VII laid siege to Jerusalem and Hyrcanus was forced to sue for peace. Hyrcanus insisted that one of the terms be that Jews be permitted to continue to live under their ancestral laws. Antiochus' terms imposed a handover of weapons, imposition of tribute and a partial restoration of the Seleucid garrison in the Akra. In addition, Hyrcanus had to provide hostages as a guarantee of good faith and pay 500 talents.[140] Hyrcanus' attitude to Rome may be inferred by his actions. The main evidence is his sending envoys to Rome to seek backing for his military exploits. Three Roman documents are quoted by Josephus, which historians believe refer to Roman diplomatic relations under John Hyrcanus I. These documents are the Fannius Decree (Jos. *Ant.* 13.259–266), the Valerius Decree (Jos. *Ant.* 14.144–148) and the Pergamum Decree (Jos. *Ant.* 14. 247–255). These decrees are presented with an accompanying commentary dealing with their authenticity and their date. Many have found it difficult to find chronological markers for these documents. I discuss the Valerius Decree later and consider it to belong to 47 BCE under Hyrcanus II. Now I shall discuss the Fannius Decree and the Pergamum Decree.

### *The Fannius Decree*

Josephus reports (*Ant.* 13.259) that Hyrcanus, the High Priest, wished to revive (ἀνανεώσασθαι) the friendship with the Romans and sent an embassy to Rome with a letter from himself. In response, the senate made friendship with him. Then follows the text of a senatorial decree. The text in Jos. *Ant.* 13.260–264 reads as follows:

> [260] 'Fannius son of Marcus, praetor convened the senate on the 8th day before the Ides of February in the Comitium, Lucius Mallius son of Lucius of the Menena tribe and Gaius Sempronius son of Gaius of the Falerna tribe being present, regarding the matters presented by Simon son of Dositheus and Apollonius son of Alexander and Diodorus son of Jason, excellent and worthy men sent by the Jewish people, [261] who also spoke of their existing friendship and alliance with the Romans and of public affairs such as their request that Joppa and its harbours and Gezer and Pegae and whatever

other cities and territories which Antiochus took from them in war, contrary to the decree of the senate, be restored to them; [262] and that royal troops not be permitted to march through their territory or that of their subjects; that the laws made by Antiochus during that war, contrary to the decree of the senate, be annulled; [263] and that the Romans send envoys to bring about the restitution of the places taken from the Jews by Antiochus, and to estimate the value of the territory damaged in war; and also that they give letters to the Jewish envoys for the kings and free cities to ensure their safety on their return home. [264] Regarding these matters, therefore, it has been decreed to renew friendship and alliance with these worthy men who have been sent by a worthy and friendly people. [265] Regarding the letters, however, they replied that they would deliberate on them when the senate should have leisure from its own affairs, and that they would see to it that no similar injustice should be done them in the future, and also that the praetor, Fannius, should give them money from the public treasury for their return home. [266] Accordingly, Fannius dismissed the Jewish envoys in this manner, giving them money from the public treasury and a senatorial decree to those who were to conduct them on their way and furnish them with a safe return home.

The cited document purports to be the text of a senatorial decree. There are many extant decrees known from inscriptions that provide a template for the form and content of these decrees. The order and phraseology is standard. Mommsen first isolated the constituent elements.[141] Moehring and Sherk follow him in their listing of the sections and their contents with opening and closing formulas.[142] Table 7.2 adopts Moehring's listings of the sections of a typical *senatus consultum* with his schema demonstrating how far a given document complies with the typical pattern.

From the decree we learn that three Jewish envoys spoke in the senate and reminded the senators of the current status of their friendship with Rome. They requested the return of the territory captured by King Antiochus, the imposition of a prohibition on Seleucid troops crossing their territory or that of their allies, the annulment of Antiochus' decisions, and the return of land from Antiochus and payment of war damages. The senate decided to revive friendship, to deliberate at their leisure on the demands of the Jewish ambassadors, to provide public funds for the envoys' return journey, and to give them a safe conduct letter.

The name Fannius, son of Marcus, praetor, is attested in Rome. The *gens Fannia* appears in the second century BCE.[143] This Fannius M. f. is generally identified as the son of M. Fannius C. f. (*RE* 14),[144] the brother of the consul of 161 BCE, C. Fannius Strabo (*RE* 20).[145] Münzer identifies Fannius with Fannius (*RE* 7) and dates his praetorship to 133 BCE and the embassy to between 133 and 131 BCE.[146] Others place the date of his praetorship in 127/6 BCE.[147]

The meeting of the senate in the Comitium refers merely to the Curia in the northwestern section of the Forum where the majority of senatorial meetings were held.[148] One should note that 'Comitium' is not found in the manuscripts

*Table 7.2* Comparison of the Fannius Decree with the standard form of a senatorial decree (*senatus consultum*)

| *Standard form for a senatus consultum* | *The Fannius Decree (Jos. Ant. 13.260–264)* | *Degree of compliance*[a] |
|---|---|---|
| I Prescript | | |
| (a) name and rank of the presiding magistrate/s | Fannius, the son of Marcus, praetor | + |
| (b) *senatus consuluit* τη συγκλὴτῳ συνεβουλεύσατο | Βουλὴν συνὴγαγε | / |
| (c) day and month of meeting | eighth day before the Ides of March | + |
| (d) place | in the Comitium | + |
| (e) names of the witnesses introduced by the phrase *scribendo adfuerunt* γραφομένῳ παρῆσαν | Lucius Mellius and Gaius Sempronius παρόντας | / |
| II Theme | | |
| (a) *relatio: quod* [name of *relator*] *uerba fecit de* [or *ut*] περί ὧν ὁ δεῖνα ἐποιὴσατο περὶ [or ὅπως] | περὶ ὧν ἐπρέσβευσε Σίμων . . . καὶ Διόδωρος . . . οἱ καὶ διελέχθησαν περὶ φιλίας . . . | + |
| (b) résumé of the events or motives that prompted the *relator* to bring the matter before the senate | ὅπως τε' Ιόππη . . . ἔλαβον' Αντίοχος | + |
| (c) concluding formula *d(e) e(a) r(e) i(ta) c(ensuereunt)* περὶ τούτοῦ πράγματος οὕδοξεν serves as an introduction to III | ἔδοξεν οὖν περὶ τούτων ταῦτα | + |
| III The Decree Proper | | |
| In *indirect* speech or introduced by *ut (uti)* | ἀζανεώσασθαι φιλίαν . . . | + |
| IV Mark of approval: formal expression of the vote c(ensuere) ἔδοξεν | | 0 |

Note

a + signifies full compliance; / signifies basic agreement with some difference in detail; 0 means the section is missing.

and is reconstructed from several different corrupt readings: Κόππῳ, Κόμπῳ and Κομπίῳ.[149]

It is difficult to identify a Lucius Mallius, son of Lucius of the tribe Menenia. There is no Mallius attested in this period. The closest is L. Mallius (*RE* 5), who was consul in 202 BCE and still alive in 167 BCE.[150] In Greek manuscripts, Mallius and Manlius were often confused. Münzer, therefore, identifies L. Mallius with L. Manlius (*RE* 27), who was quaestor in 168 BCE and thus a member of the senate at this time.[151] Some suggest Mallius is to be identified with L. Manlius Torquatus, quaestor 113 or 112 BCE.[152] The name of the tribe is disputed. The Greek text, as given by Niese, reads Mentina. Ritschl emended the name to Tromentina.[153]

Gaius Sempronius, son of Gaius of the Falerna tribe, is generally identified as C. Sempronius C. f. C. n. Tuditanus (*RE* 92).[154] His consulship for 129 BCE is attested, but his earlier career has to be reconstructed. Münzer suggests a quaestorship in 145 BCE, a curule aedileship in 135 BCE and the praetorship in 132 BCE.[155] A certain C. Sempronius C. f. also from the Falerna tribe is attested the *senatus consultum de agris Pergamenis* of 129 BCE.[156] There is no doubt that he was a senator at the time of the Jewish embassy.

The document mentions two witnesses. According to Sherk, the number of witnesses commonly listed down to the middle of the first century BCE is two or three.[157] It is said that by the time of Caesar there were ten or more witnesses to a *senatus consultum*.[158] The evidence for the Caesarian period from non-Jewish sources is based on two documents: one inscription (Sherk no. 26) and a letter of Cicero (*Fam.* 8.8.5). For the second century, several inscriptions are very incomplete: however, they do indicate that four or more witnesses were present.[159] Not much significance may be derived from the numbers of witnesses attached to Caesar's decrees. As Gelzer noted, Caesar announced his decisions in the senate and the names of witnesses included those who were not present and knew nothing about the decree.[160] It may be that the two names we see here were witnesses actually present, as apart from inflated lists of names. In any case, the evidence is too scanty to permit firm judgements based on the numbers of witnesses to date the document.[161]

Named Jewish envoys did not take part in previous embassies to Rome: only the father of Diodorus, Jason, may have been an envoy to Rome in 162 BCE.

The document mentions an 'existing friendship and alliance'. The Jewish envoys speak of an already-existing friendship in §261. However, the senate decrees to revive (ἀνανεώσασθαι) the ties of friendship in §264. A possible solution first put forward by Mendelssohn in 1875 is that a prior approach to Rome was made (to be found in the Pergamum Decree: Jos. *Ant.* 14.248–250) that re-established the diplomatic ties.[162] The revival of those ties could be made by the senate, indicating a strengthening of ties usually when the envoys presented a situation of some urgency or gravity.[163]

The decree refers to territory that Antiochus seized in war. Antiochus VII invaded Judaea in 134 BCE and the war lasted for over a year.[164] Hyrcanus made a settlement, thus ending the war in 132 BCE, as can be judged by the minting of Seleucid coins in Jerusalem from 132 BCE.[165] Both dates for the praetorship of C. Fannius are post-134 BCE, in 133 BCE or 127/26 BCE. The first date of 133 BCE would coincide with the middle of the war. The second date falls after the death of Antiochus VII in 129 BCE, during the reign of Demetrius II. Thus we can rule out a date before Antiochus VII laid siege to Jerusalem.[166] Rajak suggests a date during the siege of Jerusalem. This requires emending the text slightly in section 262 from καὶ ὅπως τὰ κατὰ τὸν πόλεμον ἐκεῖνον ψηφισθέντα ὑπὸ Ἀντιόχου παρὰ τὸ τῆς συγκλήτου δόγμα ἄκυρα γένηται, to read καὶ ὅπως τὰ κατὰ τὸν πόλεμον ἐκεῖνον ψηφισθέντα ὑπε\r Ἀντιόχου παρὰ τὸ τῆς συγκλήτου δόγμα ἄκυρα γένηται. This would permit her suggestion that a senatorial decree in favour of the Jews was obtained during the siege of Jerusalem, thus explaining the sudden decision of Antiochus VII to come to terms with Hyrcanus.[167] We shall return to Rajak's reconstruction of senatorial embassies under Hyrcanus I in the context of the Pergamum Decree. Suggestions that Antiochus is to be identified with Antiochus IX Cyzicenus, because he too invaded Judaea c. 113 BCE, fail on the basis of the date of Fannius' praetorship. Seeman suggests that the embassy was sent after the death of Antiochus VII to annul his seizures before the next king could claim the lands as his.[168]

We read that the envoys were to be provided with letters for kings and free peoples for their safe return. The senate granted the normal courtesies extended to returning envoys.[169]

Historians are divided over the date of this document. Some wish to attribute the decree to 110 BCE.[170] Ritschl wanted to date both it and the Pergamum Decree to the reign of Antiochus Sidetes – that is, between 138 and 129 BCE.[171] Reinach considered the Pergamum Decree to be even older.[172] These dates do not accord with the placement of the text in Josephus' *Antiquities*: it is inserted between an account of Hyrcanus' conquests beginning in 129 BCE, and the civil war between Antiochus VIII Grypus and Antiochus IX Cyzicenus – that is, before 114 BCE. After the death of Antiochus VII in 129 BCE, Josephus reports that Hyrcanus revolted from the Seleucids, refusing to give them aid and nullifying his status as friend or subject.[173]

According to Roman criteria, Hyrcanus was now autonomous and eligible for diplomatic relations.[174] A date of 134–132 BCE for the decree would be impossible since Hyrcanus had just been defeated and had become a tributary subject of the Seleucids.[175] It is important to note that this document reports an already-existing friendship between Rome and Judaea.[176] Supporting a later date is the mention of Fannius, the praetor (*strategos*). The only attested Fannius in the period 129–114 is C. Fannius, the consul of 122 BCE.[177] The date of his praetorship is unknown, but estimates vary from 133 to 127/6 BCE. With a two-year interval required between the holding of the praetorship and the consulship, Fannius' praetorship would have fallen between 125–124 BCE.[178] Some would date the decree to the consulship of Fannius.[179] There are two objections: first, in this period, consul is always rendered in Greek as *strategos hupatos*; second, such a date would cause the Seleucid king to be identified with Antiochus VIII Grypus, who had no attested contact with Judaea.[180] Therefore, 129 BCE appears to satisfy both the historical background and the practices of Roman *Völkerrecht*.

In conclusion, the Fannius Decree is a genuine Roman *senatus consultum*, conforming as it does to the form and content of such decrees. Details in the decree are factual, according to what we know of Roman politicians at the time and Roman practice. The names of the three Romans mentioned in the decree, the presiding official and the two witnesses, can all be found attested in the period c. 133–122 BCE. The senate is said to meet in the most common location where it held its meetings. The specifics of the requests of the Jewish envoys accord also with the results of the invasion of Judaea from 133 to 132 BCE. If, as Seeman suggests, the embassy was in Rome in 129 BCE, prompted by the death of Antiochus VII, this date could go some way to explaining the reluctance of the senate to give an immediate answer. Their waiting may have been connected with the dynastic turmoil after Antiochus VII's death, when Demetrius II came to the throne and was faced with a rival, Alexander II Zabinas. The senate may have been waiting to see how events in Syria played out in order to decide whether one or none of the men would be recognised by the senate as king of Syria.

### *The Valerius Decree*

As evidence for Roman diplomatic relations, Josephus quotes a senatorial decree of Lucius Valerius at *Ant.* 14.145–148. The text reads as follows:

> [145] Lucius Valerius, the son of Lucius, the praetor, consulted with the senate on the Ides of December, in the temple of Concordia. There were present at the writing of this decree Lucius Coponius, the son of Lucius of the Collina tribe and Papirius of the Quirina tribe. [146] Whereas Alexander the son of Jason, Numenius the son of Antiochus and Alexander the son of Dositheus, envoys of the Jews and worthy man and allies, have discussed the matter of reviving the goodwill and friendship which they formerly maintained with the Romans, [147] and have brought a shield of gold, as a token of the alliance, valued at fifty thousand pieces of gold; and have asked that letters be given to them, to the autonomous cities and to the kings in order that their country and ports may be secure and suffer no harm, [148] it has been decreed to form friendship and goodwill with them, and to provide them with all the things which they have requested, and to accept the shield which they have brought. This took place in the ninth year of Hyrcanus the high priest and ethnarch, in the month of Panemus.

Three Jewish envoys spoke in the senate, requesting a revival of their friendship with Rome. As a token of their submission, they brought a gold shield of substantial value. The senate decided to accept the gift and to accept them into the friendship of the Roman people. The senators also decided to supply the envoys with letters to kings and free cities, warning them not to harm Judaea or its ports. The cited document purports to be the text of a senatorial decree. Using a template for the form and content of these decrees designed by Moehring, Table 7.3 demonstrates how far a given document complies with the typical pattern.

It was Ritschl in 1875 who first decided to re-date this document from the time of Hyrcanus II, where Josephus had placed it, to the period of Hyrcanus I.[181] Many scholars have remarked on the similarity of the contents of the Lucius letter in 1 Macc. 15.16–24 to a senatorial decree (*senatus consultum*) recorded by Josephus at *Ant.* 14.145–148, which he includes among documents dating from the time of Julius Caesar in 47 BCE. Both mention that the Romans granted the Jews friendship, that the Jewish ambassadors (with similar names) brought a gold shield as a gift to the Romans, and that guarantees of peace and security for Jews were sent in a circular letter to many places around the eastern Mediterranean and further

*Table 7.3* Comparison of the Lucius Decree with the standard form of a senatorial decree (*senatus consultum*)
περὶ ὧν ὁ δεῖνα ἐποιήσατο περὶ [or ὅπως]

| *Standard form for senatus consultum* | *The Lucius Decree (Jos. Ant. 14. 145–148)* | *Degree of compliance*[a] |
|---|---|---|
| I Prescript | | |
| (a) name and rank of the presiding magistrate/s | Lucius Valerius, the praetor | + |
| (b) *senatus consuluit* τῃ συγκλήτῳ συνεβουλεύσατο | συνεβουλεύσατο τῇ συγκλήτῳ | + |
| (c) day and month of meeting | Ides of December | + |
| (d) place | Temple of Concordia | + |
| (e) names of the witnesses introduced by the phrase *scribendo adfuerunt* γραφομένῳ παρῆσαν | Lucius Coponius, son of Lucius of the Collina tribe and Papirius of the Quirina tribe γραφομένῷ τῷ δόγματι παρῆσαν | + |
| II Theme | | |
| (a) *relatio: quod* [name of *relator*] *uerba fecit de* [or *ut*] περὶ ὧν ὁ δεῖνα ἐποιήσατο περὶ [or ὅπως] | περὶ ὧν᾽ Αλεξανδρος . . . διελέχθησαν | / |
| (b) résumé of the events or motives that prompted the *relator* to bring the matter before the senate | wish to revive friendship and presentation of a gold shield | + |
| (c) concluding formula *d(e) e(a) r(e) i(ta) c(ensuereunt)* περὶ τούτου τοῦ πράγματος οὓδοξεν serves as an introduction to III | ἔδοξε συνθέσθαι φιλίαν καὶ χάριτας αὐτούς | + |
| III The Decree Proper | | + |
| In *indirect* speech or introduced by *ut (uti)* | to form friendship and to provide the envoys with all they requested | |
| IV Mark of approval: formal expression of the vote c(ensuere) ἔδοξεν | | 0 |

Note

a + signifies full compliance; / signifies basic agreement with some difference in detail; 0 means the section is missing.

east. There are, however, sufficient differences to allow that they represent two separate embassies.[182] Elsewhere I have shown how another document cited by Josephus, the Fannius letter (Jos. *Ant.* 14.233), was placed with documents dating to 49 BCE, and although Niese re-dated it to 161 BCE, we should consider that Josephus gave it the correct chronological position in his *Antiquities*. In a similar vein, there are reasons for the senatorial decree of Lucius Valerius (Jos. *Ant.* 14.145–148) to retain its date in the 47 BCE, as will be demonstrated.[183]

The proposer of the decree in Josephus is a certain L. Valerius, son of Lucius. How to identify him depends on which date one prefers for the document. If the decree cited in Josephus is taken out of its context and re-dated in the time of John Hyrcanus I, one would need to find a praetor who held office around 142 BCE with the *praenomen*, Lucius. Some have suggested L. Valerius Flaccus, consul in 131 BCE.[184] The difficulty with this suggestion is that it requires a very long time to have lapsed between his praetorship and consulship. As Sievers points out, such an interval was rare but not unprecedented: he cites one example where there was a gap of 45 years between the holding of the two offices.[185] However, if we accept that the senatorial decree belongs to the year 47 BCE, it is necessary to search for a L. Valerius in the 40s BCE, who was a στρατηγὸς or praetor, as in Jos. *Ant.* 14.145. We have no assured names of the praetors for 47 BCE.[186] The elections were postponed until Julius Caesar's return to Rome, which did not take place until the autumn. Consequently those elected served only three months in office.[187] We know, however, of a certain L. Valerius Acisculus, mint-master in 45 BCE. He was probably tribune of the plebs in this period.[188] However, although the name fits, the question of whether he was praetor in 47 BCE must remain open, as we have no evidence for the names of the successful candidates for praetor for that year.

The *senatus consultum* mentions that the session of the senate was held in the Temple of Concordia. Mommsen raised the question whether this temple was standing in 142 BCE.[189] Suggestions that the temple was the *aedicula* of Cn. Flaccus fail to take into account that this was not an inaugurated *templum* that was necessary for meetings of the senate.[190] Likewise the Temple of Concordia of Camillus, if it was ever built, was not an inaugurated space. The temple would have been the one vowed in 366 BCE by Camillus (Plut. *Cam.* 42), but archaeological excavations in 1983 have found no trace of a temple under the Temple to Concordia built in 121 BCE by L. Opimius.[191] The physical evidence must make us discard a date of 142 BCE for the senatorial decree.[192] However, for 47 BCE there is ample evidence that the temple was much used for meetings of the senate, after the Curia Hostilia had burned down in the riots of 52 BCE following the funeral of the popular agitator Clodius. Nine meetings of the senate are recorded in the Temple of Concordia between 63 and 39 BCE: two in 63, one each in 58 and 57, three in 44, and one each in 43 and 39.[193]

Proof of the authenticity of the *senatus consultum* quoted by Josephus is to be found in another name in the document, a certain Lucius Coponius, son of Lucius of the Colline tribe, who was present at the drafting of the decree. The name is correct in its details.[194] The family hailed from Tibur.[195] The first point to note is that the name only comes to prominence in the Late Republic. There is only one Coponius from an earlier period and he is a T. Coponius, the grandfather of the brothers C. and T. Coponius whose careers spanned the 50s and 40s BCE.[196] There was a member of the *gens* who was alive in 91 BCE and another who worked as a sculptor on the statues in the theatre of Pompey during the 50s BCE.[197] A certain Coponius (with no *praenomen* known) features as an aid to the Syrian governor at the time of Herod.[198] Two other Coponii lived during the imperial period.[199]

Münzer claimed that the L. Coponius L. f. of the *senatus consultum* in Josephus is otherwise unattested.[200] He was under the impression that one should search only in 142 BCE. If we look in the 40s BCE, we find a certain C. Coponius, an ex-Pompeian who was proscribed in 43 BCE by the Triumvirate.[201] He is the grandson of T. Coponius, who won Roman citizenship through a successful prosecution of a Roman senator in the extortion court (see p. 254). A coin attests to the praetorship of the grandson in 49 BCE, with legend *C. Coponius pr(aetor)*.[202] He was certainly a senator by 47 BCE.

The document mentions a certain Papirius of the Quirina tribe. The *gens* Papiria had a strong connection with the tribe of Quirina. Their most famous forebear, L. Papirius Cursor (*RE* 53), had instituted the worship of the god Quirinus in 293 BCE.[203] Broughton identifies the Papirius in the Valerius Decree as C. (Papirius?) Maso (*RE* 59).[204] There is, however, a C. Papirius Carbo, who would have been a senator in 47 BCE. He was tribune of the plebs c. 67 BCE, received consular insignia for a successful prosecution after 67 BCE, and was praetor c. 62 BCE.[205] Between 61–59 BCE, he was propraetor in Bithynia.[206]

The names of the ambassadors in the decree differ from those sent to Rome in the time of Simon. His embassy is recorded as having only one ambassador, a certain Numenius, mentioned without a patronymic.[207] The embassy of Hyrcanus II had three: Alexander, the son of Jason; Numenius, the son of Antiochus; and Alexander, son of Doritheus.[208] The father of Numenius seems to have had an odd name for a Jew. Admittedly, this Antiochus would have been born before Antiochus IV came to the throne. His name would have carried no negative associations.[209]

A golden shield is mentioned in this decree. A date in 47 BCE would suggest that the gift was given to Caesar at a time during the civil war when he was desperate for funds. The financial emergency was particularly acute in 47 BCE, such that when Julius Caesar returned from the East he passed a raft of measures to bring in cash. He legislated, for example, that those who had taken over property in Rome belonging to Pompeians would now have to pay.[210] The shield accords well with Caesar's desperate need for funds at this time. It should be considered as a contribution to his war funds, hence the extravagant amount.

The document mentions circular letters without specifying the destinations or recipients. In the Lucius letter, the detailed list has been considered a demarcation of the extension of Roman influence.[211] By 47 BCE it was only all too well known how much of the East had come under Roman sway and there was no need to be specific. Lastly, Hyrcanus is referred to as High Priest and Ethnarch. These were the titles that Hyrcanus II had received from Pompey in 63 BCE and which were confirmed by Julius Caesar.[212] By contrast Hyrcanus I did not use the title ethnarch.[213]

The passage in Josephus ends with another date, the month of Panemos from the Macedonian calendar. Questions have been raised concerning its appropriateness in a Roman document that should identify the years by the names of the two consuls elected each year. The first to raise the incongruity of a Macedonian month at the end of the senatorial decree was Mendelssohn, in 1875, who used the reference to the Macedonian calendar to discredit the document or to say that it was not part of the original Roman document but was added on. This view has become widely accepted.[214] There is something very wrong with the information in the sentence, ταῦτα ἐγένετο ἐπὶ Ὑρκανοῦ ἀρχιερέως καὶ ἐθνάρχου ἔτους ἐνάτου μηνὸς Πανέμου. The ninth year of Hyrcanus' rule, starting from 63 BCE, would place the document in 53/52 BCE. Stern suggested the possibility that εἰκοστοῦ may have appeared before ἐνάτου and since dropped out of the manuscript so that it would read, 'in the twenty-ninth year of Hyrcanus'. With this emendment, it is possible to arrive at the date 47 BCE, taking 29 years from the date that Hyrcanus became High Priest in 76 BCE.[215] To accept this suggestion renders it unnecessary to move the document to the period of Hyrcanus I.

The date given in the senatorial decree is the Ides of December. The first step is to convert this date into the two possible dates for the document c. 140 BCE and 47 BCE. For the mid-second century BCE, according to Bennett's calculations 1 December fell on the following dates:[216]

1 December in 142 BCE fell on 30 November (Julian)

1 December in 141 BCE fell on 19 November (Julian)

1 December in 140 BCE fell on 2 December (Julian)

1 December in 139 BCE fell on 22 November (Julian)

1 December in 138 BCE fell on 12 November (Julian).

In 47 BCE the Roman calendar was running three months ahead because of the lack of intercalation for several years.[217] In 47 BCE, December (Roman) equates to September (Julian). Therefore, to find a calendar with the month of Panemos it ought to equate to November c. 142/39 BCE (Julian) or to September 47 BCE (Julian) in order to synchronise with the Ides of December.

The task now becomes discerning whether it is possible to synchronise this date with any of the Macedonian calendars or calendars operating with months named in the Macedonian fashion with this Roman date either in c. 140 BCE at the time of Hyrcanus I or in 47 BCE at the time of Hyrcanus II. In the mid-second century BCE there were three main calendars in the eastern Mediterranean that used Macedonian month names: these were the Macedonian calendar, the Seleucid Macedonian calendar (or the Syro-Macedonian calendar)[218] and the Ptolemaic calendar. The latter two were based on local calendars, with the months given Macedonian names. In the second century, according to the Macedonian calendar, Panemos fell in June (Julian).[219] The Seleucid Macedonian calendar correlated Macedonian months to the Babylonian calendar starting in 323 BCE. In this calendar, Panemos was equated with the Babylonian month of Simanu, the third month of the year. The New Year fell on 3 April (Julian) and Panemos began on 25/26 June (Julian).[220] As this was not a fixed calendar, the date of the New Year day could vary resulting in different dates for 1 Panemos. Bennet has calculated these dates and according to his calculations:[221]

1 Panemos in 142 BCE fell on 24 May (Julian)

1 Panemos in 141 BCE fell on 11 June (Julian)

1 Panemos in 140 BCE fell on 31 May (Julian)

1 Panemos in 139 BCE fell on 19 June (Julian).

In neither of these two calendars does the month of Panemos fall in November (Julian) in the second century BCE so that it would synchronise with the Roman month of December. For the mid-first century we are looking for Panemos that falls in September (Julian). According to the same tables computed by Bennet, Simanu (Panemos) in 47 BCE falls on 23 May (Julian). This date also does not synchronise with the Roman date.

It remains to examine the Ptolemaic Egyptian calendar.[222] This calendar was introduced by Alexander the Great and his successors. The native Egyptian calendar did not fall out of use and both systems were in operation simultaneously until the two calendars were merged. The Egyptian civil calendar of 12 months of 30 days with five epagomenal days was retained, but the names of the months were changed to Macedonian names. The first reform came in the reign of Ptolemy II Philadelphus (285/84–247/46 BCE), in which Panemos was the fifth month of the year equated with the Egyptian month of Tybi.[223] The second reform came in 119/18 BCE, when Ptolemy VIII Euergetes II introduced a new calendar in which Panemos was the ninth month equated with the Egyptian month of Pachon.[224] This Alexandrian calendar became the model for the calendars of Gaza, Ascalon and Arabia. In Gaza and Ascalon the Macedonian month names were applied in the known order, but the new year began in the autumn.[225] The Ptolemaic calendar was in operation until the new calendar of Augustus was introduced into Egypt. Bennet has calculated the Julian dates for the start of each month for several centuries.

For the dates that might be appropriate if the document belongs to Hyrcanus I, his results are that in 142 BCE 1 Tybi fell on 26 January (Julian) and from 141–138 BE 1 Tybi fell on 25 January (Julian). On these calculations the Ptolemaic calendar does not synchronise with the Roman date of the Ides of December during the mid-second century. Does the date refer to Panemos in 47 BCE? In that year, the opening of the Egyptian calendar of 1 Thoth fell on 4 September (Julian).[226] With Panemos being the ninth month, it would fall on May (Julian).[227] The Ptolemaic dates for the mid-second century and for the mid-first century do not harmonise with the Roman date of the Ides of December (September (Julian)).

There were, nevertheless, other calendars using Macedonian month names in operation not in the second century but in the mid-first century. In the areas of the Levant conquered by Pompey, there were cities that he declared free and autonomous and from that time they began their own versions of the Macedonian calendar. Later other cities were given grants of autonomy from Caesar in 48 BCE and their calendars began from that date. After Caesar's reform of the Roman calendar, many of these were in synchronisation with the Macedonian calendar where Panemos fell in July (Julian) (September (Roman)). Among these were the calendars of Tyre, Ascalon, Sidon, Antioch and Lycia.[228]

An understanding of Panemos as the month from a calendar from the Greek-speaking East at the time of Caesar does not appear feasible. Another possibility has been raised that the month, Panemos, refers to the period when Caesar was in Syria in 47 BCE.[229] Caesar arrived in Syria from Alexandria in early June (Roman) – that is, late March (Julian).[230] If we accept the date from Ioannes Malalas, a sixth-century CE Byzantine writer, Caesar entered Antioch on 23 Artemisius, which equates to 28 June (Roman) or 16 April (Julian), and departed on 3 July (Roman) – that, is 21 April 47 BCE (Julian).[231] By these calculations, Caesar spent only five days in Antioch. Caesar's time in Syria spanned 18 days from 30 March to 18 April 47 (Julian). On the basis of this reconstructed chronology, it would seem that the date on the end of the senatorial decree is not related to Caesar's time in Syria.

It has been considered a possibility that Josephus used the calendar of Antioch in converting Roman dates because Antioch was the administrative capital of the area.[232] Nicols has shown conclusively that Josephus did not convert dates into those of the calendar of Tyre because there is on average a difference of 20 days between the Julian dates and the dates if they were from the Tyrian calendar.[233] In both the calendar of Antioch and the calendar of Tyre, Panemos in 67 and 70 CE fell in July (Julian). The month for September (Julian) to represent the Ides of December was Gorpaios.[234]

We are left with the suggestion that 'Panemos' represents an archival notation made in Jerusalem of the date received.[235] That would place its reception, according to the Macedonian calendar used in the East, in May 46 (Julian), approximately July (Roman).[236] This would mean that the document took from December (Roman) 47 until July (Roman) 46 to reach Jerusalem. Seven months – that seems a rather long time.

Another suggestion has been to blame the discrepancy on an error by Josephus, who added a date with which he thought his readers would be more familiar.[237] He did not work out the exact equivalents for all his dates using a single calendrical system but used Macedonian and Jewish calendars. When he found a Roman date in his source, he simply equated the Roman month with a month from different calendars. At *BJ* 4.654 he used the Tyrian calendar.[238] At *BJ* 6.374 and 392 he uses a Jewish calendar. If Josephus just transposed December (Roman) to December (Julian) and gave it a Macedonian name, as Zack suggests, he would have written Apellaios.[239] There appears to be no good solution to explain the Macedonian month of Panemos at the end of this document.

There are three strong reasons based on evidence not previously considered in the context of the Valerius Decree to date it to 47 BCE. The first is the identification of a Valerius, Coponius and a Papirius all around 47 BCE. The second reason concerns the pairing of a Coponius and a Papirius as senatorial witnesses to the decree. The choices for dating are between the second half of the second century, which most scholars favour, and 47 BCE. In my view, a famous trial that took place in the second half of the second century precludes Coponius and Papirius co-operating with each other in any way whatsoever. The grandfather of C. Coponius (*RE* 3) was T. Coponius (*RE* 8), who gained fame through his prosecution for extortion of a C. Maso. This was the cognomen of the *gens Papiria.* Broughton identifies him as the senator of the late second century C. (Papirius?) Maso (*RE* 59).[240] The trial resulted in a successful prosecution, which gained Roman citizenship for Coponius and his family.[241] There was only one court that would result in the reward of Roman citizenship in the second century BCE, which was the extortion court. Therefore, we can date the trial to after the introduction of the court in 149 BCE through the *lex Acilia de repetundis*.[242] The infamy of Papirius' conviction was so great that it caused a hiatus in the careers of the family for a generation. Usually after trials such as this, the *inimicitia* between the families became intense. Therefore, after a trial that broke all goodwill between these two families in the second half of the second century, it would be most implausible to find them agreeing to act together in the senate as witnesses also in the second half of the second century BCE. One hundred years later, the hatred between the families may have cooled sufficiently for both of them to act in concert in the senate, but not before. For these reasons I propose a date for this document in 47 BCE, one further instance when Josephus placed his documents in the correct chronological position.

### *The Pergamum Decree (Jos. Ant. 14. 247–255)*

This document is cited by Josephus among a large collection of decrees dating to the second half of the first century BCE. The mention of Hyrcanus the High Priest in the document was associated with Hyrcanus II[243] by whoever bundled the documents together.[244] The document has been misplaced and should be assigned to the reign of Hyrcanus I, since in the letter there is mention of King Antiochus.[245] The decree reads as follows:

> [247] A decree of the Pergamenes: In the Prytany of Cratippus, on the 1st of the month of Daisios, a resolution of the magistrates: Whereas the Romans, following the lead of their forebears, have taken on dangers for the sake of the common security of all humanity and strive eagerly to establish their friends and allies in happiness and lasting peace; [248] and whereas the Judaean nation and Hyrcanus their High Priest have sent envoys to them, Strato son of Theodotus, Apollonius son of Alexander, Aeneas son of Antipater, [249] Aristoboulus son of Amyntas and Sosipater son of Philip, excellent and worthy men; and regarding the matters in accordance with which they made representations, the senate decreed regarding these matters of which they spoke: that King Antiochus, son of Antiochus, should do no wrong to the Judaeans, allies of the Romans, that he return their fortresses and harbours and territory and anything else he has seized, that they be permitted to export goods from their harbours [250] and that no one, whether king or people, exporting goods from the territory or harbours of the Judaeans be untaxed, save only Ptolemy, king of the Alexandrians, since he is our ally and friend; that the

> garrison in Joppa be expelled, just as they have requested. [251] And Lucius Pettius, an excellent and worthy man of our Council, commanded that we should see to it that these things were observed just as the senate has decreed, and that provision should be made for the safe return home of the envoys. [252] We have also received Theodorus into the Council and assembly, hearing from him the letter and the decree of the senate. And since he, speaking with great zeal, made manifest both the virtue and magnanimity of Hyrcanus, [253] how he was a benefactor both to all and, in particular, to those who approached him, we have deposited the documents in our public archives and have passed a resolution that we, as allies of the Romans, should do everything on the Judaeans' behalf dictated by the decree of the senate. [254] And Theodorus, having given the letter to us, also begged of our magistrates to send to Hyrcanus the copy of the resolution and envoys who would make plain the zeal of our people and who would exhort him to both maintain and enhance his friendship with us, and that he always be the cause of some worthy thing, [255] mindful that he will receive fitting recompense and also that in the time of Abraham, who was the father of all the Hebrews, our forefathers were their friends, just as we find in [our] documents.

The Jewish envoys visited Pergamum on their way home from Rome, perhaps because of the existence of a Jewish community there.[246] The Council invited the Jewish envoys to their meeting and heard their account of the meeting in the Roman Senate. Following their speech, the Council decided to pass their own decree that would demonstrate their loyalty to Rome with praise for the Romans' concern for their allies. We find in the decree the names of the five Jews who made up the embassy with the notation that they were specifically sent to Rome by Hyrcanus, the High Priest. The senate decided that Antiochus should not harm the Judaeans, that he should restore the territories he captured, that the Judaean ports be opened for trade, that customs duties be imposed, that Ptolemy of Egypt should be exempt from these duties, and that the Seleucid garrison be expelled.

The words 'a decree of the Pergamenes' is a note from the archives giving the provenance of the decree. Without this, the city whose Boule passed the decree would be unknown. There is no reference to Pergamum in the text of the decree itself. The source of the Roman documents cited by Josephus is considered to have derived from the archives of cities in Asia Minor.[247]

The date is given as 'in the prytany of Cratippus on the 1st of the month of Daisios'. The prytany of Cratippus is attested in an inscription from Pergamum, which is undated.[248] The Pergamenes used the Macedonian calendar in which Daisios represents the month of May.

In this document we find praise of the Romans, which is a common feature of inscriptions from the Greek-speaking East. The Romans are referred to as the common benefactors. In an inscription from 88 BCE, the people of Aphrodisias proclaim, for example, that without Roman leadership they would not chose to live.[249]

With five envoys, this is the largest Judaean legation attested. Apollonius, son of Alexander appears in the Valerius Decree. In addition, we find new individuals

*Table 7.4* Comparison of the Pergamum Decree with the standard form of a senatorial decree (*senatus consultum*)

| *Standard form for senatus consultum* | *The Pergamum Decree* | *Degree of compliance*[a] |
|---|---|---|
| I Prescript | | |
| (a) name and rank of the presiding magistrate/s | | 0 |
| (b) *senatus consuluit* τῃ συγκλήτῳ συνεβουλεύσατο | | 0 |
| (c) day and month of meeting | | 0 |
| (d) place | | 0 |
| (e) names of the witnesses introduced by the phrase *scribendo adfuerunt* γραφομένῳ παρῆσαν | | 0 |
| II Theme | | |
| (a) *relation: quod* [name of *relator*] *uerba fecit de* [or *ut*] περὶ ὧν ὁ δεῖνα ἐποιήσατο περι [or ὅπως] | | 0 |
| (b) résumé of the events or motives that prompted the *relator* to bring the matter before the senate | | 0 |
| (c) concluding formula *d(e) e(a) r(e) i(ta) c(ensuereunt)* περὶ τούτου τοῦ πράγματος οὗδοξεν serves as an introduction to | The senate decreed regarding these matters of which they spoke ἐδογμάτισεν ἡ σύγκλητος | + |
| III The Decree Proper | | |
| In *indirect* speech or introduced by *ut (uti)* | Not introduced by *ut* and not in indirect speech: section 250 | / |
| IV Mark of approval: formal expression of the vote *c(ensuere)* ἔδοξεν | | 0 |

Note

a + signifies full compliance; / signifies basic agreement with some difference in detail; 0 means the section is missing.

chosen to represent Judaea. Striking is the name, Aeneas, son of Antipater. On the one hand, one wonders whether this was a nod to Rome, referencing their ancestral founder, or to Ilium (Troy) in Pergamum, and why this individual was chosen to represent Judaea.[250] On the other hand, some have suggested that the name Aeneas was a way of affirming the Greek identity of the Seleucids, and by implication those who had lived in the Seleucid Empire.[251] Aeneas is also found mentioned in 1 Macc. 12.16 and 14.22. Apollonius, son of Alexander appears as an envoy to Rome in the time of Hyrcanus I in the Fannius Decree.[252] Seeman suggests that the new envoys may indicate a lack of connection with other embassies and hence no relation to other senatorial decrees.[253]

The Seleucid king is styled 'King Antiochus, son of Antiochus'. The only Seleucid king in the time of John Hyrcanus I who could be styled thus is Antiochus IX (Cyzicenus), who was the son of Antiochus VII. We may rule out Antiochus VII, who was the son of Demetrius I, and also Antiochus VIII, who was the son of Demetrius II. Josephus' placement of the document among those from the time of Hyrcanus II cannot be possible as the only King Antiochus at that time was Antiochus XIII, who only controlled Antioch and was in no position to invade Judaea. Numismatic evidence confirms the hold that Antiochus IX had over the coastal area between Ascalon and Tripolis between 113 and 104 BCE, which would confirm the information in the decree that Antiochus had placed a garrison in Joppa.[254]

A certain Lucius Pettius is said to have been 'of our Council'. The name, however, is Oscan, attested in the second century BCE from an inscription from Delos.[255] The Lucius in this document is identified as L. Pettius (*RE* 3).[256] There is a question whether he was a member of the Pergamene Boule or whether he was a Roman senator in Pergamum on a Roman commission.[257] Reinach emended τῆς βουλῆς to τῇ βουλῇ so that it would read that Pettius gave orders to the Council, not that he was a member of the Council.[258]

Theodorus was a common Jewish name in the Graeco-Roman period in Judaea and in the Diaspora.[259] An Alexander, son of Theodorus was an envoy for Hyrcanus II and is mentioned in three senatorial decrees from the Triumviral period by Josephus.[260] The identity of Theodorus is unclear from the document. He is not named as an envoy, but neither is he a Pergamene because he was honoured with the right of being part of the Council and Assembly of Pergamum. It would appear that the council was granting him honorary citizenship. He appears to have been a forceful advocate for Hyrcanus. Theodorus' praise of Hyrcanus, however, is in conventional general terms ('the virtue and magnanimity of Hyrcanus', 'he was a benefactor to all in general') and does not display any special knowledge of the Jewish leader sufficient to warrant the claim that he possessed an intimate knowledge of the High Priest.[261] Trebilco suggests that Theodorus may have been a prominent member of the Jewish community in Pergamum.[262]

Ties of friendship with Pergamum are accompanied by the customary claims of ancestral kinship. The Pergamenes express the hope that the ties projected back to Abraham will remain. Proof of kinship with the Jews, they assert, could be found in their own documents. Gruen remarks on the similarity of this claim to be found in the Letter of Areus in connection with Spartan–Jewish ties of kinship. He finds it implausible that the Pergamenes would have included ties with 'Abraham, who was father of all the Hebrews' in their own decree and considers that it was inserted by unspecified Jews.[263] Nevertheless, we may assume some prior contact due to the reference to a document in the archives of the Pergamenes.[264]

In this document the Jews are already considered as friends and allies of the Romans. The decree testifies to the mutual aid the Romans expected between two of their allies as seen in the provision for tax exemptions for Ptolemy from Hyrcanus. Rajak wishes to separate the references to a decree of the senate from the rest of the document and date it to the middle of the siege of Jerusalem by Antiochus VII c. 133/32 BCE.[265] This would place the decree at the time of Antiochus VII. The difficulty is that the senatorial decree mentions a King Antiochus, son of Antiochus, but Antiochus VII was the son of Demetrius. The date of the document lies in the reign of Antiochus IX, the son of Antiochus – that is, between 114 and 103 BCE –, with some preferring a more specific date of 113/2 BCE or 105 BCE.[266]

The decree presents authentic information about Pergamum, its political institutions, its calendar and its relationship to Rome. It came probably from an archive from Asia Minor. The Jewish legation is larger than any previously sent to Rome, with five members, four of whose names are new. The changing of the guard in Jewish diplomacy suggests a date later than 129 BCE. The senate's reference to King Antiochus, son of Antiochus permits a date in the reign only of Antiochus IX, with preference for early in his rule.

## Breaking the ties

Every Hasmonaean leader from Judas, Jonathan, Simon and John Hyrcanus sent embassies to Rome, each of which was despatched after military victories over the Seleucids (as did Judas Maccabaeus), sufficient to meet the conditions of the Romans that they were autonomous and, therefore, eligible to establish diplomatic ties in their own right. In the period after Judas' death, first Jonathan and then Simon defeated the Seleucids on the battlefield and gave birth to Judaean independence from Syria. The struggle was to maintain it.

John Hyrcanus sent his last embassy to Rome in c. 113 BCE (or 105 BCE), but this seems to have been the last until Pompey arrived in Syria. Until Rappaport's study, there had been no explanation for the lack of contact with Rome under Alexander Jannaeus. Since the First Book of Maccabees concludes with the account of John Hyrcanus, it makes no mention of any embassies during the reign of Alexander Jannaeus, and Josephus passes over in silence on relations at Rome at this time, whereas elsewhere he is eager to present documents to show such ties whenever he can. It is difficult to imagine that he would ignore an embassy to Rome if one had existed.[267]

Certain behaviour disqualified an ally from being a friend (*amicus*) of the Roman people. Here I present those actions of John Hyrcanus and Alexander Jannaeus that cut them off from Rome. It is not a case of their having neglected or severed relations; rather, the senate no longer considered them worthy to be a friend of the Roman people. Friends of the Roman people did not associate with pirates. Such actions placed one outside the norms of civilised legal norms, not to be trusted, not competent to make a treaty that involved oath-taking. An ally of Rome could not make any alliance (a treaty or friendship) with others without Roman authorisation, especially outside the Roman *imperium*. To do so immediately voided any diplomatic ties with Rome.[268] These two Jewish rulers did not conform to the behaviour that Rome expected from her allies. In this section I examine first the Hasmonaean contact with the Parthians and secondly their ties to the Cilician pirates.

***The Parthians***

The historical context of Hasmonaean ties to the Parthians involves the Parthian Empire's expansion into the Seleucid Empire at the same time the Hasmonaean state was in formation. The large Jewish presence in Babylonia may have facilitated the development of early relations between Judaea and Parthia.[269] The Jews in Babylonia and Media had readily accepted Parthian rule over that of the Seleucids and, in Media, over the Seleucid rebel, Timarchos.[270] Both had a shared interest in promoting a weakening, if not collapse, of the Seleucid Empire.[271] The timing of the Maccabaean revolt had indirectly assisted Parthia, for it had diverted Seleucid military resources from the East and had taken pressure off the Parthian king, Mithridates I (165–132 BCE), who looked especially to the west to expand his influence. He extended his reach into Media between 161 and 155 BCE.[272]

By 141 BCE, Mithridates had captured the royal capital of Seleucia. The Parthian king had to withdraw, probably because of an incursion on his eastern border; the rest of his reign was consumed with campaigns in central and southern Parthia.[273] Mithridates left a general in charge of his forces in Syria. This Parthian force was able to capture Demetrius II, the Syrian king, not long after Mithridates departed.[274] The Parthians established themselves in Susa, which, according to numismatic evidence, they had captured probably in 151–150 BCE.[275] On the death of Mithridates in 138/37 BCE, his son Phraates II became king.[276] Demetrius was still held by the Parthians despite several unsuccessful escape attempts. Meanwhile Antiochus VII had taken the Syrian throne and by 130 BCE he mounted a campaign against the Parthians to free Demetrius. He did this not so much to restore him to the throne as to eliminate him; for as long as Demetrius lived, Antiochus VII would always be regarded as a caretaker (or worse, as a usurper).[277] Jewish forces under the generalship of their leader John Hyrcanus joined the campaign. Antiochus and his army met with initial success, winning three battles against the Parthians. Trouble began when Antiochus decided to winter in Media instead of returning to Syria. His large force had to be billeted in many Median cities, an action that only exacerbated anti-Seleucid hatred, leading to these cities turning on the Seleucid soldiers. Antiochus VII opted to meet the Parthians in battle, but was overwhelmed and killed along with his own son.[278] These events form the background to early contact between the Hasmonaeans and the Parthians.

The first reported contact between Judaea and the Parthians came in 130–129 BCE during the Median campaign, in which Hyrcanus I, as part of the terms to end the siege of Jerusalem, had agreed to take part with Antiochus VII. The evidence for this contact comes to us from two Jewish sources: Josephus and the Tannaitic sources in the Talmud. Evidence on the Parthians in this period from classical writers was once plentiful, but their works are no longer extant. Histories of the Parthians were composed in antiquity by Arrian, Asinius Quadratus, Quintus Dellius and Crepereius Calpurnianus of Pompeiopolis.[279] Perhaps the most influential of these histories was the *Parthica*, a lost work in four books by Apollodorus of Armetica, who lived in the Parthian Empire during the first century BCE and who was the first to write a monograph on the subject. He formed around himself an influential circle of writers who undertook to compose Parthian histories.[280] The testimony of Josephus (*Ant.* 13. 250–253) is as follows:

> On this we have the testimony of several writers, also of Nicolaus of Damascus, who writes as follows: 'After defeating Indates, the Parthian general, and setting up a victory monument at the Lycus river, Antiochus (VII) remained there two days at the request of the Jew Hyrcanus because of a festival of his ancestors during which Jews are forbidden to travel. Nor does he speak falsely of this; for the festival of Shavuot had arrived following the Sabbath, and (Jews) are not permitted to travel either on the Sabbath or on a festival.' But when Antiochus joined battle with Arsaces, the King of Parthia, he lost a great deal of this army, and he himself was slain . . . .

Pucci draws attention to an inconsistency in this account. If Hyrcanus and his troops halted for a few days, why did Antiochus VII continue on without them? And why did Hyrcanus not only not help, but also escape death while the king did not? He even took advantage of Antiochus' death to attack Syria.[281] Josephus (*Ant.* 254–255) writes:[282]

> But when Hyrcanus heard of the death of Antiochus, he presently made an expedition against the cities of Syria, hoping to find them destitute of fighting men, and of such who were able to defend them.

A passage from the Talmud refers to an attack by the Jews on Antioch at about this time.[283] Josephus does not provide information on how Hyrcanus and his army managed to return to Syria safely. His troops appear not to have had to fight the Parthians on the way back.

An interpolation in the *Book of Josippon* may provide an explanation. It reports treachery on the part of Hyrcanus, who deliberately concealed his intentions to Antiochus VII and betrayed him, afterwards forming an alliance with the Parthians.[284] It must be remembered that Hyrcanus was not a willing ally of Antiochus VII. After the Syrian king had captured Jerusalem, participation in this campaign was part of the king's terms.[285] Josephus (*Ant.* 13.250) says that Hyrcanus accompanied Antiochus VII on his campaign against the Parthians as a Seleucid vassal. The text from Josippon revealing the Parthian–Hyrcanus alliance reads as follows:

> Then Ashraq, king of Persia, despatched a secret message to King Hyrcanus saying: 'Know you not that the Persians built your Temple and upheld the stronghold of your honour? Why do you now harm us with your might, seeing that we have not been guilty in your regard? Don't you [all] know that the pernicious Greeks defiled both your Temple and your country and still do so to this day? What benefit can you expect from them or their alliance? Let us combat your enemies and destroy them, for Persia's hate will serve you better than Greece's love. As for the evil you have wrought against us, we are aware

> that you have acted so not freely but in dread of your enemy. We shall therefore not hold it against you but shall make an alliance with you. Once you have withdrawn from his side, this enemy of yours will find himself utterly defenceless; we shall destroy him and live together in security.' Hyrcanus sent Ashraq a message assenting to his offer. Advancing therefrom, Hyrcanus and Antiochus then completed a two-day march, and when the third day came, Hyrcanus said to Antiochus: 'Proceed alone with the Greek forces and strike the Persian camp, and I shall follow after you and surprise him and his troops when he is least expecting it.' The idea pleased him, so he marched on alone with his army without awaiting Hyrcanus, King of Judah, so low was his esteem for the king of Persia's valour. So he smote Ashraq, king of Persia, and struggled with him, and on that day, all the Greek warriors were laid low on the field of battle and not a single soul survived. Antiochus himself ended his days on that occasion, for he too fell in battle. When Hyrcanus saw that Antiochus was no more, he ceased his sorties against Ashraq and concluded a pact with him and there was peace.[286]

How can we evaluate the historicity of this episode? In the Josephus passage is found a quotation from Nicolaus of Damascus, who reported the reason that Hyrcanus and his army did not join the fateful and decisive battle. The origin of his information is from a source that was not favourable for the Jews. Suspicion falls on Posidonius, who was known to be anti-Semitic and pro-Seleucid.[287] Josephus' telling of the episode makes no mention of any alliance between Hyrcanus and the Parthian king, Phraates. This may have been a case of Josephus exercising some censorship because, in his day, he wanted to emphasise the loyalty of the Jews as allies and to omit examples of previous treacherous behaviour – especially any ties to the Parthians, who were enemies of Rome at the time Josephus was writing.[288] Two reasons for scepticism concerning any Parthian–Jewish alliance at this time are, first, that Josephus does not mention it, probably due to the apologetic nature of his work, and secondly, due to the ingrained rejection among scholars of late sources.[289] The date of the *Book of Josippon* has been placed in the first half of the tenth century.[290] We can trace this over-cautiousness back to Scalinger in the early seventeenth century, who rejected all late writers.[291] In Jewish studies, as compared with Classical studies, the value of the *Book of Josippon* as evidence has been recognised since the late nineteenth century.[292] Many more scholars following Flusser would be prepared to admit that the author was a serious historian.[293] What could have been the sources of the author of the *Book of Josippon* and how reliable are they? Trieber considered that the author used Jason of Cyrene, Josephus and Nicolaus of Damascus.[294] Also among his sources was the Second Book of Maccabees.[295] But this does not help identify the source of the interpolation. These interpolations were placed in the text sometime before 1160. Flusser, after his examinations of these inserted passages, has concluded that, indeed, some have historical merit. Their source, he suggests, was a Byzantine *chronikon* that had used a reliable ancient source translated into Hebrew.[296]

Placing the two sources side by side, we have a picture of a reluctant Hyrcanus, forced to join the Syrian eastern expedition, who, at the crucial moment of battle, opts out, citing the need to celebrate a religious festival. The Parthians, knowing of the struggle of the Jews against the Seleucids since 168 BCE, make an offer, giving the Hasmonaean army reason to stay away from the battle. When they do so, they are rewarded with an alliance with the Parthians. This episode is now accepted by a growing number of scholars.[297]

The war agreement was secret and perhaps kept as such, for the Romans appear not to have known of it at the time. Hyrcanus was able to send an embassy to Rome, possibly after the death of Antiochus VII in 129 BCE, and revive the ties of friendship. The Roman Senate would never have agreed if they had known, not because they regarded the Parthians at this stage as enemies, but because, according to Roman *Völkerrecht*, there were two principles: first, a friend of the Roman people could not make such agreements without the authorisation of Rome; secondly, one could not be allies of two different nations.[298] It was permissible to be an ally of Rome and an ally of one or more of Rome's allies: the alliances were all within the sphere of Rome's *imperium*. One could not, however, be an ally of Rome and with a nation outside the area of Roman hegemony. It was these rules that Hyrcanus broke. The penalty was to treat a transgressor as a traitor to his bonds with Rome and consider him as an enemy.[299] In addition, the man he betrayed was on good terms with the Romans. I would go so far as to suggest that Antiochus VII was an *amicus* of the Roman people. There is the possibility that his claim to the throne was recognised by Scipio Aemilianus when he toured the East c. 140 BCE and later 134 BCE Antiochus sent expensive gifts for Scipio's campaign in Spain.[300] This was the action of one who had *amicitia* with Rome. Livy informs us that these gifts were entered into the public accounts so that they could be used for the war. For a friend of Rome, one's primary obligation was to volunteer to send troops or money to help Rome at war and the Numantine War had been a particularly draining war.[301] This king, who sent gifts to the Romans, was betrayed by Hyrcanus, who left the battlefield in collusion with the enemy, it was claimed, and did not fight to save Antiochus from defeat and death. Two more embassies were sent to Rome by Hyrcanus: one after the death of Antiochus VII in 129 BCE and another somewhere between 113 and 105 BCE. Did the rumours of this disloyalty to a Roman friend ever reach Rome? There is no way of knowing whether Hyrcanus had to confront any allegations in Rome. The problem remained that, in the estimation of the Romans, Hyrcanus as a friend of Rome had not supported another friend of Rome, Antiochus VII. His behaviour resulted in the death of Antiochus. The senate cannot have been pleased with Hyrcanus once news reached Rome of these developments.

The second report of diplomatic contact between the Hasmonaeans and the Parthians is undated. The Talmud mentions in passing a goodwill visit of the Parthians to Jerusalem. Josephus does not mention this episode, which has given rise to doubts over the historicity of the delegation. That this contact forms only backdrop to the discussion would appear to argue for its authenticity.[302] The passage reads as follows:

> It was taught, three hundred *Nezirim* came up [to Jerusalem] in the time of R. Simeon bar Shetach. For one hundred and fifty of them he found a means of freeing them from their vows of *Nezirut*, while for one hundred and fifty he did not. He came to Yannai the king. He said to him, there are here three hundred *Nezirim* who require nine hundred offerings, so you give half from your funds, and I shall give half from mine. He sent him four hundred and fifty. A gossiper went forth and said to Yannai that he (Simeon) had given nothing of his funds. When Yannai the king heard, he was angered. Simeon bar Shetach was frightened and fled. After some days important men came up from the Persian Empire to Yannai the king. When they were sitting and eating they said to him, we remember that there is here a certain old man who used to say to us wise sayings. Let him teach us something. Send and summon him.[303]

Neusner considers that the story has not been invented and the small section that mentions the arrival of the Parthian ambassadors is a story that circulated separately.[304] If this is correct then we are left with the details that the ambassadors had remembered Shimon b. Shetah from some previous contact and that it cannot be securely associated with any particular Hasmonaean leader. Is it possible to date this episode? Most place this incident c. 83 BCE in the reign of Alexander Jannaeus.[305]

The visit of this Parthian delegation testifies to prior friendly connections if not diplomatic relations within fairly recent times if the old man (presumably Shimon b. Shetah) from their first visit was still living. A suggestion for a date for the incident may lie in the mention of the Pharisee Shimon b. Shetah. He is frequently said to be a contemporary of Jannaeus.[306] Support for this is found in the story in the Mishna of Shimon and Honi, the circle drawer.[307] We associate the latter with the Onias of Jos. *Ant.* 14.22.24, which is dated to 65 BCE.[308] We may have another way of finding a date for Shimon. Rabbinic sources link Queen Salome Alexandra and the Pharisee, Simon ben Shetah, as brother and sister.[309] Josephus reports that she died in 67 BCE aged 73.[310] If this is correct, she would have been born in 140 BCE. Assuming brother and sister were somewhat close in age, in 83 BCE he would have been c. 54–60 years old. The ambassadors say that he was an old man as they remember him on previous contact. Goodblatt prefers to date the embassy in the time of Agrippa I. If we calculate Shimon's age from the first year of Agrippa's reign in 11 BCE, we reach the impossible age of c. 130–120 years. Perhaps the Yannai is Hyrcanus II. Although he was High Priest from 76 BCE, he was only effectively ruler from 67 BCE. This would give an age for Shimon of c. 73 years. This coincides better with the information from the Talmudic story. In brief, the story of the Parthian embassy is later than the rule of John Hyrcanus. Even if we can sustain a date for the embassy in the reign of Hyrcanus II, there still is no independence corroboration for the account in the Talmud.

Rome's disaffection with Judaea is attributable not only to the Jews' connections with the pirates (discussed later) but also to the suspicions that John Hyrcanus had made some deal with the Parthians. It was seen in Chapter 4 that a Roman ally was expected to seek the senate's authorisation for any alliances or friendship that their ally might want to make. There is no evidence that Hyrcanus informed the Romans of the alliance and his neglect of his obligations as a friend of the Roman people put that friendship in jeopardy. He had not aided a Roman friend in war and he had abandoned Antiochus VII on the battlefield. Judaea would have been regarded as an unreliable friend and as time stretched out and there was no sign that later Hasmonaeans were ever going to correct that impression and repair any damage in relations, the Romans' view of the Judaea as a friend of the Roman people was now under suspicion. It was a short step from the loss of friendship to being placed in a state of war with Rome.[311]

The Romans showed their displeasure with Jannaeus because he had never sent ambassadors to Rome. When Diodorus reports on the delegation of Jewish notables to Pompey in Syria after his success against the pirates, they are said to have given proof of their loyalty to Rome by mentioning embassies to Rome while carefully omitting the name of Jannaeus. Hyrcanus and Aristobulus had to tread carefully as the sons of Jannaeus. Pompey postponed a decision about their dispute:

> but he strongly rebuked Hyrcanus and his associates for the lawless behaviour of the Jews and the wrongs they had committed against the Romans. He said that they deserved a stronger and harsher reprimand, but in conformity with the traditional clemency of the Romans, if they were obedient from now onwards, he would grant them forgiveness.[312]

Pompey regarded Judaea as already an enemy nation. He accused the Jews of being law-breakers and of having done injury to the Romans. This is legal language as used in the Roman procedure conducted by the fetial priests of Rome before declaring war. It refers to breaking the ties of *fides* and acting like an enemy. 'Injury' (*iniuria*) was a cause for war if demands for restitution went unanswered.[313] This is all part of the Roman view on the 'just war': war had to have a just cause and be in response to an injury.[314] In other words, Pompey was laying out the *casus belli*. Since the Jews had not been reliable as friends, the grounds for the renunciation of their friendship with the Romans existed. The Jews' disregard of the Roman hostility to the Cilician pirates could justify making war on Judaea. Herein lies the explanation for Pompey's harsh treatment of Jerusalem. The revolt of Aristobulus II against the Romans only made the Roman cause more just. The alliance with Parthia or suspicions of dealing with them had far-reaching consequences for the Jews. It accounts for the hostile attitude of the Romans and Pompey in 63 BCE.

### *The pirates*

The eastern Mediterranean coastline in the second half of the second century BCE was shared by the Egyptian Ptolemaic Empire, the Seleucid Empire, the Hasmonaean state, Rhodes and southern Anatolia, more specifically, Cilicia. The growth of piracy in Cilicia can be directly related to two factors: first, the restrictions placed on the Seleucid navy after the treaty of Apamea, which concluded Rome's war against Antiochus III; second, the weakening of the Seleucid Empire by the Parthians.[315] In this period, the Seleucid dynasty experienced many disruptions in an orderly succession to the throne, during which many failed kings and pretenders used Cilicia as a base. Such was the case for Demetrius II, Antiochus IX, Seleucus VI and Philip I, spanning a period from 144 BCE until 83 BCE.[316] The Romans saw the connection between the usurpers to the Seleucid throne and the rise of the Cilician pirates as a menacing threat to shipping in the eastern Mediterranean. The geographer Strabo (writing in the time of the emperor Tiberius) attributes the actual beginning of piracy in Cilicia in the second half of the second century to Tryphon, the leader of an insurrection against the Seleucids.[317] Whether justifiably or not, Tryphon had earned himself the reputation as the founder of Cilician piracy.[318]

Strabo (14.5.2) relates:

> The first place in Cilicia, then, to which one comes, is a stronghold, Coracesium, situated on an abrupt rock, which was used by Diodotus, called Tryphon, as a base of operations at the time when he caused Syria to revolt from the kings and was fighting it out with them, being successful at one time and failing at another. Now Tryphon was hemmed up in a certain place by Antiochus, son of Demetrius, and forced to kill himself; and it was Tryphon, together with the worthlessness of the kings who by succession were then reigning over Syria and at the same time over Cilicia, who caused the Cilicians to organize their gangs of pirates; for on account of his revolutionary attempts others made like attempts at the same time, and thus the dissensions of brethren with one another put the country at the mercy of any who might attack it.

Diodotus Tryphon used the Cilician pirates to attack the cities on the coast of Syria whose inhabitants refused to acknowledge his claim to the throne. Strabo reports that they destroyed the city of Berytus in Phoenicia as part of Tryphon's campaign of terror in the mid-140s BCE.[319]

Tryphon's career had begun as a general under Demetrius I; he joined the cause of the rebel Alexander Balas, who overthrew the king in 150 BCE. His reign was short. He was killed soon after by Demetrius II, the son of Demetrius I, c. 145 BCE. Tryphon continued to resist Demetrius II, acting as guardian for the two-year-old son of Alexander Balas, the future Antiochus VI. In 144 BCE, Tryphon killed his ward and took the throne for himself; however, he was never acknowledged by Rome. In 138 BCE, Demetrius' brother, Antiochus VII, put down Tryphon's rebellion and besieged him inside the city of Dor. Although he was able to escape, Tryphon realised his cause was lost and committed suicide at Apamea.

How did the Hasmonaeans navigate the vicissitudes of Seleucid pretenders and rivals to the throne, and what was their relationship with Tryphon, the founder of Cilician piracy? Jonathan at first gave his allegiance to Alexander Balas, receiving the title of friend of the king and general (*strategos*).[320] When the Ptolemies took advantage of the Seleucid dynastic instability in order to regain Coele-Syria in what is known as the Seventh Syrian War, Jonathan and his Judaean army fought on the side of Alexander Balas. Ptolemy VI Philometer installed Demetrius II on the throne. The new king confirmed Jonathan's titles and a deal was struck. In return for Judaean soldiers' assistance in quelling a revolt in Antioch, Demetrius promised to remove all Seleucid garrisons from Judaea. Jonathan kept his side of the bargain, but Demetrius reneged. When Tryphon rose to challenge Demetrius, Jonathan was ready to join him. Jonathan's military successes brought his army as far as the Orontes valley, but it was his fortification of Jerusalem that aroused Tryphon's suspicions. Tryphon approached Jerusalem and, unable to storm it, captured Jonathan by a ruse and had him imprisoned and then killed. Once Tryphon and his forces had evacuated Judaea, Simon, now the Hasmonaean leader, switched sides in the Seleucid power struggle, throwing in his support for Demetrius II. This king also did not reign long. During his Parthian campaign, he was captured. In his absence, Antiochus VII took the throne. In a bid to secure Simon's allegiance, the new king made him High Priest and ethnarch of Judaea.

In Roman law, pirates were considered the common enemy of all humanity, outside the laws and conventions of civilised people.[321] Piracy was regarded as the maritime equivalent of land-based banditry, both of which were outside proper legal norms.[322] We know of the Roman definition of 'civilised' from Cicero, who wrote that these were people who had a government and constitution that operated with the consent and agreement of its citizens and whose foreign policy aimed for peace through the formation of treaties.[323] With pirates there was no trust (*fides*) in any oaths (*ius iurandum*) they might make, and so one could not make treaties with them.[324] A just war (*bellum iustum*) might only be fought against a just and legitimate enemy.[325] The Cilician pirates were known for their violations of the norms of *ius gentium*.[326] Therefore, they fell outside the rules of the just war. A just war had to be declared; but against pirates, such legal niceties could be dispensed with.

From the second century on, Cilicia became the largest centre of piracy.[327] Against this background, one can well understand the increasing irritation with which the Romans would have viewed the Hasmonaean ties with Tryphon and the Cilician pirates. Tryphon, in aiding and abetting the pirates, placed himself outside the law and outside the rules of war (*ius belli*) and the law of nations (*ius gentium*). The senate's contempt for Tryphon was made plain when they accepted his gift of a gold statute and then inscribed it with the name of Antiochus VI, the ward he had ordered murdered.[328] Jonathan had been able to forge ties with Rome because he had been technically in alliance with Antiochus VI and had been taken prisoner by Tryphon. Simon had allied himself with Antiochus VII and then sent an embassy to Rome. Both had avoided being associated with the pretender to the throne who had organised the pirates in Cilicia.

Already by 229 BCE, the Romans had begun to be concerned with piracy in the Adriatic emanating from Illyria, which had been going on for some time.[329] This was the basis for the First Illyrian War, in which the Romans acted against the pirates whom Polybius calls the 'common enemy'.[330] Both this war and the Second Illyrian War were concerned with ridding the seas of pirates.[331] Rome's continued interest in keeping the sea lanes open dictated the campaign against pirates in the Balearic islands in 123 BCE.[332] By the end of the second century, piracy in Cilicia had become such a problem that the Romans sent a force under M. Antonius in 102–100 BCE to deal with it. He had ships from Rhodes and Byzantium at his disposal.[333] An inscription records the measures to be taken towards checking the prevalence of piracy in Cilicia. The law on piracy (dated to the end of 101 BCE) required letters to be sent to the kings and states allied to Rome in Anatolia, Syria and Egypt to refuse the use of their ports to pirates. The Romans clearly considered that it was the duty of their local allies to police the seas. Under this law, Cilicia became a closed military zone to be policed and subdued.[334]

The question arises why Judaea was not asked by Rome to participate in this maritime alliance against the pirates.[335] In attempting to frame a response, it may be instructive to turn to the actions of Alexander Jannaeus (103–76 BCE). Josephus reports that Jannaeus was the first of the Hasmonaeans to employ mercenaries from Cilicia.[336] Josephus speaks of the Cilicians as auxiliaries; that is to say, as soldiers in his army. It was known that Cilician pirates hired themselves out as soldiers.[337] In the war against Mithridates, Sinope was defended against the Roman general, Lucullus, by more than 8,000 Cilicians, whose leader was called an 'arch-pirate'.[338] Furthermore, the name 'Cilician' became synonymous in the Roman mind with pirates.[339] In Pompey's campaign against piracy, Metellus Creticus, when he came across Cilician soldiers, had them executed as pirates.[340] The reputation of the Jews as pirate sympathisers lingered. The principal Hasmonaean port was Joppa, and Strabo (16,2,28) informs us that it served as a base of operations for pirates and gave them asylum. He wrote concerning Joppa:

> Indeed the Judaeans have used this place as a seaport when they have gone down as far as the sea; but the seaports of robbers are obviously only robbers' dens.

Strabo had good sources and devoted much of his *Geographika* (Γεωγραφικά) to descriptions of harbours and coastlines and other maritime matters. In his view the possession of good harbours promoted piracy. Piracy and banditry are often mentioned in his work.[341]

From Strabo, we also learn that Pompey's campaign in Jerusalem and in Jaffa had as its aim to 'destroy the haunts of robbers'. By this time the Jews were regarded as pirates.[342] The reputation of the Jews for piracy created suspicion in the mind of the Romans as to their loyalty to Rome during the war against piracy that had brought Pompey to Syria.[343] It is Trogus who informs us of the acts of brigandage committed that represented piracy.[344] When Antiochus XIII asked to be restored to the Seleucid throne, he made the accusation that if he were not to be king Syria would become prey to Jewish and Arab pirates (*latrociniis*).[345] Due to this reputation, Pompey had reason to remove Joppa from the territory of

Judaea in 63 BCE and make Syria a province.[346] Even so, under the governorship of Gabinius piracy was still not eradicated.[347]

The Roman omission in the Piracy Law to request help from the Hasmonaean state against the pirates is understandable against this background. Not supporting Rome's efforts to keep the eastern Mediterranean free of pirates was not an act consistent with being a friend and ally of Rome. The Piracy Law had placed an embargo on contact with Cilicia.[348] Recruitment of Cilician pirates as mercenaries violated this embargo. This may go a long way to explaining the cessation in Roman–Jewish relations. From the Roman perspective, the friendship would immediately be terminated when the ally sided with an enemy of Rome (see Chapter 4) and flagrantly disregarded Roman legislation. The Romans had shown that, since 229 BCE, they were prepared to go to war to eradicate piracy. As a consequence, the question should not be why the Hasmonaeans ceased diplomatic contact with Rome, but why their actions proved hostile to Rome. According to the Romans, a friend of the Roman people behaved as a friend should: loyal and supporting other Roman friends and allies. The Roman Piracy Law of 100 BCE went further and instructed Roman allies in the area to do the job of policing the seas on behalf of Rome. It is instructive that Judaea, even with its own ships, was not called on to help. Friendship with Rome might be restored, but what Rome regarded as frequent betrayals would not be tolerated. The patience and forbearance of the Roman senators was not limitless.

The rising power in the East, the Parthians, had invaded the territory of a Roman ally and friend (the Seleucid king) and the Jewish army under the leadership of Hyrcanus not only did not support the king, but betrayed him by forming a wartime agreement with their enemy. For the Romans, Judaea became an enemy of the Seleucids, their ally, which rendered them also an enemy of Rome, according to the principle of Roman *Völkerrecht* that an attack on a Roman ally was, in effect, an attack on Rome itself. Ties with Parthia would not have been given Roman approval, not because they were considered enemies of Rome at this time (which they were not) but due to the inability of a Roman ally to conclude a treaty or make friendship while still maintaining their privilege of being a friend of the Roman people.[349]

Hyrcanus' hostile behaviour continued: he returned from the East and began attacking cities in Syria. In the case of the pirates, the principle was that they were outside the norms of international law, what the Romans called the *multa iura communia*, meaning the many international laws that were common to and acknowledged by all nations.[350] Alexander Jannaeus had placed himself beyond the pale in having contacts with Cilician 'pirates'.

## Conclusion

Three principles of Roman international law (*Völkerrecht*) explain the timing of embassies to Rome and the cessation of relations under Alexander Jannaeus. The first is that, in order to apply to the senate for any form of diplomatic relations, the petitioners were required to demonstrate that they were independent; that is, autonomous, non-tributary and ungarrisoned. The Jewish leaders applied to Rome the moment that they could meet these conditions. Thus, Jonathan could not send an embassy immediately he came to power in 160 BCE, only in 144/43 BCE. The senate did not require the recognition of each Jewish leader on coming to office. Jonathan needed to wait until he could throw off the vassalage under Demetrius II and score a military victory. Simon secured liberation from the Seleucids by removing the Akra from Jerusalem. His embassy was in Rome soon after, in 141 BCE. John Hyrcanus toyed with a secret alliance with the Parthians but, after that, sent an embassy to Rome in 129 BCE.

The second principle of Roman international law concerns the breaking of friendship by Rome. Hyrcanus I came under suspicion of doing a deal with the Parthians to help them defeat a Roman ally. His crime was to have two incompatible and conflicting alliances at once: friendship with Rome and the suspected friendship with Parthia.

The third principle of international law concerns the status of pirates, who, being outside international norms, were incapable of keeping sworn agreements. War against them could be undeclared and waged with no holds barred. Association with pirates rendered one liable to the same status. Thus, the employment of Cilician pirates in the army of Alexander Jannaeus tainted his rule in Roman eyes. The charge of piracy was levelled at the Jews when Pompey met with Jewish leaders in Damascus.[351]

Without the friendship of the Romans, Alexander Jannaeus could not seek aid when it would have helped against Tigranes, Demetrius III and Antiochus XII[352] and he could not send an embassy to Rome unless he was prepared to answer for consorting with pirates. It was not so much that he was actively anti-Roman, but that his actions had cut him off from Rome. The harsh treatment meted out to Jerusalem by Pompey is explicable in the terms that he himself laid out: the Jews had caused injury to Rome, they had not given any restitution (that is, correction of the situation) and the Romans were justified in interpreting the situation as a state of war that did not require a formal declaration of war. Therefore, their friendship with Rome was over and they had become the enemies of Rome. A state of war already existed when Pompey arrived and in the Roman view harsh measures were justified.

## Notes

1 I use the term 're-form' rather than renew as the latter does not necessarily carry the meaning of a break in ties, which have to be formed all over again. When the Greek text says ανανεόσασθαι, the meaning is not 'renew' but 'revive'. See Liddell and Scott (1996) 113, II, citing Thuc. 6.10.78: τὴν ἀρχήν τὴν φιλίαν τινός. This is the same context in which we find the verb in Josephus.

2 Need for *sua potestas*: Cic. *Balb.* 8.20, 11.27; Procul. *Dig.* 49.15.7.1. See Horn (1930) 7; Paradisi (1954) 5f.; Polay (1964) 106, 124; Wegner (1969) 91; Schmitt (1988) 531–532; De Martino (1973) 35, 88f., 110f., 323f., 359f. See above, pp. 107, 178–179.

3 For the Seleucid perspective, see Dąbrowa (2004) 67–68.

4 Zollschan (2002) 184–188.

5 Polyb. 18.46.15; Livy 33.32.5.

6 See p. 98.
7 1 Macc. 9.1–22; Jos. *Ant.* 12.11.6.
8 See Chapter 4.
9 1 Macc. 10.20, 10.65.
10 Polyb. 33.18.12–13.
11 Vassal: Dąbrowa (2010) 51. Recognition: Polyb. 33.18.
12 1 Macc. 11.16–20. The plan to take the Akra (see Babota (2014) 213) could not have won Jonathan an alliance with Rome; only success in shaking off the yoke of the Seleucids could do so. This was only achieved legally when Jonathan was acknowledged as ruler of Judaea by Antiochus VI (see below). New discovery of its location: see mfa.gov.il/MFA/Israel/Experience/History/Pages/Has-the-Acra-from-2000-years-ago-been-found-3-Nov-2015.aspx (accessed 13 December 2015).
13 Domingo Gygax (2013) 52. See also section on gift giving in pp. 78–82.
14 1 Macc. 11.25–28.
15 1 Macc. 11.54.
16 1 Macc. 11.57–58.
17 See Savalli-Lestrade (1998) 77–78, no. 77.
18 Seeman (2013) 433, n. 67.
19 Jos. *Ant.* 13.163.
20 Bartlett (1998) 95.
21 For the earlier literature, see Schürer (1973) 1.184–185. Representative of the sceptics would be Gruen (1996).
22 For the earlier literature, see Cardauns (1967) 317, n. 1. See most recently Nagy (2010) 110–112.
23 Amitay (2013) 88.
24 Seeman (2013) 147–149.
25 Meyer (1925) 30–31; Ginsburg (1934) 117–122; Schüller (1956) 257–268; Gutman (1958); Goldstein (1976) 457–461; Katzoff (1985) 486, n. 2; Orrieux (1989) 171–174; Cartledge and Spawforth (1989) 36–37; Rappaport (2004) 287–288. Those who consider the correspondence authentic except for the letter of Areus (1 Macc. 12.20–23): Hadas (1959) 87; Hengel (1974) 1.72, 2.50–51, 150, n. 748; Habicht (1976) 226, n. 9a; Bickerman (1988) 144; Stern (1995) 67, n. 11; Patterson (2010) 59–68; Amitay (2013).
26 Most recently Cardauns (1967); Gruen (1996); id. (1998) 265–267; id. (2011) 305–306; Bremmer (2010).
27 2 Macc. 5.9–10; Amitay (2013) 88 and n. 38. Cf. Gruen (1998) 259.
28 1 Macc. 12.16.
29 Gruen (1984) 748.
30 1 Macc. 10.76–86.
31 See above, pp. 89–90.
32 Zollschan (forthcoming) ch. 9.
33 Livy 10.12.4; Bederman (2001) 225.
34 Momigliano (1931) 148f. Embassy attributed to Simon: Timpe (1974) 149–150; Shatzman (1999).
35 Stern (1961). See Seeman's compilation (2013) 378–380.
36 2 Macc. 4.11; Zollschan (2004).
37 Jos. *Ant.* 14.145. For this date see Stern (1961).
38 Jos. *Ant.* 13.260. Date: Stern (1961) 7–11.
39 My thanks to Prof. Uriel Rappaport for this suggestion.
40 Savalli-Lestrade (1998) 78–81, 84.
41 Fischer (1970) 96ff.; Goldstein (1976) 494.
42 Gauger (1977) 179.
43 Jos. *Ant.* 13.163–165.
44 For an explanation of this term, see pp. 69–74.

45 βεβαιώσει: not just 'confirm' (as in R. Marcus' translation) but also 'to establish, to secure'. Liddell and Scott (1996) 312. See similar wording in Thuc. 1.33: τὴν ἀρχήν, τὴν φικίαν τινός.
46 Jos. *Ant.* 13.164. Dąbrowa (2010) 55, 42 suggests that the additional information supplied by Josephus may be Josephus' commentary.
47 See most recently Babota (2014) 213.
48 1 Macc. 13.36–40.
49 Jos. *Ant.* 13.213.
50 Goldstein (1976) 478; Bartlett (1998) 42.
51 Will (1982) 2.405; Fischer (1975) 193.
52 1 Macc. 13.42. See Goldstein (1976) 479; Sievers (1990) 110–111.
53 1 Macc. 13.49–52, 14.7, 36.
54 Sievers (1990) 111.
55 Consensus: Sievers (1990) 117.
56 Pina Polo (2011) 261–263.
57 1 Macc. 14.24.
58 Example: Livy 34.52.7. See Dancy (1954) 183.
59 Kappler (1936) 141.
60 Dąbrowa (2010) 58, n. 53. Date of 142: Schwartz (1993) 125; Shatzman (1999) 66.
61 The Greek is not 'renew' but 'revive'; see Liddell and Scott (1996) 113, II citing Thuc. 6.10.78, τὴν ἀρχὴν τὴν φιλίαν τινός.
62 Misplaced: Goldstein (1976) 493.
63 Mendelssohn and Ritschl (1875).
64 Zeitlin (1950) 41–42.
65 Willrich (1924) 50, 59; Giovannini and Müller (1971) 160–165; Gauger (1977) 291; Sievers (1990) 117. Authentic: Bickerman (1930) 358–360; Momigliano (1934) 215–217 (authentic except for the extradition clause and list of places where letter was to be forwarded on); Goldstein (1976) 492–500. For the earlier literature see Sievers (1990) 116–119.
66 Stern (1972) 128.
67 Sherk (1969) 1, second letter, l. 1 [= *SEG*[3] 612].
68 Goldstein (1976) 496–497 considers the use of just the *praenomen* in official documents to be common Greek practice and gives as an example Jos. *Ant.* 14.225, but in this passage only the *cognomen* is used.
69 Sherk (1969) 190; Pucci Ben Zeev (1998) 18.
70 Mason (1974) 166; Zollschan (2007b) 13–14.
71 D.H. 4.76.2.
72 Babota (2014) 11.
73 *AE* (1967) 532; Mason (1974) 166.
74 L. Caecilius Metellus Calvus (*RE* 83). Broughton (1951) 1.474, 476, n. 1. Date from Livy, *Oxyr. Per.* 54: Broughton (1951) 3.37. See also Stern (1972) 128–129.
75 Antiochus: Sherk (1969) no. 34, l. 4. Ariarathes: Sherk (1969) no. 6B l. 8. Eumenes: Sherk (1969) no. 40, l. 29.
76 *OGIS* 170, mentioned in Sievers (2005) 34, n. 6.
77 Bickerman (1930) 360.
78 Demetrius I: Polyb. 32.2.10. Tryphon: Diod. 33.28a.1.
79 Rappaport (1995) 272.
80 Rappaport (1995) 275–279.
81 1 Macc. 14.27–49.
82 Rappaport (1995) 279.
83 Momigliano (1931) 155.
84 Platner and Ashby (1929) 55–56; Gianelli (1993).
85 493 BCE: D.H. 6.94.3. Site: Coarelli (1993) 261.
86 Mossakowski (2004/2006). For *ius* in general, see Turelli (2014) 470, n. 65.

87 Goldstein (1976) 497; Rappaport (1995) 272–274.
88 Representative: Rappaport (1995) 273–274.
89 Hyrcanus II: Jos. *Ant.* 14.196. See Saulnier (1981) 179; Rajak (1984b) 117; Rappaport (1995) 280. Herod: Jos. *BJ* 1.24, 2.474; Goldstein (1976) 497.
90 Added on: Momigliano (1931) 156.
91 Goldstein (1976) 496.
92 1 Macc. 15.22–24.
93 As an example of a circular letter, the Hefzibah inscription is not comparable to the Lucius letter, as the letter in the Hefzibah inscription was circulated within the Seleucid Empire and its lower-rank officials. See Landau (1966) 61, 66, 69.
94 Philo, *Leg.* 281–282. Cited by Gauger (1990) 157–158 and n. 27.
95 Grajetzki (2011) 10.
96 Friend: Hor. *Sat.* 2.1.71–74; Gruen (1992) 280.
97 Raschke (1987) 301.
98 Jer. *Chron. Ol.* 169.3.
99 *ad regem legatus, Rhodum, Ecbatanam ac Babylonem ibo, cercurum sumam.* On Lucilius' work, see Marx (1882); Cichorius (1908) 320ff; Terzaghi (1934); Mariotti (1961); Krendkel (1972); Raschke (1987); id. (1990); Christes (2005).
100 Magie (1950) 2. 1055, n. 25; Christes (2005) 849–850. See Raschke (1979).
101 Justin. 41.6; Oros. 5.4.16; Marx (1882) 83.
102 Diod. 33.28a. Itinerary: Plut. *Mor.* 200–201; Egypt, Syria, Asia and Greece according to Cic. *Rep.* 6.11.11. See Krug (1916) 84; Knibbe (1960); Gruen (1984) 280, 714–715.
103 Astin (1959) 226.
104 Cichorius (1908) 320–322; Niese (1903) 3.270, n. 1; Krug (1916) 84; Knibbe (1960) 37 n. 11.
105 Widengren (1966) 142.
106 Dated to 96/95 BCE: Badian (1959b); Keaveney (1981) 195–198. Dated to 94/93 BCE: Dimitriev (2006); Olbrycht (2009) 173–174. Dated to 92 BCE: Lerouge (2007) 43. Failure: Plut. *Sulla* 5.8; Valgiglio (1976) n. to 5.8; Campbell (2002) 214. Against: Keaveney (1981) 196.
107 Dio 36.1–3; Keaveney (1981) 202–203.
108 Plut. *Pomp.* 33; *Apophtheg. Regum* 8; Keaveney (1981) 208; Campbell (2002) 214.
109 Dio 37.6.3; Plut. *Pomp.* 33.6.
110 64 BCE: Keaveney (1981) 209. Still in effect: Florus 1.46.4; Oros. 6.13.2. Carrhae: Plut. *Crass.* 23.7.27, 31–32.1.
111 Keaveney (1982) 419; Mattern-Parkes (2003) 389, 391.
112 Strabo 6.1.28.
113 Cic. *Fam.* 8.10.2, 8.14.14; *Att.* 5.18.11, 6.1.3, 6.1.14; Cic. *Att.* 5.21.2 *bellum Parthicum*.
114 Malitz (1984) 28.
115 App. *BC.* 2.110; Nicolaus of Damascus *FGrH* 90 F 130, 41; *Plut.* Brut. 25; *Caes.* 58; Suet. *Div. Iul.* 44.
116 Syrian situation: Sheldon (2010) 54–56; Malitz (1984) 30 and nn. 47–48.
117 For a discussion of the possible site of Sampsame with literature: Abel (1949) 269.
118 See Goldstein (1976) for the various manuscript readings.
119 Michaelis (1778) 320–322. Followed by Goldstein (1976) 498.
120 Reinach (1888) 334, n. 2.
121 Reinach (1888) 335.
122 Meineke (1849) 554.
123 Diller (1938) 333.
124 Diller (1938) 334.
125 Bouiron (2014) 788.
126 Baumgarten (1981) 33.
127 Schwartz (1993) 123–125 following Marx (1884) 68–71. Followed by Unger (1896) and Münzer (1905).

128 Mattingly (1986) 491–492.
129 Cavaignac (1951).
130 Astin (1959) 222.
131 Mattingly (1986) 492–495.
132 After censorship: Cic. *Rep.* 6.11. Before censorship: Cic. *Acad.* pr. 2–5. See Astin (1959) 221 and n. 10.
133 Mattingly (1986) 492.
134 Mattingly (1986). Cf. Broughton (1951) 1.481, n. 2.
135 Sherwin-White (1984) 57–55, 82–83. Mattingly (1986) 491.
136 Astin (1959) 226–227.
137 Regarded as a inauthentic: Giovannini and Müller (1971) 162.
138 Momigliano (1931) 156.
139 Son: 1 Macc. 16.2. Commander: 1 Macc. 13.53; Sievers (1990) 135.
140 Siege: Jos. *Ant.* 13.237, 13.241. Terms: Jos. *Ant.* 13.245–248; Sievers (1990) 136–137.
141 Mommsen (1887) 3, 2.1008. See also Daube (1956) 78–86.
142 Moehring (1975) 141–144 and Sherk (1969) 14.
143 Münzer (1907).
144 Münzer (1907) 1994.
145 Strabo: Münzer (1907) 1994–1995. Identification: Fraccaro (1926) 160. Followed by Sumner (1973) 53–55.
146 Münzer (1907) 1988, followed by Broughton (1951) 1.508, 509, n. 2. Praetorship: Münzer (1920) 439.
147 Broughton (1951) 1.508; Sumner (1973) 55.
148 Taylor and Scott (1969) 536.
149 Marcus (1933) 356.
150 Macrob. *Sat.* 2.2, 10. Münzer (1928a) 910.
151 Confusion: Münzer (1928), see L. Mallius (4) col. 910. Identification: Münzer (1928) 1159.
152 Eilers (2013) 162.
153 See Marcus (1933) 356.
154 Münzer (1923) 1441–1443; Broughton (1951) 1.498, 3.190.
155 Münzer (1923) 1441. Followed by Broughton (1951) 3.190.
156 Decree: Sherk (1969) 12, who dates the decree to 129 BCE. Eilers (2013) 162, who dates the decree to 101 BCE.
157 Sherk (1969) 7.
158 Pucci ben Zeev (1998) 131. In Caesar's time at least eight: Shatzman (2012) 57.
159 See, for example, Sherk (1969) nos. 1, 15. Lott (2012) 176 suggests that the norm for the early empire was between two and six witnesses.
160 Gelzer (1968) 290 citing Cic. *Fam.* 9.15.3–4, 13.17.1; Dio 43.27.1.
161 Cf. Pucci Ben Zeev (1998) 131; Shatzman (2012) 57, n. 109.
162 Mendelssohn (1875) 139–143. Followed by Schürer (1973) 1. 205, n. 7; Rajak (2002).
163 Heuss (1933) 46f.
164 Jos. *BJ* 1.61; *Ant.* 13.236–244. Cf. Diod. 34/35.1.1; Seeman (2013) 196.
165 Houghton et al. (2008) 391–392.
166 Smallwood (1976) 10.
167 Rajak (2002) 74–76.
168 Seeman (2013) 187.
169 Coudry (2004).
170 Reinach (1899); Willrich (1924) 63–64; Giovannini and Müller (1971) 159–160; Eilers (2013) 161–162.
171 Ritschl (1873) 610, n. 31.
172 (1899).
173 Jos. *Ant.* 13.273.
174 Stern (1961). Cf. Rajak (2002) 81–98 at 90–93.

175 Date of 134 BCE: representative: Shatzman (1999) 66–67. Against: Seeman (2013) 187.
176 Giovannini and Müller (1971) 158.
177 Broughton (1951) 1.516
178 Brennan (2000) 1.170.
179 Brennan (2000) 1.119.
180 Strategos: Mason (1974) 166. Grypus: Seeman (2013) 188.
181 Ritschl (1875) 89ff.
182 See p. 235.
183 Also expressed by Goldstein (1976) 497, without further discussion. Fannius Letter dated to 49 BCE see Zollschan (2007b). Valerius decree dated to 47 BCE also.
184 Shatzman (2012) 58.
185 Sievers (1990) 117–118, n. 60.
186 Broughton (1951) 2.287 gives the names of M. Acilius Caninus (or Caninianus) and L. Nonius Asprenas based only on estimates of when they could have held the office. He later corrected his position on the praetors of 47 BCE (3.146) after two publications appeared showing that using their commands in the civil war was not a measure that could result in sure dates for their consulships. See Sumner (1971) 260–261 and Badian (1971) 138–141.
187 Dio 42.20.4, 42.27.2, 42.55.4; Sumner (1971) 259.
188 Porph. on Hor. *Sat.* 1.2.94; Broughton (1951) 3.211. References to his coins: Broughton (1951) 2.454.
189 Mommsen (1875) 287–291. Recently revived: Shatzman (2012) 57.
190 Aedicula: Momigliano (1942) 116 and n. 1. Recently revived: Shatzman (2012) 57. Inaugurated: see Taylor and Scott (1969) 558 and n. 64.
191 App. *BC* 1.26; Varro *L.L.* 5.156. Excavations in 1983: Ferroni (1993).
192 Ritschl's discussion (in Mendelssohn and Ritschl (1875) 428–433) concerning the Temple of Concordia has now been overtaken by archaeological findings.
193 Bonnefond-Coudry (1989) 47.
194 See Momigliano (1931) 153.
195 *CIL* 14.3540.
196 The suggestion of a Q. Coponius c. 146 BCE comes from an inscription from Delphi where the *praenomen* is not given and the name 'Coponius' is restored. For the inscription and date: Münzer (1900).
197 91 BCE: Münzer (1900). 50s BCE: Varro *apud* Pliny *NH* 36.41. Robert (1900).
198 Stein (1900).
199 Q. Coponius (Münzer (1900)) and T. Coponius Maximus (von Schoeffer (1900)).
200 Münzer (1900).
201 App. *BC* 4.10, 170. *RE* 4.1215.
202 Münzer (2000) 1215. Coins: Crawford (1974) 1. 461–462, no. 444 (49 BC).
203 Livy 10.46.7–8; Palmer (1970) 165.
204 (1951) 2, Suppl., 45.
205 Broughton (1951) 2.144, 172.
206 Münzer (1949); Broughton (1951) 2.181; Fündling (2007).
207 1 Macc. 14.24.
208 Ritschl changed the name of Alexander to Antipater: (1873) 597f.
209 Sievers (2005) 41 and n. 37. In the Christian period, the name Antiochus is attested among Samaritans.
210 Cic. *Phil.* 2.71, 13.10–11; Plut. *Ant.* 10.1; App. *BC* 3.11; Dio 42.50.2. For other measures to bring in cash, see Broughton (1951) 2.286.
211 Gauger (1986) 276.
212 Jos. *Ant.* 14. 148, 151, 191, 196, 200, 226. Ben Zeev (1998) 49, nn. 13–14 for modern literature.

213 Eyal (2013) 183. See Sharon (2010) 475.
214 Mendelssohn in Mendelssohn and Ritschl (1875) 423; Abel (1949) 275; Giovannini and Müller (1971) 163.
215 Stern (1965) 159 answering the criticism of Willrich (1895) 71–72. Date 76 BCE: Jos. *B.J.* 1.106–109; *Ant.* 398–408.
216 www.tyndalehouse.com/Egypt/ptolemies/chron/roman/roman_civil.htm (accessed 13 December 2015).
217 Lack of intercalation: Cic. *Fam.* 8.6.5; Plut.*Caes*. 59. Three months ahead: Hannah (2013) 112.
218 Grumel (1958) 168–175; Samuel (1972) 139–145; Schürer (1973–1987) 588–590; Meimaris et al. (1992) 38–41.
219 Meimaris et al. (1992) 38.
220 Samuel (1972) 141–143.
221 At www.tyndalehouse.com/Egypt/ptolemies/chron/babylonian/babylonian.htm (accessed 26 August 2016).
222 The most recent treatment is Bennett (2011).
223 Samuel (1972) 149.
224 Samuel (1972) 150; Spalinger (1994) 78.
225 Meimaris (1992) 40.
226 Bickermann (1980) 120.
227 Skeat (1969) 18; Ginzel (1911) 576, table V.
228 Ideler (1825) 1. 430–439. For Sidon: Ideler (1825) 1. 434; Grumel (1958) 175; Samuel (1972) 174.
229 Judeich (1885) 106; Täubler (1913) 164; Stern (1965) 159.
230 Judeich (1885) 110–111; Schmidt (1983) 205–207. Lord (1938) 25–28 suggests Caesar arrived in Syria at the beginning of April (Julian) if travelling overland or end of March (Julian) if by sea.
231 Acceptance of date in Malalas: Holmes (1923) 3. 509. Non-acceptance: Lord (1938) 26. For the date 16 April (Julian): Judeich (1885) 106–109.
232 Nicols (1978) 55; Burgess (1999) 104.
233 Tyre: theory of Niese (1893) 194–229. Disproven: Nicols (1978) 47, table 2.
234 Nicols (1978) 47.
235 For the modern literature see Goodblatt (1994) 64. For Archival notation: Pucci Ben Zeev (1998) 402; Eilers (2008) 214.
236 Macedonian calendar: Pucci Ben Zeev (1998) 402. The intercalation of 90 days in 46 BCE to bring the Roman year in line with the solar year before Caesar could introduce his new calendar in 45 BCE makes it difficult to calculate the exact equivalents for this particular year. See chart in Ideler (1825) 1.121.
237 On Josephus' errors, the state of the original documents and Josephus' use of them as 'forensic' evidence as though in a court room see Rajak (2007) 178, 184–185.
238 Burgess (1999) 104–105.
239 Zack (forthcoming) n. 58. Apellaios: Nicols (1978) 47.
240 Broughton (1951) 2, Suppl. p. 45.
241 Cic. *Balb.* 53.
242 Badian (1961) 493; Alexander (1985) 29. For the *Lex Acilia de repetundis*: *CIL* $1^2$ 583 and Hands (1965) 225–237.
243 Fischer (1970) 9–10.
244 For the archivist, see Ben Zeev (1998) 399–405.
245 For the identification of the king as Antiochus Sidetes, see Mendelssohn (1873) 34. Followed by Giovannini and Müller (1971) 171 and n. 54.
246 Returning: Eilers (2013) 157. Community: Trebilco (2006) 8, n. 15.
247 Ben Zeev (1994) 51, 53 (Pergamene Decree), 55–59 (archives from Asia Minor).
248 Fränkel (1890) 160–164 (no. 247).

249 Sherk (1969) 59a, pp. 70–71. See Erskine (1994).
250 Osterloh considers that the name Aeneas is a reference to Troy and that it indicates the Jews' non-Greek status. See Osterloh (2008) 203.
251 Primo (2009) 94.
252 Jos. *Ant.* 13.260.
253 Seeman (2013) 197.
254 Eilers (2013) 159.
255 *Bull. Hell.* 6, no. 19, 626 and 36, no. 66, 131.
256 Münzer (1938).
257 Broughton (1951) 2, Suppl. p. 36. Roman senator: Syme (1955) 66.
258 Münzer (1938) [1381].
259 Reynolds and Tannenbaum (1987) 101.
260 Common name: Seeman (2013) 448, n. 147. Envoy: Jos. *Ant.* 14.222, 14.226, 14.307.
261 Cf. Seeman (2013) 196.
262 Trebilco (2006) 8 and n. 17.
263 Gruen (1997) 77.
264 Eilers (2013) 156.
265 Rajak (2002) 77–80.
266 114–103 BCE: Dąbrowa (2010) 72. 113/12 BCE: Bar Kochva (1996) 232; Shatzman (2012) 70. 105 BCE: Eilers (2013) 161.
267 I follow Rappaport in his explanation for the silence. See Rappaport (1968) 329–330. Against this: La Rocca (2014), who wishes to suggest that Roman–Judaean ties continued after John Hyrcanus without consideration of Roman *Völkerrecht*.
268 See above, p. 84.
269 For the influence of Jews in Babylonia, see Neusner (1965) 1.24; Diod. 34/5.1–5; Just. 36.1; Porph. *apud* Euseb. *Chronikon* (Schoene) p. 225.
270 Neusner (1965) 1.23.
271 Neusner (1965) 1.24–25.
272 Debevoise (1938) 22 and n. 97 considers that the reference in *Orac. Sibyl*, 3.303–313 refers to this period.
273 Debevoise (1938) 24.
274 Capture: 1 Macc. 14.1–3. Timing: Justin. 36.1.5–6.
275 See Debevoise (1938) 26, n. 113.
276 Date based on numismatic evidence. See Debevoise (1938) 26, n. 114.
277 Sources remember the campaign largely because they were awed by the size of the army that Antiochus VII had put together: Justin. 38.10.2; Diod. 34.17.1; Oros. 5.10.8; Posid. *FGrH* frg. 9 (IIA, p. 227); Athen. *Deipnosophistae* 12.540; Jos. *BJ* 1.50, 62.
278 For this campaign, see Justin. 38.10–42.1; Porph. *apud* Euseb. *Chronikon*, fr. 32.19; Jos. *Ant.* 13.251–252.
279 Debevoise (1938) xxxii; Nikonorov (1998) 119.
280 Strabo 2.5.12; Nikonorov (1998) 107.
281 Pucci (1981).
282 See also Jos. *BJ* 1.62.
283 Sotah 33a. See Klausner (1924) 2.74.
284 Sceptical: Dąbrowa (2010) 70, n. 13.
285 Jos. *Ant.* 13.249–252.
286 Translation from Neusner (1965) 25.
287 Pucci (1981) 336–337.
288 Pucci (1983) 17–21. Cf. Rappaport (1989) 376.
289 Josephus: Flusser (1957) 182; Rappaport (1968) 339.
290 Flusser (1953) 113. Mid-10th century: Feldman (1984a) 775.
291 Scaliger (1605).
292 Steinschneider (1893) 898; Gaster (1899) xvi–xviii; Schoesinger (1901–1906); Zeitlin (1931) 53; Flusser (1933); Baer (1949); Newmann (1953) 57; Reiner (1967) 126.

293 Flusser (1953).
294 Trieber (1895) 407–408.
295 There is a debate over whether he knew Greek. Flusser (1971) considered he did know Greek. Zeitlin (1962–1963) held that he did not know Greek.
296 Flusser (1957) 165–184.
297 Debevoise (1938) 94; Pucci (1981) and (1983); Fischer (1980) 56; Rappaport (1968) 339; id. (1989) 373–374; Atkinson (2011) 7–11.
298 See pp. 87–89.
299 Burton (2011) ch. 5.
300 Recognition: see Gruen (1984) 669–670, n. 265 for the literature. Help to Scipio in Spain: Livy *Per.* 57.
301 See pp. 86–87.
302 Neusner (1965) 25. Accepted as historical: Rappaport (1968) 343; Efron (1970) 72–73; Hackl (2010) 3.276.
303 Pal. Talmud *Brachot* 7.2. Translation: Neusner (1965) 25–26. See also Jer. Talmud, *Nazir* 5.3 and Kohelet Rabbah 7 (11) 24.
304 Neusner (1971) 97.
305 Neusner (1965) 26.
306 Goodblatt (1987) 17.
307 Mishna Ta'anit 3.8.
308 Schürer (1973) 1. 235, n. 6.
309 Sifra Beḥuqotai 1.1; Levit. Rabbah 35.10.
310 Jos. *Ant.* 13.430.
311 Burton (2011) 335.
312 Diod. 40.2.
313 Rich (2011) 209–217.
314 Cic. *Rep*. 2.17.31. On the doctrine of the 'just war', see Drexler (1959); Hausmaniger (1961); Albert (1980); Clavadetscher-Thürlemann (1985); Mantovani (1990); Loreto (2001); Calore (2003) 113 ff.; Stolfi (2009) 3.641 ff.
315 Ormond (1922) 35; Sherwin-White (1977) 69.
316 For the history of the declining years of the Seleucid Empire, see Will (1979–1982) 2.373–379, 404–413.
317 Strabo 14.5.2. See Marasco (1987) 127. Cf. Maróti (1962).
318 Cilicia as a centre of maritime power before Tryphon: De Souza (2013) 49.
319 Strabo 16.2.19. See De Souza (1999) 98.
320 1 Macc. 10.18–20.
321 Locus classicus is Cic. *de off.* 3.107: *nam pirata non est ex perduellium numero definitus, sed communis hostis omnium *** hoc nec fides debet nec ius iurandum esse commune.*
322 Ammian. 14.2.4.
323 Cic. *Phil* 4.14.
324 Pliny, *NH* 2.117.
325 Cic. *de off.* 3.108: *hostis iustus et legitimus.* Loreto (2001) 69–73.
326 Florus 1.41.3.
327 Tarwocka (2009) 31.
328 Diod. 33.28a.
329 Polyb. 2.8.1–2. Cf. Dell (1967) 357.
330 Polyb. 2.12.6. The seizure of booty in raids was common to pirates and to warfare proper, and so modern writers have found it difficult to make a distinction. Avidov would like to see the Cilicians as innocent of the charge of piracy. See Avidov (1997). Against: Rauh (2003) 178–200; Gabrielsen (2005) 400. What is missing in this debate is the definition of piracy that references their political organisation (or lack thereof).
331 Appian, *Illyr.* 3.7.8.
332 Florus 1.41.1; Oros. 5.13.1.

333 Antonius' command: Livy *Per.* 68; Cic. *de orat.* 1.82; *Brut.* 188; Obseq. 44; Trogus *Prolog.* 39; Plut. *Pomp.* 24.6. See Broughton (1946) 35–37.
334 Inscription: Hassall et al. (1976). See Jones (1926); Sherwin-White (1976b) 3–7; Shaw (1990) 220. For the problems of correlating the law from Delphi with that from Cnidos: Avidov and Timoney (1995).
335 Seeman (2013) 230 raises this question.
336 Jos. *B.J.* 1.88; *Ant.* 13.374. See Dąbrowa (2010) 81. Hyrcanus I had used mercenaries, but their origin is not known: Jos. *BJ* 1.61; *Ant.* 13.249.
337 See Ziebarth (1929) 21. Cilician pirates as mercenaries in the service of the army of Mithridates VI of Pontus: Maróti (1970) 1. 485, 488–489; De Souza (1999) 126, 159.
338 Oros. 6.3.2.
339 App. *Mithr.* 21; Strabo 14.5.2.669; Rappaport (1968) 341.
340 Dio 39.18.
341 De Souza (1999) 201.
342 Strabo 16.2.28–40. See Safrai et al. (1987) 2.677.
343 For piracy as the cause of Pompey's *iniuria* see Laqueur (1920) 149; H. Willrich in Ziebarth (1929) 37, n. 1, 114; Dobiáš (1931) 247, n.4; Rappaport (1968) 333.
344 Just. Prol. 39, 39.5.5f.; Dobiáš (1931) 247–248, n. 5.
345 Just. 40.2.4.
346 Jos. *Ant.* 14.76.
347 Dio 39.56.1.
348 Avidov (1997) 52.
349 Pucci (1982) 121.
350 Cic. *de off.* 3.108.
351 Aristobulus accused of instigating piracy: Jos. *Ant.* 14.43. Cf. Diod. 40.2 where the same charges are levelled against Hyrcanus II.
352 Seeman (2013) 227–228.

# Conclusion

One of the major outcomes of this study is re-dating the embassy to 162 BCE. The conventional order of events – that Timarchus rebelled from the Seleucids and sent a successful embassy to Rome, and that Judas, inspired by his example, also sent an embassy to Rome – needs to be reversed.

From the Book of Daniel and in the 'Eulogy to the Romans' in 1 Macc. 8.1–16, we learn that the Jews at this time regarded the Romans as the only power capable of halting the Seleucid army. The 'Eulogy to the Romans' reflects the mood after the 'Day of Eleusis', when the envoy from the Roman Senate presented a written ultimatum to Antiochus IV to withdraw his troops from Egypt. On the point of victory, the king obeyed. What a powerful message this sent around the Hellenistic world. The Romans were now the supreme power in the eastern Mediterranean.

Only *amicitia* could produce an ultimatum, because two Roman friends could not be at war with each other. The ultimatum carried consequences so dire that a king would obey. The threat of the senate renouncing friendship was enough: states and kings feared this step. Without that friendship they were left in a void, where the senate could declare war on them at any time.

The ties of *amicitia* are recognised as the most frequently used diplomatic instrument by the Romans. This study has argued for the historicity of *amicitia* relations between the Hellenistic kings of Alexander the Great, Alexander I of Epirus and the Ptolemies. The Romans learned the practice of concluding this non-legal form of relations from these Hellenistic powers.

The achievement of *amicitia* for the Jews in 162 BCE is contained in the expression 'friendship and alliance'. By 168 BCE there was little practical distinction between Roman friends and Roman allies. We read that the *amicitia* formed by Judas' envoys was renewed by later embassies. This renewal was not obligatory when a new ruler came to power. It was requested when circumstances had changed. It might be that the community wanted to make clear its loyalty when it faithfulness to Rome came under suspicion, or it might be, as in the case of the Jews, that conquest by the Seleucids had nullified their ties with Rome and the *amicitia* had to be re-formed. Rome itself could demand a renewal of *amicitia* in the preliminaries to a war to shore up the loyalties of her allies.

The Jewish concept of friendship between allies was in stark contrast to the norms of the Romans. The Jews considered that they were co-equals with their friends. In the ancient Near East, friendship was made among equals. In legal terms, the concepts also differed: for Rome, friendship was without legal form, made as it was by naming or declaring the king or community a friend of the Roman people. For the Jews, however, friendship came in the form of a treaty. Here, too, there were vast possibilities for misunderstanding.

By 162 BCE, after the conquest of Macedon, Rome had no equal. Like the Romans, the Jews believed that friends should have the same friends and enemies and not engage in treachery against their friend. Friendship was eternal unless broken by an act of disloyalty.

The doubts concerning whether the Jews entered into a treaty are heightened by the lack of similarities between the texts of Roman treaties epigraphically extant from the Greek-speaking East and the text given in 1 Macc. 8.23–32. The other pillar of the treaty hypothesis, that all divergences from this comparison of phraseology may be attributed to the multiple translation process, is shown also to be unsound. Further doubt as to whether this was a document originating from Rome or originally written in Latin, comes from an examination of the style and composition of the text. The conspicuous lack of any aid from Rome resulting from the sending of an embassy to Rome is an argument against a treaty having been concluded. This argument, while not new, remains valid. Our knowledge of the forms of Roman diplomatic relations, and how they were used, casts further doubt on the likelihood that the Jews entered into a treaty.

Before a treaty could be concluded, either *amicitia* or a declaration of *libertas* could be made by the senate. The step before a treaty was always separated by an interval of years, sometimes a short interval of five years or a longer one of up to a hundred years. Consequently, it was not Roman practice for the senate to grant, for example, *libertas* and a treaty during the same visit of an embassy.

After Judas, the later Jewish leadership sent envoys to Rome, but only after they had achieved some military success over the Seleucids such that they could answer the senate on the question of whether they were independent. After each military defeat, the diplomatic relations with Rome were nullified and had to be re-formed (not renewed).

The split with Rome came about due to Jannaeus' dealings with Cilician pirates. To the Romans, 'Cilicia' was synonymous with piracy and any Cilician soldiers captured by the Romans were executed as pirates. The Jewish leadership was not prepared to go to the senate and answer accusations that they had acted in an unfriendly manner towards the Romans. Going to the senate risked a formal renunciation of the friendship; instead, that friendship was left in limbo and as more time passed the Romans began to consider Judaea not only unreliable but hostile to Roman interests in the area.

# Bibliography


Abel, F.-M. (1949) *Les Livres des Maccabées*, Paris.

Abel, F.-M. (1952) *Histoire de Palestine*, vol. 1, Paris.

Abel, F.-M. and Starcky, J. (1961) *Les Livres des Maccabées*[3] (La Sainte Bible, 10a), Paris.

Accame, S. (1946) *Il Dominio Romano in Grecia dalla Guerra Acaica ad Augusto* (Studi Pubblicati dal R. Istituto Italiano per la storia antica, 4), Rome.

Achard, D. (1991) *La Communication à Rome*, Paris.

Adams, G.W. (2008) The Unbalanced Relationship between Ptolemy II and Pyrrhus of Epirus, in P.R. McKechnie et al. (eds) *Ptolemy II Philadelphus and His World*, Leiden, 91–102.

Ager, S.L. (1991) Rhodes: The Rise and Fall of a Neutral Diplomat, *Historia* 40.1, 10–41.

Albanese, B. (2000) 'Foedus' e 'ius iurandum'; 'pax per sponsionem', *AUPA* 46, 49–75.

Albert, S. (1980) Bellum iustum: *Die Theorie des erechten Krieges und ihre praktische Bedeutung für die auswärtigen Auseinandersetzungen Roms in republikanischer Zeit*, Kallmünz.

Albrecht, J. (1973) *Linguistik und Übersetzung* (Romanistische Arbeitschefte, 4), Tübingen.

Alessandrì, S. (1994) Le ambasceria ad Alessandro del 323 a. C.: il problema storiografico, in id. (ed.) *'Ιστορίη. Studi offerti dagli allievi a G. Nenci in onore del suo 70 compleanno*, Lecce, 21–36.

Alexander, M.C. (1985) Praemia in the Quaestiones of the Late Republic, *CP* 80.1, 20–32.

Alföldi, A. (1957) *Die Trojanische Urahnen der Römer*, Basel.

Allen, R.E. (1983) *The Attalid Kingdom: A Constitutional History*, Oxford.

Almar, K.P. (1990) *Inscriptiones Latinae: eine illustrierte Einführung in die lateinische Epigraphik* (Odense University Classical Studies, 14), Odense.

Alter, R. (1985) *The Art of Biblical Poetry*, New York.

Altheim, F. and Stiehl, R. (1966) Jesus der Galiläer, in *Die Araber in der Alten Welt*, vol. 3, Berlin, 74–97.

Amitay, O. (2013) The Correspondence in *I Maccabees* and the Possible Origins of the Judeo-Spartan Connection, *SCI* 32, 79–105.

Anderson, J.C. (1984) *The Historical Topography of the Imperial Fora* (Collection Latomus, 182), Brussels.

André, L.E.T. (1903) *Les Apocryphes de l'Ancien Testament*, Florence.

Andreussi, M. (1999) s.v. *Pomerium* in M. Steinby (ed.) *Lexicon Topographicum Urbis Romae*, vol. 4, Rome, 96–105.

Annandale-Potgieter, J. (1991) The High Priests in I Maccabees and the Writings of Josephus, *IOSCS Congress*, vol. 7, 393–429.

Arenhoevel, D. (1967) *Die Theokratie nach dem 1. und 2. Makkabäerbuch*, Mainz.

Arnaud, P. (2005) *Les routes de la navigation antique: itinéraires en Méditerranée*, Paris.

Arton, E.S. (1908) Sull'alleanza fra Giuda Maccabeo e Roma, *Rivista Israelicia* 5, 192–204.

Astin, A.E. (1959) Diodorus and the Date of the Embassy to the East of Scipio Aemilianus, *CP* 54.4, 221–227.

Atkinson, K. (2011) The Historical Chronology of the Hasmonean Period in the *War* and *Antiquities of Josephus*, in J. Pastor et al. (eds) *Flavius Josephus: Separating Fact from Fiction*, Leiden, 7–28.

Attridge, H. (1984) Historiography, in M. Stone (ed.) *Jewish Writings in the Second Temple Period: Apocrypha, Pseudepigrapha, Qumran Sectarian Writings, Philo, Josephus*, Philadelphia, 157–184.

Auer, P. and Di Luzio, A. (eds) (1984) *Interpretive Sociolinguistics* (Ergebnisse und Methoden moderner, 20), Tübingen.

Auliard, C. (2009) Cadeaux et marchandages diplomatiques à Rome jusqu'au debut de la conquête méditerranéenne, *Veleia* 26, 63–73.

Avidov, A. (1997) Were the Cilicians a Nation of Pirates?, *Mediterranean Historical Review* 10, 5–55.

Avidov, A. and Timoney, O. (1995) The *lex de provinciis praetoriis* from Delphi and Cnidos: A Revised Correlation, *Epigraphica Anatolica* 24, 7–14.

Avram, A. (1999) *Der Vertrag zwischen Rom und Kallatis: ein Beitrag zum römischen Völkerrecht*, Amsterdam.

Aymard, A. (1952) Tutelle et usurpation dans les monarchies hellénistiques: à propos d'une épisode de la sixième guerre de Syrie, *Aegyptus* 32, 85–96.

Aymard, A. (1953–1954) Autour de l'avènement d'Antiochos IV, *Historia* 2, 49–73.

Babota, V. (2014) *The Institution of the Hasmonean High Priesthood*, Leiden–Boston.

Back, H. (2005) *Karriere und Hierarchie: die römische Aristokratie und die Anfänge des* cursus honorum *in der mittleren Republik*, Berlin, 409–411.

Badian, E. (1952) The Treaty between Rome and the Achaean League, *JRS* 42, 76–80.

Badian, E. (1956) Q. Mucius Scaevola and the Province of Asia, *Athenaeum* 34, 104–123.

Badian, E. (1958) *Foreign Clientelae (264–70 B.C.)*, Oxford.

Badian, E. (1959a) Rome and Antiochus the Great: A Study in Cold War, *CPh* 54, 81–89 [= (1964) 112–139].

Badian, E. (1959b) Sulla's Cilician Command, *Athenaeum* 37, 279–304.

Badian, E. (1961) Review, Broughton, *Magistrates of the Roman Republic*, vol. 3, *Gnomon* 33.5, 492–498.

Badian, E. (1964) *Studies in Greek and Roman History*, Oxford.

Badian, E. (1965) The Date of Clitarchus, *PACA* 8, 5–11 [= (2014) *Collected Papers on Alexander the Great*, London–New York, 113–119.

Badian, E. (1969) Review of Lehmann, *Untersuchungen zur historischen Glaubwürdigkeit des Polybios*, *HZ* 208, 637–643.

Badian, E. (1970) *Titus Quinctius Flamininus: Philhellenism and Realpolitik*, University of Cincinnati, Cincinnati.

Badian, E. (1971) Two More Roman Non-Entities, *Phoenix*, 134–144.

Badian, E. (1972) Tiberius Gracchus and the Beginning of the Roman Revolution, *ANRW* 1.1, 668–731.

Badian, E. (1984) Hegemony and Independence: Prolegomena to a Study of the Relations of Rome and the Hellenistic States in the Second Century B.C., *Proceedings of the VIIth Congress of the International Federation of the Societies of Classical Studies*, I, ed. J. Harmatta, Actes du VIIe Congrès de la Fedération Internationale des Associations d'Études Classiques, vol. 1, Budapest, 397–414.

Baer, I. (1949) *The Arab Sefer Yosippon*, Jerusalem [Hebrew].
Baer, Y. (1971) Jerusalem in the Time of the Great Revolt based on the Source Criticism of Josephus and Talmudic–Midrashic Legends on the Temple's Destruction, *Zion* 36, 127–190 [Hebrew].
Baldus, C. (1998) *Regelhafte Vertragsauslegung nach Parteirollen im klassischen römischen Recht und in der modernen Völkerrechtswissenschaft*, Diss., Frankfurt.
Baldus, C. (2002) *Vestigia Pacis:* Der römische Friedensvertrag as Struktur und Ereignis, *Historia* 51.3, 298–348.
Baldwin, B. (1979) The *acta diurna, Chiron* 9, 189–203.
Baldwin, B. (1983) *Suetonius*, Amsterdam.
Balsdon, J.P.V.D. (1979) *Romans and Aliens*, London.
Baltrusch, E. (2001) Königin Salome Alexandra (76–67 v.Chr.) und die Verfassung des hasmonäischen Staates, *Historia* 50, 163–179.
Baltrusch, E. (2002) *Die Juden und das Römische Reich: Geschichte einer konfliktreichen Beziehung*, Darmstadt.
Bandelin, E. (1853) *De rebus inter Aegyptios et Romanos intercedentibus*, Diss., Halle.
Bar-Efrat, S. (1989) *Narrative Art in the Bible*, Sheffield.
Bar-Kochva, B. (1973) On the Sources and Chronology of Antiochus I's Battle against the Galatians, *PCPS* 199, 1–8.
Bar-Kochva, B. (1989) *Judas Maccabaeus: The Jewish Struggles against the Seleucids*, Cambridge.
Bar-Kochva, B. (1993) On Josephus and the Books of the Maccabees, Philology and Historiography, *Tarbiz* 62, 115–132 [Hebrew].
Bar-Kochva B. (1996) *Pseudo-Hecataeus, "On the Jews" Legitimizing the Jewish Diaspora*, Berkeley–Los Angeles–London.
Barag, D. (2000–2002) The Mint of Antiochus IV in Jerusalem: Numismatic Evidence on the Prelude to the Maccabaean Revolt, *INJ* 14, 59–77 (Plates 11–13).
Barclay, J. (1996) *Jews in the Mediterranean Diaspora from Alexander to Trajan (323 BCE – 117 CE)*, Edinburgh.
Bardon, H. (1968) *Les empereurs et les lettres latines d'Auguste à Hadrien*, Paris.
Baron, C.A. (2013) *Timaeus of Tauromenium and Hellenistic Historiography*, Cambridge.
Baronowski, D.W. (1982) *Treaties of Military Alliance between Rome and Hellenistic States in the Last Three Centuries B.C.*, Diss., University of Toronto
Baronowski, D.W. (1988) Roman Treaties with Communities of Citizens, *CQ* 38, 172–178.
Baronowski, D.W. (1990) Sub Umbra Foederis Aequi, *Phoenix* 44, 345–369.
Barré, M.L. (1983) *The God-List in the Treaty between Hannibal and Philip V of Macedon: A Study in Light of the Ancient Near East Treaty Tradition*, Baltimore.
Bartlett J.R. (1998) *1 Maccabees* (Guides to the Apocrypha and Pseudepigrapha, 5), Sheffield.
Bauman, R.A. (1967) *The Crimen Maiestatis in the Roman Republic and Augustan Principate*, Johannesburg.
Bauman, R.A. (1976) Maiestatem populi Romani comiter conservando, *Acta Juridica* 1, 19–36.
Baumgarten, A.I. (1981) *The Phoenician History of Philo of Byblos: A Commentary*, Leiden.
Bauslaugh, R.A. (1991) *The Concept of Neutrality in Classical Greece*, Berkeley.
Bean, G.E. (1948) Notes and Inscriptions from Lycia, *JHS* 68, 46–56.
Bean, G.E. (1956) Review of L. and J. Robert, *La Carie* II, *AJA* 60, 196–197.
Beauchamp, P. (1976) *L'un et L'autre Testament: Essai de Lecture*, Paris.

Bederman, D.J. (2001) *International Law in Antiquity*, Cambridge.
Beekman J., Callow J. and Kopesec M. (1981) *The Semantic Structure of Written Communication*, Dallas.
Beentjes, P.C. (2013) Friendship according to a Biblical document from the Hellenistic period, *International Journal of Philosophy and Theology* 74.1, 54–64.
Belleza, F.S. (1987) 'Mnemonic Devices and Memory Schemas', in M.A. MacDaniel and M. Pressley (eds) *Imagery and Related Mnemonic Processes: Theories, Individual Differences and Applications*, New York.
Beloch, K.J. (1880) *Der italische Bund unter Roms Hegemonie: staatsrechtliche und statistische Forschungen* (Studia Historica, 1), Leipzig.
Beloch, K.J. (1925) *Griechische Geschischte*², 4, 1, Berlin.
Ben Zeev, M. (1994) Greek and Roman Documents from Republican Times in the *Antiquities*: What was Josephus' source?, *SCI* 13, 46–59.
Bengston, H. (1950) *Griechische Geschichte: von den Anfängen bis in die römische Kaiserzeit*, Munich.
Bengston, H. (1954–1955) Randbemerkungen zu den koischen Asylieurkunden, *Historia* 3, 456–463.
Bennett, C. (2011) *Alexandria and the Moon: An Investigation into the Lunar Macedonian Calendar of Ptolemaic Egypt* (Studia Hellenistica, 52), Leuven.
Bennett, S.F. (1984) *Objective Pronominal Suffixes in Aramaic*, Diss., Yale.
Beresford, J. (2013) *The Ancient Sailing Season*, Leiden.
Bernhardt, R. (1971) *Imperium und Eleutheria*, Diss., Hamburg.
Bernhardt, R. (1998) Rom und die Städte des hellenistischen Ostens (3.–1. Jahrhundert v. Chr.), *HZ*: Sonderhefte; vol. 18, München.
Berthelot, K. (2003) Poseidonius d'Apamée et les Juifs, *JSJ* 34.2, 160–198.
Berthold, R.M. (1984) *Rhodes in the Hellenistic Age*, Ithaca.
Berve, H. (1926) *Alexanderreich auf prosopographischer Grundlage*, Munich.
Bevan, E.R. (1902) *The House of Seleucus*, vol. 2, repr. 1966, London.
Bevan, E.R. (1930) Syria and the Jews, in S.A. Cook et al. (eds) *Cambridge Ancient History*, vol. 8, *Rome and the Mediterranean: 218–133 B.C.*, Cambridge, 495–533.
Bévenot, H. (1931) *Die beiden Makkabäerbücher übersetzt und erklärt* (Die Heilige Schrift des Alten Testaments, 4.4), Bonn.
Beyer, K. (1986) *The Aramaic Language: Its Distribution and Subdivisions*, trans. J.F. Healey, Göttingen.
Beyer-Rotthoff, B. (1993) *Untersuchungen zur Aussenpolitik Ptolemaios' III*, Bonn.
Bickermann, E. (1928) Makkabäerbücher, *RE*, XIV,1, cols 779–797, Stuttgart.
Bickerman, E. (1930) Review, M.S. Ginsburg, *Rome et la Judée*, *Gnomon* 6.7, 357–360.
Bickerman, E. (1932) Bellum Antiochum, *Hermes* 67, 47–76 [= (1985) 37–68].
Bickerman, E. (1936) Review of A. Heuss, *Die Völkerrechtlichen Grundlagen der römischen Aussenpolitik in republikanischer Zeit*, *Ant. Cl.* 5, 471–474.
Bickerman, E. (1937) Note sur Polybe, *REG* 50, 217–239 [= (1985) 143–165].
Bickerman, E. (1938) *Institutions des Séleucides: Service des Antiquités*, Paris.
Bickerman, E. (1939–1944) Héliodore au temple de Jérusalem, *Annuaire de l'Institut de Philologie et d'Histoire Orientales et Slaves* 7, 5–40.
Bickerman, E.J. (1952a) *From Ezra to the last of the Maccabees: Foundations of Postbiblical Judaism*, New York.
Bickerman, E. (1952b) Hannibal's Covenant, *AJP* 73, 1–23 [= (1985) 373–397].
Bickerman, E. (1958) Autonomia: sur un passage de Thucydide (I.144.2), *RIDA* 5, 313–344 [= (1985) 421–452].

Bickerman, E.J. (1967) Daniel or the Fulfilled Prophecy, in *Four Strange Books of the Bible*, New York.
Bickerman, E.J. (1968) *Chronology of the Ancient World*, London.
Bickerman, E. (1979) *The God of the Maccabees: Studies in the Meaning and Origin of the Maccabaean Revolt*, Leiden.
Bickerman, E.J. (1980) *Chronology of the Ancient World*, rev. edn. London.
Bickerman, E. (1985) *Religions and Politics in the Hellenistic and Roman Periods*, eds E. Gabba and M. Smith, Como.
Bickerman, E. (1988) *The Jews in the Greek Age*, Cambridge, MA–London.
Billows, R. (2007) International Relations, in P. Sabin et al. (eds) *The Cambridge History of Greek and Roman Warfare*, vol. 1, Cambridge, 303–324.
Bingen, J. (2007) Ptolemy I and the Quest for Legitimacy, in id. (ed.) *Hellenistic Egypt: Monarchy, Society, Economy, Culture*, Berkeley, 15–30.
Bird, H.W. (1983) *The Breviarum* ab urbe condita *of Eutropius* (Translated Texts for Historians, 14), Liverpool.
Birley, A.R. (1984) Review of Baldwin, *Suetonius*, Wallace-Hadrill, *Suetonius: The Scholar and His Caesars*, De Coninck, *Suetonius en de archivalia*, *JRS* 74, 245–251.
Bispham, E. and Northwood, S. (2013) s.v. Acilius No. 7, in T. Cornell et al. (eds) *Fragments of the Roman Historians*, vol. 1, Oxford, 224–226.
Bittner, A. (1998) *Gesellschaft und Wirtschaft in Heraklea Pontike: eine Polis zwischen Tyrannis und Selbstverwaltung*, Bonn.
Bleicken, J. (1959) Review: H.H. Schmitt, *Rom und Rhodes*, *Gnomon* 31.5, 439–442.
Bloomer, W.M. (1992) *Valerius Maximus and the Rhetoric of the New Nobility*, London.
Bloy, D. (2012) Roman Patrons of Greek Communities before the Title πάτρων, *Historia* 61.2, 168–201.
Boas, M. (1931) Zur indirekten Caesarüberlieferung, *Rhein. Mus.* 80: 357–367.
Bohn, O. (1878) *Qua condicione juris reges socii populi Romani fuerint*, Berlin.
Bolmarcich, S. (2010) Communal Values in Ancient Diplomacy, in R. Rosen et al. (eds) *Valuing Others in Classical Antiquity*, Leiden, 113–136.
Bonnefond-Coudry, M. (1987) Transferts de fonctions et mutation idéologique: le Capitole et le forum d'Auguste, in *L'urbs: Espace urbain et histoire (I^e^ siècle av. J.-C. –IV^e^ siècles ap. J.-C.)* (Collection de l'École français de Rome, 98), Rome, 251–278.
Bonnefond-Coudry, M. (1989) *Le Sénat de la république romaine de la guerre d'Hannibal à Auguste: pratiques déliberatives et prise de decision* (Bibliotheque des Écoles françaises d'Athènes et de Rome, 273), Rome.
Bonnefond-Coudry, M. (1993) Le princeps senatus: vie et mort d'une institution républicaine, *MEFRA* 105.1, 103–134.
Bonner, R.J. (1930) The Conflict of Languages in the Roman World, *CJ* 25, 579–592.
Bonvillain, N. (1993) *Language, Culture and Communication: The Meaning of Messages*, Englewood Cliffs.
Bordi, G. (2000) L'Affresco staccato dalla chiesa di S. Adriano al Foro Romano, *Studi Romani* 35.1–2, 5–25.
Bosworth, A.B. (1972) Arrian's Literary Development, *CQ* 22.1, 163–185.
Bosworth, A.B. (1988) *From Arrian to Alexander: Studies in Historical Interpretation*, Oxford.
Bosworth, A.B. (2003) Plus ça change . . . : Ancient Historians and Their Sources, *Classical Antiquity* 22.3, 167–198.
Bouché-Leclercq, A. (1913) *Histoire des Seleucids*, vol. 1, Paris.
Bouiron, M. (2014) *L'Épitome des Ethniques de Stéphane de Byzance comme source historique: l'example de l'Europe Occidentale*, Diss., L'Université Nice Sophia Antipolis.

Bousset, W. and Gressman, H. (1926) *Die Religion des Judentums im spaethellenistischen Zeitalter*[3] (Handbuch zum neuen Testament, 02), Tübingen.

Bowman, D.A. (1989) The *formula sociorum* in the Second and First Centuries, *CJ* 75, 330–336.

Boyancé, P. (1956) La Connaissance du grec à Rome, *REL* 34, 111–131.

Boyancé, P. (1962) Fides et le serment, in M. Renard (ed.) *Hommages à Albert Grenier* (Collection Latomus, 58), Bruxelles, 329–341.

Boyancé, P. (1964a) La main de Fides, in M. Renard and R. Schilling (eds) *Hommaes à Jean Bayet* (Collection Latomus, 70), Bruxelles, 101–113.

Boyancé, P. (1964b) Les romains, peuple de la fides, *Bulletin de l'Association Guillaume Budé.* Supplement lettres d'humanité, 23, 419–435.

Boyancé, P. (1972) Fides romana et la vie internationale, in id. (ed.) *Études sur la religion romaine*, Rome, 106–119.

Braccesi, L. (1974) Roma e Alessandro il Molosso nella tradizione Liviana, *RIL* 108, 196–203.

Braccesi, L. (1975) *Alessandro e I Romani*, Bologna.

Bradshaw, J. (1981) Oral Transmission and Human Memory, *Expository Times* 92 (July), 303–307.

Brashear, W. (1981) A Greek–Latin Vocabulary, in R.S. Bagnall et al. (eds) *Proceedings of the XVI International Congress of Papyrology* (American Studies in Papyrology, 43), Chicago, 31–41.

Brassloff, S. (1902) *Zur Kenntniss des Völkerechtes in den Romanisirten Ostprovinzen des römischen Kaiserreiches*, Weimar.

Brassloff, S. (1928) *Der römische Staat und seine internationalen Beziehungen*, Wien.

Braund D. (1982) Cicero and the Greek East: Antiochus I and Ariobarzanes III, *LCM* 7, 37–39.

Braund, D. (1989) Function and Dysfunction: Personal Patronage in Roman Imperialism, in A. Wallace-Hadrill (ed.) *Patronage in Ancient Society* (Leicester–Nottingham Studies in Ancient Society, 1), London, 137–152.

Bremmer, J.N. (2010) Spartans and Jews: Abrahamic Cousins?, in M. Goodman et al. (eds) *Abraham, the Nations, and the Hagarites: Jewish, Christian and Islamic Perspectives on Kinship with Abraham*, Leiden, 59–68.

Brennan, T.C. (2000) *The Praetorship in the Roman Republic*, 2 vols, Oxford.

Briant, P. (1991) De Sardes à Suse, *Achaemenid History* 9, 67–82.

Briquel, D. (1988) Que savons-nous des *Tyrrhenica* de l'empereur?, *RFIC* 116, 448–470.

Briscoe, J. (1964) Q. Marcius Philippus and Nova Sapientia, *JRS* 54, 66–77.

Briscoe, J. (1968) Fulvii and Postumii, *Latomus* 27, 149–156.

Briscoe, J. (1969) Eastern Policy and Senatorial Politics 168–146 BC, *Historia* 18, 49–70.

Briscoe, J. (1973) *A Commentary on Livy: Books XXXI–XXXIII*, Oxford.

Briscoe, J. (1981) *A Commentary on Livy: Books XXXIV–XXXVII*, Oxford.

Briscoe, J., ed. (1986a) *Livius: Ab Urbe Condita, Libri XLI–XLV*, Stuttgart.

Briscoe, J. (1986b) Review of Gruen, *The Hellenistic World and the Coming of Rome*, *CR* 36.1, 91–96.

Briscoe, J. (2012) *A Commentary on Livy: Books 41–45*, Oxford–New York.

Brooke, G.J. (1991) The Kittim in the Qumran Pesherim, in L. Alexander (ed.) *Images of Empire* (JSOT Suppl. Series, 122), Sheffield, 135–159.

Broshi, M. and Eshel, E. (1997) The Greek King is Antiochus IV (4QHistorical Text = 4Q 248), *JJS* 48, 120–129.

Broughton, T.R.S. (1946) Notes on Roman Magistrates. I. The Command of M. Antonius in Cilicia. II. Lucullus' Commission and Pompey's Acta, *TAPA* 77, 35–43.

Broughton, T.R.S. (1951) *The Magistrates of the Roman Republic*, 3 vols (Philological Monographs, 15), American Philological Association, New York.

Broughton, T.R.S. (1987) Mistreatment of Foreign Legates and the Fetial Priests: Three Roman Cases, *Phoenix* 41, 50–62.

Brown, T.S. (1950) Clitarchus, *AJP* 7.2, 134–155.

Bruce, F.F. (1978) The Romans through Jewish Eyes, *Paganisme Judaïsme, Christianisme: influences at affrontements dans le monde antique. Mélanges offerts à Marcel Simon*, Paris, 3–12.

Brunt, P.A. (1983) *Arrian. Anabasis*, 2 vols, Cambridge, MA–London.

Brutti, M. (2006) *The Development of the High Priesthood during the pre-Hasmonean Period: History, Ideology, Theology*, Leiden.

Bruyne de, D. (1932) *Les anciennes traductions latines des Machabées* (Anecdota Maredsolana, 4), Bruges.

Büchler, A. (1899) *Tobiaden und Oniaden*, Vienna.

Burgess, R.W. (1999) *Studies in Eusebian and Post-Eusebian Chronography*, Stuttgart.

Burstein, S.M. (1980) The Aftermath of the Peace of Apamea: Rome and the Pontic War, *AJAH* 5, 1–12.

Burstein, S.M. (1985) *The Hellenistic Age from the Battle of Ipsos to the Death of Kleopatra VII*, Cambridge.

Burton, P.J. (2003) *Clientela* or *Amicitia*? Modelling Roman International Behaviour in the Middle Republic (264–146), *Klio* 85, 333–369.

Burton, P. (2011) *Friendship and Empire: Roman Diplomacy and Imperialism in the Middle Republic (353–146 BC)*, Cambridge–New York.

Burton, P. (2013) The International *amicitia* between Athens and Rome, *Antichthon* 47, 207–218.

Burton, P. (2015) Nabis, Flamininus, and the *amicitia* between Rome and Sparta, in M. Jehne and F. Pina Polo (eds) *Foreign* clientelae *in the Roman Empire*, Stuttgart.

Buturas, A. (1910) *Ein Kapitel der historischen Grammatik der griechischen Sprache. Über die gegenseitligen Beziehungen der griechischen und der fremden Sprachen, besonders über die fremden Einflüsse auf das Griechishe seit der nachklassischen Periode bis zur Gegenwart*, Leipzig.

Cabanes, P. (1976) *L'Epire de la mort de Pyrrhos à la conquête romaine (272–167 av. J.-C.)*, Paris.

Cabanes, P. (2008) Greek Colonization in the Adriatic, in G.R. Tsetskhladze (ed.) *Greek Colonization: An Account of the Greek Colonies and Other Settlements Overseas*, Leiden, 155–186.

Calderone, S. (1964) *ΠΙΣΤΙΣ – FIDES. Richerche di storia e diritto internationale nell'antichita*, Biblioteca di Helikon, Messina.

Calore, A. (2003) *Forme giuridiche del 'bellum iustum'*, Milan.

Cameron, A. (1931) Latin words in the Greek Inscriptions of Asia Minor, *AJP* 52, 232–262.

Campbell, B. (2001) Diplomacy in the Roman World (c.500 BC–AD 235), *Diplomacy and Statecraft* 12.1, 1–22.

Campbell, B. (2002) War and Diplomacy: Rome and Parthia 31 BC – AD 235, in J. Rich and G. Shipley (eds) *War and Society in the Roman World*, London–New York, 220–229.

Cappelli, A. (1928) *Lexicon Abbreviaturarum*, vol. 2, Leipzig.

Cardauns, B. (1967) Juden und Spartaner: zur hellenistich–jüdischen Literatur, *Hermes* 95, 317–324.

Cardinali, G. (1910) Ancora per i confini nella pace di Antioco, *Klio* 10, 249–251.

Carratelli, Pugliese G. (1964) *Nuovi documenti della romanizazione di Cos*, Naples.

Carruthers, M.J. (1990) *The Book of Memory: A Study in Medieval Culture*, Cambridge.
Cartledge, P. and Spawforth, A. (1989) *Hellenistic and Roman Sparta, a Tale of Two Cities*, London.
Cary, M. and Scullard, H.H. (1975) *A History of Rome down to the reign of Constantine*[3], London.
Casey, M. (1998) *Aramaic Sources of Mark's Gospel*, Cambridge.
Cassòla, F. (1962) *I gruppi politici romani nel III sec. a.C.*, Facolta di lettere e filosofia, Instituto di storia antica, n.2, Trieste.
Cassòla, F. (1968) La repubblica romana, in *Nuove questioni di storia antica*, Milan.
Casson, L. (1950) The Isis and Her Voyage, *TAPA* 81, 43–56.
Casson, L. (1971) *Ships and Seamanship in the Ancient World*, Princeton.
Casson, L. (1974) *Travel in the Ancient World*, London.
Catalano, P. (1965) *Linee del sisteme sovrannazionale romano*, vol. 1 (Memorie dell'Istituto Giuridico della Università di Torino, Serie II, memoria 119), Torino.
Cavaignac, E. (1951) À propos des monnaies de Tryphon: l'ambassade de Scipio, *Rev. Num.* ser. 5, 13, 131–138.
Charles, R.H. (1929) *A Critical and Exegetical Commentary on the Book of Daniel*, Oxford.
Christes, J. (2005) s.v. Lucilius, *BNP* vol. 7, Leiden–Boston, cols 848–850.
Ciaceri, E. (1918) *La relazioni fra Roma e l'Egitto*, Rome.
Cichorius, C. (1908) *Untersuchungen zu Lucilius*, Berlin.
Cichorius, C. (1922) *Römische Studien* (Studia historica, 80), Rome.
Cimma, M.R. (1976) *Reges socii et amici populi romani*, Milan.
Cividale, P. (2007) 'I Romani visti dall'Asia': Riflessioni sulla sezione romana della Storia di Eraclea di Memnone, in G. Urso (ed.) *Tra Oriente e Occidente: Indigeni, Greci e romani in Asia Minore*, Atti del convegno internazionale cividale del Friuli, 28–20 Sept. 2006, Pisa, 45–49.
Classen, C.J. (1965) Die Königszeit im Spiegel der Literatur der römischen Republik, *Historia*, 14, 385–403.
Clavadetscher-Thürlemann S. (1985) *Polemos dikaios und bellum iustum: Versuch einer Ideengeschichte*, Zürich–Juris.
Clinton, H.F. (1930) *Fasti Hellenici: The Civil and Literary Chronology of Greece from the 124th Olympiad to the Death of Augustus*, vol. 3, Oxford.
Coarelli, F. (1993) s.v. *Ceres, Liber, Liberaque, aedes*, in E. Steinby (ed.) *Lexicon Topographicum Urbis Romae*, vol. 1, Rome, 260–262.
Coarelli, F. (1999) s.v *senaculum*, in E. Steinby (ed.) *Lexicon Topographicum Urbis Romae*, vol. 4, Rome, 264–265.
Coates-Stephens, R. (2002) Epigraphy as Spolia: The Reuse of Inscriptions in Early Medieval Buildings, *PBSR* 70, 275–296.
Coates-Stephens, R. (2008) Notes from Rome, *PBSR* 76, 299–307.
Cody, J.M. (1973) New Evidence for the Republican *Aedes Vestae*, *AJA* 77, 43–50.
Cohen, G.M. (1994) The 'Antiochenes in Jerusalem' Again, in D.J.A. Clines and P.R. Davies (eds) *Pursuing the Text: Studies in Honor of Ben Zion Wacholder* (JSOT Suppl. Series 184), Sheffield, 243–259.
Cohen, S.J.D. (1979) *Josephus in Galilee and Rome, His Vita and Development as a Historian* (Columbia Studies in the Classical Tradition, 8), Leiden.
Colin, G. (1905) *Rome et la Grèce de 200 à 146 ans avant J.-C.*, Paris.
Collins, J.J. (1981) *Daniel, First Maccabees, Second Maccabees*, OTM 16, Wilmington, DE.
Collins, J.J. (1993) *Daniel: A Commentary on the Book of Daniel*, Minneapolis.
Collins, J.J. (1998) *Jewish Wisdom in the Hellenistic Age*, Edinburgh.

Collins, J.J. (1999) *The Hellenization of Jerusalem in the Pre-Maccabean Era* (International Rennert Guest Lecture Series, 6), Jerusalem.

Collins, J.J. (2001) Current Issues in the Study of Daniel, in J.J. Collins and P.W. Flint (eds) *The Book of Daniel: Composition and Reception*, Leiden–Boston–Köln, 1–15.

Collins, J.J. (2005) Cult and Culture: The Limits of Hellenization in Judea, in id. (ed.) *Jewish Cult and Hellenistic Culture: Essays on the Jewish Encounter with Hellenism and Roman Rule*, Leiden, 21–43.

Condurachi, E. (1970) Kotys, Rome et Abdère, *Latomus* 29, 581–594.

Conrad, C.F. (2004) *Augusto Augurio: Rerum Humanarum et Divinarum. Commentationes in Honorem Jerzy Linderski*, Stuttgart.

Coppola, A. (1993) *Demetrio di Faro* (Problemi e ricerche di storia antica, 15), Rome.

Coppola, A. (1994) Memorie romane e ambascerie troiane, *Hesperia*, 4, 177–186.

Corcoran, S. (2013) State Correspondence in the Roman Empire: Imperial Communication from Augustus to Justinian, in K. Radner (ed.) *State Correspondence in the Ancient World: From New Kingdom Egypt to the Roman Empire*, Oxford, 172–209.

Corley, J. (2002) *Ben Sira's Teaching on Friendship*, Providence RI.

Coşkun, A. (2008) Anhang: Rückkehr zum Vertragscharakter der *amicitia*? Zu einer alt-neuen Forschungskontroverse, in id. (ed.) *Freundschaft und Gefolgschaft in den auswärtigen Beziehungen der Römer (2. Jahrhundert v. Chr. – 1. Jahrhundert n. Chr.)*, Frankfurt am Main, 11–28.

Corbier, M. (1974) *L'Aerarium Saturni et l'aerarium militare*, Rome.

Coudry, M. (2004) Contrôle et traitement des ambassadeurs étrangers sous la république romaine, in C. Moatti (ed.) *La mobilité des personnes en Mediterranée de l'Antiquité à l'époque moderne: procédure de contrôle et documents d'identification*, Rome, 529–565.

Cowley, A. (1923) *Aramaic Papyri of the Fifth Century B.C.*, Oxford.

Craven, T. (1983) *Artistry and Faith in the Book of Judith*, SBLDS 70, Chico CA.

Crawford, M.H. (1973) Foedus and Sponsio, *PBSR* 41, 1–7.

Crawford, M.H. (1974) *Roman Republican Coinage*, 2 vols, Cambridge.

Crawford, M.H. (ed.) (1996) *Roman Statutes*, vol. 1, Institute of Classical Studies, School of Advanced Study, University of London.

Crook, J.A. (1956/7) Suetonius ab epistulis, *PCPhS* n.s. 4, 18–22.

Culham, P. (1984) Tablets and Temples: Documents in Republican Rome, *Provenance, Journal of the Society of Georgia Archivists* 11, 15–31.

Culham, P. (1989) Archives and Alternatives in Republican Rome, *CP* 84.2, 100–115.

Culham, P. (1996) Fraud, Fakery and Forgery: The Limits of Roman Information Technology, *Ancient World* 27, 172–183.

Dąbrowa, E. (2004) De l'assujettissement à l'independence: observations sur les relations entre les Séleucides et les Maccabées (de 152 à 114 av. J.-C.), *Electrum* 8, 67–84.

Dąbrowa, E. (2010) *The Hasmoneans and the Homogenity of Their State*, Krakow.

Dąbrowa, E. (forthcoming) The Seleucids, Rome and the Jews (134–76 BCE), 1–12.

Dahlheim, W. (1965) *Deditio und societas: Untersuchungen zur Entwicklung der römischen Aussenpolitik in der Blütezeit der Republik*, Diss., Munich.

Dahlheim, W. (1968) *Struktur und Entwicklung des römischen Völkerrechtes im 3 und 2. Jahrhundert v. Chr.* (Kommission für alte geschichte und epigraphik des Deutschen Archäologischen Instituts Vestigia. Beiträge zur alten Geschichte, Band 8), Munich.

Dahlheim, W. (1977) *Gewalt und Herrschaft: die provinziale Herrschaftssystem der römisches Republik*, Berlin.

Dalman, G. (1898) *Die Worte Jesu: mit Berücksichtigung des nachkanonischen jüdischen schriftums und der aramäischen Sprache*, book 1. Einleitung und wichtige Begriffe, Leipzig.

Dalman, G. (1902) *The Words of Jesus Considered in the Light of Post-Biblical Jewish Writings and the Aramaic Language*, vol. 1, *Introduction and Fundamental Ideas*, Edinburgh.

Dancy, J.C. (1954) *A Commentary on I Maccabees*, Oxford.

Daube, D. (1956) *Forms of Roman Legislation*, Oxford.

Daux, G. (1936) *Delphes au II*[e] *et au I*[e] *siècle depuis l'abaissement de l'Étolie jusqu'à la paix romaine, 191 – 31av. J.-C.*, Paris.

Davaze, V. (2013) *Memnon, historien d'Héraclée du Pont*, PhD Diss., Université du Maine.

David, M. (1946) The Treaties between Rome and Carthage and Their Significance for Our Knowledge of Roman International Law, in M. David et al. (eds) *Symbolae ad Jus et Historiam Antiquitatis pertinentes Juliano Christiano Van Oven dedicatae*, Leiden, 231–250.

Davies, P.R. (1991) Daniel in the Lion's Den, in L. Alexander (ed.) *Images of Empire* (JSOT Suppl. Series, 122), Sheffield, 160–178.

Davies, P.R. (2000) If the Lord's Annointed Had Lived, *Bibl. Interp.* 8, 151–160.

De Coninck, L. (1991) Les sources documentaires de Suétone, 'Les XII Césars': 1900–1990, *ANRW* 2.33.5, Berlin, 3675–3700.

De Libero, L. (1997) *Ut eodem quos populus Romanus amicos atque hostes habeant.* Die Freund–Feind–Klausel in den Beziehungen Roms zu griechischen und Italischen Staaten, *Historia* 46.3, 270–305.

De Martino, F. (1973) *Storia della costituzzione romana*[2], vol. 2, Naples.

De Ruggiero, E. (1961–1962) *Dizionario Epigrafico di Antichità romane*, vols 1 and 3, Rome.

De Sanctis G. (1907–1917) *Storia dei Romani*, vols 2 and 3, 1 (Il pensiero storico: 038, La nuova Italia), Turin–Florence.

De Souza, P. (1999) *Piracy in the Graeco-Roman World*, Cambridge.

De Souza, P. (2013) Who Are You Calling Pirates?, in M.C. Hoff and R.F. Townsend (eds) *Rough Cilicia: New Historical and Archaeological Approaches* (Proceedings of an International Conference, Lincoln, Nebraska, October 2007), Oxford–Oakville, 43–54.

De Visscher, F. (1945) Le Statut juridique des nouveaux citoyens romains et l'inscription de Rhosos, *Ant. Class.* 29–59.

De Visscher, F. (1947) *Le régime romain de la noxalitë: De la responsibilité individuelle*, Brussels.

Debevoise, N.C. (1938) *A Political History of Parthia*, Chicago–London.

Degrassi, A. (ed.) (1937) *Inscriptiones Italiae*, vol. 13, Fasc. 3, Rome.

Degrassi, A. (1962) Le Dediche di popoli e re Asiatici al popolo Romano e a Giove Capitolino, in *Scritti vari di antichità*, vol. 1, A cura del Comitato D'Onore, Rome, 415–444 [= (1951–1952) *Bulletino della Commissione Archeologica communale di Roma* 17, 19–47].

Deissmann, A.G. (1895) *Bibelstudien: Beiträge, zumeist aus den Papyri und Inschriften, zur Geschichte der Sprache, des Schriftums und der Religion des hellenistischen Judentums und des Urchristentums*, Marburg.

Delcor, M. (1967) Le Temple d'Onias en Egypte, *RB* 75, 188–203.

Delcor, M. (1989) The Apocrypha and Pseudepigrapha of the Hellenistic Period, in W.D. Davies and L. Finkelstein (eds) *The Cambridge History of Judaism, vol. 2. The Hellenistic Age*, Cambridge, The Book of the Maccabees, 456–470.

Delcor, M. (1991) L'Éloge des Romains d'après I Mac 8, *Henoch* 13, 19–28.

Delehay, H. (1961) *The Legends of the Saints: An Introduction to Hagiography*, trans. V.M. Crawford, Notre Dame.

Dell, H.J. (1967) The Origins and Nature of Illyrian Piracy, *Historia* 16, 344–358.

Derow, P.S. (1970) *Rome and the Greek World from the Earliest Contacts to the End of the First Illyrian War*, Diss., Princeton.
Derow, P.S. (1973) The Roman Calendar 190–168 B.C., *Phoenix* 27, 345–356.
Derow, P.S. (1991) Pharos and Rome, *ZPE* 88, 261–270.
Dietrich, J. (2014) Friendship with God: Old Testament and Ancient Near East Perspectives, *Scandinavian Journal of the Old Testament* 28.2, 157–171.
Diller, A. (1938) The Tradition of Stephanus Byzantius, *TAPA* 69, 333–348.
Dimitriev, S. (2006) Cappadocian Dynastic Arrangements on the Eve of the First Mithridatic War, *Historia* 55, 285–297.
Dimitriev, S. (2011a) Antiochus III: A Friend of the Roman People, *Klio* 93, 104–130.
Dimitriev, S. (2011b) *The Greek Slogan of Freedom and Early Roman Politics in Greece*, Malden.
Dobiáš, J. (1931) Les premiers rapports des Romains avec les Parthes et l'occupation de la Syrie, *Archiv Orientalni* 3, 215–256.
Domingo Gygax, M. (2013) Gift-Giving and Power Relationships in Greek Social Praxis and Public Discourse, in M. Satlow (ed.) *The Gift in Antiquity*, New York, 45–60.
Dommershausen W. (1985) *1 Makkabäer 2 Makkabäer: die Neue Echter Bibel Kommentar zum alten Testament mit der Einheitsübersetzung*, Echter, Würzburg.
Donati, A. (1965) I Romani nell'Egeo: i documenti dell'età repubblicana, *Epigraphica* 27, 3–59.
D'Onofino C. (1988) *Visitiamo Roma mille anni fa: la città dei Mirabilia*, Rome.
Doran, R. (1977) *Studies in the Style and Literary Character of 2 Maccabees*, Diss., Harvard.
Doran, R. (1979) 2 Maccabees and 'Tragic History', *HUCA* 50, 107–114.
Doran, R. (1981) *Temple Propaganda: The Purpose and Character of 2 Maccabees* (The Catholic Biblical Quarterly Monograph Series, 12), Washington.
Doran, R. (1987) Jewish Hellenistic Historians before Josephus, *ANRW* 2.20.2, 246–297.
Dorsey, D.A. (1999) *The Literary Structure of the Old Testament*, Grand Rapids, MI.
Drew-Bear, T. (1972) Three *Senatus Consulta* concerning the Province of Asia, *Historia* 21, 75–87.
Drexler, H. (1959) Bellum Iustum, *Rh.Mus.* n.s. 102, 97–140.
Droysen, J.G. (1877–1878) *Geschichte des Hellenismus*, Hamburg (French translation).
Drüner H. (1896) *Untersuchungen über Josephus*, Diss., Marburg.
Dubuisson, M. (1981) Problèmes du bilinguisme romain, *LEC* 49, 27–45.
Dubuisson, M. (1982) Grecs et Romains: le conflit linguistique, *L'Histoire* 50 (November), 21–29.
Dubuisson, M. (1982) Y a-t-il une politique linguistique romaine?, *Ktèma* 7, 187–210.
Dubuisson, M. (1983) Some Aspects of Graeco-Roman Relations: The Attitude of Roman Administration towards Language Use, Xenophobia and Disparaging Words in Latin and Greek, *Prudentia* 15, 35–47.
Dubuisson, M. (1984) La traduction en grec des concepts romains et la vision grecque de Rome: problèmes et perspective, in P. Achard (ed.) *Histoire et linguistique*, Paris, 213–224.
Dubuisson, M. (1985) *Le Latin de Polybe: les implications historiques d'un cas de bilinguisme*, Paris.
Duchesne, L. (1904) L'auteur des *Mirabilia*, *MEFRA* 24, 479–489.
Dueck, D. (1999) The Date and Method of Composition of Strabo's 'Geography', *Hermes* 27.4, 467–478.
Dueck, D. (2006) Memnon of Herakleia on Rome and the Romans, in T.B. Nielsen (ed.) *Rome and the Black Sea Region*, Aarhus, 43–62.

Dulkeit, G. and Schwarz, F. (1970) *Römische Rechtsgeschichte*[5], München.

Dumézil, G. (1956) Remarques sur le 'ius fetiale', *REL* 34, 93–111.

Dumézil, G. (1974) *La religion romaine archaique*[2], part 4, Paris.

Dunbabbib, J. (1985) The Maccabees as Exemplars in the Tenth and Eleventh Centuries, in K. Walsh and D. Wood (eds) *The Bible in the Medieval World*, Oxford, 31–41.

Eckstein, A.M. (1987) *Senate and General: Individual Decision-Making and Roman Foreign Relations 264–194 BC*, Berkeley.

Eckstein, A.M. (1988) Rome, the War with Perseus, and Third Party Mediation, *Historia* 37, 414–444.

Eckstein, A.M. (1991) Pharos and Rome, *ZPE* 88, 261–270.

Eckstein, A.M. (1999a) Glabrio and the Aetolians: A Note on *Deditio*, *TAPA* 125, 271–289.

Eckstein, A.M. (1999b) Pharos and the Question of Roman Treaties of Alliance in the Greek East in the Third Century B.C.E., *CP* 94, 395–418.

Eckstein, A.M. (2006) *Mediterranean Anarchy, Interstate War, and the Rise of Rome*, Berkeley.

Eckstein, A.M. (2008) *Rome enters the Greek East: From Anarchy to Hierarchy in the Hellenistic Mediterranean, 230–170 B.C.*, Oxford.

Edmondson, J. (1993) *Instrumenta imperii*: Law and Imperialism in Republican Rome, in B. Halpern and D.W. Hobson (eds) *Law, Politics and Society in the Ancient Mediterranean World*, Sheffield, 156–192.

Efron J. (1970) Shimon ben Shetah and Alexander Jannaeus, in M. Dorman et al. (eds) *In Memory of Gedaliahu Alon: Essays in Jewish History and Philology*, Tel Aviv, 69–132 [Hebrew].

Ehrimes, K.M. (1949) *Ancient Sparta: A Re-examination of the Evidence*, Manchester.

Eichert, O. (1882) *Vollständiges Wörterbuch zur Philippischen Geschichte des Justinus*, Hannover.

Eilers, C. (2003) Josephus' Caesarian *Acta*: History of a Dossier, Paper to SBL Conference.

Eilers, C. (2008) Forgery, Dishonesty, and Incompetence in Josephus' *Acta*: The Decree of Athens (*AJ* 14, 149–155), *ZPE* 166, 211–217.

Eilers, C. (2013) Diplomacy and the Integration of the Hasmonean State, in S.L. Ager and R. A. Faber (eds) *Belonging and Isolation in the Hellenistic World*, Toronto–Buffalo–London, 155–165.

Eisenmann, R.H. (1983) *Maccabees, Zadokites, Christians and Qumran: A New Hypothesis of Qumran Origins*, Leiden, 1055.

Elvers, K.-L. (2005) Iulius I. 11, *Brill's New Pauly*, vol. 6. Leiden.

Elwyn, S. (1993) Interstate Kinship and Roman Foreign Policy, *TAPA* 123, 261–286.

Epstein, I. (trans.) (1935) *The Babylonian Talmud*, Seder Nezikin, London.

Ermini, L. Pani (1974) *Corpus della Scultura altomedievale*, vol. 7, *La raccolta dei Fori Imperiali*, pt. 2, Spoleto.

Errington, R.M. (1987) Θεὰ 'Ρώμη und römischer Einfluss südlich des Mäanders im 2. Jh. v. Chr., *Chiron* 17, 97–118.

Errington, R.M. (1989) Rome and Greece to 205 BC, *CAH*[2] 8. 81–106.

Erskine, A. (1991) Hellenistic Monarchy and Roman Political Invective, *CQ* 41, 106–120.

Erskine, A. (1994) The Romans as Common Benefactors, *Historia* 43.1, 70–87.

Erskine, A. (2001) *Troy between Greece and Rome: Local Tradition and Imperial Power*, Oxford.

Erskine, A. (2002) Life after Death: Alexandria and the Body of Alexander, *Greece and Rome* 49, 163–179.

Ettelson, H.W. (1925) The Integrity of I Maccabees, *Transactions of the Connecticut Academy of Arts and Sciences* 27, 249–384.

Eyal, R. (2013) *The Hasmoneans: Ideology, Archaeology, Identity* (Journal of Ancient Judaism. Supplements, 10), Göttingen.

Ewald, H. (1878) *The History of Israel*, trans. J.E. Carpenter, London.

Fabricius, W. (1888) *Theophanes von Mytilene und Quintus Dellius als Quellen der Geographie des Strabon*, Diss., Strassburg.

Fassberg, S.E. (1993) Hebraisms in the Aramaic Documents from Qumran, in T. Muraoka (ed.) *Studies in Qumran Aramaic* (Abr-Nahrain Suppl. 3), Louvain, 48–69.

Favaloro, G. (1925) *Il Tramonto dell'Imperialismo nell'antica Siria con un esame storico-critico sui IV Libri dei Maccabei*, Reggio Calabria.

Federici, E.V. (1899) *Regesto del monastero di S. Silvestro de Capite*, Rome.

Feldman, L.H. (1984a) Flavius Josephus Revisited: The Man, His Writings and His Significance, *ANRW* 2.21.2, 763–862.

Feldman, L.H. (1984b) *Josephus and Modern Scholarship*, Berlin.

Feldman, L.H. (1994) Josephus' Portrayal of the Hasmoneans compared with I Macc., in Parente, F. (ed.) *Josephus and the History of the Greco-Roman Period: Essays in Memory of Morton Smith*, Leiden, 41–68 [= (1996) *Studies in Hellenistic Judaism*, Leiden, 137–163].

Ferrari, G. (1957) *Early Roman Monasteries: Notes for the History of the Monasteries and Convents at Rome from the V through the X Century* (Pontificio Istituto di archeologia cristiano), Vatican City.

Ferrary, J.-L. (1985) La Lex Antonia de Termessibus, *Athenaeum* 63, 419–457.

Ferrary, J.-L. (1988) *Philhellénisme et impérialisme: aspectes idéologiques de la conquête romaine du monde hellénistique, de la second guerre de macédoine à la guerre contre Mithridate* (Bibliothèque des écoles français d'Athènes et de Rome, 271), Paris–Rome.

Ferrary, J.-L. (1990) Traités et domination romaine dans le monde hellénique, in L. Canfora et al. (eds) *I trattati nel mondo antico: forma ideologia funzione* (Istituto Gramsci, Seminario di Antichistica), 217–235.

Ferrary, J.-L. (1995) Ius fetiale et diplomatie, in E. Frézouls and A. Jacquemin (eds) *Les Relations Internationales*, Actes du Colloque de Strasbourg 15–17 Juin 1993 (Université des Sciences humaines de Strasbourg, Travaux du Centre de recerche sur le proche-Orient et la Grèce antique, 13), Paris, 411–432.

Ferrenbach, V. (1895) *Die amici populi romani republikanischer Zeit*, Diss., Strassbourg.

Ferroni, A.M. (1993) s.v *Concordia, aedes*, in E. Steinby (ed.) *Lexicon Topographicum Urbis Romae*, vol. 1, Rome, 316–320.

Fiori, R. (1996) *Homo Sacer, Dinamica politico costituzionali di una sanzione giuridico-religiosa* (Università di Roma 'La Sapienza', Pubblicazioni dell'Istituto di diritto romano e dei diritti dell'oriente mediterraneo), Naples.

Fischer, T. (1970) *Untersuchungen zum Partherkrieg Antiochus' VII im rahmen der Seleukidengeschichte*, Tübingen.

Fischer, T. (1975) Zum jüdischen Verfassungsstreit vor Pompejus (Diodor 40,2), *ZDPV* 91, 46–49.

Fischer, T. (1980) *Seleukiden und Makkabäer, Beiträge zur Seleukidengeschichte und zu den politischen Ereignissen in Judäa während der 1. Hälfe des 2. Jahrhunderts v. Chr.*, Bochum.

Fischer, T. (1992) Maccabees, the Books of, in D.N. Freedman (ed.) *The Anchor Bible Dictionary*, New York–London, 439–454.

Fitzmyer, J. (1971) *The Genesis Apocryphon of Qumran Cave I* (Biblica and Orientalia, 18A) Rome.

Fitzmyer, J. (1974) Some Notes on Aramaic Epistolography, *JBL* 93, 201–225.

Fitzmyer, J. (1979) *A Wandering Aramean: Collected Aramaic Essays* (SBL Monograph Series, 25), Chico, CA.

Flintoff, E. (1976) Varro in the Works of John of Lydia, in *Atti congresso internazionale studi varroniani*, Riete, 365–377.

Flower, H.I. (2008) Remembering and Forgetting Temple Destruction: The Destruction of the Temple of Jupiter Optimus Maximus in 83 BC, in G. Gardner and K.L. Osterloh (eds) *Antiquity in Antiquity: Jewish and Christian Pasts in the Greco-Roman World*, Tübingen, 74–92.

Flower, M. (2002) Alexander and Panhellenism, in A.B. Bosworth and E. Baynham (eds) *Alexander the Great in Fact and Fiction*, Oxford–New York, 96–135.

Flurl, W. (1969) *Deditio in Fidem: Untersuchungen zu Livius und Polybios*, Diss., Munich.

Flusser, D. (1933) *The Author of the Book of Josippon*, *Zion* 17, 114–117.

Flusser, D. (1953) The Author of the Book of Josippon: His Personality and His Age, *Zion* 18, 109–126 [Hebrew].

Flusser, D. (1957) An 'Alexander Geste' in a Parma MS, *Tarbiz* 26, 181–183 [Hebrew].

Flusser, D. (1971) s.v. Josippon, in C. Roth and G. Wigoder (eds) *Encyclopaedia Judaica*, vol. 10, Jerusalem, 296–298.

Foley, J.M. (1999) What's in a Sign?, in E.A. Mackay (ed.) *Signs of Orality: The Oral Tradition and Its Influence in the Greek and Roman World*, Leiden–Boston–Köln, 1–27.

Fornara, C.W. (1983) *Translated Documents of Greece and Rome: Archaic Times to the End of the Peloponnesian Wars*, Cambridge.

Forsythe, G. (1999) *Livy and Early Rome: A Study in Historical Method and Judgement*, Stuttgart.

Forsythe, G. (2005) *A Critical History of Early Rome: From Prehistory to the First Punic War*, Berkeley.

Forte, B. (1972) *Rome and the Romans as the Greeks Saw Them*, Papers and Monographs of the American Academy in Rome, Rome.

Fraccaro, P. (1926) Ancora sulla questione dei Fannii, *Athenaeum* 4.3, 153–160.

Fraenkel, E. (1916) Zur geschichte des Wortes *Fides*, *Rhein. Mus.* n.s. 71, 187–199.

Franga, L. (1988) À propos de l'epitomé de Justin, *Latomus* 47, 868–874.

Fränkel, M. (1890) *Die Inschriften von Pergamon I: Bis zum Ende der Königszeit*, Berlin.

Frankfort, T. (1961) La date de l'autobiographie de Flavius Josèphe et des oeuvres de Justus de Tibèriade, *Rev. Belge de Philol. et d'Hist.* 39, 36–58.

Fraser, P.M. (1967) The Alexandrian View of Rome, *Bull. de la Societé archéologique* 42, 1–16.

Fraser, P. (1972) *Ptolemaic Egypt*, vol. 1, Oxford.

Fredericksen, M.W. (1965) The Republican Municipal Laws: Errors and Drafts, *JRS* 55, 183–195.

Freundenthal, J. (1874–75) *Hellenistische Studien: Alexander Polyhistor und die von ihm erhaltenen Reste jüdischer und samaritanischer Geschichtswerke*, Hellenistische Studien 001–002 (Jahresbericht des jüdisch–theologischen Seminars Fraenkelscher Stiftung), Breslau.

Freyburger, G. (1982) Fides et potestas, πίστις et ἐπιτροπή, *Ktèma* 7, 177–185.

Freyburger, G. (1986) *Fides: étude sémantique et religieuse depuis les origines jusqu'à l'époque augustéene*, Paris.

Frezza, P. (1938) Le Forme federative e la struzzura dei rapporti internazionali nell'antico diritto romano, *SDHI* 4, 363–428.

Frezza, P. (1955) L'età classica della costituzione repubblicana, *Labeo* 1, 320–336.

Frezza, P. (1967) In tema di relazioni internazionali nel mondo greco-romano, *SDHI* 33, 337–358.

Frezza, P. (1969) Le relazioni internazionali di Roma nel terzo e secondo secolo a. Cr., *SDHI* 35, 341–360.

Friezer, E. (1959) Interregnum and Patrum Auctoritas, *Mnemosyne* ser. 4, 12.4, 301–329.

Fündling, J. (2007) C. Papirius Carbo [I.7], *BNP* vol. 10, col. 485.

Gabba, E. (1973) *Esercito e società nella tarda Repubblica Romana*, Florence.

Gabba, E. (1976) Sulla valorizzazione politica delle origini troiane di Roma, in M. Sordi (ed.) *I canali della propaganda nel momdo antico* (CISA, 40), Milan, 84–101.

Gabba, E. (1989) The Growth of Anti-Judaism and the Greek Attitude towards the Jews, in L. Finkelstein and W.D. Davies (eds) *The Cambridge History of Judaism, vol. 2, The Hellenistic Age*, Cambridge, 614–656.

Gabrielson, V. (1993) Rhodes and Rome after the Third Macedonian War, in P. Bilde (ed.) *Centre and Periphery in the Hellenistic World*, Aarhus, 132–161.

Gabrielsen, V. (2005) Piracy and the Slave Trade, in A. Erskine (ed.) *A Companion to the Hellenistic World*, Oxford, 389–404.

Gafni, I.M. (1989) Josephus and I Maccabees, in L.H. Feldman and G. Hata (eds) *Josephus, the Bible and History*, Detroit, 116–131.

Gagarin, M. (1999) The Orality of Greek Oratory, in E.A. Mackay (ed.) *Signs of Orality: The Oral Tradition and its Influence in the Greek and Roman World*, Leiden–Boston–Köln, 163–180.

Gallet, L. (1937) Essai sur le senatus-consulte 'de Aesclépiade sociisque', *RHDFE* 16, 242–293, 387–425.

Galsterer, H. (1976) *Herrschaft und Verwaltung im republikanischen Italien: die Beziehungen Roms zu den italischen Gemeinden vom Latinerfrieden 338 v. Chr. bis zum Bundesgenossenkrieg 91 v. Chr.* (Münchener Beiträge zur Papyrusforschung und antiken Rechtsgeschichte, Heft 068), Munich.

Ganzert, J. (1996) *Der Mars-Ultor-Tempel auf dem Augustusforum in Rom*, Mainz am Rhein.

Ganzert, J. and Kockel, V. (1988) Augustusforum und Mars-Ultor-tempel, in M.R. Hofter (ed.) *Kaiser Augustus und die verlorene Republik*, Berlin, 149–199.

Garoufalias, P. (1979) *Pyrrhus, King of Epirus*, London.

Gascou, J. (1994) L'utilization de documents de première main dans les *Vies des Douze Césars de Suétone*, *Vita Latina* 133, 7–21.

Gasperini, L. (1967) *Quaderni di Archeologia della Libia*, vol. 5, Rome.

Gaster, M. (1899) *The Chronicles of Jerahmeel*, London.

Gauger, J.-G. (1977) *Beiträge zur jüdischen Apologetik* (Bonner biblische Beiträge, 49), Köln–Bonn.

Gauger, J.-D. (1986) Zur Rekonstrktion der römisch–jüdischen Beziehungen im 2. Jh. v. C., in H. Kalcyk et al. (eds) *Studien zur alten Geschichte: Siegfried Lauffer zum 70. Geburtstag*, Rome, 1.263–291.

Gauger, J.-D. (1990) Überlegung zum *programma* Antiochos' III. für den Tempel und die Stadt Jerusalem (Ios. ant. Iud. 12.145–146) und zum Problem jüdischer Listen, *Hermes* 188, 150–164.

Gehman, H.S. (1914) *The Interpreters of Foreign Languages Among the Ancients: A Study based on Greek and Latin Sources*, Diss., University of Pennsylvania.

Gehman, H.S. (1951) The Hebrew Character of Septuagint Greek, *VT* 1, 81–167.

Gehrke, H.-J. (1982) Der siegreiche König. Überlegung zur hellenistischen Monarchie, *AKG* 64, 247–277.

Geiger, A. (1857) *Urschrift und Übersetzungen der Bibel in ihrer Abhängigkeit von der innern Entwicklung des Judentums*, Breslau.

Geiger, J. (1984) The History of Judas Maccabaeus: One Aspect of Hellenistic Historiography, *Zion* 49, 1–8 [Hebrew].
Geiger, J. (1985–1988) Form and Content in Jewish–Hellenistic Historiography, *SCI* 8–9, 120–129.
Gelzer, M. (1968) *Caesar: Politician and Statesman*, trans. P. Needham, Cambridge.
Gelzer, M. (1969) *The Roman Nobility*, trans. R. Seager, New York.
Gensel, P. (1907) *RE* 6A, s.v. Eutropius (10), cols 1521–1527.
Gera, D. (1998) *Judaea and Mediterranean Politics 219 to 161 B.C.E.* (Brill's Series in Jewish Studies, 8), Leiden.
Geraty, L.T. (1975) The Khirbet el-Kôm Bilingual Ostrakon, *BASOR* 220, 55–61.
Gerhardsson, B. (1961) *Memory and Manuscript: Oral Tradition and Written Transmission in Rabbinic Judaism and Early Christianity* (Acta Seminarii Neotestamentici Upsaliensis, 22), Copenhagen.
Gerkan, A.V. (1927) Der Grabungen im Augustusforum, *Gnomon* 3.1, 58–60.
Gianelli, G. (1993) s.v. *Arx*, in E. Steinby (ed.) *Lexicon Topographicum Urbis Romae*, vol. 1, Rome, 127–129.
Ginsburg, M.S. (1928) *Rome et la Judée: contribution à l'histoire de leurs relations politiques*, Paris.
Ginsburg, M.S. (1934) Sparta and Judea, *CP* 29, 117–122.
Ginzel, F.K. (1911) *Handbuch der mathematischen und technischen Chronologie*, vol. 2, Leipzig.
Giovannini, A. (2000) Le droit fécial et la déclaration de guerre de Rome à Carthage en 218 avant J.-C., *Athenaeum* 88, 69–116.
Giovannini, A. and Müller, H. (1971) Die Beziehungen zwischen Rom und den Juden im 2. Jh. v. Chr., *Mus. Helv.* 28, 156–171.
Gizewski, C. (2005) *s.v.* Interrex, *Brill's New Pauly* 6, Boston–Leiden, cols 871–872.
Glare, P. (1982) *Oxford Latin Dictionary*, Oxford.
Gold, B.K. (1985) Pompey and Theophanes of Mytilene, *AJP* 106, 312–327.
Goldstein, J.A. (1966) The Syriac Bill of Sale from Dura-Europas, *JNES* 25, 1–16.
Goldstein, J.A. (1975) The Hasmoneans: The Dynasty of God's Resistor's, *Harv.Th.Rev.* 68, 53–57.
Goldstein, J.A. (1976) *I Maccabees: A New Translation with Introduction and Commentary* (The Anchor Bible, 41), Garden City NY.
Goldstein, J.A. (1983) *II Maccabees: A New Translation with Introduction and Commentary* (The Anchor Bible, 41), Garden City NY.
Goodblatt, D.M. (1987) Agrippa I and Palestinian Judaism in the First Century, *Jewish History* 2.1, 7–32.
Goodblatt, D.M. (1994) *The Monarchic Principle: Studies in Jewish Self-Government in Antiquity*, Tübingen.
Goodman, M. (1999) Jewish History and Roman History: Changing Methods and Preoccupations, in A. Oppenheimer and E. Müller-Luckner (eds) *Jüdische Geschichte in hellenistisch–römischer Zeit* (Schriften des Historischen Kollegs, Kolloquien 44), Munich, 75–83.
Goodspeed, E.J. (1942) The Possible Aramaic Gospel, *JNES* I, 315–340.
Goodyear, F. (1982) Pompeius Trogus and the Oxford Latin Dictionary, *LCM* 7, 13–14.
Gow, A.S.F. and Page, D.L. (1965) *The Greek Anthology: Hellenistic Epigrams*, Cambridge.
Grabbe, L.L. (1991) Maccabean Chronology: 167–4 or 168–165 BCE?, *JBL* 110, 59–74.
Grabbe, L.L. (2000) *Judaic Religion in the Second Temple Period: Belief and Practice from the Exile to Yavneh*, London–New York.

Graetz, H. (1906) *Geschichte der Juden von den ältesten Zeiten bis auf die Gegenwart*, 3. 2, *Geschichte der Judäer von dem Tode Juda Makkabi's bis zum Untergang des jüdischen Staates*[5], Leipzig.
Grainger, J.D. (2002) *The Roman War of Antiochus the Great*, Leiden.
Grainger, J.D. (2007/2009) *Alexander the Great Failure: The Collapse of the Macedonian Empire*, London–New York.
Grainger, J.D. (2010) *The Syrian Wars*, Leiden.
Grajetzki, W. (2011) *Greeks and Parthians in Mesopotamia and Beyond, 331 BC – AD 224*, Bristol.
Grant, M. (1946) *From Imperium to Auctoritas*, London.
Grant, M. (1973) *The Jews in the Roman World*, London.
Greenhalgh, M. (1989) *The Survival of Roman Antiquities in the Middle Ages*, London.
Grimal, P. (1986) Les élements philosophiques dans l'idée de monarchie à Rome à la fin de la Republic, in L.G. Kidd (ed.) *Fondation Hardt pour l'étude de l'antiquité classique: entretiens sur l'antiquité classique*, vol. 32, Geneva, 233–281.
Grimm, C.L.W. (1853) *Das erste Buch der Maccabäer* (Kurzgefasstes exegetisches; Handbuch zu den Apokryphen des Alten Testaments, 3), Leipzig.
Grimm, C.L.W. (1857) *Das zweite, dritte und vierte Buch der Maccabäer*, Leipzig.
Grimm, W. (1874) Ueber I Macc. VIII und XV, 16–21 nach Th. Mommsen's u. Fr. Ritschl's Forschungen, *Zeitschrift f. wiss. Theol.*, 17, 231–238.
Grueber, H.A. (1910) *Coins of the Roman Republic in the British Museum*, British Museum, London.
Gruen, E.S. (1975) Rome and Rhodes in the Second Century BC: A Historiographical Study, *CQ* 25, 58–81.
Gruen, E.S. (1976) Rome and the Seleucids in the Aftermath of Pydna, *Chiron* 6, 73–95.
Gruen, E.S. (1978) The Consular Elections for 216 B.C. and the Veracity of Livy, *Calif. Stud. Class. Ant.* 11, 61–74.
Gruen, E.S. (1982) Greek πίστις and Roman Fides, *Athenaeum* 60, 50–68.
Gruen, E.S. (1984) *The Hellenistic World and the Coming of Rome*, Berkeley–Los Angeles–London.
Gruen, E.S. (1992) *Culture and Identity in Republican Rome*, Ithaca.
Gruen, E.S. (1996) The Purported Jewish–Spartan Affiliation, in R.W. Wallace and E.M. Harris (eds) *Transitions to Empire. Essays in Greco-Roman History 360–146 BC in Honour of E. Badian*, Norman–London, 254–269.
Gruen, E.S. (1997) Jewish Legends in a Hellenistic Context, in P. Cartledge et al. (eds) *Hellenistic Constructs: Essays in Culture, History and Historiography*, Berkeley, 72–104.
Gruen, E.S. (1998) *Heritage and Hellenism: The Reinvention of Jewish Tradition*, Berkeley.
Gruen, E.S. (2002) *Diaspora: Jews amidst Greeks and Romans*, Cambridge, MA–London.
Gruen, E.S. (2011) *Rethinking the Other in Antiquity*, Princeton.
Grumel, V. (1958) *La chronologie*, Paris.
Grundy, G.B. (1917) *Murray's Classical Atlas*[2], London.
Grundy, R.H. (1964) The Language Milieu of First-Century Palestine, *JBL* 83, 404–408.
Grzybek, E. (1980) Roms Bündnis mit Byzanz (Tac. 12, 62), *Mus. Helv.* 37, 50–59.
Gsell, S. (1913–1929) *Histoire ancienne de l'Afrique du Nord*, 8 vols, Paris.
Guarducci, M. (ed.) (1942) *Inscriptiones Creticae: Opera et consilio Friderici Halbherr collectae*, vol. 3, *Tituli Cretae orientalis*, Rome, no. 10, 106–111.
Guerrieri Borsoi, M.B. (1998) La chiesa della Santissima Annunziata al foro Augusto, *B.A.* 83, 33–48.

Gundel, H.G. (1963) Der Begriff Maiestas in politischen Denken der römischen Republik, *Historia* 12, 281–320.
Gutberlet, C. (1927) *Das zweite Buch der Machabäer: übersetzt und erklärt*, Münster.
Gutmann, J. (1932) art., Josephus Flavius, *Encyclopedia Judaica*, Berlin.
Gutman, Y. (1958) The Correspondence with Sparta, in id. (ed.) *The Beginnings of Jewish–Hellenistic Literature*, Jerusalem, vol. 1, 75–94 [Hebrew].
Gutman, Y. (1963) Eupolemus, the son of John, in id. (ed.) *The Beginnings of Jewish–Hellenistic Literature*, Jerusalem [Hebrew], vol. 2, 108–111.
Habicht, C. (1976) *2. Makkabäerbuch* (Jüdische Schriften aus hellenistisch–römischer Zeit, 1), Gütersloh.
Habicht, C. (1982) *Studien zur Geschichte Athens in hellenistischer Zeit*, Göttingen.
Habicht, C. (1989) The Seleucids and Their Rivals, in A.E. Astin et al. (eds) *The Cambridge Ancient History*, VIII$^2$, *Rome and the Mediterranean to 133 B.C.*, Cambridge, 324–387.
Habicht, C. (1997) *Athens from Alexander to Antony*, trans. D.L. Schneider, Cambridge MA.
Hadas, M. (1959) *Hellenistic Culture: Fusion and Diffusion*, New York.
Hadas-Lebel, M. (1987) L'évolution de l'image de Rome auprès des Juifs en deux siècles de relations judéo-romaines – 164 à +70, *ANRW*, 2.20.3, 715–856.
Hackl, U. et al. (eds) (2010) *Quellen zur Geschichte des Partherreiches*, 3 vols, Göttingen.
Hahn, L. (1906) *Rom und Romanismus im griechish–römischen Osten: mit besonderer Berücksichtigung der Sprache, bis auf die Zeit Hadrians*, Leipzig.
Hahn, L. (1907) Zum Sprachenkampf im römischen Reich bis auf die Zeit Justinians, *Philologus*, Suppl. 10, 677–718.
Hamilton, B. (1961) The City of Rome and the Eastern Churches in the Tenth Century, *Orientalia Christiana Periodica* 27, 5–26.
Hamilton, C.D. (1979) *Sparta's Bitter Victories: Politics and Diplomacy in the Corinthian War*, Ithaca.
Hamilton, J.R. (1961) Cleitarchus and Aristobulus, *Historia* 10.4, 448–458.
Hammer, R.J. (1976) *The Book of Daniel* (The Cambridge Bible Commentary), Cambridge.
Hammond, N.G.L. (1967) *Epirus: The Geography, the Ancient Remains, the History and the Topography of Epirus and Adjacent Areas*, Oxford.
Hammond, N.G.L. (1972) *A History of Macedonia*, vol. 1, Oxford.
Hammond, N.G.L. (1983) *Three Historians of Alexander the Great*, Cambridge.
Hammond, N.G.L. (1988) Which Ptolemy Gave Troops and Stood as Protector of Pyrrhus' Kingdom?, *Historia* 37.4, 404–413.
Hammond, N.G.L. and Walbank, F.W. (1988) *A History of Macedonia*, vol. 3, Oxford.
Hands, A.R. (1965) The Political Background of the 'Lex Acilia de repetundis', *Latomus* 24.2, 225–237.
Hanhart, R. (1959) *Maccabaeorum liber II*, Septuaginta: Vetus Testamentum Graecum; Auctoritate Academiae Litterarum Gottingensis 9/2, Göttingen.
Hanhart, R. (1964) Zur Zeitrechnung des I. und II Makkabäerbuches, *Beihefte zur Zeitschrift für die Alttestamentliche Wissenschaft* 88, 55–96.
Hannah, R. (2013) *Greek and Roman Calendars: Construction of Time in the Classical World*, Bristol.
Hansen, E.V. (1972) *Attalids of Pergamum*$^2$, Ithaca.
Hantos, T. (1983) *Das römische Bundesgenossensystem in Italien*, Munich.
Hardy, F.W. (1983) *An Historicist Perspective on Daniel 11*, MA Diss., Andrews University.
Harmand, L. (1957) *Le Patronat sur les collectivés publiques*, Paris.

Hassall, M., Crawford, M. and Reynolds, J. (1974) Rome and the Eastern Provinces at the End of the Second Century BC: The So-called 'Piracy Law' and a New Inscription from Cnidos (*Fouilles de Delphes*, III, 4, no. 37), *AJA* (1972, 64–65) *JRS* 64, 195–220.

Hatch, E. and Redpath, R.A. (1998) *A Concordance to the Septuagint and other Greek Versions of the Old Testament*[2], Grand Rapids MI.

Hausmaniger, H. (1961) *'Bellum iustum' und 'iusta causa belli' im älteren römischen Recht, Österr. Zeitschr. f. öffentl. Recht* 11, 335–345.

Havelock, E.A. (1963) *Preface to Plato*, Cambridge, MA.

Hayne, L. (1996) Caesar and Lentulus Crus, *Acta Classica* 39, 72–76.

Hayward, R. (1982) The Jewish Temple at Leontopolis: A Reconsideration, *JJS* 33, 429–443.

Heftner, H. (1997) *Der Aufstieg Roms vom Pyrrhoskrieg bis zum Fall von Karthago (280–146 v. Chr.)*, Regensburg.

Heinen, H. (1972) Die politischen Beziehungen zwischen Rom und dem Ptolemäerreich von ihren Anfängen bis zum Tag von Eleusis (273–168 v. Chr.), *ANRW* 1.1, 633–659.

Heinze, R. (1929) Fides, *Hermes* 64, 140–166.

Hengel, M. (1969) *Judentum und Hellenismus: Studien zu ihrer Begegnung unter besonderer Berücksichtigung Palästinas bis zur Mitte des 2.Jh. v. Chr.* (Wissenschaftliche Untersuchungen zum neuen Testament, 10), Tübingen.

Hengel, M. (1974) *Judaism and Hellenism*, trans. J. Bowden, 2 vols, London.

Hengel, M. (1989) The Interpretation of Judaism and Hellenism in the Pre-Maccabean Period, in L. Finkelstein and W.D. Davies (eds) *The Cambridge History of Judaism, vol. 2, The Hellenistic Age*, Cambridge, 167–228.

Henry, R. (1965) *Photius, Bibliothèque*, Paris.

Henten, J.W. van (1997) *The Maccabaean Martyrs as Saviours of the Jewish People: A Study of 2 and 4 Maccabees* (Suppl. JSJ, 57), Leiden.

Henten, J.W. van (2006) Judas the Maccabee's Dream (2 Macc. 15: 11–16) and the Egyptian King's Sickle Sword, *Zutot* 4, 8–15.

Henze, W. (1892) *De Civitatibus Liberis quae fuerunt in provinciis populi Romani*, Berlin.

Herklotz, I. (2000) *Gli eredi di Costantino: il papato, il Laterano e la propaganda visiva nel XII secolo*, Rome.

Herman, G. (1987) *Ritualised Friendship and the Greek City*, Cambridge.

Hermann, P. (1965) Antiochos der Grosse und Teos, *Anadolu* 9, 29–160.

Herzfeld, L. (1863) *Geschichte des Volkes Jisrael von der Zerstörung des ersten Tempels bis zur Einsetzung des Makkabäers Schimon zum hohen Priester und Fürsten*[2], book 2, Leipzig.

Heurgon, J. (1969) *Rome et la Méditerranée occidentale jusqu'aux guerrres puniques*, Paris.

Heuss, A. (1933) *Die Völkerrechtlichen Grundlagen der römischen Aussenpolitik in republikanischer Zeit* (Klio Beiheft 31, Neue Folge, Heft 18), Leipzig.

Heuss, A. (1934) Abschluss und Beurkundung des griechischen und römischen Staatsvertrages, *Klio* 27, 14–53, 218–257.

Heuss, A. (1937) *Stadt und Herrscher des Hellenismus in ihren Staats – und völkerrechtlichen Beziehungen* (Klio Beiheft 39, Neue Folge, Heft 26, Leipzig).

Higgins, C.M. (2009) *Popular and Imperial Response to Earthquakes in the Roman Empire*, Diss., Ohio University.

Hinrichs, F.-T. (1966) Die *lex agraria* des Jahres 111 v. Chr., *ZSS* 83, 252–307.

Hody, H. (1711) *Histoire critique*, vol. 1, Paris.

Hof, P. van't (1955) *Bijdrage tot de kennis van Antiochus IV Epiphanes konig van Syrië*, Amsterdam.

Hoffmann, W. (1934) *Rom und die griechische Welt im 4. Jahrhundert*, Leipzig.

Hölkeskamp, K.-J. (2000) *Fides-deditio in fidem-dextra data et accepta*: Recht, Religion und Ritual in Rom, in C. Bruun (ed.) *The Roman Middle Republic: Politics, Religion and Historiography c.400–133 B.C.* (Acta Instituti Romani Finlandiae, 23), Rome, 223–249.

Holleaux, M. (1898) Epigraphica, *REG* 11, 250–278.

Holleaux, M. (1902) Le Prétendu traité de 306 entre les Rhodiens et les Romains, in *Mélanges Perrot*, Paris, 183–190.

Holleaux, M. (1908) La chronologie de la cinquième guerre de Syrie, *Klio* 8, 267–281.

Holleaux, M. (1917) Textes Gréco-Romains, *REA* 19, 77–97.

Holleaux, M. (1918) *ΣΤΡΑΤΗΓΟΣ ΥΠΑΤΟΣ: étude sur la traduction en grec du titre consulaire*, Paris.

Holleaux, M. (1921) *Rome, la Grèce et les monarchies hellénistiques au III^e^ siècle avant J.-C.*, Paris.

Holleaux, M. (1924) Fragment de sénatus-consulte trouvé à Corfu, *BCH* 48, 381–398.

Holleaux, M. (1930) Rome and Macedon: The Romans against Philip, in S.A. Cook et al. (eds) *The Cambridge Ancient History*, vol. 8, *Rome and the Mediterranean 218–133 B.C.*, Cambridge, 138–98.

Holleaux, M. (1942) Études d'épigraphie et d'histoire grecques, vol. 3, Paris.

Holleaux, M. (1957) La clause territoriale du traité d'Apamée, in L. Robert (ed.) *Études d'épigraphique et d'histoire grecque* (Academie des inscriptions et belles lettres), Paris, 208–243.

Holmes, T. Rice (1923) *The Roman Republic and the Founder of the Empire*, vol. 3, New York.

Hölscher, G. (1904) *Die Quellen des Josephus fur die Zeit vom Exil bis zum judischen Kriege*, Leipzig.

Hölscher, G. (1906) Bemerkungen zur Topographie Palästinas, *ZDPV* 29, 135–136.

Horn, H. (1930) *Foederati: Untersuchungen zur Geschichte ihrer Rechtsstellung im Zeitalter der römischen Republik und des frühen Principats*, Diss., Frankfurt.

Horsnaes, H.W. (2002) *The Cultural Development in North Western Lucania c. 600–273 BC*, Rome.

Houghton, A. et al. (eds) (2008) *Seleucid Coins: A Comprehensive Catalogue. Part 2: Seleucus IV through Antiochus XIII*, vol. 1, New York.

Howlett, D.R. (1995) *The Celtic Latin Tradition of Biblical Style*, Dublin.

Humm, M. (2006) Rome face à la menace d'Alexandre le Grand, in E. Caire and S. Pittia (eds) *Guerre et Diplomatie romaines, IV^e^–III^e^ siècles av. J.-C. Pour un réexamen des sources*, Aix-en Provance, 175–196.

Hurley, D.W. (ed.) (2001) *Suetonius: Diuus Claudius*, Cambridge.

Huss, W. (2001) *Ägypten in hellenistischer Zeit*, Munich.

Huzar, E.G. (1966) Egyptian Influences on Roman Coinage in the Third Century, *CJ* 61.8, 337–346.

Huzar, E. (1984) Claudius: The Erudite Emperor, *ANRW* 2.32.1, 611–650.

Ideler, L. (1825) *Handbuch der mathematischen und technischen Chronologie*, 2 vols, Berlin.

Ilari, V. (1974) *Gli italici nelle strutture militari romani*, Università di Roma, Milan.

Instinsky, H.U. (1964) Schwurszene und Coniuratio, *Jahrbuch für Numismatik und geldgeschichte* 14, 83–87.

Jacoby, F. (1907) Eupolemos (No. 11), *RE* 6, cols 1227–1229.

Jacoby, F. (1923) *Die Fragmente der griechischen Historiker*, vol. 2, B, Berlin (repr. 1962, Leiden).

Jahn, J. (1970) *Interregnum und Wahldiktatur*, Kallmunz.
Jal, P. (1983) But et technique d'abréviateurs latins: Justin et les abréviateurs de Valère Maxime, *BSNAF* 26 Jan., 39–44.
Janke, M. (1938) *Historische Untersuchungen zu Memnon von Heraklea*, Würzburg.
Jeffers, J.S. (1999) *The Greco-Roman World of the New Testament Era: Exploring the Background of Early Christianity*, Downers Grove IL.
Jepsen, A. and Hanhart, R. (1964) *Untersuchungen zur Israeitisch–Jüdischen Chronologie* (BZAW, 88), Berlin.
Johannsen, K. (1971) *Die* lex agraria *des Jahres 111 v. Chr.*, Diss., Munich.
Johnson, A.C., Coleman P.R. and Bourne F.C. (1961) *Ancient Roman Statutes*, Austin.
Jones, H.S. (1926) A Roman Law concerning Piracy, *JRS* 16, 155–173.
Jordan, H. (1871) *Topographie der Stadt Rom in Alterthum*, vol. 2. Berlin.
Joüon, P. (1922) Quelques hébraisms de syntaxe dans le premier livre des Maccabées, *Biblica* 3, 204–206.
Jouguet, P. (1937) Les débuts du règne de Ptolémée Philométor et la sixième guerre syrienne, d'après un mémoire de M. Walter Otto, *Revue de Philologie, de littérature et d'histoire anciennes*, 11 (3rd series), 193–238.
Judeich, W. (1885) *Caesar im Orient; kritische Übesicht der Ereignisse vom 9. August 48 v. Chr. bis Oktober 47*, Leipzig.
Juster, J. (1914) *Les Juifs dans l'empire romain; leur condition juridique, economique et sociale*, vol. 1, Paris.
Kahrstedt, U. (1913) *Geschichte der Karthager*, Berlin.
Kaibel, G. (1890) *Inscriptiones Italiae et Siciliae* (Inscriptiones Graecae), Prüssische Akademie der Wissenschaften, Berlin.
Kaimo, I. (1979) *The Romans and the Greek Language* (Comm. Hum. Litt., 64), Helsinki.
Kallet-Marx, R.M. (1995) *Hegemony to Empire: The Development of the Roman* Imperium *in the East from 148 to 62 B.C.*, Berkeley.
Kamphausen, A. (1900) Das zweite Buch der Makkabäer, in E. Kautzsch (ed.) *Die Apokryphen und Pseudepigraphen des Alten Testaments*, Tübingen, vol. 1, 81–118.
Kappler, W. (1936) *Septuaginta, vol. IX, 1, Maccabaeorum liber I*, Göttingen.
Kappler, W. and Hanhart, R. (1976) *Maccabaeorum liber II*, Göttingen.
Kappler, W. and Hanhart, R. (1959) *Maccabaeorum libri I–IV*, Göttingen.
Kaser, M. (1942) Die Typen des römischen Bodenrechts, *ZSS* 62, 1–81.
Kaser, M. (1993) *Ius gentium*, Köln–Weimar–Wienn.
Kasher, A. (1990) *Jews and Hellenistic Cities in Eretz-Israel* (Texte und Studien zum antiken Judentum, 21), Tübingen.
Katzoff, R. (1985) Jonathan and Late Sparta, *AJP* 106, 485–489.
Keaveney, A. (1981) Roman Treaties with Parthia circa 95–64 B.C., *AJP* 102.2, 195–212.
Keaveney, A. (1982) The King and the War-Lords: Romano-Parthian Relations circa 64–53 B.C., *AJP* 103.4, 412–428.
Keerl, P. F. (1852) *Die Apokryphen des Alten Testaments*, Leipzig.
Keil, C.F. (1875) *Commentar über die Bücher der Makkabäer*, Leipzig.
Keil, V. (1985) Onias III.: Märtyrer oder Tempelgründer?, *ZAW* 97, 221–233.
Kienast, D. (1968) Entstehung und Aufbau des römischen Reiches, *ZSS RA* 85, 330–367.
Kienast, D. (1984) Die Anfänge der römischen Provinzialordnung in Sizilien, in V. Napoli (ed.) *Sodalitas: Scritti in onore di Antonio Guarino*, vol. 1, 105–123.
Kieweler, H.V. (1992) *Ben Sira zwischen Judentum und hellenismus: eine kritische Auseinandersetzung mit Th. Middendorp*, Vienna.

Kinney, D. (2007) Fact and Fiction in the *Mirabilis urbis Romae*, in E. Carragain and C. Neumann de Vegvar (eds) *Roma Felix: Formation and Reflections of Medieval Rome*, Burlington, 234–252.

Kippenberg, H.G. (1986) Die jüdischen Überlieferungen πάτριοι νόμοι, in R. Faber and R. Schlesier (eds) *Die Restauration der Götter: Antike Religion und Neo-Paganismus*, Würzburg, 45–60.

Klausner, J. (1924) *Israelite History*, Jerusalem [Hebrew].

Klausner, T. (1974) *Aurum Coronarium: Gesammelte Arbeiten zur Liurgiegeschichte, Kirchengeschichte und Christlichen Archäologie*, Münster.

Kloesel, H. (1935) *Libertas*, Diss., Breslau.

Kloos, R. M. (1979) Die frühmittelalteriche lateinische Epigraphik, in *La cultura in Italia fra Tardo Antico e Alto Medioevo* (Atti del convegno tenuto a Roma, consiglio nazionale delle richerche, dal 12 al 16 novembre 1979, Rome, 1979), vol. 2, Rome, 893–901.

Klose, P. (1972) *Die völkerrechtliche Ordnung der hellenistischen Staatenwelt in der Zeit von 280 bis 168 v. Chr: Ein Beitrag zur Geschichte des Völkerrechts*, Munich.

Klotz, A. (1923) s.v. *senaculum*, *RE* 2A, cols 1453–1454.

Klotz, A. (1940) *Livius und seine Vorgänger*, Leipzig–Berlin.

Klotz, A. (1953) Caesar und Livius, *Rhein. Mus.* 96, 62–67.

Knabenbauer, J. (1907) *Commentarius in duos libros Machabaeorum*, Paris.

Knibb, M. (2001) The Book of Daniel in its Context, in J.J. Collins and P.W. Flint (eds) *The Book of Daniel: Composition and Reception*, Leiden, 16–35.

Knibbe, D. (1960) Die Gestandtschaftsreise des jüngeren Scipio Africanus im Jahre 140 v. Chr.: eine Höhepunkt der Weltreichspolitik Roms im 2 Jahrhundert, *Jahreshefte des Österrechischen Archäologischen Instituts* 45, 36–37.

Koehler, L. and Baumgartner, W. (2001) *The Hebrew and Aramaic Lexicon of the Old Testament*, trans. M.E.J. Richardson, vol. 1, Leiden.

Kolbe, W. (1926) *Beiträge zur syrischen und jüdischen Geschichte* (Beiträge zur Wissenschaft vom Alten Testament NF 10), Berlin–Stuttgart–Leipzig.

Konstan, D. (1997) *Friendship in the Classical World*, Cambridge.

Kontorini, V. (1983) Rome et Rhodes au tournant de IIIe s. av. J.-C. d'après une Inscription Inedite de Rhodes, *JRS* 73, 24–32.

Kooij, A. van der (2001) The Septuagint of Psalms and the First Book of Maccabees, in R.J.V. Hiebert et al. (eds) *The Old Greek Psalter: Studies in Honour of Albert Pietersma* (JSOT Suppl. Series 332), Sheffield, 229–247.

Kooij, A. van der (2012) The Claim of Maccabaean Leadership and the Use of Scripture, in B. Eckhardt (ed.) *Jewish Identity and Politics between the Maccabees and Bar Kochva: Groups, Normativity and Rituals*, Leiden, 29–49.

Korn, G.B. (1972) An Apollonian Embassy to Rome, *Latomus* 32.3, 570–574.

Kornemann, E. (1920) Die letzen Ziele der Politik Alexander des Groβen, *Klio* 16, 213–218.

Koskenniemi, H. (1956) *Studien zur Idee und Phraseologie des griechischen Briefes bis 400 n. Chr.*, Helsinki.

Kostial, M. (1995) *Kriegerisches Rom? Zur Frage von Unvermeidbarkeit und Normalität Militärischer Konflikte in der Römischen Politik*, Stuttgart.

Kosters, W.H. (1878) De Polemiek van het tweede boek der Makkabeën, *Theologisch Tÿdschrift* 12, 491–558.

Kratz, R. (2001) The Visions of Daniel, in J.J. Collins and P.W. Flint (eds) *The Book of Daniel: Composition and Reception*, Leiden, 91–113.

Krendkel, W.A. (1972) Zur Biographie des Lucilius, *ANRW* 1.2, Berlin, 1240–1259.
Krug, E. (1916) *Die Senatsboten der römischen Republik*, Breslau.
Kubitschek, W. (1894) *RE* 1.1, s.v. *acta*, no. 5, *Acta urbis*, cols 285–301.
Kuhlmey, C.G.A. (1840) *Eupolemi fragmenta proleomenis et commentario instructa*, Diss., Berlin.
Kunkel, W. (1966) *An Introduction to Roman Legal and Constitutional History*, Oxford.
Kürçer, A. et al. (2012) An Assessment of the Earthquakes of Ancient Troy, NW Anatolia, Turkey, Tectonics – Recent Advances, Prof. Evgenii Sharkov (ed.), at http://www.intechopen.com/books/tectonics-recent-advances/an-assessment-of-the-earthquakes-of-ancient-troy-nw-Anatolia-turkey (accessed 26 August 2016).
Kutscher, E.Y. (1974) *The Language and Linguistic Background of the Complete Isaiah Scroll (STD) 6*, Leiden.
Kutscher, E.Y. (1982) *A History of the Hebrew Language*, Jerusalem.
Kylie McCarter, P. (1992) The Mystery of the Copper Scroll, in H. Shanks (ed.) *Understanding the Dead Sea Scrolls*, New York, 227–241.
Kytzler, B. (1989) *Fidus Interpres*: The Theory and Practice of Translation in Classical Antiquity, *Antichthon* 23, 42–50.
La Penna, A. (1953) *Librei dei Maccabei* (La Sacra Bibbia), Marietti.
La Penna, A. (1965) Διαθήκη e συνθήκη nei libri dei Maccabei, *Biblica*, 46, 149–180.
La Penna A. (1981) Mobilità dei modelli etici e relativismo dei valori: da Cornelio Nepote a Valerio Massimo e alla *Laus Pisonis*, in A. Giardina and A. Schiavone (eds) *Società romana e produzione schiavistica*, 3 (Modelli etici, diritto e traformazioni sociali), Rome–Bari, 193–198.
La Rocca, S. (2014) The Roman Republic and Hasmonean Judaea, *Athenaeum* 102.1, 47–78.
La Roche J. (1892) *Commentar zu Homers Odysée*, Prague.
Lacocque, A. (1979) *The Book of Daniel*, Atlanta.
Ladouceur, D.J. (1983) The Language of Josephus, *JSJ* 14, 18–38.
Lampela, A. (1998) *Rome and the Ptolemies of Egypt: The Development of Their Political Relations, 273–80 B.C.* (Commentationes Humanarum Litterarum, 111), Helsinki.
Lancel, S. (1985) Y-a-t-il une africitas?, *REL 63*, 161–182.
Lanciani, R. (1890a) *L'Itinerario di Einsiedeln e l'Ordine di Benedetto Canonico*, Rome.
Lanciani, R. (1890b) La cloaca massima, *B.Com.* n.s. 3, 95–102.
Lanciani, R.A. (1892) *Ruins and Excavations of Ancient Rome*, Boston–New York.
Landau, Y.H. (1966) A Greek Inscription found near Hefzibah, *IEJ* 16, 54–70.
Lapide, P. (1975) Insights from Qumran into the languages of Jesus, *R.Q.* 8, 4, 483–501.
Laqueur, R. (1904) *Kritische Untersuchungen zum zweiten Makkabäerbuch*, Strassburg.
Laqueur, R. (1920) *Der jüdische Historiker Flavius Josephus: ein biographischer Versuch auf neuer quellenkritischer Grundlage*, Giessen.
Laqueur, R. (1926) *RE* 13, s.v. Lokalchronik, cols 1098–1102.
Laqueur, R. (1927) Griechische Urkunden in der jüdisch–hellenistischen Literatur, *Historische Zeitschrift* 136, 229–252.
Laqueur, R. (1932) *RE* 4A.2, s.v. Synkellos (1), 1388–1410.
Larivière, L. (1892) *Des traités conclus par Rome avec les rois étrangers*, Paris.
Larsen, J.A.O. (1935) Was Greece Free between 196 and 146 B.C.?, *CP* 30, 193–214.
Larsen, J.A.O. (1937) The Peace of Phoenice and the Outbreak of the Second Macedonian War, *CP* 32, 15–31.
Larsen, J.A.O. (1956) The Araxa Inscription and the Lycian Confederacy, *CP* LI, 151–169.

Larsen, J.A.O. (1970) Review, W. Dahlheim: (1968) *Struktur und Entwicklung des römischen Völkerrechtes im 3 und 2. Jahrhundert v. Chr.*, *JRS* 60, 218–219.

Lasch, R. (1908) *Der Eid. Entstehung und Beziehung zu Glaube und Brauch der Naturvolker: eine Ethnologische Studie*, Stuttgart.

Last, D.M. and Ogilvie, R.M. (1958) Claudius and Livy, *Latomus* 17, 476–487.

Last, H. (1954) Rome and the Empire, in S.A. Cook et al. (eds) *The Cambridge Ancient History*, vol. 11, *The Imperial Peace A.D. 70–192*, Cambridge, 435–478.

Laticheff, B. (1882) Inscriptions de Narthakion, *BCH* 6, 356–387.

Lazenby, J.F. (1978) *Hannibal's War*, Warminster.

Leech, H.B. (1877) *An Essay on Ancient International Law*, Dublin.

Lehmann, G.A. (1967) *Untersuchungen zur historischen Glaubwürdigkeit des Polybios* (Fontes et Commentationes, Heft 5), Münster.

Lehmann-Haupt, C.F. (1902) Ptolemaios II. und Rom, *Klio* 2, 347–348.

Lehmann-Haupt, C.F. (1903) Der erste syrische Krieg und die Weltage um 275–272 v. Chr., *Klio* 3, 496–547.

Leone, R. and Margiotta, A. (2007) *Fori Imperiali. Demolizioni e scavi. Fotografie 1924/1940*, Milan.

Lenschau, Th. (1940) Timarchus (6a), in *RE*. Suppl. 7, col. 1574.

Lerouge, C. (2007) *L'image des Parthes dans le monde gréco-romain: du début du Ier siècle av. J.-C. jusqu'à la fin du Haut-Empire romain*, Stuttgart.

Lesaffer, R.C.H. (2002) *Amicitia* in Renaissance peace and alliance treaties (1450–1530), *J. of Hist. of Intern Law* 4.1, 77–99.

Lévêque, P. (1957) *Pyrrhos* (Bibliothéque des écoles français d'Athènes et de Rome, 185) Paris.

Levick, B. (1983) The *senatus consultum* from Larinum, *JRS* 73, 97–115.

Levick, B. (2013) Claudius no. 75, in T. Cornell et al. (eds) *Fragments of the Roman Historians*, vol. 1, Oxford, 509–513.

Lewis, C.T. and Short, C. (1966) *A Latin Dictionary*, Oxford.

Lewis, N. (1950) Ad Livium 42.29.5: Appendicule à Eulaeos et Lénaeos, *J. Juristic Papyrology*, 4, 265–266.

Lewis, R.G. (1993) Imperial Biography: Augustus to Hadrian, *ANRW* 2.34.1, 629–706.

Liddell, H.G. and Scott, R. (1996) *Greek–English Lexicon*, 9th rev. edn, Oxford.

Liebmann-Frankfort T. (1969) Rome et le conflit judéo-syrien (164–161) avant notre ère, *L'Antiquité Classique* 38, 101–120.

Limentani, I. Calabi (1970) Sul non saper leggere le epigrafi classiche nei secoli XI e XIII: sulla scoperta graduale delle abbreviazioni epigrafiche, *Acme* 23, 253–281.

Linderski, J. (1986) The Augural Law, *ANRW* 2.16.3, 2146–2312.

Lintott, A. (1978) The Capitoline Dedications to Jupiter and the Roman Empire, *ZPE* 30, 137–144.

Lintott, A.W. (1992) *Judicial Reform and Land Reform in the Roman Republic: A New Edition with Translation and Commentary*, Cambridge.

Liou-Gille, B. (1998) *Une lecture 'religieuse' de Tite-Live I: cultes, rites, croyances de la Rome archäique*, Paris.

Lombardi, G. (1947) *Sul concetto di 'ius gentium'*, Rome.

Lord, L.E. (1938) The date of Julius Caesar's Departure from Alexandria, *JRS* 28, 19–40.

Loreto, L. (2001) *Il bellum iustum e i suoi equivoci: Cicerone ed una componente della rappresentazione romana del Völkerrecht antico*, Naples.

Lott, J.B. (2012) *Death and Dynasty in Early Imperial Rome: Key Sources, with Text, Translation and Commentary*, Cambridge.

Lundbom, J.R. (1996) The *Inclusio* and Other Framing Devices in Deuteronomy LXXVIII, *VT* 46, 296–315.

Luraschi, G. (1979) *Foedus, Ius Latii, Civitas: aspetti costituzionali della romanizzazione in Transpadana* (Studi nelle scienze giuridiche e sociale, 29), Padua.

Ma, J. (1999) *Antiochus III and the Cities of Asia Minor*, Oxford.

McCarthy, D.J. (1966) Plagues and Sea of Reeds: Exodus 5–14, *JBL* 85, 137–158.

McCreesh, T.P. (1991) *Biblical Sound and Sense: Poetic Sound Patterns in Proverbs 10–29* (JSOT Suppl. Series, 129), Sheffield.

McDonald, A.H. (1967) The Treaty of Apamea (188 B.C.), *JRS* 57, 1–8.

Macé, A. (1900) *Essai sur Suétone*, Paris.

Maetzke, G. (1991) La struttura stratigrafica nell'area N.O. del Foro Romano come appare dai recenti interventi di scavo, *Archeologia Medievalia* 18, 43–200.

Magdelain, A. (1943) *Essai sur les origines de la sponsio*, Diss., TEPAC, Paris.

Magie, D. (1939) Rome and the City-States of Western Asia Minor from 200 to 133 B.C., in W.M. Calder and J. Keil (eds) *Anatolian Studies Presented to W.H. Buckler*, Manchester, 161–185.

Magie, D. (1950) *Roman Rule in Asia Minor*, 2 vols, Princeton.

Maiuri, A. (1925) *Nuova Silloge Epigrafica di Rodi e Cos*, Florence.

Malitz, J. (1984) Caesars Partherkrieg, *Historia* 33.1, 21–59.

Malitz, J. (1994) Claudius (*FGrH* 276): der Prinzeps als Gelehrter, in V.M. Strocka (ed.) *Die Regierungszeit des Kaisers Claudius*, Mainz, 133–144.

Mandell, S. (1991) Did the Maccabees Believe That They Had a Valid Treaty with Rome?, *CBQ* 53, 202–220.

Manganaro, G. (1964) Città di Sicilia e santuari panhellenici nel III e II sec. A.C., *Historia* 13, 414–439.

Manigk, A. (1927) Societas, *RE* vol. 3A, 1, cols 772–781, Stuttgart.

Manimanis, V., Theodosiou, E. and Dimitrijevic, M. (2012) The Geographers of the Byzantine Period, *European Journal of Science and Theology* 18.4, 23–40.

Manni, E. (1949) L'Egitto tolemaico nei suoi rapporti politici con Roma, *Riv. Filol.* 27, 79–106.

Manni, E. (1956) Sulle più antiche relazioni fra Roma e il mondo ellenistico, *PP* 11, 180–181.

Manni, E. (1962) Alessandro il Molosso e la sua spedizione in Italia, *Studi Salentini* 14, 344–352.

Mantovani, M. (1990) Bellum iustum. *Die idee der gerechten Krieges in der römischen Kaiserzeit*, Bern–Frankfurt am Main–New York.

Marasco, C. (1987) Roma e la pirateria cilicia, *Riv. Stor. It.* 99, 122–135.

Marchetti, P. (1973) La Marche du Calendrier romain de 203 à 190 (années Varr. 551–564), *AC* 42, 473–496.

Marchetti, P. (1976) La Marche du Calendrier romain et la Chronologie à l'Époque de la Bataille de Pydna, *BCH* 100, 401–423.

Marchetti Longhi, G. (1943–1944) Apollinar, Senatus ad Apollinis e Curia Pompeja, *Acc. Rom. Arch.* 20, 383–445.

Marcus, R. (1933) *Josephus*, vol. 7 (LCL), Harvard–London.

Mariani, B. (1965) L'allianza e l'amicizia dei Maccabei con i Romani sotto l'aspetto teocratico, *Divinitas* 9, 75–104.

Mariotti, L. (1961) *Studi Luciliani*, Florence.

Maróti, E. (1962) Diodotos Tryphon et la piratie, *Acta Antiqua Academiae Scientiarum Hungaricae* 10, 187–194.

Maróti, E. (1970) Die Rolle der Seeraüber in der Zeit des Mithridatischen Krieges, in L. de Rosa (ed.) *Ricerche storiche ed economische in memoria di Corrado Barbagallo*, vol. 1, Naples, 479–493.

Marshall, A.J. (1968) Friends of the Roman People, *AJP* 89.1, 39–55.

Martin, R.A. (1974) *Syntactical Evidence of Semitic Sources in Greek Documents* (Septuagint and Cognate Studies, 3), Cambridge, MA.

Martola, N. (1984) *Capture and Liberation: A Study in the Composition of the First Book of Maccabees*, Acta Academiae Aboensis, Abo.

Marx, F. (1882) *Studia Luciliana*, Diss., Bonn.

Marx, F. (1884) Animaduersiones criticae in Scipionis Aemiliani historian et C. Gracchi orationem aduersus Scipionem, *Rhein. Mus*. 39, 65–72.

Masi, A. (1961) s.v. *foedus*, in A. Azara and E. Eula (eds) *Novissimo Digesto Italiano*, Turin.

Mason, G.M. (1987) Senacula and Meeting Places of the Roman Senate, *CJ* 83.1, 39–50.

Mason, H.J. (1970) The Roman Government in Greek Sources, *Phoenix* 24, 150–159.

Mason, H.J. (1974) *Greek Terms for Roman Institutions: A Lexicon and Analysis* (American Studies in Papyrology, 013), Toronto.

Mason, S. (1991) *Flavius Josephus on the Pharisees: A Composition-Critical Study*, Leiden.

Mastino, A. (1978) *Il 'giornalismo' nell'antica Roma: gli Acta urbis*, Urbino.

Mattern-Parkes, S.P. (2003) The Defeat of Crassus and the Just War, *CW* 96.4, 387–396.

Matthaei, L. (1907) On the Classification of Roman Allies, *CQ* 1, 182–204.

Mattingly, H. (1950) Zephyritis, *AJA* 54, 26–128.

Mattingly, H.B. (1969) The Two Republican Laws of the Tabula Bembina, *JRS* 59, 129–143.

Mattingly, H.B. (1983) Rome's Earliest Relations with Byzantium, Heraclea Pontica and Callatis, in A.G. Poulter (ed.) *Ancient Bulgaria*, vol. 1, Nottingham, 239–252.

Mattingly, H.B. (1986) Scipio Aemilianus' Eastern Embassy, *CQ* 36.2, 491–495.

Matz, D. (2012) *Voices of Ancient Greece and Rome: Contemporary Accounts of Daily Life*, Santa Barbara, CA.

Mayer, E. (1961) *Römischer Staat und Staatsgedanke*, Darmstadt.

Mazzotta, M.C. (2013) L'*interregnum* a Roma, *Politica antica: Rivista di prassi e cultura politica nel mondo greco e romano* 3, 51–79.

Mederer, E. (1936) *Die Alexanderlegenden bei den älttesten Alexander Historikern* (Würzburger Studien, 8), Stuttgart.

Mehl, A. (1986) *Seleukos Nikator und sein Reich*, Studia Hellenistica 28, Louvain.

Meimaris, Y.E. et al. (1992) *Chronological Systems in Roman–Byzantine Palestine and Arabia: The Evidence of the Dated Greek Inscriptions* (Melethmata, 17), Athens–Paris.

Meineke, A. (1849) *Stephani Byzantii ethnicorum quae supersunt*, Berlin.

Meister, K. (1999) Memnon aus Herakleia 5, *DNP* 7, 1205–1206.

Mellor, R. (1975) *ΘΕΑ ΡΩΜΗ: The Worship of the Goddess Roma in the Greek World* (Hypomnemata, 42), Göttingen.

Mellor, R. (1978) The Dedications on the Capitoline Hill, *Chiron* 8, 319–330.

Mendels, D. (2004) *Memory in Jewish Pagan and Christian Societies of the Graeco-Roman World: Fragmented Memory–Comprehensive Memory–Collective Memory*, London.

Mendels, D. (2005) The Formation of an Historical Canon of the Greco-Roman Period: From the Beginnings to Josephus, in G. Lembi and J. Sievers (eds) *Josephus and Jewish History in Flavian Rome and Beyond*, Leiden, 3–19.

Mendelssohn, L. (1873) *De senati consulti Romanorum ab Josepho Antiq. XIV 8,5 relati temporibus commentatio*, Diss., Leipzig.

Mendelssohn, L. (1875) Senati Consulta Romanorum quae sunt in Josephi Antiquitatibus, *ASPL* 5, 83–288.
Mendelssohn, L. and Ritschl, F. (1875) Nochmals der römische Senatsbeschluss bei Josephus Ant. XIV, 8, 5, *Rhein. Mus.* 30, 419–435.
Meneghini, R. and Valenziani, R.S. (1996) Episodi di trasformazione del paesaggio urbano nella Roma altomedievale attraverso l'analisi di due contesti: un isolata in piazza dei cinqucento e l'area dei Fori Imperiali, *Archeologia Medievale* 23, 53–99.
Meneghini, R. and Valenziani, R.S. (2007) *I Fori Imperiali: gli scavi del Comune di Roma (1991–2007)*, Rome.
Menge, H. (2000) *Lehrbuch der lateinischen Syntax und Semantik*, Darmstadt.
Metzger, B. (1957) *An Introduction to the Apocrypha*, New York.
Meyer, E. (1922) *Caesars Monarchie und das Prinzipat des Pompejus*[3], Stuttgart.
Meyer, E. (1924) *Kleine Schriften*, Halle.
Meyer, E. (1925) *Ursprung und Anfänge des Christentums*, book 2[5], Stuttgart.
Meyer, E. (1964) *Römischer Staat und Staatgedanke*[3], Zürich–Stuttgart.
Meyer, E.A. (2004) *Legitimacy and Law in the Roman World:* Tabulae *in Roman Belief and Practice*, Cambridge.
Michaelis, J.D. (1778) *Deutsche Übersetzung des ersten Buchs der Maccabäer*, Göttingen–Leipzig.
Michel, J.H. (1980) L'extradition du général en droit romain, *Latomus* 39.3, 675–693.
Michel, O. and Bauernteind, O. (1960) *De Bello Judaico* I, Wissenschaftliche Buchgesellschaft, Darmstadt.
Michels, A.K. (1968) *The Calendar of the Roman Republic*, Princeton.
Middendorp, T. (1973) *Die Stellung Jesu Ben Siras zwischen Judentum und Hellenismus*, Leiden.
Miedema, N.R. (1996) 'Mirabilia Romae': *Untersuchungen zu ihrer Überlieferung*, Tübingen.
Milard, A.R. (1994) King Solomon's Gold Shields, in J.C. Exum and D.M. Coogan (eds) *Scripture and Other Artefacts: Essays on the Bible and Archaeology in Honor of P.J. King*, Westminster, 286–295.
Milik, J. (ed.) (1977) *Discoveries in the Judaean Desert* 6, Oxford.
Millar, F. (1984) The Political Character of the Classical Roman Republic, 200–151 B.C., *JRS* 74, 1–19.
Millar, F. (1992) *Emperor in the Roman World (31 BC–AD337)*, Cornell.
Mitchell, L.G. (1997) Φιλία, εὔνοια and Greek Interstate Relations, *Antichthon* 31, 28–44.
Mitchell, S. (2005) The Treaty between Rome and Lycia of 46 BC (MS 2070), *Papyrologica Florentina* 35, 164–259.
Mittag, P.F. (2006) *Antiochus IV Epiphanes: eine politische Biographie*, Berlin.
Moehring, H.R. (1975) The *Acta pro Judaeis* in the *Antiquities* of Flavius Josephus: A Study in Hellenistic and Modern Apologetic Historiography, in J. Neusner (ed.) *Christianity, Judaism and other Greco-Roman Cults: Studies for Morton Smith at Sixty*, vol. 3, Leiden, 133–157.
Moffat, J. (1913) 2 Maccabees, in R.H. Charles (ed.) *Apocrypha and Pseudepigrapia of the Old Testament in English*, vol. 1, Oxford, 125–154.
Momigliano, A. (1931) *Prime linee di storia della tradizione maccabaica*, Torino.
Momigliano, A. (1934) Ricerche sull'organizzazione della Guidea sotto il dominio romano (63 a.C. – 70 d. C.), *ANSP* 2, 3, 183–221, 349–396.
Momigliano, A. (1942) Camillus and Concord, *CQ* 36, 111–120.
Momigliano, A. (1961) *Claudius, the Emperor and his Achievement*[2], Cambridge.

Momigliano, A. (1975) The Second Book of Maccabees, *CP* 50, 81–88.

Momigliano, A. (1980) The Date of the First Book of Maccabees, in id. (ed.) *Sesto contributo alla storia degli studi classici e del mondo antico*, vol. 2, Rome, 561–566.

Momigliano, A. (1982) Review of Gauger's *Beiträge zur jüdischen Apologetik*, *CP* 77, 258–261.

Mommsen, Th. (1860) *Über das römische Munzwesen*, Berlin.

Mommsen, Th. (1864a) Das römische Gastrecht und die römische Clientel, in id. (ed.) *Römische Forschungen*, vol. 1, Berlin, 319–390.

Mommsen, Th. (1864b) Ueber den princeps senatus, *RhM*, 19, 455–457.

Mommsen, Th. (1868) *Römische Geschichte*, book $1^1$, Berlin.

Mommsen, Th. (1875) Der Senatsbeschluss Josephus Ant. XIV, 8, 5, *Hermes* 9, 282–291.

Mommsen, Th. (1879) *Römische Forschungen*, vols 1 and 2, Berlin.

Mommsen, Th. (1887) *Römisches Staatsrecht*, vols 1–3, Leipzig.

Mommsen, Th. (1903) *Römische Geschichte*, vol. $1^7$, Berlin.

Montgomery, J.A. (1927) *A Critical and Exegetical Commentary on the Book of Daniel* (International Critical Commentary), Edinburgh.

Mooren, L. (1979) (ed.) Antiochus IV: Epiphanes und das ptolemäische Königtum, in *Actes du XV^e^ Congrès Intern. de Papyrologie*, Brussel, 78–86.

Mora, F. (1999) *Fasti e schemi cronologici: la riorganizzione annalistica del passato remoto romano* (Historia Einzelschriften, 125), Stuttgart.

Moretti, L. (1950) Una Nuova Iscrizione da Araxa, *Riv. di Fil.* 78, 326–350.

Mørkholm, O. (1964) The Accession of Antiochus I of Syria, *ANS MN* 11, 63–76.

Mørkholm, O. (1966) *Antiochus IV of Syria* (Classica et Medievalia, Dissertationes 8), Copenhagen.

Morton, J. (2001) *The Role of the Physical Environment in Ancient Greek Seafaring*, Leiden.

Mossakowski, W. (2004/2006) Concept of Asylum (Asylum, confugium) in Ancient Rome, *Pomoerium* 5, 53–57.

Mottershead, J. (1986) *Suetonius, Claudius*, Bristol.

Moulton, R.G. (1899) *The Literary Study of the Bible*$^2$, New York.

Mouritsen, H. (2001) *Plebs and Politics in the Late Republic*, Cambridge.

Münzer, F. (1900) *RE* 4.1, s.v. Coponius (3), col. 1215.

Münzer, F. (1901) *RE* 4, s.v Coponius (3) col. 1215.

Münzer, F. (1905) Anmerkungen zur neuern Liviusepitome, *Klio* 5, 135–140.

Münzer, F. (1907) *RE* 6.2, s.v. C. Fannius Strabo C. f. C. n. (20), cols 1994–1995.

Münzer, F. (1909) *RE* 6.2, s.v. Fannius (1)–(22), cols 1986–1995.

Münzer, F. (1920) Die Fanniusfrage, *Hermes 55*, 427–442.

Münzer, F. (1923) *RE* 2A.2, s.v. Sempronius (5) and (92) col. 1361, 1441–1443.

Münzer, F. (1928a) *RE* 14.1, s.v. Mallius (4), col. 910.

Münzer, F. (1928b) *RE* 14.1, s.v. Manlius (27), cols 1159.

Münzer, F. (1938) *RE* 19.2, s.v. Pettius, col. 1381.

Münzer, F. (1949) *RE* 18.3, Papirius (35), cols 1021–1022.

Münzer, F. (1999) *Roman Aristocratic Parties and Families*, trans. T. Ridley, Baltimore.

Muraoka, T. (1998) *Hebrew/Aramaic Index to the Septuagint*, Grand Rapids, MI.

Nagy, V.K. (2010) Die Beziehung der Makkabäer zu fremden Nationen: die Bündnisse mit Rome und Sparta, in G.G. Xeravits and J. Dušek (eds) *The Stranger in Ancient and Mediaeval Jewish Tradition*, Rome, 107–117.

Neatby, L.H. (1950) Romano-Egyptian Relations during the Third Century B.C., *TAPA* 81, 89–98.

Nelis, J.T. (1972) *I Makkabeeën*. Da Boeken van het oede Testaement, Deel VI/Boek 1A, Roermond.

Nenci, G. (1953) *Pirro: aspirazioni egemoniche ed equilibrio mediterraneo*, Torino.

Nenci, G. (1958) L'ambasceria romana di Alessandro, in id. (ed.) *Introduzione alle Guerre persiane e altri saggi di storia antica*, Pisa, 261–281.

Neumann, K.J. (1894) *RE* 1.2, s.v. *amicus* (3), cols 1831–1833, Stuttgart.

Neusner, J. (1965) *A History of the Jews in Babylonia*, 5 vols, Leiden.

Neusner, J. (1971) *The Rabbinic Traditions about the Pharisees before 70*, vol. 1, *The Masters*, Leiden.

Newmann, A.A. (1953) *Josippon and the Apocrypha: Landmarks and Goals*, Philadelphia.

Nicolet, C. (1977) *Rome et la Conquête du Monde Méditerraneén, vol. 1. Les Structures de l'Italie romaine*, Nouvelle Clio 008, Paris.

Nicolet, C. (1994) Documents fiscaux et géographie dans la Rome ancienne, in *La mémoire perdue: à la recherche des aarchives oubliées, publiques et privées, de la Rome antique*, Paris, 149–172.

Nicols, J. (1978) *Vespasian and the* Partes Flavianae, Wiesbaden.

Niese, B. (1892) *Flavii Iosephi opera: Antiquitates Iudaicae*, vol. 3, Berlin.

Niese, B. (1893) Zur Chronologie des Josephus, *Hermes* 28, 194–229.

Niese, B. (1899) *Geschichte der griechischen und makedonischen Staaten seit der Schlacht bei Chaeronea*, vol. 2. *Vom Jahre 281 v. Chr. bis zur Begründung der römischen Osten 188 v. Chr.*, Gotha.

Niese, B. (1900) Kritik der beiden Makkabäerbücher, *Hermes* 35, 268–307, 453–527.

Niese, B. (1903) *Geschichte der griechischen und makedonischen Staaten seit der Schlacht bei Chaeronea*, Gotha.

Niese, B. (1906) Eine Urkunde aus der Makkabaerzeit, in C. Bezold (ed.) *Orientalische Studien Th. Noldeke um siebzigsten Geburststag gewidmet*, book 2, Giessen, 817–829.

Niese, B. (1914) Josephus, in J. Hastings (ed.) *Encyclopaedia of Religion and Ethics*, vol. 7, Edinburgh 569–579.

Nikonorov, V.P. (1998) Apollodorus of Artemita and the Date of his *Parthica* Revisited, in E. Dąbrowa (ed.) *Ancient Iran and the Mediterranean World* (Electrum: Studies in Ancient History, 2), Krakow, 107–122.

Nissen, H. (1863) *Kritische Untersuchungen über die Quellen der vierten und fünften Dekade des Livius*, Berlin.

Nissen, H. (1870) Der Caudinische Friede, *Rh.Mus.* 25, 1–65.

Nodet, E. (1999) *Baptême et résurrection: le témoignage de Josèphe*, Paris.

Nodet, E. (2005) *La crise maccabéene: historiographies juivre et traditions bibliques*, Paris.

Norden, E. (1901) Vergils *Aeneid* im Lichte ihrer Zeit, *Neue Jahrb. für das kl. Altert.* 7, 256–260.

Norden, E. (1959) *Die germanische Urgeschichte in Tacitus Germania*, Stuttgart.

Nörr, D. (1969) *Imperium und Polis in der hohen Prinzipatszeit* (Münchener Beiträge zur Papyrusforschung und antiken Rechtsgeshichte, 50), Munich.

Nörr, D. (1989) *Aspekte des römischen Völkerrechts: die Bronzetafel von Alcántara* (Bayerische Akademie der Wissenschaften philosophisch–historisch Klasse N.F. Heft 101), Munich.

Nuffelen, P. van (2002) Name Game: Hellenistic Historians and Royal Epithets, in id. (ed.) *Faces of Hellenism: Studies in the History of the Eastern Mediterranean (4th century B.C.–5th century A.D.)*, Leuven–Paris–Walpole, MA, 93–111.

Nussbaum, A. (1954) *A Concise History of the Law of Nations*, New York.

Oesterley, W.O.E. (1913) The First Book of Maccabees, in R.H. Charles (ed.) *The Apocrypha and Pseudepigrapha of the Old Testament in English*, vol. 1, Oxford, 67–123.
Oesterley, W.O.E. (1915) *The Books of the Apocrypha*, London.
Ogilvie, R.M. (1965) *A Commentary on Livy Books 1–5*, Oxford.
Olbrycht, M.J. (2009) Mithridates VI Eupator and Iran, in J.M. Hœjte (ed.) *Mithridates VI Eupator and the Pontic Kingdom*, Aarhus, 163–190.
Olmstead, A.T. (1942) Could an Aramaic Gospel be Written?, *JNES* 1, 41–75.
Ong, W. (1982) *Orality and Literacy: The Technologizing of the Word*, London–New York.
Oost, S.I. (1953) The Roman Calendar in the Year of Pydna (168 B.C.), *CP* 48, 217–230.
Oost, S.I. (1954) *Roman Policy in Epirus and Acarnania in the Age of the Conquest of Greece* (Arnold Foundations Series, n.s. v. 004), Dallas.
Orlin, E.M. (2002) Foreign Cults in Republican Rome: Rethinking the Pomerial Rule, *MAAR* 47, 1–18.
Ormond, H.A. (1922) The Campaigns of Servilius Isauricus against the Pirates, *JRS* 12, 35–56.
Ormerod, H.A. (1924) *Piracy in the Ancient World*, Baltimore.
Orrieux, C. (1989) La 'parente' entre Juifs et Spartiates, in R. Lonis (ed.) *L'étranger dans le monde grec*, Nancy, 169–191.
Östenberg, I. (2009) *Staging the World: Spoils, Captives and Representations in the Roman Triumphal Procession*, Oxford.
Osterloh, K.L. (2008) Judea, Rome and the Hellenistic Oikoumene, in E. Iricinschi et al. (eds) *Heresy and Identity in Late Antiiquity*, Tübingen, 168–206.
Otto, W. (1934) Zur Geschichte der Zeit des 6. Ptolemäers, *Abh-München.* 11, 1–147.
Packard, D.W. (1968) *A Concordance to Livy*, 4 vols, Cambridge MA.
Pagola Torregaray, E. (2006) Los espacios de la diplomacia en la Roma republicana, *Caesarodunum* 40, 223–258.
Pais, E. (1920) *Storia critica di Roma durante i primi cinque secoli*, vol. 4, Rome.
Palmer, R.E. (1970) *The Archaic Community of the Romans*, Cambridge.
Paltiel, E. (1982) Antiochus Epiphanes and Roman Politics, *Latomus*, 41, 229–254.
Panessa, G. (1981) Contributo epigrafico da Demetriade alla conoscenza dei rapporti magneto-tessalici, in S. Castaldi (ed.) *Studi sui rapporti interstatali nel mondo antico*, Pisa, 239–249.
Panessa, G. (1999) Philiai. *L' amicizia nelle relazioni interstatali dei Greci. I. Dalle origini alla fine della guerra del peloponneso*, Pisa.
Paradisi, B. (1947) L''amicitia' internationale nell'alto medio evo, in A. Gemelli (ed.) *Scritti in onore di Contardo Ferrini: pubblicati in occasione della sua beatificazione*, vol. 1, Pubblicazione dell'Università Cattolica del S. Cuore, Milan, 178–225.
Paradisi, B. (1951) L'amitié internationale: les phases critiques de son ancienne histoire, *Recueil des Cours, Academie de droit international*, 78, 329–378.
Paradisi, B. (1954) Dai foedera iniqua alla crisobulle bizantine, *SDHI* 20, 5f.
Parente, F. (1994) Onias III's Death and the Founding of the Temple of Leontopolis, in F. Parente and J. Sievers (eds) *Josephus and the History of the Greco-Roman Period: Essays in Memory of Morton Smith* (Studia Post-Biblica, 41), Leiden, 69–98.
Parente, F. (1995) Le témoinage de Théodore de Mopsueste sur le sort d'Onias III et la fondation du temple de Léontopolis, *REJ* 4, 429–436.
Parker, J.E. (1997) Report from Rome: The Imperial Fora, a Retrospective, *American Journal of Archaeology* 101, 307–30.

Parker, R.A. and Dubberstein, R.A. (1956) *Babylonian Chronology 626 B.C. – A.D. 75*, Providence.

Parunak, H.V.D. (1979) *Structural Studies in Ezekiel*, Diss., Ann Arbor MI.

Passerini, A. (1935a) Il Testo del *foedus* di Roma con Callatis, *Athenaeum* n.s. 13, 57–72.

Passerini, A. (1935b) Roma e l'Egitto durante la terza guerra macedonica, *Athenaeum* 13, 317–342.

Paton, W.R. and Hicks, E.L. (1891) *The Inscriptions of Cos*, Oxford, repr. 1990, Hildesheim.

Patterson, L.L. (2010) *Kinship Myth in Ancient Greece*, Austin TX.

Pearson, C.L. (1960) *The Lost Histories of Alexander the Great*, Oxford.

Pearson, L. (1962) Pliny, 'Nat. Hist' III.57, *Mnemosyne* 15.1, 46–47.

Peremans, W. and van't Dack, E. (1972) Sur les rapports de Rome avec les Lagides, *ANRW* 1.1, 610–667.

Perrin, B. (1968) *Plutarch's Lives*, vol. 7, Cambridge, MA–London.

Petzold, K.-E. (1972) Die beiden ersten römisch–karthagischen Verträge und das *Foedus Cassianum*, *ANRW* 1.2, 364–414.

Petzold, K.-E. (1992) Griechischer Einfluss auf die Anfänge römischer Ostpolitik, *Historia* 41.2, 205–245.

Petzold, K.-E. (1999) Die Freiheit der Griechen und die Politik der *nova sapientia*, *Historia* 48, 61–93.

Petrochilos, N. (1974) *Roman Attitudes to the Greeks*, Athens.

Phillipson, C. (1911) *The International Law and Custom of Ancient Greece and Rome*, vol. 2, London.

Piganiol, A. (1937) Histoire romaine (1930–1935), *Rev. Hist.* 181, 40–98.

Piganiol, A. (1950) Venire in Fidem, *Revue Internationale des droits de l'antiquité* 5, 339–347.

Pina Polo, F. (2011) *The Consul at Rome: The Civil Functions of the Consuls in the Roman Republic*, Cambridge–New York.

Platner, S.B. and Ashby, T. (1929) *A Topographical Dictionary of Ancient Rome*, London.

Poddighe, E. (2013) 'Neutrality', in R.S. Bagnall et al. (eds) *The Encyclopedia of Ancient History*, vol. 9, Oxford, 4760–4761.

Polay, E. (1964) *Differenzierung der Gesellschaftsnormen im antiken Rom*, Budapest.

Porten, B. (1967) The Structure and Theme of the Solomon Narrative (I Kings 3–11), *HUCA*, 93–128.

Porten, B. (1983) The Address Formulae in Aramaic Letters: A New Collation of Cowley 17, *Revue Biblique* 90, 396–415.

Portier-Young, A. (2010) Languages of Identity and Obligation: Daniel as a Bilingual Book, *VT* 60, 98–115.

Posner, E. (1972) *Archives in the Ancient World*, Cambridge, MA.

Powell, T.G.E. (1958) *The Celts* (Ancient Peoples and Places, 006), New York.

Power, T. (2010) Pliny, Letters 5.10 and the Literary Career of Suetonius, *JRS* 100, 140–162.

Prandi, L. (1996) *Fortuna e realtà dell'opera di Clitarcho*, Stuttgart.

Preaux, C. (1931) *L'economie royale des Lagides*, Brussels.

Preiser, W. (1963) *Die Völkerrechtsgeschichte, ihre Aufgaben und ihre Methode*, Frankfurt am Main.

Premerstein, A. von (1924) *RE* 12, s. v. Legatus, cols 1133–1149.

Preminger, A. and Greenstein, E.L. (eds) (1986) *The Hebrew Bible in Literary Criticism*, New York.

Price, M.J. (1991) *The Coinage in the Name of Alexander the Great and Philip Arrhidaeus*, vol. 1, Zurich–London.

Primo, A. (2009) *La storiografia sui Seleucidi*, Pisa.

Pucci, M. (1981) An Unknown Source on a Possible Treaty between Hyrcanus I and the Parthians, *Zion* 46.4, 331–338 [Hebrew].

Pucci, M. (1982) On the Tendentiousness of Josephus' Historical Writing, in U. Rappaport (ed.) *Josephus Flavius: Historian of Eretz-Israel in the Hellenistic Period*, Jerusalem, 117–129 [Hebrew].

Pucci, M. (1983) Jewish–Parthian Relations in Josephus, in L.I. Levine (ed.) *The Jerusalem Cathedra: Studies in the History, Archaeology, Geography and Ethnography of the Land of Israel*, vol. 3, Jerusalem–Detroit, 13–25.

Pucci Ben Zeev, M. (1994) Greek Documents from Republican Times in the *Antiquities:* What was Josephus' Source?, *SCI* 13, 46–59.

Pucci Ben Zeev, M. (1996) Polybius, Josephus and the Capitol in Rome, *JSJ* 27, 21–30.

Pucci Ben Zeev, M. (1998) *Jewish Rights in the Roman World: The Greek and Roman Documents Quoted by Josephus Flavius*, Tübingen.

Pulci Doria, L.B. (1975) Recenti studi su Pompeo Trogo, *PP* 30, 468–477.

Purcell, N. (2013) On the Significance of East and West in Today's 'Hellenistic' History: Reflections on Symmetrical Worlds, Reflecting through World Symmetries, in J.R.W. Prag and J.C. Quinn (eds) *The Hellenistic West: Rethinking the Ancient Mediterranean*, Cambridge, 367–390.

Qimron, E. (1992) Observations on the History of Early Hebrew (1000 B.C.E.–200 C.E.) in the Light of the Dead Sea Documents, in D. Dimant and U. Rappaport (eds) *The Dead Sea Scrolls: Forty Years of Research*, Leiden–New York–Köln, 349–361.

Rabin, C. (1976) Hebrew and Aramaic in the First Century, in S. Safrai and M. Stern (eds) *The Jewish People in the First Century*, vol. 1, pt 2, 1007–1039.

Radicke, J. (1999) *Imperial and Undated Authors: A Biography*, Leiden.

Raggi, A. (2001) Senatus consultum de Asclepiade Clazomenio sociisque, *ZPE* 135, 73–116.

Rajak, T. (1984a) *Josephus: The Historian and his Society*, Philadelphia.

Rajak, T. (1984b) Was There a Roman Charter for the Jews?, *JRS* 74, 107–123.

Rajak, T. (1986) The Sense of History in Jewish Intertestamental Writing, in J. Moor et al. (eds) *Crises and Perspectives*, Leiden, 124–145.

Rajak, T. (2002) Roman Intervention in a Seleucid Siege of Jerusalem? in *The Jewish Dialogue with Greece and Rome; Studies in Cultural and Social Interaction*, Leiden, 65–81.

Rajak, T. (2007) Document and Rhetoric in Josephus: Revisiting the 'Charter' for the Jews, in S.J.S. Cohen and J.J. Schwartz (eds) *Studies in Josephus and the Varieties of Ancient Judaism*, Leiden–Boston, 177–189.

Ramsey, G. (2013) Review: A.M. Eckstein, *Rome Enters the Greek East*, 2012 (re-issue), *BMCR* (online), July 2013.

Rappaport, U. (1968) La Judée et Rome pendant le regne d'Alexandre Jannée, *REJ* 127, 329–345.

Rappaport, U. (1989) The Jews between the Romans and the Parthians, in D.H. French and C.S. Lightfoot (eds) *The Eastern Frontier of the Roman Empire*, Proceedings of a colloquium held in Ankara in Sept. 1988 (BAR International Series, 553), Oxford, 373–381.

Rappaport, U. (1992) Apocalyptic Vision and Preservation of Historical Memory, *JSJ* 23, 217–226.

Rappaport, U. (1993) The Hellenistic World as Seen by the Book of Daniel, in G. Sed-Rajna (ed.) *Rashi: 1040–1900: Hommage à Ephraim E. Urbach*, Paris, 71–79.

Rappaport, U. (1995) The Extradition Clause in I Maccabees, XV, 21, in K. van Lerberghe and A. Schoors (eds) *Immigration and Emigration within the Ancient Near East: Festschrift E. Lipinski* (Orientalia Lovaniensia Analecta, 65) Leuven, 272–283.

Rappaport, U. (1996) A Note on the Use of the Bible in 1 Maccabees, in M.E. Stone and E.G. Chazan (eds) *Biblical Perspectives: Early Use and Interpretation of the Bible in the Light of the Dead Sea Scrolls* (Proceedings of the First International Symposium of the Orion Center for the Study of the Dead Sea Scrolls and Associated Literature), Leiden, 175–179.

Rappaport, U. (2001) I Maccabees, in J. Barton and J. Muddiman (eds) *The Oxford Bible Commentary*, Oxford–New York, 711–734.

Rappaport, U. (2004) *The First Book of Maccabees: Introduction, Hebrew Translation and Commentary*, Jerusalem [Hebrew].

Rappaport, U. (2007) Lysias: An Outstanding Politician, in S.J.D. Cohen and J.J. Schwartz (eds) *Studies in Josephus and the Varieties of Ancient Judaism*, Leiden–Boston, 169–175.

Raschke, W.J. (1979) The Chronology of the Early Books of Lucilius, *JRS* 69, 78–89.

Raschke, W.J. (1987) Arma pro amico: Lucilian Satire at the Crisis of the Roman Republic, *Hermes* 115, 299–318.

Raschke, W.J. (1990) The Virtue of Lucilius, *Latomus* 4.9, 352–369.

Rauh, N.K. (2003) *Merchants, Sailors and Pirates in the Roman World*, Stroud.

Rawlings, H.R. (1976) Antiochus the Great and Rhodes, 197–191 B.C., *AJAH*, 1, 2–28.

Rawson, E. (1975) Caesar's Heritage: Hellenistic Kings and their Roman Equals, *JRS* 65, 148–159.

Ray, J.D. (1976) *Archive of Ḥor*, London.

Raynolds, J. (1611) *Censura librorum apocryphorum veteris testamenti, adversum pontifios, imprimis Robertum Bellarminum: praelectionibus ducentis et quinquaginta posthumis in academia Oxoniensi tractata*, Oppenheim.

Reger, G. (1999) The Relations between Rhodes and Caria from 246 to 167 B.C., in V. Gabrielsen et al. (eds) *Hellenistic Rhodes: Politics, Culture and Society* (Studies in Hellenistic Civilization, 9), Aarhus, 76–97.

Regev, E. (2013) *The Hasmoneans: Ideology, Archaeology, Identity*, Göttingen.

Reiter, W. (1988) *Aemilius Paullus, Conqueror of Greece*, London.

Reinach, T. (1888) Villes méconnues, *REG* 1, 333–335.

Reinach, T. (1899) Antiochus Cyzicene et les Juifs, *REJ* 38, 161–171.

Reinach, A.-J. (1911) Inscriptions d'Itanos, *REG* 24, 377–425.

Reinach, Th. (1895) *Mithridates Eupator: Roi de Pont*$^2$, Bibliothèque d'archéologie, d'art et d'histoire ancienne, Paris.

Reinach, Th. (1899) Antiochus Cyzicène et les Juifs, *REJ* 38, 161–171.

Reinach, Th. (1902) *L'histoire des monnaies: esssai de numismatique ancienne*, Paris.

Reiner, J. (1967) The English Yosippon, *JQR* 58.2, 126–142.

Reymond, E.D. (2014) *Qumran Hebrew: An Overview of Orthography, Phonology, and Morphology*, Atlanta.

Reynolds, J. (1982) *Aphrodisias and Rome* (JRS Monograph), London.

Reynolds, J.M. and Tannenbaum, R. (1987) *Jews and God-Fearers at Aphrodisias: Greek Inscriptions with Commentary* (PCPhS Suppl. 12), Cambridge.

Ricci, C. (1911) Per l'isolamento e la redenzione dei resti dei Fori Imperiale, *Bollettino d'Arte* 5.12, 445–55.

Ricci, C. (1926) Foro di Augusto: La Scala Mortuorum, *Capitolium* 2, 4–9.

Ricci, C. (1930) Il Foro d'Augusto e la casa dei cavalieri di Rodi, *Capitolium* 6, 157–189.

Rich, J. R. (1984) Roman Aims in the First Macedonian War, *PCPS* 21, 126–180.

Rich, J.R. (1989) Patronage and Interstate Relations, in A. Wallace-Hadrill (ed.) *Patronage in Ancient Society*, London, 117–135.

Rich, J. R. (2011) The *Fetiales* and Roman International Relations, in J.H. Richardson and F. Santangelo (eds) *Priests and State in the Roman World*, Stuttgart, 187–242.

Rich, J. R. (2015) Appian, Polybius and the Romans' War with Antiochus the Great: A Study in Appian's Sources and Methods, in K. Welch (ed.) *Appian's Roman History: Empire and Civil War*, Swansea, 65–123.

Rich, J.W. (1976) *Declaring War in the Roman Republic in the Period of Transmarine Expansion* (Collection Latomus, 149), Brussels.

Richardson, J. (1992) Review: D. Nörr's *Aspekte des römischen Völkerrechts: die Bronzetafel von Alcántara*, *JRS* 82, 241.

Richter, H.E. (1938) Übersetzen und Übersetzungen in der römischen Literatur, Diss., Erlangen.

Rife, J.M. (1933) The Mechanics of Translation Greek, *JBL* 52, 244–252.

Rigsby, K.J. (1996) *Asylia: Territorial Inviolability in the Hellenistic World*, Berkeley–Los Angeles–London.

Ritschl, F. (1873) Eine Berichtigung der republicanischen Consularfasten, *Rh. Mus.* n.s. 28, 586–614.

Ritschl, F. (1875) Gesammtbearbeitung der josephinischen Urkunden, 5, 89ff.

Ritter, H.-W. (1965) *Diadem und Königsherrschaft: Untersuchungen zu Zeremonien und Rechtsgrundlagen des Herrschaftsantritts bei den Persen, bei Alexander dem Groben und im Hellenismus*, Munich–Berlin.

Rizzo, F.P. (1974) *La consanguinitas degli Iliensi*, in *Studi ellenistico-romani*, Palermo, 83–88.

Robert, C. (1900) *RE* 12, s.v. Coponius (1), col. 1214.

Robert, J. and Robert, L. (1954) *Le Carie: histoire et geographie historique avec recueil des inscriptions antiques* (Libraire d'Amerique et d'Orient), vol. 2, Paris.

Robert, J. and Robert, L. (1984) Bulletin épigraphique, *REG* 97, 461.

Robert, L. (1940) *Hellenica: recueil d'épigraphie, de numismatique et d'antiquités grecques*, Limoges.

Robert, L. (1969) *Opera minora selecta*, vol. 1, Amsterdam.

Roberto, U. (2003) Diplomazia greca ed ἐλευθερία dei Macccabei: Demetrio I, Bacchide e Gionata, *Mediterraneo Antico* 6, 795–824.

Robinson, O.F. (1997) *The Sources of Roman Law: Problems and Methods for Ancient Historians*, London–New York.

Rochette, B. (1996) *Fides Interpretes* La Traduction orale à Rome, *Anc. Soc.* 27, 73–89.

Rochette, B. (1997) *Le Latin dans le monde grec* (Coll. Latomus, 233), Bruxelles.

Roller, D.W. (2013) *Through the Pillars of Herakles: The Greco-Roman Exploration of the Atlantic*, London–New York.

Rongy, H. (1938–1939) L'Historicité du premier livre des Macchabées, *Revue Ecclésiastique de Liège* 30, 230–244.

Rood, T. (1998) Thucydides and his Predecessors, at http://www.dur.ac.uk/Classics/histos/1998/rood.html (accessed 26 August 2016).

Ros, J.G.A. (1940) *Studie van het Bijbelgrieksch van Hugo Grotius to Adolf Deissmann*, Nijmegen.

Rosenne, S. (1999) The Influence of Judaism on the Development of International Law: An Assessment, in M.V. Janis et al. (eds) *Religion and International Law*, Leiden, 63–94.

Rosenstein, N. (1986) *Imperatores Victi*: The Case of C. Hostilius Mancinus, *Class. Ant.* 5, 230–252.

Rossi, G.B. (1888) *Inscriptiones Christianae Urbis Romae*, vol. 2, pt 1, Rome.
Rostovtzeff, M.I. (1941) *The Social and Economic History of the Hellenistic World*, 2 vols, Oxford.
Roth, O. (1914) *Rom und die Hasmonäer, Untersuchungen zu den jüdisch–römischen Urkunden im ersten Makkabäerbuche und in Josephus' Jüdischen Altertumern XIV* (Beiträge zur Wissenschaft von Alten Testament, 17), Leipzig.
Rubin, D.C. (1995) *Memory in Oral Traditions: The Cognitive Psychology of Epic, Ballads, and Counting-out Rhymes*, New York–Oxford.
Rüpke, J. (2008) *Fasti sacerdotum*, Oxford–New York.
Rushforth, G. McN. (1919) Magister Gregorius De Mirabilibus Urbis Romae: A New Description of Rome in the Twelfth Century, *JRS* 9, 14–48.
Russo, F. (2014) The Function of the Trojan Myth in Early Roman Expansionism in Greece and Asia Minor, in V. Cojocaru et al. (eds) *Interconnectivity in the Mediterranean and Pontic World during the Hellenistic and Roman Periods*, Cluj–Napoca, 581–602.
Rutledge, S. (2012) *Ancient Rome as a Museum: Power, Identity, and the Culture of Collecting*, Oxford.
Ryan, F.X. (1998) *Rank and Participation in the Republican Senate*, Stuttgart.
Saastamoinen, T. (2006) The Use of History in Late Medieval Guidebooks to Rome (Paper to the XIV International Economic History Congress, Helsinki, 21 August), 1–8, at helsinki.fi/iehc2006/papers2/saastamoinen.pdf (accessed 26 August 2016).
Sacks, K.S. (1994) Diodorus and His Sources: Conformity and Creativity, in S. Hornblower (ed.) *Greek Historiography*, Oxford, 213–232.
Sáenz-Badillos, A. (1993) *A History of the Hebrew Language*, trans. J. Elwolde, Cambridge.
Safrai, S. et al. (1987) *The Jewish People in the First Century: Historical Geography, Political History, Social, Cultural and Religious Life and Institutions*, 2 vols, Assen.
Saint-Denis, E. de (1947) Mare Clausum, *REL* 25, 196–214.
Salvatorelli, L. (1938) *Storia d'Italia*, vol. 3. Milan.
Samuel, A.E. (1972) *Greek and Roman Chronology: Calendars and Years in Classical Antiquity*, Munich.
Sands, P.C. (1908) *The Client Princes of the Roman Empire under the Republic*, Cambridge.
Santangelo, F. (2007) *Sulla, the Elites and Empire: A Study of Roman Policies in Italy and the Greek East*, Leiden.
Saulnier, C. (1981) Lois romaines sur les Juifs selon Flavius Josèphe, *RB* 88, 161–198.
Saulnier, C. (1994) La Cité hellénistique de Jérusalem à l'époque du grand prêtre Jason, *Transeuphratène*, 7, 83–92.
Saumagne, C. (1927) Sur la loi agraire de 111, *Rev. Phil.* 53, 50–80.
Savalli-Lestrade, I. (1998) Des 'amis' des rois aux 'amis' des Romains: amité et engagement politique dans les cités grecques à l'époque hellénistique (III$^{e}$—I$^{er}$ s. av. J.-C.), *RPh* 72, 65–86.
Scafuro, A.C. (1987) Prusias II of Bithynia and Third Party Arbitration, *Historia* 36, 28–37.
Scaliger, J.-J. (1605) *Elenchus Trihaeresii Nicolai Serarii*, Franeker.
Schachermeyr, F. (1949) *Alexander der Grosse*, Graz–Salzburg–Wien.
Schäfer, P. (2003) *The History of the Jews in the Greco-Roman World*, rev. edn, London–New York.
Schalit, A. (1933) When Did Josephus Write His *Autobiography*?, *Zion* 5, 174–187 [Hebrew].
Schanz, M. and Hosius, C. (1935) *Geschichte der römischen Literatur bis zum Gesetzgebungswerk des Kaisers Justinian* (Handbuch der Altertumswissenschaft, 8,2) vol. 2, Munich.

Schaumberger, J. (1955) Die neue Seleukiden-Liste BM 35603 und die Makkabäische Chronologie, *Biblica* 36, 423–435.

Scheid, J. (2007) Sacrifices for Gods and Ancestors, in J. Rüpke (ed.) *A Companion to Roman Religion*, Oxford, 263–271.

Schiff, A. (1905) *RE* 5.2, s.v. Eleusis (4), cols 2339–2342.

Schlatter, A. (1891) *Jason von Kyrene: ein Beitrag zu seiner Wiederherstellung* (FS der Theologischen Fakultät zu Greifswald zu Ehren der Fünfundzwanzigjährigen Jubelfeier ihres Seniors), Munich.

Schmidt, O.E. (1983) *Der Briefwechsel des M. Tullius Cicero von seinem Prokonsulat in Cilicien bis zu Caesars Ermordung*, Leipzig.

Schmitt, H.H. (1957) *Rom und Rhodos: Geschichte ihrer politischen Beziehungen seit der ersten Beruhrung bis zum Aufgehen des Inselstaater im römischen Weltreich* (Münchener Beiträge zur Papyrusforschung und antiken Rechtsgeschichte Heft 040), Munich.

Schmitt, H.H. (1964) *Untersuchunngen zur Geschichte Antiochos' der Grossen und seiner Zeit*,Wiesbaden.

Schmitt, H.H. (1969) *Die Staatsverträge des Altertums Bd. 3: die Verträge der griechisch–römischen Welt von 338–200 v. Chr.*, Munich.

Schmitt, H.H. (1988) Forme della vita interstatale nell'antichità, *Storica Critica* 25, 529–546.

Schoeffer, V. von (1900) *RE* 12, s.v. Coponius (10), col. 1216.

Schoesinger, M. (1901–1906) s.v. Joseph Ben Gorion, *The Jewish Encyclopedia*, 7.259 –260.

Schuler, C. (2007) Ein Vertrag zwischen Rom und den Lykien, in id. (ed.) *Griechische Epigraphik in Lykien*, Vienna, 51–79.

Schüller S. (1956) Some Problems Connected with the Supposed Common Ancestry of Jews and Spartans and Their Relations during the Last Three Centuries B.C., *JSS* 1, 257–268.

Schultze, J. (1862) *Quaestiones Lydianae*, Greifswald.

Schunck, K.-D. (1980) I. Makkabäerbuch *Historische und legendarische Erzählungen*, JSHRZ, bk 1, Gütersloh.

Schürer, E. (1909) *Geschichte des jüdischen Volkes im zeitalter Jesu Christu*[4], vol. 3, Leipzig.

Schürer, E. (1973–1987) *The History of the Jewish People in the Age of Jesus Christ (175 B.C. – A.D. 135)*, 3 vols, rev. edn, eds G. Vermes et al., Edinburgh.

Schwartz, D.R. (1982) Apollonius, son of Menestheus: Whose Ambassador?, *AJAH* 7, 45–52.

Schwartz, D.R. (1983) Josephus and Nicolaus on the Pharisees, *JSJ* 14.2, 157–171.

Schwartz, D.R. (1990) On Drama and Authenticity in Philo and Josephus, *SCI* 10, 113–129.

Schwartz, D.R. (1993) Scipio's Embassy and Simon's Ambassadors (I Maccabees 15), *SCI* 12, 114–126.

Schwartz, D.R. (2002) Rome and the Jews: Josephus on 'Freedom' and 'Autonomy', in A.K. Bowman et al. (eds) *Representations of Empire: Rome and the Mediterranean World* (Proceedings of the British Academy, 114), Oxford, 65–81.

Schwartz, D.R. (2008) *2 Maccabees*, Berlin.

Schwartz, E. (1903) *RE* 5.1, s.v. Diodorus (38), Diodorus von Agyrion, 689–690.

Schwartz, S. (1995) Language, Power and Identity in Ancient Palestine, *Past and Present* 148, 3–47.

Schwartz, S. (2005) A God of Reciprocity: Torah and Social Relations in an Ancient Mediterranean Society, in J.-J. Aubert and Z. Várhelyi (eds) *A Tall Order: Writing the Social History of the Ancient World*, Munich–Leipzig, 3–36.

Schwartz, S. (2009) *Were the Jews a Mediterranean Society? Reciprocity and Solidity in Ancient Judaism*, Princeton.
Schwegler, A. (1870) *Römische Geschichte*, vol. 2, Berlin.
Scramuzza, V.M. (1971) *The Emperor Claudius* (Studia Historia, 93), Rome.
Scullard, H.H. (1970) *Scipio Africanus: Soldier and Politician*, London.
Seager, R. (1979) *Pompey: A Political Biography*, Oxford.
Seel, O. (1972a) *Die Praefatio des Pompeius Trogus*, Erlanger Forschungen R.A., vol. 3, Erlangen.
Seel, O. (1972b) *Eine römische Weltgeschichte: Studien zum Text der Epitome des Iustinus und zur Historik des Pompeius Trogus*, Nürnberg.
Seel, O. (1982) Pompeius Trogus und das Problem der Universalgeschichte, *ANRW* 2.30.2, 1363–1423.
Seeman, C. (2013) *Rome and Judea in Transition: Hasmonean Relations with the Roman Republic and the Evolution of the High Priesthood*, New York–Washington.
Segre, M. (1993) *Iscrizioni di Cos*, vol. 1, Monografie della Scuola archaeologica di Atene e delle missioni Italiane in oriente, Rome.
Sérandour, A. (2000) Hébreu et araméen dans la bible, *REJ* 159.3–4, 345–355.
Sharon, N. (2010) The Title *Ethnarch* in Second Temple Judea, *JSJ* 41, 472–493.
Shatzman, I. (1992) The Hasmoneans in Greco-Roman Historiography, *Zion* 57, 5–64 [Hebrew].
Shatzman, I. (1999) The Integration of Judaea into the Roman Empire, *SCI* 18, 49–84.
Shatzman, I. (2002) Aspects of Violence and Cruelty at Rome, *Historia* 9, 23–94 [Hebrew].
Shatzman, I. (2012) The Expansionist Policy of John Hyrcanus and His Relations with Rome, in G. Urso (ed.) *Iudaea Socia–Iudaea Capta*, Atti del convegno internazionale Cividale del Friuli, 22–24 settembre, Pisa, 29–77.
Shaw, B.D. (1990) Bandit Highlands and Lowland Peace: The Mountains of Isauria-Cilicia, *J. of Econ. and Social History of the Orient* 33.2, 199–233.
Sheldon, R.M. (2010) *Rome's Wars in Parthia: Blood in the Sand*, London–Portland, OR.
Sherk, R.K. (1965) *Senatus Consultum de Tabenis*, *GRBS* 6, 295–300.
Sherk, R.K. (1969) *Roman Documents from the Greek East*, Senatus consulta *and* Epistulae *to the age of Augustus*, Baltimore.
Sherk, R.K. (1984) *Rome and the Greek East to the Death of Augustus*, Cambridge.
Sherwin-White, A.N. (1973a) *The Roman Citizenship*$^2$, Oxford.
Sherwin-White, A.N. (1973b) The Tabula of Banasa and the Constitutio Antoniniana, *JRS* 63, 86–98.
Sherwin-White, A.N. (1976) Rome, Pamphylia and Cilicia, 133–70 BCE, *JRS* 66, 1–14.
Sherwin-White, A.N. (1977) Roman Involvement in Anatolia, 167–188 BC, *JRS* 67, 62–75.
Sherwin-White, A.N. (1984) *Roman Foreign Policy in the East 168 B.C. to A.D. 1*, London.
Sherwin-White, S. (1976) A Note on Three Coin Inscriptions, *ZPE* 21.2, 183–188.
Sherwin-White, S. (1978) *Ancient Cos: An Historical Study from the Dorian Setlement to the Imperial Period* (Hypomnemata: Untersuchungen zur antike und zu ihrem nachleben Heft 51), Göttingen.
Sherwin-White, S. and Kuhrt, A. (1993) *From Samarkhand to Sardis: A New Approach to the Seleucid Empire*, London.
Sievers, J. (1990) *The Hasmoneans and their Supporters: From Mattathias to the Death of John Hyrcanus I* (SFSHJ, 6), Atlanta.
Sievers, J. (2001a) Josephus, First Maccabees, Sparta, the Three *haireseis* – and Cicero, *JSJ* 32, 241–251.

Sievers, J. (2001b) *Synopsis of the Greek Sources for the Hasmonean Period: 1–2 Maccabees and Josephus* (War I and Antiquities, 12–14), Rome.

Sievers, J. (2005) What's in a Name? Antiochus in Josephus' 'Bellum Judaicum', *JJS* 56.1, 34–47.

Silvagni, A. (1921) Nuovo ordimamento delle sillogi epigrafiche di Roma anteriori al secolo XI, *Dissertazioni della Pontificia Accademia romana di archeologia*, ser. 2, 15, 181–229.

Silving, H. (1959) The Oath: I, *The Yale Law Journal* 68, 1329–1390.

Sisti-Zambrini, F. (ed.) (2004) Arriano, *Anabasi di Alessandro*, Milan.

Skeat, T.C. (1969) *The Reigns of the Ptolemies*², Munich.

Skidmore, C. (1996) *Practical Ethics for Roman Gentlemen: The Work of Valerius Maximus*, Exeter.

Small, J.P. (1997) *Wax Tablets of the Mind: Cognitive Studies of Memory and Literacy in Classical Antiquity*, London and New York.

Smallwood, E.M. (1976) *The Jews under Roman Rule*, Leiden.

Smith, M. (1978) Rome and the Maccabaean Conversions: Notes on I Macc. 8, in E. Bammel (ed.) *Donum Gentilicum: New Testament Studies in Honour of D. Daube*, Oxford, 1–7.

Smith, M. (1996) Were the Maccabees Priests?, in S.J.D. Cohen (ed.) *Studies in the Cult of Yahweh, Studies in Historical Method, Ancient Israel, Ancient Judaism*, vol. 1 (Religions in the Ancient World, 130/1), Leiden, 320–325.

Snowdon, M. (2014) 'In the Friendship of the Romans': Melitaia, Narthakion and Greco-Roman Interstate Friendship in the Second Century BCE, *Historia* 63, 422–444.

Sorabji, R. (1972) *Aristotle on Memory*, London.

Sokoloff, M. (1974) *The Targum to Job from Qumran Cave XI*, Ramat Gan.

Sordi, M. (1952) Il Valore politico del trattato fra i romani e i guidei nel 161 a. C., *Acme* 5, 509–519.

Sordi, M. (1965) Alessandro e I Romani, *RIL* 99, 4, 445–452 [= M. Sordi (ed.) (2002) *Scritti di storia romana*, Milan, 153–170].

Sordi, M. (1975) L'elogio dei Romani nel I libro dei Maccabei, in *Storiografia e propaganda*, vol. 3, Milan, 95–104.

Sordi, M. (1983) Le lettura dei Romani a Seleuco per gli Iliensi, in id. (ed.) *Studi in onore di Cesare Sanfilippo*, Milan, 719–727.

Sordi, M. (1985) *Pax Deorum* e libertà religiosa nella storia di Roma, in P. Voci (ed.) *La Pace nel mondo antico*, Milan, 146–154.

Spaer, A. (1984) Ascalon: From Royal Mint to Autonomy, in A. Houghton et al. (eds) *Studies in Honor of Leo Mildenberg*, 229–239, plates 35–37.

Spalinger, A.J. (1994) *Revolutions in Time: Studies in Ancient Egyptian Calendrics*, San Antonio TX.

Spolsky, B. (1985) Jewish Multilingualism in the First Century: An Essay in Historical Sociolinguistics, in J.A. Fishman (ed.) *Readings in the Sociology of Jewish Languages*, Leiden, 35–50.

Stählin, O. (1920) in W. von Christ (ed.) *Griechischer Litteraturgeschichte*⁶ (Handbuch der klassischen Altertums-Wissenschaft, 007), vol. 2, Munich.

Staveley, E.S. (1954) The Conduct of Elections during an 'Interregnum', *Historia* 3.2, 193–211.

Stein, A. (1900) *RE* 4.1, s.v. Coponius (2), col. 1214.

Steinschneider, M. (1893) *Die Hebräischen Übersetzungen des Mittelalters*, Berlin.

Sterling, G.E. (1992) *Historiography and Self-Definition: Josephus, Luke–Acts and Apologetic Historiography*, Leiden.

Stern, M. (1960) The Death of Onias III, *Zion* 25, 1–16 [Hebrew].
Stern, M. (1961) The Relations between Judaea and Rome during the Rule of John Hyrcanus, *Zion*, 26, 1–22 [Hebrew].
Stern, M. (1968) The Books of Maccabees, in *Biblical Encyclopedia*, vol. 5, Bialik Institute, Jerusalem, 286–304 [Hebrew].
Stern, M. (1972) *Documents on the History of the Hasmonean Revolt*², Tel Aviv [Hebrew].
Stern M. (1973) Die Urkunden, in J. Maier and J. Schreiner (eds) *Literature und Religion des Frühjudentums: eine Einfürung*, Würzburg, 181–199.
Stern, M. (1974) *Greek and Latin Authors on Jews and Judaism*, vol. 1, Jerusalem.
Stern, M. (1976) The Jews in Greek and Latin Literature, in S. Safrai and M. Stern (eds) *The Jewish People in the First Century*, Philadelphia, 1101–1159.
Stern, M. (1986) The Treaty between Judaea and Rome in 161 BCE, *Zion* 51, 3–28 [Hebrew].
Stern, M. (1995) *Hasmonean Judaea in the Hellenistic World: Chapters in Political History*, ed. D.R. Schwartz, Jerusalem.
Stolfi, E. (2009) *Configurazioni della guerra e concetto di* 'díkaios pólemos' *nell'esperienza greca: alcune osservazioni*, in *Studi in onore di Remo Martini*, vol. 3, Milan, 641ff–688.
Storm, C. (1992) Freiheit als Geschenk? Identische Mechanismem in der Darstellung des römischen Freiheitsbegriffs nach Kynoskephalai und Pydna, *G.B.* 18, 65–86.
Stouder, G. (2009) Création de l'éspace diplomatique à Rome à l'époque médio-républicaine, *Veleia* 29, 173–185.
Strasburger, H. (1965) Poseidonius on Problems of the Roman Empire, *JRS* 55, 40–53.
Sumner, G.V. (1971) Lex annalis under Caesar, *Phoenix*, 246–271.
Sumner, G.V. (1973) *The Orators in Cicero's* Brutus: *Prosopography and Chronology* (Phoenix Suppl., 11), Toronto.
Sumner, G.V. (1978) The 'Piracy Law' from Delphi, *GR&BS* 19, 211–225.
Sündermeier, A. (1896) *Quaestiones chronographicae ad Eusebii et Hieronymi chronica spectantes*, Bremen.
Susemihl, F. (1891–1892) *Geschichte der griechischen Litteratur in der Alexandrinzeit*, vol. 2, Leipzig (repr. 1965, Hildesheim).
Susini, G.C. (1982) *Epigrafia romana*, Rome.
Swain, J.W. (1944) Antiochus Epiphanes and Egypt, *CP* 39, 73–94.
Syme, R. (1955) Missing Senators, *Historia* 4, 52–71.
Syme, R. (1961) Who was Vedius Pollio?, *JRS* 51, 23–30.
Syme, R. (1980) Biographers of the Caesars, *MusHelv.* 37, 104–128 [= A.R. Birley (ed.) (1984) *Roman Papers*, vol. 3, Oxford, 1251–1274].
Syme, R. (1981) The Travels of Suetonius Tranquillus, *Hermes* 109, 105–117 [= A.R. Birley (ed.) (1984) *Roman Papers*, vol. 3, Oxford, 1337–1349].
Taillardat, J. (1982) Φιλότης, Πίστις et Foedus, *REG* 95, 1–14.
Tal, A. (2001) Is there a raison d'être for an Aramaic targum in a Hebrew-speaking society?, *REJ* 160, 357–378.
Talbert, R.J.A. (1984) *The Senate of Imperial Rome*, Princeton.
Talmon, S. (1991) Oral Tradition and Written Transmission, or the Heard and the Seen Word in Judaism of the Second Temple Period, in H. Wansborough (ed.) *Jesus and the Oral Gospel Tradition*, Sheffield, 121–158.
Tarn, W.W. (1921) Alexander's ὑπομνήματα and the 'World Kingdom', *JHS* 41.1, 1–17.
Tarn, W.W. (1948) *Alexander the Great*, Cambridge.
Tarn, W.W. (1950) *Alexander the Great: Sources and Studies*, Cambridge.
Tarn, W.W. (1952) *Hellenistic Civilization*, Cleveland.

Tarwocka, A. (2009) *Romans and the Pirates: Legal Perspective*, Warsaw.

Täubler, E. (1913) *Imperium Romanum: Studien zur Entwicklungsgeschichte des römischen Reichs*, vol. 1, Leipzig–Berlin.

Täubler, E. (1921) *Die Vorgeschichte des zweiten punischen Kriegs*, Berlin.

Taylor, L.R. (1931) *The Divinity of the Roman Emperor*, Middleton.

Taylor, L.R. (1942) Caesar's Colleagues in the Pontifical College, *AJP* 63, 385–412.

Taylor, L.R. and Scott, R.T. (1969) Seating Space in the Roman Senate and the *Senatores Pediarii*, *TAPA* 100, 529–582.

Tcherikover, V. (1930) The Documents in the Second Book of Maccabees, *Tarbiz* 1, 31–45 [Hebrew].

Tcherikover, V. (1959) *Hellenistic Civilization and the Jews*, trans. S. Appelbaum, Philadelphia.

Terzaghi, N. (1934) *Lucilio*, Turino.

Thackeray, H. St.J. (1904) Josephus, in J. Hastings (ed.) *A Dictionary of the Bible*, vol. 5, Edinburgh, 461–473.

Thackeray, H. St.J. (1929) *Josephus: The Man and the Historian*, New York.

Thackeray, H. St.J. (1976) *Josephus*, vol. 2, *The Jewish War*, books 1–3, London.

Thein, A.G. (2014) Capitoline Jupiter and the Historiography of Roman World Rule, *Histos* 8, 284–319.

Thompson, D.J. (1988) *Memphis under the Ptolemies*, Princeton.

Thompson, J.D. (2002) *A Critical Concordance to the Apocrypha: I Maccabees, Book 1* (The Computer Bible, 98), Lewiston.

Timpe, D. (1962) Herrschaftsidee und Klientstaatenpolitik in Sallusts Bellum Jugurthinum, *Hermes* 90, 334–375.

Timpe, D. (1974) Der römische Vertrag mit den Juden von 161 v. Chr. *Chiron* 4, 133–152.

Toebelmann, F. (1927) *Römishe Gebalke*, Heidelberg.

Toki, K. (1977) The Dates of the First and Second Books of Maccabees, *AJBI* 3, 69–83.

Torrey, C.C. (1902) Maccabees (First Book), in T.K. Cheyne and J.S. Black (eds) *Encycyclopedia Biblica*, vol. 3, London, cols. 2857–2869.

Torrey, C.C. (1945) *The Apocryphal Literature*, New Haven.

Touloumakos, J. (1988) Zum römischen Gemeindepatronat im griechischen Osten, *Hermes* 116, 304–324.

Tov, E. (1988) The Septuagint, in M.J. Mulder (ed.) *Mikra: Text, Translation, Reading and Interpretation of the Hebrew Bible in Ancient Judaism and Early Christianity*, Philadelphia, 161–188.

Townend, G.B. (1959) The Date of Composition of Suetonius' Caesars, *CQ* n.s. 9, 285–293.

Toynbee, A.J. (1965) *Hannibal's Legacy: The Hannibalic War's Effects on Roman Life*, vol. 1, London.

Trahman, C.R. (1951) The Attitude of the Roman Administration toward Greek and Latin, *CB* 27, 51–57.

Trebilco, P.R. (2006) *Jewish Communities in Asia Minor*, Berkeley.

Treves, F. (1953) *Il Mito di Alessandro e la Roma di Augusto*, Milan–Naples.

Trieber, K. (1895) Zur Kritik des Gorionides, *Nachrichten von der Königlichen Gesellschaft der Wissenschaften zu Göttingen, philol.-hist. Klasse*, vol. 4, 381–408.

Triepel, H. (1943) *Die Hegemonie: ein Buch von fünrenden Staaten*[2], Stuttgart.

Trundle, M. (2008) Kings and Contracts in the Hellenistic World, in P.R. McKechnie et al. (eds) *Ptolemy II Philadelphus and His World*, Leiden, 103–118.

Tupet, A.M. (1976) *La magie dans la poésie latine*, Paris.

Turelli, G. (2011) *'Audi Iuppiter': il collegio dei feziali nell'esperienza giuridica romana*, Milan.

Turelli, G. (2014) Fetialis religio: una riflessione su religione e diritto nell'esperienza romana, in S. Randazzo (ed.) *Religione e Diritto Romano: la cogenza del rito*, Le Tricase, 449–494.

Turner, N. (1962) *The Interpreter's Dictionary of the Bible*, New York.

Tuval, M. (2013) *From Jerusalem Priest to Roman Jew*, Tübingen.

Twyman, B.L. (1984) The Consular Elections for 216 B.C. and the Lex Maenia de Patrum Auctoritate, *CP* 79.4, 285–294.

Unger, G.F. (1896) Umfang und Anordnung der Geschichte des Poseidonius, *Philol.* 55, 73–122.

Urbrock, W.J. (1972) Formula and Theme in the Song-Cycle of Job, in L.C. McGaughy (ed.) *SBL Proceedings*, vol. 2, Missoula, 459–487.

Valentini, R. and Zucchetti, G. (eds) (1940–1954) *Codice topografico della città di Roma*, vol. 3, Rome.

Valenzani, R.S. (2007) Un nuovo paessaggio urbano: il Foro di Augusto/Pantano di S. Basilio, in R. Meneghini and R. Santangelo Valenzani (eds) *I Fori Imperiali: Gli Scavi del Comune di Roma (1991–2007)*, Rome, 125–158.

Valgiglio, E. (1976) *Plutarco, Praecepta gerendae rei publicae*, Milan.

Valvo, A. (2001) Formula amicorum, commercium amicitiae, φιλιας κοινωνια, in M. Bertinelli and L. Piccirilli (eds) *Serta antiqua et mediaevalia*, vol. 4, Rome, 133–145.

VanderKam, J.C. (1990) People and High Priesthood in Early Maccabean Times, in W.H. Propp et al. (eds) *The Hebrew Bible and its Interpreters*, Winona Lake, 205–225.

VanderKam, J.C. (2004) *From Joshua to Caiaphas: High Priest after the Exile*, Minneapolis.

van't Dack, E. (1963) A studiis, a bybliothecis, *Historia* 12, 177–184.

Vegetius, R.F. (1885) *Epitoma rei militaris*, ed. C. Lang, Leipzig.

Vermes, G. (1975) Ancient Rome in Post-Biblical Literature, in id. (ed.) *Post-Biblical Jewish Studies*, Leiden, 215–224.

Vermes, G. (1996) The Leadership of the Qumran Community, the Sons of Zadok, Priests, Congregation, in H. Cancik et al. (eds) *Geschichte–Tradition–Reflexion: Festschrift für Martin Hengel*, vol. 1, Tübingen, 381–384.

Versnel, H.S. (1976) Two Types of Roman *Devotio*, *Mnemosyne* 29.4, 365–410.

Vidal-Naquet, P. (1978) *Rome et la conquête du monde méditerranéen. 2 Genèse d'un empire*, Paris.

Viereck, P. (1888) *Sermo graecus quo senatus populusque Romanus magistratusque populi Romani usque ad Tiberii Caesaris aetatem in scriptis publicis usi sunt examinatur*, Göttingen.

Viereck, P. (1909) Die Festsetzung der Grenze im Frieden des Antiochus, *Klio* 9, 371–375.

Visscher, F. de (1946a) Le deditio internationale et l'affaire des Fourches Caudines, *CRAI* 90.1, 82–95.

Visscher, F. de (1946b) *Le Régime romain de la Noxalité de la vengeance collective à la responsabilité individuelle*, Brussels.

Vogt, J. (1976) Empire Building and a Common Language in the Roman Republic, *CF* 30, 107–126.

Volkmann, H. (1925) Demetrius I und Alexander I von Syrien, *Klio* 19, 373–412.

Volkmann, H. (1959a) *RE* 23.2, s.v. Ptolemaios II, cols 1645–1667.

Volkmann, H. (1959b) *RE* 23.2, s.v. Ptolemaios (19) 1651.

Volkmann, H. (1959c) *RE* 23.2 s.v. Ptolemaios VI. Philometor, cols 1702–1719.

Vollmer, D. (1990) *Symploke, das Übergreifen der römischen Expansion auf den griechischen Österreich*, Stuttgart.
Vossius, I. (1687) *Antiquité des temps rétablie et défendue contre les Juifs*, Paris.
Wacholder, B. (1962) *Nicolaus of Damascus*, Berkeley.
Wacholder, B. (1974) *Eupolemus: A Study of Judaeo-Greek Literature*, Cincinnati.
Wachsmuth, C. (1895) *Einleitung in das Studium der alten Geschichte*, Leipzig.
Walbank, F.W. (1936) The Accession of Ptolemy V: A Study in Chronology, *Journal of Egyptian Archaeology* 22, 20–34.
Walbank, F.W. (1963) Polybius and Rome's Eastern Policy, *JRS* 53, 1–13.
Walbank, F.W. (1972) Nationality as a Factor in Roman History, *HSCP* 76, 145–168.
Walbank, F.W. (1967–1979) *A Historical Commentary on Polybius*, 3 vols, Oxford.
Walek, Th. (1925) La politique romaine en Grèce et dans l'Orient hellénistique au IIIe siècle, *Rev. Phil.* 49, 118–142.
Walker, T.A. (1899) *A History of the Law of Nations*, Cambridge.
Wallace-Hadrill, T. (1983) *Suetonius: The Scholar and His Caesars*, London.
Walsh, J.J. (1996) Flamininus and the Propaganda of Liberation, *Historia* 45.3, 344–363.
Walsh, J.T. (2001) *Style and Structure in Biblical Hebrew Narrative*, Collegeville, MN.
Walton, B. (1964) *Biblia Sacra Polyglotta*, vol. 4, Graz, Austria.
Walton, F.R. (1956) Notes on Diodorus, *AJP* 77, 408–414.
Walton, F.R. (1957) *Diodorus Siculus*, vol. 11, London.
Wardle, D. (1998) *Valerius Maximus: Memorable Deeds and Sayings Book I: Translated with Introduction and Commentary*, Oxford.
Warmington, E.H. (1935) *Remains of Old Latin*, vol. 4, London.
Warrior, V.M. (1996) *The Initiation of the Second Macedonian War: An Explication of Livy Book 31*, Stuttgart.
Wasserstein, A. (1993) Notes on the Temple of Onias at Leontopolis, *Illinois Classical Studies*, 18, 119–129.
Water, R. van de (1999–2000) Reconsidering Paleographic and Radiocarbon Dating of the Dead Sea Scrolls, *RQ* 19.3–4, 423–439.
Watson, A. (1993) *International Law in Archaic Rome: War and Religion*, Baltimore–London.
Watson Selby, J. (1853) *Justin, Cornelius Nepos and Eutropius, Literally Translated, with Notes and a General Index*, London.
Watters, W.R. (1976) *Formula Criticism and the Poetry of the Old Testament* (Beiheft zur Zeitschrift für alttestamentliche Wissenschaft, 138), Berlin
Weber, E. (1972) Die trojanische Abstammung der Römer als politisches Argument, *Weiner Studien* 85, 213–225.
Wegner, A. (1936) *Geschichte des Völkerrecht*, Stuttgart.
Wegner, M. (1969) *Untersuchungen zu den lateinischen Begriffen* socius *und* societas (Hypomnemata, 21), Göttingen.
Weinfeld, M. (1973) Covenant Terminology in the Ancient Near East and Its Influence on the West, *JAOS* 93.2, 190–199.
Welles, C. B. (1965) Greek Liberty, *JJP* 15, 29–47.
Welles, C.B. (1966) *Royal Correspondence in the Hellenistic Period: A Study in Greek Epigraphy* (Studia Historica, 028), Rome.
Wellhausen, J. (1907) *Israelische und Judische Geschichte*[6], Berlin.
Wengler, P. (1963) Die Abgrenzung zwischen völkerrechtlichen und nichtvölkerrechtlichen Normen im internationalen Verkehr, in C.J. Arnholm et al. (eds) *Legal Essays presented to Frede Castberg*, Oslo, 332–352.

Werner, R. (1987) *Alexander der Molosser in Italien*, in W. Will and J. Heinrichs (eds) *Zu Alexander der Grosse: Festschrift G. Wirth zum 60. Geburtstag*, Amsterdam, 335–390.

Wernsdorff, G. (1747) *Commentatio historico-critica de fide historica librorum Maccabaicorum*, Vratislavia.

Westall, R. (2011) Rome and Ptolemaic Egypt: Initial Contacts, in P. Buzi et al. (eds) *Aegyptiaca et Coptica: Studi in onore di Sergio Pernigotti*, Oxford, 349–360.

Wheeler, E.L. (1984) Sophistic Interpretations and Greek Treaties, *GRBS* 25, 253–274.

Whitehead, J.D. (1974) *Early Aramaic Epistolography: The Arsames Correspondence*, Diss., University of Chicago.

Widengren, G. (1966) Iran and Israel in Parthian Times with Special Regard to the Ethiopian Book of Enoch, *Temenos* 2, 139–177.

Wiedermann, T. (1986) The *Fetiales*: A Reconsideration, *CQ* 36, 478–490.

Wieseler, K. (1877) Einige Bemerkungen zu den römischen Urkunden bei Josephus Ant. 12.10, 148 and 14.10, *Theologische Studien und Kriten*, 50, 281–298.

Wilcken, U. (1931) *Alexander der Grosse*, Leipzig.

Will, E. (1972) Rome et les Séleucides, *ANRW* 1.1, 590–632.

Will, E. (1979–1982) *Histoire politique du monde hellénistique (323–30 av. J.-C.)*$^2$, vols 1 and 2, Nancy.

Willems, P. (1878–1885) *Le Sénat de la république romaine*, Louvain (repr. 1968, Aarlen).

Williams, C. (2008) Friends of the Roman People: Some Remarks on the Language of *Amicitia*, in A. Coşkun (ed.) *Freundschaft und Gefolgschaft in den auswärtigen Beziehungen der Römer (2. Jahrhundert v.Chr. – 1. Jahrhundert n. Chr.)*, Frankfurt am Main, 29–44.

Williams, D.S. (1996) *The Structure of 1 Maccabees* (The Catholic Biblical Quarterly Monograph Series, 31), Washington.

Williamson, C. (1987) Monuments of Bronze: Roman Legal Documents on Bronze Tablets, *Class. Ant.* 6, 160–183.

Williamson, C. (1995) The Display of Law and Archival Practice in Rome, in H. Solin and O. Salomies (eds) *Acta colloquii epigraphici Latini*, Helsinki, 239–252.

Willrich, H. (1895) *Juden und Griechen vor der makkabäischen Erhebung*, Göttingen.

Willrich, H. (1899) Alabanda und Rom zur Zeit des ersten Krieges gegen Mithradates, *Hermes* 34, 305–311.

Willrich, H. (1900) *Judaica: Forschung zur hellenistisch-jüdischen Geschichte und Literatur*, Göttingen.

Willrich, H. (1903) Caligula, *Klio* 3, 397–470.

Willrich, H. (1924) *Urkundenfälschung in der hellenistisch-jüdischen Literatur*, Göttingen.

Wilson, V.M. (1997) *Divine Symmetries: The Art of Biblical Narrative*, Lantham–New York–London.

Winckler, H. (1901) Die Juden und Rom, in id. (ed.) *Altorientalische Forschungen*, Dritte Reihe, I, in *Kritische Schriften*, Berlin, 97–134.

Wirszubski, C. (1950) *Libertas as a Political Ideal during the Late Republic and the Early Empire*, Cambridge.

Wischmeyer, O. (1995) *Die Kultur des Buches Jesus Sirach*, Berlin–New York.

Wise, M.O. (2005) 4Q245 (PSAN'AR) and the High Priesthood of Judas Maccabaeus, *DSD* 12, 313–364.

Wiseman, J. (1979) Corinth and Rome. I: 228 B.C.–A.D. 267, *ANRW* 2.7.1, 438–548.

Wissowa, G. (1912) *Religion und Kultus der Römer*, Munich.

Wolff, S.R. and Finkielsztein, G. (2009) Two Hellenistic Lead Weights of the Tanit Series, in J.D. Schloen (ed.) *Exploring the Longue Durée: Essays in Honor of Lawrence E. Stager*, Winona Lake, 497–506.

Worthington, I. (2014a) *Alexander the Great: Man and God*, London–New York.

Worthington, I. (2014b) *By the Spear: Philip II, Alexander the Great, and the Rise and Fall of the Macedonian Empire*, Oxford.

Worthington, I. (2014–2017) *Brill's New Jacoby* [= *BNJ*] online.

Wünsch, R. ed. (1903) *De magistratibus populi Romani*, vol. 3, Leipzig.

Yardley, J.C. and Develin, R. (1994) *Justin: The Epitome of the Philippic History of Pompeius Trogus*, Atlanta.

Yardley, J.C. and Heckel, W. (1997) *Justin: Epitome of the Philippic History of Pompeius Trogus*, vol. 1, Oxford.

Yardley, J.C. and Hoyos, D. (2013) *Livy: Rome's Italian Wars, Books 6–10*, Oxford.

Yarrow, L.M. (2006) *Historiography at the End of the Republic: Provincial Perspectives on Roman Rule*, Oxford.

Yates, F.A. (1966) *The Art of Memory*, London.

Yoder, P. (1971) A–B Pairs and Oral Composition in Hebrew Poetry, *VT* 21, 470–489.

Yoshimura, T. (1984) Zum römischen *libertas*–Begriff in der Aussenpolitik im zweiten Jahrhundert vor Chr., *AJAH* 9, 1–22.

Zack, A. (2007) *Studien zum 'Römischen Völkerrecht' Kriegserklärung, Kriegsbeschluss, Beeidung und Ratification zwischenstaatlicher Verträge, internationale Freundschaft und Feindschaft während der römischen Republik bis zum Beginn des Prinzipats*,[2] Göttingen.

Zack, A. (2012) Forschungen über die rechtlichen Grundlagen der römischen Außenbe ziehungen während der Republik bis zum Beginn des Prinzipats. II. Teil: Fragen an Varro de lingua Latina 5,33: die augurale Ordnung des Raumes, *Göttinger Forum für Altertumswissenschaft* 15, 61–128.

Zack, A. (2013) Forschungen über die rechtlichen Grundlagen der römischen Außenbeziehungen während der Republik bis zum Beginn des Prinzipats. III. Teil: Der personenrechtliche Status der amici, socii und amici et socii und die formula amicorum und formula sociorum, *Göttinger Forum für Altertumswissenschaft* 16, 63–113.

Zack, A. (2015a) Das Thema, der Begriff des 'Vertrages', die Opposition der Abhandlung, Rückblick auf die Teile III und IV der 'Forschungen' und die Thesen des VI. Teils der 'Forsuchungen', *Göttingen Forum für Altertumswissenschaft* 18, 27–82.

Zack, A. (2015b) Forschungen über die rechtlichen Grundlagen der römischen Außenbeziehungen während der Republik bis zum Beginn des Prinzipats. VI. Teil: Die juristische Form und der rechtliche Gehalt der intergesellschaftlichen *amicitia* und *amicitia et societas* mit Rom. Erster Abschnitt: die Begrifflichkeit und die aus ihr zu erschließende Systematik der rechtlichen Formen, *Göttinger Forum für Altertumswissenschaft* 18, 115–178,

Zack, A. (forthcoming) C. Iulius Caesar and Hyrkanus II. Der Zusammenhang und die chronologische Abfolge der bei Falvius Josephus ant. 14,8,5 [145–148] und ant. 14,10,2–10 [190–222] referierten und ganz oder teilweise zitierten Dokumente (48–47 v,Chr.), ein Vorschlag, *Electrum, Journal of Ancient History*, 2017.

Zeitlin, S. (1931) *Josephus on Jesus*, Philadelphia.

Zeitlin, S. (1950) *The First Book of Maccabees*, trans. S. Tedesche, New York.

Zeitlin, S. (ed.) (1954) *The Second Book of Maccabees*, trans. S. Tedesche, New York.

Zeitlin, S. (1962–1963) Josippon, *JQR* 53, 277–297.

Ziebarth, E. (1929) *Beiträge zur Geschichte des Seeraubs und Seehandels in alten Griechenland*, Hamburg.
Zeigler, K. (1936) *RE* 6A.1, art. Timarchos (5), col. 1238.
Ziegler, K. (1941) *RE* 20, s.v. Photius, cols 662–737.
Ziegler, K.-H. (1972) Das Völkerrecht der römischen Republik, *ANRW* 1.2, 68–114.
Ziegler, K.-H. (1982) Amicus et Socius Populi Romani, *Labeo* 28, 61–67.
Ziegler, K.-H. (1995) Conclusion and Publication of International Treaties in Antiquity, *Israel Law Review* 29, 233–249.
Zilken, F. (1909) *De Inscriptionibus Latinis Graecis Bilinguibus: quaestiones selectae*, Diss., Bonn.
Zimmermann, F. (1975) *Biblical Books Translated from the Aramaic*, New York.
Zlotnick, D. (1984–5) Memory and the Integrity of the Oral Tradition, *JANES* 16–17, 229–241.
Zlotnick, D. (1988) *The Iron Pillar: Mishnah, Redaction, Form and Content*, Jerusalem.
Zollschan, L.T. Greenlees- (1997) *A Study in Roman–Maccabaean Relations*, M.A. Diss., Deakin University, Melbourne.
Zollschan, L.T. (2002) Macedonian Libertas, *The Classical Bulletin* 78.2, 177–202.
Zollschan, L. (2003) Roman Diplomatic Procedure and the Senate's Response to the Jewish Embassy of 161 BCE, in M. Ben-Zeev and D. Gera (eds) *The Path of Peace: Studies in Honour of Israel Ben Shalom*, Beersheva, *1–*31.
Zollschan, L.T. (2004) The Earliest Jewish Embassy to the Romans: 2 Macc.4:11?, *JJS* 55, 37–44.
Zollschan, L. Greenlees-, (2005) *Roman Diplomacy and the Jewish Embassy of 161 BCE*, Ph.D. Diss., Ben-Gurion University of the Negev, Beersheva, Israel.
Zollschan, L.T. (2005) Senate's Response to the Jewish Embassy of 161 BCE, in M. Ben-Zeev and D. Gera (eds) *The Path of Peace: Studies in Honor of Israel Ben Shalom*, Jerusalem, 1–31.
Zollschan, L. T. (2007a) Orality and the Politics of Roman Peacemaking, in C. Cooper (ed.) *Politics of Orality*, Leiden, 171–190.
Zollschan, L.T. (2007b) The Date of the Fannius Letter: Jos. Ant. 14.233, *JSJ* 38, 9–38.
Zollschan, L.T. (2008) Justinus 36.3.9 and Roman–Judaean Diplomatic Relations in 161 BCE, *Athenaeum* 96, 153–171.
Zollschan, L.T. (2011) The Ritual Garb of the Fetial Priests, *Mus. Helv.* 68, 47–67.
Zollschan, L.T. (2012a) The Longevity of the Fetial College, in O. Tellegen-Couperus (ed.) *Roman Law and Roman Religion*, Leiden–Boston, 119–144.
Zollschan, L.T. (2012b) The Roman Bronze Tablet in the Church of San Basilio in Rome, *Classica et Mediaevalia* 63, 217–245.
Zollschan, L.T. (forthcoming) *The Fetial Priests of Rome*.
Zorat, M. (1966) Delfi, Turi e Tarento (per la storia della Magna Graecia nel IV secolo), in L. Braccesi (ed.) *Hesperia 7: Studi sulla Grecita e Occidente*, Rome, 99–110.
Zucchi, A. (1940) Il monastero della SS. Annunziata e le chiesa S. Basilio ai Pantani, in id. (ed.) *Roma domenicana: note storiche*, vol. 2, Florence, 3–40.

# Index

Note: Where subheadings for entries refer to chapter/verse numbers they have been made bold for legibility.

Made in the USA
Las Vegas, NV
31 October 2024

10666574R00195